Sociology Full Circle

Sociology Full Circle

Contemporary Readings on Society

Second Edition

edited by
William Feigelman

Nassau Community College

Praeger Publishers
New York

To My Parents

Published in the United States of America in 1976
by Praeger Publishers, Inc.
111 Fourth Avenue, New York, N.Y. 10003

This is the second edition
of a book originally published
in 1972 by Praeger Publishers, Inc.

© 1972, 1976 by Praeger Publishers, Inc.

Second printing, 1976

Library of Congress Cataloging in Publication Data

Feigelman, William, comp.
Sociology full circle.

Includes bibliographies.
1. Sociology—Addresses, essays, lectures.
I. Title.
HM51.F42   1976   301'.08   74-9400
ISBN 0-275-22260-8
ISBN 0-275-89210-7 pbk.

Printed in the United States of America

Contents

PREFACE   vii

1. THE NATURE OF SOCIOLOGY   3

The Promise   *C. Wright Mills*   6
Anti-Minotaur: The Myth of a Value-free Sociology
  Alvin W. Gouldner   14
Body Ritual Among the Nacirema   *Horace Miner*   22

2. CULTURE   28

Sexual Modesty, Social Meanings, and the Nudist Camp
  Martin S. Weinberg   32
One Hundred Per Cent American   *Ralph Linton*   37
Steel Axes for Stone-Age Australians   *Lauriston Sharp*   39
Cultural Components in Responses to Pain   *Mark Zborowski*   51

3. SOCIAL ORGANIZATION   64

The Folk Society   *Robert Redfield*   67
Queue Culture: The Waiting Line as a Social System   *Leon Mann* 79
Antidote to Alienation: Learning to Belong   *Melvin Seeman*   91

4. SOCIALIZATION   100

Erik Erikson's Eight Ages of Man   *David Elkind*   105
Changing the Game from "Get the Teacher" to "Learn"
  *Robert L. Hamblin, David Buckholdt, Donald Bushell,
  Desmond Ellis, and Daniel Ferritor*   114
The Split-Level American Family   *Urie Bronfenbrenner*   127
The Chinese Indoctrination Program for Prisoners of War
  Edgar H. Schein   139

5. SOCIAL STRATIFICATION   161

The New Egalitarianism   *Herbert J. Gans*   165
Programmed for Social Class: Tracking in High School
  Walter E. Schafer, Carol Olexa, and Kenneth Polk   173
Sociology of Christmas Cards   *Sheila K. Johnson*   186
The Culture of Poverty   *Oscar Lewis*   192

6. MINORITIES   203

Discriminating to End Discrimination   *Nina Totenberg*   208
The Social Construction of the Second Sex   *Jo Freeman*   218

Men and Jobs *Elliot Liebow*   231
An Advocate of Black Power Defines It *Charles V. Hamilton*   241

7. THE FAMILY   253

The Attempt to Abolish the Family in Russia
  Nicholas S. Timasheff   257
Cultural Contradictions and Sex Roles: The Masculine Case
  Mirra Komarovsky   266

8. DEVIANCE   279

Tearoom Trade: Impersonal Sex in Public Places
  Laud Humphreys   285
On Being Sane in Insane Places *D. L. Rosenhan*   303

9. POLITICAL SOCIOLOGY   321

The Social and Psychological Aspects of Chieftainship
  in a Primitive Tribe *Claude Lévi-Strauss*   327
The World Behind Watergate *Kirkpatrick Sale*   339

10. SOCIAL CHANGE   354

The Population Explosion: Facts and Fiction *Paul R. Ehrlich*   360
The Anabaptist Explosion *William F. Pratt*   367
Toward a Theory of Revolution *James C. Davies*   377
Communes in Cities *Rosabeth Moss Kanter*   391

Preface

The object of this collection of essays, as of most anthologies in introductory sociology, is to give the student some notion of the scope and intellectual range of the discipline while presenting examinations in some depth of certain selected issues and topics generally explored in the introductory course. At the same time, the anthology, it is hoped, will make sociology real to the student by giving him a clearer idea of what the sociologist does, how sociological research is actually conducted, and how the sociologist applies seemingly abstract concepts to illuminate our understanding of social phenomena.

One bothersome problem I have noted in many anthologies is that they seem to take little account of the intellectual potentialities and interests of the beginning sociology student. Although the collection may be fairly representative in presenting what is being done and has been done by sociologists, most of what is offered seems to be directed toward professional sociologists rather than beginning students. The classroom performance can often create bridges of understanding across this chasm, but more frequently the student is left with a feeling that sociology consists of a great deal of verbal hocus-pocus overladen with statistics.

What I have attempted to do in this book is to select materials that are highly readable, straightforward, and inherently interesting to the beginner, including both the student who plans to specialize in the field and the student who does not expect to go beyond the introductory course. Moreover, these selections, it is hoped, will be comprehensible and appealing not only to undergraduates in a four-year college but to junior- and community-college students as well. Although several of the selections have been taken from such professional sociological journals as *The American Sociological Review*, *The American Journal of Sociology*, and *Social Problems*, several come from more popular sources such as *The New York Times Magazine*,

Saturday Review Society/Trans-action, and *Natural History.* The authors represented are all outstanding social scientists; a number of the works included are prizewinning efforts.

Most of the selections have been extensively tested with students to assess their readability and appeal. With virtually no exceptions, questionnaire responses have indicated uniformly high interest in and acceptance of the articles among students who reviewed them.

In order to stimulate interest in, and appreciation of, the discipline, several areas of sociological inquiry are emphasized. Considerable attention has been devoted to the sociology of social problems—that is, examining contemporary and topical issues in a sociological way, sometimes in their own right and sometimes as part of larger or more basic social processes. In our increasingly complex world, we look more and more to the sociologist to provide answers to such social questions as alienation, the generation gap, youth culture, the crisis of overpopulation, black power, women's liberation, economic and political conflict, the disruptive consequences of technological change, courtship and family patterns, and the like.

Another dimension highlighted here is the cross-cultural approach. Many of the selections either were written by anthropologists or concern preliterate peoples and their problems. If we want to develop a systematic understanding of human society, we must take its total variety and diversity into account. By studying the social institutions and cultural patterns of so-called primitives, we may be able to observe social forms in a purer, more elemental state, in a way that better illuminates their dynamics, than would be the case if we observed our own complex and heterogeneous social world. The cross-cultural perspective also enables us to develop and test hypotheses about the interrelatedness of social forms as we compare societies on various axes. From the data provided by cross-cultural research, we may one day derive a meaningful picture of the origins of society, its present situation, how it is changing, and how the transformations may affect our lives in the future.

Still another focus of this collection is what might be called the sociology of the absurd. A number of the essays deal with ostensibly off-beat or bizarre subjects—nudists, queueing up for football games, sending Christmas cards. Sociological understanding can be obtained from a study of all human behavior, eccentric as well as conventional. Exploring seemingly absurd questions may enable us to clarify our understanding of important social forms and may give us insight into workings of society that previously seemed obscure. Only by encouraging free-ranging curiosity can we acquire truly imaginative sociological insight.

The selections also represent the most important theoretical and methodological approaches to the study of society—functionalism, conflict theory, social-exchange theory, and symbolic interactionism. The styles of research represented include questionnaire and interview surveys, participant and direct-observation research, census studies, intervention research, and sociohistorical analysis—all of which involve a variety of sampling and statistical-analytical procedures.

In arranging this collection, we have made certain more or less arbitrary decisions regarding the particular chapters in which the articles appear. It should be understood, however, that many articles have ramifications for other topics as well. The introduction to each chapter indicates other articles in the book that might be assigned in connection with the subject under study. The instructor, of course, may wish to assign these essays in still another order.

It is hoped that these selections will convey to the student not only the range of subject matter and techniques of the professional sociologist but also some sense of the wonder and fascination sociologists experience as they study society and group behavior.

Sociology Full Circle

1. The Nature of Sociology

INTRODUCTION

What is sociology? What benefits can it provide for mankind? How does one conduct sociological research? What important moral, socio-political, and methodological problems are involved in being a sociologist? The selections in this opening chapter explore some of these questions related to the basic characteristics of sociology and ways of doing social research.

Sociology may be defined as the scientific study of human society. The sociologist's interest is in human relationships: how they arise, how they persist, how they change. Unlike the psychologist, who studies individual behavior, the sociologist is interested in human interaction. Groups, in all their myriad forms, represent the distinctive focus of sociology. The range of human relationships explored by the sociologist is limitless. The behavior of the most respected and the most despised members of society, of the most ordinary and the most extraordinary people—all fall within the province of the sociologist.

The assertion that sociology is "scientific" carries with it a number of implications. It means that one of the sociologist's primary goals is the identification of regularities in group behavior. The sociologist seeks to establish a systematic body of knowledge about human society in the form of logically interrelated sets of hypotheses and theories that are directly verifiable and capable of accurately predicting social action.

To obtain systematic knowledge about society, the sociologist uses the so-called scientific method. This involves adopting a speculative attitude; everything is open to doubt until it is proved, and nothing is taken for granted. Moreover, the regularities presumed by the social scientist must be capable of being substantiated empirically (directly observable) and thus capable of convincing any rational man. Furthermore, the scientist is obliged to suspend his prejudices and predilections and to examine questions about society impartially and dispassionately.

Among the most significant benefits of sociological knowledge is that, by helping people to see clearly what their society is and what it can become, it affords them the opportunity to pursue their goals in rational, intelligent, and effective ways. It also gives them a vision of the manifold consequences of their beliefs and actions and helps them to choose among them.

Moreover, a knowledge of sociology provides man with a viewpoint, a way of looking at his world, of examining his society critically. A sociological perspective prods him to peer behind the commonplace rituals, conventions, and traditions of his culture. A sociological perspective can thus be unsettling; nevertheless, it yields a broadening vista of human life and engenders an appreciation of the infinite variety of human potentialities.

Some of the many benefits of sociological inquiry are suggested in the late C. Wright Mills's essay "The Promise," an excerpt from his well-known book *The Sociological Imagination*. Mills contends that in the contemporary world—where urban-industrial man finds himself torn from his traditional moorings—a sociological imagination has become indispensable for individual well-being.

We can trace sociological analysis in Western history back as early as ancient Greece, specifically to the writings of the Sophists. However, it was not until 1839, in the work of Auguste Comte, that the term "sociology" was first used. Although Comte defined sociology much as it is conceived today, the major corpus of Comte's work was not in keeping with his view of the discipline; for the most part, it represented a social-philosophical, nonempirical approach.

The positivist furor of the late nineteenth century, with its devotion to science and its commitment to the notion of unremitting evolution toward progress, provided the take-off point for the development of sociology. The development has dramatically accelerated during this century. Notwithstanding several notable exceptions, much early sociological research was, like Comte's, of the "armchair theory" variety. However, sociological study during the twentieth century, particularly in America, has had a decidedly empirical orientation.

The idea of a value-free sociology is one of the legacies of its positivist roots. From the early days of sociology until fairly recently, almost all sociologists argued that in order to maintain scientific objectivity the social scientist must avoid advocacy. Many social scientists believed that any expression of value judgment would necessarily hamper the scientist's ability to study society impartially and would ultimately result in a kind of pseudosociological analysis representing narrow self-interest or political partisanship.

This doctrine has recently been subjected to considerable re-examination. In "Anti-Minotaur: The Myth of a Value-free Sociology," Alvin Gouldner argues that the value-free ideal has frequently been propounded to mask moral indifference, crass commercialism, and political conservatism. Gouldner suggests that expression of the social scientist's interests, beliefs, and values is both unavoidable and necessary. As the social scientist selects problems for study, he inevitably suggests his own biases and beliefs. Also, once a social-science product is presented to society, it is viewed as favoring the interests of some groups and disfavoring those of others. Gouldner argues that it is one thing for the scientist to suspend his moral judgment in the interest of scientific precision and objectivity; it is quite another for him to be indifferent to the ways in which his research bears on the human predicament and how it might be applied to human affairs. Accepting Mills's notion that the modern world has made a sociological imagination indispensable, Gouldner maintains that the sociologist has a public responsibility to address existing social problems, both by identifying their origins and by attempting to ameliorate them. Although most contemporary sociologists agree with the former objective, it should be noted that a sizable number of others do not share his advocacy of social amelioration.

Sociology, like the other behavioral sciences, involves several methodological problems not found in the physical sciences. These problems hinge on the central fact that the subject of sociological study is mankind. Unlike the laboratory scientist studying animals or inanimate things, the sociologist can never perfectly control his subject; no one will permit another to rearrange his life completely for a scientific experiment. Secondly, in studying society we are usually studying ourselves, our families, our intimate friends, and other groups of whom we may have formed very definite evaluations. Can we suspend our attitudes and moral judgments so that they do not distort our analysis? While studying ourselves, can we be scientifically objective? In "Body Ritual Among the Nacirema," Horace Miner suggests, in a most amusing and thoughtful manner, that transcending the precepts of our own culture, studying a group dispassionately on its own terms, may be an insurmountable task. He leads us to wonder whether the stranger has a distinct advantage over the native in social research. Because his moral investments in the culture are less great, he may be better able to suspend his judgment in the interest of scientific objectivity.

Social-science research involves, first, the selection of a problem for study and the formulation of hypotheses. In the next step, the scientist painstakingly observes and records data relevant to the hypotheses, possibly examining official records, collecting interviews, or directly observing his sample or group. The data are then organized or classified; at this point, statistical computations are performed if necessary. Then, the scientist generalizes from his findings, indicates whether they confirm or refute his original hypotheses, and determines whether they add anything to established theory or suggest its revision. Finally, he makes his work public; he puts his findings on record, complete with data and procedures, so that his work can be repeated by others, tested, and added to the cumulative fund of knowledge.

There are many ways in which sociologists study society, including direct observation, interviewing, questionnaire surveys, the study of official records, content analysis (inferring social trends from popular literature, films, songs, or other such cultural items), and correlation analysis (examining data to find whether change in the amount of one variable is accompanied by comparable change in the amount of another). A variety of research designs are employed, including case studies, sampling surveys, and applications and variations of the "classical" experimental design (observing differences between a group exposed to an experimental manipulation and a control group, similar in every respect with the exception of the experimental condition).

Sociological curiosity has led to the exploration of a broad and diverse range of problems and questions about human society. In the chapters that follow, we shall attempt to provide an overview of both the types of questions explored and the methods and techniques used in sociological research.

The Sociological Imagination

The Promise*
C. Wright Mills

Nowadays, men often feel that their private lives are a series of traps. They sense that, within their everyday worlds, they cannot overcome their troubles, and, in this feeling, they are often quite correct: What ordinary men are directly aware of and what they try to do are bounded by the private orbits in which they live; their visions and their powers are limited to the close-up scenes of job, family, neighborhood; in other milieux, they move vicariously and remain spectators. And the more aware they become, however vaguely, of ambitions and of threats, that transcend their immediate locales, the more trapped they seem to feel.

Underlying this sense of being trapped are seemingly impersonal changes in the very structure of continent-wide societies. The facts of contemporary history are also facts about the success and the failure of individual men and women. When a society is industrialized, a peasant becomes a worker; a feudal lord is liquidated or becomes a businessman. When classes rise or fall, a man is employed or unemployed; when the rate of investment goes up or down, a man takes new heart or goes broke. When wars happen, an insurance salesman becomes a rocket launcher; a store clerk, a radar man; a wife lives alone; a child grows up without a father. Neither the life of an individual nor the history of a society can be understood without understanding both.

Yet, men do not usually define the troubles they endure in terms of historical change and institutional contradiction. The well-being they enjoy, they do not usually impute to the big ups and downs of the societies in which they live. Seldom aware of the intricate connection between the patterns of their own lives and the course of world history, ordinary men do not usually know what this connection means for the kinds of men they are becoming and for the kinds of history-making in which they might take part. They do not possess the quality of mind essential to grasp the interplay of man and society, of biography and history, of self and world. They cannot cope with their personal troubles in such ways as to control the structural transformations that usually lie behind them.

Surely, it is no wonder. In what period have so many men been so totally exposed at so fast a pace to such earthquakes of change? That Americans have not known such catastrophic changes as have the men and women of other societies is due to historical facts that are now quickly becoming "merely history." The history that now affects every man is world history. Within this scene and this period, in the course of a single generation, one-sixth of mankind is transformed from all that is feudal and backward into all that is modern, advanced, and fearful. Political colonies are freed; new and less visible forms of imperialism, installed. Revolutions occur; men feel the intimate grip of new kinds of authority. Totalitarian societies rise, and are smashed to bits—or succeed fabulously. After two centuries of ascendancy, capitalism is shown up as only one way to make society into an industrial apparatus. After two centuries of hope, even formal democracy is restricted to a quite small portion of mankind. Everywhere in the underdeveloped world, ancient ways of life are broken up and vague expectations become urgent demands. Everywhere in the overdeveloped world, the means of authority and of violence become total in scope and bureaucratic in form. Humanity itself now lies before us, the supernation at either pole concentrating its most coordinated and massive efforts upon the preparation of World War III.

The very shaping of history now outpaces the ability of men to orient themselves in accordance with cherished values. And which values? Even when they do not panic, men often sense that older ways of feeling and thinking have collapsed, and that newer beginnings are ambiguous to the point of moral stasis. Is it any wonder that ordinary men feel they cannot cope with the larger worlds with which they are so suddenly confronted?

That they cannot understand the meaning of their epoch for their own lives? That—in defense of selfhood—they become morally insensible, trying to remain altogether private men? Is it any wonder that they come to be possessed by a sense of the trap?

It is not only information that they need—in this Age of Fact, information often dominates their attention and overwhelms their capacities to assimilate it. It is not only the skills of reason that they need—although their struggles to acquire these often exhaust their limited moral energy.

What they need, and what they feel they need, is a quality of mind that will help them to use information and to develop reason in order to achieve lucid summations of what is going on in the world and of what may be happening within themselves. It is this quality, I am going to contend, that journalists and scholars, artists and publics, scientists and editors are coming to expect of what may be called the sociological imagination.

The sociological imagination enables its possessor to understand the larger historical scene in terms of its meaning for the inner life and the external career of a variety of individuals. It enables him to take into account how individuals, in the welter of their daily experience, often become falsely conscious of their social positions. Within that welter, the framework of modern society is sought, and within that framework the psychologies of a variety of men and women are formulated. By such means, the personal uneasiness of individuals is focused upon explicit troubles, and the indifference of publics is transformed into involvement with public issues.

The first fruit of this imagination—and the first lesson of the social science that embodies it—is the idea that the individual can understand his own experience and gauge his own fate only by locating himself within his period, that he can know his own chances in life only by becoming aware of those of all individuals in his circumstances. In many ways, it is a terrible lesson; in many ways, a magnificent one. We do not know the limits of man's capacities for supreme effort or willing degradation, for agony or glee, for pleasurable brutality or the sweetness of reason. But in our time we have come to know that the limits of "human nature" are frighteningly broad. We have come to know that every individual lives, from one generation to the next, in some society; that he lives out a biography, and that he lives it out within some historical sequence. By the fact of his living he contributes, however minutely, to the shaping of this society and to the course of its history, even as he is made by society and by its historical push and shove.

The sociological imagination enables us to grasp history and biography and the relations between the two within society. That is its task and its promise. To recognize this task and this promise is the mark of the classic social analyst. It is characteristic of Herbert Spencer—turgid, polysyllabic, comprehensive; of E. A. Ross—graceful, muckraking, upright; of Auguste Comte and Emile Durkheim; of the intricate and subtle Karl Mannheim. It is the quality of all that is intellectually excellent in Karl Marx; it is the clue to Thorstein Veblen's brilliant and ironic insight, to Joseph Schumpeter's many-sided constructions of reality; it is the basis of the psychological sweep of W. E. H. Lecky no less than of the profundity and clarity of Max Weber. And it is the signal of what is best in contemporary studies of man and society.

No social study that does not come back to the problems of biography, of history, and of their intersections within a society has completed its intellectual journey. Whatever the specific problems of the classic social analysts, however limited or however broad the features of social reality they have examined, those who have been imaginatively aware of the promise of their work have consistently asked three sorts of questions:

1. What is the structure of this particular society as a whole? What are its essential components, and how are they related to one another? How does it differ from other varieties of social order? Within it, what is the meaning of any particular feature for its continuance and for its change?

2. Where does this society stand in human history? What are the mechanics by which it is changing? What is its place within, and its meaning for, the development of humanity as a whole? How does any particular feature we are examining affect, and how is it affected by, the historical period in which it moves? And this period—what are its essential features? How does it differ from other periods? What are its characteristic ways of history-making?

3. What varieties of men and women now prevail in this society and in this period? And what varieties are coming to prevail? In what ways are they selected and formed, liberated and repressed, made sensitive and blunted? What kinds of "human nature" are revealed in the conduct and character we observe in this society in this period? And what is the meaning for "human nature" of each and every feature of the society we are examining?

Whether the point of interest is a great power state or a minor literary mood, a family, a prison, a creed—these are the kinds of questions the best social analysts have asked. They are the intellectual pivots of classic studies of man in society—and they are the questions inevitably raised by any mind possessing the sociological imagination. For that imagination is the capacity to shift from one perspective to another—from the political to the psychological; from examination of a single family to comparative assessment of the national budgets of the world; from the theological school to the military establishment; from considerations of an oil industry to studies of contemporary poetry. It is the capacity to range from the most impersonal and remote transformations to the most intimate features of the human self—and to see the relations between the two. Back of its use, there is always the urge to know the social and historical meaning of the individual in the society and in the period in which he has his quality and his being.

That, in brief, is why it is by means of the sociological imagination that men now hope to grasp what is going on in the world, and to understand what is happening in themselves as minute points of the intersections of biography and history within society. In large part, contemporary man's self-conscious view of himself as at least an outsider, if not a permanent stranger, rests upon an absorbed realization of social relativity and of the transformative power of history. The sociological imagination is the most fruitful form of this self-consciousness. By its use, men whose mentalities have swept only a series of limited orbits often come to feel as if suddenly awakened in a house with which they had only supposed themselves to be familiar. Correctly or incorrectly, they often come to feel that they can now provide themselves with adequate summations, cohesive assessments, comprehensive orientations. Older decisions that once appeared sound now seem to them products of a mind unaccountably dense. Their capacity for astonishment is made lively again. They acquire a new way of thinking, they experience a transvaluation of values: In a word, by their reflection and by their sensibility, they realize the cultural meaning of the social sciences.

Perhaps the most fruitful distinction with which the sociological imagination works is between the "personal troubles of milieu" and the "public issues of social structure." This distinction is an essential tool of the sociological imagination and a feature of all classic work in social science.

Troubles occur within the character of the individual and within the range of his immediate relations with others; they have to do with his self and with those limited areas of social life of which he is directly and personally aware. Accordingly, the statement and the resolution of troubles properly lie within the individual as a biographical entity and within the scope of his immediate milieu—the social setting that is directly open to his personal experience and, to some extent, his willful activity. A trouble is a private matter: Values cherished by an individual are felt by him to be threatened.

Issues have to do with matters that transcend these local environments of the individual and the range of his inner life. They have to do with the organization of many such milieux into the institutions of a historical society as a whole, with the ways in which various milieux overlap and interpenetrate to form the larger structure of social and historical life. An issue is a public matter: Some value cherished by publics is felt to be threatened. Often, there is a debate about what that value really is and about what it is that really threatens it. This debate is often without focus, if only because it is the very nature of an issue, unlike even widespread trouble, that it cannot very well be defined in terms of the immediate and everyday environments of ordinary men. An issue, in fact, often involves a crisis in institutional arrangements, and often, too, it involves what Marxists call "contradictions" or "antagonisms."

In these terms, consider unemployment. When, in a city of 100,000, only one man is unemployed, that is his personal trouble, and for its relief we properly look to the character of the man, his skills, and his immediate opportunities. But when, in a nation of 50 million employees, 15 million men are unemployed, that is an issue, and we may not hope to find its solution within the range of opportunities open to any one individual. The very structure of opportunities has collapsed. Both the correct statement of the problem and the range of possible solutions require us to consider the economic and political institutions of the society, and not merely the personal situation and character of a scatter of individuals.

Consider war. The personal problem of war, when it occurs, may be how to survive it or how to die in it with honor; how to make money out of it; how to climb into the higher safety of the military apparatus; or how to contribute to the war's termination. In short, according to one's values, to find a set of milieux and within it to survive the war or make one's death in it meaningful. But the structural issues of war have to do with its causes; with what types of men it throws up into command; with its effects upon economic and political, family and religious institutions, with the unorganized irresponsibility of a world of nation-states.

Consider marriage. Inside a marriage, a man and a woman may experience personal troubles; but, when the divorce rate during the first four years of marriage is 250 out of every 1,000 attempts, this is an indication of a structural issue having to do with the institutions of marriage and the family and other institutions that bear upon them.

Or consider the metropolis—the horrible, beautiful, ugly, magnificent sprawl of the great city. For many upper-class people, the personal solution to the problem of the city is to have an apartment with private garage under it in the heart of the city, and, forty miles out, a house by Henry Hill, garden by Garrett Eckbo, on a hundred acres of private land. In these two controlled environments—with a small staff at each end and a private helicopter connection—most people could solve many of the problems of personal milieux caused by the facts of the city. But all this, however splendid, does not solve the public issues that the structural fact of the city poses. What should be done with this wonderful monstrosity? Break it all up into scattered units, combining residence and work? Refurbish it as it stands? Or, after evacuation, dynamite it and build new cities according to new plans in new places? What should those plans be? And who is to decide and to accomplish whatever choice is made? These are structural issues; to confront them and to solve them requires us to consider political and economic issues that affect innumerable milieux.

Insofar as an economy is so arranged that slumps occur, the problem of unemployment becomes incapable of personal solution. Insofar as war is inherent in the nation-state system and in the uneven industrialization of the world, the ordinary individual in his restricted milieu will be powerless —with or without psychiatric aid—to solve the troubles this system or lack of system imposes upon him. Insofar as the family as an institution turns women into darling little slaves and men into their chief providers and unweaned dependents, the problem of a satisfactory marriage remains incapable of purely private solution. Insofar as the overdeveloped megalopolis and the overdeveloped automobile are built-in features of the overdeveloped society, the issues of urban living will not be solved by personal ingenuity and private wealth.

What we experience in various and specific milieux, I have noted, is often caused by structural changes. Accordingly, to understand the changes of many personal milieux, we are required to look beyond them. And the number and variety of such structural changes increase as the institutions within which we live become more embracing and more intricately connected with one another. To be aware of the idea of social structure and to use it with sensibility is to be capable of tracing such linkages among a great variety of milieux. To be able to do that is to possess the sociological imagination.

What are the major issues for publics and the key troubles of private individuals in our time? To formulate issues and troubles, we must ask what values are cherished yet threatened, and what values are cherished and supported, by the characterizing trends of our period. In the case both of threat and of support, we must ask what salient contradictions of structure may be involved.

When people cherish some set of values and do not feel any threat to them, they experience *well-being*. When they cherish values but *do* feel them to be threatened, they experience a crisis—either as a personal trouble or as a public issue. And, if all their values seem involved, they feel the total threat of panic.

But suppose people are neither aware of any cherished values nor experience any threat? That is the experience of *indifference*, which, if it seems to involve all their values, becomes apathy. Suppose, finally, they are unaware of any cherished values, but still are very much aware of a threat? That is the experience of *uneasiness, of anxiety*, which, if it is total enough, becomes a deadly, unspecified malaise.

Ours is a time of uneasiness and indifference—not yet formulated in such ways as to permit the work of reason and the play of sensibility. Instead of troubles—defined in terms of values and threats—there is often the misery of vague uneasiness; instead of explicit issues, there is often merely the beat feeling that all is somehow not right. Neither the values threatened nor whatever threatens them has been stated; in short, they have not been carried to the point of-decision. Much less have they been formulated as problems of social science.

In the 1930's, there was little doubt—except among certain deluded business circles—that there was an economic issue that was also a pack of personal troubles. In these arguments about the "crisis of capitalism," the formulations of Marx and the many unacknowledged reformulations of his work probably set the leading terms of the issue, and some men came to understand their personal troubles in these terms. The values threatened were plain to see and cherished by all; the structural contradictions that threatened them also seemed plain. Both were widely and deeply experienced. It was a political age.

But the values threatened in the era after World War II are often neither widely acknowledged as values nor widely felt to be threatened. Much private uneasiness goes unformulated; much public malaise and many decisions of enormous structural relevance never become public issues. For those who accept such inherited values as reason and freedom, it is the uneasiness itself that is the trouble; it is the indifference itself that is the issue. And it is this condition, of uneasiness and indifference, that is the signal feature of our period.

UNEASINESS
AND
APATHY
TODAY

All this is so striking that it is often interpreted by observers as a shift in the very kinds of problems that need now to be formulated. We are frequently told that the problems of our decade, or even the crises of our period, have shifted from the external realm of economics and now have to do with the quality of individual life—in fact, with the question of whether there is soon going to be anything that can properly be called individual life. Not child labor but comic books, not poverty but mass leisure, are at the center of concern. Many great public issues as well as many private troubles are described in terms of the "psychiatric"—often, it seems, in a pathetic attempt to avoid the large issues and problems of modern society. Often, this statement seems to rest upon a provincial narrowing of interest to the Western societies, or even to the United States—thus ignoring two-thirds of mankind; often, too, it arbitrarily divorces the individual life from the larger institutions within which that life is enacted, and which on occasion bear upon it more grievously than do the intimate environments of childhood.

Problems of leisure, for example, cannot even be stated without considering problems of work. Family troubles over comic books cannot be formulated as problems without considering the plight of the contemporary family in its new relations with the newer institutions of the social structure. Neither leisure nor its debilitating uses can be understood as problems without recognition of the extent to which malaise and indifference now form the social and personal climate of contemporary American society. In this climate, no problems of the "private life" can be stated and solved without recognition of the crisis of ambition that is part of the very career of men at work in the incorporated economy.

It is true, as psychoanalysts continually point out, that people do often have the "increasing sense of being moved by obscure forces within themselves that they are unable to define." But it is *not* true, as Ernest Jones asserted, that "man's chief enemy and danger is his own unruly nature and the dark forces pent up within him." On the contrary: "Man's chief danger" today lies in the unruly forces of contemporary society itself, with its alienating methods of production, its enveloping techniques of political domination, its international anarchy—in a word, its pervasive transformations of the very "nature" of man and the conditions and aims of his life.

It is now the social scientist's foremost political and intellectual task—for here the two coincide—to make clear the elements of contemporary uneasiness and indifference. It is the central demand made upon him by other cultural workmen—by physical scientists and artists, by the intellectual community in general. It is because of this task and these demands, I believe, that the social sciences are becoming the common denominator of our cultural period, and the sociological imagination, our most needed quality of mind.

* * *

Is Sociology Value-free?

Anti-Minotaur: The Myth of a Value-free Sociology*

Alvin W. Gouldner

This is an account of a myth created by and about a magnificent minotaur named Max—Max Weber, to be exact; his myth was that social science should and could be value-free. The lair of this minotaur, although reached only by a labyrinthian logic and visited only by a few who never return, is still regarded by many sociologists as a holy place. In particular, as sociologists grow older they seem impelled to make a pilgrimage to it and to pay their respects to the problem of the relations between values and social science.

Considering the perils of the visit, their motives are somewhat perplexing. Perhaps their quest is the first sign of professional senility; perhaps it is the last sigh of youthful yearnings. And perhaps a concern with the value problems is just a way of trying to take back something that was, in youthful enthusiasm, given too hastily.

In any event, the myth of a value-free sociology has been a conquering one. Today, all the powers of sociology, from Parsons to Lundberg, have entered into a tacit alliance to bind us to the dogma that "Thou shalt not commit a value judgment," especially as sociologists. Where is the introductory textbook, where the lecture course on principles, that does not affirm or imply this rule?

In the end, we cannot disprove the existence of minotaurs, who, after all, are thought to be sacred precisely because, being half-man and half-bull, they are so unlikely. The thing to see is that a belief in them is not so much untrue as it is absurd. Like Berkeley's argument for solipsism, Weber's brief for a value-free sociology is a tight one and, some say, logically unassail-

* From *Social Problems,* vol. 9, no. 3 (Winter, 1962). Reprinted by permission of The Society for the Study of Social Problems.

able; yet, it, too, is absurd. Both arguments appeal to reason but ignore experience.

I do not here wish to enter into an examination of the *logical* arguments involved, not because I regard them as incontrovertible, but because I find them less interesting to me as a sociologist. Instead, what I will do is to view the belief in a value-free sociology in the same manner that sociologists examine any element in the ideology of any group. This means that we will look upon the sociologist just as we would any other occupation, be it the taxicab driver, the nurse, the coal miner, or the physician. In short, I will look at the belief in a value-free sociology as part of the ideology of a working group and from the standpoint of the sociology of occupations.

The image of a value-free sociology is more than a neat intellectual theorem demanded as a sacrifice to reason; it is also a felt conception of a role and a set of more or less shared sentiments as to how sociologists should live. We may be sure that it became this not simply because it is true or logically elegant, but, also, because it is somehow useful to those who believe in it. Applauding the dancer for her grace is often the audience's way of concealing its lust.

That we are in the presence of a group myth, rather than a carefully formulated and well-validated belief appropriate to scientists, may be discerned if we ask, just what is it that is believed by those holding sociology to be a value-free discipline? Does the belief in a value-free sociology mean that, in point of fact, sociology is a discipline actually free of values, and that it successfully excludes all nonscientific assumptions in selecting, studying, and reporting on a problem? Or does it mean that sociology should do so? Clearly, the first is untrue, and I know of no one who even holds it possible for sociologists to exclude completely their nonscientific beliefs from their scientific work; and, if this is so, on what grounds can this impossible task be morally incumbent on sociologists?

Does the belief in a value-free sociology mean that sociologists cannot, do not, or should not make value judgments concerning things outside their sphere of technical competence? But what has technical competence to do with the making of value judgments? If technical competence does provide a warrant for making value judgments, then there is nothing to prohibit sociologists from making them within the area of their expertise. If, on the contrary, technical competence provides no warrant for making value judgments, then, at least, sociologists are as free to do so as anyone else; their value judgments are at least as good as anyone else's—say, a twelve-year-old child's. And, if technical competence provides no warrant for making value judgments, then what does?

I fear that there are many sociologists today who, in conceiving social science to be value-free, mean widely different things; that many hold these beliefs dogmatically without having examined seriously the grounds upon which they are credible; and that some few affirm a value-free sociology ritualistically without having any clear idea of what it might mean. Weber's own views on the relation between values and social science are scarcely identical with some held today. While Weber saw grave hazards in the sociologist's expression of value judgments, he also held that these might be voiced if caution were exercised to distinguish them from statements of fact. If Weber insisted on the need to maintain scientific objectivity, he also warned that this was altogether different from moral indifference.

Not only was the cautious expression of value judgments deemed permissible by Weber, but, he emphasized, these were positively mandatory under certain circumstances. Although Weber inveighed against the professorial "cult of personality," we might also remember that he was not against all value-imbued cults, and that he himself worshipped at the shrine of individual responsibility. A familiarity with Weber's work on these points would only be embarrassing to many who today affirm a value-free sociology in his name.

What, to Weber, was an agonizing expression of a highly personal faith, intensely felt and painstakingly argued, has today become a hollow catechism, a password, and a good excuse for no longer thinking seriously. It has become increasingly the trivial token of professional respectability, the caste mark of the decorous; it has become the gentleman's promise that boats will not be rocked. Rather than showing Weber's work the respect that it deserves, by carefully re-evaluating it in the light of our own generation's experience, we reflexively reiterate it even as we distort it to our own purposes. Ignorance of the gods is no excuse; but it can be convenient. For, if the worshipper never visits the altar of his god, then he can never learn whether the fire still burns there, or whether the priests, grown fat, are simply sifting the ashes.

The needs that the value-free conception of social science serves are both personal and institutional. Briefly, my contention will be that one of the main institutional forces facilitating the survival and spread of the value-free myth was its usefulness in maintaining both the cohesion and the autonomy of the modern university, in general, and the newer social science disciplines, in particular. There is little difficulty, at any rate, in demonstrating that these were among the motives originally inducing Max Weber to formulate the conception of a value-free sociology.

This issue might be opened at a seemingly peripheral and petty point; namely, when Weber abruptly mentions the problem of competition among professors for students. Weber notes that professors who do express a value stand are more likely to attract students than those who do not and are, therefore, likely to have undue career advantages. In effect, this is a complaint against a kind of unfair competition by professors who pander to student interests. Weber's hope seems to have been that the value-free principle would serve as a kind of "Fair Trades Act" to restrain such competition.

This suggests that one of the latent functions of the value-free doctrine is to bring peace to the academic house, by reducing competition for students, and, in turn, it directs us to some of the institutional peculiarities of German universities in Weber's time. Unlike the situation in the American university, career advancement in the German university was then felt to depend too largely on the professor's popularity as a teacher; indeed, at the lower ranks, the instructor's income was directly dependent on student enrollment. As a result, the competition for students was particularly keen, and it was felt that the system penalized good scholars and researchers in favor of attractive teaching. In contrast, of course, the American system has been commonly accused of overstressing scholarly publication, and the typical complaint is that good teaching goes unrewarded, and that you must "publish or perish." In the context of the German academic system, Weber was raising no trivial point when he intimated that the value-free doctrine would reduce academic competition. He was linking the doctrine to guild problems and anchoring this lofty question to academicians' earthy interests.

Weber also opposed the use of the lecture hall as an arena of value affirmation by arguing that it subjects the student to a pressure he is unable to evaluate or resist adequately. Given the comparatively exalted position of the professor in German society, and given the one-sided communication inherent in the lecture hall, Weber did have a point. His fears were, perhaps, all the more justified if we accept a view of the German "national character" as being authoritarian—in Nietzsche's terms, a combination of arrogance and servility. But these considerations do not hold with anything like equal cogency in more democratic cultures such as our own. For, here, not only are professors held in more modest esteem, but the specific ideology of education itself stresses the desirability of student initiative and participation, and there is more of a systematic solicitation of the student's "own" views in small "discussion" sections. There is little student servility to complement and encourage occasional professorial arrogance.

When Weber condemned the lecture hall as a forum for value affirmation, he had in mind most particularly the expression of political values. The point of Weber's polemic is not directed against all values with equal sharpness. It was not the expression of aesthetic or even religious values that Weber sees as most objectionable in the university but, primarily, those of politics. His promotion of the value-free doctrine may, then, be seen not so much as an effort to amoralize as to depoliticize the university and to remove it from the political struggle. The political conflicts then echoing in the German university did not entail comparatively narrow differences, such as those now between Democrats and Republicans in the United States. Weber's proposal of the value-free doctrine was, in part, an effort to establish a *modus vivendi* among academicians whose political commitments were often intensely felt and in violent opposition.

Under these historical conditions, the value-free doctrine was a proposal for an academic truce. It said, in effect, if we all keep quiet about our political views, then we may all be able to get on with our work. But, if the value-free principle was suitable in Weber's Germany, because it served to restrain political passions, is it equally useful in America today, where not only is there pitiable little difference in politics, but men often have no politics at all? Perhaps the need of the American university today, as of American society more generally, is for more commitment to politics and for more diversity of political views. It would seem that now the national need is to take the lid off, not to screw it on more tightly.

Given the historically unique conditions of nuclear warfare, where the issue would not be decided in a long-drawn-out war requiring the sustained cohesion of mass populations, national consensus is no longer, I believe, as important a condition of national survival as it once was. But, if we no longer require the same degree of unanimity to fight a war, we do require a greater ferment of ideas and a radiating growth of political seriousness and ·variety within which alone we may find a way to prevent war. Important contributions to this have been made and may further be made by members of the academic community, perhaps especially by its social-science sector. The question arises, however, whether this group's political intelligence can ever be adequately mobilized for these purposes so long as it remains tranquilized by the value-free doctrine.

Throughout his work, Weber's strategy is to safeguard the integrity and freedom of action of both the state, as the instrument of German national policy, and the university, as the embodiment of a larger Western tradition of rationalism. He feared that the expression of political value judgments in the university would provoke the state into censoring the university and would imperil its autonomy. Indeed, Weber argues that professors are not entitled to freedom from state control in matters of values, since these do not rest on their specialized qualifications.

This view will seem curious only to those regarding Weber as a liberal in the Anglo-American sense: that is, as one who wishes to delimit the state's powers on behalf of the individual's liberties. Actually, however, Weber aimed not at curtailing but at strengthening the powers of the German state and making it a more effective instrument of German nationalism. It would seem, however, that an argument contrary to the one he advances is at least as consistent; namely, that professors are, like all others, entitled and perhaps obligated to express their values. In other words, professors have a right to profess. Rather than being made the objects of special suspicion and special control by the state, they are no less (and no more) entitled than others to the trust and protection of the state.

In a *Realpolitik* vein, Weber acknowledges that the most basic national questions cannot ordinarily be discussed with full freedom in government universities. Since the discussion there cannot be completely free and all-sided, he apparently concludes that it is fitting that there should be no discussion at all, rather than risk partisanship. But this is too pious by far. Even Socrates never insisted that all views must be at hand before the dialogue could begin. Here again, one might as reasonably argue to the contrary, that one limitation of freedom is no excuse for another. Granting the reality of efforts to inhibit unpopular views in the university, it seems odd to prescribe self-suppression as a way of avoiding external suppression. Suicide does not seem a reasonable way to avoid being murdered. It appears, however, that Weber was so intent on safeguarding the autonomy of the university and the autonomy of politics that he was willing to pay almost any price to do so, even if this led the university to detach itself from one of the basic intellectual traditions of the West—the dialectical exploration of the fundamental purposes of human life.

Insofar as the value-free doctrine is a mode of ensuring professional autonomy, it does not, as such, entail an interest peculiar to the social sciences. In this regard, as a substantial body of research in the sociology of occupations indicates, social scientists are kin to plumbers, house painters, or librarians. Most, if not all, occupations seek to elude control by outsiders and manifest a drive to maintain exclusive control over their practitioners.

Without doubt, the value-free principle did enhance the autonomy of sociology; it was one way in which our discipline pried itself loose—in some modest measure—from the clutch of its society, in Europe freer from political party influence, in the United States freer of ministerial influence. In both places, the value-free doctrine gave sociology a larger area of autonomy in which it could steadily pursue basic problems rather than journalistically react to passing events, and it gained more freedom to pursue questions uninteresting either to the respectable or to the rebellious. It made sociology freer—as Comte had wanted it to be—to pursue all its own theoretical implications. The value-free principle did, I think, contribute to the intellectual growth and emancipation of our enterprise.

There was another kind of freedom that the value-free doctrine also allowed: It enhanced a freedom from moral compulsiveness and permitted a partial escape from the parochial prescriptions of the sociologist's local or native culture. Above all, effective internationalization of the value-free principle has always encouraged at least a temporary suspension of the moralizing reflexes built into the sociologist by his own society. From one perspective, this, of course, has its dangers—a disorienting normlessness and moral indifference. From another standpoint, however, the value-free principle might also have provided a moral as well as an intellectual opportunity. Insofar as moral reactions are only suspended and not aborted, and insofar as this is done in the service of knowledge and intellectual discipline, then, in effect, the value-free principle strengthened Reason (or Ego) against the compulsive demands of a merely traditional morality. To this degree, the value-free discipline provided a foundation for the development of more reliable knowledge about men and, also, established a breathing space within which moral reactions could be less mechanical and in which morality could be reinvigorated.

The value-free doctrine thus had a paradoxical potentiality: It might enable men to make better value judgments rather than none at all. It could encourage a habit of mind that might help men in discriminating between their punitive drives and their ethical sentiments. Moralistic reflexes suspended, it was now more possible to sift conscience with the rod of reason and to cultivate moral judgments that expressed a man's total char-

BENEFITS of VALUE-FREE

acter as an adult person; he need not now live quite so much by his past parental programming but in terms of his more mature present.

The value-free doctrine could have meant an opportunity for a more authentic morality. It could and sometimes did aid men in transcending the morality of their "tribe" by opening themselves to the diverse moralities of unfamiliar groups and by seeing themselves and others from the standpoint of a wider range of significant cultures.

Doubtless, there were some who did use the opportunity thus presented; but there were also many who used the value-free postulate as an excuse for pursuing their private impulses to the neglect of their public responsibilities and who, far from becoming more morally sensitive, became morally jaded. Insofar as the value-free doctrine failed to realize its potentialities, it did so because its deepest impulses were—as we shall note later—dualistic; it invited men to stress the separation and not the mutual connectedness of facts and values; it had the vice of its virtues. In short, the conception of a value-free sociology has had diverse consequences, not all of them useful or flattering to the social sciences.

On the negative side, it may be noted that the value-free doctrine is useful both to those who want to escape from the world and to those who want to escape into it. It is useful to those young, or not so young, men who live off sociology rather than for it, and who think of sociology as a way of getting ahead in the world by providing them with neutral techniques that may be sold on the open market to any buyer. The belief that it is not the business of a sociologist to make value judgments is taken, by some, to mean that the market on which they can vend their skills is unlimited. From such a standpoint, there is no reason why one cannot sell one's knowledge to spread a disease just as freely as he can to fight it. Indeed, some sociologists have had no hesitation about doing market research designed to sell more cigarettes, although well aware of the implication of recent cancer research. In brief, the value-free doctrine of social science was sometimes used to justify the sale of one's talents to the highest bidder and is, far from new, a contemporary version of the most ancient sophistry.

In still other cases, the image of a value-free sociology is the armor of the alienated sociologist's self. Although C. Wright Mills may be right in saying this is the Age of Sociology, not a few sociologists, Mills included, have felt estranged and isolated from their society. They feel impotent to contribute usefully to the solution of its deepening problems, and, even when they can, they fear that the terms of such an involvement require them to submit to a commercial debasement or a narrow partisanship, rather than contributing to a truly public interest.

Many sociologists feel themselves cut off from the larger community of liberal intellectuals, in whose satire they see themselves as ridiculous caricatures. Estranged from the larger world, they cannot escape in fantasies of posthumous medals and by living huddled behind self-barricaded intellectual ghettoes. Self-doubt finds its anodyne in the image of a value-free sociology, because this transforms their alienation into an intellectual principle; it evokes the soothing illusion, among some sociologists, that their exclusion from the larger society is a self-imposed duty rather than an externally imposed constraint.

Once committed to the premise of a value-free sociology, such sociologists are bound to a policy that can only alienate them further from the surrounding world. Social science can never be fully accepted in a society, or by a part of it, without paying its way; this means it must manifest both its relevance and its concern for the contemporary human predicament. Unless the value relevance of sociological inquiry is made plainly evident, unless there are at least some bridges between it and larger human hopes and purposes, it must inevitably be scorned by laymen as pretentious word-mongering. But the manner in which some sociologists conceive the value-free doctrine disposes them to ignore current human problems and to huddle together like old men seeking mutual warmth. "This is not our job," they say, "and if it were we would not know enough to do it. Go away, come back when we're grown up," say these old men. The issue, however, is not whether we know enough; the real questions are whether we have the courage to say and use what we do know and whether anyone knows more.

* * *

The problem of a value-free sociology has its most poignant implications for the social scientist in his role as educator. If sociologists ought not to express their personal values in the academic setting, how, then, are students to be safeguarded against the unwitting influence of these values that shape the sociologist's selection of problems, his preferences for certain hypotheses or conceptual schemes, and his neglect of others? For these are unavoidable; and, in this sense, there is and can be no value-free sociology. The only choice is between an expression of one's values, as open and honest as it can be this side of the psychoanalytical couch, and a vain ritual of moral neutrality that, because it invites men to ignore the vulnerability of reason to bias, leaves it at the mercy of irrationality.

If truth is the vital thing, as Weber is reputed to have said on his death-bed, then it must be all the truth we have to give, as best we know it, being painfully aware, and making our students aware, that even as we offer it we may be engaged in unwitting concealment rather than revelation. If we would teach students how science is made, really made rather than as publicly reported, we cannot fail to expose them to the whole scientist by whom it is made, with all his gifts and blindnesses, with all his methods and his values as well. To do otherwise is to usher in an era of spiritless technicians who will be no less lacking in understanding than they are in passion, and who will be useful only because they can be used.

In the end, even these dull tools will build, through patient persistence and cumulation, a technology of social science strong enough to cripple us. Far as we are from a sociological atomic bomb, we already live in a world of the systematic brainwashing of prisoners of war and of housewives with their advertising-exacerbated compulsions; and the social-science technology of tomorrow can hardly fail to be more powerful than today's.

It would seem that social science's affinity for modeling itself after physical science might lead to instruction in matters other than research alone. Before Hiroshima, physicists also talked of a value-free science; they, too, vowed to make no value judgments. Today, many of them are not so sure. If, today, we concern ourselves exclusively with the technical proficiency of our students and reject all responsibility for their moral sense, or lack of it, then we may someday be compelled to accept responsibility for having trained a generation willing to serve in a future Auschwitz. Granted that science always has inherent in it both constructive and destructive potentialities, it does not follow that we should encourage our students to be oblivious to the difference. Nor does this in any degree detract from the indispensable norms of scientific objectivity; it merely insists that these differ radically from moral indifference.

* * *

Problems in Doing Sociological Research

Body Ritual Among the Nacirema*
Horace Miner

The anthropologist has become so familiar with the diversity of ways in which different peoples behave in similar situations that he is not apt to be surprised by even the most exotic customs. In fact, if all of the logically possible combinations of behavior have not been found somewhere in the world, he is apt to suspect that they must be present in some yet undescribed tribe. This point has, in fact, been expressed with respect to clan organization by Murdock (1949:71). In this light, the magical beliefs and practices of the Nacirema present such unusual aspects that it seems desirable to describe them as an example of the extremes to which human behavior can go.

Professor Linton first brought the ritual of the Nacirema to the attention of anthropologists twenty years ago (1936:326), but the culture of this people is still very poorly understood. They are a North American group living in the territory between the Canadian Cree, the Yaqui and Tarahumare of Mexico, and the Carib and Arawak of the Antilles. Little is known of their origin, although tradition states that they came from the east. Ac-

* Reproduced by permission of the American Anthropological Association from *American Anthropologist,* vol. 58, no. 3 (1956), pp. 503–7.

cording to Nacirema mythology, their nation was originated by a culture hero, Notgnihsaw, who is otherwise known for two great feats of strength— the throwing of a piece of wampum across the river Pa-To-Mac and the chopping down of a cherry tree in which the Spirit of Truth resided.

Nacirema culture is characterized by a highly developed market economy that has evolved in a rich natural habitat. While much of the people's time is devoted to economic pursuits, a large part of the fruits of these labors and a considerable portion of the day are spent in ritual activity. The focus of this activity is the human body, the appearance and health of which loom as a dominant concern in the ethos of the people. While such a concern is certainly not unusual, its ceremonial aspects and associated philosophy are unique.

The fundamental belief underlying the whole system appears to be that the human body is ugly, and that its natural tendency is to debility and disease. Incarcerated in such a body, man's only hope is to avert these characteristics through the use of the powerful influences of ritual and ceremony. Every household has one or more shrines devoted to this purpose. The more powerful individuals in the society have several shrines in their houses, and, in fact, the opulence of a house is often referred to in terms of the number of such ritual centers it possesses. Most houses are of wattle and daub construction, but the shrine rooms of the more wealthy are walled with stone. Poorer families imitate the rich by applying pottery plaques to their shrine walls.

While each family has at least one such shrine, the rituals associated with it are not family ceremonies but are private and secret. The rites are normally only discussed with children, and then only during the period when they are being initiated into these mysteries. I was able, however, to establish sufficient rapport with the natives to examine these shrines and to have the rituals described to me.

The focal point of the shrine is a box or chest, which is built into the wall. In this chest are kept the many charms and magical potions without which no native believes he could live. These preparations are secured from a variety of specialized practitioners. The most powerful of these are the medicine men, whose assistance must be rewarded with substantial gifts. However, the medicine men do not provide the curative potions for their clients but decide what the ingredients should be and then write them down in an ancient and secret language. This writing is understood only by the medicine men and by the herbalists who, for another gift, provide the required charm.

The charm is not disposed of after it has served its purpose but is placed in the charm-box of the household shrine. As these magical materials are specific for certain ills, and the real or imagined maladies of the people are many, the charm-box is usually full to overflowing. The magical packets are so numerous that people forget what their purposes were and fear to use them again. While the natives are very vague on this point, we can only assume that the idea in retaining all the old magical materials is that their presence in the charm-box, before which the body rituals are conducted, will in some way protect the worshipper.

Beneath the charm-box is a small font. Each day, every member of the family, in succession, enters the shrine room, bows his head before the charm-box, mingles different sorts of holy waters in the font, and proceeds with a brief rite of ablution. The holy waters are secured from the Water Temple of the community, where the priests conduct elaborate ceremonies to make the liquid ritually pure.

In the hierarchy of magical practitioners, and below the medicine men in prestige, are specialists whose designation is best translated "holy-mouth-men." The Nacirema have an almost pathological horror of, and fascination with, the mouth, the condition of which is believed to have a supernatural influence on all social relationships. Were it not for the rituals of the mouth, they believe that their teeth would fall out, their gums bleed, their jaws shrink, their friends desert them, and their lovers reject them. They also believe that a strong relationship exists between oral and moral characteristics. For example, there is a ritual ablution of the mouth for children that is supposed to improve their moral fiber.

The daily body ritual performed by everyone includes a mouth-rite. Despite the fact that these people are so punctilious about care of the mouth, this rite involves a practice that strikes the uninitiated stranger as revolting. It was reported to me that the ritual consists of inserting a small bundle of hog hairs into the. mouth, along with certain magical powders, and then moving the bundle in a highly formalized series of gestures.

In addition to the private mouth-rite, the people seek out a holy-mouth-man once or twice a year. These practitioners have an impressive set of paraphernalia, consisting of a variety of augers, awls, probes, and prods. The use of these objects in the exorcism of the evils of the mouth involves almost unbelievable ritual torture of the client. The holy-mouth-man opens the client's mouth and, using the above-mentioned tools, enlarges any holes that decay may have created in the teeth. Magical materials are put into these holes. If there are no naturally occurring holes in the teeth, large sections of one or more teeth are gouged out so that the supernatural substance can be applied. In the client's view, the purpose of these ministrations is to arrest decay and to draw friends. The extremely sacred and traditional character of the rite is evident in the fact that the natives return to the holy-mouth-men year after year, despite the fact that their teeth continue to decay.

It is to be hoped that, when a thorough study of the Nacirema is made, there will be careful inquiry into the personality structure of these people. One has but to watch the gleam in the eye of a holy-mouth-man, as he jabs an awl into an exposed nerve, to suspect that a certain amount of sadism is involved. If this can be established, a very interesting pattern emerges, for most of the population shows definite masochistic tendencies. It was to these that Professor Linton referred in discussing a distinctive part of the daily body ritual that is performed only by men. This part of the rite involves scraping and lacerating the surface of the face with a sharp instrument. Special women's rites are performed only four times during each lunar month, but what they lack in frequency is made up in barbarity. As part of this ceremony, women bake their heads in small ovens for about an hour. The theoretically interesting point is that what seems to be a preponderantly masochistic people have developed sadistic specialists.

The medicine men have an imposing temple, or *latipso,* in every community of any size. The more elaborate ceremonies required to treat very sick patients can be performed only at this temple. These ceremonies involve not only the thaumaturge but a permanent group of vestal maidens who move sedately about the temple chambers in distinctive costume and headdress.

The *latipso* ceremonies are so harsh that it is phenomenal that a fair proportion of the really sick natives who enter the temple ever recover. Small children whose indoctrination is still incomplete have been known to resist attempts to take them to the temple, because "that is where you go to die." Despite this fact, sick adults are not only willing but eager to undergo the protracted ritual purification, if they can afford to do so. No matter how ill the supplicant or how grave the emergency, the guardians of many temples will not admit a client if he cannot give a rich gift to the custodian. Even after one has gained admission and survived the ceremonies, the guardians will not permit the neophyte to leave until he makes still another gift.

The supplicant entering the temple is first stripped of all his or her clothes. In everyday life, the Nacirema avoids exposure of his body and its natural functions. Bathing and excretory acts are performed only in the secrecy of the household shrine, where they are ritualized as part of the body-rites. Psychological shock results from the fact that body secrecy is suddenly lost upon entry into the *latipso.* A man whose own wife has never seen him in an excretory act suddenly finds himself naked and assisted by a vestal maiden while he performs his natural functions into a sacred vessel. This sort of ceremonial treatment is necessitated by the fact that the excreta are used by a diviner to ascertain the course and nature of the client's sickness. Female clients, on the other hand, find their naked bodies are subjected to the scrutiny, manipulation, and prodding of the medicine men.

Few supplicants in the temple are well enough to do anything but lie on their hard beds. The daily ceremonies, like the rites of the holy-mouth-men, involve discomfort and torture. With ritual precision, the vestals awaken their miserable charges each dawn and roll them about on their beds of pain while performing ablutions, in the formal movements of which the maidens are highly trained. At other times, they insert magic wands into the supplicant's mouth or force him to eat substances that are supposed to be healing. From time to time, the medicine men come to their clients and jab magically treated needles into their flesh. The fact that these temple ceremonies may not cure, and may even kill, the neophyte in no way decreases the people's faith in the medicine men.

There remains one other kind of practitioner, known as a "listener." This witch doctor has the power to exorcise the devils that lodge in the heads of people who have been bewitched. The Nacirema believe that parents bewitch their own children. Mothers are particularly suspected of putting a curse on children while teaching them the secret body rituals. The counter-magic of the witch doctor is unusual in its lack of ritual. The patient simply tells the "listener" all his troubles and fears, beginning with the earliest difficulties he can remember. The memory displayed by the Nacirema in these exorcism sessions is truly remarkable. It is not uncommon for the patient to bemoan the rejection he felt upon being weaned as a babe, and a few individuals even see their troubles going back to the traumatic effects of their own birth.

In conclusion, mention must be made of certain practices that have their base in native esthetics, but which depend upon the pervasive aversion to the natural body and its functions. There are ritual fasts to make fat people thin and ceremonial feasts to make thin people fat. Still other rites are used to make women's breasts larger if they are small, and smaller if they are large. General dissatisfaction with breast shape is symbolized in the fact that the ideal form is virtually outside the range of human variation. A few women afflicted with almost inhuman hypermammary development are so idolized that they make a handsome living by simply going from village to village and permitting the natives to stare at them for a fee.

Reference has already been made to the fact that excretory functions are ritualized, routinized, and relegated to secrecy. Natural reproductive functions are similarly distorted. Intercourse is taboo as a topic and scheduled as an act. Efforts are made to avoid pregnancy by the use of magical materials or by limiting intercourse to certain phases of the moon. Conception is actually very infrequent. When pregnant, women dress so as to hide their condition. Parturition takes place in secret, without friends or relatives to assist, and the majority of women do not nurse their infants.

Our review of the ritual life of the Nacirema has certainly shown them to be a magic-ridden people. It is hard to understand how they have managed to exist so long under the burdens they have imposed upon themselves. But even such exotic customs as these take on real meaning when they are viewed with the insight provided by Malinowski when he wrote (1948:70):

> Looking from far and above, from our high places of safety in the developed civilization, it is easy to see all the crudity and irrelevance of magic. But without its power and guidance early man could not have mastered his practical difficulties as he has done, nor could man have advanced to the higher stages of civilization.

REFERENCES

LINTON, RALPH. *The Study of Man* (New York: D. Appleton-Century Co., 1936).

MALINOWSKI, BRONISLAW. *Magic, Science, and Religion* (Glencoe, Ill.: The Free Press, 1948).

MURDOCK, GEORGE P. *Social Structure* (New York: The Macmillan Co., 1949).

1. SUGGESTIONS FOR FURTHER READING

BATES, ALAN. *The Sociological Enterprise* (Boston: Houghton Mifflin, 1967).*
BENSMAN, JOSEPH, ARTHUR VIDICH, and MAURICE STEIN (eds.). *Reflections on Community Studies* (New York: John Wiley & Sons, 1964).
BERGER, PETER. *Invitation to Sociology* (Garden City, N.Y.: Doubleday, 1963).*
CAMERON, WILLIAM. *Informal Sociology* (New York: Random House, 1961).*
DOUGLAS, JACK (ed.). *The Relevance of Sociology* (New York: Appleton, 1970).*
FESTINGER, LEON, and DANIEL KATZ (eds.). *Research Methods in the Behavioral Sciences* (New York: Holt, Rinehart, 1953).
GOODE, W. J., and P. K. HATT. *Methods of Social Research* (New York: McGraw-Hill, 1952).
GOULDNER, ALVIN. *The Coming Crisis of Western Sociology* (New York: Basic Books, 1970).*
HAMMOND, PHILLIP (ed.). *Sociologists at Work* (New York: Basic Books, 1964).*
HINKLE, ROSCOE, and GISELLA HINKLE. *Development of Modern Sociology* (New York: Random House, 1954).*
HUGHES, H. STUART. *Consciousness and Society* (New York: Random House, 1961).*
INKELES, ALEX. *What Is Sociology?* (Englewood Cliffs, N.J.: Prentice-Hall, 1964).*
KAPLAN, ABRAHAM. *The Conduct of Inquiry* (San Francisco: Chandler, 1964).*
MADGE, JOHN. *Origins of Scientific Sociology* (New York: The Free Press, 1962).*
MARTINDALE, DON. *The Nature and Types of Sociological Theory* (Boston: Houghton Mifflin, 1960).
MILLS, C. WRIGHT. *The Sociological Imagination* (New York: Oxford University Press, 1959).*
NISBET, ROBERT. *The Sociological Tradition* (New York: Basic Books, 1966).
PARSONS, TALCOTT, *et al.* (eds.). *Theories of Society* (New York: The Free Press, 1961).
SHOSTAK, ARTHUR. *Putting Sociology to Work: Case Studies in the Application of Sociology to Modern Social Problems* (New York: David McKay, 1974).*
———— (ed.). *Sociology in Action* (Homewood, Ill.: Dorsey Press, 1966).*
TANUR, JUDITH, *et al. Statistics: A Guide to the Unknown* (San Francisco: Holden-Day, 1972).*
TIMASHEFF, NICHOLAS. *Sociological Theory: Its Nature and Growth* (New York: Random House, 1961).
ZITO, GEORGE. *Methodology and Meanings: Varieties of Sociological Inquiry* (New York: Praeger, 1975).*

* *Available in paperback.*

2. Culture

INTRODUCTION

Among laymen, culture is generally conceived of as the "finer things in life"—art, music, literature, philosophy. For the social scientist, however, the term has a much broader meaning. Anthropologist Clyde Kluckhohn states that it denotes the "distinctive way of life of a group of people" or a "design for living."[1] The classic definition of culture is Edward Tylor's: "Culture is that complex whole which includes knowledge, belief, art, morals, custom and other capabilities acquired by man as a member of society."[2]

Most definitions of culture include the following characteristics:

1. *Culture is socially shared.* Cultural patterns are socially transmitted by members of a group to one another, thus creating pressure toward uniformity of social behavior.
2. *Culture is learned.* Culture is not instinctive or inborn; it is not part of man's biological apparatus. All animals learn to some extent, but it is man's substantially greater learning ability that makes him the only animal able to acquire culture.
3. *Culture is transmitted from one generation to the next.* Man inherits a social tradition. Thus, culture is cumulative; it permits each new generation to build on the achievements of preceding generations.
4. *Culture enhances adaptation.* It serves to accommodate man to the demands of his biological nature and his physical environ-

[1] Clyde Kluckhohn, "The Study of Culture," in Daniel Lerner and Harold Lasswell (eds.), *The Policy Sciences* (Stanford, Calif.: Stanford University Press, 1951), p. 86.
[2] Edward Tylor, *The Origins of Culture* (New York: Harper & Row, 1958), p. 1.

ment. It is culture that furnishes man with the technical means to overcome the obstacles in his environment.

As Tylor has indicated, the components of culture are numerous and include knowledge, beliefs, technology, customs (the actual patterns of behavior shared by members of a group), norms (the ideal patterns for behavior, the rules that specify appropriate and inappropriate behavior), values, ideologies (systems of belief about the social world that are strongly rooted in specific sets of values and interests), and artifacts (everything man-made a people may possess, from primitive stone tools and pottery to electronic data-processing machines and television sets).

Norms may be classified in various ways. In his highly influential book *Folkways*, published in 1906, William Graham Sumner distinguished two main types of norms—folkways and mores. Folkways are norms that the members of a society do not regard as extremely important and that may be violated without severe punishment. For example, most rules of social etiquette are folkways; greeting another person without attempting to shake hands or using inappropriate eating utensils while dining might elicit social disapproval, but it is not likely to be intense.

Mores, on the other hand, are norms that are regarded as extremely important and that, if violated, will bring severe punishment. Many marriage rules are among the mores; the social rule of sexual fidelity in marriage, monogamy, and the taboos against incest are all mores.

Laws are distinguished from folkways and mores in that laws are institutionalized, maintained and enforced by specially designated agents of society; in contrast, folkways and mores are maintained and enforced by public sentiment. Laws vary in intensity from the weakly sanctioned codes governing the licensing of pets to the strongly sanctioned statutes concerned with the punishment for murder. There tends to be a general correspondence in society between the folkways and mores, on the one hand, and the laws, on the other. The most effective laws are grounded in the mores; for example, whether particular communities have antibigamy statutes is of less significance than the fact that injunctions against bigamy are firmly embedded in the mores. When the mores and the laws are discrepant, one or more of the following causes are indicated: rapid social change, group conflict or normative dissensus, totalitarian social control. The current controversy over the illegal status of marijuana possession and use reflects such a gap between the laws and the mores of a sizable group in society.

Many social scientists hold the view that the culture of a people is not simply an agglomeration of specific beliefs, values, customs, and the like but the integration of these components into some meaningful whole embodying a dominant set or direction, which may be called the ethos of a society. This should not be interpreted to mean that every culture possesses a similar degree of coherence around a central theme. Rather, the components of a culture are subject to a strain toward consistency, exhibiting varying degrees of integration.

The notion of a *subculture* (a subgroup whose patterns of thinking, feeling, and acting depart from those of the larger group) would appear to be antithetical to the conception of cultural integration. Yet, in many ways, all subcultures, no matter how insulated or alienated from the surrounding society they may be, find that their cultural patterns are influenced and shaped by the dominant culture. For example, in Martin Weinberg's "Sexual Modesty, Social Meanings, and the Nudist Camp," we learn that, although nudism is obviously at odds with the dominant morality, many of the specific norms governing nudist behavior appear to involve various puritanical elements. For the nudist, it seems, these social codes alleviate personal feelings of guilt and anxiety over nonconformity; thus, they represent an attempt to reconcile nudism with the values of the dominant, non-nudist society.

The study of culture invariably leads us to examine other cultures and to consider people whose way of life is different from our own. One's precepts, standards, and commitments to one's own social world are likely to affect the judgments one makes of others. The tendency to evaluate other cultures in terms of one's own, to consider one's own group superior to all others, is called *ethnocentrism*. For the anthropologist, ethnocentrism can have most adverse consequences, transforming attempts at analytic description into self-congratulatory moralism. Horace Miner's "Body Ritual Among the Nacirema," which appears in Chapter 1, shows very clearly how ethnocentrism can distort one's perceptions and thus entirely prevent scientific objectivity. In the realm of human relations, ethnocentrism tends to lead to resistance to social change, intolerance, misunderstanding, and group conflict.

Of enormous significance in attempts to understand other cultures is the viewpoint of *cultural relativity* (the principle that every culture must be judged on its own terms, that moral judgments are always relative to the standards of a given culture). This view, of course, is the converse of ethnocentrism. The fact that much of our own culture was formed by contact with other cultures over time supports the relativity approach. Ralph Linton's "One Hundred Per Cent American" indicates several of the sources of the so-called American way. His discussion raises the issue of the quantity of culture that is a result of *innovation* (additions to knowledge and the use of knowledge in novel forms) as compared with the amount that is due to *diffusion* (the process by which culture traits spread from one social unit to another). It, appears that innovation accounts for a minor portion of the cultural whole, that the great bulk of culture is a product of diffusion. Linton estimates that no more than 10 per cent of the material objects used by any people represents its own inventions.

Diffusion is a two-way process. For example, the Anglo-Americans owe to the Indians of the Americas their knowledge of corn, potato, tomato, peanut, tobacco, chocolate, pineapple, and many other plant foods. Had the Indians not domesticated these plants, it is doubtful that Anglo-Americans would have done so, for they would probably have introduced the crops they were familiar with from Europe. From the Indians, Anglo-Americans also learned much about woodcraft, canoes, and rubber, among many other inventions, as well as the use of numerous medicinal plants, including quinine. In turn, the Indians owe to the Anglo-Americans their knowledge of metallurgy, the rifle, and countless other innovations. The process of assimilation, therefore, has reciprocal consequences.

As the traits of one culture are diffused to another, various consequences ensue. In some places the recipient group may benefit from the new elements; in others innovations may have unsettling and disorganizing implications. Lauriston Sharp's research among the Yir Yiront of Australia very cogently demonstrates the unforeseen disruptive consequences that may arise from the introduction of new technology in a culture. The adoption of steel axes among the Yir Yiront served to undermine their status system and the harmonious relationships they previously enjoyed with their neighbors.

Sharp's research constitutes a warning to social planners that they must take adequate account of the cultures in which they work if any social good is to result. No matter how well-intentioned the planners may be, there is always the danger that they may fail to pay sufficient heed to the needs and wishes of those they are trying to help. Modern transportation and communication methods coupled with industrial society's ever growing need for resources and markets are likely to have similarly disorganizing consequences for the few aboriginal peoples still extant. Perhaps, in more instances than we would care to admit, the best help industrial peoples might offer the aborigine is not to intrude on his culture at all.

Culture influences, shapes and modifies the physiological functioning of the individual, as well as his use of material objects. Physiologist W. B. Cannon has argued that a person's conviction that he is the victim of witchcraft can cause so great a disturbance of autonomic functioning as to result in death. The experience of menstrual cramps or morning sickness during pregnancy may be a result of cultural beliefs; Margaret Mead, for example, reported that she could discover no instances of morning sickness among the Arapesh of New Guinea. Similarly, Ford and Beach have noted that, for the majority of men in our society, ejaculation occurs within two minutes after the beginning of intercourse, whereas, among the Marquesans, every man learns early in life to control his reflexes so as to permit maintenance of an erection and continuation of coitus for as long as desired.

Within our own society, we can observe the influence of culture on the biological functioning of subgroups. Mark Zborowski, in "Cultural Components in Responses to Pain," finds important differences among "WASP," Italian, and Jewish patients in their reactions to the pain caused, in most cases, by the same illnesses. On the basis of this research, we can observe the pervasive effects of culture, which influences virtually every aspect of our experience.

Cultures and Subcultures

Sexual Modesty, Social Meanings, and the Nudist Camp*

Martin S. Weinberg

* * *

THE NUDIST CAMP

The ideology of the nudist camp provides a new definition of the situation regarding nudity, which, in effect, maintains that

NUDIST IDEOLOGY

1. Nudism and sexuality are unrelated
2. There is nothing shameful about exposing the human body
3. The abandonment of clothes can lead to a feeling of freedom and natural pleasure
4. Nude activities, especially full bodily exposure to the sun, leads to a feeling of physical, mental, and spiritual well-being

These definitions are sustained by nudists to a remarkable degree, illustrating the extent to which adult socialization can function in changing long-maintained meanings; in this case, regarding the exposure of one's nude body in heterosexual situations. The tremendous emphasis on covering the sexual areas, and the relation between nudism and sexuality that exists in the outside society, however, suggest that the nudist definition of the situation might, at times, be quite easily called into question. The results of the field work and formal interviews indicate how the social organization of the nudist camp has developed a system of norms that contributes to sustaining the official definition of the situation. Since the major concern of this paper

* From *Social Problems*, vol. 12, no. 3 (Winter, 1965), 314–18. Reprinted by permission of The Society for the Study of Social Problems.

is modesty, we will restrict our discussion to the first two declarations of nudist ideology (i.e., that nudism and sexuality are unrelated, and that there is nothing shameful about exposing the human body). These are also the elements that lead to the classification of nudists as deviant. The normative proscriptions that contribute to the maintenance of this definition of the situation will be described.

Organizational precautions. Organizational precautions are initially taken in the requirements for admission to a nudist camp. Most camps do not allow unmarried individuals, especially single men, or allow only a small quota of singles. Those camps that do allow male-singles may charge up to 35 per cent higher rates for the single's membership than is charged for the membership of an entire family. This is intended to discourage single memberships, but, since the cost is still relatively low in comparison to other resorts, this measure is not very effective. It seems to do little more than create resentment among the singles. By giving formal organizational backing to the definition that singles are not especially desirable, it also might be related to the social segregation of single and married members that is evident in nudist camps.

An overabundance of single men is recognized by the organization as threatening the definition of nudism that is maintained. The presence of singles at the camp is suspected to be for purposes other than the "nudist way of life" (e.g., to gape at the women). Such a view may call into question the denied relation between nudity and sexuality.

Certification by the camp owner is also required before anyone is admitted on the camp grounds. This is sometimes supplemented by three letters of recommendation in regard to the character of the applicant. This is a precaution against admitting those "social types" who might conceivably discredit the ideology of the movement.

A limit is sometimes set on the number of trial visits that can be made to the camp; that is, visits made without membership in some camp or inter-camp organization. In addition, a limit is usually set on the length of time one is allowed to maintain oneself clothed. These rules function to weed out those guests whose sincere acceptance of the "nudist" definition of the situation is questionable.

Norms regarding interpersonal behavior. Norms regarding patterns of interpersonal behavior are also functional for the maintenance of the organization's system of meanings. The existence of these norms, however, should be recognized as formally acknowledging that the nudist definition of the situation could become problematic unless precautions were taken.

No staring. This rule functions to prevent any overt signs of "overinvolvement." In the words of a nonnudist who is involved in the publication of a nudist magazine, "They all look up to the heavens and never look below." This pattern of civil inattention[1] is most exaggerated among the females,

[1] See Erving Goffman, *Behavior in Public Places* (New York: The Free Press, 1963), p. 84.

who manage the impression that there is absolutely no concern or awareness that the male body is in an unclothed state. Women often recount how
they expect everyone will look at them when they are nude, only to find that
no one communicates any impression of concern when they finally do get up
their nerve and undress. One woman told the writer: "I got so mad because
my husband wanted me to undress in front of other men that I just pulled
my clothes right off thinking everyone would look at me." She was amazed
(and somewhat disappointed) when no one did. Thus, even though nudists
are immodest in their behavior by "showing" their bodies, . . . "looking
at" immodesty is controlled; external constraints prohibit staring.

> (Have you ever observed or heard about anyone staring at someone's
> body while at camp?)[2] I've heard stories—particularly about men that
> stare. Since I heard these stories, I tried not to, and even done away
> with my sunglasses after someone said, half-joking, that I hide behind
> sunglasses to stare. Toward the end of the summer, I stopped wearing
> sunglasses. And you know what? It was a child who told me this.

No sex talk. Sex talk, or telling "dirty" jokes, is not common in the nudist
camp. The owner of one of the most widely known camps in the Midwest
told the writer: "It is usually expected that members of a nudist camp will
not talk about sex, politics, or religion." Or, in the words of one single-
male: "It is taboo to make sexual remarks here." Verbal immodesty was
not experienced by the writer during his period of field work. Interview
respondents who mentioned that they had discussed or talked about sex
qualified this by stating that such talk was restricted to close friends, was of
a "scientific" nature, or, if a joke, was of a "cute" sort. Verbal immodesty
. . . is not common to the nudist camp.

When respondents were asked what they would think of someone who
breached this norm, they indicated that such behavior would cast doubt on
the actor's acceptance of the nudist definition of the situation:

> One would expect to hear less of that at camp than at other places.
> (Why's that?) Because you expect that the members are screened in
> their *attitude for nudism*—and this isn't one who prefers sexual jokes.
>
> They probably don't belong there. They're there to see what they
> can find to observe. (What do you mean?) Well, their mind isn't on
> being a nudist, but to see so-and-so nude.

Body contact is taboo. Although the degree to which this rule is enforced
varies among camps, there is at least some degree of informal enforcement.
Nudists mention that one is particularly careful not to brush against anyone
or have any body contact, because of the way it might be interpreted. The
following quotation illustrates the interpersonal precautions taken: "I stay
clear of the opposite sex. They're so sensitive, they imagine things." One
respondent felt that this taboo was simply a common-sense form of
modesty: "Suppose one had a desire to knock one off or feel his wife—
modesty or a sense of protocol prohibits you from doing this." When asked

[2] Interview questions and probes have been placed in parentheses.

to conceptualize a breakdown in this form of modesty, a common response was:

> They are in the wrong place. (How's that?) That's not part of nudism. (Could you tell me some more about that?) I think they are there for some sort of sex thrill. They are certainly not there to enjoy the sun.

If any photographs are taken for publication in a nudist magazine, the subjects are allowed to have only limited body contact. As one female nudist said: "We don't want anyone to think we're immoral." Outsiders' interpretations of body contact among nudists would cast doubt on the nudist definition of the situation or the characteristics set forth as the "nudist way of life."

A correlate of the body contact taboo is the prohibition of dancing in the nude. This is verbalized by nudist actors as a separate rule, and it is often the object of jest by members. This indication of "organizational strain" can be interpreted as an instance in which the existence of the rule itself brings into question the nudist definition of the situation; that is, that there is no relationship between nudism and sexuality. The following remark acknowledges this: "This reflects a contradiction in our beliefs. But it's self-protection. One incident and we'd be closed." Others define dancing in the nude as an erotic overture that would incite sexual arousal. Such rationalizations are common to the group. . . .

Alcoholic beverages are not allowed in American camps. This rule also functions in controlling any breakdown in inhibitions that could lead to "aggressive-erotic" overtures. Even those respondents who told the writer that they had "snuck a beer" before going to bed went on to say, however, that they fully favored the rule. The following quotation is representative of nudists' thoughts:

> Anyone who drinks in camp is jeopardizing their membership and they shouldn't. Anyone who drinks in camp could get reckless. (How's that?) Well, when guys and girls drink, they're a lot bolder— they might get fresh with someone else's girl. That's why it isn't permitted, I guess.

Rules regarding photography. Taking photographs in a nudist camp is a sensitive matter. Unless the individual is an official photographer (i.e., one photographing for the nudist magazines), the photographer's definition of the situation is sometimes suspect, especially when one hears such remarks as the following: "Do you think you could open your legs a little more?"

There may be a general restriction on the use of cameras, and, when cameras are allowed, it is expected that no pictures will be taken without the subject's permission. Members especially tend to blame the misuse of cameras on single men. As one nudist said: "You always see the singles poppin' around out of nowhere snappin' pictures." In general, however, control is maintained, and any infractions that might exist are not blatant or obvious. Any overindulgence in taking photographs would communicate an overinvolvement in the nude state of the alters and bring doubt on the denied connection between nudism and sexuality. This, like staring, . . . is controlled by the norms of the nudist camp.

The official photographers who are taking pictures for nudist magazines recognize the impression communicated by forms of immodesty other than nudity, that is, for the communication of sexuality. In regard to . . . erotic overtures . . . the following statement of an official photographer is relevant: "I never let a girl look straight at the camera. It looks too suggestive. I always have her look off to the side."

Accentuation of the body is suspect as being incongruent with the ideology of nudism. The internalization of the previously discussed principles of nudist ideology would be called into question by such accentuation. Thus, one woman who had shaved her pubic area was labeled as disgusting by those members who talked to the writer about it. Women who blatantly sit in an "unladylike" manner are similarly typed. In the words of one female nudist:

> It's no more nice to do than when you are dressed. I would assume they have a purpose. (What's that?) Maybe to draw someone's attention sexually. I'd think it's bad behavior, and it's one thing that shouldn't be done, especially in a nudist camp. (Why's that?) Because it could lead to trouble or some misfortune. (Could you tell me some more about that?) It could bring up some trouble or disturbance among those who noticed it. It would not be appreciated by "true nudists."

Unnatural attempts at covering any area of the body are similarly ridiculed, since they call into question the actor's acceptance of the definition that there is no shame in exposing any area of the human body. If such behavior occurs early in one's nudist career, however, it is responded to mostly with smiles. The actor is viewed as not yet able to get over the initial difficulty of disposing of "outsiders'" definitions.

Communal toilets are also related to the ideological view that there is nothing shameful about the human body or its bodily functions. Although all camps do not have communal toilets, the large camp at which the writer spent the majority of his time did have such a facility, which was labeled "Little Girls Room and Little Boys Too." The stalls were provided with three-quarter-length doors. The existence of this combined facility helped, however, to sustain the nudist definition of the situation by the element of consistency: If you are not ashamed of any part of your body, or of any of its natural body functions, why do you need separate toilets? Thus, even the physical ecology of the nudist camp is designed in a way that will be consistent with the organization's definition of modesty.

CONSEQUENCES OF A BREAKDOWN IN CLOTHING MODESTY

In the introductory section of this paper, it was stated that common-sense actors anticipate breakdowns in clothing modesty to result in rampant sexual interest, promiscuity, embarrassment, jealousy, and shame. The field work and interview data from this study, however, indicate that such occurrences are not common to the nudist camp. The social organization of the nudist camp provides a system of meanings and norms that negate these consequences.

hyp NOT
upheld

CONCLUSIONS

Our results make possible some general conclusions regarding modesty: (1) Covering the body through the use of clothes is not a necessary condition for a pattern of modesty to exist, nor is it required for tension management and social control of latent sexual interests. Sexual interests are very adequately controlled in nudist camps; in fact, those who have visited nudist camps agree that sexual interests are controlled to a much greater extent than they are on the outside. Clothes are also not a sufficient condition for a pattern of modesty; the manipulation of clothes and fashion in stimulating sexual interest is widely recognized. (2) Except for clothing immodesty, . . . all . . . forms of modesty are maintained in a nudist camp (e.g., not looking, not saying, not communicating erotic overtures). This suggests that the latter proscriptions are entirely adequate in achieving the functions of modesty when definitions regarding the exposure of the body are changed. (3) When deviance from the institutionalized patterns of modesty is limited to one cell of our typology, (i.e., clothing is dispensed with), and the definition of the situation is changed, the typically expected consequence of such a breakdown in this normative pattern does not occur. Rampant sexual interest, promiscuity, embarrassment, jealousy, and shame were not found to be typical of the nudist camp.

Cultural Diffusion

One Hundred Per Cent American*
Ralph Linton

* * *

Our solid American citizen awakens in a bed built on a pattern that originated in the Near East but that was modified in Northern Europe before it was transmitted to America. He throws back covers made from cotton, domesticated in India, or linen, domesticated in the Near East, or wool from sheep, also domesticated in the Near East, or silk, the use of which was dis-

* From: *The Study of Man: An Introduction,* by Ralph Linton. Copyright 1936 by D. Appleton-Century Company, Inc. © 1964 by Meredith Corporation. Reprinted by permission of Appleton-Century-Crofts, Educational Division, Meredith Corporation.

covered in China. All of these materials have been spun and woven by processes invented in the Near East. He slips into his moccasins, invented by the Indians of the Eastern woodlands, and goes to the bathroom, whose fixtures are a mixture of European and American inventions, both of recent date. He takes off his pajamas, a garment invented in India, and washes with soap, invented by the ancient Gauls. He then shaves—a masochistic rite that seems to have been derived from either Sumer or ancient Egypt.

Returning to the bedroom, he removes his clothes from a chair of southern European type and proceeds to dress. He puts on garments whose form originally derived from the skin clothing of the nomads of the Asiatic steppes, puts on shoes made from skins tanned by a process invented in ancient Egypt and cut to a pattern derived from the classical civilizations of the Mediterranean, and ties around his neck a strip of bright-colored cloth that is a vestigial survival of the shoulder shawls worn by the seventeenth-century Croatians. Before going out for breakfast, he glances through the window, made of glass invented in Egypt, and, if it is raining, puts on overshoes made of rubber discovered by the Central American Indians and takes an umbrella, invented in Southeastern Asia. Upon his head he puts a hat made of felt, a material invented in the Asiatic steppes.

On his way to breakfast, he stops to buy a paper, paying for it with coins, an ancient Lydian invention. At the restaurant, a whole new series of borrowed elements confronts him. His plate is made of a form of pottery invented in China. His knife is of steel, an alloy first made in southern India; his fork, a medieval Italian invention; and his spoon, a derivative of a Roman original. He begins breakfast with an orange, from the eastern Mediterranean, a canteloupe from Persia, or perhaps a piece of African watermelon. With this he has coffee, an Abyssinian plant, with cream and sugar. Both the domestication of cows and the idea of milking them originated in the Near East, while sugar was first made in India. After his fruit and first coffee, he goes on to waffles, cakes made by a Scandinavian technique from wheat domesticated in Asia Minor. Over these he pours maple syrup, invented by the Indians of the Eastern woodlands. As a side dish, he may have the egg of a species of bird domesticated in Indochina, or thin strips of the flesh of an animal domesticated in Eastern Asia that have been salted and smoked by a process developed in Northern Europe.

When our friend has finished eating, he settles back to smoke, an American Indian habit, consuming a plant domesticated in Brazil in either a pipe, derived from the Indians of Virginia, or a cigarette, derived from Mexico. If he is hardy enough, he may even attempt a cigar, transmitted to us from the Antilles by way of Spain. While smoking, he reads the news of the day, imprinted in characters invented by the ancient Semites upon a material invented in China by a process invented in Germany. As he absorbs the accounts of foreign troubles, he will, if he is a good, conservative citizen, thank a Hebrew deity in an Indo-European language that he is 100 per cent American.

* * *

The Multifold Consequences of Cultural Change

Steel Axes for Stone-Age Australians[*]

Lauriston Sharp

Like other Australian aboriginals, the Yir Yoront group, which lives at the mouth of the Coleman River on the west coast of Cape York Peninsula, originally had no knowledge of metals. Technologically their culture was of the Old Stone Age or Paleolithic type. They supported themselves by hunting and fishing and obtained vegetables and other materials from the bush by simple gathering techniques. Their only domesticated animal was the dog; they had no cultivated plants of any kind. Unlike some other aboriginal groups, however, the Yir Yoront did have polished stone axes hafted in short handles, which were most important in their economy.

Towards the end of the nineteenth century metal tools and other European artifacts began to filter into the Yir Yoront territory. The flow increased with the gradual expansion of the white frontier outward from southern and eastern Queensland. Of all the items of Western technology thus made available, the hatchet, or short-handled steel axe, was the most acceptable to and the most highly valued by all aboriginals.

In the mid 1930s an American anthropologist lived alone in the bush among the Yir Yoront for thirteen months without seeing another white man. The Yir Yoront were thus still relatively isolated and continued to live an essentially independent economic existence, supporting themselves entirely by means of their Old Stone-Age techniques. Yet their polished stone axes were disappearing fast and being replaced by steel axes, which came to them in considerable numbers, directly or indirectly, from various European sources to the south.

What changes in the life of the Yir Yoront still living under aboriginal conditions in the Australian bush could be expected as a result of their increasing possession and use of the steel axe?

THE COURSE OF EVENTS

Events leading up to the introduction of the steel axe among the Yir Yoront begin with the advent of the second known group of Europeans to reach the shores of the Australian continent. In 1623 a Dutch expedition landed

* Reproduced by permission of the Society for Applied Anthropology from *Human Organization*, vol. 11, no. 2 (Summer, 1952), pp. 17–22.

on the coast where the Yir Yoront now live. In 1935 the Yir Yoront were still using the few cultural items recorded in the Dutch log for the aboriginals they encountered. To this cultural inventory the Dutch added beads and pieces of iron, which they offered in an effort to attract the frightened "Indians." Among these natives metal and beads have disappeared, together with any memory of this first encounter with whites.

The next recorded contact in this area was in 1864. Here there is more positive assurance that the natives concerned were the immediate ancestors of the Yir Yoront community. These aboriginals had the temerity to attack a party of cattlemen who were driving a small herd from southern Queensland through the length of the then unknown Cape York Peninsula to a newly established government station at the northern tip. Known as the Battle of the Mitchell River, this was one of the rare instances in which Australian aboriginals stood up to European gunfire for any length of time. A diary kept by the cattlemen records that:

> Ten carbines poured volley after volley into them from all directions, killing and wounding with every shot with very little return, nearly all their spears having already been expended. . . . About 30 being killed, the leader thought it prudent to hold his hand, and let the rest escape. Many more must have been wounded and probably drowned, for 59 rounds were counted as discharged.

The European party was in the Yir Yoront area for three days; they then disappeared over the horizon to the north and never returned. In the almost three-year-long anthropological investigation conducted some seventy years later—in all the material of hundreds of free-association interviews, in texts of hundreds of dreams and myths, in genealogies, and eventually in hundreds of answers to direct and indirect questioning on just this particular matter—there was nothing that could be interpreted as a reference to this shocking contact with Europeans.

The aboriginal accounts of their first remembered contact with whites begin in about 1900 with references to persons known to have had sporadic but lethal encounters with them. From that time on whites continued to remain on the southern periphery of Yir Yoront territory. With the establishment of cattle stations (ranches) to the south, cattlemen made occasional excursions among the "wild black-fellows" in order to inspect the country and abduct natives to be trained as cattleboys and "house girls." At least one such expedition reached the Coleman River where a number of Yir Yoront men and women were shot for no apparent reason.

About this time the government was persuaded to sponsor the establishment of three mission stations along the 700-mile western coast of the peninsula in an attempt to help regulate the treatment of natives. To further this purpose a strip of coastal territory was set aside as an aboriginal reserve and closed to further white settlement.

In 1915, an Anglican mission station was established near the mouth of the Mitchell River, about a three-day march from the heart of the Yir Yoront country. Some Yir Yoront refused to have anything to do with the mission, others visited it occasionally, while only a few eventually settled more or less permanently in one of the three "villages" established at the mission.

Thus the majority of the Yir Yoront continued to live their old self-supporting life in the bush, protected until 1942 by the government reserve and the intervening mission from the cruder realities of the encroaching new order from the south. To the east was poor, uninhabited country. To the north were other bush tribes extending on along the coast to the distant Archer River Presbyterian mission with which the Yir Yoront had no contact. Westward was the shallow Gulf of Carpentaria, on which the natives saw only a mission lugger making its infrequent dry-season trips to the Mitchell River. In this protected environment for over a generation the Yir Yoront were able to recuperate from shocks received at the hands of civilized society. During the 1930s their raiding and fighting, their trading and stealing of women, their evisceration and two- or three-year care of their dead, and their totemic ceremonies continued, apparently uninhibited by Western influence. In 1931 they killed a European who wandered into their territory from the east, but the investigating police never approached the group whose members were responsible for the act.

As a direct result of the work of the Mitchell River mission, all Yir Yoront received a great many more Western artifacts of all kinds than ever before. As part of their plan for raising native living standards, the missionaries made it possible for aboriginals living at the mission to earn some Western goods, many of which were then given or traded to natives still living under bush conditions; they also handed out certain useful articles gratis to both mission and bush aboriginals. They prevented guns, liquor, and damaging narcotics, as well as decimating diseases, from reaching the tribes of this area, while encouraging the introduction of goods they considered "improving." As has been noted, no item of Western technology available, with the possible exception of trade tobacco, was in greater demand among all groups of aboriginals than the short-handled steel axe. The mission always kept a good supply of these axes in stock; at Christmas parties or other mission festivals they were given away to mission or visiting aboriginals indiscriminately and in considerable numbers. In addition, some steel axes as well as other European goods were still traded in to the Yir Yoront by natives in contact with cattle stations in the south. Indeed, steel axes had probably come to the Yir Yoront through established lines of aboriginal trade long before any regular contact with whites had occurred.

RELEVANT FACTORS

If we concentrate our attention on Yir Yoront behavior centering about the original stone axe (rather than on the axe—the object—itself) as a cultural trait or item of cultural equipment, we should get some conception of the role this implement played in aboriginal culture. This, in turn, should enable us to foresee with considerable accuracy some of the results stemming from the displacement of the stone axe by the steel axe.

The production of a stone axe required a number of simple technological skills. With the various details of the axe well in mind, adult men could set about producing it (a task not considered appropriate for women or children). First of all a man had to know the location and properties of several natural resources found in his immediate environment: pliable wood for a handle, which could be doubled or bent over the axe head and bound tightly; bark, which could be rolled into cord for the binding; and gum, to fix the stone head in the haft. These materials had to be correctly gathered, stored, prepared, cut to size and applied or manipulated. They were in plentiful supply and could be taken from anyone's property without special permission. Postponing consideration of the stone head, the axe could be made by any normal man who had a simple knowledge of nature and of the technological skills involved, together with fire (for heating the gum), and a few simple cutting tools—perhaps the sharp shells of plentiful bivalves.

The use of the stone axe as a piece of capital equipment used in producing other goods indicates its very great importance to the subsistence economy of the aboriginal. Anyone—man, woman, or child—could use the axe; indeed, it was used primarily by women, for theirs was the task of obtaining sufficient wood to keep the family campfire burning all day, for cooking or other purposes, and all night against mosquitoes and cold (for in July, winter temperature might drop below 40°). In a normal lifetime a woman would use the axe to cut or knock down literally tons of firewood. The axe was also used to make other tools or weapons, and a variety of material equipment required by the aboriginal in his daily life. The stone axe was essential in the construction of the wet-season, domed huts which keep out some rain and some insects; of platforms which provide dry storage; of shelters which give shade in the dry summer when days are bright and hot. In hunting and fishing and in gathering vegetable or animal food the axe was also a necessary tool, and in this tropical culture, where preservatives or other means of storage are lacking, the natives spend more time obtaining food than in any other occupation—except sleeping. In only two instances was the use of the stone axe strictly limited to adult men: for gathering wild honey, the most prized food known to the Yir Yoront; and for making the secret paraphernalia for ceremonies. From this brief listing of some of the activities involving the use of the axe, it is easy to understand why there was at least one stone axe in every camp, in every hunting or fighting party, and in every group out on a "walk-about" in the bush.

The stone axe was also prominent in interpersonal relations. Yir Yoront men were dependent upon interpersonal relations for their stone axe heads, since the flat, geologically recent, alluvial country over which they range provides no suitable stone for this purpose. The stone they used came from quarries 400 miles to the south, reaching the Yir Yoront through long lines of male trading partners. Some of these chains terminated with the Yir Yoront men, others extended on farther north to other groups, using Yir Yoront men as links. Almost every older adult man had one or more regular trading partners, some to the north and some to the south. He provided his partner or partners in the south with surplus spears, particularly fighting spears tipped with the barbed spines of sting ray, which snap into vicious fragments when they penetrate human flesh. For a dozen such spears, some of which he may have obtained from a partner to the north, he would receive one stone axe head. Studies have shown that the sting-ray-barb spears increased in value as they moved south and farther from the sea. One hundred and fifty miles south of Yir Yoront one such spear may be exchanged for one stone axe head. Although actual investigations could not be made, it was presumed that farther south, nearer the quarries, one sting-ray-barb spear would bring several stone axe heads. Apparently people who acted as links in the middle of the chain and who made neither spears nor axe heads would receive a certain number of each as a middleman's profit.

Thus trading relations, which may extend the individual's personal relationships beyond that of his own group, were associated with spears and axes, two of the most important items in a man's equipment. Finally, most of the exchanges took place during the dry season, at the time of the great aboriginal celebrations centering about initiation rites or other totemic ceremonials which attracted hundreds and were the occasion for much exciting activity in addition to trading.

Returning to the Yir Yoront, we find that adult men kept their axes in camp with their other equipment, or carried them when traveling. Thus a woman or child who wanted to use an axe—as might frequently happen during the day—had to get one from a man, use it promptly, and return it in good condition. While a man might speak of "my axe," a woman or child could not.

This necessary and constant borrowing of axes from older men by women and children was in accordance with regular patterns of kinship behavior. A woman would expect to use her husband's axe unless he himself was using it; if unmarried, or if her husband was absent, a woman would go first to her older brother or to her father. Only in extraordinary circumstances would she seek a stone axe from other male kin. A girl, a boy, or a young man would look to a father or an older brother to provide an axe for their use. Older men, too, would follow similar rules if they had to borrow an axe.

It will be noted that all of these social relationships in which the stone axe had a place are pair relationships and that the use of the axe helped to define and maintain their character and the roles of the two individual participants. Every active relationship among the Yir Yoront involved a definite and accepted status of superordination or subordination. A person could have no dealings with another on exactly equal terms. The nearest approach to equality was between brothers, although the older was always superordinate to the younger. Since the exchange of goods in a trading relationship involved a mutual reciprocity, trading partners usually stood in a brotherly type of relationship, although one was always classified as older than the other and would have some advantage in case of dispute. It can be seen that repeated and widespread conduct centering around the use of the axe helped to generalize and standardize these sex, age, and kinship roles both in their normal benevolent and exceptional malevolent aspects.

The status of any individual Yir Yoront was determined not only by sex, age, and extended kin relationships, but also by membership in one of two dozen patrilineal totemic clans into which the entire community was divided. Each clan had literally hundreds of totems, from one or two of which the clan derived its name, and the clan members their personal names. These totems included natural species or phenomena such as the sun, stars, and daybreak, as well as cultural "species": imagined ghosts, rainbow serpents, heroic ancestors; such eternal cultural verities as fires, spears, huts; and such human activities, conditions, or attributes as eating, vomiting, swimming, fighting, babies and corpses, milk and blood, lips and loins. While individual members of such totemic classes or species might disappear or be destroyed, the class itself was obviously ever present and indestructible. The totems, therefore, lent permanence and stability to the clans, to the groupings of human individuals who generation after generation were each associated with a set of totems which distinguished one clan from another.

The stone axe was one of the most important of the many totems of the Sunlit Cloud Iguana clan. The names of many members of this clan referred to the axe itself, to activities in which the axe played a vital part, or to the clan's mythical ancestors with whom the axe was prominently associated. When it was necessary to represent the stone axe in totemic ceremonies, only men of this clan exhibited it or pantomimed its use. In secular life, the axe could be made by any man and used by all; but in the sacred realm of the totems it belonged exclusively to the Sunlit Cloud Iguana people.

Supporting those aspects of cultural behavior which we have called technology and conduct is a third area of culture which includes ideas, sentiments, and values. These are most difficult to deal with, for they are latent and covert, and even unconscious, and must be deduced from overt actions and language or other communicating behavior. In this aspect of the culture lies the significance of the stone axe to the Yir Yoront and to their cultural way of life.

The stone axe was an important symbol of masculinity among the Yir Yoront (just as pants or pipes are to us). By a complicated set of ideas the axe was defined as "belonging" to males, and everyone in the society (except untrained infants) accepted these ideas. Similarly spears, spear throwers, and fire-making sticks were owned only by men and were also symbols of masculinity. But the masculine values represented by the stone axe were constantly being impressed on all members of society by the fact that females borrowed axes but not other masculine artifacts. Thus the axe stood for an important theme of Yir Yoront culture: the superiority and rightful dominance of the male, and the greater value of his concerns and of all things associated with him. As the axe also had to be borrowed by the younger people it represented the prestige of age, another important theme running through Yir Yoront behavior.

To understand the Yir Yoront culture it is necessary to be aware of a system of ideas which may be called their totemic ideology. A fundamental belief of the aboriginal divided time into two great epochs: (1) a distant and sacred period at the beginning of the world when the earth was peopled by mildly marvelous ancestral beings or culture heroes who are in a special sense the forebears of the clans; and (2) a period when the old was succeeded by a new order which includes the present. Originally there was no anticipation of another era supplanting the present. The future would simply be an eternal continuation and reproduction of the present which itself had remained unchanged since the epochal revolution of ancestral times.

The important thing to note is that the aboriginal believed that the present world, as a natural and cultural environment, was and should be simply a detailed reproduction of the world of the ancestors. He believed that the entire universe "is now as it was in the beginning" when it was established and left by the ancestors. The ordinary cultural life of the ancestors became the daily life of the Yir Yoront camps, and the extraordinary life of the ancestors remained extant in the recurring symbolic pantomimes and paraphernalia found only in the most sacred atmosphere of the totemic rites.

Such beliefs, accordingly, opened the way for ideas of what *should be* (because it supposedly *was*) to influence or help determine what actually *is*. A man called Dog-chases-iguana-up-a-tree-and-barks-at-him-all-night had that and other names because he believed his ancestral alter ego had also had them; he was a member of the Sunlit Cloud Iguana clan because his ancestor was; he was associated with particular countries and totems of this same ancestor; during an initiation he played the role of a dog and symbolically attacked and killed certain members of other clans because his ancestor (conveniently either anthropomorphic or kynomorphic) really did the same to the ancestral alter egos of these men; and he would avoid his mother-in-law, joke with a mother's distant brother, and make spears in a certain way because his and other people's ancestors did these things. His behavior in these specific ways was outlined, and to that extent determined for him, by a set of ideas concerning the past and the relation of the present to the past.

But when we are informed that Dog-chases-etc. had two wives from the Spear Black Duck clan and one from the Native Companion clan, one of them being blind, that he had four children with such and such names, that he had a broken wrist and was left-handed, all because his ancestor had exactly these same attributes, then we know (though he apparently didn't) that the present has influenced the past, that the mythical world has been somewhat adjusted to meet the exigencies and accidents of the inescapably real present.

There was thus in Yir Yoront ideology a nice balance in which the mythical was adjusted in part to the real world, the real world in part to the ideal

pre-existing mythical world, the adjustments occurring to maintain a fundamental tenet of native faith that the present must be a mirror of the past.
Thus the stone axe in all its aspects, uses, and associations was integrated
into the context of Yir Yoront technology and conduct because a myth, a
set of ideas, had put it there.

THE OUTCOME

The introduction of the steel axe indiscriminately and in large numbers into
the Yir Yoront technology occurred simultaneously with many other changes.
It is therefore impossible to separate all the results of this single innovation.
Nevertheless, a number of specific effects of the change from stone to steel
axes may be noted, and the steel axe may be used as an epitome of the increasing quantity of European goods and implements received by the aboriginals and of their general influence on the native culture. The use of the
steel axe to illustrate such influences would seem to be justified. It was one
of the first European artifacts to be adopted for regular use by the Yir
Yoront, and whether made of stone or steel, the axe was clearly one of the
most important items of cultural equipment they possessed.

The shift from stone to steel axes provided no major technological difficulties. While the aboriginals themselves could not manufacture steel axe
heads, a steady supply from outside continued; broken wooden handles
could easily be replaced from bush timbers with aboriginal tools. Among
the Yir Yoront the new axe was never used to the extent it was on mission
or cattle stations (for carpentry work, pounding tent pegs, as a hammer,
and so on); indeed, it had so few more uses than the stone axe that its practical effect on the native standard of living was negligible. It did some jobs
better, and could be used longer without breakage. These factors were sufficient to make it of value to the native. The white man believed that a shift
from steel to stone axe on his part would be a definite regression. He was
convinced that his axe was much more efficient, that its use would save
time, and that it therefore represented technical "progress" towards goals
which he had set up for the native. But this assumption was hardly borne
out in aboriginal practice. Any leisure time the Yir Yoront might gain by
using steel axes or other Western tools was not invested in "improving the
conditions of life," nor, certainly, in developing aesthetic activities, but in
sleep—an art they had mastered thoroughly.

Previously, a man in need of an axe would acquire a stone axe head
through regular trading partners from whom he knew what to expect and
was then dependent solely upon a known and adequate natural environment
and his own skills or easily acquired techniques. A man wanting a steel axe,
however, was in no such self-reliant position. If he attended a mission festi-
val when steel axes were handed out as gifts, he might receive one either by
chance or by happening to impress upon the mission staff that he was one of
the "better" bush aboriginals (the missionaries definition of "better" being
quite different from that of his bush fellows). Or, again almost by pure

chance, he might get some brief job in connection with the mission which would enable him to earn a steel axe. In either case, for older men a preference for the steel axe helped change the situation from one of self-reliance to one of dependence, and a shift in behavior from well-structured or defined situations in technology or conduct to ill-defined situations in conduct alone. Among the men, the older ones whose earlier experience or knowledge of the white man's harshness made them suspicious were particularly careful to avoid having relations with the mission, and thus excluded themselves from acquiring steel axes from that source.

In other aspects of conduct or social relations, the steel axe was even more significantly at the root of psychological stress among the Yir Yoront. This was the result of new factors which the missionary considered beneficial: the simple numerical increase in axes per capita as a result of mission distribution, and distribution directly to younger men, women, and even children. By winning the favor of the mission staff, a woman might be given a steel axe which was clearly intended to be hers, thus creating a situation quite different from the previous custom which necessitated her borrowing an axe from a male relative. As a result a woman would refer to the axe as "mine," a possessive form she was never able to use of the stone axe. In the same fashion, young men or even boys also obtained steel axes directly from the mission, with the result that older men no longer had a complete monopoly of all the axes in the bush community. All this led to a revolutionary confusion of sex, age, and kinship roles, with a major gain in independence and loss of subordination on the part of those who now owned steel axes when they had previously been unable to possess stone axes.

The trading-partner relationship was also affected by the new situation. A Yir Yoront might have a trading partner in a tribe to the south whom he defined as a younger brother and over whom he would therefore have some authority. But if the partner were in contact with the mission or had other access to steel axes, his subordination obviously decreased. Among other things, this took some of the excitement away from the dry-season fiestalike tribal gatherings centering around initiations. These had traditionally been the climactic annual occasions for exchanges between trading partners, when a man might seek to acquire a whole year's supply of stone axe heads. Now he might find himself prostituting his wife to almost total strangers in return for steel axes or other white-man's goods. With trading partnerships weakened, there was less reason to attend the ceremonies, and less fun for those who did.

Not only did an increase in steel axes and their distribution to women change the character of the relations between individuals (the paired relationships that have been noted), but a previously rare type of relationship was created in the Yir Yoront's conduct towards whites. In the aboriginal society there were few occasions outside the immediate family when an individual would initiate action to several other people at once. In any average group, in accordance with the kinship system, while a person might be superordinate to several people to whom he could suggest or command action, he was also subordinate to several others with whom such behavior would be tabu. There was thus no overall chieftainship or authoritarian leadership of any kind. Such complicated operations as grass-burning animal drives or totemic ceremonies could be carried out smoothly because each person was aware of his role.

On both mission and cattle stations, however, the whites imposed their conception of leadership roles upon the aboriginals, consisting of one person in a controlling relationship with a subordinate group. Aboriginals called together to receive gifts, including axes, at a mission Christmas party found themselves facing one or two whites who sought to control their behavior for the occasion, who disregarded the age, sex, and kinship variables of which the aboriginals were so conscious, and who considered them all at one subordinate level. The white also sought to impose similar patterns on work parties. (However, if he placed an aboriginal in charge of a mixed group of post-hole diggers, for example, half of the group, those subordinate to the "boss," would work while the other half, who were superordinate to him, would sleep.) For the aboriginal, the steel axe and other European goods came to symbolize this new and uncomfortable form of social organization, the leader-group relationship.

The most disturbing effects of the steel axe, operating in conjunction with other elements also being introduced from the white man's several subcultures, developed in the realm of traditional ideas, sentiments, and values. These were undermined at a rapidly mounting rate, with no new conceptions being defined to replace them. The result was the erection of a mental and moral void which foreshadowed the collapse and destruction of all Yir Yoront culture, if not, indeed, the extinction of the biological group itself.

From what has been said it should be clear how changes in overt behavior, in technology and conduct, weakened the values inherent in a reliance on nature, in the prestige of masculinity and of age, and in the various kinship relations. A scene was set in which a wife, or a young son whose initiation may not yet have been completed, need no longer defer to the husband or father who, in turn, became confused and insecure as he was forced to borrow a steel axe from them. For the woman and boy the steel axe helped establish a new degree of freedom which they accepted readily as an escape from the unconscious stress of the old patterns—but they, too, were left confused and insecure. Ownership became less well defined with the result that stealing and trespassing were introduced into technology and conduct. Some of the excitement surrounding the great ceremonies evaporated and they lost their previous gaiety and interest. Indeed, life itself became less interesting, although this did not lead the Yir Yoront to discover suicide, a concept foreign to them.

The whole process may be most specifically illustrated in terms of totemic system, which also illustrates the significant role played by a system of ideas, in this case a totemic ideology, in the breakdown of a culture.

In the first place, under pre-European aboriginal conditions where the native culture has become adjusted to a relatively stable environment, few, if any, unheard of or catastrophic crises can occur. It is clear, therefore, that the totemic system serves very effectively in inhibiting radical cultural changes. The closed system of totemic ideas, explaining and categorizing a well-known universe as it was fixed at the beginning of time, presents a considerable obstacle to the adoption of new or the dropping of old culture traits. The obstacle is not insurmountable and the system allows for the minor variations which occur in the norms of daily life. But the inception of major changes cannot easily take place.

Among the bush Yir Yoront the only means of water transport is a light wood log to which they cling in their constant swimming of rivers, salt creeks, and tidal inlets. These natives know that tribes 45 miles farther north have a bark canoe. They know these northern tribes can thus fish from midstream or out at sea, instead of clinging to the river banks and beaches, that they can cross coastal waters infested with crocodiles, sharks, sting rays, and Portuguese men-of-war without danger. They know the materials of which the canoe is made exist in their own environment. But they also know, as they say, that they do not have canoes because their own mythical ancestors did not have them. They assume that the canoe was part of the ancestral universe of the northern tribes. For them, then, the adoption of the canoe would not be simply a matter of learning a number of new behavioral skills for its manufacture and use. The adoption would require a much more difficult procedure; the acceptance by the entire society of a myth, either locally developed or borrowed, to explain the presence of the canoe, to associate it with some one or more of the several hundred mythical ancestors (and how decide which?), and thus establish it as an accepted totem of one of the clans ready to be used by the whole community. The Yir Yoront have not made this adjustment, and in this case we can only say that, for the time being at least, ideas have won out over very real pressures for technological change. In the elaborateness and explicitness of the totemic ideologies we seem to have one explanation for the notorious stability of Australian cultures under aboriginal conditions, an explanation which gives due weight to the importance of ideas in determining human behavior.

At a later stage of the contact situation, as has been indicated, phenomena unaccounted for by the totemic ideological system begin to appear with regularity and frequency and remain within the range of native experience. Accordingly, they cannot be ignored (as the "Battle of the Mitchell" was apparently ignored), and there is an attempt to assimilate them and account for them along the lines of principles inherent in the ideology. The bush Yir Yoront of the mid-thirties represent this stage of the acculturation process. Still trying to maintain their aboriginal definition of the situation, they accept European artifacts and behavior patterns, but fit them into their totemic system, assigning them to various clans on a par with original totems. There is an attempt to have the myth-making process keep up with these cultural changes so that the idea system can continue to support the rest of the culture. But analysis of overt behavior, of dreams, and of some of the new myths indicates that this arrangement is not entirely satisfactory, that the native clings to his totemic system with intellectual loyalty (lacking any substitute ideology), but that associated sentiments and values are weakened. His attitudes towards his own and towards European culture are found to be highly ambivalent.

All ghosts are totems of the Head-to-the-East Corpse clan, are thought of as white, and are of course closely associated with death. The white man, too, is closely associated with death, and he and all things pertaining to him are naturally assigned to the Corpse clan as totems. The steel axe, as a totem, was thus associated with the Corpse clan. But as an "axe," clearly linked with the stone axe, it is a totem of the Sunlit Cloud Iguana clan. Moreover, the steel axe, like most European goods, has no distinctive origin myth, nor are mythical ancestors associated with it. Can anyone, sitting in the shade of a *ti* tree one afternoon, create a myth to resolve this confusion? No one has, and the horrid suspicion arises as to the authenticity of the origin myths, which failed to take into account this vast new universe of the white man. The steel axe, shifting hopelessly between one clan and the other, is not only replacing the stone axe physically, but is hacking at the supports of the entire cultural system.

The aboriginals to the south of the Yir Yoront have clearly passed beyond this stage. They are engulfed by European culture, either by the mission or cattle station subcultures or, for some natives, by a baffling, paradoxical combination of both incongruent varieties. The totemic ideology can no longer support the inrushing mass of foreign culture traits, and the myth-making process in its native form breaks down completely. Both intellectually and emotionally a saturation point is reached so that the myriad new traits which can neither be ignored nor any longer assimilated simply force the aboriginal to abandon his totemic system. With the collapse of this system of ideas, which is so closely related to so many other aspects of the native culture, there follows an appallingly sudden and complete cultural disintegration, and a demoralization of the individual such as has seldom been recorded elsewhere. Without the support of a system of ideas well devised to provide cultural stability in a stable environment, but admittedly too rigid for the new realities pressing in from outside, native behavior and native sentiments and values are simply dead. Apathy reigns. The aboriginal has passed beyond the realm of any outsider who might wish to do him well or ill.

Returning from the broken natives huddled on cattle stations or on the fringes of frontier towns to the ambivalent but still lively aboriginals settled on the Mitchell River mission, we note one further devious result of the introduction of European artifacts. During a wet-season stay at the mission, the anthropologist discovered that his supply of toothpaste was being depleted at an alarming rate. Investigation showed that it was being taken by old men for use in a new toothpaste cult. Old materials of magic having failed, new materials were being tried out in a malevolent magic directed towards the mission staff and some of the younger aboriginal men. Old males, largely ignored by the missionaries, were seeking to regain some of their lost power and prestige. This mild aggression proved hardly effective, but perhaps only because confidence in any kind of magic on the mission was by this time at a low ebb.

For the Yir Yoront still in the bush, a time could be predicted when personal deprivation and frustration in a confused culture would produce an overload of anxiety. The mythical past of the totemic ancestors would disappear as a guarantee of a present of which the future was supposed to be a stable continuation. Without the past, the present could be meaningless and the future unstructured and uncertain. Insecurities would be inevitable. Reaction to this stress might be some form of symbolic aggression, or withdrawal and apathy, or some more realistic approach. In such a situation the missionary with understanding of the processes going on about him would find his opportunity to introduce his forms of religion and to help create a new cultural universe.

The Effect of Culture on the Individual

Cultural Components in Responses to Pain *
Mark Zborowski

This paper reports on one aspect of a larger study: that concerned with discovering the role of cultural patterns in attitudes toward, and reactions to, pain that is caused by disease and injury—in other words, responses to spontaneous pain. . . .

* * *

In setting up the research, we were interested not only in the purely theoretical aspects of the findings in terms of possible contribution to the understanding of the pain experience in general; we also had in mind the practical goal of a contribution to the field of medicine. In the relationship between the doctor and his patient, the respective attitudes toward pain may play a crucial role, especially when the doctor feels that the patient exaggerates his pain, while the patient feels that the doctor minimizes his suffering. The same may be true, for instance, in a hospital where the members of the medical and nursing staff may have attitudes toward pain different from those held by the patient, or when they expect a certain pattern of behavior

* From *The Journal of Social Issues,* vol. 8, no. 4 (1953), pp. 16–31. Reprinted by permission of The Society for the Psychological Study of Social Issues.

according to their cultural background, while the patient may manifest a behavior pattern that is acceptable in his culture. These differences may play an important part in the evaluation of the individual pain experience, in dealing with pain at home and in the hospital, in administration of analgesics, etc. Moreover, we expected that this study of pain would offer opportunities to gain insight into related attitudes toward health, disease, medication, hospitalization, medicine in general, etc.

With these aims in mind, the project was set up at the Kingsbridge Veterans Hospital, Bronx, New York, where four ethnocultural groups were selected for an intensive study. These groups included patients of Jewish, Italian, Irish, and "Old American" stock. Three groups—Jews, Italians, and Irish—were selected because they were described by medical people as manifesting striking differences in their reaction to pain. Italians and Jews were described as tending to "exaggerate" their pain, while the Irish were often depicted as stoical individuals who are able to take a great deal of pain. The fourth group, the "Old Americans," were chosen because the values and attitudes of this group dominate in the country and are held by many members of the medical profession and by many descendants of the immigrants, who, in the process of Americanization, tend to adopt American patterns of behavior. The members of this group can be defined as White, native-born individuals, usually Protestant, whose grandparents, at least, were born in the United States, and who do not identify themselves with any foreign group, either nationally, socially, or culturally.

The Kingsbridge Veterans Hospital was chosen because its population represents roughly the ethnic composition of New York City, thus offering access to a fair sample of the four selected groups, and also because various age groups were represented among the hospitalized veterans of World War I, World War II, and the Korean War. In one major respect, this hospital was not adequate, namely, in not offering the opportunity to investigate sex differences in attitude toward pain. This aspect of research will be carried out in a hospital with a large female population.

In setting up this project, we were mainly interested in discovering certain regularities in reactions and attitudes toward pain characteristic of the four groups. Therefore, the study has a qualitative character, and the efforts of the researchers were not directed toward a collection of material suitable for quantitative analysis. The main techniques used in the collection of the material were interviews with patients of the selected groups, observation of their behavior when in pain, and discussion of the individual cases with doctors, nurses, and other people directly or indirectly involved in the pain experience of the individual. In addition to the interviews with patients, "healthy" members of the respective groups were interviewed on their attitudes toward pain; because, in terms of the original hypothesis, those attitudes and reactions that are displayed by the patients of the given cultural groups are held by all members of the group, regardless of whether or not they are in pain, although in pain these attitudes may come more sharply into focus. In certain cases, the researchers have interviewed a member of the patient's immediate family in order to check the report of the patient on his pain experience, and in order to find out what are the attitudes and reactions of the family toward the patient's experience.

These interviews, based on a series of open-ended questions, were focused upon the past and present pain experiences of the interviewee. However, many other areas were considered important for the understanding of this experience. For instance, it was felt that complaints of pain may play an important role in manipulating relationships in the family and the larger social environment. It was also felt that, in order to understand the specific reactive patterns in controlling pain, it is important to know certain aspects of child-rearing in the culture, relationships between parents and children, the role of infliction of pain in punishment, the attitudes of various members of the family toward specific expected, accepted pain experiences, and so on. The interviews were recorded on wire and transcribed verbatim for an ultimate detailed analysis. The interviews usually lasted for approximately two hours, the time being limited by the condition of the interviewee and by the amount and quality of his answers. When it was considered necessary, an interview was repeated. In most of the cases, the study of the interviewee was followed by informal conversations and by observation of his behavior in the hospital.

The information gathered from the interviews was discussed with members of the medical staff, especially in the areas related to the medical aspects of the problem, in order to get their evaluation of the pain experience of the patient. Information as to the personality of the patient was checked against results of psychological testing by members of the psychological staff of the hospital when these were available.

The discussion of the material presented in this paper is based on interviews with 103 respondents, including 87 hospital patients in pain and 16 healthy subjects. According to their ethno-cultural background, the respondents are distributed as follows: "Old Americans," 26; Italians, 24; Jews, 31; Irish, 11; and others, 11. In addition, there were the collateral interviews and conversations noted above with family members, doctors, nurses, and other members of the hospital staff.

With regard to the pathological causes of pain, the majority of the interviewees fall into the group of patients suffering from neurological diseases, mainly herniated discs and spinal lesions. The focusing upon a group of patients suffering from a similar pathology offered the opportunity to investigate reactions and attitudes toward spontaneous pain that is symptomatic of one group of diseases. Nevertheless, a number of patients suffering from other diseases were also interviewed.

This paper is based upon the material collected during the first stage of study. The generalizations are to a great extent tentative formulations on a descriptive level. There has been no attempt as yet to integrate the results with the value system and the cultural pattern of the group, although here and there there will be indications to the effect that they are part of the culture pattern. The discussions will be limited to main regularities within three groups, namely, the Italians, the Jews, and the "Old Americans." Factors related to variations within each group will be discussed after the main prevailing patterns have been presented.

PAIN AMONG PATIENTS OF JEWISH AND ITALIAN ORIGIN

As already mentioned, the Jews and Italians were selected mainly because interviews with medical experts suggested that they display similar reactions to pain. The investigation of this similarity provided the opportunity to check a rather popular assumption that similar reactions reflect similar attitudes. The differences between the Italian and Jewish cultures are great enough to suggest that, if the attitudes are related to cultural pattern, they will also be different, despite the apparent similarity in manifest behavior.

Members of both groups were described as being very emotional in their responses to pain. They were described as tending to exaggerate their pain experience and being very sensitive to pain. Some of the doctors stated that, in their opinion, Jews and Italians have a lower threshold of pain than members of other ethnic groups, especially members of the so-called Nordic group. This statement seems to indicate a certain confusion as to the concept of the threshold of pain. According to people who have studied the problem of the threshold of pain—for instance, Harold Wolff and his associates—the threshold of pain is more or less the same for all human beings regardless of nationality, sex, or age.

In the course of the investigation, the general impressions of doctors were confirmed to a great extent by the interview material and by the observation of the patients' behavior. However, even a superficial study of the interviews has revealed that, although reactions to pain appear to be similar, the underlying attitudes toward pain are different in the two groups. While the Italian patients seemed to be mainly concerned with the immediacy of the pain experience and were disturbed by the actual pain sensation that they experienced in a given situation, the concern of patients of Jewish origin was focused mainly upon the symptomatic meaning of pain and upon the significance of pain in relation to their health, welfare, and, eventually, for the welfare of the families. The Italian patient expressed, in his behavior and in his complaints, the discomfort caused by pain as such, and he manifested his emotions with regard to the effects of this pain experience upon his immediate situation in terms of occupation, economic situation, and so on; the Jewish patient expressed primarily his worries and anxieties as to the extent to which the pain indicated a threat to his health. In this connection, it is worth mentioning that one of the Jewish words to describe strong pain is *yessurim*, a word that is also used to describe worries and anxieties.

Attitudes of Italian and Jewish patients toward pain-relieving drugs can serve as an indication of their attitude toward pain. When in pain, the Italian calls for pain relief and is mainly concerned with the analgesic effects of the drugs that are administered to him. Once the pain is relieved, the Italian patient easily forgets his sufferings and manifests a happy and joyful disposition. The Jewish patient, however, often is reluctant to accept the drug, and he explains this reluctance in terms of concern about the effects of the drug upon his health in general. He is apprehensive about the habit-forming aspects of the analgesic. Moreover, he feels that the drug relieves his pain only temporarily and does not cure him of the disease that may cause the pain. Nurses and doctors have reported cases in which patients would hide the pill that was given to them to relieve their pain and would prefer to suffer. These reports were confirmed in the interviews with the patients. It was also observed that many Jewish patients, after being relieved from pain, often continued to display the same depressed and worried behavior, because they felt that, although the pain was currently absent, it may recur as long as the disease was not cured completely. From these observations, it appears that, when one deals with a Jewish and an Italian patient in pain, in the first case it is more important to relieve the anxieties with regard to the sources of pain, while in the second it is more important to relieve the actual pain.

Another indication as to the significance of pain for Jewish and Italian patients is their respective attitudes toward the doctor. The Italian patient seems to display a most confident attitude toward the doctor, which is usually reinforced after the doctor has succeeded in relieving pain; whereas the Jewish patient manifests a skeptical attitude, feeling that the fact that the doctor has relieved his pain by some drug does not mean at all that he is skillful enough to take care of the basic illness. Consequently, even when the pain is relieved, he tends to check the diagnosis and the treatment of one doctor against the opinions of other specialists in the field. Summarizing the difference between the Italian and Jewish attitudes, one can say that the Italian attitude is characterized by a present-oriented apprehension with regard to the actual sensation of pain, and the Jew tends to manifest a future-oriented anxiety as to the symptomatic and general meaning of the pain experience.

It has been stated that the Italians and Jews tend to manifest similar behavior in terms of their reactions to pain. As both cultures allow for free expression of feelings and emotions by words, sounds, and gestures, both the Italians and Jews feel free to talk about their pain, complain about it, and manifest their sufferings by groaning, moaning, crying, etc. They are not ashamed of this expression. They admit willingly that, when they are in pain, they do complain a great deal, call for help, and expect sympathy and assistance from other members of their immediate social environment, especially from members of their family. When in pain, they are reluctant to be alone and prefer the presence and attention of other people. This behavior, which is expected, accepted, and approved by the Italian and Jewish cultures, often conflicts with the patterns of behavior expected from a patient by American or Americanized medical people. Thus, they tend to describe the behavior of the Italian and Jewish patients as exaggerated and overemotional. The material suggests that they do tend to minimize the actual pain experiences of the Italian and Jewish patients, regardless of whether they have the objective criteria for evaluating the actual amount of pain that the patient experiences. It seems that the uninhibited display of reaction to pain as manifested by the Jewish and Italian patients provokes distrust in American culture instead of provoking sympathy.

Despite the close similarity between the manifest reactions among Jews and Italians, there seem to be differences in emphasis, especially with regard to what the patient achieves by these reactions and as to the specific manifestations of these reactions in the various social settings. For instance, they differ in their behavior at home and in the hospital. The Italian husband, who is aware of his role as an adult male, tends to avoid verbal complaining at home, leaving this type of behavior to the women. In the hospital, where he is less concerned with his role as a male, he tends to be more verbal and more emotional. The Jewish patient, on the contrary, seems to be more calm in the hospital than at home. Traditionally, the Jewish male does not emphasize his masculinity through such traits as stoicism, and he does not equate verbal complaints with weakness. Moreover, the Jewish culture allows the patient to be demanding and complaining. Therefore, he tends more to use his pain in order to control interpersonal relationships within the family. Although similar use of pain to manipulate the relationships between members of the family may be present also in some other cultures, it seems that, in the Jewish culture, this is not disapproved, while in others it is. In the hospital, one can also distinguish variations in the reactive patterns among Jews and Italians. Upon his admission to the hospital, and in the presence of the doctor, the Jewish patient tends to complain, ask for help, be emotional even to the point of crying. However, as soon as he feels that adequate care is given to him, he becomes more restrained. This suggests that the display of pain reaction serves less as an indication of the amount of pain experienced than as a means to create an atmosphere and setting in which the pathological causes of pain will be best taken care of. The Italian patient, on the other hand, seems to be less concerned with setting up a favorable situation for treatment. He takes for granted that adequate care will be given to him, and, in the presence of the doctor, he seems to be somewhat calmer than the Jewish patient. The mere presence of the doctor reassures the Italian patient, while the skepticism of the Jewish patient limits the reassuring role of the physician.

To summarize the description of the reaction patterns of the Jewish and Italian patients, the material suggests that, on a semiconscious level, the Jewish patient tends to provoke worry and concern in his social environment as to the state of his health and the symptomatic character of his pain, while the Italian tends to provoke sympathy toward his suffering. In one case, the function of the pain reaction will be the mobilization of the efforts of the family and the doctors toward a complete cure, while, in the second case, the function of the reaction will be focused upon the mobilization of effort toward relieving the pain sensation.

On the basis of the discussion of the Jewish and Italian material, two generalizations can be made: (1) *Similar reactions to pain manifested by members of different ethnocultural groups do not necessarily reflect similar attitudes to pain.* (2) *Reactive patterns similar in terms of their manifestations may have different functions and serve different purposes in various cultures.*

PAIN AMONG PATIENTS OF "OLD AMERICAN" ORIGIN

There is little emphasis on emotional complaining about pain among "Old American" patients. Their complaints about pain can best be described as reporting on pain. In describing his pain, the "Old American" patient tries to find the most appropriate ways of defining the quality of pain, its localization, duration, etc. When examined by the doctor, he gives the impression of trying to assume the detached role of an unemotional observer who gives the most efficient description of his state for a correct diagnosis and treatment. The interviewees repeatedly state that there is no point in complaining and groaning and moaning, etc., because "it won't help anybody." However, they readily admit that, when pain is unbearable, they may react strongly, even to the point of crying, but they tend to do it when they are alone. Withdrawal from society seems to be a frequent reaction to strong pain.

There seem to be different patterns in reacting to pain, depending on the situation. One pattern, manifested in the presence of members of the family, friends, etc., consists of attempts to minimize pain, to avoid complaining and provoking pity; when pain becomes too strong, there is a tendency to withdraw and express freely such reactions as groaning, moaning, etc. A different pattern is manifested in the presence of people who, on account of their profession, should know the character of the pain experience, because they are expected to make the appropriate diagnosis, advise the proper cure, and give the adequate help. The tendency to avoid deviation from certain expected patterns of behavior plays an important role in the reaction to pain. This is also controlled by the desire to seek approval on the part of the social environment, especially in the hospital, where the "Old American" patient tries to avoid being a "nuisance" in the ward. He seems to be, more than any other patient, aware of an ideal pattern of behavior that is identified as "American," and he tends to conform to it. This was characteristically expressed by a patient who answered the question how he reacts to pain by saying, "I react like a good American."

An important element in controlling the pain reaction is the wish of the patient to cooperate with those who are expected to take care of him. The situation is often viewed as a team composed of the patient, the doctor, the nurse, the attendant, etc., and, in this team, everybody has a function and is supposed to do his share in order to achieve the most successful result.

Emotionality is seen as a purposeless and hindering factor in a situation that calls for knowledge, skill, training, and efficiency. It is important to note that this behavior is also expected by American or Americanized members of the medical or nursing staff, and the patients who do not fall into this pattern are viewed as deviants, hypochondriacs, and neurotics.

As in the case of the Jewish patients, the American attitude toward pain can be best defined as a future-oriented anxiety. The "Old American" patient is also concerned with the symtomatic significance of pain, which is correlated with a pronounced health-consciousness. It seems that the "Old American" is conscious of various threats to his health that are present in his environment and therefore feels vulnerable and is prone to interpret his pain sensation as a warning signal indicating that something is wrong with his health and therefore must be reported to the physician. With some exceptions, pain is considered bad and unnecessary and therefore must be immediately taken care of. In those situations where pain is expected and accepted, such as in the process of medical treatment or as a result of sports activities, there is less concern with the pain sensation. In general, however, there is a feeling that suffering pain is unnecessary when there are means of relieving it.

Although the attitudes of the Jewish and "Old American" patients can be defined as pain anxiety, they differ greatly. The future-oriented anxiety of the Jewish interviewee is characterized by pessimism or, at best, by skepticism, while the "Old American" patient is rather optimistic in his future-orientation. This attitude is fostered by the mechanistic approach to the body and its functions and by the confidence in the skill of the experts, which are so frequent in the American culture. The body is often viewed as a machine that has to be well taken care of, be periodically checked for disfunctioning, and, eventually, when out of order, be taken to an expert who will "fix" the defect. In the case of pain, the expert is the medical man who has the "know-how" because of his training and experience and therefore is entitled to full confidence. An important element in the optimistic outlook is faith in the progress of science. Patients with intractable pain often stated that, although at the present moment the doctors do not have the "drug," they will eventually discover it, and they will give the examples of sulfa, penicillin, etc.

The anxieties of a pain-experiencing "Old American" patient are greatly relieved when he feels that something is being done about it in terms of specific activities involved in the treatment. It seems that his security and confidence increase in direct proportion to the number of tests, X-rays, examinations, injections, etc., that are given to him. Accordingly, "Old American" patients seem to have a positive attitude toward hospitalization, because the hospital is the adequate institution that is equipped for the necessary treatment. While a Jewish and an Italian patient seem to be disturbed by the impersonal character of the hospital and by the necessity of being treated there instead of at home, the "Old American" patient, on the contrary, prefers the hospital treatment to the home treatment, and neither he nor his family seems to be disturbed by hospitalization.

To summarize the attitude of the "Old American" toward pain, he is disturbed by the symptomatic aspect of pain and is concerned with its incapacitating aspects, but he tends to view the future in rather optimistic colors, having confidence in the science and skill of the professional people who treat his condition.

SOME SOURCES OF INTRAGROUP VARIATION

In the description of the reactive patterns and attitudes toward pain among patients of Jewish and "Old American" origin, certain regularities have been observed for each particular group, regardless of individual differences and variations. This does not mean that each individual in each group manifests the same reactions and attitudes. Individual variations are often due to specific aspects of pain experience, to the character of the disease that causes the pain, or to elements in the personality of the patient. However, there are also other factors that are instrumental in provoking these differences, and that can still be traced back to the cultural backgrounds of the individual patients. Such variables as the degree of Americanization of the patient, his socio-economic background, education, and religiosity may play an important role in shaping individual variations in the reactive patterns. For instance, it was found that the patterns described are manifested most consistently among immigrants, while their descendants tend to differ in terms of adopting American forms of behavior and American attitudes toward the role of the medical expert, medical institutions, and equipment in controlling pain. It is safe to say that the further the individual is from the immigrant generation, the more American is his behavior. This is less true for the attitudes toward pain, which seem to persist to a great extent even among members of the third generation, and even though the reactive patterns are radically changed. A Jewish or Italian patient born in this country of American-born parents tends to *behave* like an "Old American" but often expresses *attitudes* similar to those that are expressed by the Jewish or Italian people. They try to appear unemotional and efficient in situations where the immigrant would be excited and disturbed. However, in the process of the interview, if a patient is of Jewish origin, he is likely to express attitudes of anxiety as to the meaning of his pain, and, if he is an Italian, he is likely to be rather unconcerned about the significance of his pain for his future.

The occupational factor plays an important role when pain affects a specific area of the body. For instance, manual workers with herniated discs are more disturbed by their pain than are professional or business people with a similar disease because of the immediate significance of this particular pain for their respective abilities to earn a living. It was also observed that headaches cause more concern among intellectuals than among manual workers.

The educational background of the patient also plays an important role in his attitude with regard to the symptomatic meaning of a pain sensation. The more educated patients are more health-conscious and more aware of pain as a possible symptom of a dangerous disease. However, this factor plays a less important role than might be expected. The less educated "Old American" or Jewish patient is still more health-conscious than the more educated Italian. On the other hand, the less educated Jew is as much worried about the significance of pain as the more educated one. The education of the patient seems to be an important factor in fostering specific reactive patterns. The more educated patient, who may have more anxiety with regard to illness, may be more reserved in specific reactions to pain than an unsophisticated individual, who feels free to express his feelings and emotions.

THE TRANSMISSION OF CULTURAL
ATTITUDES TOWARD PAIN

In interpreting the differences that may be attributed to different socio-economic and education backgrounds, there is enough evidence to conclude that these differences appear mainly on the manifest and behavioral level, whereas attitudinal patterns toward pain tend to be more uniform and to be common to most of the members of the group, regardless of their specific backgrounds.

These attitudes toward pain and the expected reactive patterns are acquired by the individual members of the society from the earliest childhood, along with other cultural attitudes and values that are learned from the parents, parent-substitutes, siblings, peer groups, etc. Each culture offers to its members an ideal pattern of attitudes and reactions, which may differ for various subcultures in a given society, and each individual is expected to conform to this ideal pattern. Here, the role of the family seems to be of primary importance. Directly and indirectly, the family environment affects the individual's ultimate response to pain. In each culture, the parents teach the child how to react to pain, and, by approval or disapproval, they promote specific forms of behavior. This conclusion is amply supported by the interviews. Thus, the Jewish and Italian respondents are unanimous in relating how their parents, especially mothers, manifested overprotective and overconcerned attitudes toward the child's health, participation in sports, games, fights, etc. In these families, the child is constantly reminded of the advisability of avoiding colds, injuries, fights, and other threatening situations. Crying in complaint is responded to by the parents with sympathy, concern, and help. By their overprotective and worried attitude, they foster complaining and tears. The child learns to pay attention to each painful experience and to look for help and sympathy, which are readily given to him. In Jewish families, where not only a slight sensation of pain but also each deviation from the child's normal behavior is looked upon as a sign of illness, the child is prone to acquire anxieties with regard to the meaning and significance of these manifestations. The Italian parents do not seem to be concerned with the symptomatic meaning of the child's pains and aches, but, instead, there is a great deal of verbal expression of emotions and feelings of sympathy toward the "poor child" who happens to be in discomfort because of illness or because of an injury in play. In these families, a child is praised when he avoids physical injuries and is scolded when he does not pay enough attention to bad weather, to drafts, or when he takes part in rough games and fights. The injury and pain are often interpreted to the child as punishment for the wrong behavior, and physical punishment is the usual consequence of misbehavior.

In the "Old American" family, the parental attitude is quite different. The child is told not to "run to mother with every little thing." He is told to take pain "like a man," not to be a "sissy," not to cry. The child's participation in physical sports and games is not only approved but is also strongly stimulated. Moreover, the child is taught to expect to be hurt in sports and games and is taught to fight back if he happens to be attacked by other boys. However, it seems that the American parents are conscious of the threats to the child's health, and they teach the child to take immediate care of any injury. When hurt, the right thing to do is not to cry and get emotional but to avoid unnecessary pain and prevent unpleasant consequences by applying the proper first-aid medicine and by calling a doctor.

Often, attitudes and behavior fostered in a family conflict with those patterns that are accepted by the larger social environment. This is especially true in the case of children of immigrants. The Italian or Jewish immigrant parents promote patterns that they consider correct, while the peer groups in the street and in the school criticize this behavior and foster a different one. In consequence, the child may acquire the attitudes that are part of his home-life but may also adopt behavior patterns that conform to those of his friends.

The direct promotion of certain behavior described as part of the child-rearing explains only in part the influence of the general family environment and the specific role of the parents in shaping responses to pain. They are also formed indirectly by observing the behavior of other members of the family and by imitating their responses to pain. Moreover, attitudes toward pain are also influenced by various aspects of parent-child relationship in a culture. The material suggests that differences in attitudes toward pain in Jewish, Italian, and "Old American" families are closely related to the role and image of the father in the respective cultures in terms of his authority and masculinity. Often, the father and mother assume different roles in promoting specific patterns of behavior and specific attitudes. For example, it seems that, in the "Old American" family, it is chiefly the mother who stimulates the child's ability to resist pain, thus emphasizing his masculinity. In the Italian family, it seems that the mother is the one who inspires the child's emotionality, while, in the Jewish family, both parents express attitudes of worry and concern that are transmitted to the children.

Specific deviations from expected reactive and attitudinal patterns can often be understood in terms of a particular structure of the family. This became especially clear from the interviews of two Italian patients and one Jewish patient. All three subjects revealed reactions and attitudes diametrically opposite to those that the investigator would expect on the basis of his experience. In the process of the interview, however, it appeared that one of the Italian patients was adopted into an Italian family, found out about his adoption at the age of fourteen, created a phantasy of being of Anglo-Saxon origin because of his physical appearance, and, accordingly, began to eradicate everything "Italian" in his personality and behavior. For instance, he denied knowledge of the Italian language, despite the fact that he always spoke Italian in the family, and even learned to abstain from smiling, because he felt that being happy and joyful is an indication of Italian origin. The other Italian patient lost his family at a very early age because of family disorganization and was brought up in an Irish foster home. The Jewish patient consciously adopted a "non-Jewish" pattern of behavior and attitude because of strong sibling rivalry. According to the respondent, his brother, a favored son in the immigrant Jewish family, always manifested "typical" Jewish reactions toward disease, and the patient, who strongly disliked the brother and was jealous of him, decided to be "completely different."

2. SUGGESTIONS FOR FURTHER READING

BARNOUW, VICTOR. *Culture and Personality* (Homewood, Ill.: Dorsey Press, 1963).

BECKER, HOWARD. *Outsiders* (New York: The Free Press, 1963).*

BENEDICT, RUTH. *Patterns of Culture* (Boston: Houghton Mifflin, 1961).*

CHILDE, V. GORDON. *Man Makes Himself* (New York: New American Library, 1952).*

FOSTER, GEORGE. *Traditional Societies and Technological Change* (New York: Harper & Row, 1973).*

GEERTZ, CLIFFORD. *Interpretation of Cultures* (New York: Basic Books, 1974).

GRABURN, NELSON. *Eskimos Without Igloos* (Boston: Little, Brown, 1969).*

HALL, EDWARD T. *The Silent Language* (Garden City, N.Y.: Doubleday, 1959).*

HAYS, H. R. *From Ape to Angel* (New York: Alfred A. Knopf, 1958).*

HENRY, JULES. *Culture Against Man* (New York: Random House, 1963).*

HOEBEL, E. ADAMSON. *The Law of Primitive Man* (Cambridge, Mass.: Harvard University Press, 1954).*

HUNT, ROBERT (ed.). *Personalities and Cultures* (Garden City, N.Y.: Natural History Press, 1967).*

KLUCKHOHN, CLYDE. *Mirror for Man* (New York: McGraw-Hill, 1949).*

LEWIS, OSCAR. *Children of Sanchez* (New York: Random House, 1961).*

———. *Tepoztlán* (New York: Holt, Rinehart, 1960).*

LINTON, RALPH. *The Study of Man* (New York: D. Appleton-Century, 1936).*

MALINOWSKI, BRONISLAW. *Argonauts of the Western Pacific* (New York: E. P. Dutton, 1961).*

MEAD, MARGARET (ed.). *Cultural Patterns and Technical Change* (Paris: UNESCO, 1953).*

————. *New Lives for Old* (New York: William Morrow, 1953).*

————. *Sex and Temperament in Three Primitive Societies* (New York: William Morrow, 1935).*

ROSENBERG, B., and D. WHITE (eds.). *Mass Culture* (Glencoe, Ill.: The Free Press, 1957).*

RUESCH, HANS. *Top of the World* (New York: Pocket Books, 1951).*

SHAPIRO, HARRY (ed.). *Man, Culture and Society* (New York: Oxford University Press, 1960).*

SUMNER, WILLIAM G. *Folkways* (Boston: Ginn, 1906).*

TURNBULL, COLIN. *The Mountain People* (New York: Simon & Schuster, 1972).*

* *Available in paperback.*

3. Social Organization

INTRODUCTION

Sociologists use the term "social structure" or "social organization" to refer to the orderly or patterned way in which individuals and groups of people relate to one another in society. In any given society, social organization involves the assignment of different functions to different people and the relation of these functions to one another and to the group purposes.

To illustrate social organization: Think of a metropolitan hospital that serves the health-care needs of thousands of patients daily. During an average day, the hospital receives many requests for admission. Some patients require ambulance service. The patient population requires a wide variety of medical ministrations, as well as food, bed changes, and the like. If the entire hospital staff had to deliberate as to who would do what and how every time a request for any of these services developed, it is doubtful whether many of the patients would receive much health care. The social organization of the hospital, by its differentiation and coordination of functions—admission personnel, ambulance drivers, physicians, nurses, dieticians, social workers, and so forth—stabilizes interaction between staff and patients in a manner that makes the provision of health care possible.

As we focus on the structure of groups and individuals within a society, we can discern a network of statuses (positions occupied by members of society) and roles (the functions these people are expected to perform according to the cultural norms shared by the members). For example, within the hospital society we find the status or position of nurse; this position has a variety of roles associated with it, such as taking patients' temperatures and administering medication.

Any individual may be said to have various statuses; for example, the same man may be professor, father, taxpayer, patient. As these examples suggest, status is always relational or reciprocal. Without its complement—professor-student, father-child—status would be meaningless. Role defines the rights, obligations, and privileges of a person who occupies a particular status. It tells a person what he ought to do in his positions of professor, father, and so forth; to whom he has obligations; and upon whom he has a rightful claim.

In the course of performing his many roles, a person is subject to conflicting pressures and strains that arise because different and inconsistent kinds of behavior are required by his different statuses. For example, a "working wife" has role obligations toward her family and toward her job. Should a member of her family become ill, she would feel the obligation to care for him and yet, at the same time, the obligation to perform her work role.

Often, role strains and conflicts are built into a single role. Consider, for example, the role of a military officer. Success in this role requires, on the one hand, a relationship of friendship and intimacy with his men, which can stimulate them to perform effectively; yet, at the same time, the role requires impersonal judgment and command, which discourage the development of friendship and personal loyalty. The individual subjected to role conflict is confronted with a dilemma: How should he behave? As people move in ever wider social circles, performing more roles than ever before, the likelihood of role strain and role conflict will inevitably increase.

It has been suggested that, without the interrelated system of roles and statuses of social organization, the number of decisions that social life requires would be totally overwhelming to the individual. Yet, social organization can conceivably become a straitjacket, impeding the individual from adapting to changing circumstances or conditions. Culture provides the script, and social organization casts the players in the ongoing, yet ever changing, drama of social life. To put this in another way, social organization coordinates the social relationships among persons and groups into a meaningful pattern, which, if the group or society is to persist, must respond to the changing needs of the group and to the changing pressures from the physical and social environment.

The transition from rural to urban society probably represents the single most sweeping and comprehensive reordering of social relationships that has taken place in the history of human society. It has been examined by a great number of sociologists from the nineteenth century to the present. Henry S. Maine called this change the transition from status to contract; Ferdinand Toennies saw it as a movement from Gemeinschaft (commune) to Gesellschaft (society); Émile Durkheim referred to it as a shift from mechanical solidarity to organic solidarity. Robert Redfield's essay on "The Folk Society" explores several dimensions of this movement from rural, or folk, to urban society.

In folk society, a man's family membership was a paramount factor in his social placement; in the wake of industrialization, his role in the process of production, his occupation, has now assumed the pivotal position. Where status in society was once ascriptive (based on given characteristics such as family, age, and sex), it is now predominantly achieved (based on the accomplishments of the individual).

Urban society is a social world in which many of our encounters are transitory, instrumental (merely a means to some other end), and nonintimate; in which group memberships are formal and secondary (relationships that are specialized, unemotional, and impersonal, involving a limited aspect of one's personality); and in which roles are delimited and segmented. The values of the urban, industrial world are oriented toward the future, highlight the rational and scientific, and are essentially secular.

Many critics of the modern world have argued that urban society exhibits severe social disorganization. They claim that the kind of behavior that prompted thirty-odd New Yorkers several years ago to "mind their own business" when Katherine Genovese, screaming for help within earshot of them, was assaulted and murdered is symptomatic of some of the social-disorganizational tendencies of urban society. Sociologists refer to this condition as anomie (normlessness), analogous to the notion of political deregulation—anarchy.

Yet, the urban scene may not be so disorganized as many people argue. Recently, sociologists have been devoting much attention to the normative order and social organization governing the urban scene. One result of this research is Leon Mann's "Queue Culture: The Waiting Line as a Social System," which demonstrates that, despite intense competition among avid soccer fans for the relatively few general-admission seats, there has evolved a rather elaborate, widely understood, and highly effective social system governing the distribution of tickets. This normative order is quite antithetical to the idea of anomie. More studies of the urban scene, particularly of public places, may lead to greater understanding of social rules and structures in our present-day experience.

Another significant aspect of the study of social organization is bureaucracy. Although bureaucratic organization in the layman's view generally refers to a government agency or "red tape" (administrative rigidity), the term has a different meaning for the sociologist. A bureaucracy, as defined by Max Weber, is any organization in which (1) the regular activities are distributed in a fixed way as official duties; (2) the arrangement of offices follows the principle of hierarchy; (3) operations are governed by a consistent system of abstract rules and represent the application of these rules to particular cases; (4) the ideal official conducts his office in a spirit of formalistic impersonality; and (5) employment is based on technical qualifications, is protected against arbitrary dismissal, and constitutes a career with promotions based on seniority or achievement.

When Weber studied bureaucracy, well over fifty years ago, he was convinced that its technical efficiency would lead to its increasing expansion. This prediction has so far proved accurate, despite the many dehumanizing features of bureaucracy, its discouragement of individual initiative, its susceptibility to rigidity, and its inability to cope with changing and unique conditions. Many social scientists argue that this continuing bureaucratic development has had an atomizing effect on human relationships, ushering in a protototalitarian period in which most people experience feelings of powerlessness, insignificance, and alienation. Melvin Seeman, in "Antidote to Alienation: Learning to Belong," discusses this viewpoint and suggests a number of ways in which man might reassume his social involvement.

Social Organization in Folk and Urban Societies

The Folk Society*
Robert Redfield

*　　*　　*

"The conception of a 'primitive society' which we ought to form," wrote Sumner, "is that of small groups scattered over a territory."[1] The folk society is a small society. There are no more people in it than can come to know each other well, and they remain in long association with each other. Among the Western Shoshone, the individual parental family was the group, which went about, apart from other families, collecting food; a group of families would assemble and so remain for a few weeks, from time to time, to hunt together; during the winter months, such a group of families would form a single camp.[2] Such a temporary village included perhaps a hundred people. The hunting or food-collecting bands considered by Steward, representing many parts of the world, contained, in most cases, only a few score people.[3] A Southwestern pueblo contained no more than a few thousand persons.

[1] W. G. Sumner, *Folkways* (Boston: Ginn & Co., 1907), p. 12.

[2] Julian Steward, *Basin-Plateau Aboriginal Sociopolitical Groups* (Smithsonian Institution, Bureau of American Ethnology, Bull. 120 [Washington: Government Printing Office, 1938]), pp. 230–34.

[3] Julian Steward, "Economic and Social Basis of Primitive Bands," *Essays in Anthropology Presented to A. L. Kroeber* (Berkeley: University of California Press, 1936), pp. 341–42.

* From *American Journal of Sociology*, vol. 52, no. 4 (January, 1947), 293–308. Copyright © 1947, University of Chicago. Reprinted by permission.

The folk society is an isolated society. Probably there is no real society whose members are in complete ignorance of the existence of people other than themselves; the Andamanese, although their islands were avoided by navigators for centuries, knew of outsiders and occasionally came in contact with Malay or Chinese visitors.[4] Nevertheless, the folk societies we know are made up of people who have little communication with outsiders, and we may conceive of the ideal folk society as composed of persons having communication with no outsider.

This isolation is one half of a whole of which the other half is intimate communication among the members of the society. A group of recent castaways is a small and isolated society, but it is not a folk society; and, if the castaways have come from different ships and different societies, there will have been no previous intimate communication among them, and the society will not be composed of people who are much alike.

May the isolation of the folk society be identified with the physical immobility of its members? In building this ideal type, we may conceive of the members of the society as remaining always within the small territory they occupy. There are some primitive peoples who have dwelt from time immemorial in the same small valley, and who rarely leave it.[5] Certain of the pueblos of the American Southwest have been occupied by the same people or their descendants for many generations. On the other hand, some of the food-collecting peoples, such as the Shoshone Indians and certain aborigines of Australia, move about within a territory of very considerable extent; and there are Asiatic folk groups that make regular seasonal migrations hundreds of miles in extent.

It is possible to conceive of the members of such a society as moving about physically without communicating with members of other groups than their own. Each of the Indian villages of the midwest highlands of Guatemala is a folk society distinguishable by its customs and even by the physical type of its members from neighboring villages; yet, the people are great travelers, and, in the case of one of the most distinct communities, Chichicastenango, most of the men travel far and spend much of their time away from home.[6] This does not result, however, in much intimate communication between those traveling villagers and other peoples. The gypsies have moved about among the various peoples of the earth for generations, and yet they retain many of the characteristics of a folk society.

Through books, the civilized people communicate with the minds of other people and other times, and an aspect of the isolation of the folk society is the absence of books. The folk communicate only by word of mouth; therefore, the communication upon which understanding is built is

[4] A. R. Radcliffe-Brown. *The Andaman Islanders* (Cambridge: At the University Press, 1933), pp. 6–9.

[5] A. L. Kroeber, *Handbook of Indians of California* (Smithsonian Institution, Bureau of American Ethnology, Bull. 78 [Washington: Government Printing Office, 1925]) p. 13.

[6] Robert Redfield, "Primitive Merchants of Guatemala," *Quarterly Journal of Inter-American Relations,* I, no. 4, 42–56.

only that which takes place among neighbors, within the little society itself. The folk has no access to the thought and experience of the past, whether of other peoples or of their own ancestors, such as books provide. Therefore, oral tradition has no check or competitor. Knowledge of what has gone before reaches no further back than memory and speech between old and young can make it go; behind "the time of our grandfathers," all is legendary and vague. With no form of belief established by written record, there can be no historical sense, such as civilized people have, no theology, and no basis for science in recorded experiment. The only form of accumulation of experience, except the tools and other enduring articles of manufacture, is the increase of wisdom that comes as the individual lives longer; therefore, the old, knowing more than the young can know until they, too, have lived that long, have prestige and authority.

The people who make up a folk society are much alike. Having lived in long intimacy with one another and with no others, they have come to form a single biological type. The somatic homogeneity of local, inbred populations has been noted and studied. Since the people communicate with one another and with no others, one man's learned ways of doing and thinking are the same as another's. Another way of putting this is to say that, in the ideal folk society, what one man knows and believes is the same as what all men know and believe. Habits are the same as customs. In real fact, of course, the differences among individuals in a primitive group and the different chances of experience prevent this ideal state of things from coming about. Nevertheless, it is near enough to the truth for the student of a real folk society to report it fairly well by learning what goes on in the minds of a few of its members, and a primitive group has been presented, although sketchily, as learned about from a single member. The similarity among the members is found also as one generation is compared with its successor. Old people find young people doing, as they grow up, what the old people did at the same age, and what they have come to think right and proper. This is another way of saying that, in such a society, there is little change.

The members of the folk society have a strong sense of belonging together. The group that an outsider might recognize as composed of similar persons different from members of other groups is also the group of people who see their own resemblances and feel correspondingly united. Communicating intimately with each other, each has a strong claim on the sympathies of the others. Moreover, against such knowledge as they have of societies other than their own, they emphasize their own mutual likeness and value themselves as compared with others. They say of themselves "we" as against all others, who are "they."[7]

Thus, we may characterize the folk society as small, isolated, nonliterate, and homogeneous, with a strong sense of group solidarity. Are we not soon to acknowledge the simplicity of the technology of the ideal folk society? Something should certainly be said about the tools and tool-making of this generalized primitive group, but it is not easy to assign a meaning to

[7] Sumner, *op. cit.,* pp. 13–15.

"simple," in connection with technology, that will do justice to the facts as known from the real folk societies. The preciseness with which each tool, in a large number of such tools, meets its needs in the case of the Eskimo, for example, makes one hesitate to use the word "simple." Some negative statements appear to be safe: Secondary and tertiary tools—tools to make tools—are relatively few as compared with primary tools; there is no making of artifacts by multiple, rapid, machine manufacture; there is little or no use of natural power.

There is not much division of labor in the folk society: What one person does is what another does. In the ideal folk society, all the tools and ways of production are shared by everybody. The "everybody" must mean "every adult man" or "every adult woman," for the obvious exception to the homogeneity of the folk society lies in the differences between what men do and know and what women do and know. These differences are clear and unexceptional (as compared with our modern urban society, where they are less so). "Within the local group there is no such thing as a division of labor save as between the sexes," writes Radcliffe-Brown about the Andaman Islanders. ". . . Every man is expected to be able to hunt pig, to harpoon turtle and to catch fish, and also to cut a canoe, to make bows and arrows and all the other objects that are made by men."[8] So, all men share the same interests and have, in general, the same experience of life.

We may conceive, also, of the ideal folk society as a group economically independent of all others: The people produce what they consume and consume what they produce. Few, if any, real societies are completely in this situation; some Eskimo groups, perhaps, most closely approach it. Although each little Andamanese band could get along without getting anything from any other, exchange of goods occurred between bands by a sort of periodic gift-giving.

The foregoing characterizations amount, roughly, to saying that the folk society is a little world off by itself, a world in which the recurrent problems of life are met by all its members in much the same way. This statement, while correct enough, fails to emphasize an important, perhaps the important, aspect of the folk society. The ways in which the members of the society meet the recurrent problems of life are conventionalized ways; they are the results of long intercommunication within the group in the face of these problems; and these conventionalized ways have become interrelated within one another so that they constitute a coherent and self-consistent system. Such a system is what we mean in saying that the folk society is characterized by a "culture." A culture is an organization or integration of conventional understandings. It is, as well, the acts and the objects, insofar as they represent the type characteristic of that society, that express and maintain these understandings. In the folk society, this integrated whole, this system, provides for all the recurrent needs of the individual from birth to death and of the society through the seasons and the years. The society is

8 Radcliffe-Brown, *op. cit.*, p. 43.

to be described, and distinguished from others, largely by presenting this system.

This is not the same as saying, as was said early in this paper, that, in the folk society, what one man does is the same as what another man does. What one man does in a mob is the same as what another man does, but a mob is not a folk society. It is, so far as culture is concerned, its very antithesis.[9] The members of a mob (which is a kind of "mass") each do the same thing, it is true, but it is a very immediate and particular thing, and it is done without much reference to tradition. It does not depend upon and express a great many conventional understandings related to one another. A mob has no culture. The folk society exhibits culture to the greatest conceivable degree. A mob is an aggregation of people doing the same simple thing simultaneously. A folk society is an organization of people doing many different things successively as well as simultaneously. The members of a mob act with reference to the same object of attention. The members of a folk society are guided in acting by previously established comprehensive and interdependent conventional understandings; at any one time, they do many different things, which are complexly related to one another, to express collective sentiments and conceptions. When the turn comes for the boy to do what a man does, he does what a man does; thus, although in the end the experiences of all individuals of the same sex are alike, the activities of the society, seen at a moment of time, are diverse, while interdependent and consistent.

The Papago Indians, a few hundred of them, constituted a folk society in southern Arizona. Among these Indians, a war party was not so simple a thing as a number of men going out together to kill the enemy. It was a complex activity involving everybody in the society, before, during, and after the expedition, and dramatizing the religious and moral ideas fundamental to Papago life.[10] Preparation for the expedition involved many practical or ritual acts on the part of the immediate participants, their wives and children, previously successful warriors, and many others. While the party was away, the various relatives of the warriors had many things to do or not to do—prayer, fasting, preparation of ritual paraphernalia, etc. These were specialized activities, each appropriate to just that kind of relative or other category of person. So, the war was waged by everybody. These activities, different and special as they were, interlocked, so to speak, with each other to make a large whole, the society-during-a-war-expedition. And all these specialized activities obeyed fundamental principles, understood by all and expressed and reaffirmed in the very forms of the acts—the gestures of the rituals, the words of songs, the implied or expressed explanations and admonitions of the elders to the younger people. All understood that the end in view was the acquisition by the group of the supernatural

[9] Herbert Blumer, "Mass Behavior and the Motion Picture," *Publications of the American Sociological Society,* XXIX, no. 3 (August, 1935), 115–27.
[10] Ruth Underhill, *The Autobiography of a Papago Woman* ("American Anthropological Association, Memoirs," no. 46 [1936]).

power of the slain enemy. This power, potentially of great positive value, was dangerous, and the practices and rituals had as their purposes, first, the success of the war party and, then, the draining off of the supernatural power acquired by the slaying into a safe and "usable" form.

We may say, then, that, in the folk society, conventional behavior is strongly patterned: It tends to conform to a type or a norm. These patterns are interrelated in thought and in action with one another, so that one tends to evoke others and to be consistent with the others. Every customary act among the Papago when the successful warriors return is consistent with and is a special form of the general conceptions held as to supernatural power. We may still further say that the patterns of what people think should be done are closely consistent with what they believe is done, and that there is one way, or a very few conventional ways, in which everybody has some understanding, and some share, of meeting each need that arises.[11] The culture of a folk society is, therefore, one of those wholes that is greater than its parts. Gaining a livelihood takes support from religion, and the relations of men to men are justified in the conceptions held of the super-natural world or in some other aspect of the culture. Life, for the member of the folk society, is not one activity and then another and different one; it is one large activity out of which one part may not be separated without affecting the rest.

A related characteristic of the folk society was implied when it was declared that the specialized activities incident to the Papago war party obeyed fundamental principles understood by all. These "principles" had to do with the ends of living, as conceived by the Papago. A near-ultimate good for the Papago was the acquisition of supernatural power. This end was not questioned; it was a sort of axiom in terms of which many lesser activities were understood. This suggests that we may say of the folk society that its ends are taken as given. The activities incident to the war party may be regarded as merely complementarily useful acts—aspects of the division of labor. They may also, and more significantly, be seen as expressions of un-questioned common ends. The folk society exists not so much in the ex-change of useful functions as in common understandings as to the ends given. The ends are not stated as matters of doctrine but are implied by the many acts that make up the living that goes on in the society. Therefore, the morale of a folk society—its power to act consistently over periods of time and to meet crises effectively—is dependent not upon discipline exerted by force or upon devotion to some single principle of action but to the con-currence and consistency of many or all of the actions and conceptions that make up the whole round of life. In the trite phrase, the folk society is a "design for living."

What is done in the ideal folk society is done not because somebody or some people decided, at once, that it should be done but because it seems "necessarily" to flow from the very nature of things. There is, moreover,

[11] Ralph Linton, *The Study of Man* (New York: D. Appleton–Century Co., 1936), chap. 16, esp. p. 283.

no disposition to reflect upon traditional acts and consider them objectively and critically. In short, behavior in the folk society is traditional, spontaneous, and uncritical. In any real folk society, of course, many things are done as a result of decision as to that particular action, but as to that class of actions tradition is the sufficient authority. The Indians decide now to go on a hunt; but it is not a matter of debate whether or not one should, from time to time, hunt.

The folkways are the ways that grow up out of long and intimate association of men with each other; in the society of our conception, all the ways are folkways. Men act with reference to each other by understandings that are tacit and traditional. There are no formal contracts or other agreements. The rights and obligations of the individual do not come about by special arrangement; they are, chiefly, aspects of the position of the individual as a person of one sex or the other, one age group or another, one occupational group or another, and as one occupying just that position in a system of relationships that are traditional in the society. The individual's status is thus, in large part, fixed at birth; it changes as he lives, but it changes in ways that were "foreordained" by the nature of his particular society. The institutions of the folk society are of the sort that has been called "crescive"; they are not of the sort that is created deliberately for special purposes, as was the juvenile court. So, too, law is made up of the traditional conceptions of rights and obligations and the customary procedures whereby these rights and obligations are assured; legislation has no part in it.

If legislation has no part in the law of the ideal folk society, neither has codification, still less jurisprudence. Radin has collected material suggesting the limited extent to which real primitive people do question custom and do systematize their knoweldge.[12] In the known folk societies, they do these things only to a limited extent. In the ideal folk society, there is no objectivity and no systematization of knowledge as guided by what seems to be its "internal" order. The member of this mentally constructed society does not stand off from his customary conduct and subject it to scrutiny apart from its meaning for him as that meaning is defined in culture. Nor is there any habitual exercise of classification, experiment, and abstraction for its own sake, least of all for the sake of intellectual ends. There is common practical knowledge, but there is no science.

Behavior in the folk society is highly conventional, custom fixes the rights and duties of individuals, and knowledge is not critically examined or objectively and systematically formulated; but it must not be supposed that primitive man is a sort of automaton in which custom is the mainspring. It would be as mistaken to think of primitive man as strongly aware that he is constrained by custom. Within the limits set by custom, there is invitation to excel in performance. There is lively competition, a sense of opportunity, and a feeling that what the culture moves one to do is well worth doing. "There is no drabness in such a life. It has about it all the allurements of

[12] Paul Radin, *Primitive Man as Philosopher* (New York: D. Appleton–Century Co., 1927).

personal experience, very much one's own, of competitive skill, of things well done."[13] The interrelations and high degree of consistency among the elements of custom that are presented to the individual declare to him the importance of making his endeavors in the directions indicated by tradition. The culture sets goals that stimulate action by giving great meaning to it.[14]

It has been said that the folk society is small, and that its members have lived in long and intimate association with one another. It has also been said that, in such societies, there is little critical or abstract thinking. These characteristics are related to yet another characteristic of the folk society: Behavior is personal, not impersonal. A "person" may be defined as that social object which I feel to respond to situations as I do, with all the sentiments and interests that I feel to be my own; a person is myself in another form, his qualities and values are inherent within him, and his significance for me is not merely one of utility. A "thing," on the other hand, is a social object that has no claim upon my sympathies, that responds to me, as I conceive it, mechanically; its value for me exists insofar as it serves my end. In the folk society, all human beings admitted to the society are treated as persons; one does not deal impersonally ("thing-fashion") with any other participant in the little world of that society. Moreover, in the folk society much besides human beings is treated personally. The pattern of behavior that is first suggested by the inner experience of the individual—his wishes, fears, sensitivenesses, and interests of all sorts—is projected into all objects with which he comes into contact. Thus, nature, too, is treated personally: The elements, the features of the landscape, the animals, and especially anything in the environment that, by its appearance or behavior, suggests that it has the attributes of mankind—to all these are attributed qualities of the human person.[15]

In short, the personal and intimate life of the child in the family is extended, in the folk society, into the social world of the adult and even into inanimate objects. It is not merely that relations in such a society are personal; it is also that they are familial. The first contacts made as the infant becomes a person are with other persons; moreover, each of these first persons, he comes to learn, has a particular kind of relation to him that is associated with that one's genealogical position. The individual finds himself fixed within a constellation of familial relationships. The kinship connections provide a pattern in terms of which, in the ideal folk society, all personal relations are conventionalized and categorized. All relations are personal. But relations are not, in content of specific behavior, the same for everyone. As a mother is different from a father, and a grandson from a nephew, so are these classes of personal relationship, originating in genealogical connection, extended outward into all relationships whatever. In this sense, the folk society is a familial society. Lowie[16] has demonstrated the

[13] A. A. Goldenweiser, "Individual, Pattern and Involution," *Essays in Honor of A. L. Kroeber* (Berkeley: University of California Press, 1936), p. 102.

[14] Ruth Benedict, *Patterns of Culture* (Boston: Houghton Mifflin, 1934).

[15] Ruth Benedict, "Animism," *Encyclopaedia of the Social Sciences*.

[16] Robert H. Lowie, *The Origin of the State* (New York: Harcourt, Brace, 1927), pp. 51–73.

qualification that is to be introduced into the statement of Maine[17] that the primitive society is organized in terms of kinship rather than territory. It is true that the fact that men are neighbors contributes to their sense of belonging together. But the point to be emphasized in understanding the folk society is that, whether mere contiguity or relationship as brother or as son is the circumstance uniting men into the society, the result is a group of people among whom prevail the personal and categorized relationships that characterize families as we know them, and in which the patterns of kinship tend to be extended outward from the group of genealogically connected individuals into the whole society. The kin are the type persons for all experience.

This general conception may be resolved into component or related conceptions. In the folk society, family relationships are clearly distinguished from one another. Very special sorts of behavior may be expected by a mother's brother of his sister's son, and this behavior will be different from that expected by a father's brother of his brother's son. Among certain Australian tribes, animals killed by a hunter must be divided so that nine or ten certain parts must be given to nine or ten corresponding relatives of the successful hunter—the right ribs to the father's brother, a piece of the flank to the mother's brother, and so on.[18] The tendency to extend kinship outward takes many special forms. In many primitive societies, kinship terms and kinship behavior (in reduced degree) are extended to persons not known to be genealogically related at all, but who are nevertheless regarded as kin. Among the central Australians, terms of relationship are extended "so as to embrace all persons who come into social contact with one another. . . . In this way the whole society forms a body of relatives."[19] In the folk society, groupings that do not arise out of genealogical connection are few, and those that do exist tend to take on the attributes of kinship. Ritual kinship is common in primitive and peasant societies in the forms of blood brotherhood, godparental relationships, and other ceremonial sponsorships.[20] These multiply kinship connections; in these cases, the particular individuals to be united depend upon choice. Furthermore, there is frequently a recognizedly fictitious or metaphorical use of kinship terms to designate more casual relationships, as between host and guest or between worshipper and deity.[21]

The real primitive and peasant societies differ very greatly as to the forms assumed by kinship. Nevertheless, it is possible to recognize two main types. In one of these, the connection between husband and wife is emphasized, while neither one of the lineages, matrilineal or patrilineal, is singled out as

[17] Henry Maine, *Ancient Law* (London: J. Murray, 1861).

[18] A. W. Howitt, *The Native Tribes of Southeastern Australia* (New York: Macmillan, 1904), p. 759.

[19] A. R. Radcliffe-Brown, "Three Tribes of Western Australia," *Journal of the Royal Anthropological Institute,* XLIII, 150–51.

[20] Benjamin Paul, "Ritual Kinship: With Special Reference to Godparenthood in Middle America" (Ph.D. thesis, University of Chicago, 1942).

[21] E. C. Parsons, *Notes on Zuni,* Part II ("American Anthropological Association Memoirs," IV, no. 4 [1917]).

contrasted with the other. In such a folk society, the individual parental family is the social unit, and connections with relatives outside this family are of secondary importance. Such family organization is common where the population is small, the means of livelihood are by precarious collection of wild food, and larger units cannot permanently remain together because the natural resources will not allow it. But, where a somewhat larger population remains together, either in a village or in a migratory band, there often, although by no means always, is found an emphasis upon one line of consanguine connection rather than the other with subordination of the conjugal connection.[22] There results a segmentation of the society into equivalent kinship units. These may take the form of extended domestic groups or joint families (as in China) or may include many households of persons related in part through recognized genealogical connection and in part through the sharing of the same name or other symbolic designation (in the latter case, we speak of the groups as clans). Even in societies where the individual parental family is an independent economic unit, as in the case of the eastern Eskimo, husband and wife never become a new social and economic unit with the completeness that is characteristic of our own society. When a marriage in primitive society comes to an end, the kinsmen of the dead spouse assert upon his property a claim they have never given up.[23] On the whole, we may think of the family among folk peoples as made up of persons consanguinely connected. Marriage is, in comparison with what we in our society directly experience, an incident in the life of the individual who is born, brought up, and dies with his blood kinsmen. In such a society, romantic love can hardly be elevated to a major principle.

Insofar as the consanguine lines are well defined (and, in some cases, both lines may be of importance to the individual),[24] the folk society may be thought of as composed of families rather than of individuals. It is the familial groups that act and are acted upon. There is strong solidarity within the kinship group, and the individual is responsible to all his kin as they are responsible to him. "The clan is a natural mutual aid society. . . . A member belongs to the clan, he is not his own; if he is wrong, they will right him; if he does wrong, the responsibility is shared by them."[25] Thus, in folk societies wherein the tendency to maintain consanguine connection has resulted in joint families or clans, it is usual to find that injuries done by an individual are regarded as injuries against his kinship group, and the group takes the steps to right the wrong. The step may be revenge regulated by custom or a property settlement. A considerable part of primitive law exists in the regulation of claims by one body of kin against another. The fact that

[22] Ralph Linton, *The Study of Man* (New York: D. Appleton-Century, 1936), p. 159.

[23] Ruth Benedict, "Marital Property Rights in Bilateral Societies," *American Anthropologist,* XXXVIII, no. 3 (July–September, 1936), 368–73.

[24] Peter Murdock, "Double Descent," *American Anthropologist,* XLII (new ser.), no. 4, pt. 1 (October–December, 1940), 555–61.

[25] Edwin W. Smith and Andrew Murray Dale, *The Ila-Speaking Peoples of Northern Rhodesia* (London: Macmillan, 1920), I, 296.

the folk society is an organization of families rather than an aggregation of individuals is further expressed in many of those forms of marriage in which a certain kind of relative is the approved spouse. The customs by which, in many primitive societies, a man is expected to marry his deceased brother's widow or a woman to marry her deceased sister's husband express the view of marriage as an undertaking between kinship groups. One of the spouses having failed by death, the undertaking is to be carried on by some other representative of the family group. Indeed, in the arrangements for marriage —the selection of spouses by the relatives, in bride-price, dowry, and in many forms of familial negotiations leading to a marriage—the nature of marriage as a connubial form of social relations between kindreds finds expression.

It has been said in foregoing paragraphs that behavior in the folk society is traditional, spontaneous, and uncritical, that what one man does is much the same as what another man does, and that the patterns of conduct are clear and remain constant throughout the generations. It has also been suggested that the congruence of all parts of conventional behavior and social institutions with each other contributes to the sense of rightness that the member of the folk society feels to inhere in his traditional ways of action. In the well-known language of Sumner, the ways of life are folkways; furthermore, the folkways tend to be also mores—ways of doing or thinking to which attach notions of moral worth. The value of every traditional act or object or institution is, thus, something that the members of the society are not disposed to call into question; and, should the value be called into question, the doing so is resented. This characteristic of the folk society may be briefly referred to by saying that it is a sacred society. In the folk society, one may not, without calling into effect negative social sanctions, challenge as valueless what has come to be traditional in that society.

Presumably, the sacredness of social objects has its source, in part at least, in the mere fact of habituation; probably the individual organism becomes early adjusted to certain habits, motor and mental, and to certain associations between one activity and another or between certain sense experiences and certain activities, and it is almost physiologically uncomfortable to change or even to entertain the idea of change. There arises "a feeling of impropriety of certain forms, of a particular social or religious value, or a superstitious fear of change."[26] Probably the sacredness of social objects in the folk society is related also to the fact that, in such well-organized cultures, acts and objects suggest the traditions, beliefs, and conceptions that all share. There is reason to suppose that, when what is traditionally done becomes less meaningful because people no longer know what the acts stand for, life becomes more secular.[27] In the repetitious character of conventional action (aside from technical action), we have ritual; in its expressive character, we have ceremony; in the folk society, ritual tends also

[26] Franz Boas, *Primitive Art* (Oslo, 1927), p. 150.
[27] Robert Redfield, *The Folk Culture of Yucatan* (Chicago: University of Chicago Press, 1941), p. 364.

to be ceremonious, and ritual-ceremony tends to be sacred, not secular.

The sacredness of social objects is apparent in the ways in which, in the folk society, such an object is hedged around with restraints and protections that keep it away from the commonplace and the matter-of-fact.[28] In the sacred, there is alternatively, or in combination, holiness and dangerousness. When the Papago Indian returned from a successful war expedition, bringing the scalp of a slain Apache, the head-hairs of the enemy were treated as loaded with a tremendous "charge" of supernatural power; only old men, already successful warriors and purified through religious ritual, could touch the object and make it safe for incorporation into the home of the slayer. Made into the doll-like form of an Apache Indian, it was, at last, after much ceremonial preparation, held for an instant by the members of the slayer's family, addressed in respect and awe by kinship terms, and placed in the house, there to give off protective power.[29] The Indians of San Pedro de la Laguna, Guatemala, recognize an officer, serving for life, whose function it is to keep custody of ten or a dozen Latin breviaries printed in the eighteenth century and to read prayers from one or another of these books on certain occasions. No one but this custodian may handle the books, save his assistants on ceremonial occasions, with his permission. Should anyone else touch a book, he would go mad or be stricken with blindness. Incense and candles are burnt before the chest containing the books, yet the books are not gods —they are objects of sacredness.[30]

In the folk society, this disposition to regard objects as sacred extends, characteristically, even into the foodstuffs of the people. Often, the foodstuffs are personified as well as sacred. " 'My granduncle used to say to me,' explained a Navajo Indian, ' "if you are walking along a trail and see a kernel of corn, pick it up. It is like a child lost and starving." According to the legends, corn is just the same as a human being, only it is holier. . . . When a man goes into a cornfield, he feels that he is in a holy place, that he is walking among Holy People. . . . Agriculture is a holy occupation. Even before you plant you sing songs. You continue this during the whole time your crops are growing. You cannot help but feel that you are in a holy place when you go through your fields and they are doing well.' "[31] In the folk society, ideally conceived, nothing is solely a means to an immediate practical end. All activities, even the means of production, are ends in themselves, activities expressive of the ultimate values of the society.

[28] Émile Durkheim, *The Elementary Forms of the Religious Life* (London: Allen & Unwin, 1926).

[29] Underhill, *op. cit.,* p. 18.

[30] Benjamin Paul, unpublished MS.

[31] W. W. Hill, *The Agricultural and Hunting Methods of the Navaho Indians* ("Yale University Publications in Anthropology," no. 18 [New Haven: Yale University Press, 1938]), p. 53.

* * *

The Social Organization of Public Gatherings

Queue Culture: The Waiting Line as a Social System*

Leon Mann

* * *

THE STUDY

Every Saturday afternoon in the month of September, over 100,000 specta-tors crowd into a stadium in Melbourne, Australia, to watch the "world series" of Australian rules football.

On August 15, 1967, approximately 10,000 people formed twenty-two queues outside the Melbourne Football Stadium to buy 14,000 sets of tick-ets for the four games. It was the last opportunity to get tickets, because mail applications for the bulk of the tickets had been oversubscribed weeks before. A great many of the 10,000 faced disappointment, because most queuers usually buy the full allotment of two adult and two children's tickets.

From 6 A.M. until 8 A.M., when the selling windows opened, a team of nine research assistants, male psychology majors from the University of Mel-bourne, conducted short, standard interviews with 216 people in ten of the twenty-two queues. Each interviewer was randomly assigned a queue. Starting with the first person in line, the procedure was to approach every tenth person. The request was brief and informal: "I am from the Univer-sity, and we are doing a study of how people feel about the queues. Would you care to answer a few questions?" Only two refusals were encountered; with the exception of one queue, all interviews were completed by 8 A.M., when the lines began to move. Questions covered attitudes toward the sys-tem of queueing, evidence of pushing in and place keeping, arrangements to make the task of queueing more pleasant, as well as estimates of position in line and chances of getting a ticket. Interviewers also made notes on their observations of the physical shape of the queues and on their impressions of the mood and morale of the people in them. Data from the Melbourne stadium are the main source of evidence cited in this paper.

Members of the research team also conducted interviews and made ob-servations in the club queues at suburban Collingwood, Carlton, and Rich-mond, each of which had allocations of 1,000 tickets for club members.

* From *American Journal of Sociology,* vol. 74, no. 3 (November, 1969), 340–54. Copyright © 1969, University of Chicago. Reprinted by permission.

Data gathered from the club queues provide additional evidence presented in this paper.

THE QUEUE TRADITION

The system of selling seat bookings for the football finals several weeks before the start of the series was first introduced in 1956. Before 1956, people queued outside the stadium on the day of the game, and "first in" took the best seats. Over the years, because of the large increase in the number of football followers, the queue system became accepted as the only workable method for selling tickets. Although there were complaints from the public, the great overnight queues became a regular event at the end of a Melbourne winter. And, as the queues took on an institutional character, increasing numbers of veterans began to regard them as a kind of cherished tradition or ritual. For example, even during the regular season, although it was possible to get choice seats two hours before the commencement of most Saturday games, long queues formed outside stadiums on Friday, perhaps to train for the big one in August.

The queue of 1965 was perhaps the most remarkable, for in that year 25,000 people waited for 12,500 tickets, some of them for over a week, in mud and drizzling rain. Queuers erected a shantytown of tents and caravans outside the stadium, and conditions, according to the Melbourne town clerk, rapidly became "squalid and unhygienic." In 1966, to prevent a recurrence of the shantytown, the Melbourne City Council banned tents and camping equipment from the queues and prohibited the lighting of fires. Also, queues or assemblies were not allowed outside the stadium until twenty hours before ticket sales started. The city council regulations made the wait for tickets colder, but much shorter, and accordingly, it was decided to retain them the following year.

In the 1967 queues, our interviewers noted that people improvised tents by tying tarpaulins to the side of barricades and brought stretchers, sleeping bags, and supplies of liquor to make themselves comfortable during the wait. Even after a cold night in the open, 26 per cent of the respondents claimed they were happy with the queue system. Only the aged and those who had to go straight to work felt very unhappy about their night out. In 1966, when a sample of 122 queuers were interviewed on a mild afternoon before the ticket windows opened, 47 per cent reported satisfaction with this method of selling tickets.

At Collingwood, the Melbourne City Council regulations did not apply, and accommodations in the first part of the queue resembled a refugee camp. The first three families in line, numbering approximately thirty men, women, and children, pitched a bedouin tent on the sidewalk fronting the ticket box and settled down to a six-day wait around a blazing camp fire. Some enthusiasts moved out of their homes and took up formal residence in the queue. Five days before tickets went on sale, the general secretary of Collingwood, Gordon Carlyon, received a letter addressed to "Mr. Alfred McDougall, c/o Queue outside Collingwood Football Ground, Collingwood,

3066." The *Melbourne Herald* of August 8, 1967, reported that Mr. Carlyon threaded his way through beds and tents on the sidewalk outside the stadium to deliver the letter. Melbournians had not only started to tolerate queues but actually seemed to be enjoying them. One woman outside the Melbourne stadium was heard to remark: "People are always knocking queues; what I would like to know is what people like myself would do without them" (*Melbourne Age,* August 16, 1967).

It seems that the means behavior, that is, lining up to get tickets for the event, almost becomes an end in itself, with its own intrinsic rewards and satisfactions. What does queueing mean, and why has it become an important occasion in the lives of these people? The answer lies partly in the publicity and recognition given to the queuers and partly in the challenge and excitement. For several days in August, the attention of Melbourne and its mass media is focused on the brave queues outside its stadium. To be able to claim, in football-mad Melbourne, that one has stood through the night and obtained tickets earns the kind of kudos and respect that must have been given to those who fought at Agincourt. And there are other pleasures. Outside the stadium, something of a carnival atmosphere prevails. The devotees sing, sip warm drinks, play cards, and huddle together around the big charcoal braziers. If he has come as part of a large group, or a cheer squad, the aficionado enjoys a brief taste of communal living and the chance to discuss and debate endlessly the fine points of the game. Above all, football fans regard the great queue as an adventure, an unusual and yet traditional diversion at the end of a Melbourne winter, as the football season approaches its exciting climax.

PROFILE OF THE QUEUER

The typical queuer is male, not yet twenty-five years of age, lives in a working-class suburb, and probably has absented himself from work to wait in line. Together with three friends, he has waited for at least fifteen hours to get tickets to watch his club play in the finals. He cannot explain why he likes football, but he has followed his team faithfully since childhood. He claims he would still be queueing even if his team were not playing, but the scarcity of supporters of nonfinals teams in the queue indicates that this is not likely. He has not counted the number of people ahead of him and has no real idea of the number of tickets for sale to the queue. He is fairly confident that he will get tickets, and he does not seem very unhappy about the queue system.

THE PROFESSIONAL QUEUER

When demand exceeds supply, it is inevitable that ticket speculators move into the queue in search of supplies for the flourishing market in hard-to-get tickets.

The Australian football queue contains two kinds of speculators: groups of highly organized people, hired at a fee to wait and buy tickets for large business concerns; and small-time operators, who resell their two tickets to the highest bidder. Often, the speculators are university students, whose earnings help to pay tuition fees. Two days before ticket sales opened at the Melbourne stadium, twenty students flew from Tasmania to the mainland to join the queue. The airline company, which hired them to buy the tickets, also provided free return flights, accommodation at a leading hotel, and taxis during their stay (*Melbourne Herald,* August 12, 1967). An advertising agency engaged Melbourne University students to stand in line for one dollar an hour each, the tickets to be given away as prizes. Other students, operating as free-lance scalpers, asked an outraged public fifty dollars for $5.60 tickets, and had no difficulty getting their price.[1]

It is difficult to estimate the number of speculators in the football queues, as most people would be reluctant to admit to this kind of activity, but it was apparent from the number of advertisements for tickets in the "Wanted to Sell" columns of the Melbourne newspapers that a large proportion of queuers turned professional in the week following the ticket sales.

In the Melbourne stadium lines, very few people actually counted their position, perhaps because they believed there was no point in it, since there was no accurate information available about the number of tickets available to each line (Mann and Taylor, 1969). In club queues, however, a different set of conditions obtained. There was usually a single mammoth queue (at Richmond it included over 3,000 people and ringed the perimeter of the stadium). Most important, the number of tickets on sale was well publicized, and, therefore, it was possible to make a fairly accurate estimate of the chances of getting tickets, if the person had accurate information about his position in line. Accordingly, the estimates of position in the club queues were somewhat more accurate than at the stadium, because people either had taken the trouble to count the number ahead or had consulted with a queue "counter." Queue counters are boys who count the queue at regular intervals if it is long and winding. Queue counters, like ticket speculators, "invent" businesses to go along with what began simply as a necessary social act. At Carlton, a group of boys went backward and forward during the night, counting the queue, and, at Richmond, the counters turned professional and, for a fee (ten cents), gave each customer up-to-date information on the number of people ahead and behind, as well as topical news and gossip.

THE PRE-QUEUE

A queue is a line of persons waiting in turn to be served, according to order of arrival. But the act of queueing involves more than the acquisition of a right to prior service because of early arrival. To validate this priority, the person must also spend time in the queue, not only to show late-comers that he occupies a given position but also to demonstrate that his right to

[1] Speculation in the physical position itself is not found in Australian queues, as it is in waiting lines for Broadway hit shows. At smash hits, it is not unusual for people to make a business of getting in line early in order to sell their advanced positions to late-comers for a large fee (*Life,* September 24, 1956).

priority is confirmed by an unquestionable willingness to undergo further suffering to get the commodity.

If all that is required to reserve a place in a queue is the act of registering order of arrival, everyone would make an effort to be present at the time of queue formation. This would lead either to uncontrolled competition and hostility at the time of registration or, more probably, the formation of pre-queues to establish recognition of the right to priority in the official queue.

The pre-queue is an unofficial line that forms spontaneously before the official, recognized queue is allowed to form. The Melbourne football queues were not allowed to form until 3 P.M. of the afternoon before the sale of tickets. To enforce this regulation, police erected a perimeter of barricades around the wall of the stadium. Nevertheless, hundreds of people gathered in the park hours before queueing was officially allowed to start and, without police direction or intervention, spontaneously formed lines outside the barricades. At 3 P.M., when the barricades were removed, they folded their chairs and, keeping the lines intact, filed in perfect order to the ticket windows to commence the official seventeen-hour wait. The formation of a pre-queue, in this instance, almost certainly functioned to prevent an explosive situation, which could have occurred had people failed to sort themselves into some kind of recognized order before the official line started. The lack of competition for positions among the early-comers can be explained in terms of the reward-cost structure in the first part of the line. There is little to be gained from being first, rather than twentieth or fiftieth (all are virtually guaranteed a ticket), but there is much to be lost if aggressive competition leads to physical damage and general disorder.

SERVING TIME IN QUEUES

There is a curious dilemma in the overnight queue. If there is a unanimous willingness to respect the order of arrival, it is pointless to require everyone to spend an uncomfortable night in the open. But, if large numbers absent themselves, those remaining to protect the queue from outsiders will feel that their greater inputs of time and suffering now outweigh the merits of early arrival and entitle them to priority of service. Also, they will feel no responsibility for minding the places of people who, by their absence, are in no position to offer reciprocal place-minding services. In recognition of the conflicting considerations of unnecessary suffering caused by continuous oc-cupancy, and the necessity to validate one's position by spending some time in residence, various arrangements are made that function to lessen the ordeal while protecting the rights of early-comers. Usually, the arrangements represent a compromise that allows the queuer to take brief leaves of absence while retaining undisputed rights of re-entry.

In Australian football lines, "time-out" is accomplished by two informal arrangements. Early-comers, who usually come in groups of four or five, often organize a "shift system," in which members spend one hour on with four hours off. One person can hold up to four places until the relief reports back to take over as group custodian. In our survey, an average of 39 per cent of respondents in the first 100 of every queue reported that they had organized a shift system; in the latter part of the queue, only 24 per cent reported participation in a shift system. Sometimes, the system involves a large group of people who share not only place-keeping duties but also facilities for eating, sleeping, and entertainment. The *Melbourne Herald* of August 15, 1967, described a seventeen-year-old girl, one of twelve people who took turns to leave the queue to eat and sleep in one of the few trailers found outside the Melbourne stadium. The same newspaper carried a story of a young scalper who combined business with pleasure: "I was one of a group of 20 students who stood together all night in the queue outside the ground. We were well organized. A couple of us kept our positions, and the others went out on the town" (*Melbourne Herald,* August 22, 1967).

It is rare for queuers at the head of the line to come alone; 94 per cent of the respondents questioned in the first 100 of every line reported that they had come with others. However, a large minority toward the end of each line came alone; while their need for time-outs was less pressing, they also made arrangements to cover brief absences, if necessary. It is an accepted practice to "stake a claim" in a queue by leaving some item of personal property. One can keep a place in a line with a labeled box, folding chair, haversack, or sleeping bag for quite long periods. The object stands for the person and his place, symbolism reminiscent of burial customs of the ancient Egyptians.[2] During the early hours of waiting, when many people were enjoying a carefree game of football in the surrounding park, the queues often consisted of one part people to two parts inanimate objects. The norm in leaving position markers is that one must not be absent for periods longer than two to three hours. In the Collingwood queue of 1966, irate late-comers, who noticed that many people in the middle of the queue had not made an appearance for most of the day, spontaneously seized their boxes and burnt them. The late-comers were protesting the violation of the principle of serving time to earn occupancy of a position. In the ensuing melee, scores of people made significant advances in their positions. Because arrangements for absence from the football queue are of necessity extremely informal, inefficiency and abuse often occur. To ensure protection of their valued positions, some do not trust the shift or marker systems but prefer to keep a constant vigil, which lasts the entire life of the queue.

 First come, first served, the fundamental concept of queueing, is a basic principle of the behavior referred to as distributive justice (Homans 1961). There is a direct correspondence between inputs (time spent waiting) and outcomes (preferential service). Generally, if a person is willing to invest large amounts of time and suffering in an activity, people who believe there should be an appropriate fit between effort and reward will respect his right to priority. We have seen, however, that the principle of distributive justice

[2] Markers such as notebooks, coats, newspapers, and umbrellas are often used to defend a "reserved" space in public places, such as a crowded cafeteria or study hall (Sommer, 1969).

is elaborated to encompass the need for leaves of absence in marathon queues. In recognition of the fact that continuous residence in the line imposes great hardship, members come to an agreement on the minimum inputs of time necessary to validate occupancy of a position. It is reasonable to claim that rules regulating time spent in and out of the line are the essential core of the queue culture.[3]

QUEUE JUMPING

Place-keeping and pushing in violate the principle of first come, first served. When people at the end of a queue feel certain that the violation does not jeopardize their own chances of obtaining the commodity, there is likely to be some irritation but no attempt to eject the offender. Stronger measures are likely, however, if people at the tail end believe that the lengthening of the line worsens their prospects of receiving service.

Since there is a great deal at stake, football queuers are especially annoyed by any attempt to jump the queue, and they adopt a variety of physical and social techniques to keep people in line. At certain times in the life of the queue when police supervision was minimal, queuers had to devise their own constraints. The most extreme constraint was physical force. During the early hours of August 15, five men were taken to hospitals after four separate brawls broke out in the ticket lines (*Melbourne Herald,* August 15, 1967). The strategic placement of barriers acts as a constraint against would-be infiltrators. It was observed that people in the middle of the queue worked together to erect barricades from material left in the park. Keeping close interperson distance also serves to maintain the "territory" in the face of would-be intruders. At times of maximum danger, and in the hour before the ticket windows opened, there was a visible bunching together, or shrinkage, in the physical length of the queue, literally a closing of the ranks. The exercise of effective social constraints depends on the capacity for cohesive action on the part of the queuers. At the stadium, whenever outsiders approached the head of the queue, they were intimidated by vociferous catcalls and jeering. Ordinarily, this mode of protecting the queue was successful during daylight, the pressure of concerted disapproval inhibiting all but the boldest. During the hours of darkness, social pressure proved less effective; the knowledge that one cannot be seen easily undermines social pressure and shaming as a technique.

Despite these constraints, many late-comers attempted to push in, and it was apparent that some succeeded. Letters to the newspapers by disappointed queuers testified to the activity of queue jumpers. One man who

[3] Queue systems with inbuilt guarantees of distributive justice are to be found in both the United States and the U.S.S.R. At the weekly line for tickets to the Metropolitan Opera in New York, an unofficial "keeper of the list" registers applicants in order of arrival, assigns numbers, and checks names when the queuers appear for roll call every three hours (*New Yorker,* January 14, 1967). In Moscow, when scarce goods go on sale, a series of queue custodians take turns "standing guard" and list the names of interested customers as they arrive throughout the night (Levine, 1959, pp. 338–39).

missed out in the Carlton queue claimed that he had been dislodged from 185th to 375th place in the span of two hours. When asked "Has anyone tried to push in?" respondents in every part of each queue reported that they had witnessed attempts to jump the queue, but only in a minority of cases had the intruder been ejected. According to the reports of our respondents, the act of intrusion was usually met with passivity rather than a physically hostile response, especially toward the end of the line, where people came alone and were not organized for dealing with intruders. Yet, when asked what they would do if someone tried to crash the queue immediately in front of them, respondents were almost unanimous in claiming that they would resort to physical force.

According to our respondents' reports, pushing in occurred most often near the tail of the queue. This seems puzzling at first, for, if someone is going to risk pushing in, it seems sensible to try at the front, where there is a greater certainty of getting tickets. However, we must bear in mind the more effective policing at the front, as well as the decreased risk toward the rear of the queue, where, in absolute numbers, fewer people are put out by the violation and, hence, there is less likelihood of concerted action. In brief, opposition to a queue jumper decreases as a function of the number of people whose chances of getting tickets are affected by the intrusion; at the end of the line, there are very few such people. Ironically, however, it is these people, regardless of where pushing in occurs, who stand to lose most by the infraction, because their chances of getting tickets are put in even greater jeopardy.

Why does the queue fail to act in unison to dismiss the queue jumper? To some extent, the varying interests of people in different parts of the queue provide an answer. People at the front of the queue do not care particularly about pushing in that occurs behind them, because they do not suffer from the intrusion. Of course, if queue jumping becomes widespread, the early-comers show concern, because their positions may be threatened by late-comers who realize that the entire line is vulnerable. But, usually, they have nothing to gain and much to lose from becoming involved in policing the queue. It is surprising, however, that people after the point of intrusion do not act together to expel the violator, since they all suffer equally by the loss of a place. It seems that responsibility for evicting a trespasser falls squarely on the shoulders of the person who is the immediate victim of the violation, that is, the person directly behind the violator. Those farther back may jeer and catcall, but the immediate victim is expected to take the initiative in ejecting the queue jumper. The reasoning seems to be that the victim, either through his passive looks or careless surveillance of his territory, must have given some encouragement to the queue jumper, so he is now obliged to handle the situation without causing unpleasantness for other people.

The reluctance of queuers to exert physical action against queue jumpers may also be related to the nature of informal versus formal organization of the queue. In any informal queue, there are many signs of organizational control, role prerogatives, and orderly behavior, which are almost exactly the same as those in well-organized queues, where there is real policing and monitoring of the line. Therefore, people will assume that the informal queue will function in much the same way as the organized queue. When acts of pushing in and disorder occur, members of the queue realize they were mistaken and jeer spontaneously, exert informal pressure, and make threats to preserve their positions. If verbal constraints fail, physical violence emerges as a last resort. At this point, there is a reluctance to pursue the matter further, because more may be lost from physical action than from a small loss in position. The person who jumps the queue could be desperate, and the immediate victim anticipates the possibility that a struggle could cause injury and damage. If the police action is unsuccessful, the person is made to look foolish in the eyes of the onlookers. It is also possible that, if the struggle sets off a widespread melee, he stands to lose more than face and position. Therefore, if verbal censure fails, members of the queue fall back on a conspiracy of silence to ignore minor violations. Resorting to physical violence seems to represent a kind of public acknowledgment that the queue is no longer organized and under control. Once this happens, a grave danger exists that people in less favorable positions, as well as outsiders, will take advantage of what is then recognized to be a helpless, unorganized queue. To prevent this, occasional minor infractions, if they are not met successfully by verbal threats and jeering, are seldom handled by physical threats and violence. The use of physical methods, especially if they prove unsuccessful, are a signal to others that the queue organization is about to disintegrate completely, and this may actually serve to encourage an epidemic of queue jumping.

One reason for the prevalence of pushing in, and the failure to exert effective action against it, is the confusion that exists between illegal acts of entry and the somewhat more acceptable act of place-keeping. Because place-keeping occurs fairly frequently, it is not always clear whether an individual who moves boldly into a line is attempting to crash the queue or is merely joining his group. Therefore, many are reluctant to challenge the entry of outsiders during the early hours of the queue. Although the custom of place-keeping is a cause of friction, only informal rules have been formulated to regulate its practice. Of the respondents, 29 per cent believed that it is permissible to keep a place for someone, and that people behind would not care. However, only a handful of queuers admitted to actually keeping a place for someone. People do not admit freely to place-keeping, because the newcomer usually makes his appearance only in the last hour before tickets go on sale, and people already in line are likely to be very resentful.

THE QUEUE AS A SOCIAL SYSTEM

The queue, although made up of numerous groups of strangers gathered together temporarily, emerges as an embryonic social system with a set of norms for controlling conflict.

Parsons (1951) maintains that social systems develop spontaneously whenever two or more people come into some stabilized, patterned mode of interaction. He lists three properties of any social system: (1) two or more actors occupying differentiated statuses or positions and performing differentiated roles; (2) some organized pattern governing the relationships of the members, describing their rights and obligations with respect to one another; and (3) some set of common norms and values, together with various types of shared cultural objects and symbols.

The long, overnight queue has all three characteristics of a social system. While the queue may not directly allocate different statuses or roles to its members, the members themselves assume different roles. In and around every queue there is a host of people—professional and hired speculators, queue counters, custodians, vigilantes, people, and officials—performing a variety of queue-related tasks.

The other two properties of a social system—an organized pattern of relationships and a set of common norms—are readily identifiable in the queue. Order of arrival governs the relationship among members, while the shift system and the practice of time-outs controls the network of rights and obligations. Moreover, there are shared norms about the desirability of distributive justice, as reflected in the set of rules regulating place-keeping and pushing in.

Interactive systems, such as the queue, develop within the matrix of a long-established sociocultural system that defines roles, normative standards, and goals. When a large number of people gather together and priority of service has value, a line is formed. All members bring to the new queue a host of ideas about the roles they should play, and develop firm notions about the way in which deviant behavior should be punished. Roles in the queue are drawn from, and are molded by, the institutional system of the larger society. The precise form of social organizations, the sharing and division of labor inherent in the shift system, the preferred modes of policing the queue, the development of businesses and ticket speculation, the notion that one must earn one's place in line by spending time in it, even the very reason for queueing itself, reflects the character of the surrounding society.

The culture of the queue also draws upon, and incorporates elements in, the broader culture. The importance of time as a value in Western society is reflected in the emphasis placed on serving time, and restrictions on time-outs. The way in which people orient themselves toward a scarce commodity, their preference for cooperation, the entrepreneurial zeal they display in scalping tickets and charging fees for counting the queue, is a function of broad-culture patterns, as well as the way society has taught them to behave.

The queue, moreover, is subject to sanctioning pressure from outside officials and onlookers, who try to bring it into conformity with societal expectations. Ultimately, of course, each queue has to work out its own final set of mutual adjustments, in which socially prescribed rules about queueing are modified and embellished in various ways. A prime example of these adjustments is to be found in the various interpretations of the rules governing leaves of absence from the line.

While the queue system is embedded in a larger social matrix, it is also composed of many subsystems—groups, cliques, and coacting individuals—whose physical presence reinforces the very idea or concept of a line.

According to Parsons and Smelser (1957), there are four functional problems, or imperatives, faced by every social system: goal attainment, adaptation, integration, and latency. The queue, even though it is a relatively minor, short-lived social system, must confront these four problems.

The problem of goal attainment is to keep the system moving steadily toward the collective goal of its members—in this case, the purchase of tickets in an orderly manner, with a minimum of unpleasantness. Before the system can move toward this goal, however, a host of instrumental and technical problems must be solved. Many of the problems are external to the queue, in the sense that they are not under the control of its members; for example, the seller (not the customer) must decide when and where people should be allowed to queue, how many lines should be formed, how many tickets will be made available, what limitation will be placed on the number of tickets sold to each customer, and so on. But the question of how to begin the queue, especially if people have gathered before the official starting time, is a problem left to the members themselves. As we have seen, the football fans solved this difficulty by forming a prequeue, which became the officially recognized queue when the barriers to the ticket boxes were lowered.

Adaptation is the problem of bringing facilities and resources to the system that enable it to come to terms with the environment. One aspect of adaptation is the active manipulation of the environment. Thus, queuers formed their line along concrete paths, constructed barriers out of material found in the park, erected shelters by tying tarpaulins to the barriers, built fires, and even brought in trailers, to make their temporary living quarters as comfortable as possible.

Manipulation of the system itself to blend with the environment is another aspect of adaptation. For the most part, the queue, rather than a single file of people, consisted of numerous knots of people, two and three abreast, who sat side by side to facilitate efficient communication and social interaction.

The integrative problem, perhaps the most distinctive in any social system, is concerned with the maintenance of appropriate emotional and social ties among members of the system. In order to achieve its goals, the system must establish and maintain a high degree of solidarity and cohesion. In the queue, cohesion is achieved by establishing informal rules, which are kept sufficiently general to allow individual members to adjust to the normative pattern. Those who stay out too long, and therefore are unable to make the line viable, are sanctioned, or lose their place. In a sense, this represents a form of turn taking; if the queue structure is to be preserved, only some members can be permitted to take leaves of absence at any one time.

The group or clique, by means of the shift system, regulates turn taking for its members, and this ensures continuity of the line. The group, since it is the carrier of queue culture, brings a high level of solidarity to the line.

At the head of the line, the group takes on the characteristics of a community. Large family groups share eating, rest, and recreational facilities, and time spent together serves to strengthen the feelings of community. It is likely that the major factor underlying the effective policing of the head and middle regions of the line is the presence of large, coordinated groups. The breakdown of defense against intruders in the end part of every line can be attributed primarily to the fragmented, isolated nature of the membership.

But, even in parts of the line where organized groups are less prominent, individuals trade on a mutual trust that allows them to ask one another to "mind my place" and feel confident that they will be vouched for when they return from a brief leave of absence. The latency function is reflected in two related but different problems—pattern maintenance and tension management.

Pattern maintenance is the problem faced by an individual in reconciling the conflicting norms and demands imposed by his participation in the queue. Many members experience role conflicts arising out of their obligations to the queue and to their family or work roles. As we have seen, some queuers solve the problem by moving their entire family into the line. Others are faced with a different kind of dilemma: whether or not to keep a place for friends. The member who fails to commit himself to the queue norms is subject to considerable social pressure. If rules governing leaves of absence are not observed, the member is likely to find himself no longer part of the queue.

Tension management is the related problem of maintaining a level of commitment sufficient to perform the required role. To cope with tension and fatigue, members introduce a variety of entertainments in and around the line, such as pick-up games, story and joke telling, and beer parties. Time-out from the queue is, however, the major mode of tension management.

The queue system is mostly concerned with the problem of pattern maintenance and tension management because these are the most significant from the viewpoint of continuous participation and control. Of course, at critical times in the life of the queue, the other three functional problems require attention. Indeed, all four must be solved if the system is to continue in the state of equilibrium necessary for control and order.

* * *

CONCLUSION

This paper described how patterned regularities in behavior and attitudes emerge to regulate life in an overnight football queue. Although arrangements made to control behavior in the queue are informal, they are clearly identifiable, and it is appropriate to regard them as constituting a kind of culture. The queue, which possesses the characteristics of a social system, attempts to solve the set of functional problems confronted by every social system.

Our major findings were: (1) the growth of a queue tradition in which large numbers of people return annually to share the experience of waiting for tickets overnight in the open; (2) an increasing professionalization of the queue, marked by an influx of speculators and middlemen who profit by the increased demand for tickets; (3) the formation of unofficial prequeues to recognize the priority of people who arrived before the start of the official queue; (4) elaboration of the principle of first come, first served to control the amount of time spent in and out of the queue ("shift" and "marker" systems, which control "time-outs," were developed to regulate leaves of absence from the line); and (5) social constraints, and less often physical constraints, used to control queue jumping and to govern the practice of place-keeping.

It is appropriate to conclude that queueing behavior, a neglected area of social research, could be a rich source of ideas for students of crowd behavior, judgmental processes, cross-national differences, and the influence of cultural values on public behavior.

REFERENCES

HALL, E. T. *The Hidden Dimension* (New York: Doubleday, 1964).
————. *The Silent Language* (New York: Doubleday, 1959).
HOMANS, G. C. *Social Behavior: Its Elementary Forms* (New York: Harcourt, Brace, 1961).
LEVINE, I. R. *Main Street, U.S.S.R.* (New York: Doubleday, 1959).
MANN, L., AND K. F. TAYLOR. "Queue Counting: The Effect of Motives Upon Estimates of Numbers in Waiting Lines," *Journal of Personality and Social Psychology,* XII (1969), 95-103.
PARSONS, T. *The Social System* (New York: The Free Press, 1951).
PARSONS, T., AND NEIL J. SMELSER. *Economy and Society* (New York: The Free Press, 1957).
SOMMER, R. *Personal Space* (Englewood Cliffs, N.J.: Prentice-Hall, 1969).

Social-Organizational Problems in Modern Society

Antidote to Alienation: Learning to Belong[*]

Melvin Seeman

Most of us in the United States now live in the great, faceless conglomerates of population—the large metropolitan areas with their strung-out suburban

* From *Trans-action,* vol. 3, no. 5 (May–June, 1966), 34–39. Copyright © 1966 by Trans-action, Inc., New Brunswick, New Jersey.

belts—where who one's neighbors are is largely a matter of accident, and it usually doesn't pay to get closely involved with them, because they keep changing. Parents and children are close—perhaps even closer than before—as long as they live in the same house; but older generations and other relatives drift away, take jobs in other cities, go to retirement homes, have their own interests and associates. Often, it seems painful but realistic to conclude that, in the last analysis, you and your family are alone, and the only ones you can really count on for help and support are yourselves. No one else cares.

The American legend has it that not much more than a generation ago it used to be very different. Our fathers lived, mostly, in a golden age of belonging, in the traditional tree-shaded small town or closely-knit neighborhood (complete with the *Saturday Evening Post* version of a colonial-style church at the end of the block). Everyone was friendly and solicitous, and, in the case of need, neighbors by the tens and cousins by the dozens would come running.

For most of us, this dream, to the extent that it ever was real, is dead.

It is the dominant theme of "mass theory" in social psychology that such social and personal ties cannot be cut or seriously weakened without major damage—both to us and to the democratic process. Torn loose from so many of our emotional supports and roots—from the guidelines that remind us who we are and what we are worth—we must, so the theme goes, become prey increasingly to feelings of isolation, helplessness, and alienation.

But a theme is not yet a theory. It becomes a theory by being specific about processes—by describing the step-by-step development from cause to effect. How do the feelings of isolation, helplessness, and alienation come about, and what is their consequence? Mass theory becomes useful when it combines (1) history and social structure with (2) a description of the psychological effects of that structure, those alienative effects that, in turn, lead to (3) predicted behavior. *Alienation* is the center and the key to mass theory—it is produced by the structure of society, and it produces distinctive behavior.

To describe this process in greater detail:

• *Historically* and *structurally,* the old roots and close relationships have practically disappeared and have been replaced by anonymity and impersonality in social and personal life and by bureaucracy and mechanization at work.

• *Psychologically,* this must result in *alienation.* Alienation can take a number of forms: feelings of powerlessness, rootlessness, lack of standards and beliefs, and "self-estrangement" (having no clear idea of your personality or place, not even "belonging" to yourself).

• Alienation, in turn, results in *alienated behavior,* such as political passivity, racial and religious prejudice, taking part in movements that promise to usher in the millenium (but have little immediate or practical effect), and the like.

SUCCESS AND FAILURE

Since personal alienation is the key element, psychological theory is crucial to its understanding. In trying to understand and explain these psychological processes, I have found the social-learning theory of Julian B. Rotter very helpful (*Social Learning and Clinical Psychology,* Prentice-Hall, 1954). Rotter's principal contention is that human behavior depends on (1) the degree to which a person *expects* that the behavior will have a successful outcome, and (2) the *value* of that success to the person trying to achieve it. If these factors are powerful, separately or together, the behavior is most likely to occur. Specifically, if a person expects that learning something will help him achieve some goal, or he values that goal, he is more likely to learn.

Rotter's theory helps clarify the different meanings of alienation. Let us concentrate on what is probably the most important aspect of alienation in mass society—feelings of *powerlessness,* a person's belief that there is little he can do to bring about what he wants. People conceive of success and failure as being not only due to *external* factors—those that work on a man essentially from the outside and are usually considered beyond his control (luck, fate, "city hall," or "they")—but also *internal* factors, coming from within, which often do give him some control (skills, motives, determination, work).

Rotter and his co-workers argue that most experimental studies in learning usually unwittingly emphasize *external* control—the experimenter himself controls most of the pressures and conditions of the situation, and the subject is really not independent at all. If the subject could feel that he had some personal control over the learning, could relate it to his own needs and self-respect, then the patterns and amounts of learning might be very different.

A number of recent studies have supported this principle. These studies show that, when the same learning task is performed in two separate ways, with two sets of instructions—one, for instance, emphasizing the skill and energy required from the learner, and the other stressing the luck or chance aspect of the task (*internal* versus *external* control)—there are striking differences in learning and retention. A person will definitely learn *less* from experiences he conceives to be dominated by others, or by chance, which he feels he cannot influence.

This finding parallels the argument of the followers of mass theory that the isolated individual in "the lonely crowd," subordinated to, and intimidated by, bureaucracy, becomes convinced of his powerlessness and gives up learning about those things that might affect his future. As a specific example, he becomes apathetic and indifferent to politics—"You can't fight city hall."

Thus, mass-society theory and Rotter's social-learning theory agree that those persons with greater feelings of powerlessness will not learn as much or as well as those who feel they exercise some control over the factors that influence their lives.

UNIVERSAL ALIENATION

The statement that feelings of powerlessness inhibit knowledge is a basic conclusion about human beings. If true, it should be true not only of a few people but of many; not only of those in our country but in other nations as well. It should be true not only about one type of learning but throughout a wide spectrum of learning situations. Providing always, of course, that the learning is *relevant to control*—that it seems to the learner to be giving him a tool he can use to change his condition. Thus, an unemployed man learning how and where best to apply for a job is acquiring *control-relevant* information—while one learning baseball batting averages is not. The alienated can presumably learn escapist and irrelevant information as quickly as anyone—perhaps more quickly.

To test the hypothesis that the connection between feelings of powerlessness and inhibition of learning was generally true of mankind, we conducted several studies on powerlessness and alienation:

- in different institutions (a hospital and a reformatory);
- with different degrees of belonging to a work organization (unorganized versus unionized workers in Columbus, Ohio);
- and in different nations (Sweden and the United States).

Although specific items used in the several studies (hospital, reformatory, Columbus, and Sweden) varied somewhat, in all cases the person was offered a choice between an expression of mastery and one of powerlessness. For example:

- "Many times I feel that I have little influence over the things that happen to me," or, "I do not believe that chance and luck are very important in my life";
- "Becoming a success is a matter of hard work; luck has little or nothing to do with it," or, "Getting a job depends mainly on being in the right place at the right time."

The study of the hospital, published by John W. Evans and myself in the *American Sociological Review* (1962), and of the reformatory in *American Journal of Sociology* (1963), may be considered as a pair. They were both done in the United States. They sought to find out how feelings of powerlessness are related to lack of knowledge and information, in places where knowledge and information might give the individual some understanding and control of his fate. The hospital study dealt with tuberculosis patients; we found that those with the strongest feelings of powerlessness knew less about health matters than those not so alienated. In the reformatory study, inmates with greater feelings of helplessness learned relatively little when given information about parole, even though it might have helped shorten their confinement.

A third American study with Arthur G. Neal (*American Sociological Review,* 1964), was designed to test whether, as predicted, members of a formal occupational organization, such as a union or professional association, would feel less powerless than nonmembers. In form and feeling (if not always in fact) joining a vocational association apparently dedicated to a common goal should give a member some feeling of control over his job destiny and perhaps over broader socio-economic matters as well. Mass theory postulates that the great centers of power—government and the major corporations—are rapidly increasing in size and impersonality. At the same time, and as a consequence, jobs are becoming more specialized, more interchangeable, and the workers are moving more and more from job to job and city to city. This breakdown of personal identification with his work is supposed to make the worker feel more insignificant, expendable, and isolated ("just another cog"). The labor organizations that mediate between him and the great bureaucracies should therefore become more and more important to him, especially as a means of providing him with some sense of control.

ORGANIZED FOR POWER

We picked at random about 800 adult male names from the Columbus, Ohio, city directory, and mailed questionnaires to them designed to explore this relationship between union membership and feelings of powerlessness. About 57 per cent answered—245 manual workers and 216 nonmanuals.

The results of the Columbus study were definite. When factors such as age, income, education, and type of job are equal, unorganized workers *do* feel more powerless. This was true of both manual and nonmanual workers. (The powerlessness was a little greater for workers who changed jobs most often.) Further, these results were *specific* to powerlessness; that is, a test of the workers' generalized unhappiness (anomie) showed that the unorganized do not feel significantly more despairing about everything (or even most things) than the organized—it is apparently a rather specific sense of *mastery,* but not of well-being in general, that organization membership provides.

On the basis of the Columbus study, we could state that feelings of powerlessness do arise among unorganized workers in the United States. But a further demonstration seemed necessary, one that could combine all three elements—organization, powerlessness, and knowledge—into a single study; that could show whether these findings were peculiar to America; and that could concentrate on a broader field than health or corrections—the field of politics and international affairs.

Accordingly, a study was designed for Sweden to fulfill these needs and was carried out by interview (in Swedish) with a sample of the male work force in Malmo. (Malmo is Sweden's third largest city, population about 240,000, with a heavy concentration of commercial and seaport occupations.) A random sample of males aged twenty to seventy-nine was drawn from the official register maintained by government authorities. A total of 558 workers were interviewed.

The interview contained questions on three major variables:

- *Feelings of powerlessness*: (The individual's expectations of control), proferring the usual choice between items expressing mastery and powerlessness.
- *Organization membership*: Apart from simple membership in a union or other work organization, evidence was gathered on (1) the person's *degree* of participation and (2) his *involvement* in organizations outside of work.
- *Political knowledge*: A sixteen-item information test dealt with both Swedish politics and international affairs.

When the Swedish data had been collected, checked, and evaluated, the differences were found to be consistently and significantly as predicted: *High feelings of powerlessness and low political knowledge were found together among the unorganized workers.* Second, there was a relatively small but predictable difference between those who were officials and those who were simply members of unions.

MASTER OF THE POLITICAL SHIP

These results are clearly consistent with the learning- and mass-society theses. But, before they can be accepted without question, other complicating factors must be eliminated. What about education? Could differences in education be the real underlying cause of the differences in feelings of powerlessness? What about other factors, such as age or job prestige? A close examination of the data, correcting for education and other elements, makes the result even more emphatic. In Sweden, as in the United States, neither education nor other differences obliterated the trend. High powerlessness among the workers appeared to flow from lack of union membership and was intimately related to low political knowledge.

The officers of unions were shown to have the lowest feelings of powerlessness and to be highest in political knowledge. But was this due to the fact that they were *officers* and, therefore, a special kind of member (and also, perhaps, a special breed of cat with different personality characteristics); or was it primarily because they were more involved—"more engaged" —in the affairs of the union and, therefore, more capable of exerting control? Would other "more engaged" members (who were nonofficers) also be less alienated and have greater capacity for learning control-relevant information?

"Engaged" members, we decided, would be those who attended meetings regularly, considered the union to be important in their lives, and thought individual members were important and influential in the union. Pitting the scores of such rank-and-file members against the "less engaged," we found a parallel with the over-all comparison of organized versus unorganized workers. The relationship is modest but consistent: The greater the personal involvement in union meetings and affairs, the less the feelings of powerlessness; and, for the manual workers (who would generally tend to have less education), involvement and amount of political knowledge go together as well. (This picture calls to mind the old socialist ideal of the politically wise proletarian who spent much time in study and discussion of the political and economic factors that controlled his life and then organized to do something about them.)

We found, too, that the person's *interest* in political affairs is part of the same picture. Of course, those with more interest in politics have greater knowledge of it; but more important here is the fact that strong feelings of powerlessness go along with low interest. Those who do not feel mastery do not develop interest and do not learn.

This interest, or lack of it, is directly related to union membership—to belonging to an organization that could exert job control. Organized workers were significantly more interested in political affairs than the nonunion workers. And this interest, again, was *specific* to what we call *control-relevant* information. The unorganized were *not* totally withdrawn or apathetic; they were just as interested as the organized workers in personal and local affairs and in discussing their work. But the unorganized felt powerless to control their larger destinies—and politics and international affairs represented these larger destinies.

So far, these conclusions agree with both learning theory and mass theory. Men with little hope for success feel powerless; lose interest in, and have difficulty learning, control-relevant information.

However, it must be recalled that Rotter's learning theory made a distinction between a person's *expectation* that he can achieve a goal and the *value* he places on that goal. Theoretically, at least, a person will not try very earnestly for a goal he does not value, no matter how sure he is he can get it; contrariwise, he may try very hard, even with little hope of achievement, if he wants the goal badly enough.

In the American reformatory study, knowledge that might have helped the inmate have some control over his future (parole information) and non-control knowledge (descriptive information about the institution) were both offered to the inmates tested. We split the subjects into two groups—those who tended to conform to what prison authorities wanted of them, who seemed to value the officially approved goals and behavior set for them (working hard, obeying regulations, making no trouble, trying to meet parole requirements), and those who would not conform. We reasoned that, if the inmate did not value parole (as part of the prison system) very highly, then whether or not he believed he could achieve it was not very important in determining whether he would learn parole information; however, if he did value parole, his expectation (or lack of it) that he could determine his own life should affect how much he would study and learn about parole. The results were consistent with this view: Generally, those inmates who valued the conventional standards of how to get ahead in the reformatory world, who "conformed," learned more of the parole information than did the "unconventionals." But even in this conforming group, those who felt powerless learned less. We may conclude, then, that both the *value* of the goal and the *expectation* of achieving it will be reflected in how much learning a man will acquire that relates to the goal.

RISING EXPECTATIONS

Summarizing the over-all conclusions of all four studies:

• *Powerlessness and organization*: A person's feelings of self-reliance and power are tied up with whether he belongs to an organization that has some control over his occupational destiny. If he does belong to such an organization—union, business, or professional association—his further feelings of mastery are directly tied up with how actively he works in it—whether he has some control over *its* destiny.

• *Powerlessness and learning*: The ability to learn and retain knowledge that has some connection with control over an individual's future (politics, parole, or health information) is also directly affected by belonging to a union or other relevant organization, and to a person's alienation. To the extent that he feels powerless to affect his future, he will not learn as well what he needs to know to affect it. And he will not be as interested in it—he may even reject it.

To the degree that he *expects* to achieve his goal, he will attend to the associated learning; to the degree that he *values* the goal, he will also be oriented to learn.

• The connection between organization membership and powerlessness holds true from nation to nation—it is as true in Sweden, for example, as in the United States.

• The connection between powerlessness and learning holds true through many different kinds of organizations (reformatories, hospitals, unions) and many different kinds of control information (parole and health information, politics, international affairs).

These studies are perhaps more important for what they promise than for what they presently accomplish. The promise is that controlled studies of this kind, carried out in various cultures and settings, can establish the validity of arguments and theories about contemporary life that depend upon the idea of alienation. There is much literature of this kind, both inside and outside of social science; and it deals with a wide range of subjects—for example, mass movements, intergroup prejudice, mass communication, and politics. It is a literature that touches a powerful array of basic human values: normlessness and trust, meaninglessness and understanding, self-estrangement and integrity.

The promise is that we can concern ourselves with such large questions about the individual in modern society and test long-held theories that have highly practical consequences—learning what it really means, under various circumstances, to exert control, to sink roots, to find understanding, or even to be oneself.

3. SUGGESTIONS FOR FURTHER READING

BERNE, ERIC. *Games People Play* (New York: Grove Press, 1964).*

BLAU, PETER. *Bureaucracy in Modern Society* (New York: Random House, 1971).*

————. *Exchange and Power in Social Life* (New York: John Wiley & Sons, 1964).

DURKHEIM, ÉMILE. *Division of Labor in Society* (Glencoe, Ill.: The Free Press, 1957).*

ETZIONI, AMITAI. *Modern Organizations* (Englewood Cliffs, N.J.: Prentice-Hall, 1964).*

FARB, PETER. *Man's Rise to Civilization* (New York: E. P. Dutton, 1968).*

GERMANI, GINO. *Modernization, Urbanization and the Urban Crisis* (Boston: Little, Brown, 1973).*

GERTH, H. H., and C. WRIGHT MILLS (eds.). *From Max Weber* (New York: Oxford University Press, 1946).*

GOFFMAN, ERVING. *Behavior in Public Places* (New York: The Free Press, 1963).*

————. *Presentation of Self in Everyday Life* (Garden City, N.Y.: Doubleday, 1959).*

GREER, SCOTT. *Social Organization* (New York: Random House, 1955).*

JOSEPHSON, ERIC, and MARY JOSEPHSON (eds.). *Man Alone: Alienation in Modern Society* (New York: Dell, 1962).*

LOFLAND, LYN. *A World of Strangers: Order and Action in Urban Public Places* (New York: Basic Books, 1974).

MERTON, ROBERT. *Social Theory and Social Structure* (Glencoe, Ill.: The Free Press, 1957).

MURDOCK, GEORGE P. *Social Structure* (Glencoe, Ill.: The Free Press, 1949).*

OLMSTEAD, MICHAEL. *The Small Group* (New York: Random House, 1959).*

REDFIELD, ROBERT. *The Folk Culture of Yucatan* (Chicago: University of Chicago Press, 1941).

SERVICE, ELMAN. *Primitive Social Organization* (New York: Random House, 1962).*

STEIN, M., A. VIDICH, and D. WHITE (eds.). *Identity and Anxiety* (Glencoe, Ill.: The Free Press, 1960).*

SUTTLES, GERALD. *The Social Construction of Communities* (Chicago: University of Chicago Press, 1972).*

WHYTE, WILLIAM F. *Street-Corner Society* (Chicago: University of Chicago Press, 1943).*

WHYTE, WILLIAM H., JR. *The Organization Man* (New York: Simon & Schuster, 1956).*

WOLFF, KURT (ed.). *The Sociology of George Simmel* (Glencoe, Ill.: The Free Press, 1950).

* *Available in paperback.*

4. Socialization

INTRODUCTION

Socialization is the process by which an individual learns how to become a functioning member of his society by internalizing appropriate behavior patterns, values, and attitudes as well as acquiring necessary skills and information.

Socialization begins at birth. In due course, the child learns to take part in group life and to embody to some degree the values of his society and of groups within it. Socialization also continues into adult life. In response to his ever changing web of group affiliations and his inexorable movement through the life cycle, the individual inevitably participates in new social forms and institutions, learns new disciplines, and develops new values.

Many theories have been conceived to explain the process by which socialization occurs. Some have been derived from the observation of normal children in our society; others, from study of the emotionally disturbed; others, from laboratory experiments with children and animals; and still others, from the study of preliterate peoples. Piecing together the various theories may yield a broader, more comprehensive understanding of the nature of socialization.

Personality is an important concept in many theories of socialization. It is defined as a relatively organized and enduring structure of habits, feelings, attitudes, and predispositions to behave. The individual's personality is very much a product of the social and cultural forces impinging on him as well as of his biological inheritance.

Sigmund Freud's psychoanalytic theory, derived from the clinical study of emotionally disturbed individuals, has had enormously far-reaching effects on contemporary views of socialization. Freud was among the first to highlight the importance of the irrational, morbid, and emotional side of man's nature. He emphasized the cruciality of early childhood experiences in shaping the individual's later behavior and responses. Freud conceived of the psychosexual development of personality as a series of progressive resolutions of conflicts associated with the oral, anal, and genital areas of the body and related to weaning, toilet training, and the acquisition of socially accepted patterns for the expression of sexual drives.

Freud thought of the personality as divided into three segments; the id (unconscious, instinctual drives and wishes), the ego (the rational, conscious part of personality), and the superego (conscience, the person's conception of morality). Freud's theory, especially as it developed in his later years, held that the ego acted as mediator between the demands made by the id and the restrictions dictated by the superego. While contemporary psychoanalysts have modified many facets of Freudian theory, most acknowledge its fundamental insights into man's perennial dilemma—the conflict between his basic wants and his sense of right. David Elkind's essay on "Erik Erikson's Eight Ages of Man" suggests many parallels between Freud's psychoanalytic theory and that of a distinguished post-Freudian psychoanalyst. However, Erikson feels that personality development continues throughout the whole life cycle. He also believes that the personality is shaped at different stages of life by important resolutions the individual makes about how to orient himself to the world. To Freud, parents exerted the most important influence on the personality of the child. Erikson expands the influencing forces to include spouses, friends, peers, and others.

In sharp contrast to psychoanalysis, behaviorism focuses on the individual organism and its capacity to learn. The basic precepts of behaviorism are straightforward: (1) Overt behavior is the main, if not the exclusive, interest of the behavioral scientist; attitudes and subjective experience are ignored or given low priority. (2) Behavior is conceived in terms of stimulus and response; the learning process involves conditioning (attaching the desired responses to various stimuli through a system of reward and punishment), which is effective because, in general, the human organism seeks to maximize pleasure and minimize pain. (3) Aside from essential physiological needs, such as those for food, water, and sleep, the newborn infant exhibits considerable plasticity; he can learn almost anything.

Since it has developed mainly through laboratory work, behaviorist research is ordinarily more precise and controlled than psychoanalysis. For example, it is often possible to measure the extent of a drive or to regulate the strength of a stimulus. Behaviorism—or operant conditioning, as many of its contemporary adherents call it—has been best illuminated by research with animals and young children or with adults when the situations are relatively simple. Consider, for example, the rather impressive results obtained by Robert Hamblin and his associates in their behavior-modification research. "Changing the Game from 'Get the Teacher' to 'Learn'" strongly suggests that it may be totally unwarranted to apply a "hopeless" prognosis to many hyper-aggressive, infantile, and autistic children. However, behaviorism's critics take issue with the behaviorists' dismissal of subjective phenomena as things to be ignored because they cannot be measured quantitatively. Behaviorism has also been faulted for its inability to explain successfully social situations involving self-judgment, ambivalent feelings, and complex motivations. But, whatever its shortcomings, behaviorism has encouraged social scientists to formulate operational definitions (definitions whose meaning inheres in a set of operations or objective measurements) and to test their hypotheses in ways that can be replicated by other scientists.

Still another perspective on the socialization process is offered by the social-role theory, developed by George Herbert Mead. Social-role theory highlights social interaction and role-playing in the development of the adult person. The focal point of socialization concerns the acquisition of a self (the aspect of the individual's personality that consists of his awareness and feelings about his own personal and social identity). Mead divided the self into two parts: the "I" and the "me." The "I" represents the spontaneous, active, expressive part of the person—the unique, natural, and innovative part. The "me" represents the reflexive, subjective, and conventional part of the person; it represents the internalized demands of society and the individual's awareness of these demands. The "I" appears first; the "me" develops later, after the individual has learned the rules and expectations of his society. The "me" acts as a censor of the "I"; it is based originally on the demands and expectations of parents and subsequently on the rules and expectations of society. Mead's conceptions of the "I" and the "me" are directly comparable to Freud's notions of the id and the superego.

According to Mead, the self develops in three distinct stages. In the first, or "preparatory," stage, the child does not have the ability to perceive his own behavior; he imitates specific actions. When his action comes close to social expectations, adults reward the behavior, thus encouraging the child to repeat this pattern.

In the second, or "play," stage, the child plays at specific roles: He links together specific behaviors that are identified with a given position and its expectations. For example, the girl plays at being a mother; she strokes her doll, attempts to feed it, puts it to bed, reprimands it for crying, etc.

In the third, or "game," stage, the child acquires the ability to respond to several people at the same time. In baseball, for example, the player does not act out a highly specific individual role; he must continually adapt his behavior to the needs of the team as a whole, to the specific situations that arise in the game, while bearing in mind the rules of the game. At this point, Mead would say that the individual is responding to the "generalized other," the organized community or group that gives the person his unity of self. By slow degrees, the child learns to take the point of view not only of his parents and friends but of the organized society as a whole.

Mead's theory is highly abstract and, therefore, does not lend itself readily to empirical verification. However, there have been several researches[1] that have succeeded in quantifying key assumptions of Mead's viewpoint, thereby offering support for the theory. Thus, we see that social-role theory can be quantified and empirically tested. Perhaps future research will be able to explore other aspects of the theory, further extending our knowledge of the socialization process.

Throughout the world, the family is the most significant socializing agent for most people. Without doubt, in our own society the parent-child relationship is the most critical for the formation of individual personality and character. As industrialization has developed in the Western world, it has reduced to a certain extent the importance of the role the family enacts in the socialization process. Many skills that were once transmitted in the home are now conveyed at the university, school, office, or plant. But, although educational and economic institutions have eclipsed the family in the occupational and status preparation of the individual, the family is still supreme in the moral training of the person, for character development.

Nevertheless, the family exerts an all-pervasive influence on the behavior of the individual. Mark Zborowski's study in Chapter 2 suggests the importance of the family in shaping responses to pain. In Chapter 7, the reader will find more discussion of this question along with an examination of the family as a basic social institution in its own right.

After World War II, hundreds of thousands of American families began migrating from the overcrowded cities to the suburbs, on the theory that suburban life was "better for the children." Now, thirty years later, with a second generation of suburbia-reared children well under way, some social scientists are wondering whether it has been so successful. Urie Bronfenbrenner does not seem to think so. His article on "The Split-Level American Family" suggests that the American suburbia-reared child has been abandoned to his peer group, deprived of interaction with adults—his parents, in particular—and overexposed to television. He suggests that this shift in the sources of socialization may lie behind the great increases in delinquency, drug use, and the development of the youth counterculture.

[1] S. Frank Miyamoto and Sanford Dornbusch, "A Test of Interactionist Hypotheses of Self-Conception," *American Journal of Sociology*, vol. 61 (March, 1956), pp. 399–403; Manford Kuhn, "Self Attitudes by Age, Sex, and Professional Training," *Sociological Quarterly*, vol. 1 (January, 1960), pp. 39–55; and E. L. Quarantelli and Joseph Cooper, "Self-Conceptions and Others: A Further Test of Meadian Hypotheses," *Sociological Quarterly*, vol. 7 (Summer, 1966), pp. 281–97.

Socialization, we have mentioned, is a lifelong process. Usually the changes taking place within the individual in his or her adult years are more gradual and of a less substantial magnitude than those that occur during childhood. For example, the individual's adjustment to a new job or to the loss of a spouse ordinarily does not produce profound alteration of his or her habits, beliefs, and values. However, there are instances when individuals undergo rapid and drastic changes as adults. Sociologists usually refer to this as *resocialization*. Such thoroughgoing change and substitution of one way of life for another, very different life style are most likely to happen when individuals have extensive experience in "total institutions." Erving Goffman, the originator of this concept, maintains that total institutions include prisons, nursing homes, military units, rehabilitation communities, monasteries, convents, and the like. Total institutions are likely to effect dramatic changes within the individual because they are all-encompassing, governing the entirety of the person's activities.

Edgar Schein's study of attempted "brainwashing" contributes a great deal toward enhancing our understanding of resocialization. The Chinese Communist indoctrination program, in its attempt to convert the American prisoners of war, appeared to apply most of the leading socialization theories. The Chinese borrowed from psychoanalysis, collecting life histories of their captives, with the purpose of promoting a reassessment and re-evaluation in light of Communist principles. Consistent with Meadian precepts, they systematically broke up the old authority structure and informal social networks, in an effort to develop a new core of "significant others" who would espouse and embrace a Marxist point of view. In line with behaviorism, they employed the systematic application of rewards and punishments to recondition the captive population. Yet, despite the extensive efforts of the Chinese, few POW's were won over; the vast majority of prisoners elected to be repatriated when the armistice was signed.

From Schein's discussion it appears that if the Chinese had had a better understanding of the American idiom, and if they could have offered material comforts more like those the Americans had been accustomed to, they would have been far more successful in gaining new adherents. Nevertheless, the brainwashing program attained some measure of success: it elicited considerable collaboration, attempted and successful escapes were exceedingly rare, and the camps were guarded with a minimum of personnel.

Theories of the Socialization Process

Erik Erikson's Eight Ages of Man*
David Elkind

At a recent faculty reception, I happened to join a small group in which a young mother was talking about her "identity crisis." She and her husband, she said, had decided not to have any more children, and she was depressed at the thought of being past the child-bearing stage. It was as if, she continued, she had been robbed of some part of herself and now needed to find a new function to replace the old one.

When I remarked that her story sounded like a case history from a book by Erik Erikson, she replied, "Who's Erikson?" It is a reflection on the intellectual modesty and literary decorum of Erik H. Erikson, psychoanalyst and professor of developmental psychology at Harvard, that so few of the many people who today talk about the "identity crisis" know anything of the man who pointed out its pervasiveness as a problem in contemporary society two decades ago.

Erikson has, however, contributed more to social science than his delineation of identity problems in modern man. His descriptions of the stages of the life cycle, for example, have advanced psychoanalytic theory to the point where it can now describe the development of the healthy personality on its own terms and not merely as the opposite of a sick one. Likewise, Erikson's emphasis upon the problems unique to adolescents and adults living in today's society has helped to rectify the one-sided emphasis on childhood as the beginning and end of personality development.

Finally, in his biographical studies, such as "Young Man Luther" and "Gandhi's Truth" (which has just won a National Book Award in philosophy and religion), Erikson emphasizes the inherent strengths of the human personality by showing how individuals can use their neurotic symptoms and conflicts for creative and constructive social purposes while healing themselves in the process.

It is important to emphasize that Erikson's contributions are genuine advances in psychoanalysis, in the sense that Erikson accepts and builds upon many of the basic tenets of Freudian theory. In this regard, Erikson differs from Freud's early co-workers, such as Jung and Adler, who, when they broke with Freud, rejected his theories and substituted their own.

* From the *New York Times Magazine*, April 5, 1970, pp. 25–27, 83–92, 110–14. Copyright © 1970/1969 by the New York Times Company. Reprinted by permission.

Likewise, Erikson also differs from the so-called neo-Freudians, such as Horney, Kardiner, and Sullivan, who (mistakenly, as it turned out) assumed that Freudian theory had nothing to say about man's relation to reality and to his culture. While it is true that Freud emphasized, even mythologized, sexuality, he did so to counteract the rigid sexual taboos of his time, which, at that point in history, were frequently the cause of neuroses. In his later writings, however, Freud began to concern himself with the executive agency of the personality, namely, the ego, which is also the repository of the individual's attitudes and concepts about himself and his world.

It is with the psychosocial development of the ego that Erikson's observations and theoretical constructions are primarily concerned. Erikson has thus been able to introduce innovations into psychoanalytic theory without either rejecting or ignoring Freud's monumental contribution.

* * *

. . . Erikson set forth the implications of his clinical observations in "Childhood and Society." In that book, the summation and integration of fifteen years of research, he made three major contributions to the study of the human ego. He posited (1) that, side by side with the stages of psychosexual development described by Freud (the oral, anal, phallic, genital, Oedipal, and pubertal), were psychosocial stages of ego development, in which the individual had to establish new basic orientations to himself and his social world; (2) that personality development continued throughout the whole life cycle; and (3) that each stage had a positive *as well as* a negative component.

Much about these contributions—and about Erikson's way of thinking—can be understood by looking at his scheme of life stages. Erikson identifies eight stages in the human life cycle, in each of which a new dimension of "social interaction" becomes possible—that is, a new dimension in a person's interaction with himself and with his social environment.

TRUST VS. MISTRUST

The first stage corresponds to the oral stage in classical psychoanalytic theory and usually extends through the first year of life. In Erikson's view, the new dimension of social interaction that emerges during this period involves basic *trust* at the one extreme and *mistrust* at the other. The degree to which the child comes to trust the world, other people, and himself depends to a considerable extent upon the quality of the care that he receives. The infant whose needs are met when they arise, whose discomforts are quickly removed, who is cuddled, fondled, played with, and talked to, develops a sense of the world as a safe place to be and of people as helpful and dependable. When, however, the care is inconsistent, inadequate, and rejecting, it fosters a basic mistrust, an attitude of fear and suspicion on the part of the infant toward the world in general and people in particular that will carry through to later stages of development.

It should be said at this point that the problem of basic trust-versus-mistrust (as is true for all the later dimensions) is not resolved once and for all during the first year of life; it arises again at each successive stage of development. There is both hope and danger in this. The child who enters school with a sense of mistrust may come to trust a particular teacher who has taken the trouble to make herself trustworthy; with this second chance, he overcomes his early mistrust. On the other hand, the child who comes through infancy with a vital sense of trust can still have his sense of mistrust activated at a later stage if, say, his parents are divorced and separated under acrimonious circumstances.

This point was brought home to me in a very direct way by a four-year-old patient I saw in a court clinic. He was being seen at the court clinic because his adoptive parents, who had had him for six months, now wanted to give him back to the agency. They claimed that he was cold and unloving, took things, and could not be trusted. He was, indeed, a cold and apathetic boy, but with good reason. About a year after his illegitimate birth, he was taken away from his mother, who had a drinking problem, and was shunted back and forth among several foster homes. Initially, he had tried to relate to the persons in the foster homes, but the relationships never had a chance to develop, because he was moved at just the wrong times. In the end, he gave up trying to reach out to others, because the inevitable separations hurt too much.

Like the burned child who dreads the flame, this emotionally burned child shunned the pain of emotional involvement. He had trusted his mother, but now he trusted no one. Only years of devoted care and patience could now undo the damage that had been done to this child's sense of trust.

AUTONOMY VS. DOUBT

Stage Two spans the second and third years of life, the period that Freudian theory calls the anal stage. Erikson sees here the emergence of autonomy. This autonomy dimension builds upon the child's new motor and mental abilities. At this stage, the child can not only walk but also climb, open and close, drop, push and pull, hold and let go. The child takes pride in these new accomplishments and wants to do everything himself, whether it be pulling the wrapper off a piece of candy, selecting the vitamin out of the bottle, or flushing the toilet. If parents recognize the young child's need to do what he is capable of doing at his own pace and in his own time, then he develops a sense that he is able to control his muscles, his impulses, himself, and, not insignificantly, his environment—the sense of autonomy.

When, however, his caretakers are impatient and do for him what he is capable of doing himself, they reinforce a sense of shame and doubt. To be sure, every parent has rushed a child at times, and children are hardy enough to endure such lapses. It is only when caretaking is consistently overprotective and criticism of "accidents" (whether these be wetting, soiling, spilling, or breaking things) is harsh and unthinking that the child develops an excessive sense of shame with respect to other people and an excessive sense of doubt about [his] own abilities to control his world and himself.

If the child leaves this stage with less autonomy than shame or doubt, he will be handicapped in his attempts to achieve autonomy in adolescence and adulthood. Contrariwise, the child who moves through this stage with his sense of autonomy buoyantly outbalancing his feelings of shame and doubt is well prepared to be autonomous at later phases in the life cycle. Again, however, the balance of autonomy to shame and doubt set up during this period can be changed in either positive or negative directions by later events.

It might be well to note, in addition, that too much autonomy can be as harmful as too little. I have in mind a patient of seven who had a heart condition. He had learned very quickly how terrified his parents were of any signs in him of cardiac difficulty. With the psychological acuity given to children, he soon ruled the household. The family could not go shopping, or for a drive, or on a holiday if he did not approve. On those rare occasions when the parents had had enough and defied him, he would get angry and his purple hue and gagging would frighten them into submission.

Actually, this boy was frightened of this power (as all children would be) and was really eager to give it up. When the parents and the boy came to realize this, and to recognize that a little shame and doubt were a healthy counterpoise to an inflated sense of autonomy, the three of them could once again assume their normal roles.

INITIATIVE VS. GUILT

In this stage (the genital stage of classical psychoanalysis), the child, age four to five, is pretty much master of his body and can ride a tricycle, run, cut, and hit. He can thus initiate motor activities of various sorts on his own and no longer merely responds to or imitates the actions of other children. The same holds true for his language and fantasy activities. Accordingly, Erikson argues that the social dimension that appears at this stage has *initiative* at one of its poles and *guilt* at the other.

Whether the child will leave this stage with his sense of initiative far outbalancing his sense of guilt depends to a considerable extent upon how parents respond to his self-initiated activities. Children who are given much freedom and opportunity to initiate motor play such as running, bike riding, sliding, skating, tussling, and wrestling have their sense of initiative reinforced. Initiative is also reinforced when parents answer their children's questions (intellectual initiative) and do not deride or inhibit fantasy or play activity. On the other hand, if the child is made to feel that his motor activity is bad, that his questions are a nuisance, and that his play is silly and stupid, then he may develop a sense of guilt over self-initiated activities in general that will persist through later life stages.

INDUSTRY VS. INFERIORITY

Stage Four is the age period from six to eleven, the elementary-school years (described by classical psychoanalysis as the *latency phase*). It is a time during which the child's love for the parent of the opposite sex and rivalry with the same-sexed parent (elements in the so-called family romance) are quiescent. It is also a period during which the child becomes capable of deductive reasoning and of playing and learning by rules. It is not until this period, for example, that children can really play marbles, checkers, and other "take turn" games that require obedience to rules. Erikson argues that the psychosocial dimension that emerges during this period has a sense of *industry* at one extreme and a sense of *inferiority* at the other.

The term industry nicely captures a dominant theme of this period, during which the concern with how things are made, how they work, and what they do predominates. It is the Robinson Crusoe age, in the sense that the enthusiasm and minute detail with which Crusoe describes his activities appeals to the child's own budding sense of industry. When children are encouraged in their efforts to make, do, or build practical things (whether it be to construct creepy crawlers, tree houses, or airplane models—or to cook, bake, or sew), are allowed to finish their products, and are praised and rewarded for the results, then the sense of industry is enhanced. But parents who see their children's efforts at making and doing as "mischief," and as simply "making a mess," help to encourage in children a sense of inferiority.

During these elementary-school years, however, the child's world includes more than the home. Now social institutions other than the family come to play a central role in the developmental crisis of the individual. (Here Erikson introduced still another advance in psychoanalytic theory, which heretofore concerned itself only with the effects of the parents' behavior upon the child's development.)

A child's school experiences affect his industry-inferiority balance. The child, for example, with an I.Q. of 80 to 90 has a particularly traumatic school experience, even when his sense of industry is rewarded and encouraged at home. He is "too bright" to be in special classes, but "too slow" to compete with children of average ability. Consequently, he experiences constant failures in his academic efforts that reinforce a sense of inferiority.

On the other hand, the child who had his sense of industry derogated at home can have it revitalized at school through the offices of a sensitive and committed teacher. Whether the child develops a sense of industry or inferiority, therefore, no longer depends solely on the caretaking efforts of the parents but on the actions and offices of other adults as well.

IDENTITY VS. ROLE CONFUSION

When the child moves into adolescence (Stage Five—roughly, the ages twelve to eighteen), he encounters, according to traditional psychoanalytic theory, a reawakening of the family-romance problem of early childhood.

His means of resolving the problem is to seek and find a romantic partner of his own generation. While Erikson does not deny this aspect of adolescence, he points out that there are other problems as well. The adolescent matures mentally as well as physiologically, and, in addition to the new feelings, sensations, and desires he experiences as a result of changes in his body, he develops a multitude of new ways of looking at and thinking about the world. Among other things, those in adolescence can now think about other people's thinking and wonder about what other people think of them. They can also conceive of ideal families, religions, and societies, which they then compare with the imperfect families, religions, and societies of their own experience. Finally, adolescents become capable of constructing theories and philosophies designed to bring all the varied and conflicting aspects of society into a working, harmonious, and peaceful whole. The adolescent, in a word, is an impatient idealist who believes that it is as easy to realize an ideal as it is to imagine it.

Erikson believes that the new, interpersonal dimension that emerges during this period has to do with a sense of *ego identity* at the positive end and a sense of *role confusion* at the negative end. That is to say, given the adolescent's newfound integrative abilities, his task is to bring together all of the things he has learned about himself as a son, student, athlete, friend, Scout, newspaper boy, and so on, and integrate these different images of himself into a whole that makes sense and that shows continuity with the past while preparing for the future. To the extent that the young person succeeds in this endeavor, he arrives at a sense of psychosocial identity, a sense of who he is, where he has been, and where he is going.

In contrast to the earlier stages, where parents play a more or less direct role in the determination of the result of the developmental crises, the influence of parents during this stage is much more indirect. If the young person reaches adolescence with, thanks to his parents, a vital sense of trust, autonomy, initiative, and industry, then his chances of arriving at a meaningful sense of ego identity are much enhanced. The reverse, of course, holds true for the young person who enters adolescence with considerable mistrust, shame, doubt, guilt, and inferiority. Preparation for a successful adolescence, and the attainment of an integrated psychosocial identity, must, therefore, begin in the cradle.

Over and above what the individual brings with him from his childhood, the attainment of a sense of personal identity depends upon the social milieu in which he or she grows up. For example, in a society where women are to some extent second-class citizens, it may be harder for females to arrive at a sense of psychosocial identity. Likewise, at times, such as the present, when rapid social and technological change breaks down many traditional values, it may be more difficult for young people to find continuity between what they learned and experienced as children and what they learn and experience as adolescents. At such times, young people often seek causes that give their lives meaning and direction. The activism of the current generation of young people may well stem, in part at least, from this search.

When the young person cannot attain a sense of personal identity, because of either an unfortunate childhood or difficult social circumstances, he shows a certain amount of *role confusion*—a sense of not knowing what he is, where he belongs, or whom he belongs to. Such confusion is a frequent symptom in delinquent young people. Promiscuous adolescent girls, for example, often seem to have a fragmented sense of ego identity. Some young people seek a "negative identity," an identity opposite to the one prescribed for them by their family and friends. Having an identity as a "delinquent," or as a "hippie," or even as an "acid head," may sometimes be preferable to having no identity at all.

In some cases, young people do not seek a negative identity so much as they have it thrust upon them. I remember another court case in which the defendant was an attractive sixteen-year-old girl who had been found "tricking it" in a trailer located just outside the grounds of an Air Force base. From about the age of twelve, her mother had encouraged her to dress seductively and to go out with boys. When she returned from dates, her sexually frustrated mother demanded a kiss-by-kiss, caress-by-caress description of the evening's activities. After the mother had vicariously satisfied her sexual needs, she proceeded to call her daughter a "whore" and a "dirty tramp." As the girl told me, "Hell, I have the name, so I might as well play the role."

Failure to establish a clear sense of personal identity at adolescence does not guarantee perpetual failure. And the person who attains a working sense of ego identity in adolescence will of necessity encounter challenges and threats to that identity as he moves through life. Erikson, perhaps more than any other personality theorist, has emphasized that life is constant change, and that confronting problems at one stage in life is not a guarantee against the reappearance of these problems at later stages or against the finding of new solutions to them.

INTIMACY VS. ISOLATION

Stage Six in the life cycle is young adulthood—roughly, the period of courtship and early family life that extends from late adolescence till early middle age. For this stage, and the stages described hereafter, classical psychoanalysis has nothing new or major to say. For Erikson, however, the previous attainment of a sense of personal identity and the engagement in productive work that marks this period give rise to a new interpersonal dimension of *intimacy* at the one extreme and *isolation* at the other.

When Erikson speaks of intimacy, he means much more than lovemaking alone; he means the ability to share with, and care about, another person without fear of losing oneself in the process. In the case of intimacy, as in the case of identity, success or failure no longer depends directly upon the parents but only indirectly as they have contributed to the individual's success or failure at the earlier stages. Here, too, as in the case of identity, social conditions may help or hinder the establishment of a sense of intimacy. Likewise, intimacy need not involve sexuality; it includes the relationship between friends. Soldiers who have served together under the most dangerous circumstances often develop a sense of commitment to one another that exemplifies intimacy in its broadest sense. If a sense of intimacy is not established with friends or a marriage partner, the result, in Erikson's view, is a sense of isolation—of being alone without anyone to share with or care for.

GENERATIVITY VS. SELF-ABSORPTION

This stage—middle age—brings with it what Erikson speaks of as either *generativity* or *self-absorption,* and stagnation. What Erikson means by generativity is that the person begins to be concerned with others beyond his immediate family, with future generations and the nature of the society and world in which those generations will live. Generativity does not reside only in parents; it can be found in any individual who actively concerns himself with the welfare of young people and with making the world a better place for them to live and to work [in].

Those who fail to establish a sense of generativity fall into a state of self-absorption, in which their personal needs and comforts are of predominant concern. A fictional case of self-absorption is Dickens's Scrooge in "A Christmas Carol." In his one-sided concern with money and in his disregard for the interests and welfare of his young employe, Bob Cratchit, Scrooge exemplifies the self-absorbed, embittered (the two often go together) old man. Dickens also illustrated, however, what Erikson points out: namely, that unhappy solutions to life's crises are not irreversible. Scrooge, at the end of the tale, manifested a sense both of generativity and of intimacy that he had not experienced before.

INTEGRITY VS. DESPAIR

Stage Eight in the Eriksonian scheme corresponds roughly to the period when the individual's major efforts are nearing completion, and when there is time for reflection—and for the enjoyment of grandchildren, if any. The psychosocial dimension that comes into prominence now has *integrity* on [the] one hand and *despair* on the other.

The sense of integrity arises from the individual's ability to look back on his life with satisfaction. At the other extreme is the individual who looks back upon his life as a series of missed opportunities and missed directions; now, in the twilight years, he realizes that it is too late to start again. For such a person, the inevitable result is a sense of despair at what might have been.

These, then, are the major stages in the life cycle as described by Erikson. Their presentation, for one thing, frees the clinician to treat adult emotional problems as failures (in part at least) to solve genuinely adult personality crises and not, as heretofore, as mere residuals of infantile frustrations and conflicts. This view of personality growth, moreover, takes some of the onus off parents and takes account of the role that society and the person himself play in the formation of an individual personality. Finally, Erikson has offered hope for us all by demonstrating that each phase of growth has its strengths as well as its weaknesses, and that failures at one stage of development can be rectified by successes at later stages.

The reason that these ideas, which sound so agreeable to "common sense," are, in fact, so revolutionary has a lot to do with the state of psychoanalysis in America. As formulated by Freud, psychoanalysis encompassed a theory of personality development, a method of studying the human mind, and, finally, procedures for treating troubled and unhappy people. Freud viewed this system as a scientific one, open to revision as new facts and observations accumulated.

The system was, however, so vehemently attacked that Freud's followers were constantly in the position of having to defend Freud's views. Perhaps because of this situation, Freud's system became, in the hands of some of his followers and defenders, a dogma upon which all theoretical innovation, clinical observation, and therapeutic practice had to be grounded. That this attitude persists is evidenced in the recent remark by a psychoanalyst that he believed psychotic patients could not be treated by psychoanalysis because "Freud said so." Such attitudes, in which Freud's authority rather than observation and data is the basis of deciding what is true and what is false, has contributed to the disrepute in which psychoanalysis is widely held today.

Erik Erikson has broken out of this scholasticism and has had the courage to say that Freud's discoveries and practices were the start and not the end of the study and treatment of the human personality. In addition to advocating the modifications of psychoanalytic theory outlined above, Erikson has also suggested modifications in therapeutic practice, particularly in the treatment of young patients. "Young people in severe trouble are not fit for the couch," he writes. "They want to face you, and they want you to face them, not as a facsimile of a parent, or wearing the mask of a professional helper, but as a kind of over-all individual a young person can live with or despair of."

Erikson has had the boldness to remark on some of the negative effects that distorted notions of psychoanalysis have had on society at large. Psychoanalysis, he says, has contributed to a widespread fatalism—"even as we were trying to devise, with scientific determinism, a therapy for the few, we were led to promote an ethical disease among the many."

*   *   *

There is now more and more teaching of Erikson's concepts in psychiatry, psychology, education, and social work in America and in other parts of the world. His description of the stages of the life cycle are summarized in major textbooks in all of these fields, and clinicians are increasingly looking at their cases in Eriksonian terms.

Research investigators have, however, found Erikson's formulations somewhat difficult to test. This is not surprising, inasmuch as Erikson's conceptions, like Freud's, take into account the infinite complexity of the human personality. Current research methodologies are, by and large, still not able to deal with these complexities at their own level, and distortions are inevitable when such concepts as "identity" come to be defined in terms of responses to a questionnaire.

Likewise, although Erikson's life stages have an intuitive "rightness" about them, not everyone agrees with his formulations. Douvan and Adelson, in their book *The Adolescent Experience,* argue that, while his identity theory may hold true for boys, it doesn't for girls. This argument is based on findings that suggest that girls postpone identity consolidation until after marriage (and intimacy) have been established. Such postponement occurs, say Douvan and Adelson, because a woman's identity is partially defined by the identity of the man whom she marries. This view does not really contradict Erikson's, since he recognizes that later events, such as marriage, can help to resolve both current and past developmental crises. For the woman, but not for the man, the problems of identity and intimacy may be solved concurrently.

Objections to Erikson's formulations have come from other directions as well. Robert W. White, Erikson's good friend and colleague at Harvard, has a long-standing (and warm-hearted) debate with Erikson over his life stages. White believes that his own theory of "competence motivation," a theory that has received wide recognition, can account for the phenomenon of ego development much more economically than can Erikson's stages. Erikson has, however, little interest in debating the validity of the stages he has described. As an artist, he recognizes that there are many different ways to view one and the same phenomenon and that a perspective that is congenial to one person will be repugnant to another. He offers his stage-wise description of the life cycle for those who find such perspectives congenial and not as a world view that everyone should adopt.

* * *

Changing the Game from "Get the Teacher" to "Learn"*

Robert L. Hamblin, David Buckholdt, Donald Bushell, Desmond Ellis, and Daniel Ferritor

Almost any educator of experience will assure you that it is next to impossible—and often actually impossible—to teach normal classroom subjects to

* From *Trans-action,* vol. 6, no. 3 (January, 1969). Copyright © January, 1969, by Trans-action, Inc., New Brunswick, New Jersey.

children who have extreme behavior problems, or who are "too young." Yet, at four experimental classrooms of the Central Midwestern Regional Educational Laboratories (CEMREL), we have been bringing about striking changes in the behavior and learning progress of just such children.

In the eighteen months of using new exchange systems and working with different types of problem children, we have seen these results:

• Extraordinarily aggressive boys, who had not previously responded to therapy, have been tamed.

• Two-year-olds have learned to read about as fast and as well as their five-year-old classmates.

• Four ghetto children, too shy, too withdrawn to talk, have become better than average talkers.

• Several autistic children, who were either mute or could only parrot sounds, have developed functional speech, have lost their bizarre and disruptive behavior patterns, and their relationships with parents and other children have improved. All of these children are on the road to normality.

Our system is deceptively simple. Superficially, in fact, it may not even seem new—although, in detail, it has never been tried in precisely this form in the classroom before. In essence, we simply reinforce "good" behavior and nonpunitively discourage "bad" behavior. We structure a social exchange so that as the child progresses, we reinforce this behavior—give him something that he values, something that shows our approval. Therefore, he becomes strongly motivated to continue his progress. To terminate bizarre, disruptive, or explosive patterns, we stop whatever has been reinforcing that undesirable behavior—actions or attention that teachers or parents have unwittingly been giving him in exchange, often in the belief that they were punishing and thus discouraging him. Study after study has shown that, whenever a child persists in behaving badly, some adult has, perhaps inadvertently, been rewarding him for it.

"Socialization" is the term that sociologists use to describe the process of transforming babies—who can do little but cry, eat, and sleep—into adults who can communicate and function rather effectively in their society. Socialization varies from culture to culture, and, while it is going on all around us, we are seldom aware of it. But when normal socialization breaks down, "problems" occur—autism, nonverbal or hyperaggressive behavior, retardation, delinquency, crime, and so on.

The authors, after years of often interesting but, by and large, frustrating research, realized that the more common theories of child development (Freudian, neo-Freudian, the developmental theories of Gesell and Piaget, and a number of others) simply do not satisfactorily explain the socialization process in children. Consequently, in desperation we began to move toward the learning theories and then toward the related exchange theories of social structure. Since then, working with problem children, our view has gradually been amplified and refined. Each experimental classroom has given us a different looking glass. In each, we can see the child in different conditions, and can alter the conditions that hinder his socialization into a civilized, productive adult capable of happiness.

By the time they become students, most children love to play with one another, to do art work, to cut and paste, to play with Playdoh, to climb and swing on the playground, and so on. Most preschools also serve juice and cookie snacks and some have television sets or movies. There is, consequently, no dearth of prizes for us to reward the children [with] for good behavior. The problem is not in finding reinforcers but in managing them.

THE BASIC SYSTEM: TOKEN EXCHANGE

One of the simplest and most effective ways, we found, was to develop a token-exchange system. The tokens we use are plastic discs that children can earn. A child who completes his arithmetic or reading may earn a dozen tokens, given one by one as he proceeds through the lessons. And at the end of the lesson period comes the reward.

Often it is a movie. The price varies. For four tokens, a student can watch while sitting on the floor; for eight, he gets a chair; for twelve, he can watch while sitting on the table. Perhaps the view is better from the table—anyway, the children almost always buy it, if they have enough tokens. But, if they dawdled so much that they earned fewer than four, they are "timed out" into the hall while the others see the movie. Throughout the morning, therefore, the children earn, then spend, then earn, then spend.

This token-exchange system is very powerful. It can create beneficial changes in a child's behavior, his emotional reactions, and, ultimately, even his approach to life. But it is not easy to set up, nor simple to maintain.

At the beginning, the tokens are meaningless to the children; so, to make them meaningful, we pair them with M&M candies or something similar. As the child engages in the desired behavior (or a reasonable facsimile), the teacher gives him a "Thank you," an M&M, and a token. At first, the children are motivated by the M&M's and have to be urged to hold on to the tokens; but then they find that the tokens can be used to buy admission to the movie, Playdoh, or other good things. The teacher tells them the price and asks them to count out the tokens. Increasingly, the teacher "forgets" the M&M's. In two or three days, the children get no candy, just the approval and the tokens. By then, they have learned.

There are problems in maintaining a token exchange. Children become disinterested in certain reinforcers if they are used too frequently and, therefore, in the tokens that buy them. For instance, young children will work very hard to save up tokens to play with Playdoh once a week; if they are offered Playdoh every day, the charm quickly fades. Some activities—snacks, movies, walks outdoors—are powerful enough to be used every day.

As noted, the children we worked with had different behavior problems, reflecting various kinds of breakdowns in the socialization process. Each experiment we conducted concentrated on a particular type of maladjustment or a particular group of maladjusted children to see how a properly structured exchange system might help them. Let us look at each experiment, to see how each problem was affected.

AGGRESSION

Unfortunately, our world reinforces and rewards aggressive behavior. Some cultures and some families are open and brazen about it—they systematically and consciously teach their young that it is desirable, and even virtuous, to attack certain other individuals or groups. The child who can beat up the other kids, on the playground is sometimes respected by his peers and perhaps by his parents; the soldier achieves glory in combat. The status, the booty, or the bargaining advantages that come to the aggressor can become reinforcement to continue and escalate his aggressions.

In more civilized cultures, the young are taught not to use aggression, and we try to substitute less harmful patterns. But, even so, aggression is sometimes reinforced unintentionally—and the consequences, predictably, are the same as if the teaching [was] deliberate.

In the long run, civilized cultures are not kind to hyperaggressive children. A recent survey in England, for instance, found that the great majority of teachers felt that aggressive behavior by students disturbed more classrooms than anything else and caused the most anxiety among teachers. At least partly as a result, the dropout rates for the hyperaggressives was two and a half times as great as for "normals," and disproportionate numbers of hyperaggressives turned up in mental clinics.

The traditional treatment for aggressive juveniles is punishment—often harsh punishment. This is not only of dubious moral value, but generally it does not work.

We took seriously—perhaps for the first time—the theory that aggression is a type of exchange behavior. Boys become aggressive because they get something for it; they continue to be aggressive because the rewards are continuing. To change an aggressive pattern in our experimental class at Washington University, therefore, we had to restructure appropriately the exchange system in which the boys were involved.

As subjects, we (Ellis and Hamblin) found five extraordinarily aggressive four-year-old boys, all referred to us by local psychiatrists and social workers who had been able to do very little with them. Next, we hired a trained teacher. We told her about the boys and the general nature of the experiment—then gave her her head. That is, she was allowed to use her previous training during the first period—and this would provide a baseline comparison with what followed after. We hoped she would act like the "typical teacher." We suspect that she did.

LET'S PLAY "GET THE TEACHER"

The teacher was, variously, a strict disciplinarian, wise counselor, clever arbitrator, and sweet peacemaker. Each role failed miserably. After the eighth day, the average of the children was 150 sequences of aggression per day! Here is what a mere four minutes of those sequences were like:

Mike, John, and Dan are seated together, playing with pieces of Play-doh. Barry, some distance from the others, is seated and also is playing with Playdoh. The children, except Barry, are talking about what they are making. Time is 9:10 A.M. Miss Sally, the teacher, turns toward the children and says, "It's time for a lesson. Put your Playdoh away." Mike says "Not me." John says "Not me." Dan says "Not me." Miss Sally moves toward Mike. Mike throws some Playdoh in Miss Sally's face. Miss Sally jerks back, then moves forward rapidly and snatches Playdoh from Mike. Puts Playdoh in her pocket. Mike screams for Playdoh, says he wants to play with it. Mike moves toward Miss Sally and attempts to snatch the Playdoh from Miss Sally's pocket. Miss Sally pushes him away. Mike kicks Miss Sally on the leg. Kicks her again and demands the return of his Playdoh. Kicks Miss Sally again. Picks up a small steel chair and throws it at Miss Sally. Miss Sally jumps out of the way. Mike picks up another chair and throws it more violently. Miss Sally cannot move in time. Chair strikes her foot. Miss Sally pushes Mike down on the floor. Mike starts up. Pulls over one chair. Now another [and] another. Stops a moment. Miss Sally is picking up chairs, Mike looks at Miss Sally. Miss Sally moves toward Mike. Mike runs away.

John wants his Playdoh. Miss Sally says "No." He joins Mike in pulling over chairs and attempts to grab Playdoh from Miss Sally's pocket. Miss Sally pushes him away roughly. John is screaming that he wants to play with his Playdoh. Moves toward phonograph. Pulls it off the table; lets it crash onto the floor. Mike has his coat on. Says he is going home. Miss Sally asks Dan to bolt the door. Dan gets to the door at the same time as Mike. Mike hits Dan in the face. Dan's nose is bleeding. Miss Sally walks over to Dan, turns to the others, and says that she is taking Dan to the washroom, and that, while she is away, they may play with the Playdoh. Returns Playdoh from pocket to Mike and John. Time: 9:14 A.M.

Wild? Very. These were barbarous little boys who enjoyed battle. Miss Sally did her best, but they were just more clever than she, and they *always* won. Whether Miss Sally wanted to or not, they could always drag her into the fray and just go at it harder and harder until she capitulated. She was finally driven to their level, trading a kick for a kick and a spit in the face for a spit in the face.

What Miss Sally did not realize [was] that she had inadvertently structured an exchange where she consistently reinforced aggression. First, as noted, whenever she fought with them, she *always lost*. Second, more subtly, she reinforced their aggressive pattern by giving it serious attention—by looking, talking, scolding, cajoling, becoming angry, even striking back. These boys were playing a teasing game called "Get the Teacher." The more she showed that she was bothered by their behavior, the better they liked it, and the further they went.

These interpretations may seem farfetched, but they are borne out dramatically by what happened later. On the twelfth day, we changed the conditions. First, we set up the usual token exchange to reinforce cooperative behavior. This was to develop or strengthen behavior that would replace aggression. Any strong pattern of behavior serves some function for the individual, so the first step in getting rid of a strong, disruptive pattern is substituting another one that is more useful and causes fewer problems. Not only therapy, but simple humanity dictates this.

First, the teacher had to be instructed in how *not to reinforce* aggression. Contrary to all her experience, she was asked to turn her back on the aggressor and, at the same time, to reinforce others' cooperation with tokens. Once we were able to coach her and give her immediate feedback over a wireless-communication system, she structured the exchanges almost perfectly. The data show the crucial changes: a gradual increase in cooperation from about 56 to about 115 sequences per day, and a corresponding decrease in aggression from 150 to about 60 sequences!

These results should have been satisfactory, but we were new at this kind of experimentation and nervous. We wanted to reduce the frequency of aggression to a "normal" level, to about 15 sequences a day. So we restructured the exchange system. We simply made sure that aggression would always be punished. The teacher was told to *charge* tokens for any aggression.

To our surprise, the frequency of cooperation remained stable, about 115 sequences per day; but aggression *increased* to about 110 sequences per day! Evidently, the boys were still playing "Get the Teacher," and the fines were enough reinforcement to increase aggression.

So, instead of fining the children, the teacher was again told to ignore aggression by turning her back and giving attention and tokens only for cooperation. The frequency of aggression went down to a nearly "normal" level—about 16 sequences per day—and cooperation increased to about 140 sequences.

Then, as originally planned, the conditions were again reversed. The boys were given enough tokens at the beginning of the morning to buy their usual supply of movies, toys, and snacks, and these were not used as reinforcers. The teacher was told to do the best she could. She was not instructed to return to her old pattern, but, without the tokens and without our coaching, she did—and with the same results. Aggression increased to about 120 sequences per day, and cooperation decreased to about 90. While this was an improvement over [the situation] before the boys had ever been exposed to the token exchange, it was not good. The mixture of aggression and cooperation was strange, even weird, to watch.

When the token exchange was restructured and the aggression no longer reinforced, the expected changes recurred—with a bang. Aggression decreased to seven sequences on the last day, and cooperation rose to about 181 sequences. In "normal" nursery schools, our observations have shown that five boys can be expected to have 15 aggression sequences and 60 cooperation sequences per day. Thus, from extremely aggressive and uncooperative, our boys had become less aggressive and far more cooperative than "normal" boys.

Robert L. Hamblin et al.   119

Here is an example of their new behavior patterns, taken from a rest period—precisely the time when the most aggressive acts had occurred in the past:

All of the children are sitting around the table, drinking their milk; John, as usual, has finished first. Takes his plastic mug and returns it to the table. Miss Martha, the assistant teacher, gives him a token. John goes to cupboard, takes out his mat, spreads it out by the blackboard, and lies down. Miss Martha gives him a token. Meanwhile, Mike, Barry, and Jack have spread their mats on the carpet. Dan is lying on the carpet itself, since he hasn't a mat. Each of them gets a token. Mike asks if he can sleep by the wall. Miss Sally says "Yes." John asks if he can put out the light. Miss Sally says to wait until Barry has his mat spread properly. Dan asks Mike if he can share his mat with him. Mike says "No." Dan then asks Jack. Jack says "Yes," but, before he can move over, Mike says "Yes." Dan joins Mike. Both Jack and Mike get tokens. Mike and Jack get up to put their tokens in their cans. Return to their mats. Miss Sally asks John to put out the light. John does so. Miss Martha gives him a token. All quiet now. Four minutes later—all quiet. Quiet still, three minutes later. Time: 10:23 A.M. Rest period ends.

The hyperaggressive boys actually had, and were, double problems; they were not only extremely disruptive, but they were also washouts as students. Before the token system, they paid attention to their teacher only about 8 per cent of the lesson time. The teacher's system of scolding the youngsters for inattention and taking their attention for granted with faint approval, if any, did not work at all. To the pupils, the "Get the Teacher" game was much more satisfying.

After the token exchange was started, it took a long, long time before there was any appreciable effect. The teacher was being trained from scratch, and our methods were then not very good. However, after we set up a wireless-communication system that allowed us to coach the teacher from behind a one-way mirror and to give her immediate feedback, the children's attention began to increase. Toward the end, it leveled off at about 75 per cent—from 8 per cent! After the token exchange was taken out, attention went down to level off at 23 per cent; put back in, it shot back up to a plateau of about 93 per cent. Like a roller coaster: 8 per cent without, to 75 with, to 23 without, to 93 with.

NORMAL CHILDREN

These results occurred with chronic, apparently hopeless hyperaggressive boys. Would token exchange also help "normal," relatively bright upper-middle-class children? Sixteen youngsters of that description—nine boys and seven girls, ranging from two years nine months to four years nine months—

were put through an experimental series by Bushell, Hamblin, and Denis Stoddard in an experimental preschool at Webster College. All had about a month's earlier experience with the token-exchange system.

At first, the study hour was broken up into 15-minute periods, alternating between the work that received tokens and the play or reward that the tokens could be used for. Probably because the children were already familiar with token exchange, no great increase in learning took place. On the twenty-second day, we decided to try to increase the learning period, perhaps for the whole hour. The time spent in studying went up rapidly and dramatically—almost doubling—from 27 to level off at 42 minutes.

[Then] the token exchange was taken out completely. The teachers still gave encouragement and prepared interesting lessons as before. The rewards —the nature walks, snacks, movies, and so on—were retained. But, as in a usual classroom, they were given to the children free instead of being sold. The children continued at about the same rate as before for a few days. But, after a week, attention dropped off slowly, then sharply. On the last day, it was down to about 15 minutes—one-third the level of the end of the token period.

[Finally], the token exchange was reinstituted. In only three days, attention snapped back from an average of 15 minutes to 45 minutes. However, by the end of [this period], the students paid attention an average of 50 of the available 60 minutes.

A comparison of the record of these normals with the record of the hyperaggressive boys is interesting. The increase in attention brought by the token exchange, from about 15 minutes to 50, is approximately threefold for the normal children; but for the hyperaggressive boys—who are disobedient and easily distracted—it is about elevenfold, from 8 per cent to 93 per cent of the time. Not only was the increase greater, but the absolute level achieved was higher. This indicates strongly, therefore, that the more problematic the child, the greater may be the effect of token exchange on his behavior.

The high rates of attention were not due to the fact that each teacher had fewer children to work with. Individualized lessons were not enough. Without the token exchange, even three teachers could not hold the interest of 16 children two to four years old—at least not in reading, writing, and arithmetic.

Praise and approval were not enough as rewards. The teachers, throughout the experiment, used praise and approval to encourage attention; they patted heads and said things like "Good," "You're doing fine," and "Keep it up"; yet, when the token exchange was removed, this attention nevertheless ultimately declined by two-thirds. Social approval is important but not nearly so powerful as material reinforcers.

Finally, it is obvious that, if the reinforcers (movies, snacks, toys, or whatever) do not seem directly connected to the work, they will not sustain a high level of study. To be effective with young children, rewards must occur in a structured exchange in which they are given promptly as recompense and thus are directly connected to the work performed.

Robert L. Hamblin et al.   121

THE VERY YOUNG CHILD

According to accepted educational theory, a child must be about six and a half before he can comfortably learn to read. But is this really true, or is it merely a convenience for the traditional educational system? After all, by the time a normal child is two and a half, he has learned a foreign language —the one spoken by his parents and family; and he has learned it without special instruction or coaching. He has even developed a feel for the rules of grammar, which, by and large, he uses correctly. It is a rare college student who becomes fluent in a foreign language with only two and a half years of formal training—and our college students are supposed to be the brightest of our breed. Paul Goodman has suggested that, if children learn to *speak* by the same methods that they learn to *read,* there might well be as many nonspeakers now as illiterates.

What if the problem is really one of motivation? If we structured an exchange that rewarded them, in ways they could appreciate, for learning to read, couldn't they learn as readily as five-year-olds?

We decided that, for beginners, the number of words a child can read is the best test of reading ability. In an experiment designed by Hamblin, Carol Pfeiffer, Dennis Shea, and June Hamblin, and administered at our Washington University preschool, the token-exchange system was used to reward children for the number of words each learned. The two-year-olds did about as well as the five-year-olds; their sight vocabularies were almost as large.

There was an interesting side effect: At the end of the school year, all but one of these children tested at the "genius" level. On Stanford-Binet individual tests, their I.Q. scores increased as much as 36 points. It was impossible to compute an average gain only because three of the children "topped out" —made something in excess of 149, the maximum score possible.

In general, the lower the measured I.Q. at the start, the greater the gain— apparently as a result of the educational experience.

THE NONVERBAL CHILD

What happens when ghetto children are introduced into a token-exchange system? At our Mullanphy Street preschool, 22 Afro-American children— aged three to five—attend regularly. All live in or near the notorious Pruitt-Igoe Housing Project and most come from broken homes. When the school began, the teachers were unenthusiastic about a token exchange, so we let them proceed as they wished. The result was pandemonium. About half of the children chased one another around the room, engaged in violent arguments, and fought. The others withdrew; some would not even communicate.

After the third day, the teachers asked for help. As in the other experimental schools, we (Buckholdt and Hamblin) instructed them to ignore aggressive-disruptive behavior and to reward attention and cooperation with social approval and the plastic tokens, later to be exchanged for such things as milk, cookies, admission to the movies, and toys. The children quickly caught on, the disruptions diminished, and cooperation increased. Within three weeks of such consistent treatment, most of the children took part in the lessons, and disruptive behavior had become only an occasional problem. All of this, remember, without punishment.

Our attention was then focused upon the children with verbal problems. These children seldom started conversations with teachers or other students, but they would sometimes answer questions with a word or perhaps two. This pattern may be unusual in the middle classes but is quite common among ghetto children. Our research has shown that children so afflicted are usually uneducable.

As we investigated, we became convinced that their problem was not that they were unable to talk as much as that they were too shy to talk to strangers—that is, to nonfamily. In their homes, we overheard most of them talking brokenly but in sentences. Consequently, we set up a token exchange for them designed specifically to develop a pattern of talking with outsiders, especially teachers and school children.

As it happened, we were able to complete the experiment with only four children. During the baseline period (before the tokens were used), the four children spoke only in about 8 per cent of the 15-second sampling periods. In [the next phase], the teachers gave social approval and tokens *only* for speaking; nonverbalisms, like pointing or headshaking, would not be recognized or reinforced. . . .

[Then] we reversed the conditions by using a teacher new to the school. The rate of talking dropped off immediately, then increased unevenly until it occurred in about 23 per cent of the sample periods.

[Then] the new teacher reintroduced the token exchange for talking, and once more there was a dramatic rise: The speaking increased much more rapidly than the first time, ending up at about 60 per cent. (This more rapid increase is known as the Contrast Effect. It occurs in part, perhaps, because the children value the token exchange more after it has been taken away.)

In the final test, we again took out the token exchange and introduced yet another new teacher. This time the drop was small, to 47 per cent.

We followed the children for three months after the end of the experiment. Their speech level remained at 48 per cent, with little drop-off. This compares with the 40 per cent talking rate for our other ghetto children and the 42 per cent rate for upper-middle-class children at the Washington University preschool.

Frequency of speech, however, was not the only important finding. . . . By the end of [the experiment] they spoke in sentences, used better syntax, and frequently started conversations.

Mothers, teachers, and neighbors all reported that the children were much more friendly and assertive. But some claimed that the children now talked too much! This could reflect individual bias; but there was little doubt that at least one child, Ben, had become an almost compulsive talker.

He was given to saying hello to everyone he met and shaking their hands. So, we terminated the experiment—what would have happened to Ben had we started *another* exchange?

This experiment shows that token exchange can bring on permanent behavior change, but that the culture must reinforce the new behavior. Talking is important in our culture, and so is reading; therefore, they are reinforced. But other subjects—such as mathematics beyond simple arithmetic— are not for most people. For behavior to change permanently, it must be reinforced at least intermittently.

AUTISM

The problems of autistic children usually dwarf those of all other children. To the casual observer, autistic children never sustain eye contact with others but appear to be self-contained—sealed off in a world of their own. The most severe cases never learn how to talk, although they sometimes echo or parrot. They remain dependent upon mother and become more and more demanding. They develop increasingly destructive and bizarre behavior problems. Finally, between five and ten years old, autistic children ordinarily become unbearable to their families, and, at that point, they are almost invariably institutionalized. Until recently, at least, this meant a rear ward to vegetate in until they died.

The breakthrough in therapy for autism came in 1964, when Dr. Ivar Lovaas and Dr. Montrose Wolfe, and a graduate student, now Dr. Todd Risley, simultaneously developed therapy systems using well-established principles of operant conditioning. They were particularly successful with those children who randomly echoed or imitated words or sentences (this is called echolalia).

The therapy systems we have designed, developed, and tested, though similar in some ways to those developed by Lovaas, Wolfe, and Risley, are quite different in others. First, we do not use punishment or other negative stimuli. We simply terminate exchanges that reinforce the autistic patterns and set up exchanges that reinforce normal patterns. Second, our children are not institutionalized; they live at home and are brought to the laboratory for 20 minutes to three hours of therapy per day. Third, as soon as possible —usually within months—we get the children into classrooms where a therapist works with four or five at a time. Fourth, we train the mother to be an assistant therapist—mostly in the home but also in the laboratory. These changes were introduced for several reasons but primarily in the hope of getting a better, more permanent cure for autism.

THE ETIOLOGY OF AUTISM

Is autism hereditary, as many believe? Our studies indicate that this is not the important question. Many mental faculties, including I.Q., have some physiological base. But the real issue is how much physiologically based potential is socially realized, for good or bad. As far as we can tell, the exchanges that intensify autism get structured inadvertently, often by accident; but, once started, a vicious cycle develops that relentlessly drives the child further into autism.

When autism starts, the mother often reacts by babying the child, trying to anticipate his every need before he signals. Thus, normal communication is not reinforced, and the child never learns to work his environment properly. But, even if he doesn't know how to get what he wants through talking, he does learn, through association, that his oversolicitous and anxious mother will always respond if he acts up violently or bizarrely enough. And she must, if only to punish. He thus learns to play "Get mother's attention"; and this soon develops into "Get mother exasperated but stop just short of the point where she punishes and really hurts." Here is an example (observed by Ferritor in the first of a series of experiments by the Laboratory's staff, not reported here):

Larry is allowed to pick out his favorite book. His mother then atttempts to read it to him; but he keeps turning the pages, so she can't. He gets up and walks away from the table. The mother then yells at him to come back. He *smiles* (a sign of pleasure usually, but not always, accompanies reinforcement). Mother continues to talk to the child to try to get him back for the story. Finally, he comes over to the table and takes the book away from her. She lets him and goes back to the bookcase for another book. He then sits down, and she begins to read. He tries to get up, but his mother pulls him back. Again. Again. She holds him there. He gets away and starts walking around the room. Goes to the toy cabinet. Mother gets up to go over and take a toy away from him. He sits on the floor. The mother comes over and sits down by him. He gets up and goes over by the door and opens it and tries to run out. She tells him he has to stay. He *smiles*. She resumes reading. He gets up and starts walking around the table. She grabs him as he comes by. He *smiles*.

A clinical psychologist who had tested Larry did not diagnose him as autistic but as an educable mental retardate with an I.Q. of perhaps 30. Yet, he had gaze aversion, and we suspected that Larry, like other autistics, was feigning inability as a way of getting what he wanted from his mother and then from other adults. He began to respond to the attractive exchanges that we structured for him, and, as we did, he began to tip his hand. For example, at one point when his mother was being trained to be an assistant therapist, the following incident occurred:

Mrs. C. told Larry that, as soon as he strung some beads, he could have gum from the gum machine that was across the room. For about 10 minutes, he fumbled, he whined—all the time crying—saying "I can't." Finally, he threw the beads at his mother. Eventually, the mother had the good sense to leave the room, saying, "As soon as you string those beads, you can have your gum." With his mother out of the room, according to our observers, he sat right down and, in less than 30 seconds, filled a string with beads with no apparent trouble.

Just two weeks later, after the mother had been through our ten-day training program, they again had a "story time." The mother begins by immediately asking Larry questions about this book (the same book used a few weeks before). He responds to every question. She gives approval for every correct answer. Then she tries to get him to say "That is a duck." He will not say it intelligibly but wants to turn the page. Mother says, "As soon as you say 'duck,' you may turn the page." Larry says "Duck" and turns the page. He *smiles*.

After seven minutes, Larry is still sitting down. They have finished one book and are beginning a second.

Most autistic children play the game "Look at me, I'm stupid" or "Look at me, I'm bizarre." These are simply attention-getting games that most adults repeatedly reinforce. Man is not a simple machine; he learns, and, as he develops his abilities, he develops stronger and stronger habits. Thus, once these inadvertent exchanges get established, the child becomes more and more dependent, more and more disruptive, more and more bizarre, more and more alienated from the positive exchanges that are structured in his environment. What is sad is that the parents and the others in the child's life sense that something is terribly wrong, but the more they do, the worse the situation becomes.

It seems to those of us who have been involved in these experiments from the beginning that the exchange techniques and theories we have used have without question demonstrated their effectiveness in treating and educating problem children. Watching these children as they go peacefully and productively about their lessons toward the end of each experimental series is both an exhilarating and a humbling experience. It is almost impossible to believe that so many had been written off as "uneducable" by professionals, that without this therapy and training—or something similar—most would have had dark and hopeless futures.

But it is not inevitable that so many hyperaggressive or environmentally retarded ghetto children become dropouts or delinquents; it is not inevitable that so many autistic children, saddest of all, must vegetate and die mutely in the back wards of mental hospitals.

Recent Trends in American Socialization Patterns

The Split-Level American Family*
Urie Bronfenbrenner

Children used to be brought up by their parents.

It may seem presumptuous to put that statement in the past tense. Yet it belongs to the past. Why? Because *de facto* responsibility for upbringing has shifted away from the family to other settings in the society, where the task is not always recognized or accepted. While the family still has the primary moral and legal responsibility for developing character in children, the power or opportunity to do the job is often lacking in the home, primarily because parents and children no longer spend enough time together in those situations in which such training is possible. This is not because parents don't want to spend time with their children. It is simply that conditions of life have changed.

To begin with, families used to be bigger—not in terms of more children so much as more adults—grandparents, uncles, aunts, cousins. Those relatives who didn't live with you lived nearby. You often went to their houses. They came as often to yours, and stayed for dinner. You knew them all—the old folks, the middle-aged, the older cousins. And they knew you. This had its good side and its bad side.

On the good side, some of these relatives were interesting people, or so you thought at the time. Uncle Charlie had been to China. Aunt Sue made the best penuche fudge on the block. Cousin Bill could read people's minds (according to him). And all these relatives gave you Christmas presents.

But there was the other side. You had to give Christmas presents to all your relatives. And they all minded your business throughout the years. They wanted to know where you had been, where you were going, and why. If they didn't like your answers, they said so (particularly if you had told them the truth).

Not just your relatives minded your business. Everybody in the neighborhood did. Again, this had its two sides.

If you walked on the railroad trestle, the phone would ring at your house. Your parents would know what you had done before you got back home. People on the street would tell you to button your jacket, and ask why you weren't in church last Sunday.

* From *The Saturday Review,* October 7, 1967, pp. 60–66. Copyright 1967 Saturday Review, Inc.

But you also had the run of the neighborhood. You were allowed to play in the park. You could go into any store, whether you bought anything or not. They would let you go back of the store to watch them unpack the cartons and to hope that a carton would break. At the lumber yard, they let you pick up good scraps of wood. At the newspaper office, you could punch the linotype and burn your hand on the slugs of hot lead. And, at the railroad station (they had railroad stations then), you could press the telegraph key and know that the telegraphers heard your dit-dah-dah all the way to Chicago.

These memories of a gone boyhood have been documented systematically in the research of Professor Herbert Wright and his associates at the University of Kansas. The Midwestern investigators have compared the daily life of children growing up in a small town with the lives of children living in a modern city or suburb. The contrast is sobering. Children in a small town get to know well a substantially greater number of adults in different walks of life and, in contrast to their urban and suburban agemates, are more likely to be active participants in the adult settings that they enter.

As the stable world of the small town has become absorbed into an ever shifting suburbia, children are growing up in a different kind of environment. Urbanization has reduced the extended family to a nuclear one with only two adults, and the functioning neighborhood—where it has not decayed into an urban or rural slum—has withered to a small circle of friends, most of them accessible only by motor car or telephone. Whereas the world in which the child lived before consisted of a diversity of people in a diversity of settings, now, for millions of American children, the neighborhood is nothing but row upon row of buildings inhabited by strangers. One house, or apartment, is much like another, and so are the people. They all have about the same income and the same way of life. And the child doesn't even see much of that, for all the adults in the neighborhood do is come home, have a drink, eat dinner, mow the lawn, watch TV, and sleep. Increasingly often, today's housing projects have no stores, no shops, no services, no adults at work or play. This is the sterile world in which many of our children grow, the "urban renewal" we offer to the families we would rescue from the slums.

Neighborhood experiences available to children are extremely limited nowadays. To do anything at all—go to a movie, get an ice cream cone, go swimming, or play ball—they have to travel by bus or private car. Rarely can a child watch adults working at their trades. Mechanics, tailors, or shopkeepers are either out of sight or unapproachable. A child cannot listen to gossip at the post office as he once did. And there are no abandoned houses, barns, or attics to break into. From a young point of view, it's a dull world.

Hardly any of this really matters, for children aren't home much, anyway. A child leaves the house early in the day, on a schoolbound bus, and it's almost suppertime when he gets back. There may not be anybody home when he gets there. If his mother isn't working, at least part-time (more than a third of all mothers are), she's out a lot—because of social obligations, not just friends—doing things for the community. The child's father leaves home in the morning before the child does. It takes the father an hour and a half to get to work. He's often away weekends, not to mention absences during the week.

If a child is not with his parents or other adults, with whom does he spend his time? With other kids, of course—in school, after school, over weekends, on holidays. In these relationships, he is further restricted to children of his own age and the same socio-economic background. The pattern was set when the old neighborhood school was abandoned as inefficient. Consolidated schools brought homogeneous grouping by age, and the homogenizing process more recently has been extended to segregate children by levels of ability; consequently, from the preschool years onward the child is dealing principally with replicas of the stamp of his own environment. Whereas social invitations used to be extended to entire families on a neighborhood basis, the cocktail party of nowadays has its segregated equivalent for every age group down to the toddlers.

It doesn't take the children very long to learn the lesson adults teach: Latch onto your peers. But, to latch, he must contend with a practical problem. He must hitch a ride. Anyone going in the right direction can take him. But, if no one is going in that direction just then, the child can't get there.

The child who can't go somewhere else stays home and does what everybody else does at home: He watches TV. Studies indicate that American youngsters see more TV than children in any other country do. By the late 1950's, the TV-watching figure had risen to two hours a day for the average five-year-old, three hours a day during the watching peak age period of twelve to fourteen years.

In short, whereas American children used to spend much of their time with parents and other grownups, more and more waking hours are now lived in the world of peers and of the television screen.

What do we know about the influence of the peer group, or of television, on the lives of young children? Not much.

The prevailing view in American society (indeed, in the West generally) holds that the child's psychological development, to the extent that it is susceptible to environmental influence, is determined almost entirely by the parents and within the first six years of life. Scientific investigators—who are, of course, products of their own culture, imbued with its tacit assumptions about human nature—have acted accordingly. Western studies of influences on personality development in childhood overwhelmingly take the form of research on parent-child relations, with the peer group, or other extraparental influences, scarcely being considered.

In other cultures, this is not always so. A year ago, at the International Congress of Psychology in Moscow, it was my privilege to chair a symposium on "Social Factors in Personality Development." Of a score of papers presented, about half were from the West (mostly American) and half from the Socialist countries (mostly Russian). Virtually without exception, the Western reports dealt with parent-child relationships; those from the Soviet

Union and other East European countries focused equally exclusively on the influence of the peer group or, as they call it, the children's collective.

Some relevant studies have been carried out in our own society. For example, I, with others, have done research on a sample of American adolescents from middle-class families. We have found that children who reported their parents away from home for long periods of time rated significantly lower on such characteristics as responsibility and leadership. Perhaps because it was more pronounced, absence of the father was more critical than that of the mother, particularly in its effect on boys. Similar results have been reported in studies of the effects of father-absence among soldiers' families during World War II, in homes of Norwegian sailors and whalers, and in Negro households with missing fathers, both in the West Indies and in the United States. In general, father absence contributes to low motivation for achievement, inability to defer immediate for later gratification, low self-esteem, susceptibility to group influence, and juvenile delinquency. All of these effects are much more marked for boys than for girls.

The fact that father-absence increases susceptibility to group influence leads us directly to the question of the impact of the peer group on the child's attitudes and behavior. The first—and, as yet, the only—comprehensive research on this question was carried out by two University of North Carolina sociologists, Charles Bowerman and John Kinch, in 1959. Working with a sample of several hundred students from the fourth to the tenth grades in the Seattle school system, these investigators studied age trends in the tendency of children to turn to parents versus peers for opinion, advice, or company in various activities. In general, there was a turning point at about the seventh grade. Before that, the majority looked mainly to their parents as models, companions, and guides to behavior; thereafter, the children's peers had equal or greater influence.

Although I can cite no documentation from similar investigators since then, I suspect the shift comes earlier now and is more pronounced.

In the early 1960's, the power of the peer group was documented even more dramatically by James Coleman in his book *The Adolescent Society*. Coleman investigated the values and behaviors of teen-agers in eight large American high schools. He reported that the aspirations and actions of American adolescents were primarily determined by the "leading crowd" in the school society. For boys in this leading crowd, the hallmark of success was glory in athletics; for girls, it was the popular date.

Intellectual achievement was, at best, a secondary value. The most intellectually able students were not those getting the best grades. The classroom wasn't where the action was. The students who did well were "not really those of highest intelligence, but only the ones who were willing to work hard at a relatively unrewarded activity."

The most comprehensive study relevant to the subject of our concern here was completed only a year ago by the same James Coleman. The data were obtained from more than 600,000 children in grades one to twelve in 4,000 schools carefully selected as representative of public education in the United

States. An attempt was made to assess the relative contribution to the child's intellectual development (as measured by standardized intelligence and achievement tests) of the following factors: (1) family background (e.g., parents' education, family size, presence in the home of reading materials, records, etc.); (2) school characteristics (e.g., per pupil expenditure, classroom size, laboratory and library facilities, etc.); (3) teacher characteristics (e.g., background, training, years of experience, verbal skills, etc.); and (4) characteristics of other children in the same school (e.g., their background, academic achievement, career plans, etc.).

Of the many findings of the study, two were particularly impressive; the first was entirely expected, the second somewhat surprising. The expected finding was that home background was the most important element in determining how well the child did at school, more important than any of all aspects of the school that the child attended. This generalization, while especially true for Northern whites, applied to a lesser degree to Southern whites and Northern Negroes, and was actually reversed for Southern Negroes, for whom the characteristics of the school were more important than those of the home. The child apparently drew sustenance from wherever sustenance was most available. Where the home had most to offer, the home was the most determining; but where the school could provide more stimulation than the home, the school was the more influential factor.

The second major conclusion concerned the aspects of the school environment that contributed most to the child's intellectual achievement. Surprisingly enough, such items as per pupil expenditure, number of children per class, laboratory space, number of volumes in the school library, and the presence or absence of ability grouping were of negligible significance. Teacher qualifications accounted for some of the child's achievement. But by far the most important factor was the pattern of characteristics of the other children attending the same school. Specifically, if a lower-class child had schoolmates who came from advantaged homes, he did reasonably well; but, if all the other children also came from deprived backgrounds, he did poorly.

What about the other side of the story? What happens to a middle-class child in a predominantly lower-class school? Is he pulled down by his classmates? According to Coleman's data, the answer is no; the performance of the advantaged children remains unaffected. It is as though good home background had immunized them against the possibility of contagion.

This is the picture so far as academic achievement is concerned. How about other aspects of psychological development? Specifically, how about social behavior—such qualities as responsibility, consideration for others, or, at the opposite pole, aggressiveness or delinquent behavior? How are these affected by the child's peer group?

The Coleman study obtained no data on this score. Some light has been shed on the problem, however, by an experiment that my Cornell colleagues and I recently carried out with school children in the United States and in the Soviet Union. Working with a sample of more than 150 sixth-graders (from six classrooms) in each country, we placed the children in situations in which we could test their readiness to engage in morally disapproved behavior, such as cheating on a test, denying responsibility for property damage, etc. The results indicated that American children were far more ready to take part in such actions.

The effect of the peer group (friends in school) was quite different in the two societies. When told that their friends would know of their actions, American children were even more willing to engage in misconduct. Soviet youngsters showed just the opposite tendency. In their case, the peer group operated to support the values of the adult society, at least at their age level.

We believe these contrasting results are explained, in part, by the differing role of the peer group in the two societies. In the Soviet Union, *vospitanie,* or character development, is regarded as an integral part of the process of education, and its principal agent—even more important than the family—is the child's collective in school and out. A major goal of the Soviet educational process, beginning in the nursery, is "to forge a healthy, self-sufficient collective" that, in turn, has the task of developing the child into a responsible, altruistic, and loyal member of a socialist society. In contrast, in the United States, the peer group is often an autonomous agent relatively free from adult control and uncommitted—if not outrightly opposed—to the values and codes of conduct approved by society at large. Witness the new phenomenon of American middle-class vandalism and juvenile delinquency, with crime rates increasing rapidly not only for teen-agers but for younger children as well.

How early in life are children susceptible to the effects of contagion? Professor Albert Bandura and his colleagues at Stanford University have conducted some experiments that suggest that the process is well developed at the preschool level. The basic experimental design involves the following elements. The child finds himself in a familiar playroom. As if by chance, in another corner of the room a person is playing with toys. Sometimes this person is an adult (teacher), sometimes another child. This other person behaves very aggressively. He strikes a large Bobo doll (a bouncing, inflated figure), throws objects, and mutilates dolls and animal toys, with appropriate language to match. Later on, the experimental subject (i.e., the child who "accidentally" observed the aggressive behavior) is tested by being allowed to play in a room containing a variety of toys, including some similar to those employed by the aggressive model. With no provocation, perfectly normal, well-adjusted preschoolers engage in aggressive acts, not only repeating what they observed but elaborating on it. Moreover, the words and gestures accompanying the actions leave no doubt that the child is living through an emotional experience of aggressive expression.

It is inconvenient to use a live model every time. Thus, it occurred to Bandura to make a film. In fact, he made two, one with a live model and a second film of a cartoon cat that said and did everything the live model had said and done. The films were presented on a TV set left on in a corner of the room, as if by accident. When the children were tested, the TV film turned out to be just as effective as real people. The cat aroused as much aggression as the human model.

As soon as Bandura's work was published, the television industry issued a statement calling his conclusions into question on the interesting ground that the children had been studied "in a highly artificial situation," since no parents were present either when the TV was on or when the aggressive behavior was observed. "What a child will do under normal conditions cannot be projected from his behavior when he is carefully isolated from normal conditions and the influences of society," the statement declared. Bandura was also criticized for using a Bobo doll (which, the TV people said, is "made to be struck") and for failing to follow up his subjects after they left the laboratory. Since then, Bandura has shown that only a ten-minute exposure to an aggressive model still differentiates children in the experimental group from their controls (children not subjected to the experiment) six months later.

Evidence for the relevance of Bandura's laboratory findings to "real life" comes from a subsequent field study by Dr. Leonard Eron, now at the University of Iowa. In a sample of more than 600 third-graders, Dr. Eron found that the children who were rated most aggressive by their classmates were those who watched TV programs involving a high degree of violence.

At what age do people become immune from contagion to violence on the screen? Professor Richard Walters, of Waterloo University in Canada, and his associate, Dr. Llewellyn Thomas, showed two movie films to a group of thirty-four-year-old hospital attendants. Half of these adults were shown a knife fight between two teen-agers from the picture *Rebel Without a Cause*; the other half saw a film depicting adolescents engaged in art work. Subsequently, all the attendants were asked to assist in carrying out an experiment on the effects of punishment in learning.

In the experiment, the attendants gave an unseen subject an electric shock every time the subject made an error. The lever for giving shocks had settings from zero to ten. To be sure the assistant understood what the shocks were like, he was given several, not exceeding the level of four, before the experiment. Since nothing was said about the level of shocks to be administered, each assistant was left to make his own choice. The hospital attendants who had seen the knife-fight film gave significantly more severe shocks than those who had seen the art-work film. The same experiment was repeated with a group of twenty-year-old females. This time, the sound track was turned off, so that only visual cues were present. But neither the silence nor the difference in sex weakened the effect. The young women who had seen the aggressive film administered more painful shocks.

These results led designers of the experiment to wonder what would happen if no film were shown and no other deliberate incitement were introduced in the immediate setting of the experiment. Would the continuing emotional pressures of the everyday environment of adolescents—who see more movies and more TV and are called on to display virility through aggressive acts in teen-age gangs—provoke latent brutality comparable to that exhibited by the older people under direct stimulation of the movie of the knife fight?

Fifteen-year-old high school boys were used to test the answer to this question. Without the suggestive power of the aggressive film to step up their feelings, they pulled the shock lever to its highest intensities (levels eight to ten). A few of the boys made such remarks as "I bet I made that fellow jump."

Finally, utilizing a similar technique in a variant of what has come to be known as the "Eichmann experiment," Professor Stanley Milgram, then at Yale University, set up a situation in which the level of shock to be administered was determined by the lowest level proposed by any one of three "assistants," two of whom were confederates of Milgram and were instructed to call for increasingly higher shocks. Even though the true subjects (all adult males) could have kept the intensity to a minimum simply by stipulating mild shocks, they responded to the confederates' needling and increased the degree of pain they administered.

All of these experiments point to one conclusion: At all age levels, pressure from peers to engage in aggressive behavior is extremely difficult to resist, at least in American society.

Now, if the peer group can propel its members into antisocial acts, what about the opposite possibility? Can peers also be a force for inducing constructive behavior?

Evidence on this point is not so plentiful, but some relevant data exist. To begin with, experiments on conformity to group pressure have shown that the presence of a single dissenter—for example, one "assistant" who refuses to give a severe shock—can be enough to break the spell, so that the subject no longer follows the majority. But the only research explicitly directed at producing moral conduct as a function of group experience is a study conducted by Muzafer Sherif and his colleagues at the University of Oklahoma and known as the "Robber's Cave Experiment." In the words of Elton B. McNeil:

> War was declared at Robber's Cave, Oklahoma, in the summer of 1954 (Sherif et al., 1961). Of course, if you have seen one war you have seen them all, but this was an interesting war, as wars go, because only the observers knew what the fighting was about. How, then, did this war differ from any other war? This one was caused, conducted, and concluded by behavioral scientists. After years of religious, political, and economic wars, this was, perhaps, the first scientific war. It wasn't the kind of war that an adventurer could join just for the thrill of it. To be eligible, ideally, you had to be an eleven-year-old, middle-class, American, Protestant, well-adjusted boy who was willing to go to an experimental camp.

Sherif and his associates wanted to demonstrate that, within the space of a few weeks, they could produce two contrasting patterns of behavior in this group of normal children. First, they could bring the group to a state of intense hostility, and then completely reverse the process by inducing a spirit of warm friendship and active cooperation. The success of their efforts can be gauged by the following two excerpts describing the behavior of the boys after each stage had been reached. After the first experimental treatment of the situation was introduced,

good feeling soon evaporated. The members of each group began to call their rivals "stinkers," "sneaks," and "cheaters." They refused to have anything more to do with individuals in the opposing group. The boys . . . turned against buddies whom they had chosen as "best friends" when they first arrived at the camp. A large proportion of the boys in each group gave negative ratings to all the boys in the other. The rival groups made threatening posters and planned raids, collecting secret hoards of green apples for ammunition. To the Robber's Cave came the Eagles, after a defeat in a tournament game, and burned a banner left behind by the Rattlers; the next morning, the Rattlers seized the Eagles' flag when they arrived on the athletic field. From that time on, name-calling, scuffles, and raids were the rule of the day.

. . . In the dining-hall line, they shoved each other aside, and the group that lost the contest for the head of the line shouted "Ladies first!" at the winner. They threw paper, food, and vile names at each other at the tables. An Eagle bumped by a Rattler was admonished by his fellow Eagles to brush "the dirt" off his clothes.

But, after the second experimental treatment,

. . . The members of the two groups began to feel more friendly to each other. For example, a Rattler whom the Eagles disliked for his sharp tongue and skill in defeating them became a "good egg." The boys stopped shoving in the meal line. They no longer called each other names and sat together at the table. New friendships developed between individuals in the two groups.

In the end, the groups were actively seeking opportunities to mingle, to entertain and "treat" each other. They decided to hold a joint campfire. They took turns presenting skits and songs. Members of both groups requested that they go home together on the same bus, rather than on the separate buses in which they had come. On the way, the bus stopped for refreshments. One group still had $5, which they had won as a prize in a contest. They decided to spend this sum on refreshments. On their own initiative, they had invited their former rivals to be their guests for malted milks.

How were each of these effects achieved? Treatment One has a familiar ring:

. . . To produce friction between the groups of boys, we arranged a tournament of games: baseball, touch football, a tug-of-war, a treasure hunt, and so on. The tournament started in a spirit of good sportsmanship. But, as the play progressed, good feeling soon evaporated.

How does one turn hatred into harmony? Before undertaking this task, Sherif wanted to demonstrate that, contrary to the views of some students of human conflict, mere interaction—pleasant social contact between antagonists—would not reduce hostility.

> . . . we brought the hostile Rattlers and Eagles together for social events: going to the movies, eating in the same dining room, and so on. But, far from reducing conflict, these situations only served as opportunities for the rival groups to berate and attack each other.

How was conflict finally dispelled? By a series of stratagems, of which the following is an example:

> . . . Water came to our camp in pipes from a tank about a mile away. We arranged to interrupt it and then called the boys together to inform them of the crisis. Both groups promptly volunteered to search the water line for trouble. They worked together harmoniously, and, before the end of the afternoon, they had located and corrected the difficulty.

On another occasion, just when everyone was hungry and the camp truck was about to go to town for food, it developed that the engine wouldn't start, and the boys had to pull together to get the vehicle going.

To move from practice to principle, the critical element for achieving harmony in human relations, according to Sherif, is joint activity in behalf of a *superordinate goal*. "Hostility gives way when groups pull together to achieve overriding goals which are real and compelling for all concerned."

Here, then, is the solution for the problems posed by autonomous peer groups and rising rates of juvenile delinquency. Confront the youngsters with some superordinate goals, and everything will turn out fine.

What superordinate goals can we suggest? Washing dishes and emptying wastebaskets? Isn't it true that meaningful opportunities for children no longer exist?

This writer disagrees. Challenging activities for children can still be found; but their discovery requires breaking down the prevailing patterns of segregation identified earlier in this essay—segregation not merely by race (although this is part of the story) but, to an almost equal degree, by age, class, and ability. I am arguing for greater involvement of adults in the lives of children and, conversely, for greater involvement of children in the problems and tasks of the larger society.

We must begin by desegregating age groups, ability groups, social classes, and, once again, engaging children and adults in common activities. Here, as in Negro-white relations, integration is not enough. In line with Sherif's findings, contact between children and adults, or between advantaged and disadvantaged, will not of itself reduce hostility and evoke mutual affection and respect. What is needed, in addition, is involvement in a superordinate goal, common participation in a challenging job to be done.

Where is a job to be found that can involve children and adults across the dividing lines of race, ability, and social class?

Here is one possibility: Urbanization and industrialization have not done away with the need to care for the very young. To be sure, "progress" has brought us to the point where we seem to believe that only a person with a master's degree is truly qualified to care for young children. An exception is made for parents, and for babysitters, but these are concessions to practicality; we all know that professionals could do it better.

It is a strange doctrine. For, if present-day knowledge of child development tells us anything at all, it tells us that the child develops psychologically as a function of reciprocal interaction with those who love him. This reciprocal interaction need be only of the most ordinary kind—caresses, looks, sounds, talking, singing, playing, reading stories—the things that parents, and everybody else, have done with children for generation after generation.

Contrary to the impression of many, our task in helping disadvantaged children through such programs as Head Start is not to have a "specialist" working with each child but to enable the child's parents, brothers, sisters, and all those around him to provide the kinds of stimulations that families ordinarily give children but that can fail to develop in the chaotic conditions of life in poverty. It is for this reason that Project Head Start places such heavy emphasis on the involvement of parents, not only in decision-making but in direct interaction with the children themselves, both at the center and (especially) at home. Not only parents but teen-agers and older children are viewed as especially significant in work with the very young; for, in certain respects, older siblings can function more effectively than adults. The latter, no matter how warm and helpful they may be, are, in an important sense, in a world apart; their abilities, skills, and standards are so clearly superior to those of the child as to appear beyond childish grasp.

Here, then, is a context in which adults and children can pursue together a superordinate goal, for there is nothing so "real and compelling to all concerned" as the need of a young child for the care and attention of his elders. The difficulty is that we have not yet provided the opportunities—the institutional settings—that would make possible the recognition and pursuit of this superordinate goal.

The beginning of such an opportunity structure, however, already exist in our society. As I have indicated, they are to be found in the poverty program, particularly those aspects of it dealing with children: Head Start, which involves parents, older children, and the whole community in the care of the very young; Follow Through, which extends Head Start into the elementary grades, thus breaking down the destructive wall between the school, on the one hand, and parents in the local community, on the other; Parent and Child Centers, which provide a neighborhood center where all generations can meet to engage in common activities in behalf of children, etc.

The need for such programs is not restricted to the nation's poor. So far as alienation of children is concerned, the world of the disadvantaged simply reflects in more severe form a social disease that has infected the entire society. The cure for the society as a whole is the same as that for its sickest segment. Head Start, Follow Through, Parent and Child Centers are all needed by the middle class as much as by the economically less favored. Again, contrary to popular impression, the principal purpose of these programs is not remedial education but the giving to both children and their families of a sense of dignity, purpose, and meaningful activity, without which children cannot develop capacities in any sphere of activity, including the intellectual.

Service to the very young is not the only superordinate goal potentially available to children in our society. The very old also need to be saved. In segregating them in their own housing projects and, indeed, in whole communities, we have deprived both them and the younger generations of an essential human experience. We need to find ways in which children once again can assist and comfort old people and, in return, gain insight to character development that occurs through such experiences.

Participation in constructive activities on behalf of others will also reduce the growing tendency to aggressive and antisocial behavior in the young, if only by diversion from such actions and from the stimuli that instigate them. But, so long as these stimuli continue to dominate the TV screen, those exposed to TV can be expected to react to the influence. Nor, as we have seen, is it likely that the TV industry will be responsive to the findings of research or the arguments of concerned parents and professionals. The only measure that is likely to be effective is pressure where it hurts most. The sponsor must be informed that his product will be boycotted until programing is changed.

My proposals for child rearing in the future may appear to some as a pipe dream, but they need not be a dream. For, just as autonomy and aggression have their roots in the American tradition, so have neighborliness, civic concern, and devotion to the young. By re-exploring these last, we can rediscover our moral identity as a society and as a nation.

Change During Adulthood:
A Study of Attempted "Brainwashing"

The Chinese Indoctrination Program for Prisoners of War*

Edgar H. Schein

In this article I shall try to present an account of the "typical" experiences of U.N. prisoners of war in Chinese Communist hands and to interpret these experiences in a social-psychological framework. Before the return of U.N. prisoners, the "confessions" of such prominent men as Cardinal Mindszenty and William Oatis had already aroused considerable interest in so-called brainwashing. This interest was heightened by the widespread rumors of collaboration among U.N. prisoners of war in Korea. Following their repatriation in August, 1953, a rash of testimonial articles appeared in the weekly magazines, some attempting to show that the Chinese Communist techniques were so terrifying that no one could withstand them, others roundly condemning the collaborative activities of the so-called progressives as having been selfishly motivated under conditions in which resistance was possible. These various accounts fall short because they are too emotionally charged to be objective, and because they fail to have any generality, since they are usually based on the personal experiences of only one man.

The data upon which this article is based were gathered in an attempt to form a generalized picture of what happened to the average man from the time he was captured until the time he was repatriated. The data were collected during August, 1953, at Inchon, Korea, where the repatriates were being processed, and on board the U.S.N.S. *General Black* in transit to the United States from September 1 to September 16. The method of collecting the data was, in the main, by intensive interviews conducted in Inchon, where the author was a member of one of the processing teams.

Of approximately twenty repatriates selected at random at different stages of the repatriation, each was asked to tell in chronological order and in as great detail as possible what had happened to him during his captivity. Emphasis was placed on what the Chinese or North Koreans *did* in their handling of the prisoners and how the men reacted. The men were particularly encouraged to relate the reactions of *others,* in order to avoid arousing

* From *Psychiatry*, vol. 19 (1956), pp. 149–72.

anxiety or guilt over their own behavior and thereby blocking the flow of memories. The interviews varied in length from two to four hours. . . .

The picture presented is not to be viewed as the experience of any single person, nor as the experience of all men. Rather, it represents a composite or typical account which, in all its details, may or may not have been true for any one prisoner.

THE PRISONER-OF-WAR EXPERIENCE

Capture, the March, and Temporary Camps. U.N. soldiers were captured by the Chinese and North Koreans at all stages of the Korean conflict, although particularly large groups were captured during November and December, 1950. The conditions under which men were captured varied widely. Some men were captured by having their positions overrun or surrounded; others ran into road blocks and were cut off; still others fought for many days on a shifting front before they succumbed. The situation in the front lines was highly fluid, and there was a good deal of confusion on both sides. When a position was overrun, the men often scattered and became disorganized.

While the initial treatment of prisoners by the North Koreans was typically harsh and brutal—they often took the prisoner's clothing, gave him little if any food, and met any resistance with immediate severe punishment or death—the Chinese, in line with their over-all indoctrination policy, often tried to create an atmosphere of friendliness and leniency. Some men reported that their Chinese captors approached them with outstretched hands, saying, "Congratulations! You've been liberated." It was made clear to the man that he could now join forces with other "fighters for peace." Often the Chinese soldiers pointed out to their captives how lucky they were not to have been captured by the North Koreans. Some men reported incidents of Chinese beating off North Koreans who were "trying to hurt" American prisoners, or of punishing their own guards for being too rough or inconsiderate. The men were usually allowed to keep their clothing, and some consideration was given to the sick and wounded. However, the food and medical attention were only slightly better than that provided by the North Koreans.

For the first six to twenty-four hours after capture, a man was usually in a state of dazed shock, unable to take any kind of integrated action and, later, unable to report any kind of feeling he had had during this period. Following this, he expected death or torture at the hands of his captors, for rumors that this would happen had been widely circulated in the front lines, often based on stories of men who had fallen into North Korean hands. These fears were, however, quickly dispelled by the friendly attitude of the Chinese soldiers; and this friendly attitude with the emphasis on "peace" was the first and perhaps most significant step in making the prisoner receptive to the more formal indoctrination which was to come later. . . .

The men were collected behind the lines and were marched north in groups of varying sizes. The men marched only at night, averaging about twenty miles, and were kept under strict cover in the daytime. Conditions on the march were very hard. Most men reported having great difficulty eating strange and badly prepared foods; however, they were often reminded, whether true or not, that they were getting essentially the same rations as the average Chinese foot soldier. Medical care was almost non-existent, but this too was depicted as being equally true for Chinese soldiers because of supply shortages. Almost all the men had diarrhea, many had dysentery, and most of them suffered from exposure. Every day would find a few more dead.

Although the columns were not well guarded, few escapes were attempted because the men were too weak, did not know the terrain, were on the whole poorly organized, and were afraid of the North Koreans. The few who did escape were almost always returned to the group within a short time.

During these one- to two-week marches the men became increasingly disorganized and apathetic. They developed a slow plodding gait, called by one man a "prisoner's shuffle." Lines of authority tended to break down, and the prevailing attitude was "every man for himself." Open competition for food, clothing, and shelter made the maintenance of group ties almost impossible. Everything that happened tended to be frustrating and depriving, yet there was no ready outlet for hostility, and no opportunity for constructive resistance. The only *realistic* goal was to get to prison camp where, it was hoped, conditions would be better.

Uppermost in the men's minds were fantasies of food—memories of all the good meals they had had in the past, or plans for elaborate menus in the future. The only competing fantasies concerned loved ones at home, or cars, which seemed symbolically to represent the return to their homes and to freedom.

Arrival at one of the temporary camps was usually a severe disappointment. Many men reported that the only thing that had kept them going on the march was the hope of improved conditions in the camp; but they found the food as bad as ever, living conditions more crowded than before, and a continued lack of consideration for the sick and wounded. Moreover, there was now nothing to do but sit and wait. The news given the men was mostly false, playing up Communist military victories, and was, of course, particularly demoralizing. Many of the men became extremely apathetic and withdrawn, and according to some reports these apathy states sometimes became so severe as to result in death.

The Chinese continually promised improvements in conditions or early repatriation, and failures of these promises to materialize were blamed on obstructions created by U.N. air activity or lack of "cooperation" among the prisoners. It was always made clear that only certain prisoners could hope to get a break: those who "did well," "cooperated," "learned the truth," and so on. The Chinese distributed propaganda leaflets and required the men to sing Communist songs. Apparently even guards were sensitized to finding potential collaborators among the prisoners by observing their reactions to such activities. Outright indoctrination was not attempted on the marches and in the temporary camps, but those men who finally reached one of the permanent camps were ill-prepared physically and psychologically for the indoctrination pressures they were about to face.

Life in the Permanent Prisoner-of-War Camp. Most of the permanent camps were parts of small Korean villages, often split into several compounds in different parts of the village. The camps were sometimes surrounded by a fence, by barbed wire, or by natural barriers, although sometimes not enclosed at all. While guards were posted at key places, they were not sufficiently plentiful to prevent escapes or excursions to other parts of the village. The camp usually consisted of a series of mud huts in which the men slept on the floor or on straw matting, and a schoolhouse or other permanent building which was used as administrative headquarters, for lectures, and for recreation. The various Chinese officer and enlisted billets were usually scattered through the village. Mess and latrine facilities were very inadequate, and conditions were crowded, but far better than in the temporary camps.

In camp the men were segregated by race, nationality, and rank, and were organized into companies, platoons, and squads. The squads varied in size from ten to fifteen men, who usually shared the same living area. No formal organization was permitted among the prisoners; thus, the Chinese put their own personnel in charge of the platoons and companies, and appointed certain prisoners as squad leaders without consideration of rank.

Although the daily routine in camp varied, the average prisoner arose at dawn, was required to do calisthenics for an hour or more, was assigned to various details—such as gathering wood, carrying water, cooking, repairing roads, burying other prisoners, and general maintenance of the camp—and then was given a breakfast of potato soup or some form of cereal at around 8:00 A.M. The rest of the morning and afternoon was usually spent on indoctrination or details. Whether there was a midday meal depended on the attitude of the prisoner, the supply of food, and the general state of the political situation. The main meal was served around 5:00 P.M. and usually consisted of vegetables, grains, rice, and occasional bits of pork fat or fish. For men on such a meager diet, details involving many miles of walking or very hard work were especially exhausting.

Recreation varied with the camp and with the political situation. During the first year or so, a heavy emphasis was placed on indoctrination, and recreation was restricted to reading Communist literature, seeing propaganda films, and playing such games as checkers and chess. As the truce talks progressed and repatriation became a possibility, conditions in the camps improved generally. Less emphasis was placed on indoctrination and more leeway was given to the prisoners to engage in recreation of their own choice. . . .

There are few data available concerning the sexual activities of the prisoners. There were Korean women available in the villages, but the men seldom visited them. Reports of homosexuality were very infrequent.

THE INDOCTRINATION PROGRAM

All of these conditions in the permanent camp were, in actual practice, interlocked with the indoctrination program. This program cannot be viewed as a collection of specific techniques routinely applied, but rather as the creation of a whole set of social conditions within which certain techniques operated. Whether the Chinese manipulation of the social setting to create certain effects was intentional can only be conjectured; intentional or not, it was an important factor in such success as the indoctrination program achieved.

The Removal of Supports to Beliefs, Attitudes, and Values. On matters of opinion, people tend to rely primarily on the opinions of others for determination of whether they themselves are "right" or "wrong"—whether these opinions of others are obtained through mass media of communication or through personal interaction. All of the prisoners' accustomed sources of information concerning daily events on a local, national, or international level were cut off by the Chinese, who substituted their own, usually heavily biased, newspapers, radio broadcasts, and magazines. *The Daily Worker* from various cities was available in the camp libraries, as were numerous magazines and journals from China, Poland, Russia, and Czechoslovakia. The radio news broadcasts heard usually originated in China. And the camp headquarters had no scruples concerning accuracy in the news announcements made over the camp public-address system.

The delivery of mail from home was systematically manipulated; the evidence indicates that all mail which contained information about the war or the truce talks, or which contained favorable personal news, was withheld, while letters containing no general information, or bad personal news, were usually delivered.

Personal contact with visitors from outside the camps was very limited, mainly restricted to Communist news correspondents. For most prisoners, there was simply no way to find out accurately what was going on in the world.

The Chinese also attempted to weaken the means of consensual validation by undermining personal contacts among the men. First of all, the men were segregated by race, apparently in order to put special indoctrination pressure on members of certain minorities, especially Negroes. The men were also segregated by rank, in what appeared to be a systematic attempt to undermine the internal structure of the group by removing its leaders. . . .

The Chinese emphasized that rank was no longer of any significance; the entire group was now part of a wider "brotherhood"—the earlier mentioned "fighters for peace"—in which, under communism, everyone was to be equal.

The Chinese sometimes put particularly young or inept prisoners in command of the squads to remind the men that former bases of organization no longer counted. While such a procedure aroused only resistance and hostility in most of the prisoners, undoubtedly a few malcontents welcomed the opportunity to gain occupancy of the favored positions that had never been available to them before.

There was also persistent emphasis on undermining all friendships, emotional bonds, and group activities. For instance, the Chinese prohibited all forms of religious expression and ruthlessly persecuted the few chaplains or others who tried to organize or conduct religious services. Bonds to loved ones at home were weakened by the withholding of mail, as the Chinese frequently pointed out to the men that the lack of mail meant that their friends and relatives no longer cared for them.

The systematic use of Chinese spies and also informers from prisoner ranks made it possible for the Chinese to obtain detailed information about almost all activities going on in camp. The men reported that the Chinese were forever sneaking around their quarters and listening to conversations or observing activities from hidden posts, and they also knew that some of their number were acting as informers. These circumstances helped to create a feeling of general distrust, and the only fully safe course was to withdraw from all intimate interaction with other prisoners.

When any semblance of effective organization appeared spontaneously among the men, the Chinese would usually immediately remove and segregate the leaders or key figures; and informal groups which might have supported resistance activities were also usually systematically broken up. The few that were not broken up either were not effective or died because of lack of internal support, thus indicating that this system of social control was highly effective. Usually groups were formed for one of three purposes —to plan for and aid in escapes, to prevent men from collaborating, or for social reasons. According to most reports, the groups organized around escape were highly ineffective. Usually such groups were quickly liquidated by being physically broken up. A few poorly planned escapes were attempted, but the marginal diet, the strangeness of the surrounding terrain, and the carefully built-up fear of the North Koreans all served to minimize escapes. When an escape did occur, the Chinese usually recovered the man easily by offering a bag of rice to anyone turning him in. The groups organized to keep men from collaborating, or to retaliate against them if they did, were usually composed of some of the more outspoken and violent resisters. . . .

A few groups remained intact even though the Chinese knew about them, perhaps because the Chinese did not consider them very dangerous, or because their leaders, as spokesmen for the prisoners, provided a valuable sounding board whenever the Chinese wanted to know how the group would react to certain changes in policy. . . .

Various other groupings of men existed, some, such as the squad, for administrative reasons, others to support various Chinese enterprises. Soon after capture, the Chinese made a concerted effort to recruit men for a number of "peace committees" whose purpose it was to aid in the indoctrination by conducting personal interviews with resistant prisoners and to deter any resistance activity. They also were charged with such propaganda missions as the preparation of leaflets, peace petitions, and scripts for radio broadcasts—all under the guise of running such innocuous camp activities as recreation. An intercamp peace organization was also formed to draw up peace appeals and petitions to be submitted to the United Nations, carrying, of course, the endorsement of a large number of prisoners. . . .

Each camp also had a number of other committees operating under the peace committee. They were responsible for the daily routine affairs of the camp, such as sanitation, food, recreation, study, and entertainment. The number of noncollaborators who were allowed to be members appeared to depend on the mood of the Chinese and the degree to which they wanted to keep in touch with prisoner opinions. It is likely that with the general improvement in camp conditions in 1952 and 1953, the membership of the various committees became more representative. The peace committees were, by then, largely defunct; they had been exploited as much as possible by the Chinese and no longer served any function in their propaganda campaigns.

Various social groups formed by pro's were left intact—perhaps as a reminder to other prisoners that one way to enter into meaningful relationships with others was through common political activities for the Communists.

One of the most significant facts about the few types of groups that did exist in camp is that they were highly unstable from an internal point of view because of the possible presence of informers and spies. Mutual distrust existed especially in the peace committees and in groups sanctioned by the Chinese, because no member was ever sure whether any other member was really a pro or was just pretending to "go along." If a man was pretending, he had to hide this carefully lest a real pro turn him in to the Chinese. Yet a man who sincerely believed in the Chinese peace effort had to hide this fact from others who might be pretenders, for fear they might harm him directly or blacklist him for the future, at the same time convincing other pro's that he really was sincere.

The members of resistance groups and social groups also had to be wary of each other, because they never knew whether the group had been infiltrated by spies and informers. Furthermore, the fact that the group might be broken up at any time tended to keep any member from becoming too dependent on, or close to, another.

From the point of view of this analysis, the most important effect of the social isolation which existed was the consequent emotional isolation which prevented a man from validating any of his beliefs, attitudes, and values through meaningful interaction with other men at a time when these were under heavy attack from many sources, and when no accurate information was available.

Direct Attacks on Beliefs, Attitudes and Values. The chief method of direct indoctrination was a series of lectures that all prisoners had to attend at some time during their imprisonment. These lectures were given daily and lasted from two to three hours. Each camp had one or more political instructors who read the lectures from a prepared text. Often one instructor read while another seemed to follow a second copy of the text, as if to make sure that the right material was being presented. The lectures were direct, simple, black-and-white propaganda. They attacked the United Nations and particularly the United States on various political, social, and economic issues, at the same time glorifying the achievements of the Communist countries, and making strong appeals for "peace."

Most men reported that the anti-American material was naïve and seldom based on adequate or correct information about the United States. . . .

The constant hammering at certain points, combined with all the other techniques used—and in a situation where the prisoners had no access to other information—made it likely that many of the Chinese arguments did filter through enough to make many of the men question some of their former points of view. It is also likely that any appeal for "peace," no matter how false, found a receptive audience among combat-weary troops, especially when it was pointed out that they were fighting on foreign soil and were intervening in a civil war which was "none of their business." . . .

Another direct technique was the distribution of propaganda leaflets and the showing of Communist films glorifying the accomplishments of the Communist regime in Russia and China, and pointing out how much more had been done by communism for the peasant and laborer than by the capitalist system. While such films might have been highly ineffectual under ordinary circumstances, they assumed considerable importance because of the sheer lack of any other audio-visual material.

Perhaps the most effective attack on existing values, beliefs, and attitudes was the use of testimonials from prisoners who were ostensibly supporting Communist enterprises. These included peace petitions, radio appeals, speeches, and confessions. The use of such testimonials had a double effect in that it further weakened group ties while presenting pro-Communist arguments. As long as the men unanimously rejected the propaganda, each of them could firmly hold to the position that his beliefs must be right, even if he could not defend them logically. However, *if even one other man became convinced, it was no longer possible to hold this position.* Each man was then required to begin examining his beliefs and was vulnerable to the highly one-sided arguments that were repeatedly presented.

Of particular importance were the germ-warfare confessions which were extracted from a number of Air Force officers and enlisted men. The Chinese made a movie of one or two of the officers giving their testimony to the "international" commission which they had set up to investigate the problem, and showed this movie in all the camps. Furthermore, one or two of the officers personally went from camp to camp and explained how U.N. forces had used these bombs; this made a powerful impression on many men who had, until then, dismissed the whole matter as a Chinese propaganda project. The great detail of the accounts, the sincerity of the officers, the fact that they were freely going from camp to camp and did not look as if they were then or had previously been under any duress made it difficult for some men to believe that the accounts could be anything but true.

Indirect Attacks on Beliefs, Attitudes, and Values. In the direct attacks which I have been discussing, the source of propaganda was external. In the indirect attacks, a set of conditions was created in which each prisoner of war was encouraged to participate in a way that would make it more possible for him to accept some of the new points of view. One attempt to accomplish this was by means of group discussions following lectures.

Most lectures ended with a series of conclusions—for example, "The South Koreans started the war by invading North Korea," or "The aim of the capitalist nations is world domination." The men were then required to break up into squads, go to their quarters, and discuss the material for periods of two hours or more. At the end of the discussion each squad had to provide written answers to questions handed out during the lecture—the answers, obviously, which had already been provided in the lecture. To "discuss" the lecture thus meant, in effect, to rationalize the predetermined conclusions.

A monitor was assigned to each squad to "aid" the men in the discussion, to make sure that they stayed on the proper topic, and to collect the answers and make sure that they were the "right" ones. Initially, the monitor for most squads was an English-speaking Chinese, but whenever possible the Chinese turned the job over to one of the squad members, usually the one who was most cooperative or sympathetic to the Communist point of view. If one or more members of the squad turned in "wrong" answers—for example, saying that the North Koreans had invaded South Korea—the entire squad had to listen to the lecture again and repeat the group discussion. This procedure might go on for days. The Chinese never tired of repeating the procedure over and over again, apparently believing that group discussion had a better chance of success in converting men to their point of view than individual indoctrination.

The success of such discussions often depended on the degree of supervision. If the monitor was lax, the groups would talk about anything but the required material. But a prisoner-of-war monitor who was actively pro-Communist or a Chinese who had a good understanding of English idiom might obtain considerable discussion. Even when an issue was actively discussed, in many cases it probably reinforced the U.N. position by providing an opportunity for the men to obtain some consensual validation. . . .

A second means of indirect attack was interrogation. Interrogations were carried on during all stages of internment, but their apparent function and the techniques utilized varied from time to time. Almost all men went through lengthy and repetitive military interrogations, but failure to answer questions seldom led to severe physical punishment. Instead, various psychological pressures were applied. For instance, all information supplied was cross-checked against earlier interrogations and against the information from other men. If an answer did not tally with other information, the respondent had to explain the discrepancy. Continuous pressure to resolve contrary answers often forced a man to tell the truth.

The Chinese tried to create the impression that they could obtain *any* information from *anyone* by the following interrogation technique: If a man continued to refuse to answer a question, despite great fatigue and continued repetition of the question, the interrogator would suddenly pull out a notebook and point out to the man the complete answer to the question, sometimes in astonishingly accurate detail. The interrogation would then move on to a new topic and the same procedure would be repeated, until the man could not assess whether there was indeed *anything* that the Chinese did *not* know. In most cases the man was told that others had already given information or "confessed," so why should he hold back and suffer?

A further technique was to have the man write out the question and then the answer. If he refused to write it voluntarily, he was asked to copy it from the notebooks, which must have seemed like a harmless enough concession. But the information which he had copied could then be shown to another man as evidence that he had given information of his own volition. Furthermore, it could be used to blackmail him, because he would have a hard time proving that he had merely copied the material.

Another type of interrogation to which almost all men were subjected involved primarily nonmilitary information. The Chinese were very curious about all aspects of life in the Western world and asked many questions about it, often in great detail. They also endeavored, by means of printed forms, to obtain a complete personal history from each prisoner, with particular emphasis on his social-cultural background, his class status, his and his parents' occupational histories, and so on. The purpose was apparently to determine which prisoners' histories might predispose them toward the Communist philosophy and thus make them apt subjects for special indoctrination.

Most men did not give accurate information. Usually the prisoner filled out the form in terms of fictitious characters. But later he would be required to repeat the entire procedure and would usually be unable to remember his earlier answers. He would then be confronted with the discrepancies and would be forced into the fatiguing activity of having to invent justification after justification to resolve them.

If and when the Chinese felt that they had obtained a relatively true account, it was used in discussion between the interrogator and the prisoner to undermine the prisoner's beliefs and values. Various points in the life history were used to show a man the "errors" of his past life—for example, that he or his parents had been ruthless capitalists exploiting workers, yet had really received only meager benefits from such exploitation. The Chinese were particularly interested in any inconsistencies in the life histories and would focus discussion on them in order to bring to light the motivations involved. Whenever possible, any setbacks that a man had experienced economically or socially were searchingly analyzed, and the blame was laid on the capitalistic system.

The fact that many men were unclear about why they were fighting in Korea was a good lever for such discussions. The interrogator or instructor could point out the basic injustices of foreign intervention in a civil war, and simultaneousiy could arouse longings for home and the wish that the United Nations had never taken up the fight in the first place. It was not difficult to convince some men that being in Korea was unfair to the Koreans, to themselves, and to their families who wanted them home.

Interrogations might last for hours, days, or even weeks. In some cases the interrogator lived with his subject and tried to create an atmosphere of warmth and friendliness. The main point seemed to be to get the prisoner talking, no matter what he was talking about. The discussions sometimes became effective didactic sessions because of the friendly relationship which the interrogator built up. If there were any weaknesses or inconsistencies in a man's belief systems, once he lowered his guard and began to examine them critically, he was in danger of being overwhelmed by the arguments of the instructor. This did not, of course, occur typically. For many men such critical self-evaluation served as a reinforcement to their own beliefs and actually enabled them to expose weaknesses in the Communist arguments.

Another effective technique for getting the men to question their own beliefs and values was to make them confess publicly to wrongdoings and to "criticize" themselves. Throughout the time that the men were in camp they were required to go through these rituals over and over again, no matter how trivial the offense. These offenses usually were infractions of camp rules. Soon after the men had arrived in permanent camp they were given copies of the camp rules and were required to sign a statement that they would abide by them. Most of the men were far too hungry and cold to read several pages of script covering every aspect of camp life in such minute detail that it was practically impossible not to break one of the rules from time to time. For example, an elaborate set of rules governed where in camp a man was allowed to expectorate.

Sooner or later a minor or major infraction of the rules would occur. The man would be immediately brought up before the camp commander, where his offense would be condemned as a serious crime—one for which he, the commander would point out, could be severely punished, if it were not for the lenient Chinese policy. In line with the great show which the Chinese made of treating the prisoner as a responsible person, the fact that he had agreed in writing to abide by the rules would be emphasized. The prisoner could not now say that he had not read the rules, for this would expose him to further embarrassment. The camp commander would then ask whether the man would admit that he had broken the rule, whether he was sorry that he had done so, and whether he would promise not to behave in such a "criminal" manner in the future. If the offender agreed, which seemed at the time to be harmless enough and an easy way to get off, he would be asked to write out a confession.

Sometimes this ended the matter. But frequently the man was required to read his confession to a group of prisoners and to follow it by "self-criticism," which meant that the description of the wrong deed had to be analyzed in terms of the wrong *idea* that lay behind it, that the self had to be "deeply and sincerely" criticized in terms of a number of reasons why the idea and deed were "wrong," and that an elaborate set of promises about future conduct had to be made, along with apologies for the past. Such public self-effacement was a humiliating and degrading experience, and it set a bad precedent for other men who had been attempting to resist getting caught in this net.

Writing out confessions, reading them, and criticizing oneself for minor misconduct in camp did not seem too great a concession at first when viewed against the possibility of physical punishment, torture, or imprisonment. However, these techniques could become a psychological torture once the initial concession had been made. A man who had broken a rule and had gone through the whole ritual of criticism would shortly afterward break another rule, which would arouse increased hostility on the part of the Chinese and lead to correspondingly greater demands for confession and self-criticism. Men who had confessed at first to trivial offenses soon found themselves having to answer for relatively major ones.

It should be pointed out, however, that the prisoners found numerous ways to obey the letter but not the spirit of the Chinese demands. For example, during public self-criticism sessions they would often emphasize the wrong words in the sentence, thus making the whole ritual ridiculous: "I am sorry I called Comrade Wong *a no-good son-of-a-bitch.*" Another favorite device was to promise never to "get caught" committing a certain crime in the future. Such devices were effective because even those Chinese who knew English were not sufficiently acquainted with idiom and slang to detect subtle ridicule.

There is also some evidence that the Chinese used enforced idleness or solitary confinement to encourage prisoners to consider the Communist point of view. One of the few activities available, in such circumstances, was to read Communist literature and books by Western authors who directly or indirectly attacked capitalism. The camp libraries were wholly made up of such literature. Those who did not have the strength or inclination to go on physically taxing details found themselves with no alternative but to spend their them reading pro-Communist material. In addition, some read because they felt so emotionally isolated from other prisoners that they could enjoy only solitary activities.

The Eliciting of Collaboration by Rewards and Punishments. For a number of propaganada purposes the Chinese seemed to want certain men to cooperate in specific ways, without caring whether they accepted communism or not. These men did not seem to enjoy as much status as other pro's and were cast off by the Chinese as soon as they had ceased to be useful. Such collaboration was elicited directly by a system of rewards and incentives on the one hand, and threats and punishments on the other. . . .

It was made clear to all prisoners, from the time of their capture on, that cooperation with the Chinese would produce a more comfortable state of affairs, while noncooperation or open resistance would produce a continuing marginal existence. Which rewards were of primary importance to the men varied with their current condition. On the marches and in the temporary camps physical conditions were so bad that more food, any medication, any clothing or fuel, better and less crowded living conditions, and the like constituted a powerful reward. Promises of early repatriation, or at least of marked improvement of conditions in the permanent camps, were powerful incentives which were chronically exploited.

In the permanent camps there was some improvement in the physical conditions, so that basic necessities became less effective incentives. The promise of early repatriation continued to be a great incentive, however, despite the fact that it had been promised many times before without result. Communicating with the outside world now became a major concern. To let those at home know they were alive, some prisoners began to collaborate by making slanted radio broadcasts or filling their letters with propaganda or peace appeals in order to make sure that they were sent.

As conditions continued to improve, some of the luxury items and smaller accessories to living assumed greater significance. Cigarettes, combs, soap, candy, small items of clothing, a cup of hot tea, a drink of liquor, fresh fruit, and other items of this kind were sought avidly by some men. Obtaining such items from the Chinese was inextricably linked with the degree to which the prisoner was willing to "cooperate." Any tendency toward "cooperation" was quickly followed by an increase in material rewards and promises for the future.

In some cases rewards were cleverly linked with participation in the indoctrination. For example, highly valued prizes such as cigarettes or fresh fruit were offered for essays dealing with certain aspects of world politics. The winning entries were published in the camp newspaper or magazine. Usually the winning entry was selected on the basis of its agreement with a Communist point of view. . . . In order to retain these special privileges—and having in any case incurred the hostility or even ostracism of their own group—some of these men continued to collaborate, rationalizing that they were not really harming the U.N. cause. They became self-appointed secret agents and attempted to infiltrate the Chinese hierarchy to gather "intelligence information," in which capacity they felt that they could actually aid the U.N. cause.

Among the most effective rewards used by the Chinese were special privileges and certain symbolic rewards, such as rank and status in the prison hierarchy. Perhaps the most important of the privileges was freedom of movement; the pro's had free access to the Chinese headquarters and could go into town or wherever they wished at any time of the day or night. They were given certain preferred jobs, such as writing for the camp newspaper, and were excused from the more unpleasant chores around the camp. They were often consulted by the Chinese in various policy matters. They received as a status symbol a little peace dove to be worn in the lapel or a Mao Tse-tung button which served as an identification badge. And many rewards were promised them for the future; they were told that they were playing a vital role in the world-wide movement for "peace," and that they could enjoy positions of high rank in this movement if they stayed and continued to work for it.

If one askes why men "fell" for this kind of line—why they were able to believe this kind of promise—one must look to the circumstances described earlier. These men had no sources of contrary information to rely on, and once they had collaborated even a little they were ostracized by their buddies, thus losing the support of the group which might have kept them from collaborating further.

Just as the probability of collaborative behavior could be increased through the use of rewards, the probability of resistance could be decreased through negative or painful stimulation. Usually threats of punishment were used when prisoners refused to "cooperate," and actual punishment was meted out for more aggressive resistance. Threats of death, nonrepatriation, torture, reprisals against families, reduction in food and medication, and imprisonment were all used. While the only one of these threats which was carried out with any degree of consistency was imprisonment, which sometimes involved long periods of solitary confinement, the other threats were nevertheless very effective and the possibility that they might be carried out seemed very real. Especially frightening was the prospect of nonrepatriation, which seemed a likely possibility before the prisoner lists were exchanged at Panmunjom. The threat of death was also effective, for the men knew that they could be killed and listed officially as having died of heart failure or the like. With regard to food and medication, the men could not determine whether they were actually being punished by having these withheld, or whether the meager supply was merely being reserved for "deserving" prisoners.

An effective threat with officers was that of punishing the whole group for which the officer was responsible if he personally did not "cooperate." The incidence of such group punishment was not revealed in the accounts, but it is clear that if an officer did "cooperate" with the Chinese, he was able both to relieve his own fears and to rationalize his cooperation as being the only means of saving the men for whom he was responsible.

Reinforcing all these threats was the vague but powerful fear of the unknown; the men did not know what they were up against in dealing with the Chinese and could not predict the reactions of their captors with any degree of reliability. The only course that led to a consistent reduction in such tension was participation in Chinese enterprises.

Overt punishment varied with the offense, with the political situation, and with the person administering it. Shortly after capture there were numerous incidents of brutality, most of them committed by North Koreans. During early interrogations the Chinese frequently resorted to minor physical punishment such as face-slapping or kicking when answers were not forthcoming, but a prisoner who continued to be silent was usually dismissed without further physical punishment.

Physical punishments in permanent camps had the effect of weakening rather than injuring the men. They varied from severe work details to such ordeals as standing at attention for long periods; being exposed to bright lights or excessive cold; standing on tiptoe with a noose around the neck; being confined in the "cage," a room too small to allow standing, sitting, or lying down; being thrown in the "hole," a particularly uncomfortable form of solitary confinement; or being kept in filthy surroundings and denied certain essentials for keeping clean. Those who were *chronically* uncooperative were permanently segregated from the rest of the group and put into special camps where more severe forms of discipline backed by harsher punishments were in effect. Basically, the "lenient policy" applied only to those men whom the Chinese hoped they could use.

More common forms of punishment for minor infractions were social in character, intended to degrade or embarrass the prisoner in front of his fellows. Public confessions and self-criticisms were the outstanding forms of such punishment, with blackmail being frequently used if a prisoner had once collaborated to any extent. There is *no* evidence that the Chinese used any drugs or hypnotic methods, or offered sexual objects to elicit information, confessions, or collaborative behavior. Some cases of severe physical torture were reported, but their incidence is difficult to estimate.

General Principles in All Techniques. Several general principles underlay the various phases of the Chinese indoctrination, which may be worth summing up at this point. The first of these was *repetition*. One of the chief characteristics of the Chinese was their immense patience in whatever they were doing; whether they were conducting an interrogation, giving a lecture, chiding a prisoner, or trying to obtain a confession, they were always willing to make their demand or assertion over and over again. Many men pointed out that most of the techniques used gained their effectiveness by being used in this repetitive way until the prisoner could no longer sustain his resistance. A second characteristic was the *pacing of demands*. In the various kinds of responses that were demanded of the prisoners, the Chinese always started with trivial, innocuous ones and, as the habit of responding became established, gradually worked up to more important ones. Thus after a prisoner had once been "trained" to speak or write out trivia, statements on more important issues were demanded of him. This was particularly effective in eliciting confessions, self-criticism, and information during interrogation.

Closely connected with the principle of pacing was the principle of constant *participation* from the prisoner. It was never enough for the prisoner to listen and absorb; some kind of verbal or written response was always demanded. Thus if a man would not give original material in question-and-answer sessions, he was asked to copy something. Likewise, group discussions, autobiographical statements, self-criticisms, and public confessions all demanded an active participation by the prisoner.

In their propaganda campaign the Chinese made a considerable effort *to insert their new ideas into old and meaningful contexts.* In general this was not very successful, but it did work for certain prisoners who were in some way not content with their lot in the United States. The obtaining of auto-biographies enabled each interrogator to determine what would be a signifi-cant context for the particular person he was dealing with, and any mis-fortune or setback that the person had suffered served as an ideal starting place for undermining democratic attitudes and instilling communistic ones.

No matter which technique the Chinese were using, they always struc-tured the situation in such a way that the correct response was followed by some form of *reward,* while an incorrect response was immediately followed by *threats* or *punishment.* The fact that the Chinese had complete control over material resources and had a monopoly of power made it possible for them to manipulate hunger and some other motives at will, thereby giving rewards and punishments their meaning.

Among the various propaganda techniques employed by the Chinese, their use of *prestige suggestion* was outstanding. The average prisoner had no way of disputing the germ-warfare confessions and testimonials of Air Force officers, or the conclusions of an investigation of the germ-warfare charges by ostensibly impartial scientists from many nations.

Among the positive propaganda appeals made, the most effective was probably the *plea for peace.* The Chinese presented an antiwar and laissez-faire ideology which strongly appealed to the war-weary combat soldier.

In addition, the Chinese used a number of *manipulative tricks,* which were usually successful only if the prisoner was not alert because of fatigue or hunger. One such trick was to require signatures, photographs, or per-sonal information for a purpose which sounded legitimate, then using them for another purpose. Some prisoners reported that they were asked to sign "camp rosters" when they first arrived in camp and later found that they had actually signed a peace petition.

In essence, the prisoner-of-war experience in camp can be viewed as a series of problems which each man had to solve in order to remain alive and well integrated. Foremost was the problem of physical privation, which powerfully motivated each man to improve his living conditions. A second problem was to overcome the fears of nonrepatriation, death, torture, or reprisals. A third problem was to maintain some kind of cognitive integra-tion, a consistent outlook on life, under a set of conditions where basic values and beliefs were strongly undermined and where systematic confu-sion about each man's role in life was created. A fourth problem was to maintain a valid position in a group, to maintain friendship ties and concern for others under conditions of mutual distrust, lack of leadership, and sys-tematically created social disorganization. The Chinese had created a set of conditions in which collaboration and the acceptance of communism led to a resolution of conflicts in all these areas.

REACTIONS TO THE INDOCTRINATION

It is very difficult to determine after the fact what happened in this highly complex and novel situation—what it was really like for the men who had to spend several years in the Chinese prisoner-of-war camps. Each set of experiences had a highly personal and unique flavor to it, making generalized conclusions difficult.

I may illustrate the problem by discussing *ideological change* and *collaboration*. Both of these were responses to the indoctrination, broadly conceived, *but neither necessarily implies the other*. It was possible for a man to collaborate with the enemy without altering his beliefs, and it was equally possible for a man to be converted to communism to some degree without collaborating.

Obviously, it is necessary to define these responses, even though any precise definition will to some degree distort the actual events. *Collaboration* may be defined as any kind of behavior which helped the enemy: signing peace petitions, soliciting signatures for peace petitions, making radio appeals, writing radio scripts, writing false information home concerning conditions in the camps (or recording statements to this effect), writing essays on communism or working for the Communist-controlled newspaper, allowing oneself to be photographed in "rigged" situations, participating in peace rallies or on peace committees, being friendly with the enemy, asking others to cooperate with the enemy, running errands for the enemy, accepting special privileges or favors, making false confessions or pro-enemy speeches, informing on fellow prisoners, divulging military information, and so on. . . .

Ideological change may be defined as a reorganization of political beliefs, which could vary from acquiring mild doubts concerning some aspects of the democratic ideology to the complete abandonment of this ideology and a total embracing of communism. The latter I shall label *conversion*. The problem of measuring the *degree* of ideological change is complicated by the lack of good behavioral criteria for measuring such a process of reorganization of beliefs. One might be tempted to say that anyone could be termed a convert who actively attempted to convince others of the worth of communism, who took all the advanced courses in camp, and who was able to demonstrate in his overt behavior a disregard for democratic values. But such behavior might also characterize a relatively intelligent man who had begun to read Communist literature out of boredom, only to find that both his friends and the Chinese took this as evidence of his genuine interest in communism. He might then be ostracized by his friends and pressed into collaboration by the Chinese, who, it was rumored, severely punished anyone who deceived them.

Of all the prisoners, twenty-one refused repatriation; one might assume that these represent the total number of converts, but such a criterion is inadequate on at least two grounds. On the one hand, some converts would undoubtedly have been sent back to the United States to spread communism and form a potential fifth column. On the other hand, some collaborators who had not changed ideologically might have been afraid to return, knowing that court-martial proceedings and personal degradation probably awaited them. . . .

Thus it is more difficult to determine how the prisoners responded to indoctrination techniques ideologically than it is to determine what overt collaboration occurred. What the prisoners *did* is, relatively speaking, a matter of fact; why they did it is a matter of conjecture. . . .

THE EFFECTIVENESS OF THE INDOCTRINATION TECHNIQUES

By disrupting social organization and by the systematic use of reward and punishment, the Chinese were able to elicit a considerable amount of collaboration. This is not surprising when one considers the tremendous effort the Chinese made to discover the weak points in individual prisoners, and the unscrupulousness with which they manipulated the environment. Only a few men were able to avoid collaboration altogether—those who adopted a completely negativistic position from the moment of capture without considering the consequences for themselves or their fellow prisoners. At the same time the number of men who collaborated to a sufficient extent to be detrimental to the U.N. cause was also very small. The majority collaborated at one time or another by doing things which seemed to them trivial, but which the Chinese were able to turn to their own advantage. Such behavior did not necessarily reflect any defection from democratic values or ideology, nor did it necessarily imply that these men were opportunists or neurotics. Often it merely represented poor judgment in evaluating a situation about which they had little information, and poor foresight regarding the reactions of the Chinese, other prisoners, and people back home.

The extent to which the Chinese succeeded in converting prisoners of war to the Communist ideology is difficult to evaluate because of the previously mentioned hazards in measuring ideological change, and because of the impossibility of determining the *latent* effects of the indoctrination. In terms of *overt* criteria of conversion or ideological change, one can only conclude that, considering the effort devoted to it, the Chinese program was a failure. Only a small number of men decided to refuse repatriation—possibly for reasons other than ideological change—and it was the almost unanimous opinion of the prisoners that most of the pro's were opportunists or weaklings. One can only conjecture, of course, the extent to which prisoners who began to believe in communism managed to conceal their sympathies from their fellows and the degree to which repatriates are now, as a result of their experience, predisposed to find fault with a democratic society if they cannot make a go of it.

It is difficult to determine whether to attribute this relative failure of the Chinese program to the inadequacy of their principles of indoctrination, to their technical inefficiency in running the program, or to both these factors.

In actual practice the direct techniques used were usually ineffective because many of the Chinese instructors were deficient in their knowledge of Western culture and the English language. Many of their facts about America were false, making it impossible for them to obtain a sympathetic audience, and many of their attempts to teach by means of group discussion failed because they were not sensitive to the subtle ways in which prisoners managed to ridicule them by sarcasm or other language devices. The various intensive pressures brought to bear on single prisoners and the fostering of close personal relationships between prisoner and instructor were far more effective in producing ideological change, but the Chinese did not have nearly enough trained personnel to indoctrinate more than a handful of men in this intensive manner.

The technique of breaking up both formal and spontaneous organization was effective in creating feelings of social and emotional isolation, but it was never sufficiently extended to make the prisoners completely dependent on the Chinese. As long as the men lived and "studied" together, there remained opportunities for consensual validation and thus for resisting indoctrination. However, as a means of social control this technique was highly effective, in that it was virtually impossible for the prisoners to develop any program of organized resistance or to engineer successful commuciation with the outside by means of escapes or clandestine sending out of information.

The most powerful argument against the intellectual appeal of communism was the low standard of living which the men observed in the Korean villages in which they lived. The repatriates reported that they were unable to believe in a system of values which sounded attractive on paper but which was not practiced, and they were not impressed by the excuse that such conditions were only temporary.

Most men returned from prison camp expressing a strong anti-Communist feeling and a conviction that their eyes had, for the first time, been opened to the real dangers of communism. . . .

In summary, it can be said that the Chinese were successful in eliciting and controlling certain kinds of behavior in the prisoner population. They were less successful in changing the beliefs of the prisoners. Yet this lack of success might have been due to the inefficiency of a program of indoctrination which could have been highly effective had it been better supported by adequate information and adequately trained personnel.

Collaboration with the enemy occurs to a greater or lesser extent in any captive population. It occurred in the Japanese and German prisoner-of-war camps during World War II. But never before have captured American soldiers faced a *systematic effort* to make them collaborate and to convert them to an alien political ideology. The only precedent in recent history was the handling of political prisoners by the Nazis. . . . By means of extreme and degrading physical and psychological torture the Nazis attempted to reduce the prison population to an "infantile" state in which the jailer would be viewed with the same awe as the child views his father. Under these conditions, the prisoners tended in time to identify with the punitive authority figures and to incorporate many of the values they held, especially with respect to proper behavior in camp. They would curry the favor of the guards, would imitate their style of dress and speech, and would attempt to make other prisoners follow camp rules strictly.

It is possible that such a mechanism also operated in the Chinese prison camps. However, the Nazis attempted, by brutal measures, to reduce their prisoners to docile slave laborers, while the Chinese attempted, by using a "lenient policy" and by treating the prisoners as men in need of "education," to obtain converts who would actively support the Communist point of view. Only those prisoners who showed themselves to be "backward" or "reactionary" by their inability to see the fundamental "truths" of communism were treated punitively.

The essence of this novel approach is to gain complete control over those parts of the physical and social environment which sustain attitudes, beliefs, and values, breaking down interactions and emotional bonds which support the old beliefs and values, and building up new interactions which will increase the probability of the adoption of new beliefs and values. If the only contacts a person is permitted are with persons who *unanimously* have beliefs different from his own, it is very likely that he will find at least some among them with whom, because of growing emotional bonds, he will identify and whose beliefs he will subsequently adopt.

Is the eliciting of collaborative behavior in itself sufficient to initiate the process of ideological change? One might assume that a person who had committed acts consonant with a new ideology might be forced to adopt this ideology in order to rationalize his behavior. This might happen especially if the number of possible rationalizations were limited. The situation in the prison camps, however, allowed the men to develop rationalizations which did not necessarily involve Communist premises. Furthermore, it is likely that whatever rationalizations are adopted, they will not acquire the permanence of beliefs unless supported by social reinforcements. When the prisoners reentered the democratic setting, most of them gave up whatever Communist premises they might have been using to rationalize their collaboration and found new rationalizations that attempted to explain, from the standpoint of democratic premises, why they had collaborated. Apart from the technical difficulties the Chinese experienced in running their indoctrination program, they were never able to control social interactions to a sufficient extent to reinforce in meaningful social relationships the Communist rationalizations for collaboration.

Taken singly, there is nothing new or terrifying about the specific techniques used by the Chinese; they invented no mysterious devices for dealing with people. Their method of controlling information by controlling the mass media of communication has been a well-known technique of totalitarian governments throughout history. Their system of propagandizing by means of lectures, movies, reading materials, and testimonials has its counterparts in education and in advertising. Group discussions and other methods requiring participation have their counterparts in education and in psychiatry. The possibility that group discussion may be fundamentally superior to lectures in obtaining stable decisions by participants has been the subject of extensive research in American social psychology. The Chinese methods of interrogation have been widely used in other armies, by the police, by newspaper reporters, and by others interested in aggressively eliciting information. Forced confessions and self-criticism have been widely used techniques in religious movements as a basis for conversion or as a device to perpetuate a given faith. The control of behavior by the manipulation of reward and punishment is obviously the least novel of all the techniques, for men have controlled each other in this way since the beginning of history.

Thus the only novelty in the Chinese methods was the attempt to *use a combination of all these techniques and to apply them simultaneously* in order to gain complete control over significant portions of the physical and social environment of a group of people. . . .

4. SUGGESTIONS FOR FURTHER READING

BANDURA, A., and R. WALTERS. *Social Learning and Personality Development* (New York: Holt, Rinehart, 1963).

BECKER, HOWARD, *et al. Boys in White* (Chicago: University of Chicago Press, 1961).

BERKOWITZ, LEONARD. *Aggression: A Social Psychological Study* (New York: McGraw-Hill, 1962).

BLAU, ZENA SMITH. *Old Age in a Changing Society* (New York: Franklin Watts, 1973).*

BRIM, O., and S. WHEELER. *Socialization After Childhood* (New York: John Wiley & Sons, 1966).*

BRONFENBRENNER, URIE. *Two Worlds of Childhood: U.S. and U.S.S.R.* (New York: Russell Sage, 1970).

COLEMAN, JAMES. *The Adolescent Society* (New York: The Free Press, 1961).*

ELKIN, FREDERICK. *The Child and Society* (New York: Random House, 1960).*

ERIKSON, ERIK. *Childhood and Society* (New York: W. W. Norton, 1950).*

FREUD, SIGMUND. *Civilization and Its Discontents* (Garden City, N.Y.: Doubleday, 1958).*

GOFFMAN, ERVING. *Asylums* (Garden City, N.Y.: Doubleday, 1961).*

GOLDSTEIN, J. A., ANNA FREUD, and A. SOLNIT. *Beyond the Best Interests of the Child* (New York: The Free Press, 1973).*

HALL, CALVIN. *A Primer of Freudian Psychology* (New York: New American Library, 1954).*

HOLLINGSHEAD, AUGUST. *Elmtown's Youth* (New York: John Wiley & Sons, 1949).*

MEAD, MARGARET. *Coming of Age in Samoa* (New York: William Morrow, 1928).*

MILLER, D., and G. SWANSON. *Inner Conflict and Defense* (New York: Schocken Books, 1966).*

NEILL, A. S. *Summerhill* (New York: Hart, 1960).*

PIAGET, JEAN. *The Moral Judgement of the Child* (London: Kegan Paul, 1932).*

SIDEL, RUTH. *Women and Child Care in China* (New York: Hill & Wang, 1972).*

SKINNER, B. F. *Beyond Freedom and Dignity* (New York: Alfred A. Knopf, 1971).

SPIRO, MELFORD. *Children of the Kibbutz* (New York: Schocken Books, 1965).*

STRAUSS, ANSELM (ed.). *The Social Psychology of George Herbert Mead* (Chicago: University of Chicago Press, 1934).*

* *Available in paperback.*

5. Social Stratification

INTRODUCTION

An important aspect of the social organization of society involves social stratification—the hierarchical ranking of positions in the social order according to unequal shares of socially valued rewards. Every society has some degree of social stratification. Even in the smallest, simplest, most primitive societies, there is some social ranking according to sex, age, and kinship differences, or differences in hunting or fishing proficiency. Evidence confirming rudimentary social stratification in very primitive societies can be found in the essay on the Nambikuara bands of Brazil's northwestern Mato Grosso in Chapter 9, "Political Sociology." The author, Claude Levi-Strauss, suggests that the Nambikuara chief's privilege of having several wives, which is denied to all other members of the group, may be an essential inducement to perform necessary leadership tasks. Differentially distributed rewards, in this manner, can contribute to social maintenance. In their functional theory of stratification,[1] Davis and Moore advance a very similar view with more formal theoretical precision. As societies grow in complexity, and as they acquire some economic surplus, they inevitably develop a relatively stable, enduring, and heritable system of social ranks.

Once a society arrives at the high degree of social-organizational complexity characteristic of the mass, urban-industrial social order, this hierarchy of social ranks becomes so deeply embedded that it seems impossible to eliminate it. It appears that, notwithstanding the efforts of those in socialist or Communist societies—and of some in the capitalistic West—to eliminate class distinctions, they continue to exist.

[1] K. Davis and W. Moore, "Some Principles of Stratification," *American Sociological Review*, vol. 10 (April, 1945), pp. 242–49.

Furthermore, stratification systems are very similar throughout modern industrial society. Perhaps the best that can be hoped for is movement in the direction of narrowing the gap between the haves and the have-nots. In speaking of our own society, Herbert Gans, in "The New Egalitarianism," suggests that while the American class structure has not yet changed significantly, the recent upsurge of political activism among a number of currently subjugated groups may substantially reduce inequality in the future. Gans emphasizes the need to adhere to an individualistic approach in seeking to reduce inequality if the changes are to be widely supported.

Sociologists generally distinguish three main types of stratification systems: caste, estate, and class societies. A caste system consists of an array of closed social groups that exhibit a fixed order of superiority and inferiority. Intimate association, mobility, and intermarriage between castes are forbidden. The system is sanctioned by religion and the mores. One's caste position is based on ascription (birth). India best exemplifies a caste society.

An estate system of social stratification is based on hereditary relationships to land. Each estate constitutes a distinct stratum (a group of individuals and families who share similar social rank), whose rights and obligations are defined and sanctioned by law. Although mobility is possible, changes in status are unusual. The best-known example of an estate system is that of medieval Europe.

A class system, by contrast, is based primarily upon differences in wealth and income. There are no legal restraints on the movement of individuals and families from one class to another, although such movement may be difficult. Social classes are not closed social groups; they are aggregates of persons with similar amounts of income and property and similar sources of income. Positions in the class order, ideally, are based on achievement. The class system of stratification is found in most modern industrial societies.

These definitions suggest the possibility of social mobility in class society and its diminished likelihood in the caste order. However, some mobility actually occurs in caste societies as a result of changes in science and technology, in economic structures, in educational arrangements, in ideologies, or in the structure of authority and power; some castes may move up in status, others down. For example, a shoemaker subcaste, consisting of a group of highly skilled craftsmen, could experience a loss in status with the importation of mass-produced, low-cost shoes. Or a local subcaste may be able to accumulate sufficient wealth to buy land, thus entering a more highly valued occupation than the one it was in. Mobility in caste society, when it occurs, generally involves group mobility. Geographical mobility is also likely to affect social mobility in a caste system. A person who leaves his local village subcaste, moves to a city, and enters a secular occupation may find that his old social rank has a higher evaluation in his new community; the anonymity of the city facilitates social mobility.

In presumably open class societies, on the other hand, many, if not most, social ranks are passed from one generation to the next. The son of a railway porter is considerably less likely to become socially prominent than the kin of a Rockefeller or a Roosevelt. Within actual societies, there are both caste and class elements; societies can be conceived of as situated along a continuum exhibiting varying degrees of class or caste features. The estate society represents a type situated between these extremes but decidedly closer to the caste end of the continuum.

A social class is defined as a group of people who share a more or less similar rank and some similarity of behavior and values. Most laymen believe that income or wealth is the best indicator of social position. In fact, the best index of social rank depends, in part, on the phenomena being studied. If we were studying political attitudes, a subjective index of social class (the class a person thinks he belongs to) might be most useful in determining how he will vote. On the other hand, if differences in family size are being investigated, an objective method (class measured by education, occupation, or income) might yield the best results. If we had to commit ourselves to a single best indicator of social rank, however, the choice would be occupation. Occupation suggests a person's wealth or income, the degree of his authority and control over others, his education and specialized training, and who his close associates and friends are likely to be—all of which factors come much closer to indicating his total life-style and life chances than a merely economic criterion.

Studies of occupational rank over time indicate that the prestige of various occupations remains relatively stable in industrial society. The National Opinion Research Corporation conducted two studies, in 1947 and 1963, to find out the prestige granted to various occupational positions. A sample of nearly 3,000 Americans was asked to rate 90 occupations as having excellent, good, average, somewhat below average, or poor general standing. The answers were weighted so as to yield a score from 1 to 100 for each occupation. In 1963, Supreme Court justice received 94, the highest ranking; physician, 93; college professor, 90; trained machinist, 75; mail carrier, 66; filling-station attendant, 51; and the lowest category, shoeshiner, 34. These were substantially the same as the findings in 1947. Moreover, these studies found considerable agreement among respondents on the relative standings of various occupational categories. Cross-national comparisons, including data from several underdeveloped nations, also show little variation in the prestige ranking of occupations. These findings strongly suggest that there is a relatively fixed hierarchy of prestige associated with the positions and institutions of industrial society.

Belonging to a particular social class has dramatic consequences for one's life chances. Greater likelihood of infant mortality, shorter life expectancy, more physical and mental illness, malnutrition, and less adequate health care are characteristic of the lower social classes. The higher in the class scale we go, the taller, healthier, and heavier are the members and the higher their scores on IQ tests. Those lower on the social scale are more likely to be arrested and convicted for crimes and less likely to receive the degree of justice and legal protection accorded to those at the top. And they have much more limited educational opportunities than those available to the rich. The study by Schafer, Olexa, and Polk shows how the poor are sorted out of the high school world and shuttled into the more limited horizons of vocational programs.

The net effect of these and other life-chance differences among the classes ultimately reduces social mobility from one generation to the next. The children of the lower classes are encouraged to assume positions at the lower social levels; the uppers, at the top.

Class membership affects almost everything a person does, thinks, and believes. What his politics is, how actively he promotes it, where and how he lives, what he does in his leisure time, who his associates and friends are, what he reads, his religious participation, his organizational memberships, the size of his family—these are only a few of an infinity of matters affected by class membership. We note in Sheila Johnson's "Sociology of Christmas Cards" that even so trivial and seemingly unimportant a matter as selecting and sending Christmas cards is affected by social class. Johnson's work suggests that, by assuming the life-styles of their social superiors, individuals hope to encourage their own social mobility. What one does is not only an indicator of where one is located in the status hierarchy; it also indicates where one expects to be heading.

One of the results of cross-national social-stratification studies has been the development of the concept of a culture of poverty. Although there is much controversy concerning its existence and components, according to one of its advocates, the late Oscar Lewis, the subculture of poverty consists of a distinctive and remarkably stable and persistent way of life, passed down from generation to generation and involving a sense of alienation, lack of effective participation in the institutions of society, antipathy and cynicism toward the caretakers of society (i.e., the police, government officials, the church), precarious family relationships, early initiation into sex, a trend toward mother-centered families, and a privatized, helpless, dependent, and hedonistic outlook. Lewis argues, in "The Culture of Poverty," that these characteristics are accompaniments of the processes of urbanization and industrialization, and that they are associated with capitalistic society. Although the culture of poverty exists on a small scale in the United States and other highly urbanized and industrialized nations, it is widespread among transitional societies.

Stratification Trends in American Society

The New Egalitarianism*

Herbert J. Gans

Although the fundamental idea of the Declaration of Independence is that "all men are created equal," Americans traditionally have been more interested in life, liberty, and the pursuit of happiness than in the pursuit of equality. In the last decade, however, their interests have begun to shift, and equality may be on its way to becoming as significant as liberty in the hierarchy of American goals.

The shift began approximately on the day in 1955 when Mrs. Rose Parks of Montgomery, Alabama, decided that she was no longer willing to sit in the rear of a bus. Much has been written about the ensuing political and social unrest, but few observers have emphasized that the revolts of the blacks, the young, and others have a common theme: the demand for greater equality by the less than equal. Blacks have agitated for racial equality through black power; students, in high schools as well as in colleges, have demanded more power on the campus; teen-agers have begun to claim the sexual freedom now available to young adults, and in less public ways they—and even younger children—have sought more equality within the family. And, of course, many women are now demanding equality with men, and homosexuals with heterosexuals.

Similar developments have been occurring in the economy and the polity. Wage workers have begun to demand guaranteed annual incomes and the other privileges that salaried workers enjoy. Public employees have struck for wage equity with workers in private industry. Assembly-line workers have sought better working conditions and more control over the operation of the line. Enlisted men have called for reductions in the power of officers.

In politics the 1960s saw the emergence of the drive for community control—attempts by urban residents to obtain more power over their neighborhoods. Subsequently, community control broadened into a movement to reduce the power of bureaucracies at all levels of government and of professionals over their clients; for example, of doctors over patients, teachers over parents, and planners over home owners. Consumers have called for more control over what goods are to be produced and sold, environmentalists over how they are to be produced. Stockholders have demanded a greater role in the decisions taken by management.

* From *Saturday Review,* May 6, 1972, pp. 43–46. Reprinted by permission.

Few of these demands have been explicitly phrased in terms of equality; most of those making the demands have spoken of autonomy and democracy. Many have actually asked for more liberty. Still, if all of these demands are put together, they mean more income for some and higher costs for others, more power for some and less for others. If the demands were heeded, the eventual outcome would be greater over-all equality.

No one can accurately predict whether or not these demands will be heeded, but egalitarian ideas are cropping up with increased frequency among politicians and in the media. Senator Fred Harris's populist presidential campaign, which called for some income redistribution, was short-lived, but Senator George McGovern has proposed a comprehensive tax reform program along the same lines, and Governor George Wallace occasionally injects egalitarian notions into his campaign speeches. Widely read journalists, such as Tom Wicker, Jack Newfield, and *New Republic*'s TRB, have talked and written about the need for equality. In March an article entitled "Equality" appeared in *Fortune;* it sought, rather gingerly, to prepare the business community for a more egalitarian future.

The current interest in equality cannot be explained away as the plaints of discontented minorities and newly radicalized public figures. It stems from the fact that America's is, and always has been, a very unequal society. Take the distribution of income. The poorest fifth of the U.S. population receives only 4 per cent of the nation's annual income, and the next poorest fifth, only 11 per cent, while the richest fifth gets about 45 per cent, and the 5 per cent at the top, over 20 per cent. Inequality of assets is even greater: 1 per cent of the people control more than one-third of the country's wealth. Although many Americans now own some stocks, 2 per cent of all individual stockholders own about two-thirds of stocks held by individuals.

The same inequality exists in the business world. Of the almost two million corporations in America, one-tenth of 1 per cent controls 55 per cent of the total corporate assets; 1.1 per cent controls 82 per cent. At the other end of the spectrum, 94 per cent of the corporations own only 9 per cent of the total assets. Even the public economy is unequal, for the poor pay a larger share of their incomes for taxes than other groups; people earning less than $2,000 pay fully half of their incomes in direct and indirect taxes as compared with only 45 per cent paid by those earning $50,000 or more. Moderate income groups are not much better off; people earning $8,000–$10,000 a year pay only 4 per cent less of their income than those making $25,000–$50,000.

Of course, the poor get something back from the government through welfare and other subsidies, but then so do the affluent, especially through indirect subsidies in the guise of tax policies, such as the oil-depletion allowance, crop supports, and tax exemptions granted to municipal-bond purchasers. Philip Stern, author of *The Great Treasury Raid* and himself a multimillionaire, recently described these subsidies as "a welfare program that reverses the usual pattern and gives huge welfare payments to the su-perrich but only pennies to the very poor." Stern estimated that the annual subsidies came to $720,000 per family for people with million-dollar in-comes, $650 per family for the $10,000–$15,000 middle-income group, and $16 per family for the under-$3,000 poor.

Political inequality is also rampant. For example, since about 13 per cent of the population is poor in terms of the official poverty line, an egalitarian political system would require that almost fifty congressmen and thirteen senators be representatives of the poor. This is not the case, however, even though big business, big labor, and even less numerous sectors of the popu-lation have their unofficial representatives in both houses of Congress. While Supreme Court action has finally brought about the one-man, one-vote principle in electing these representatives, the seniority system main-tains the traditional pattern of inequality, and so a handful of congressmen and senators, many from rural districts, still hold much of the real power on Capitol Hill. Affluent individuals and well-organized interest groups in effect have more than one vote per man because they have far greater ac-cess to their elected representatives than the ordinary citizen and because they can afford to hire lobbyists who watch out for their interests and even help to write legislation.

These patterns of inequality are not new; although America has some-times been described as a nation of equals and as a classless society, these are simply myths. To be sure, America never had the well-defined classes or estates that existed in Europe, but from its beginning it has nevertheless been a nation of unequals. For example, in 1774, among the minority of Philadelphians affluent enough to pay taxes, 10 per cent owned fully 89 per cent of the taxable property. Over the last two hundred years the degree of economic inequality has been reduced somewhat, but in the last sixty years —since reliable statistics on income distribution have become available— that distribution has changed little.

Although the ideal of a nation of equals has existed in American life from the beginning, it has, in fact, never been pursued very energetically in either the economy or the polity. Even the ideal that every boy could be president of the United States or chairman of the board of General Motors has rarely been achieved; most of our presidents have been rich, and studies of the origins of American businessmen show that in the nineteenth century, as now, the large majority have themselves been sons of businessmen.

Nevertheless, over the last two hundred years most Americans seem to have put up quietly with the prevailing inequality. Today, however, the traditional patience with inequality has disappeared, and for three reasons.

First, many Americans are now beginning to realize that the frontier, by which I mean the opportunity to strike out on one's own and perhaps to strike it rich, is closing down. The literal frontier in the West was closed before the turn of the century, but until recently, other frontiers were still thought to be open. Rural people hoped that they could become independent by saving up for a farm; factory workers, by going into business, perhaps opening a gas station or small workshop; and middle-class people, by entering the independent professions.

Today these hopes have begun to disappear, for the family farm is economically obsolete, the small store cannot compete with the chain, and the independent professions now consist more and more of salaried employees. Of course, there are still exceptions, and every year a few well-publicized individuals strike it rich, but their small number only proves the rule. Most Americans now realize that they will spend their working lives as employees and that they can best improve their fortunes by making demands on their employers and, because the government's role in the economy is rapidly increasing, on their political representatives.

Second, as people have voiced more political demands, they have also become less patient with political inequality, particularly with their increasing powerlessness as bureaucracies and corporations continue to get bigger. Indeed, many of the demands for change that sprang up during the 1960s were fledgling attempts to fight powerlessness and to redress the political imbalance.

Third, the affluence of the post-World War II era has enabled many Americans to raise their incomes to a point where they are no longer preoccupied solely with making ends meet. As a result, new expectations have emerged, not only for a higher standard of living but also for improvements in the quality of life and for greater power to control one's destiny. And, more than ever before, people believe that the economy and the government should help them achieve their new expectations.

What people demand is not necessarily what they will get, as the lingering recession of the last few years and the continuation of the war in Vietnam have persuasively demonstrated. Still, the demands associated with the equality revolution will not recede, and if America is to have any chance of becoming a more stable society, it must also become a more egalitarian society.

Once upon a time inequality helped to make America great. The country was built out of the energy of restless entrepreneurs, the labor supplied by the unequal, and the capital generated from both. Today, however, inequality is a major source of social instability and unrest and is even a cause of the rising rates of crime, delinquency, and social pathology—alcoholism, drug addiction, and mental illness, for example. The conventional wisdom maintains that crime and pathology are caused largely by poverty, but during the 1960s poverty declined while crime and pathology increased. In these same years, however, inequality did not decrease; by some estimates, it actually grew worse.

One conventional measure of inequality is the number of people who earn less than half of a country's median family income. In the United States between 1960 and 1970, when this median rose from $5,620 to $9,870, the number earning half the median dropped only 1 per cent—from 20 to 19. One can also define inequality by measuring how far the poor are from the median income. In 1960 income at the poverty line, earned only by the richest of the poor, came to 50 per cent of the median; by 1970 it came to only 40 per cent. In other words, during the decade the poverty line rose far more slowly than the median income, and the inequality gap between the poor and the median earners actually widened by a full 20 per cent.

This gap is not just economic, however; it also produces social and emotional consequences. Inequality gives rise to feelings of inferiority, which in turn generate inadequacy and self-hate or anger. Feelings of inadequacy and self-hate, more than poverty, account for the high rates of pathology; anger results in crime, delinquency, senseless violence—and, of course, in political protest as well. But inequality also has less dramatic consequences. For example, because they cannot afford to dress their children properly, some poor mothers refuse to send them to school; shabby clothes may protect a youngster from the elements—a flour sack made into a suit or dress will do that—but shabby clothes also mark the child as unequal, and mothers want to protect their children from this label even at the cost of depriving them of schooling.

The social and emotional consequences of inequality are also felt by moderate-income people, especially the almost 40 per cent of Americans who earn above the poverty line but below the median income. For example, many young factory workers now realize, as their fathers could not afford to realize, that they hold unpleasant jobs without much chance of advancement or escape, and that much blue-collar work is inferior to white-collar jobs, which are now the norm in the American economy. In fact, the pathology and the protest normally associated with the poor is beginning to develop among factory workers as well. Hard drugs are now showing up in blue-collar neighborhoods, and strikes over working conditions . . . are increasing in number and intensity.

Indeed, if the most serious inequalities in American life are not corrected, people who feel themselves to be most unequal are likely to find new ways of getting even with America. New kinds of school, factory, and office disturbances, ghetto unrest, and dropping out of the system can be expected, and more crime in middle-class urban neighborhoods and suburbs is likely, for crime has always been a way by which at least some poor people can obtain a primitive kind of income redistribution when society pays no heed to their inequality.

Inequality does not harm only the unequal; it hurts the entire society. The past ten years have demonstrated the fragility of the American political fabric, but the social fabric is also weak. Old sources of stability have disappeared, as has much of the traditional American culture that once provided satisfactions even under inegalitarian conditions. The small towns and rural areas that gave people a sense of rootedness, which compensated them for their poverty, are being depleted by out-migration. In the cities the ethnic groups, which maintained the peasants' necessary resignation to European inequality and provided group cohesion and a close-knit family life as compensation, are now Americanized. (Although a revival of ethnic identity may be taking place currently, the old cultures are not being resuscitated, for the new ethnic identity is political and actually calls for more equality for ethnics.) Increasingly, Americans today are members of a single mainstream culture, partly urban, partly suburban, and distinguished primarily by differences in income and education. The mainstream culture pursues values long identified with the American way of life, mainly individual and familial comforts, security, and self-improvement, but it strives for ever higher levels of these, and with ever rising expectations that they will be achieved. As a result, mainstream culture rejects traditional rural, ethnic, and other values that call for modest expectations of comfort, security, and self-improvement and that thus accept the prevailing inequality.

The continued rise in expectations makes it likely that America will enter a period of greater economic and political conflict, for, when almost everyone has higher expectations, there must inevitably be conflict over how these expectations are to be met and just whose expectations are to be met first and foremost.

America has always endured conflict, of course; after all, economic competition is itself a form of conflict. But conflict can tear society apart unless it can be resolved constructively. This is possible only if the participants in the conflict have, and feel they have, a chance to get what they want or, when this is not feasible, to get about as much as everyone else—if, in other words, the conflict ends in a compromise that meets everyone's needs as fairly as possible. But if the participants in the conflict are unequal, those with power and wealth will almost always get what they want, whether from government or from the economy.

Conflicts can best be compromised fairly if the society is more egalitarian, if differences of self-interest that result from sharp inequality of income and power can be reduced. The more egalitarian a society, the greater the similarity of interests among its citizens, and the greater the likelihood that disagreements between them can be settled through fair compromise. Also, only in a more egalitarian society is it possible to develop policies that are truly in the public interest, for only in such a society do enough citizens share enough interests so that these policies can be considered to be truly public ones.

Consequently, the time has come to start thinking about a more egalitarian America and to develop a model of equality that combines the traditional emphasis on the pursuit of liberty with the newly emerging need to reduce inequality. As Daniel Patrick Moynihan put it in the famous "Moynihan Report" of 1965, Equality of Opportunity must be transformed into Equality of Results. Equality of Opportunity simply enables people with more income and better education to win out over the less fortunate, even when the competition itself is equitable. Equality of Results means that people begin the competition more equal in these resources; therefore, the outcome is likely to be more equitable. Equality of Results does not mean absolute equality, however, either of income or of any other resource. It does mean sufficient reductions in present inequalities to erase any insurmountable handicaps in the competition.

Models or methods for achieving equality have generally been *collectivist;* they call for replacing private institutions with public agencies that will take over the allocation of resources, typically through a nationalization of industry. This approach assumes that all resources belong equally to all people and that public ownership will bring about equality. When all the people own everything, however, they really do not own anything, enabling the officials who govern in the name of the people to make themselves more equal politically and to restrict others' political liberties. This seems to be an almost inevitable outcome of collectivist policies, at least in poor countries, even though these policies have also reduced overall economic inequality.

An American equality model must be *individualist;* it must achieve enough equality to allow the pursuit of liberty to continue but not restrict equal access to liberty for others. An individualistic model of equality begins with these assumptions: that people are not ready to stop competing for material or nonmaterial gain or self-improvement; that they will not, for the sake of equality, become altruists who repress their ego-needs for the public good; and that they are not ready to surrender control over their own lives to a government, however democratic, that doles out liberty and equality through collective ownership of all resources. Consequently, an individualist model would aim for greater economic equality, not by nationalizing industry but by distributing stock ownership to larger numbers of people, as Louis Kelso, among others, has suggested.

Similarly, the model would not provide the same public or private goods and services to everyone; rather, it would attempt to equalize income and then let people decide to spend that income on goods and services of their own choosing. Nor would everyone have the same income. Instead, the model would enable people to maximize their earnings through their own efforts; it would create more equality through tax and subsidy policies, as in Sweden and Great Britain, for example. Greater equalization of incomes after taxes should not significantly reduce incentive, for even now rich people continue trying to make more money although most of the additional earnings goes to the tax collectors.

The reconciling of equality and liberty is not simple, and only a great deal of public debate can determine how it ought to be done. It is not simply a matter of giving up a little liberty for a little equality. There are many kinds of equality—economic, social, political, and sexual, among others. Which kinds are most important, how much equality is needed, and which resources, powers, rights, and privileges need to be equalized and which need to be allocated on libertarian principles must be debated.

Nevertheless, some of the basic requirements of a more egalitarian society can be outlined. The American political-bureaucratic complex must be restructured so that it will attend to the demands of average citizens rather than of those best organized to apply maximal political pressure or the largest campaign contributions. The right combination of centralization and citizen control has to be found to make this complex both effective and democratic, responsive to majority rule as well as to the rights of minorities, at state and inferior levels as well as at the federal level. Some basic services, such as health, education, legal aid, and housing, should be available to everyone at a decent level of quality, so that, for example, the poor would not be confined to slums or public housing projects but could choose from the same kind of housing as everyone else. They would obtain rent subsidies to help pay for it.

The economy must also be democratized; corporations need to become more accountable to consumers and the general public, and they must be required to shoulder the social and other indirect costs of their activities. Stock ownership has to be dispersed, taxes must be made progressive, and subsidies should be used extensively for egalitarian purposes. Unemployment and underemployment have to be eliminated and the poverty line raised so that the gaps between those at the bottom, middle, and top are reduced and so that eventually no one will earn less than 75 per cent of the median income: $7500 by today's income figures. Whether a ceiling on top incomes is economically necessary remains to be seen, although it may well be socially desirable. Even now there is considerable uproar over millionaires who pay no taxes. Nevertheless, more income equality cannot be achieved solely by redistributing some of the great wealth of the superrich; redirecting the benefits of future economic growth to the now less than equal and imposing higher taxes on the corporations and the top fifth of the population would also be necessary. Still, greater income equality can be brought about without excessive soaking of the rich; S. M. Miller has estimated that if only 10 per cent of the after-tax incomes of families earning more than $15,000 were shifted to those earning less than $4,000, the income of persons earning less than $4,000 would increase by more than half.

America is today sufficiently affluent to afford more income equality without great sacrifice by anyone. The Gross National Product is currently so high that if it were divided equally among all Americans, a family of four would receive $19,000. Part of the GNP must be used for investment, of course, but if what economists call Total Personal Income were divided up, a family of four would still receive $15,600, fully half as much again as the current median family income.

A more egalitarian America is thus economically feasible, but it would not be politically achievable without considerable political struggle. The more than equal would fight any inroads on their privileges, but even the less than equal might at first be unenthusiastic, fearful that promises would not be kept and that, as has so often happened in the past, high-sounding policy proposals would continue to result in legislation benefiting the wealthy and powerful. The less than equal would soon rally to genuinely egalitarian legislation, but the affluent would still have to be persuaded that money and privilege alone cannot buy happiness in a conflict-ridden society and that the current American malaise, from which they suffer as much as others, will disappear only with greater equality. Indeed, I am convinced that what Daniel Bell has called the postindustrial society cannot be held together unless private and public resources are shared sufficiently to give every American a fair chance in the pursuit of liberty. That is why equality is likely to become an increasingly insistent item on the agenda of American politics.

Social Class and Life Chances

Programmed for Social Class: Tracking in High School*

Walter E. Schafer, Carol Olexa, and Kenneth Polk

If, as folklore would have it, America is the land of opportunity, offering anyone the chance to raise himself purely on the basis of his or her ability, then education is the key to self-betterment. The spectacular increase in those of us who attend school is often cited as proof of the great scope of opportunity that our society offers: 94 per cent of the high school age population was attending school in 1967, as compared to 7 per cent in 1890.

Similarly, our educational system is frequently called more democratic than European systems, for instance, which rigidly segregate students by ability early in their lives, often on the basis of nationally administered examinations, such as England's "11-plus." The United States, of course, has no official national policy of educational segregation. Our students, too, are tested and retested throughout their lives and put into faster or slower classes or programs on the basis of their presumed ability, but this procedure is carried out in a decentralized fashion that varies between each city or state.

However, many critics of the American practice claim that, no matter

* From *Trans-action*, vol. 7, no. 2 (October, 1970), 39–46. Copyright © October, 1970, by Trans-action, Inc., New Brunswick, New Jersey.

how it is carried out, it does not meet the needs of the brighter and duller groups, so much as it solidifies and widens the differences between them. One such critic, the eminent educator Kenneth B. Clark, speculates: "It is conceivable that the detrimental effects of segregation based upon intellect are similar to the known detrimental effects of schools segregated on the basis of class, nationality, or race."

Patricia Cayo Sexton notes that school grouping based on presumed ability often reinforces already existing social divisions:

> Children from higher social strata usually enter the "higher quality" groups and those from lower strata the "lower" ones. School decisions about a child's ability will greatly influence the kind and quality of education he receives, as well as his future life, including whether he goes to college, the job he will get, and his feelings about himself and others.

And Arthur Pearl puts it bluntly:

> . . . "special ability classes," "basic track," or "slow learner classes" are various names for another means of systematically denying the poor adequate access to education.

In this article, we will examine some evidence bearing on this vital question of whether current educational practices tend to reinforce existing social class divisions. We will also offer an alternative aimed at making our public schools more effective institutions for keeping open the opportunities for social mobility.

EDUCATION EXPLOSION

Since the turn of the century, a number of trends have converged to increase enormously the pressure on American adolescents to graduate from high school: declining opportunity in jobs, the upgrading of educational requirements for job entry, and the diminishing needs for teen-agers to contribute to family income. While some school systems, especially in the large cities, have adapted to this vast increase in enrollment by creating separate high schools for students with different interests, abilities, or occupational goals, most communities have developed comprehensive high schools serving all the youngsters within a neighborhood or community.

In about half the high schools in the United States today, the method for handling these large and varied student populations is through some form of tracking system. Under this arrangement, the entire student body is divided into two or more relatively distinct career lines, or tracks, with such titles as college preparatory, vocational, technical, industrial, business, general, basic, and remedial. While students on different tracks may take some courses together in the same classroom, they are usually separated into entirely different courses or different sections of the same course.

School men offer several different justifications for tracking systems. Common to most, however, is the notion that college-bound students are academically more able, learn more rapidly, should not be deterred in their progress by slower, noncollege-bound students, and need courses for college preparation that noncollege-bound students do not need. By the same token, it is thought that noncollege-bound students are less bright, learn more slowly, should not be expected to progress as fast or learn as much as college-bound students, and need only a general education or work-oriented training to prepare themselves for immediate entry into the world of work or a business or vocational school.

In reply, the numerous critics of tracking usually contend that, while the college-bound are often encouraged by the tracking system to improve their performance, noncollege-bound students, largely as a result of being placed in a lower-rated track, are discouraged from living up to their potential or from showing an interest in academic values. What makes the system especially pernicious, these critics say, is that noncollege-bound students more often come from low-income and minority group families. As a result, high schools, through the tracking system, inadvertently close off opportunities for large numbers of students from lower social strata, and thereby contribute to the low achievement, lack of interest, delinquency, and rebellion that school men frequently deplore in their noncollege-track students.

If these critics are correct, the American comprehensive high school, which is popularly assumed to be the very model of an open and democratic institution, may not really be open and democratic at all. In fact, rather than facilitating equality of educational opportunity, our schools may be subtly denying it and, in the process, widening and hardening existing social divisions.

TRACKS AND WHO GETS PUT ON THEM

During the summer of 1964, we collected data from official school transcripts of the recently graduated senior classes of two Midwestern three-year high schools. The larger school, located in a predominantly middle-class, academic community of about 70,000, had a graduating class that year of 753 students. The smaller school, with a graduating class of 404, was located in a predominantly working-class, industrial community of about 20,000.

Both schools placed their students into either a college prep or a general track. We determined the positions of every student in our sample by whether he took tenth-grade English in the college prep or the general section. If he was enrolled in the college-prep section, he almost always took other college-prep sections or courses, such as advanced mathematics or foreign languages, in which almost all enrollees were also college prep.

Just how students in the two schools were assigned to—or chose—tracks is somewhat of a mystery. When we interviewed people both in the high schools and in their feeder junior highs, we were told that whether a student went into one track or another depended on various factors, such as his own desires and aspirations, teacher advice, achievement test scores, grades, pressure from parents, and counselor assessment of academic promise. One is hard put to say which of these weighs most heavily, but we must note that one team of researchers, Cicourel and Kitsuse, showed in their study of *The Educational Decision-Makers* that assumptions made by counselors about the character, adjustment, and potential of incoming students are vitally important in track assignment.

Whatever the precise dynamics of this decision, the outcome was clear in the schools we studied: socio-economic and racial background had an effect on which track a student took, quite apart from either his achievement in junior high or his ability as measured by I.Q. scores. In the smaller, working-class school, 58 per cent of the incoming students were assigned to the college-prep track; in the larger, middle-class school, 71 per cent were placed in the college-prep track. And, taking the two schools together, whereas 83 per cent of students from white-collar homes were assigned to the college-prep track, this was the case with only 48 per cent of students from blue-collar homes. The relationship of race to track assignment was even stronger: 71 per cent of the whites and only 30 per cent of the blacks were assigned to the college-prep track. In the two schools studied, the evidence is plain: Children from low-income and minority-group families more often found themselves in low-ability groups and noncollege-bound tracks than in high-ability groups or college-bound tracks.

Furthermore, this decision-point early in the students' high school careers was of great significance for their futures, since it was virtually irreversible. Only 7 per cent of those who began on the college-prep track moved down to the noncollege-prep track, while only 7 per cent of those assigned to the lower, noncollege track moved up. Clearly, these small figures indicate a high degree of rigid segregation within each of the two schools. In fact, greater mobility between levels has been reported in English secondary modern schools, where streaming—the British term for tracking—is usually thought to be more rigid and fixed than tracking in this country. (It must be remembered, of course, that, in England, the more rigid break is between secondary modern and grammar schools.)

DIFFERENCES BETWEEN TRACKS

As might be expected from the schoolmen's justification for placing students in separate tracks in the first place, track position is noticeably related to academic performance. Thirty-seven per cent of the college-prep students graduated in the top quarter of their class (measured by grade-point average throughout high school), while a mere 2 per cent of the noncollege group achieved the top quarter. By contrast, half of the noncollege-prep students fell in the lowest quarter, as opposed to only 12 per cent of the college prep.

Track position is also strikingly related to whether a student's academic performance improves or deteriorates during high school. The grade-point average of all sample students in their ninth year—that is, prior to their being assigned to tracks—was compared with their grade-point averages over the next three years. While there was a slight difference in the ninth year between those who would subsequently enter the college and noncollege tracks, this difference had increased by the senior year. This widening gap in academic performance resulted from the fact that a higher percentage of students subsequently placed in the college-prep track improved their grade-point average by the senior year, while a higher percentage of noncollege prep experienced a decline in grade-point average by the time they reached the senior year.

Track position is also related strongly to dropout rate. Four per cent of the college-prep students dropped out of high school prior to graduation, as opposed to 36 per cent of the noncollege group.

Track position is also a good indication of how deeply involved a student will be in school, as measured by participation in extracurricular activities. Out of the 753 seniors in the larger school, a comparatively small number of college-prep students—21 per cent—did not participate in any activities, while 44 per cent took part in three or more such activities. By contrast, 58 per cent, or more than half, of the noncollege group took part in no extra-curricular activities at all, and only 11 per cent of this group took part in three or more activities.

Finally, track position is strikingly related to deviance, both in and out of school. Out of the entire student body of the larger school who committed one or more serious violations of school rules during the 1963–64 year, just over one-third were college-bound, while just over one-half were noncollege-bound. (The track position of the remaining one-tenth was unknown.) Among those who committed three or more such violations, 19 per cent were college-bound compared with 70 per cent who were noncollege-bound. Among all those suspended, over one-third were college-bound while just over half were noncollege-bound. In short, the noncollege-bound students were considerably more often caught and sanctioned for violations of school rules, even though they comprised less than one-third of the student body.

Furthermore, using juvenile court records, we find that, out of the 1964 graduating class in the larger school, 6 per cent of the college-prep and 16 per cent of the noncollege-bound groups were delinquent while in high school. Even though 5 per cent of those on the noncollege track had already entered high school with court records, opposed to only 1 per cent of the college-prep track, still more noncollege-bound students became delinquent during high school than did college-prep students (11 per cent compared with 5 per cent). So, the relation between track position and delinquency is further supported.

We have seen, then, that, when compared with college-prep students, noncollege-prep students show lower achievement, great deterioration of achievement, less participation in extracurricular activities, a greater tendency to drop out, more misbehavior in school, and more delinquency outside of school. Since students are assigned to different tracks largely on the basis of presumed differences in intellectual ability and inclination for further study, the crucial question is whether assignment to different tracks helped to meet the needs of groups of students who were already different, as many educators would claim, or actually contributed to, and reinforced, such differences, as critics like Sexton and Pearl contend.

The simplest way to explain the differences we have just seen is to attribute them to characteristics already inherent in the individual students, or —at a more sophisticated level—to students' cultural and educational backgrounds.

It can be argued, for example, that the difference in academic achievement between the college and noncollege groups can be explained by the fact that college-prep students are simply brighter; after all, this is one of the reasons they were taken into college-prep courses. Others would argue that noncollege-bound students do less well in school work because of family background: They more often come from blue-collar homes, where less value is placed on grades and college, where books and help in schoolwork are less readily available, and [where] verbal expression [is] limited. Still others would contend that lower-track students get lower grades because they performed less well in elementary and junior high, have fallen behind, and probably try less hard.

Fortunately, it was possible with our data to separate out the influence of track position from the other suggested factors of social-class background (measured by father's occupation), intelligence (measured by I.Q.—admittedly not a perfectly acceptable measure), and previous academic performance (measured by grade-point average for the last semester of the ninth year). Through use of a weighted percentage technique known as test factor standardization, we found that, even when the effects of I.Q., social class, and previous performance are ruled out, there is still a sizable difference in grade-point average between the two tracks. With the influence of the first three factors eliminated, we nevertheless find that 30 per cent of the college prep, as opposed to a mere 4 per cent of the noncollege group, attained the top quarter of their class; and that only 12 per cent of the college prep, as opposed to 35 per cent of the noncollege group, fell into the bottom quarter. These figures, which are similar for boys and girls, further show that track position has an independent effect on academic achievement that is greater than the effect of each of the other three factors—social class, I.Q., and past performance. In particular, assignment to the noncollege track has a strong negative influence on a student's grades.

Looking at dropout rate, and again controlling for social-class background, I.Q., and past performance, we find that track position in itself has an independent influence that is higher than the effect of any of the other three factors. In other words, even when we rule out the effect of these three factors, noncollege-bound students still dropped out in considerably greater proportion than college-bound students (19 per cent vs. 4 per cent).

WHEN FORECASTERS MAKE THE WEATHER

So our evidence points to the conclusion that the superior academic performance of the college-bound students, and the inferior performance of the noncollege students, is partly caused by the tracking system. Our data do not explain how this happens, but several studies of similar educational arrangements, as well as basic principles of social psychology, do provide a number of probable explanations. The first point has to do with the pupil's self-image.

Stigma. Assignment to the lower track in the schools we studied carried with it a strong stigma. As David Mallory was told by an American boy, "Around here you are *nothing* if you're not college prep." A noncollege-prep girl in one of the schools we studied told me that she always carried her "general"-track books upside down because of the humiliation she felt at being seen with them as she walked through the halls.

The corroding effect of such stigmatizing is well known. As Patricia Sexton has put it, "He [the low track student] is bright enough to catch on very quickly to the fact that he is not considered very bright. He comes to accept this unflattering appraisal because, after all, the school should know."

One ex-delinquent in Washington, D.C., told one of us how the stigma from this low track affected him.

It really don't have to be the tests, but, after the tests, there shouldn't be no separation in the classes. Because, as I say again, I felt good when I was with my class, but when they went and separated us—that changed us. That changed our ideas, our thinking, the way we thought about each other, and turned us to enemies toward each other —because they said I was dumb and they were smart.

When you first go to junior high school you do feel something inside—it's like ego. You have been from elementary, to junior high, you feel great inside. You say, well daggone, I'm going to deal with the *people* here now, I am in junior high school. You get this shirt that says Brown Junior High, or whatever the name is, and you are proud of that shirt. But then you go up there and the teacher says— "Well, so-and-so, you're in the basic section, you can't go with the other kids." The devil with the whole thing—you lose—something in you—like it just goes out of you.

Did you think the other guys were smarter than you?

Not at first—I used to think I was just as smart as anybody in the school—I knew I was smart. I knew some people were smarter, and I *wanted* to go to school, I wanted to get a diploma and go to college and help people and everything. I stepped into there in junior high —I felt like a fool going to school—I really felt like a fool.

Why?

Because I felt like I wasn't a part of the school. I couldn't get on special patrols, because I wasn't qualified.

What happened between the seventh and ninth grades?

I started losing faith in myself—after the teachers kept downing me. You hear "a guy's in basic section, he's dumb," and all this. Each year—"you're ignorant—you're stupid."

Considerable research shows that such erosion of self-esteem greatly increases the chances of academic failure, as well as dropping out and causing "trouble" both inside and outside of school.

Moreover, this lowered self-image is reinforced by the expectations that others have toward a person in the noncollege group.

The self-fulfilling prophecy. A related explanation rich in implications comes from David Hargreaves' *Social Relations in a Secondary School,* a study of the psychological, behavioral, and educational consequences of the student's position in the streaming system of an English secondary modern school. In "Lumley School," the students (all boys) were assigned to one of five streams on the basis of ability and achievement, with the score on the "11-plus" examination playing the major role.

Like the schools we studied, students in the different streams were publicly recognized as high or low in status and were fairly rigidly segregated, both formally in different classes and informally in friendship groups. It is quite probable, then, that Hargreaves' explanations for the greater anti-school attitudes, animosity toward teachers, academic failure, disruptive behavior, and delinquency among the low-stream boys apply to the non-college-prep students we studied as well. In fact, the negative effects of the tracking system on noncollege-bound students may be even stronger in our two high schools, since the Lumley streaming system was much more open and flexible, with students moving from one stream to another several times during their four-year careers.

STREAMED SCHOOLS

As we noted, a popular explanation for the greater failure and misbehavior among low-stream or noncollege-bound students is that they come from homes that fail to provide the same skills, ambition, or conforming attitude as higher-stream or college-bound students. Hargreaves demonstrates that there is some validity to this position: In his study, low-stream boys more often came from homes that provided less encouragement for academic achievement and higher-level occupations, and that were less oriented to the other values of the school and teachers. Similar differences may have existed among the students we studied, although their effects have been markedly reduced by our control for father's occupation, I.Q., and previous achievement.

But Hargreaves provides a convincing case for the position that, whatever the differences in skills, ambition, self-esteem, or education commitment that the students brought to school, they were magnified by what happened to them in school, largely because low-stream boys were the victims of a self-fulfilling prophecy in their relations with teachers, with respect to both academic performance and classroom behavior. Teachers of higher-stream boys expected higher performance and got it. Similarly, boys who wore the label of stream "C" or "D" were more likely to be seen by teachers as limited in ability and troublemakers and were treated accordingly.

In a streamed school, the teacher categorizes the pupils not only in terms of the inferences he makes of the child's classroom behavior but also from the child's stream level. It is for this reason that the teacher can rebuke an "A" stream boy for being like a "D" stream boy. The teacher has learned to *expect* certain kinds of behavior from members of different streams. . . . It would be hardly surprising if "good" pupils thus became "better," and the "bad" pupils become "worse." It is, in short, an example of a self-fulfilling prophecy. The negative expectations of the teacher reinforce the negative behavioral tendencies.

A recent study by Rosenthal and Jacobson in an American elementary school lends further evidence to the position that teacher expectations influence student's performance. In this study, the influence is a positive one. Teachers of children randomly assigned to experimental groups were told at the beginning of the year to expect "unusual intellectual" gains, while teachers of the control group children were told nothing. After eight months, and again after two years, the experimental group children, the "intellectual spurters," showed significantly greater gains in I.Q. and grades. Further, they were rated by the teachers as being significantly more curious, interesting, and happy and more likely to succeed in the future. Such findings are consistent with theories of interpersonal influence and with the interactional or labeling view of deviant behavior.

If, as often claimed, American teachers underestimate the learning potential of low-track students and expect more negative attitudes and greater trouble from them, it may well be that they partially cause the very failure, alienation, lack of involvement, dropping out and, rebellion they are seeking to prevent. As Hargreaves says of Lumley, "It is important to stress that, if this effect of categorization is real, it is entirely unintended by the teachers. They do not wish to make low streams more difficult than they are!" Yet, the negative self-fulfilling prophecy was probably real, if unintended and unrecognized, in our two schools as well as in Lumley.

Two further consequences of the expectation that students in the noncollege group will learn less well are differences in grading policies and in teacher effectiveness.

Grading policies. In the two schools we studied, our interviews strongly hint at the existence of grade ceilings for noncollege-prep students and grade floors for college-bound students. That is, by virtue of being located in a college preparatory section or course, college-prep students could seldom receive any grade lower than "B" or "C," while students in noncollege-bound sections or courses found it difficult to gain any grade higher than "C," even though their objective performance may have been equivalent to a college-prep "B." Several teachers explicitly called our attention to this practice, the rationale being that noncollege-prep students do not deserve the same objective grade rewards as college-prep students, since they "clearly" are less bright and perform less well. To the extent that grade ceilings do operate for noncollege-bound students, the lower grades that result from this policy, almost by definition, can hardly have a beneficial effect on motivation and commitment.

Teaching effectiveness. Finally, numerous investigations of ability grouping, as well as the English study by Hargreaves, have reported that teachers of higher ability groups are likely to teach in a more interesting and effective manner than teachers of lower ability groups. Such a difference is predictable from what we know about the effects of reciprocal interaction between teacher and class. Even when the same individual teaches both types of classes in the course of the day, as was the case for most teachers in the two schools in this study, he is likely to be "up" for college-prep classes and "down" for noncollege-prep classes—and to bring out the same reaction from his students.

A final, and crucial, factor that contributes to the poorer performance and lower interest in school of noncollege-bound students is the relation between school work and the adult career after school.

Future payoff. Noncollege-bound students often develop progressively more negative attitudes toward school, especially formal academic work, because they see grades—and, indeed, school itself—as having little future relevance or payoff. This is not the case for college-prep students. For them, grades are a means toward the identifiable and meaningful end of qualifying for college, while among the noncollege-bound grades are seen as far less important for entry into an occupation or a vocational school. This difference in the practical importance of grades is magnified by the perception among noncollege-bound students that it is pointless to put much effort into school work, since it will be unrelated to the later world of work anyway. In a study of *Rebellion in a High School* in this country, Arthur Stinchcombe describes the alienation of noncollege-bound high school students:

> The major practical conclusion of the analysis above is that rebellious behavior is largely a reaction to the school itself and to its promises, not a failure of the family or community. High school students can be motivated to conform by paying them in the realistic coin of future advantage. Except perhaps for pathological cases, any student can be motivated to conform if the school can realistically promise something valuable to him as a reward for working hard. But for a large part of the population, especially the adolescent who will enter the male working class or the female candidates for early marriage, the school has nothing to offer. . . . In order to secure conformity from students, a high school must articulate academic work with careers of students.

Being on the lower track has other negative consequences for the student that go beyond the depressing influence on his academic performance and motivation. We can use the principles just discussed to explain our findings with regard to different rates of participation in school activities and acts of misbehavior.

TRACKS CONFORMITY AND DEVIANCE

For example, the explanations having to do with self-image and the expectations of others suggest that assignment to the noncollege-bound track has a dampening effect on commitment to school in general, since it is the school that originally categorized these students as inferior. Thus, assignment to the lower track may be seen as independently contributing to resentment, frustration, and hostility in school, leading to lack of involvement in all school activities, and finally ending in active withdrawal. The self-exclusion of the noncollege group from the mainstream of college student life is probably enhanced by intentional or unintentional exclusion by other students and teachers.

Using the same type of reasons, while we cannot prove a definite causal linkage between track position and misbehavior, it seems highly likely that assignment to the noncollege-prep track often leads to resentment, declining commitment to school, and rebellion against it, expressed in lack of respect for the school's authority or acts of disobedience against it. As Albert Cohen argued over a decade ago in *Delinquent Boys,* delinquency may well be largely a rebellion against the school and its standards by teen-agers who feel they cannot get anywhere by attempting to adhere to such standards. Our analysis suggests that a key factor in such rebellion is noncollege-prep status in the school's tracking system, with the vicious cycle of low achievement and inferior self-image that go along with it.

This conclusion is further supported by Hargreaves' findings on the effect of streaming at Lumley:

> There is a real sense in which the school can be regarded as a generator of delinquency. Although the aims and efforts of the teachers are directed toward deleting such tendencies, the organization of the school and its influence on subcultural development unintentionally foster delinquent values. . . . For low stream boys . . . , school simultaneously exposes them to these values and deprives them of status in these terms. It is at this point they may begin to reject the values because they cannot succeed in them. The school provides a mechanism through the streaming system whereby their failure is effected and institutionalized, and also provides a situation in which they can congregate together in low streams.

Hargreaves' last point suggests a very important explanation for the greater degree of deviant behavior among the noncollege-bound.

The student subculture. Assignment to a lower stream at Lumley meant a boy was immediately immersed in a student subculture that stressed and rewarded antagonistic attitudes and behavior toward teachers and all they stood for. If a boy was assigned to the "A" stream, he was drawn toward the values of teachers not only by the higher expectations and more positive rewards from the teachers themselves but from other students as well. The converse was true of lower-stream boys, who accorded each other high

Walter E. Schafer, Carol Olexa, and Kenneth Polk   183

status for doing the opposite of what teachers wanted. Because of class scheduling, little opportunity developed for interaction and friendship across streams. The result was a progressive polarization and hardening of the high- and low-stream subcultures between first and fourth years and a progressively greater negative attitude across stream lines, with quite predictable consequences.

The informal pressures within the low streams tend to work directly against the assumption of the teachers that boys will regard promotion into a higher stream as a desirable goal. The boys from the low streams were very reluctant to ascend to higher streams because their stereotypes of "A" and "B" stream boys were defined in terms of values alien to their own and because promotion would involve rejection by their low stream friends. The teachers were not fully aware that this unwillingness to be promoted to a higher stream led the high informal status boys to depress their performance in examinations. This fear of promotion adds to our list of factors leading to the formation of anti-academic attitudes among low stream boys.

Observations and interviews in the two American schools we studied confirmed a similar polarization and reluctance by noncollege-prep students to pursue the academic goals rewarded by teachers and college-prep students. Teachers, however, seldom saw the antischool attitudes of noncollege-prep students as arising out of the tracking system—or anything else about the school—but out of adverse home influences, limited intelligence, or psychological problems.

Implications. These, then, are some of the ways the schools we studied contributed to the greater rates of failure, academic decline, uninvolvement in school activities, misbehavior, and delinquency among noncollege-bound students. We can only speculate, of course, about the generalization of these findings to other schools. However, there is little reason to think the two schools we studied were unusual or unrepresentative, and, despite differences in size and social-class composition, the findings are virtually identical in both. To the extent that findings are valid and general, they strongly suggest that, through their tracking system, the schools are partly causing many of the very problems they are trying to solve and are posing an important barrier to equal educational opportunity to lower-income and black students, who are disproportionately assigned to the noncollege-prep track.

The notion that schools help cause low achievement, deterioration of educational commitment and involvement, the dropout problem, misbehavior, and delinquency is foreign and repulsive to many teachers, administrators, and parents. Yet, our evidence is entirely consistent with Kai Erikson's observation that "deviant forms of conduct often seem to derive nourishment from the very agencies devised to inhibit them."

What, then, are the implications of this study? Some might argue that, despite the negative side effects we have shown, tracking systems are essential for effective teaching, especially for students with high ability, as well as for adjusting students early in their careers to the status levels they will occupy in the adult occupational system. We contend that, however reasonable this may sound, the negative effects demonstrated here offset and call into serious question any presumed gains from tracking.

Others might contend that the negative outcomes we have documented can be eliminated by raising teachers' expectations of noncollege-track students, making concerted efforts to reduce the stigma attached to noncollege classes, assigning good teachers to noncollege-track classes, rewarding them for doing an effective job at turning on their students, and developing fair and equitable grading practices in both college-prep and noncollege-prep classes.

Attractive as they may appear, efforts like these will be fruitless so long as tracking systems, and indeed schools as we now know them, remain unchanged. What is needed [is] wholly new, experimental environments of teaching-learning-living, even outside today's public schools, if necessary. Such schools of the future must address themselves to two sets of problems highlighted by our findings: ensuring equality of opportunity for students now "locked out" by tracking, and offering—to all students—a far more fulfilling and satisfying learning process.

One approach to building greater equality of opportunity, as well as fulfillment, into existing or new secondary schools is the New Careers model. This model, which provides for fundamentally different ways of linking up educational and occupational careers, is based on the recognition that present options for entering the world of work are narrowly limited: One acquires a high school diploma and goes to work, or he first goes to college and perhaps then to a graduate or professional school. (Along the way, of course, young men must cope with the draft.)

The New Careers model provides for new options. Here, the youth who does not want to attend college, or would not qualify according to usual criteria, is given the opportunity to attend high school part time while working in a lower-level position in an expanded professional career hierarchy (including such new positions as teacher aide and teacher associate in education). Such a person would then have the options of moving up through progressively more demanding educational and work stages, and moving back and forth between the work place, the high school, and then the college. As ideally conceived, this model would allow able and aspiring persons ultimately to progress to the level of the fully certified teacher, nurse, librarian, social worker, or public administrator. While the New Careers model has been developed and tried primarily in the human-service sector of the economy, we have pointed out elsewhere that it is applicable to the industrial and business sector as well.

This alternative means of linking education with work has a number of advantages: Students can try different occupations while still in school; they can earn while studying; they can spend more time outside the four walls of the school, learning what can best be learned in the work place; less stigma will accrue to those not immediately college bound, since they, too, will have a future; studying and learning will be inherently more relevant, because it will relate to a career in which they are actively involved; teachers of such students will be less likely to develop lower expectations, because these youth, too, will have an unlimited, open-ended future; and antischool subcultures will be less likely to develop, since education will not be as negative, frustrating, or stigmatizing.

Changes of this kind imply changes in the economy as well and, therefore, are highly complicated and far-reaching. Because of this, they will not occur overnight. But they are possible, through persistent, creative, and rigorously evaluated educational, economic, and social experimentation.

Whatever the future, we hope teachers, administrators, and school boards will take one important message from our findings: What they do to students makes a difference. Through the kind of teaching-learning process they create, the schools can screen out and discourage large numbers of youth, or they can develop new means for serving the interests and futures of the full range of their students.

Social Class and Life-Style

Sociology of Christmas Cards*
Sheila K. Johnson

Anyone who has ever composed a Christmas card list has pondered the inclusion and exclusion of names on the basis of a variety of fairly explicit considerations. Shall I send so-and-so a card this year, since he didn't send me one last year? Or, I *must* send so-and-so a card this year, even though he probably won't send me one, because I want to be remembered by him. Like the decisions we make about whom to vote for, we like to think of these choices as purely individual, rational matters. Nevertheless, sociologists have demonstrated that, regardless of how and why we choose a candidate, voting behavior can be analyzed as a function of one's socio-economic status, mobility aspirations, ethnicity, and religious affiliation. Similarly, it seems likely that the patterns in which people send and receive Christmas cards can also be explained in terms of certain social characteristics, especially their social status and mobility aspirations.

This proposition first occurred to me several years ago, as I was opening some Christmas cards and noticed that there was a strange disjunction between the cards we were receiving and the ones we had sent out. About half of the cards we received were from people to whom we had also sent cards, but the other half came from people to whom we had not sent cards and to

* From *Trans-action,* vol. 8, no. 3 (January, 1971), 40–45. Copyright © January, 1971, by Trans-action, Inc., New Brunswick, New Jersey.

whom we had had no intention of sending cards, and we ourselves had sent half of our cards to people from whom we had not expected to receive (and did not receive) a card in return. When I studied the names that fell into each of these three categories, it dawned on me that the people with whom we had exchanged cards reciprocally were either relatives or people with whom we were on an equal social footing—professional friends of my husband or personal friends in different but nevertheless comparable occupations. The cards we had sent but to which we had received no reply, I discovered, went invariably to individuals whom *we* wanted to cultivate—people with regard to whom we were, in sociological terms, "upwardly mobile," such as professional acquaintances who might someday prove useful or important or social acquaintances whom we wished we knew better. By the same token, the cards we received and to which we did not reply came from individuals who wanted to cultivate us—some of my husband's graduate students and office employees, the liquor store, the hairdresser, and foreign scholars who obviously expected to visit the United States at some time in the future.

In order to test out my theory, I telephoned several friends shortly after Christmas and asked them to sort the cards they had received into two piles —reciprocals and those to whom they had not sent cards—and also to count up the number of cards they had sent "upward." (Some of the incensed replies to this request would indicate that the nature of Christmas card sending is a very touchy subject indeed.) Those of my friends who continued to speak to me and who complied with my request corroborated my theory. Several couples in their late thirties or early forties who, though of different professions, were rather similar to ourselves in their mobility aspirations and in the number of people they knew who were upwardly mobile with regard to them found that their Christmas cards could be grouped into equal thirds (one-third sent and not received, one-third sent and received, and one-third received but not sent). However, a young graduate student reported that about 70 per cent of his cards were reciprocal, with 30 per cent sent upward and none received from people who were trying to curry favor with him. This is clearly the pattern for those with their foot on the bottom rung of the status ladder. At the other end, several retired people reported that 90 per cent of their cards were reciprocal, with only 5 per cent sent upward and 5 per cent received from people who still regarded them as important. A man who had retired but taken a second job, however, reported that 70 per cent of his cards were reciprocal but that 10 per cent had been sent upward and 20 per cent had come from people trying to cultivate him.

While the percentages of cards an individual sends and receives tell us a good deal about his mobility aspirations, the fact that he sends Christmas cards at all places him rather firmly in the middle class. Members of the upper class—particularly a closed upper class to which one gains admission by birth rather than through the acquisition of wealth—have no need to send cards upward, and sending cards to other members of the upper class is a formality that many are dispensing with. In England, for example, it is increasingly common for upper-class families to place an ad in the personal columns of the London *Times* stating that Lord and Lady So-and-So send warm greetings to all their friends for Christmas and the New Year, as they will not be sending cards. (Several years ago, an upper-class English wit poked fun at these ads by placing one asking *his* friends to send him Christmas cards, as he would not be able to read the *Times* columns during December.) In the United States, because the upper class is more fluid than in England, and because the country is simply too large for all one's upper-class friends to read the same daily newspaper, the custom of sending cards among upper-class individuals has not died out. One would predict, however, that most of the private card sending of the upper class is reciprocal, and that only its business Christmas cards are sent upward, since there is always room for upward mobility in the business world.

Lower-class and working-class individuals also send few or no Christmas cards, but for entirely different reasons. Sociologists have demonstrated that lower- and working-class individuals tend to rely upon tightly knit family networks and neighbors for their friendships, and that they are less geographically mobile than the middle class. Thus, a skilled union man will probably have a large number of relatives living in the same town or same general area as he does, and he will be on friendly terms with many of his neighbors. There is no need to send these people Christmas cards, however, since he sees them nearly every day. He may be upwardly mobile in terms of his job, but this is handled by the union, and a Christmas card to the front office is not likely to do the trick. Only if he is upwardly mobile to the extent of trying to leave his stratum and become a white-collar worker may he take to sending Christmas cards to people who can help him. In that case, he may adopt other middle-class behavior patterns, such as joining various clubs and lodges, in which he will make a broader range of friends to whom he will also want to send cards at Christmas.

SENDERS AND RECIPIENTS

It is the middle class—particularly the upper middle class, consisting of high managerial and professional people—who are the Christmas card senders par excellence. These are the people who are both geographically and socially mobile—growing up in one place, going to college somewhere else, and then moving about as success in one's firm or profession seems to dictate. Kinship ties tend to be far-flung and tenuous, since it would not be advantageous to be tied down to a given area by one's aging parents or embarrassed by the sudden appearance of a lower-class cousin. Friendships are formed among social equals—at school, at work, in professional or social organizations—but these, too, change as one moves up the ladder of success or to a different section of the country. Such are the ideal conditions for the exchange of Christmas cards. Friends and relatives are scattered widely, but one wants to keep "in touch," and there are vast sources of upward mobility to be tapped.

I realize that some people will object strenuously to this analysis of their Christmas card sending and receiving. While I was attempting to collect data on the subject, several of my friends declined to cooperate on the grounds that they did not fit into the pattern I had just described to them. "Really," one of them said self-righteously, "I keep an up-to-date Christmas list, and the only people I send cards to are people who send me cards. There is no upward sending or downward receiving in our family: it's strictly reciprocal." This is pure propaganda, nurtured by the myth of absolute social equality that exists in this country. Everyone can think of some acquaintances to whom he simply *has* to send cards, regardless of whether he gets one in return. The obligatory nature of the act is the real tip-off to the social pressures at work. As for people who receive cards they were not expecting —that is, cards being sent upwards to them—and who then shamefacedly rush out on Christmas Eve to mail the forgotten sender one of theirs, they are simply insecure in their status position. Imagine the president of Chase Manhattan Bank receiving a Christmas card from the janitor and saying remorsefully, "Oh, my God, and I didn't send *him* one." Yet, thousands of people do roughly the same thing when they receive a card from someone who looks up to them. What should they do instead? The answer is nothing, except sit back and enjoy it. Of course, if the upward sender shows other indications of increased social status, it might be wise to send him a Christmas card next year, but that would depend on circumstances ranging far beyond the scope of this article.

In the film "The Diary of a Mad Housewife," the husband is shown counting the family's Christmas cards and remarking to his wife, "One hundred and fifty-three. That's fine. Three more weeks to go until Christmas, and we've already reached the half-way mark. . . . We sent out 300." He then goes on to instruct his wife to note carefully who has sent cards to them, since there's "no point" in sending cards the following year to people who have not sent them one this year. Here the authors of the film have missed a bet, however, since the husband is depicted as a social climber of the first water who would clearly insist on sending Christmas cards to certain "important" people—the same people whom he invites to his abysmal party and tries to cultivate in other ways.

In addition to scrutinizing the number of Christmas cards people send and receive for signs of social status and mobility aspirations, one can also tell a good deal about the personality of the sender by the kind of card he chooses. There may still be a few rare individuals who choose every Christmas card individually to suit the *recipient,* but for the most part those days went out with the advent of boxed cards. Somewhat more common is the tendency for people with two radically different constituencies—for example, businessmen who keep their business and private acquaintances well compartmentalized—to choose different sets of cards. However, in such cases it is not at all clear whether the two sets of cards are chosen to suit the different sets of recipients or to reflect the different personality that the businessman wishes to convey to each group—sober and elegant cards for his business acquaintances and mod, swingerish cards for his personal friends. In general, one may assume that cards reflect the sender rather than the receiver, and that a Madison Avenue executive would no more receive a museum card from his Aunt Emma in Vermont than he would send her a Hallmark Santa Claus with a rhymed poem inside.

How can one classify some of the cards that people consciously or subconsciously select to convey not only their Christmas wishes but also their personality? Among university types, whom I know best, there seem to be several distinct patterns. Well-established WASP professors tend to send museum cards or rather small studio cards of abstract design. Usually, the more powerful the professor, the smaller the card. (This appears to be a snobbish, willful inversion of the usual business pattern: the more important the executive, the bigger and more lavish the card. An academic friend argues that there are exceptions to this rule and cites Professor Henry Kissinger, from whom last year he received an absolutely gigantic Christmas card portraying both sides of the globe. I would maintain, however, that this Christmas card merely illustrates Professor Kissinger's defection from the academic ranks and his adoption of the big-business ethos of the Nixon Administration.) Jewish and youngish, slightly left-of-center professors tend to send UNICEF cards, often choosing a design that reflects their area of academic interest—India specialists send the Indian-designed card, Africa specialists send the African-designed card, and so forth. A similar tendency may be observed among government officials.

From professors who have (or think they have) artistic wives, we get hand-screened, hand-blocked, or otherwise handcrafted Christmas cards. From professors who have just had their first child we get (you guessed it) baby photographs; and from professors who are doing research abroad, we often get photos of their children in native dress. From professors abroad sans children, or from those who've been there before, we get interesting Chinese, Japanese, or Thai renderings of the nativity. (The most fascinating Thai card we ever received, from a high-ranking Thai army officer, was a photograph of the gentleman himself posed proudly beside his new Jaguar XKE. *Joyeux Noël* indeed!)

People with strong political convictions tend to remind us of these at Christmas time. Thus, we get our share of CORE and CND cards. From less political but equally morally outraged friends, we get a strange assortment of messages; cards that say on them "printed by spastics" or "designed by the deaf" and cards depicting felled redwood trees or oil-stained beaches. From our wealthier, nonacademic friends, we get cards supporting the Symphony Association and the Junior League.

In addition to all of these types of cards, we get, every year, a couple of photographs of houses. These are never from the academic world—although some professors I know live in very nice houses—because the houses displayed on Christmas cards have a special status significance. Most of the houses that I have seen on Christmas cards belonged to friends who had just retired to Florida or Hawaii, or they were the dream-come-true of people who had finally bought that acre in the country. Whatever the occasion, the house depicted is usually the visible sign of a major change in social status, and it is certainly no accident that the President's Christmas card almost always features the White House.

Finally, and perhaps hardest of all to pin down sociologically, there is the category of Christmas card known as the mimeographed Christmas letter. I would like to hold a contest sometime for the most fatuous Christmas letter, but I'm afraid I'd be deluged with entries. It is hard to attribute the Christmas letter to a particular type of person or a particular station in life, because almost everyone who has ever had an eventful year, taken an exciting trip, or accomplished a great deal has felt the urge to compose one. I have received them from internationally famous professors who were attempting to describe their world travels, from graduate students describing their Ph.D. research in the field, and from relatives recounting the latest family gossip. Perhaps mimeographed Christmas letters should be used as a vanity indicator, since they expose those among us who yielded to, rather than resisted, the pervasive temptation to blow one's own horn.

A MATTER OF TONE

The chief defect of the Christmas letter is its tone—that peculiar half-personal, half-distant note that makes most of them sound as if they were addressed to mentally defective thirteen-year-olds. This tone is the inevitable result of trying to address a single letter to a score or more of different friends. As any letter writer knows, one usually manipulates the tone of a letter to convey a certain personal image to a specific correspondent. If it is often difficult to send the same *card* to business as well as personal acquaintances because of the image to be conveyed to each group, how much more difficult to compose a letter that will ring true to a variety of recipients.

Not only is the tone of Christmas letters muddled by the lack of a clearly defined recipient, but it also often lacks the unifying voice of a single sender. Most Christmas cards can convey the status and life-style of a couple or a family as readily as they can those of an individual. But this is because cards deal in visual symbols, whereas letters traffic in words. It is always hard to believe that a mimeographed letter from "Betty and Bob" is really a joint verbal product, and so one looks for telltale "I's" and "he's" or "she's" to pin down the author. In a genuine Christmas letter, however, such slips never occur, and one is left to figure out for himself who is being the more sanctimonious from sentences that announce: "While Bob worked like a demon interviewing local politicians and village chiefs, Betty spent her time learning how to cook native dishes and teaching English to some of the wives and children." (For the full effect, one must try substituting "I" for each of the proper nouns in turn.)

There are doubtless still other sociological and psychological facets to the sending and receiving of Christmas cards. However, having said all of this, I would not want readers to conclude that I am trying to denigrate Christmas cards, or that I personally am above sending them. Far from it. Having already passed through my family-photograph, foreign, and UNICEF phases, I may even succumb to sending a Christmas letter one of these years. My card this year was a small, high-status museum number depicting a medieval knight being hoisted on his own petard. The motto on his banner reads: *Honi soit qui mal y pense.* I think it suits me rather well.

Is There a Culture of Poverty?

The Culture of Poverty[*]

Oscar Lewis

Because the research design of this study was concerned with testing the concept of a culture of poverty in different national contexts, and because this concept is helpful in understanding the Ríos family, I shall briefly summarize some of its dimensions here.

Although a great deal has been written about poverty and the poor, the concept of a culture of poverty is relatively new. I first suggested it in 1959 in my book *Five Families: Mexican Case Studies in the Culture of Poverty.* The phrase is a catchy one and has become widely used and misused. Michael Harrington used it extensively in his book *The Other America* (1961), which played an important role in sparking the national antipoverty program in the United States. However, he used it in a somewhat broader and less technical sense than I had intended. I shall try to define it more precisely as a conceptual model, with special emphasis upon the distinction between poverty and the culture of poverty. The absence of intensive anthropological studies of poor families from a wide variety of national and cultural contexts, and especially from the socialist countries, is a serious handicap in formulating valid cross-cultural regularities. The model presented here is therefore provisional and subject to modification as new studies become available.

Throughout recorded history, in literature, in proverbs, and in popular sayings, we find two opposite evaluations of the nature of the poor. Some characterize the poor as blessed, virtuous, upright, serene, independent, honest, kind, and happy. Others characterize them as evil, mean, violent, sordid, and criminal. These contradictory and confusing evaluations are also reflected in the infighting that is going on in the current war against poverty. Some stress the great potential of the poor for self-help, leadership, and community organization, while others point to the sometimes irreversible, destructive effect of poverty upon individual character and therefore emphasize the need for guidance and control to remain in the hands of the middle class, which presumably has better mental health.

These opposing views reflect a political power struggle between competing groups. However, some of the confusion results from the failure to distinguish between poverty *per se* and the culture of poverty and the tendency to focus upon the individual personality rather than upon the group—that is, the family and the slum community.

As an anthropologist, I have tried to understand poverty and its associated traits as a culture or, more accurately, as a subculture[1] with its own structure and rationale, as a way of life that is passed down from generation to generation along family lines. This view directs attention to the fact that the culture of poverty in modern nations is not only a matter of economic deprivation, of disorganization, or of the absence of something. It is also something positive and provides some rewards without which the poor could hardly carry on.

Elsewhere, I have suggested that the culture of poverty transcends regional, rural-urban, and national differences and shows remarkable similarities in family structure, interpersonal relations, time orientation, value systems, and spending patterns. These cross-national similarities are examples of independent invention and convergence. They are common adaptations to common problems.

The culture of poverty can come into being in a variety of historical contexts. However, it tends to grow and flourish in societies with the following set of conditions: (1) a cash economy, wage labor, and production for profit; (2) a persistently high rate of unemployment and underemployment for unskilled labor; (3) low wages; (4) the failure to provide social, political, and economic organization, either on a voluntary basis or by government imposition, for the low-income population; (5) the existence of a bilateral kniship system rather than a unilateral one;[2] and, finally, (6) the

---

[1] While the term "subculture of poverty" is technically more accurate, I have used "culture of poverty" as a shorter form.

[2] In a unilineal kinship system, descent is reckoned either through males or through females. When traced exclusively through males, it is called patrilineal or agnatic descent; when reckoned exclusively through females, it is called matrilineal or uterine descent. In a bilateral or cognatic system, descent is traced through males and females without emphasis on either line.

In a unilineal system, the lineage consists of all the descendants of one ancestor. In a patrilineal system, the lineage is composed of all the descendants through males of one male ancestor. A matrilineage consists of all the descendants through females of one female ancestor. The lineage may thus contain a very large number of generations. If bilateral descent is reckoned, however, the number of generations that can be included in a social unit is limited, since the number of ancestors doubles every generation.

Unilineal descent groups ("lineages" or "clans") are corporate groups in the sense that the lineage or clan may act as a collectivity: It can take blood vengeance against another descent group, it can hold property, etc. However, the bilateral kin group (the "kindred") can rarely act as a collectivity, because it is not a "group" except from the point of view of a particular individual and, furthermore, has no continuity over time.

In a unilineal system, an individual is assigned to a group by virtue of his birth. In contrast, a person born into a bilateral system usually has a choice of relatives whom he chooses to recognize as "kin" and with whom he wants to associate. This generally leads to a greater diffuseness and fragmentation of ties with relatives over time.

existence of a set of values in the dominant class that stresses the accumulation of wealth and property, the possibility of upward mobility, and thrift, and explains low economic status as the result of personal inadequacy or inferiority.

The way of life that develops among some of the poor under these conditions is the culture of poverty. It can best be studied in urban or rural slums and can be described in terms of some seventy interrelated social, economic, and psychological traits. However, the number of traits and the relationships between them may vary from society to society and from family to family. For example, in a highly literate society, illiteracy may be more diagnostic of the culture of poverty than in a society where illiteracy is widespread and where even the well-to-do may be illiterate, as in some Mexican peasant villages before the revolution.

The culture of poverty is both an adaptation and a reaction of the poor to their marginal position in a class-stratified, highly individuated, capitalistic society. It represents an effort to cope with feelings of hopelessness and despair, which develop from the realization of the improbability of achieving success in terms of the values and goals of the larger society. Indeed, many of the traits of the culture of poverty can be viewed as attempts at local solutions for problems not met by existing institutions and agencies because the people are not eligible for them, cannot afford them, or are ignorant or suspicious of them. For example, unable to obtain credit from banks, they are thrown upon their own resources and organize informal credit devices without interest.

The culture of poverty, however, is not only an adaptation to a set of objective conditions of the larger society. Once it comes into existence, it tends to perpetuate itself from generation to generation because of its effect on the children. By the time slum children are age six or seven, they have usually absorbed the basic values and attitudes of their subculture and are not psychologically geared to take full advantage of changing conditions or increased opportunities that may occur in their lifetime.

Most frequently, the culture of poverty develops when a stratified social and economic system is breaking down or is being replaced by another, as in the case of the transition from feudalism to capitalism or during periods of rapid technological change. Often, it results from imperial conquest in which the native social and economic structure is smashed and the natives are maintained in a servile colonial status, sometimes for many generations. It can also occur in the process of detribalization, such as that now going on in Africa.

The most likely candidates for the culture of poverty are the people who come from the lower strata of a rapidly changing society and are already partially alienated from it. Thus, landless rural workers who migrate to the cities can be expected to develop a culture of poverty much more readily than migrants from stable peasant villages with a well-organized traditional culture. In this connection, there is a striking contrast between Latin America, where the rural population long ago made the transition from a tribal to a peasant society, and Africa, which is still close to its tribal heritage. The more corporate nature of many of the African tribal societies, in contrast to Latin American rural communities, and the persistence of village ties tend to inhibit or delay the formation of a full-blown culture of poverty in many of the African towns and cities. The special conditions of apartheid in South Africa, where the migrants are segregated into separate "locations" and do not enjoy freedom of movement, create special problems. Here, the institutionalization of repression and discrimination tend to develop a greater sense of identity and group consciousness.

The culture of poverty can be studied from various points of view: the relationship between the subculture and the larger society; the nature of the slum community; the nature of the family; and the attitudes, values, and character structure of the individual.

1. The lack of effective participation and integration of the poor in the major institutions of the larger society is one of the crucial characteristics of the culture of poverty. This is a complex matter and results from a variety of factors that may include lack of economic resources, segregation and discrimination, fear, suspicion or apathy, and the development of local solutions for problems. However, "participation" in some of the institutions of the larger society—for example, in the jails, the army, and the public relief system—does not *per se* eliminate the traits of the culture of poverty. In the case of a relief system that barely keeps people alive, both the basic poverty and the sense of hopelessness are perpetuated rather than eliminated.

Low wages, chronic unemployment, and underemployment lead to low income, lack of property ownership, absence of savings, absence of food reserves in the home, and a chronic shortage of cash. These conditions reduce the possibility of effective participation in the larger economic system. And, as a response to these conditions, we find in the culture of poverty a high incidence of pawning of personal goods, borrowing from local moneylenders at usurious rates of interest, spontaneous informal credit devices organized by neighbors, the use of secondhand clothing and furniture, and the pattern of frequent buying of small quantities of food many times a day as the need arises.

People with a culture of poverty produce very little wealth and receive very little in return. They have a low level of literacy and education, usually do not belong to labor unions, are not members of political parties, generally do not participate in the national welfare agencies, and make very little use of banks, hospitals, department stores, museums, or art galleries. They have a critical attitude toward some of the basic institutions of the dominant classes, hatred of the police, mistrust of government and those in high position, and a cynicism that extends even to the church. This gives the culture of poverty a high potential for protest and for being used in political movements aimed against the existing social order.

People with a culture of poverty are aware of middle-class values, talk about them, and even claim some of them as their own, but, on the whole, they do not live by them. Thus, it is important to distinguish between what they say and what they do. For example, many will tell you that marriage by law, by the church, or by both, is the ideal form of marriage, but few will marry. To men who have no steady jobs or other sources of income, who do not own property and have no wealth to pass on to their children, who are present-time oriented, and who want to avoid the expense and legal difficulties involved in formal marriage and divorce, free unions or consensual marriages makes a lot of sense. Women will often turn down offers of marriage, because they feel it ties them down to men who are immature, punishing, and generally unreliable. Women feel that consensual union gives them a better break; it gives them some of the freedom and flexibility that men have. By not giving the fathers of their children legal staus as husbands, the women have a stronger claim on their children if they decide to leave their men. It also gives women exclusive rights to a house or any other property they may own.

2. When we look at the culture of poverty on the local community level, we find poor housing conditions, crowding, gregariousness, but, above all, a minimum of organization beyond the level of the nuclear and extended family. Occasionally, there are informal, temporary groupings or voluntary associations with slums. The existence of neighborhood gangs that cut across slum settlements represents a considerable advance beyond the zero point of the continuum that I have in mind. Indeed, it is the low level of organization that gives the culture of poverty its marginal and anachronistic quality in our highly complex, specialized, organized society. Most primitive peoples have achieved a higher level of sociocultural organization than our modern urban slum dwellers.

In spite of the generally low level of organization, there may be a sense of community and *esprit de corps* in urban slums and in slum neighborhoods. This can vary within a single city, or from region to region or country to country. The major factors influencing this variation are the size of the slum, its location and physical characteristics, length of residence, incidence of home and landownership (versus squatter rights), rentals, ethnicity, kinship ties, and freedom or lack of freedom of movement. When slums are separated from the surrounding area by enclosing walls or other physical barriers, when rents are low and fixed and stability of residence is great (twenty or thirty years), when the population constitutes a distinct ethnic, racial, or language group [that] is bound by ties of kinship or *compadrazgo,* and when there are some internal voluntary associations, then the sense of local community approaches that of a village community. In many cases, this combination of favorable conditions does not exist. However, even where internal organization and *esprit de corps* is at a bare minimum and people move around a great deal, a sense of territoriality develops that sets off the slum neighborhoods from the rest of the city. In Mexico City and San Juan, this sense of territoriality results from the unavailability of low-income housing outside the slum areas. In South Africa, the sense of territoriality grows out of the segregation enforced by the government, which confines the rural migrants to specific locations.

3. On the family level, the major traits of the culture of poverty are the absence of childhood as a specially prolonged and protected stage in the life cycle; early initiation into sex; free unions or consensual marriages; a relatively high incidence of the abandonment of wives and children; a trend toward female- or mother-centered families and, consequently, a much greater knowledge of maternal relatives; a strong predisposition to authoritarianism; lack of privacy; verbal emphasis upon family solidarity, which is only rarely achieved because of sibling rivalry; and competition for limited goods and maternal affection.

4. On the level of the individual, the major characteristics are a strong feeling of marginality, of helplessness, of dependence, and of inferiority. I found this to be true of slum dwellers in Mexico City and San Juan among families who do not constitute a distinct ethnic or racial group and who do not suffer from racial discrimination. In the United States, of course, the culture of poverty of the Negroes has the additional disadvantage of racial discrimination; but, as I have already suggested, this additional disadvantage contains a great potential for revolutionary protest and organization that seems to be absent in the slums of Mexico City or among the poor whites of the South.

Other traits include a high incidence of maternal deprivation, of orality, of weak ego structure; confusion of sexual identification; a lack of impulse control; a strong present-time orientation, with relatively little ability to defer gratification and to plan for the future; a sense of resignation and fatalism; a widespread belief in male superiority; and a high tolerance for psychological pathology of all sorts.

People with a culture of poverty are provincial and locally oriented and have very little sense of history. They know only their own troubles, their own local conditions, their own neighborhood, their own way of life. Usually, they do not have the knowledge, the vision, or the ideology to see the similarities between their problems and those of their counterparts elsewhere in the world. They are not class-conscious, although they are very sensitive, indeed, to status distinctions.

When the poor become class-conscious or active members of trade-union organizations, or when they adopt an internationalist outlook on the world, they are no longer part of the culture of poverty, although, they may still be desperately poor. Any movement, be it religious, pacifist, or revolutionary, that organizes and gives hope to the poor, and effectively promotes solidarity and a sense of identification with larger groups, destroys the psychological and social core of the culture of poverty. In this connection, I suspect that the civil-rights movement among the Negroes in the United States has done more to improve their self-image and self-respect than have their economic advances, although, without doubt, the two are mutually reinforcing.

The distinction between poverty and the culture of poverty is basic to the model described here. There are degrees of poverty and many kinds of poor people. The culture of poverty refers to one way of life shared by poor people in given historical and social contexts. The economic traits that I have listed for the culture of poverty are necessary but not sufficient to define the phenomena I have in mind. There are a number of historical examples of very poor segments of the population that do not have a way of life that I would describe as a subculture of poverty. Here, I should like to give four examples:

1. Many of the primitive or preliterate peoples studied by anthropologists suffer from dire poverty, which is the result of poor technology and/or poor natural resources, or of both, but they do not have the traits of the subculture of poverty. Indeed, they do not constitute a subculture, because their societies are not highly stratified. In spite of their poverty, they have a relatively integrated, satisfying, and self-sufficient culture. Even the simplest food-gathering and hunting tribes have a considerable amount of organization, bands and band chiefs, tribal councils, and local self-government—traits that are not found in the culture of poverty.

2. In India, the lower castes (the Chamars, the leather workers, and the Bhangis, the sweepers) may be desperately poor, both in the villages and in the cities, but most of them are integrated into the larger society and have their own *panchayat*[3] organizations, which cut across village lines and give them a considerable amount of power.[4] In addition to the caste system, which gives individuals a sense of identity and belonging, there is still another factor, the clan system. Wherever there are unilateral kinship systems, or clans, one would not expect to find the culture of poverty, because a clan system gives people a sense of belonging to a corporate body with a history and a life of its own, thereby providing a sense of continuity, a sense of a past and of a future.

3. The Jews of Eastern Europe were very poor, but they did not have many of the traits of the culture of poverty because of their tradition of literacy, the great value placed upon learning, the organization of the community around the rabbi, the proliferation of local voluntary associations, and their religion, which taught that they were the chosen people.

4. My fourth example is speculative and relates to socialism. On the basis of my limited experience in one socialist country—Cuba—and on the basis of my reading, I am inclined to believe that the culture of poverty does not exist in the socialist countries. I first went to Cuba in 1947 as a visiting professor for the State Department. At that time; I began a study of a sugar plantation in Melena del Sur and of a slum in Havana. After the Castro Revolution, I made my second trip to

[3] A formal organization designed to provide caste leadership.
[4] It may be that in the slums of Calcutta and Bombay an incipient culture of poverty is developing. It would be highly desirable to do family studies there as a crucial test of the culture-of-poverty hypothesis.

Cuba as a correspondent for a major magazine, and I revisited the same slum and some of the same families. The physical aspect of the slum had changed very little, except for a beautiful new nursery school. It was clear that the people were still desperately poor, but I found much less of the despair, apathy, and hopelessness that are so diagnostic of urban slums in the culture of poverty. They expressed great confidence in their leaders and hope for a better life in the future. The slum itself was now highly organized, with block committees, educational committees, party committees. The people had a new sense of power and importance. They were armed and were given a doctrine that glorified the lower class as the hope of humanity. (I was told by one Cuban official that they had practically eliminated delinquency by giving arms to the delinquents!)

It is my impression that the Castro regime—unlike Marx and Engels—did not write off the so-called lumpen proletariat as an inherently reactionary and antirevolutionary force but, rather, saw its revolutionary potential and tried to utilize it. In this connection, Frantz Fanon makes a similar evaluation of the role of the lumpen proletariat, based upon his experience in the Algerian struggle for independence. . . .

It is within this mass of humanity, this people of the shanty towns, at the core of the lumpen proletariat, that the rebellion will find its urban spearhead. For the lumpen proletariat, that horde of starving men, uprooted from their tribe and from their clan, constitutes one of the most spontaneous and most radically revolutionary forces of a colonized people.

My own studies of the urban poor in the slums of San Juan do not support the generalizations of Fanon. I have found very little revolutionary spirit or radical ideology among low-income Puerto Ricans. On the contrary, most of the families I studied were quite conservative politically and about half of them were in favor of the Republican Statehood Party. It seems to me that the revolutionary.potential of people with a culture of poverty will vary considerably according to the national context and the particular historical circumstances. In a country like Algeria, which was fighting for its independence, the lumpen proletariat was drawn into the struggle and became a vital force. However, in countries like Puerto Rico, in which the movement for independence has very little mass support, and in countries, like Mexico, that achieved their independence a long time ago and are now in their postrevolutionary period, the lumpen proletariat is not a leading source of rebellion or of revolutionary spirit.

In effect, we find that, in primitive societies and in caste societies, the culture of poverty does not develop. In socialist, fascist, and in highly developed capitalist societies with a welfare state, the culture of poverty tends to decline. I suspect that the culture of poverty flourishes in, and is generic to, the early free-enterprise stage of capitalism and that it is also endemic in colonialism.

It is important to distinguish between different profiles in the subculture of poverty, depending upon the national context in which these subcultures are found. If we think of the culture of poverty primarily in terms of the factor of integration in the larger society and a sense of identification with the great tradition of that society, or with a new emerging revolutionary tradition, then we will not be surprised that some slum dwellers with a lower per capita income may have moved further away from the core characteristics of the culture of poverty than others with a higher per capita income. For example, Puerto Rico has a much higher per capita income than Mexico, yet Mexicans have a deeper sense of identity.

I have listed fatalism and a low level of aspiration as one of the key traits for the subculture of poverty. Here, too, however, the national context makes a big difference. Certainly, the level of aspiration of even the poorest sector of the population in a country like the United States, with its traditional ideology of upward mobility and democracy, is much higher than in more backward countries like Ecuador and Peru, where both the ideology and the actual possibilities of upward mobility are extremely limited, and where authoritarian values still persist in both the urban and rural milieus.

Because of the advanced technology, high level of literacy, the development of mass media, and the relatively high aspiration level of all sectors of the population, especially when compared with underdeveloped nations, I believe that, although there is still a great deal of poverty in the United States (estimates range from thirty to fifty million people), there is relatively little of what I would call the culture of poverty. My rough guess would be that only about 20 per cent of the population below the poverty line (between six and ten million people) in the United States have characteristics that would justify classifying their way of life as that of a culture of poverty. Probably the largest sector within this group would consist of very low-income Negroes, Mexicans, Puerto Ricans, American Indians, and Southern poor whites. The relatively small number of people in the United States with a culture of poverty is a positive factor, because it is much more difficult to eliminate the culture of poverty than to eliminate poverty *per se*.

Middle-class people—and this would certainly include most social scientists—tend to concentrate on the negative aspects of the culture of poverty. They tend to associate negative valences to such traits as present-time orientation and concrete versus abstract orientation. I do not intend to idealize or romanticize the culture of poverty. As someone has said, "It is easier to praise poverty than to live in it"; yet, some of the positive aspects that may flow from these traits must not be overlooked. Living in the present may develop a capacity for spontaneity and adventure, for the enjoyment of the sensual, the indulgence of impulse, which is often blunted in the middle-class, future-oriented man. Perhaps it is this reality of the moment that the existentialist writers are so desperately trying to recapture, but which the culture of poverty experiences as natural, everyday phenomena. The frequent use of violence certainly provides a ready outlet for hostility, so that people in the culture of poverty suffer less from repression than does the middle class.

In the traditional view, anthropologists have said that culture provides human beings with a design for living, with a ready-made set of solutions for human problems, so that individuals don't have to begin all over again each generation. That is, the core of culture is its positive adaptive function. I, too, have called attention to some of the adaptive mechanisms in the culture of poverty—for example, the low aspiration level helps to reduce frustration, the legitimization of short-range hedonism makes possible spontaneity and enjoyment. However, on the whole, it seems to me that it is a relatively thin culture. There is a great deal of pathos, suffering, and emptiness among those who live in the culture of poverty. It does not provide much support or long-range satisfaction, and its encouragement of mistrust tends to magnify helplessness and isolation. Indeed, the poverty of culture is one of the crucial aspects of the culture of poverty.

The concept of the culture of poverty provides a high level of generalization that, hopefully, will unify and explain a number of phenomena viewed as distinctive characteristics of racial, national, or regional groups. For example, matrifocality, a high incidence of consensual unions, and a high percentage of households headed by women, which have been thought to be distinctive of Caribbean family organization or of Negro family life in the United States, turn out to be traits of the culture of poverty and are found among diverse peoples in many parts of the world and among peoples who have had no history of slavery.

The concept of a cross-societal subculture of poverty enables us to see that many of the problems we think of as distinctively our own or distinctively Negro problems (or that of any other special racial or ethnic group), also exist in countries where there are no distinct ethnic minority groups. This suggests that the elimination of physical poverty *per se* may not be enough to eliminate the culture of poverty, which is a whole way of life.

What is the future of the culture of poverty? In considering this question, one must distinguish between those countries in which it represents a relatively small segment of the population and those in which it constitutes a very large one. Obviously, the solutions will differ in these two situations. In the United States, the major solution proposed by planners and social workers in dealing with multiple-problem families and the so-called hard core of poverty has been to attempt slowly to raise their level of living and to incorporate them into the middle class. Wherever possible, there has been some reliance upon psychiatric treatment.

In the underdeveloped countries, however, where great masses of people live in the culture of poverty, a social-work solution does not seem feasible. Because of the magnitude of the problem, psychiatrists can hardly begin to cope with it. They have all they can do to care for their own growing middle class. In these countries, the people with a culture of poverty may seek a more revolutionary solution. By creating basic structural changes in society, by redistributing wealth, by organizing the poor and giving them a sense of belonging, of power, and of leadership, revolutions frequently succeed in abolishing some of the basic characteristics of the culture of poverty even when they do not succeed in abolishing poverty itself.

5. SUGGESTIONS FOR FURTHER READING

BALTZELL, E. DIGBY. *The Protestant Establishment* (New York: Random House, 1964).*

BENDIX, R., and S. M. LIPSET (eds.). *Class, Status and Power* (New York: The Free Press, 1966).

BOTTOMORE, TOM. *Classes in Modern Society* (New York: Pantheon, 1966).*

DAHRENDORF, RALF. *Class and Class Conflict in Industrial Society* (Stanford, Calif.: Stanford University Press, 1959).*

DAVIS, ALLISON, B. GARDNER, and M. GARDNER. *Deep South* (Chicago: University of Chicago Press, 1941).*

DJILAS, MILOVAN. *The New Class* (New York: Praeger, 1965).*

DOMHOFF, G. WILLIAM. *Who Rules America?* (Englewood Cliffs, N.J.: Prentice-Hall, 1967).*

GALBRAITH, JOHN K. *The New Industrial State* (Boston: Houghton Mifflin, 1967).*

GANS, HERBERT. *More Equality* (New York: Pantheon, 1973).*

HARRINGTON, MICHAEL. *The Other America* (New York: Macmillan, 1962).*

HELLER, CELIA (ed.). *Structured Social Inequality* (New York: Macmillan, 1969).

HODGES, HAROLD. *Social Stratification* (Cambridge, Mass.: Schenkman, 1969).

HOWE, LOUISE (ed.). *The White Majority* (New York: Random House, 1971).*

HUNTER, FLOYD. *Community Power Structure* (Chapel Hill, N.C.: University of North Carolina Press, 1953).*

JENCKS, CHRISTOPHER. *Inequality: A Reassessment of the Effect of Family and Schooling in America* (New York: Basic Books, 1973).

LEWIS, OSCAR. *La Vida* (New York: Random House, 1968).*

LIPSET, S. M., and R. BENDIX. *Social Mobility in Industrial Society* (Berkeley: University of California Press, 1959).*

LYND, ROBERT, and HELEN LYND. *Middletown* (New York: Harcourt, Brace, 1929).*

MAYER, KURT, and W. BUCKLEY. *Class and Society,* 3rd ed. rev. (New York: Random House, 1969).*

MILLS, C. WRIGHT. *The Power Elite* (New York: Oxford University Press, 1957).*

———. *White Collar* (New York: Oxford University Press, 1951).*

PIVEN, FRANCES FOX, and RICHARD A. CLOWARD. *Regulating the Poor: The Functions of Public Relief* (New York: Pantheon, 1971).*

SHOSTAK, A., and W. GOMBERG (eds.). *Blue-Collar World* (Englewood Cliffs, N.J.: Prentice-Hall, 1964).

VEBLEN, THORSTEIN. *The Theory of the Leisure Class* (New York: New American Library, 1953).*

* *Available in paperback.*

6. Minorities

INTRODUCTION

Every society is composed of a variety of groups differentiated from one another by race, national origin, religion, age, sex, kinship, economic status, political affiliation, and many other factors. Intergroup differences need not result in hostility and conflict; often, differences are more or less ignored or accepted as unimportant. However, when certain members of a given social order are singled out for distinctive treatment because of their group affiliations, intergroup animosity is likely to result.

The concept of minority, as used by sociologists, does not have any quantitative connotation. For example, the black people of the Union of South Africa vastly outnumber the white population but are decidedly a minority in the sociological sense. As we define minority, then, it is a category of people who (1) are subordinate in some way to the majority, (2) can be distinguished from the majority on the basis of physical or cultural characteristics, (3) are collectively regarded and treated as different and inferior on the basis of these characteristics, and (4) are excluded from full participation in the life of the society.[1]

Sociologists who study minorities generally distinguish between the concepts of prejudice and discrimination. Prejudice is a set of negative attitudes, feelings, and beliefs toward a particular group that has emotional weight behind it, is not readily amenable to alteration by reason or experience, and represents a predisposition to act in a particular way toward that group. Discrimination, by contrast, represents overt action involving differential treatment of individuals who belong to certain

[1] John Biesanz and Mavis Biesanz, *Introduction to Sociology* (Englewood Cliffs, N.J.: Prentice-Hall, 1969), p. 256.

groups. Generally, discrimination and prejudice go hand in hand. One who discriminates against given individuals usually harbors negative attitudes toward the groups to which they belong. Similarly, those who hold prejudicial sentiments are likely to engage in discriminatory actions. However, occasionally prejudice and discrimination are not in correspondence. Note, for example, the case of the "fair weather" white liberal who expresses his belief in equal opportunity for all people but, when a court order is issued requiring busing between his predominantly white community and an adjacent black district, keeps his own children home.

Considerable research evidence has been amassed indicating the singularly important role of primary affiliations (i.e., family and friends) in the acquisition and maintenance of racial prejudice. Prejudice is learned and sustained by the supports received from close social intimates. If conditions can be created that expand the scope and heterogeneity of one's primary-group network, then perhaps a course can be set that may eventually mitigate prejudice.

The growing corpus of research on the reactionary, anti–civil-libertarian, authoritarian, and backlash views endorsed by the white lower-middle- and working-class segments of America suggests that economic competition and the status anxieties it produces may also be significant factors in maintaining prejudice. Inasmuch as the lower-middle and working classes have thus far been among the vanguard in absorbing the effects of the continuing trend toward cybernation (they have experienced the greatest reductions of their work-weeks and more extensive unemployment), status insecurity may be at the root of their recent highly vocal manifestations of anti-minority feeling. This factor is a much more difficult matter to rectify than primary affiliation; what it requires is nothing less than wholesale changes in the American social structure. The society, and the economic institutions in particular, will require revamping before these fears can be successfully allayed.

But there are other courses to pursue as well. A great many researches, conducted over many years, show that .equal-status interaction is the most effective means of reducing prejudice. The more opportunities people of different races, religions, nationalities, and cultures have to meet and associate with one another, the more they tend to like one another and the less they tend to have negative feelings toward one another. This has been demonstrated in military organizations, in business life, in educational institutions, and in housing, as well as in other areas. If we move significantly in the direction of expanding opportunities for equal-status interaction among all groups, a path will be opened for the reduction of intergroup hostility and prejudice.

Majority-minority relationships in any given society vary within a wide range of possibilities. The majority policy might prescribe cultural pluralism—that is, a willingness on the part of the dominant group to permit cultural differences. Amalgamation is another possibility, in which the best of majority and minority patterns are blended into a new synthesis, resulting in complete fusion. Still another alternative is assimilation, in which, under varying degrees of coercion, minorities absorb the dominant patterns of the majority. Still other possibilities include segregation, expulsion, and genocide.

The discriminatory behavior implicit in coerced majority-minority relationships is influenced by numerous factors, including heterogeneity in the population, rapid social change with attendant anomie, ignorance and barriers to communication, the size and relative density of the minority-group population, direct competition and realistic conflict, the exploitative advantages of discrimination, and customs and traditions that prescribe and sustain hostility.

Intergroup relations in America today are marked by a considerable amount of conflict, confusion, and dissent, which M. Yinger calls a pattern of "subcultural anomie." Ideologically, pluralism, amalgamation, and assimilation have been touted as the dominant majority policies. In practice, however, assimilation—with occasional flourishes of force—embodied in the "melting pot" theory, and segregation have been most pervasive.

Probably the most oppressed and excluded group on the national scene today is the first American, the American Indian. Of an estimated six million people who were here at the time of the conquest of the Americas, fewer than one million survive. Of all American minorities, the Indian population has the shortest life expectancy. The average family income of Indians is approximately $5,800 per year, unemployment ranges around 40 per cent, and only one out of three adult Indians ever gets as far as completing high school.[1] Health, income, and education indices show even greater misery among the Indian population living on reservations, whose lives resemble those of landless peasants in developing nations. Living on an Indian reservation, relegated to the most arid and barren land for agricultural and livestock production, the average American Indian is totally excluded from everything that goes on in America. Everything that ever belonged to him and his forefathers has been successfully expropriated.

Our country's largest minority—51 per cent of the population—is the American female. Only recently, in the resurgence of the women's liberation movement, has the minority status of women begun to be appreciated. Jo Freeman, in "The Social Construction of the Second Sex," eloquently expounds on the subordinate position of the American female. Moreover, her essay highlights the concept of the self-fulfilling prophecy and how it applies to woman's status.

A self-fulfilling prophecy is a prediction of a social outcome that, be-

[1] *New York Times*, July 17, 1973, p. 14.

cause it is believed and acted upon as true, generates its own confirmation. The values and precepts of male-dominated America enjoin female ineptitude and incompetence. Consequently, in the socialization process women learn to develop negative conceptions of their own abilities and low achievement motivation. The most important lesson women learn is that, to be successful as women, they must fail in the socially significant areas of achievement. Thus, the full creative and productive capacity of women is stunted and circumscribed within the range of the traditionally subordinate female role.

Self-fulfilling prophecies are not limited to the case of the female minority; they are part of the experiences of all minorities. From Elliot Liebow's discussion of "Men and Jobs," we note that self-fulfilling prophecies play a most significant role in the subordination of the black American. White Americans, conceiving of the black man as "lazy, shiftless, irresponsible, immoral," and white employers especially, considering black men capable of handling only low-status, dead-end jobs, create conditions to make these prejudiced beliefs self-fulfilling. Liebow develops the position that, as the black American is subordinated in the workplace, his self-image suffers, his family life is disrupted, and his friendships become precarious. These effects, once observed, become justifications for more delimitation of opportunities.

Many whites have become frightened of and outspokenly hostile to the black man in response to the reawakened black militancy and ghetto riots of the late sixties. This militancy seems surprising to some whites in light of the gains blacks have made in recent years in such areas as income and education. Yet, many of these gains are more apparent than real. Many are counterbalanced by setbacks in other important areas. In still other areas, the old inequities remain. For example, during the period of rapid economic growth in the sixties, the gap between black and white incomes decreased somewhat, but on the average, blacks still earned less than whites had earned ten years earlier.[1] In every occupational category, black workers earn less than white workers doing the same jobs. Blacks are twice as likely to be subject to unemployment. Educational attainment provides fewer economic rewards for black Americans than for whites. There has been no slackening in housing segregation since 1900. In most parts of the country racial segregation in schools may actually have increased since 1954, when the Supreme Court ruled for school desegregation "with all deliberate speed."

Often, in a period of rising expectations, inequity develops a more disturbing character and tends to be more provocative. Otherwise, one's sights are set lower, or one is so overwhelmed by the quest for survival that protest of any kind becomes a luxury one cannot afford.

[1] Reynolds Farley and Albert Hermalin, "The 1960's: Decade of Progress for Blacks," *Demography*, vol. 9, no. 3 (August, 1972), pp. 353–67.

This phenomenon is discussed at greater length by James Davies in Chapter 10, "Social Change." Rising expectations have no doubt played a part in the development of black militancy.

For many whites, the term "black power" has a menacing connotation; it suggests that blacks have the same racist and dominating aspirations that whites have shared and implemented in America for over 300 years. However, this is not how most black leaders and the black American population conceive of black power. From Charles Hamilton's explanation, we can readily see that the realization of black power will mean not only greater well-being for the black man but a better life for all people.

The interracial tension and turbulence of the late sixties have given way to a quieter mood. There has been a shift of interest; today considerably greater attention is being paid to policies and programs that might be developed to reduce the inequities arising from discrimination. Yet, there is still much disagreement and discord over the measures that will be required to produce a more egalitarian society. For example, should school busing programs be implemented or not?

In the current ameliorist mood, "affirmative action" is frequently invoked in filling many job openings, particularly in government. Enthusiasm for affirmative action programs has remained undiminished despite several recent unfavorable court rulings. The idea of compensatory benefits to provide for past discrimination evokes considerable controversy among its supporters and detractors.

Nina Totenberg's discussion of the now celebrated DeFunis case raises most of the important arguments for and against compensatory programs. Unfortunately, those who hoped that the U.S. Supreme Court would shed light on the controversy were disappointed. The court chose not to hear the case, submitting that since DeFunis had already completed his law school education the central question of the case was no longer at issue. The adequacy of compensatory programs is another area of dispute: Do they provide restitution for those who have suffered discrimination or do they portend a new exclusionary era that seriously compromises meritocratic principles? Certainly, these questions will require a good deal more study before we can evaluate the most probable short- and long-term consequences. Yet, the questions are pressing; the fate of future generations will be sealed by decisions made today.

Toward Greater Equality in Our Pluralistic Society

Discriminating to End Discrimination*

Nina Totenberg

The two men walking across the University of Washington campus in Seattle looked like any two professors just chatting away. But they weren't. They were lawyers. Suddenly, the older gray-haired man turned to his companion and said, "You know, Jim, if the regents don't let that kid into law school, I'm going to sue the university. It'll be a big case, and I'll take it all the way to the Supreme Court if I have to. And I'll win." The younger man smiled to himself, amused at his friend's saber-rattling.

Three years later, in February, the same two men, Joe Diamond and Jim Wilson, sat on the teams at opposing tables for counsel. The place was the United States Supreme Court, and the case that had been just a seedling in 1971 had blossomed into one of the potential landmark cases of the decade. At issue is the whole concept of affirmative-action programs—programs that give preference to minority groups in such areas as school admissions and employment in order to compensate for past discrimination.

The case involves Marco DeFunis, Jr., a white, Phi Beta Kappa college graduate who was denied admission to the University of Washington Law School in 1971. DeFunis's college grades and Law School Aptitude Test scores were higher than those of thirty-six minority students—blacks, Chicanos, Indians—who were accepted by the law school. DeFunis claims he was the victim of reverse racial discrimination. He asserts that racial discrimination of any kind is a violation of his constitutional right to equal protection of the law. The university claims that "benign" discrimination—discrimination to aid historically disadvantaged minorities—is within the law. It asserts that without an affirmative-action program to aid minorities, the law school would be "lily white," and that it is the duty of the law school both to provide a diversified student body and to help correct the appalling shortage of minority lawyers in the nation.

However the Supreme Court decides the issue—and even if the Court does not decide it definitively—the case of *DeFunis v. Odegaard* (the defendant recently retired as president of the university) has brought the

* From *New York Times Magazine,* April 14, 1974, pp. 9, 36–43. © 1974 by The New York Times Company. Reprinted by permission.

Court and the nation to a painful point in history. No longer are the choices easy ones. No longer is it a simple choice of a crumbling old schoolhouse for blacks and a sparkling new school for whites; no longer is it a simple matter of a person's dark skin excluding him from a vote, or a drink at the soda fountain, or a job. The heart of American ideology is equality of opportunity and success based on individual merit. From its inception, this nation fought to undo the notion of aristocracy, at least in principle. At the same time the nation was discriminating officially and viciously against blacks and other brown-skinned groups, denying them a decent education, a decent wage, decent housing and, most of all, equal opportunity.

In 1954, the Supreme Court in its historic *Brown v. Board of Education* case pushed the country firmly down the path of racial equality. Since then, the Court, at every chance, has torn down remaining barriers to equal opportunity. But now the Court, like much of the nation, finds itself caught between two of its most cherished ideals. It must decide which is more important: to continue to do everything possible to correct the effects of centuries of racial discrimination, or to remain faithful to the American ideal of a strict merit system.

The question is so painful that it has split the traditional liberal alliance of labor, Jewish and civil-rights groups. Suddenly most of the Jewish and labor organizations are joined with big business in opposing civil-rights groups, while the government itself is split from agency to agency. Indeed, the question is so painful that it has, on occasion, brought to the surface usually repressed feelings of racism and anti-Semitism.

DeFunis himself is a Jew, though he does not argue that the university discriminated against him because of that. The reason for all the emotionalism over the case is the accumulated resentment of every white man who believes that a black or a woman was given preference over him in getting a job or a promotion. Business has always disliked affirmative action because it means constant pressure to do this or that, from the government or some other outside group. But now business has been joined for the first time by hard-core labor, predominantly white and male, which fears that affirmative action would take its jobs away. Jews have deserted the old civil-rights coalition because they see the DeFunis case as a matter of quotas, and quotas are anathema to Jews because they were used for so many centuries to keep Jews out of universities.

Marco DeFunis's journey to the Supreme Court began in 1971 when he was rejected by the University of Washington Law School for the second time. A resident of Seattle, he had received his college degree from the university and done a year of graduate work there, while working part-time for the Seattle Park Department. He had been accepted at four other law schools and had just about decided to go to the University of Oregon in Eugene, where tuition would be the same as at U.W. But there was a problem: DeFunis had lined up an office job in a Seattle law firm and neither he nor his wife, a dental assistant, could make nearly as much money in Eugene. They figured that his going to law school in Oregon would cost them about $1,500 a year in lost salaries; DeFunis's father, a furniture salesman, could give them only limited financial help.

Enter Craig Sternberg, a one-time college fraternity brother of DeFunis who was already a practicing attorney in Seattle. Sternberg offered to help, and spoke to the senior law partner in his firm about DeFunis. The partner, Josef Diamond, was intrigued—partly because the situation offended his sense of rightness, and partly because he had a couple of well-to-do clients who had children not as qualified as DeFunis who were having trouble getting into law school. Diamond took over the DeFunis case. After numerous unsuccessful meetings with the law-school dean, the admissions committee chairman and the board of regents, he brought a lawsuit. Following a trial in a local court, the judge issued an order compelling the university to admit DeFunis to the 1971 freshman class. The university complied and then appealed to the Washington State Supreme Court, which reversed the ruling of the trial judge.

By this time, DeFunis was well into law school; he thought the university would probably let him stay, and wasn't enthusiastic about appealing. After all, being called the "house bigot" wasn't much fun; there were at least a couple of incidents, his lawyer says, when DeFunis walked into the library and encountered a group of black students who pointed him out as a bigot and promptly got up and left. But despite his uncomfortable position, DeFunis agreed to press his case when Diamond noted that the university was then legally free to throw him out. An appeal was brought to the Supreme Court and Justice William O. Douglas issued an order that has kept him in school until the present.

Now twenty-five years old, he is expected to graduate in May. His legal education, however, will be far more expensive than he ever anticipated. Attorney Diamond is not charging his young client a fee. Just costs. But those add up to from $10,000 to $12,000 by Diamond's estimate. Why was Marco DeFunis, this Phi Beta Kappa, *magna cum laude* college graduate, forced to go to court to get into law school? The facts are fascinating and give a rare insight into the admissions process.

In 1971 more than 1,600 students applied for the 150 student slots in the U.W. freshman law-school class. The Law School Admissions Committee, consisting of five faculty members and two students, used a preliminary system of ranking students according to their numerical records. A student's undergraduate junior-senior grade point average was combined with his Law School Aptitude Test (L.S.A.T.) score under a formula that was supposed to yield his Predicted First-Year Average (P.F.Y.A.). Applicants with P.F.Y.A.'s above 77 were almost automatically accepted. Those with P.F.Y.A.'s below 74.5 were generally rejected. The group scoring between 74.5 and 77 was put aside for later review. Two basic exceptions were made regarding P.F.Y.A.'s under 74.5: All returning veterans who had previously been enrolled in the law school could re-enroll; and all minority students' files were held for further evaluation.

Marco DeFunis's junior-senior grade point average was 3.71 out of a possible 4. He took the L.S.A.T.'s three times, getting 512, 566 and 668; the scores were averaged. His P.F.Y.A. was 76.23—in the middle-ground between 74.5 and 77.

Thus, when the preliminary accepting and rejecting was completed, De-Funis was still in the running, along with the others in the middle group, a few applicants with P.F.Y.A.'s above 77 about whom the admissions committee had doubts, and all the minority applicants. More subjective criteria then began to operate: the quality of the applicant's work in difficult, analytical seminars; his recommendations; the standards of the school he attended; his past employment; his extracurricular activities, and his racial or ethnic background.

The minority students, however, were essentially isolated into a separate class and evaluated in regard to each other, rather than as part of the group as a whole. All the minority applicants considered had P.F.Y.A.'s that indicated passing grades in law school, but only six had grades higher than DeFunis. Also given some weight among the minority applicants was their participation and progress in one of the Council on Legal Education (CLEO) summer schools. CLEO is a government-funded program, sponsored by the American Bar Association and other legal groups, which provides summer training schools and financial assistance to disadvantaged students seeking admission to law school.

By the time the admissions process was finished, 330 applicants had been offered admission to the University of Washington Law School (including 44 minority students); and 150 of them had accepted (including 18 minority students). Of the 330 offered admission, 74 had lower P.F.Y.A.'s than DeFunis (36 of these were minority students, 22 returning servicemen, and 16 applicants considered deserving of admission on the basis of other information in their files). But Marco DeFunis wasn't the only high-scoring white candidate rejected; 29 applicants with scores higher than his were also turned down.

DeFunis was not helped by a recommendation written by his college adviser which, while commending him for his goal orientation, worried that he demonstrated "the slight tendency of not caring upon whom he might step in the process. . . ." To what degree, this comment hurt him is not known. Moreover, it is possible (though not likely) that there were other factors against him that have not come out. He made the law-school's waiting list, but he was in the fourth quartile, and only students in the first two quartiles were eventually offered admission. Why the fourth quartile? Richard Roddis, dean of the law school, says, "It wasn't anything negative, but when you are down to shaving things so closely, it's just a matter of his not having pluses other people did." Other school authorities indicated such activities as work in political campaigns and community-action programs were considered pluses.

The courts that have ruled on the case agree with DeFunis that some minority students were admitted with P.F.Y.A.'s "so low that had they been white their applications would have been summarily denied." But what is pictured as a grand gulf between various P.F.Y.A.'s turns out, upon analysis, to be narrow indeed. For example, take a hypothetical applicant who received the same L.S.A.T. score as DeFunis the first time he took it, but who did not retake the test, and who had college grades identical to DeFunis's except that he took four different and more difficult courses than DeFunis, earning B's where DeFunis earned A's; such a student would have had a P.F.Y.A. of 74.46, well below the cut-off point for most whites and almost 2 points lower than DeFunis's. Thus, the differences among applicants often were minuscule, and the fact that a student was black, or Chicano, or Indian was a big plus on his side. Women, and most Asian groups, were not included in the minority preference program, because they had achieved adequate representation in the student body without any special treatment. Women, for example, represented 25 per cent of the applicants but 30 per cent of those accepted.

Special treatment, however, is what the DeFunis case is all about. It is such a crucial and emotional issue that more than two dozen friend-of-the-court briefs were filed for and against DeFunis on behalf of more than 100 organizations. Arrayed on his side are most of the big Jewish organizations, the Chamber of Commerce, the A.F.L.-C.I.O., the National Association of Manufacturers, and several groups of Polish and Italian lawyers. Leading the pro-DeFunis forces is the B'nai B'rith Anti-Defamation League, which for the past two decades has fought alongside civil-rights groups in race cases and now finds itself on the other side. The B'nai B'rith brief, written by constitutional scholars Philip Kurland and Alexander Bickel, socks its point home hard:

If the Constitution prohibits exclusion of blacks and other minorities on racial grounds, it cannot permit exclusion of whites on racial grounds. For it must be the exclusion on racial grounds which offends the Constitution, and not the particular skin color of the person excluded.

For at least a generation, the lesson of the great decisions of the [Supreme] Court and the lesson of contemporary history have been the same: Discrimination on the basis of race is illegal, immoral, unconstitutional, inherently wrong and destructive of democratic society. Now this is to be unlearned and we are told that this is not a matter of fundamental principle but only a matter of whose ox is gored.

Kurland and Bickel argue that the University of Washington Law School applicants are admitted through "separate, segregated admissions procedures," with the best students chosen out of each group, that the class that entered in 1971 "was in fact two classes . . . one of minority students and the other of majority students." The two professors go on to assert that "the only justification for use by a state of a racial classification is its use to cure or alleviate specific, illegal, racial discrimination," for example when an employer proved guilty of discriminating against blacks is forced to hire blacks preferentially. But Bickel and Kurland argue that there is no evidence of past discrimination at U.W. to be remedied.

These arguments have plenty of opponents, including most of the nation's law schools and the established bar. Arrayed against DeFunis are the American Bar Association; sixty law-school deans; the Law School Admissions Council; the Association of American Law Schools; the Association of American Medical Colleges; dozens of civil-rights groups, ranging from the old, established groups like the N.A.A.C.P. to the Chicano- and women's rights groups of the nineteen seventies, and the McGovern labor coalition (including the United Auto Workers, the United Farm Workers, the United Mine Workers and the American Federation of State, County and Municipal Employes).

Advocates of affirmative action like to compare the racial situation in America to two runners, one whom has had his legs shackled for two hundred years. Suddenly, the shackles are removed, but, of course one runner is still much faster than the other. Removing the shackles doesn't make the two instantly equal in ability to compete. The previously shackled runner has to be given some advantage in order to compete effectively until he gets his legs into condition.

The University of Washington argues that the key to past cases in which the Supreme Court has struck down racial classifications and presumed them unconstitutional is the element of inferior treatment or stigmatization of racial minorities by the majority. It asserts that no such stigmatization occurs in its system of selecting students. The university concedes that some white students may be excluded from law school because of the affirmative-action program, but it maintains that its program is "necessary" to achieve an "overriding purpose"—i.e., to increase the number of minority lawyers in the state and the nation, and to provide a diversified student body that will aid both minority and majority students in their preparations for dealing with a pluralistic society. And, the university notes, had it not been for the nation's history of racial discrimination, white students would have had far more students to compete with than they do now.

Tracing the history of the Fourteenth Amendment, attorney Marian Wright Edelman, on behalf of a coalition of labor and civil-rights groups, argues that a racial classification can only be presumed unconstitutional if it disadvantages a group subject to a history of discrimination or held down by special disabilities. She contends that the Fourteenth Amendment was meant to help powerless, oppressed minorities, and that the white majority needs no such help. "One might hope that the work of the Fourteenth Amendment [guaranteeing equal protection of the laws] could be done simply by forbidding discrimination," she says. But "in the real world, the scars of past discrimination have gone too deep . . . color blindness has come to represent the long-term goal. It is now well understood, however, that our society cannot be completely color-blind in the short term if we are to have a color-blind society in the long term."

She concludes:

No doubt it is tempting to some to believe that the job is over, that now we can relax. The nineteen sixties are behind us, to be sure. But the task we set for ourselves then will not be accomplished quickly. . . . From the Congress to the Executive and down to smaller state institutions like the University of Washington Law School, Americans have grasped the tool of affirmative action and have been using it reasonably and effectively. The potential for real progress can now be seen. The question here is whether the Court will now take the tool from the hands of those who have been using it for almost a half decade now.

Also defending the University of Washington's policies is former Watergate Special Prosecutor Archibald Cox, who in his brief for Harvard University asserts that "if scholarly excellence were the sole or even predominant criterion, Harvard . . . would lose a great deal of its vitality and intellectual excellence, and the quality of its educational experience offered to all students would suffer." Cox asserts that there is no difference between admission programs that give some preference to minorities and others that give preference to athletes, musicians, farm dwellers, veterans and children of alumni.

Former Solicitor General Erwin Griswold, in a brief for the Association of American Law Schools, notes that college grades and L.S.A.T. scores do not "pick up the factors of judgment, professionalism or ethics" (a point that is certainly pertinent in the Watergate era). On the need for minorities in law school, Griswold says: "The color of a man's skin in our society still leads to the kinds of prior experience which result in differing perceptions of fact, for we can perceive 'fact' only through the lenses of our own experience." Thus, minority participation is "essential to the creation of a law-school class which can see and walk around and understand legal problems and solutions. . . ."

The N.A.A.C.P. Legal Defense and Education Fund argues that minority lawyers are the most able to perform legal services for the minority communities they come from. DeFunis's lawyers dispute that. As Joe Diamond put it during his Supreme Court argument: "I'm not ready to subscribe to the theory that minority clients are looking for minority lawyers or doctors. I think they are looking for the best-qualified lawyers and doctors to look after their needs, and I submit that they better look for the best-qualified, and not one who matches their own skin color." But minority groups respond that a white or Anglo lawyer is far less likely than a lawyer from the ghetto or barrio to understand the background of a case in those communities, to be able to locate and interview witnesses (often in Spanish or street language) and to gather material evidence.

Indisputably, there exists in the United States today an incredible shortage of minority attorneys. Only 1 per cent of the lawyers in America is black, although nearly 12 per cent of the population are black. In specific areas of the country, the situation is worse—for example in South Carolina, where there is one black lawyer for every 75,000 black citizens.

As recently as 1965, only 1.5 per cent of the law students in the country were black. For Chicanos and Indians, the statistics were even more stark.

In California, where the Chicano population is over two million, there were only three Chicano graduates from California law schools in 1969. And as of 1969, no American Indian had ever been graduated from the universities of Arizona, New Mexico or Utah, despite large Indian populations in those states. (These figures are from the 1970 *Toledo Law Review*.)

Yet while almost everyone acknowledges the deplorable lack of minority lawyers, there is wide disagreement on the remedy. Many see the U.W. policy as raising the specter of quotas. As professors Kurland and Bickel put it in their B'nai B'rith brief:

> The racial quota that is involved in this case is of particular concern to the Jewish minority in this country because of the long history of discrimination against Jews by the use of quotas. . . . After only thirty or forty years of open admissions, the universities, which for centuries set the style in excluding or restricting Jewish students, may again be able to do so.

The University of Washington insists that it has no quota system, that it merely seeks to attract a "reasonable representation" of minority students to its student body. Quota or not, just the mention of the word sends tremors throughout the Jewish community. However, one Jew who makes it clear his sympathies are not with the big Jewish organizations on this issue is Arthur Goldberg. "It is tragic that the two most persecuted minorities should fall apart on this issue," the former Supreme Court Justice says.

Arguments in the case are all very proper and legalistic. Yet, for whatever reason, the whole affirmative-action question seems to bring out the worst in Jews and blacks, and their feelings about each other. One brief filed by DeFunis's lawyers reads:

> The predominance of whites in the university law school may well be explained by a lack of inclination or aptitude on the part of blacks for studies. Any observant person knows that certain races have certain bents or inclinations. The fact that the heavyweight-boxing field is dominated by blacks does not prove that whites are excluded by discrimination. Anyone who observes professional basketball will note an exceptionally high percentage of the professional players are black. . . . By the same logic that impels the preference of less qualified minorities to achieve racial balance in law, it might be argued that special treatment should be given to whites to achieve racial balance in athletics.

For an equally embarrassing slip on the other side, one has only to read black columnist William Raspberry in the *Washington Post*:

> The fight against affirmative-action programs designed to help blacks and other minorities into the American mainstream is being led by Jews. . . . The Jewish-led assaults . . . reached their current intensity when the equal-rights fight moved from the hiring halls and government offices to the halls of academe. For a number of reasons, some cultural and some, no doubt, stemming indirectly from anti-Semitism, Jews are on America's campuses—as students and as faculty—out of all proportion

to their numbers in general society. And it may be that attempts at making the campuses more representative of the country are seen by Jews as attacks on their special preserve.

With these feelings and facts in the background, it was clearly a special day at the United States Supreme Court when arguments were heard before a packed courtroom. The justices peppered the attorneys with questions, leaving almost no time for the prepared arguments both sides had planned to present. And at one point, some of the hostility obvious in the briefs flared into the open.

The incident arose when DeFunis's lawyer, Joe Diamond, was answering questions and chose to ignore one from Justice Thurgood Marshall, the first and only black justice ever to sit on the Court, who wanted to know what specific qualifications other than grades and test scores were considered by the admissions committee. When Diamond turned back to Marshall, he said, "Now, may I answer your question—I don't remember exactly what it was." Marshall snapped, "You have my permission to forget it."

The rest of the argument was less tense, but equally lively. Justice William H. Rehnquist said to Diamond: "You're not suggesting that a law-school admissions committee has to take the 150 brightest of the applicants, or the ones who demonstrate the highest scores on a test, are you?" Diamond replied: "No. . . . I am saying that they have got to treat everybody alike . . . not treat them as two separate classes as they did here . . . If Mr. DeFunis had been black, he would have been in. He was kept out because he was white."

Washington Attorney General Slade Gorton, arguing for the university, put his case this way:

> Statistical scores . . . are not invariable and totally accurate predicters of success; nor do they solve the problem of ending the effects of racial discrimination . . . We feel that in connection with these particular minorities, the fact of discrimination against them . . . over literally hundreds of years, has had a very real effect. It means that fewer of them actually graduate from college, by percentage, than other groups in our society. It means that those who do frequently have lower grade points, and certainly have shown up with lower law-school admissions test scores. So that if we used only these mathematical determinants of admission to law school, we would continue to exclude these same minorities.

Still, Gorton argued, "We didn't admit any of them who weren't qualified."

Justice Rehnquist observed: "When you say 'qualified,' Mr. Gorton, really by the time you've diluted that phrase as much as you have in your approach to admissions, it doesn't mean a whole lot. . . ."

Gorton was undaunted. Not only were all the minority students qualified, he asserted, but they would also "contribute more" to the class as a whole and to the bar, because of their race, than would DeFunis. Chief Justice

Warren E. Burger wanted to know if the university had conducted any studies "to determine whether grades had a direct correlation with success and effectiveness in the practice of law." Gorton replied that P.F.Y.A.'s "predict nothing about the contribution you will make to the bar," or "to the law school," or "how much income you will make in the bar," or "what kind of legal career you will seek."

Late in the argument, Justice Harry Blackmun asked Diamond a question that was particularly noteworthy because of Blackmun's well-known interest in medical matters. Blackmun wanted to know if Diamond thought it would be proper for a medical school to give preference to medical-school applicants who wanted to practice in rural areas where there are few doctors. "At that level," replied Diamond, "I think an affirmative-action program . . . is good, valid, and I'm all for it. . . ."

The argument continued, and over in the seats reserved for the solicitor general and other government lawyers, there was silence. Not surprisingly, the DeFunis case has also torn the government apart. Solicitor General Robert Bork wanted to file a government brief on behalf of DeFunis, according to administration sources, but was told by the White House that the case was too controversial and that he should keep hands off. Meanwhile, several other agencies were conducting their own little campaigns. According to some reports, the Civil Service Commission, which basically operates on a merit system, wanted a brief filed on behalf of DeFunis, while the Equal Employment Opportunity Commission (E.E.O.C.) wanted one filed in behalf of the University of Washington. The E.E.O.C. actually filed a brief with the Supreme Court, but Solicitor General Bork, in an extraordinary move, wrote the Court a letter asking that the brief not be accepted. His advice was accepted, and the brief was not.

Over at the Department of Health, Education and Welfare, there also was considerable sentiment for filing a brief in behalf of the university. In fact, Washington Attorney General Gorton and his assistant, Jim Wilson, were furious that the government did not side with them.

Ironically, while the government was not supporting U.W. in its attempt to preserve affirmative-action in admissions, H.E.W. was leaning hard on the university for alleged noncompliance with affirmative action in campus hiring. The university, like 2,500 other institutions of higher learning in the United States, holds government grants and contracts and thus is required by federal law to institute "goals and timetables" for hiring more women and minorities on its faculty. School authorities resent government pressure and are battling H.E.W. over the issue.

Whatever its problems with its faculty-hiring program, the University of Washington is convinced that its admissions program is working well. Out of the eighteen minority students who began law school in 1971, fourteen are still there. On the basis of their grades and test scores, all but one of the fourteen was expected to be in the bottom quarter of the class. But at the end of their second year of law school, six were in the bottom quarter, five were in the third quarter and three in the second quarter. Of those top three, two had among the highest predicted averages of the minority group, and one had among the lowest.

Thus the university believes that many of its judgments in the selection process have been borne out. Marco DeFunis, by the way, is about in the middle of his class, according to university officials. He plans to go into general law practice when he graduates. Asked if he is sorry he brought the case, DeFunis replied, "That's my secret." (Indeed, DeFunis has kept most of his feelings secret, refusing in recent months to be interviewed or photographed by the press.)

Whatever his feelings, the Supreme Court must now make a decision in the case that bears his name—a decision that the Court can live with, that the country can live with and that will not offend the nation's sense of justice. Any ruling that would narrowly restrict affirmative-action programs would put an end to the civil-rights revolution that began twenty years ago when the High Court for the first time declared school segregation illegal. A ruling permitting "benign" discrimination could eventually come back to haunt the court, for a survey of the race cases of the past twenty years would show that many, if not most, acts of discrimination were alleged to be done benignly.

Many Court observers believe the justices might wait, declaring the DeFunis case moot, since the controversy will be resolved by the plaintiff's all-but-certain graduation. To moot the case, or in some other way duck the great issues posed by it, would give the nation more time to experiment at the state and local level. Nonetheless, a decision not to decide the great issues now, would, in its own way, be an affirmative-action by the Supreme Court to let affirmative-action programs continue unhampered—at least for the time being.

The Status of Women in America

The Social Construction of the Second Sex[*]

Jo Freeman

The passivity that is the essential characteristic of the "feminine" woman is a trait that develops in her from the earliest years. But it is wrong to assert a bio-

[*] From *Roles Women Play: Readings Toward Women's Liberation,* edited by Michele Garskof. Belmont, Calif.: Brooks/Cole, 1971. Copyright Jo Freeman. Used by permission of the author.

logical datum is concerned; it is, in fact, a destiny imposed upon her by her teachers and by society.

—*Simone de Beauvoir*

During the last thirty years, social science has paid scant attention to women, confining its explorations of humanity to the male. Research has generally reinforced the popular mythology that women are essentially nurturant, expressive, passive and men instrumental, active, aggressive. Social scientists have tended to justify these stereotypes rather than analyze their origins, their value, or their effect.

The result of this trend has been a social science that is more a mechanism of social control than of social inquiry. Rather than trying to analyze why, it has only described what. Rather than exploring how men and women came to be the way they are, it has taken their condition as irrevocably given and sought to explain this on the basis of "biological" differences.

Nonetheless, the assumption that psychology recapitulates physiology has begun to crack. William Masters and Virginia Johnson shattered the myth of woman's natural sexual passivity—on which her psychological passivity was claimed to rest. Research is just beginning in other areas, and, while evidence is being accumulated, new interpretations of the old data are being explored. What these new interpretations say is that women are the way they are because they've been trained to be that way—their motivations as well as their alternatives have been channeled by society.

This motivation is controlled through the socialization process. Women are raised to want to fill the social roles in which society needs them. They are trained to model themselves after the accepted image and to meet as individuals the expectations that are held for women as a group. Therefore, to understand how most women are socialized, we must first understand how they see themselves and are seen by others. Several studies have been done on this.

One thorough study asked men and women to choose, out of a long list of adjectives, those that most closely applied to themselves. The results showed that women strongly felt that they could accurately be described as uncertain, anxious, nervous, hasty, careless, fearful, dull, childish, helpless, sorry, timid, clumsy, stupid, silly, and domestic. On the more positive side, women felt they were understanding, tender, sympathetic, pure, generous, affectionate, loving, moral, kind, grateful, and patient. This is not a very favorable self-image, but it does correspond fairly well to the myths about what women are like. The image has some "nice" qualities, but they are not the ones normally required for the kinds of achievement to which society gives its highest rewards.

GROSS DISTORTIONS

Now, one can justifiably question both the idea of achievement and the qualities necessary for it, but this is not the place to do so. The fact remains that these standards are widely accepted, and that women have been told they do not meet them. My purpose here, then, is to look at the socialization process as a mechanism to keep them from doing so. All people are socialized to meet the social expectations held for them, and only when this process fails to work (as is currently happening on several fronts) is it at all questioned.

When we look at the *results* of female socialization, we find a strong similarity between what our society labels, even extols, as the typical "feminine" character structure and that of oppressed peoples in this country and elsewhere. In his classic study on *The Nature of Prejudice,* Gordon Allport devotes a chapter to "Traits Due to Victimization." Included are such personality characteristics as sensitivity, submission, fantasies of power, desire for protection, indirectness, ingratiation, petty revenge and sabotage, sympathy, extremes of both self and group hatred and self and group glorification, display of flashy status symbols, compassion for the underprivileged, identification with the dominant group's norms, and passivity. Allport was primarily concerned with Jews and Negroes, but his characterization is disturbingly congruent with the general profile of girls that Lewis Terman and Leona Tyler draw after a very thorough review of the literature on sex differences among young children. For girls, they listed such traits as sensitivity, conformity to social pressures, response to environment, ease of social control, ingratiation, sympathy, low levels of aspiration, compassion for the underprivileged, and anxiety. They found that girls, compared to boys, were more nervous, unstable, neurotic, socially dependent, [and] submissive; had less self-confidence, lower opinions of themselves and of girls in general; and were more timid, emotional, ministrative, fearful, and passive.

Girls' perceptions of themselves were also distorted. Although girls make consistently better school grades than boys until late high school, their opinion of themselves grows progressively worse with age, and their opinion of boys and boys' abilities grows better. Boys, however, have an increasingly better opinion of themselves and worse opinion of girls as they grow older.

These distortions become so gross that, according to Phillip Goldberg in an article in this magazine, by the time girls reach college they have become prejudiced against women. He gave college girls sets of booklets containing six identical professional articles in traditional male, female, and neutral fields. The articles were identical, but the names of the authors were not. For example, an article in one set would bear the name John T. McKay, and in another set the same article would be by-lined Joan T. McKay. Each booklet contained three articles by "women" and three by "men." Questions at the end of each article asked the students to rate the articles on value, persuasiveness and profundity and the authors for style and competence. The male authors fared better on every dimension, even such "feminine" areas as art history and dietetics. Goldberg concluded that "women are prejudiced against female professionals and, regardless of the actual accomplishments of these professionals, will firmly refuse to recognize them as the equals of their male colleagues."

This combination of group self-hate and a distortion of perceptions to justify that group self-hate is precisely typical of a minority-group character structure. It has been noted time and time again. Kenneth and Mamie Clark's finding of the same pattern in Negro children in segregated schools contributed to the 1954 Supreme Court decision that outlawed such schools. These traits, as well as the others typical of the "feminine" stereotype, have been found in the Indians under British rule, in the Algerians under the French, and in black Americans. It would seem, then, that being "feminine" is related to low social status.

This pattern repeats itself even within cultures. In giving Thematic Apperception Tests to women in Japanese villages, George De Vos discovered that those from fishing villages, where the status position of women was higher than in farming communities, were more assertive, not as guilt-ridden, and were more willing to ignore the traditional pattern of arranged marriages in favor of love marriages.

In Terman's famous fifty-year study of the gifted—a comparison of those men who conspicuously failed to fulfill their early promise with those who did—showed that the successful had more self-confidence, fewer background disabilities, and were less nervous and emotionally unstable. But, he concluded, "the disadvantages associated with lower social home status appeared to present the outstanding handicap."

SEXUAL CHARACTERISTICS

The fact that women do have lower social status than men in our society, and that both sexes tend to value men and male characteristics, values, and activities more highly than those of women, has been noted by many authorities. What has not been done is to make the connection between this status and its accompanying personality. The failure to analyze the effects and the causes of lower social status among women is surprising in light of the many efforts that have been made to uncover distinct psychological differences between men and women to account for the tremendous disparity in their social production and creativity. The Goldberg study implies that, even if women did achieve on a par with men, it would not be perceived or accepted as such, and that a woman's work must be of a much higher quality than that of a man to be given the same recognition. But these circumstances alone, or the fact that it is the male definition of achievement that is applied, are not sufficient to account for the relative failure of women to achieve. So, research has turned to male-female differences.

Most of this research, in the Freudian tradition, has focused on finding the psychological and developmental differences supposedly inherent in feminine nature and function. Despite all these efforts, the general findings of psychological testing indicate only that individual differences are greater than sex differences. In other words, sex is just one of the many character-istics that define a human being.

An examination of the work done on intellectual differences between the sexes discloses some interesting patterns, however. First of all, the statistics themselves show some regularity. Most conclusions of what is typical of one sex or the other are founded upon the performances of two-thirds of the subjects. For example, two-thirds of all boys do better on the math section of the College Board Exam than they do on the verbal section, and two-thirds of the girls do better on the verbal than the math. Robert Bales' studies show a similar distribution when he concludes that, in small groups, men are the task-oriented leaders and women are the social-emotional leaders. Not all tests show this two-thirds differential, but it is the mean about which most results of the ability tests cluster. Sex is an easily visible, differentiable, and testable criterion on which to draw con-clusions; but it doesn't explain the one-third that do not fit. The only char-acteristic virtually all women seem to have in common, besides their anat-omy, is their lower social status.

Secondly, girls get off to a very good start. They begin speaking, read-ing, and counting sooner. They articulate more clearly and put words into sentences earlier. They have fewer reading and stuttering problems. Girls are even better in math in the early school years. Consistent sex differences in favor of boys do not appear until high school age. Here, another pattern begins to develop.

During high school, girls' performance in school and on ability tests begins to drop, sometimes drastically. Although well over half of all high school graduates are girls, significantly [fewer] than half of all college stu-dents are girls. Presumably, this should mean that a higher percentage of the better female students go on to higher education, but their performance vis-à-vis boys' continues to decline.

ONLY MEN EXCEL

Girls start off better than boys and end up worse. This change in their performance occurs at a very significant point in time. It happens when their status changes, or, to be more precise, when girls become aware of what their adult status is supposed to be. It is during adolescence that peer group pressures to be "feminine" or "masculine" increase, and the concep-tions of what is "feminine" and "masculine" become more narrow. It is also at this time that there is a personal drive for conformity. And one of the norms of our culture to which a girl learns to conform is that only men excel. This was evident in Beatrice Lipinski's study on *Sex-Role Conflict and Achievement Motivation in College Women,* which showed that the-matic pictures depicting males as central characters elicited significantly more achievement imagery than those with females in them. One need only recall Asch's experiments to see how peer group pressures, armed only with our rigid ideas about "feminity" and "masculinity," could lead to a decline in girls' performance. Asch found that some 33 per cent of his subjects would go contrary to the evidence of their own senses about something as tangible as the comparative length of two lines when their judgments were at variance with those made by the other group members. All but a handful of the other 67 per cent experienced tremendous trauma in trying to stick to their correct perceptions.

When we move to something as intangible as sex role behavior, and to social sanctions far greater than the displeasure of a group of unknown experimental stooges, we can get an idea of how stifling social expectations can be. A corollary of the notion that only men can excel is the cultural norm that a girl should not appear too smart or surpass boys in anything. Again, the pressures to conform, so prevalent in adolescence, prompt girls to believe that the development of their minds will have only negative results. These pressures even affect the supposedly unchangeable I.Q. scores. Corresponding with the drive for social acceptance, girls' I.Q.'s drop below those of boys during high school, rise slightly if they go to college, and go into a steady and consistent decline when and if they become full-time housewives.

These are not the only consequences. Negative self-conceptions have negative effects. They stifle motivation and channel energies into areas more likely to get some positive social rewards. The clincher comes when the very people (women) who have been subjected to these pressures are condemned for not having striven for the highest rewards society has to offer.

A good example of this double bind is what psychologists call the "need for achievement." Achievement motivation in male college sophomores has been studied extensively. In women, it has barely been looked at. The reason for this is that women didn't fit the model social scientists set up to explain achievement in men. Nonetheless, some theories have been put forward that suggest that the real situation is not that women do not have achievement motivation but that this motivation is directed differently [from] that of men. In fact, the achievement orientation of both sexes goes precisely where it is socially directed—educational achievement for boys and marriage achievement for girls.

After considerable research on the question, James Pierce concluded that "girls see that to achieve in life as adult females they need to achieve in non-academic ways, that is, attaining the social graces, achieving beauty in person and dress, finding a desirable social status, marrying the right man. This is the successful adult woman. . . . Their achievement motivations are directed toward realizing personal goals through their relationship with men. . . . Girls who are following the normal course of development are most likely to seek adult status through marriage at an early age."

Achievement for women is adult status through marriage, not success in the usual use of the word. One might postulate that both kinds of success might be possible, particularly for the highly achievement-oriented woman.

But, in fact, the two are more often perceived as contradictory; success in one is seen to preclude success in the other.

Matina Horner recently completed a study at the University of Michigan from which she postulated a psychological barrier to achievement in women. She administered a test in which she asked undergraduates to complete the sentence "After first-term finals, Anne finds herself at the top of her medical school class" with a story of their own. A similar one for a male control group used a masculine name. The results were scored for imagery of fear of success, and Horner found that 65 per cent of the women and only 10 per cent of the men demonstrated a definite "motive to avoid success." She explained the results by hypothesizing that the prospect of success, or situations in which success or failure is a relevant dimension, are perceived as [having], and in fact do have, negative consequences for women.

While many of the choices and attitudes of women are determined by peer and cultural pressures, many other sex differences appear too early to be much affected by peer groups, and are not directly related to sex role attributes.

ANALYTIC CHILDREN

One such sex difference is spatial perception, or the ability to visualize objects out of their context. This is a test in which boys do better, although differences are usually not discernible before the early school years. Other tests, such as the Embedded Figures and the Rod and Frame Tests, likewise favor boys. They indicate that boys perceive more analytically, while girls are more contextual. Again, however, this ability to "break set" or be "field independent" also does not seem to appear until after the fourth or fifth year.

According to Eleanor Maccoby, this contextual mode of perception common to women is a distinct disadvantage for scientific production: "Girls on the average develop a somewhat different way of handling incoming information—their thinking is less analytic, more global, and more perservative [sic]—and this kind of thinking may serve very well for many kinds of functioning but it is not the kind of thinking most conducive to high-level intellectual productivity, especially in science."

Several social psychologists have postulated that the key developmental characteristic of analytic thinking is what is called early "independence and mastery training," or, as one group of researchers put it, "whether and how soon a child is encouraged to assume initiative, to take responsibility for himself, and to solve problems by himself, rather than rely on others for the direction of his activities." In other words, analytically inclined children are those who have not been subject to what Urie Bronfenbrenner calls "oversocialization," and there is a good deal of indirect evidence that such is the case. D. M. Levy has observed that "overprotected" boys tend to develop intellectually like girls. Bing found that those girls who were good at spatial tasks were those whose mothers left them alone to solve the problems by themselves, while the mothers of verbally inclined daughters insisted on helping them. H. A. Witkin similarly found that mothers of analytic children had encouraged their initiative, while mothers of nonanalytic children had encouraged dependence and discouraged self-assertion. One writer commented on these studies that "this is to be expected, for the independent child is less likely to accept superficial appearances of objects without exploring them for himself, while the dependent child will be afraid to reach out on his own, and will accept appearances without question. In other words, the independent child is likely to be more active, not only psychologically but physically, and the physically active child will naturally have more kinesthetic experience with spatial relationships in his environment."

The qualities associated with independence training also have an effect on I.Q. I. W. Sontag did a longitudinal study in which he compared children whose I.Q.'s had improved with those whose I.Q.'s had declined with age. He discovered that the child with increasing I.Q. was competitive, self-assertive, independent, and dominant in interaction with other children. Children with declining I.Q.'s were passive, shy, and dependent.

Maccoby commented on this study that "the characteristics associated with a rising I.Q. are not very feminine characteristics." When one of the people working on the Sontag study was asked about what kind of developmental history was necessary to make a girl into an intellectual person, he replied, "The simplest way to put it is that she must be a tomboy at some point in her childhood."

However, analytic abilities are not the only ones that are valued in our society. Being person-oriented and contextual in perception are very valuable attributes for many fields where, nevertheless, very few women are found. Such characteristics are also valuable in the arts and some of the social sciences. But, while women do succeed here more than in the sciences, their achievement is still not equivalent to that of men. One explanation of this, of course, is the study by Horner that established a "motive to avoid success" among women. But, when one looks further, it appears that there is an earlier cause here as well.

SONS AND DAUGHTERS

The very same early independence and mastery training that has such a beneficial effect on analytic thinking also determines the extent of one's achievement orientation. Although comparative studies of parental treatment of boys and girls are not extensive, those that have been made indicate that the traditional practices applied to girls are very different from those applied to boys. Girls receive more affection, more protectiveness, more control, and more restrictions. Boys are subjected to more achievement demands and higher expectations. In short, while girls are not always encouraged to be dependent *per se,* they are usually not encouraged to be independent and physically active. As Bronfenbrenner put it, "Such findings indicate that the differential treatment of the two sexes reflects in part a difference in goals. With sons, socialization seems to focus primarily on directing and constraining the boys' impact on the environment. With daughters, the aim is rather to protect the girl from the impact of environment. The boy is being prepared to mold his world, the girl to be molded by. it."

Bronfenbrenner concludes that the crucial variable is the differential treatment by the father, and, "in fact, it is the father who is especially likely to treat children of the two sexes differently." His extremes of affection and of authority are both deleterious. Not only do his high degrees of nurturance and protectiveness toward girls result in oversocialization," but "the presence of strong paternal . . . power is particularly debilitating. In short, boys thrive in a patriarchal context, girls in a matriarchal one."

Bronfenbrenner's observations receive indirect support from Elizabeth Douvan, who noted that "part-time jobs of mothers have a beneficial effect on adolescent children, particularly daughters. This reflects the fact that adolescents may receive too much mothering."

ANXIETY

The importance of mothers, as well as mothering, was pointed out by Kagan and Moss. In looking at the kinds of role models that mothers provide for developing daughters, they discovered that it is those women who are looked upon as unfeminine whose daughters tend to achieve intellectually. These mothers are "aggressive and competitive women who were critical of their daughters and presented themselves to their daughters as intellectually competitive and aggressive role models. It is reasonable to assume that the girls identified with these intellectually aggressive women who valued mastery behavior."

To sum up, there seems to be some evidence that the sexes have been differentially socialized with different training practices, for different goals, and with different results. If David McClelland is right in all the relationships he finds between child-rearing practices, in particular independence and mastery training, achievement motivations scores of individuals tested, actual achievement of individuals, and, indeed, the economic growth of whole societies, there is no longer much question as to why the historical achievement of women has been so low. In fact, with the dependency training they receive so early in life, the wonder is that they have achieved so much.

But this is not the whole story. Maccoby, in her discussion of the relationship of independence training to analytic abilities, notes that the girl who does not succumb to overprotection and develop the appropriate personality and behavior for her sex has a major price to pay—a price in anxiety. Some anxiety is beneficial to creative thinking, but high or sustained levels of it are damaging. Anxiety is particularly manifest in college women, and, of course, they are the ones who experience the most conflict between their current—intellectual—activities and expectations about their future—unintellectual—careers.

Maccoby feels that "it is this anxiety which helps to account for the lack of productivity among those women who do make intellectual careers." The combination of social pressures, role expectations, and parental training together tells "something of a horror story. It would appear that even when a woman is suitably endowed intellectually and develops the right temperament and habits of thought to make use of her endowment, she must be fleet of foot indeed to scale the hurdles society has erected for her and to remain a whole and happy person while continuing to follow her intellectual bent."

The reasons for this horror story must by now be clearly evident. Traditionally, women have been defined as passive creatures, sexually, physically, and mentally. Their roles have been limited to the passive, dependent, auxiliary ones, and they have been trained from birth to fit these roles. However, those qualities by which one succeeds in this society are active ones. Achievement orientation, intellectuality, analytic ability, all require a certain amount of aggression.

As long as women were convinced that these qualities were beyond them, that they would be much happier if they stayed in their place, they remained quiescent under the paternalistic system of Western civilization. But paternalism was a preindustrial scheme of life, and its yoke was partially broken by the industrial revolution. With this loosening up of the social order, the talents of women began to appear.

In the eighteenth century, it was held that no woman had ever produced anything worthwhile in literature, with the possible exception of Sappho. But, in the first half of the nineteenth century, feminine writers of genius flooded the literary scene. It wasn't until the end of the nineteenth century that women scientists of note appeared, and still later that women philosophers were found.

LORDS AT HOME

In preindustrial societies, the family was the basic unit of social and economic organization, and women held a significant and functional role within it. This, coupled with the high birth and death rates of those times, gave women more than enough to do within the home. It was the center of production, and women could be both at home and in the world at the same time. But the industrial revolution, along with decreased infant mortality, increased life span, and changes in economic organization, has all but destroyed the family as the economic unit. Technological advances have taken men out of the home, and now those functions traditionally defined as female are being taken out also. For the first time in human history, women have had to devote themselves to being full-time mothers in order to have enough to do.

Conceptions of society have also changed. At one time, authoritarian hierarchies were the norm, and paternalism was reflective of a general social authoritarian attitude. While it is impossible to do retroactive studies on feudalistic society, we do know that authoritarianism as a personality trait does correlate strongly with a rigid conception of sex roles and with ethnocentrism. We also know from ethnological data that, as W. N. Stephens wrote, there is a "parallel between family relationships and the larger social hierarchy. Autocratic societies have autocratic families. As the king rules his subjects and the nobles subjugate and exploit the commoners, so does husband tend to lord it over wife, father rule over son."

According to Roy D'Andrade, "another variable that appears to affect the distribution of authority and deference between the sexes is the degree to which men rather than women control and mediate property." He presented evidence that showed a direct correlation between the extent to which inheritance, succession, and descent-group membership were patrilineal and the degree of subjection of women.

Even today, the equality of the sexes in the family is often reflective of the economic quality of the partners. In a Detroit sample, Robert Blood and D. M. Wolfe found that the relative power of the wife was low if she did not work and increased with her economic contribution to the family. "The employment of women affects the power structure of the family by equalizing the resources of husband and wife. A working wife's husband listens to her more, and she listens to herself more. She expresses herself and has more opinions. Instead of looking up into her husband's eyes and worshipping him, she levels with him, compromising on the issues at hand. Thus her power increases and, relatively speaking, the husband's falls."

William J. Goode also noted this pattern but said it varied inversely with class status. Toward the upper strata, wives are not only less likely to work, but, when they do, they contribute a smaller percentage of the total family income than is true in the lower classes. Reuben Hill went so far as to say, "Money is a source of power that supports male dominance in the family. . . . Money belongs to him who earns it, not to her who spends it, since he who earns it may withhold it." Phyllis Hallenbeck feels more than just economic resources are involved but does conclude that there is a balance of power in every family that affects "every other aspect of the marriage division of labor, amount of adaptation necessary for either spouse, methods used to resolve conflicts, and so forth." Blood feels the economic situation affects the whole family structure. "Daughters of working mothers are more independent, more self-reliant, more aggressive, more dominant, and more disobedient. Such girls are no longer meek, mild, submissive, and feminine [as] 'little ladies' ought to be. They are rough and tough, actively express their ideas, and refuse to take anything from anybody else. . . . Because their mothers have set an example, the daughters get up the courage and the desire to earn money as well. They take more part-time jobs after school and more jobs during summer vacation."

SEX AND WORK

Herbert Barry, M. K. Bacon, and Irvin Child did an ethnohistoriographic analysis that provides some further insights into the origins of male dominance. After examining the ethnographic reports of 110 cultures, they concluded that large sexual differentiation and male superiority occur concurrently and in "an economy that places a high premium on the superior strength and superior development of motor skills requiring strength, which characterize the male." It is those societies in which great physical strength and mobility are required for survival, in which hunting and herding, or warfare, play an important role, that the male, as the physically stronger and more mobile sex, tends to dominate.

Although there are a few tasks that virtually every society assigns only to men or women, there is a great deal of overlap for most jobs. Virtually every task, even in the most primitive societies, can be performed by either men or women. Equally important, what is defined as a man's task in one society may well be classified as a woman's job in another. Nonetheless, the sexual division of labor is much more narrow than dictated by physical limitations, and what any one culture defines as a woman's job will seldom be performed by a man, and vice versa. It seems that what originated as a division of labor based upon the necessities of survival has spilled over into many other areas and lasted long past the time of its social value. Where male strength and mobility have been crucial to social survival, male dominance and the aura of male superiority have been the strongest. The latter has been incorporated into the value structure and attained an existence of its own.

Thus, male superiority has not ceased with an end to the need for male strength. As Goode pointed out, there is one consistent element in the assignment of jobs to the sexes, even in modern societies: "Whatever the strictly male tasks are, they are defined as *more honorific* [emphasis his]. . . . Moreover, the tasks of control, management, decision, appeals to the gods—in short the higher level jobs that typically do not require strength, speed or traveling far from home—are male jobs."

He goes on to comment that "this element suggests that the sexual divisions of labor within family and society come perilously close to the racial or caste restrictions in some modern countries. That is, the low-ranking race, caste, or sex is defined as not being able to do certain types of prestigious work, but it is also considered a violation of propriety if they do. Obviously, if women really cannot do various kinds of male tasks, no moral or ethical prohibition would be necessary to keep them from it."

COMPANIONSHIP

These sex role differences may have served a natural function at one time, but it is doubtful that they still do so. The characteristics we observe in women and men today are a result of socialization practices developed for the survival of a primitive society. The value structure of male superiority is a reflection of the primitive orientations and values. But social and economic conditions have changed drastically since these values were developed. Technology has reduced to almost nothing the importance of muscular strength. In fact, the warlike attitude that goes along with an idealization of physical strength and dominance is coming to be seen as dreadfully dangerous. The value of large families has also come to be questioned. The result of all these changes is that the traditional sex roles and the traditional family structures have become dysfunctional.

To some extent, patterns of child rearing have also changed. Bronfenbrenner reports that at least middle-class parents are raising both boys and girls much the same. He noted that, over a fifty-year period, middle-class parents have been developing a "more acceptant, equalitarian relationship with their children." With an increase in the family's social position, the patterns of parental treatment of children begin to converge. He likewise noted that a similar phenomenon is beginning to develop in lower-class parents, and equality of treatment is slowly working its way down the social ladder.

The changes in patterns of child rearing correlate with changes in relationships within the family. Both are moving toward a less hierarchical and more egalitarian pattern of living. As Blood has pointed out, "today we may be on the verge of a new phase in American family history, when the companionship family is beginning to manifest itself. One distinguishing characteristic of this family is the dual employment of husband and wife. . . . Employment emancipates women from domination by their husbands and, secondarily, raises their daughters from inferiority to their brothers. . . . The classic differences between masculinity and femininity are disappearing as both sexes in the adult generation take on the same roles in the labor market. . . . The roles of men and women are converging for both adults and children. As a result the family will be far less segregated internally, far less stratified into different age generations and different sexes. The old asymmetry of male-dominated, female-serviced family life is being replaced by a new symmetry."

LEFTOVER DEFINITIONS

All these data indicate that several trends are converging at about the same time. Our value structure has changed from an authoritarian one to a more democratic one, although our social structure has not yet caught up. Social attitudes begin in the family; only a democratic family can raise children to be citizens in a democratic society. The social and economic organization of society that kept women in the home has likewise changed. The home is no longer the center of society. The primary male and female functions have left it, and there is no longer any major reason for maintaining the large sex role differentiations that the home supported. The value placed on physical strength, which reinforced the dominance of men, and the male superiority attitudes that this generated have also become dysfunctional. It is the mind, not the body, that society needs now, and woman's mind is the equal of man's. The pill has liberated women from the uncertainty of child-bearing and, with it, the necessity of being attached to a man for economic support. But our attitudes toward women, and toward the family, have not changed. There is a distinct "cultural lag." Definitions of the family, conceptions of women, and ideas about social function are left over from an era when they were necessary for social survival. They have persisted into an era in which they are no longer viable. The result can only be called severe role dysfunctionality for women.

The necessary relief for this dysfunctionality must come through changes in the social and economic organization of society and in social attitudes that will permit women to play a full and equal part in the social order. With this must come changes in the family, so that men and women are not only equal but can raise their children in a democratic atmosphere. These changes will not come easily, nor will they come through the simple evolution of social trends. Trends do not move all in the same direction or at the same rate. To the extent that changes are dysfunctional with each other, they create problems. These problems will be solved not by complacency but by conscious human direction. Only in this way can we have a real say in the shape of our future and the shape of our lives.

Discrimination Against Black Americans

Men and Jobs*
Elliot Liebow

A pickup truck drives slowly down the street. The truck stops as it comes abreast of a man sitting on a cast-iron porch, and the white driver calls out, asking if the man wants a day's work. The man shakes his head, and the truck moves on up the block, stopping again whenever idling men come within calling distance of the driver. At the Carry-out corner, five men debate the question briefly and shake their heads no to the truck. The truck turns the corner and repeats the same performance up the next street. In the distance, one can see one man, then another, climb into the back of the truck and sit down. In starts and stops, the truck finally disappears.

What is it we have witnessed here? A labor scavenger rebuffed by his would-be prey? Lazy, irresponsible men turning down an honest day's pay for an honest day's work? Or a more complex phenomenon, marking the

* From *Tally's Corner,* by Elliot Liebow, copyright © 1967 by Little, Brown and Co., Inc. Used by permission of Little, Brown and Co.

intersection of economic forces, social values, and individual states of mind and body?

Let us look again at the driver of the truck. He has been able to recruit only two or three men from each twenty or fifty he contacts. To him, it is clear that the others simply do not choose to work. Singly or in groups, belly-empty or belly-full, sullen or gregarious, drunk or sober, they confirm what he has read, heard, and knows from his own experience: These men wouldn't take a job if it were handed to them on a platter.[1]

Quite apart from the question of whether or not this is true of some of the men he sees on the street, it is clearly not true of all of them. If it were, he would not have come here in the first place; or, having come, he would have left with an empty truck. It is not even true of most of them, for most of the men he sees on the street this weekday morning do, in fact, have jobs. But since, at the moment, they are neither working nor sleeping, and since they hate the depressing room or apartment they live in, or because there is nothing to do there,[2] or because they want to get away from their wives or anyone else living there, they are out on the street, indistinguishable from those who do not have jobs or do not want them. Some, like Boley, a member of a trash-collection crew in a suburban housing development, work Saturdays and are off on this weekday. Some, like Sweets, work nights cleaning up middle-class trash, dirt, dishes, and garbage, and mopping the floors of the office buildings, hotels, restaurants, toilets, and other public places dirtied during the day. Some men work for retail businesses, such as liquor stores, that do not begin the day until ten o'clock. Some laborers, like Tally, have already come back from the job, because the ground was too wet for pick and shovel, or because the weather was too cold for pouring concrete. Other employed men stayed off the job today for personal reasons: Clarence to go to a funeral at eleven this morning, and Sea Cat to answer a subpoena as a witness in a criminal proceeding.

Also on the street, unwitting contributors to the impression taken away by the truck driver, are the halt and the lame. The man on the cast-iron steps strokes one gnarled arthritic hand with the other and says he doesn't know whether or not he'll live long enough to be eligible for Social Security. He pauses, then adds matter-of-factly, "Most times, I don't care whether I do or don't." Stoopy's left leg was polio-withered in childhood. Raymond, who looks as if he could tear out a fire hydrant, coughs up blood if he bends or moves suddenly. The quiet man who hangs out in front of the Saratoga apartments has a steel hook strapped onto his left elbow. And, had

[1] By different methods, perhaps, some social scientists have also located the problem in the men themselves, in their unwillingness or lack of desire to work: "To improve the underprivileged worker's performance, one must help him to learn *to want* . . . higher social goals for himself and his children. . . . The problem of changing the work habits and motivation of [lower class] people . . . is a problem of changing the goals, the ambitions, and the level of cultural and occupational aspiration of the underprivileged worker." Allison Davis, "The Motivation of the Underprivileged Worker," in W. F. Whyte, ed., *Industry and Society* (New York: McGraw-Hill, 1946), p. 90.

[2] The comparison of sitting at home alone with being in jail is commonplace.

the man in the truck been able to look into the wine-clouded eyes of the man in the green cap, he would have realized that the man did not even understand he was being offered a day's work.

Others, having had jobs and been laid off, are drawing unemployment compensation (up to $44 per week) and have nothing to gain by accepting work that pays little more than this and frequently less.

Still others, like Bumdoodle the numbers man, are working hard at illegal ways of making money—hustlers who are on the street to turn a dollar any way they can: buying and selling sex, liquor, narcotics, stolen goods, or anything else that turns up.

Only a handful remains unaccounted for. There is Tonk, who cannot bring himself to take a job away from the corner, because, according to the other men, he suspects his wife will be unfaithful if given the opportunity. There is Stanton, who has not reported to work for four days now, not since Bernice disappeared. He bought a brand-new knife against her return. She had done this twice before, he said, but not for so long and not without warning, and he had forgiven her. But this time, "I ain't got it in me to forgive her again." His rage and shame are there for all to see, as he paces the Carry-out and the corner, day and night, hoping to catch a glimpse of her.

And, finally, there are those like Arthur, able-bodied men who have no visible means of support, legal or illegal, who neither have jobs nor want them. The truck driver, among others, believes the Arthurs to be representative of all the men he sees idling on the street during his own working hours. They are not, but they cannot be dismissed simply because they are a small minority. It is not enough to explain them away as being lazy or irresponsible, or both, because an able-bodied man with responsibilities who refuses work is, by the truck driver's definition, lazy and irresponsible. Such an answer begs the question. It is descriptive of the facts; it does not explain them.

Moreover, despite their small numbers, the don't-work-and-don't-want-to-work minority [are] especially significant, because they represent the strongest and clearest expression of those values and attitudes associated with making a living that, to varying degrees, are found throughout the street-corner world. These men differ from the others in degree rather than in kind, the principal difference being that they are carrying out the implications of their values and experiences to their logical, inevitable conclusions. In this sense, the others have yet to come to terms with themselves and the world they live in.

Putting aside, for the moment, what the men say and feel, and looking at what they actually do and the choices they make, getting a job, keeping a job, and doing well at it is clearly of low priority. Arthur will not take a job at all. Leroy is supposed to be on his job at 4:00 P.M.; but it is already 4:10, and he still cannot bring himself to leave the free games he has accumulated on the pinball machine in the Carry-out. Tonk started a construction job on Wednesday, worked Thursday and Friday, then didn't go back again. On the same kind of job, Sea Cat quit in the second week. Sweets had been working three months as a busboy in a restaurant, then quit without notice, not sure himself why he did so. A real-estate agent, saying he was more interested in getting the job done than in the cost, asked Richard to give him an estimate on repairing and painting the inside of a house, but Richard, after looking over the job, somehow never got around to submitting an estimate. During one period, Tonk would not leave the corner to take a job because his wife might prove unfaithful; Stanton would not take a job because his woman had been unfaithful.

Thus, the man-job relationship is a tenuous one. At any given moment, a job may occupy a relatively low position on the street-corner scale of real values. Getting a job may be subordinated to relations with women or to other nonjob considerations; the commitment to a job one already has is frequently shallow and tentative.

The reasons are many. Some are objective and reside principally in the job; some are subjective and reside principally in the man. The line between them, however, is not a clear one. Behind the man's refusal to take a job or his decision to quit one is not a simple impulse or value choice but a complex combination of assessments of objective reality, on the one hand, and values, attitudes, and beliefs drawn from different levels of his experience, on the other.

Objective economic considerations are frequently a controlling factor in a man's refusal to take a job. How much the job pays is a crucial question but seldom asked. He knows how much it pays. Working as a stock clerk, a delivery boy, or even behind the counter of liquor stores, drug stores, and other retail businesses pays one dollar an hour. So, too, do most busboy, car-wash, janitorial, and other jobs available to him. Some jobs, such as dishwasher, may dip as low as eighty cents an hour, and others, such as elevator operator or work in a junk yard, may offer $1.15 or $1.25. Take-home pay for jobs such as these ranges from $35 to $50 a week, but a take-home pay of over $45 for a five-day week is the exception rather than the rule.

One of the principal advantages of these kinds of jobs is that they offer fairly regular work. Most of them involve essential services and are therefore somewhat less responsive to business conditions than are some higher-paying, less menial jobs. Most of them are also inside jobs not dependent on the weather, as are construction jobs and other higher-paying outside work.

Another seemingly important advantage of working in hotels, restaurants, office and apartment buildings, and retail establishments is that they frequently offer an opportunity for stealing on the job. But stealing can be a two-edged-sword. Apart from increasing the cost of the goods or services to the general public, a less obvious result is that the practice usually acts as a depressant on the employee's own wage level. Owners of small retail establishments and other employers frequently anticipate employee stealing and adjust the wage rate accordingly. Tonk's employer explained why he was paying Tonk $35 for a 55–60 hour workweek. These men will all steal, he said. Although he keeps close watch on Tonk, he estimates that Tonk steals from $35 to $40 a week.[3] What he steals, when added to his regular earnings, brings his take-home pay to $70 or $75 per week. The employer said he did not mind this, because Tonk is worth that much to the business. But, if he were to pay Tonk outright the full value of his labor, Tonk would still be stealing $35–$40 per week, and this, he said, the business simply would not support.

This wage arrangement, with stealing built-in, was satisfactory to both parties, with each one independently expressing his satisfaction. Such a wage-theft system, however, is not as balanced and equitable as it appears. Since the wage level rests on the premise that the employee will steal the unpaid value of his labor, the man who does not steal on the job is penalized. And, furthermore, even if he does not steal, no one would believe him; the employer and others believe he steals because the system presumes it.

Nor is the man who steals, as he is expected to, as well off as he believes himself to be. The employer may occasionally close his eyes to the worker's stealing but not often and not for long. He is, after all, a businessman and cannot always find it within himself to let a man steal from him, even if the man is stealing his own wages. Moreover, it is only by keeping close watch on the worker that the employer can control how much is stolen and thereby protect himself against the employee's stealing more than he is worth. From this viewpoint, then, the employer is not in wage-theft collusion with the employee. In the case of Tonk, for instance, the employer was not actively abetting the theft. His estimate of how much Tonk was stealing was based on what he thought Tonk was able to steal despite his own best efforts to prevent him from stealing anything at all. Were he to have caught Tonk in the act of stealing, he would, of course, have fired him from the job and perhaps called the police as well. Thus, in an actual, if not in a legal, sense, all the elements of entrapment are present. The employer knowingly provides the conditions that entice (force) the employee to steal the unpaid value of his labor, but, at the same time, he punishes him for theft if he catches him doing so.

Other consequences of the wage-theft system are even more damaging to the employee. Let us, for argument's sake, say that Tonk is in no danger of entrapment; that his employer is willing to wink at the stealing, and that Tonk, for his part, is perfectly willing to earn a little, steal a little. Let us say, too, that he is paid $35 a week and allowed to steal $35. His money income—as measured by the goods and services he can purchase with it—is, of course, $70. But not all of his income is available to him for all purposes. He cannot draw on what he steals to build his self-respect or to measure his self-worth. For this, he can draw only on his earnings—the

---

[3] Exactly the same estimate as the one made by Tonk himself. On the basis of personal knowledge of the stealing routine employed by Tonk, however, I suspect the actual amount is considerably smaller.

amount given him publicly and voluntarily in exchange for his labor. His "respect" and "self-worth" income remains at $35—only half [of] that of the man who also receives $70 but all of it in the form of wages. His earnings publicly measure the worth of his labor to his employer, and they are important to others and to himself in taking the measure of his worth as a man.[4]

With or without stealing, and quite apart from any interior processes going on in the man who refuses such a job or quits it casually and without apparent reason, the objective fact is that menial jobs in retailing or in the service trades simply do not pay enough to support a man and his family. This is not to say that the worker is underpaid; this may or may not be true. Whether he is or not, the plain fact is that, in such a job, he cannot make a living. Nor can he take much comfort in the fact that these jobs tend to offer more regular, steadier work. If he cannot live on the $45 or $50 he makes in one week, the longer he works, the longer he cannot live on what he makes.[5]

Construction work, even for unskilled laborers, usually pays better, with the hourly rate ranging from $1.50 to $2.60 an hour.[6] Importantly, too, good references, a good driving record, a tenth-grade (or any high school) education, previous experience, the ability to "bring police clearance with you" are not normally required of laborers as they frequently are for some of the jobs in retailing or in the service trades.

Construction work, however, has its own objective disadvantages. It is, first of all, seasonal work for the great bulk of the laborers, beginning early

[4] Some public credit may accrue to the clever thief but not respect.

[5] It might be profitable to compare, as Howard S. Becker suggests, gross aspects of income and housing costs in this particular area with those reported by Herbert Gans for the low-income working class in Boston's West End. In 1958, Gans reports, median income for the West Enders was just under $70 a week, a level considerably higher than that enjoyed by the people in the Carry-out neighborhood five years later. Gans himself rented a six-room apartment in the West End for $46 a month, about $10 more than the going rate for long-time residents. In the Carry-out neighborhood, rooms that could accommodate more than a cot and a miniature dresser—that is, rooms that qualified for family living—rented for $12–$22 a week. Ignoring differences that really can't be ignored—the privacy and self-contained efficiency of the multiroom apartment as against the fragmented, public living of the rooming-house "apartment," with a public toilet on a floor always different from the one your room is on (no matter, it probably doesn't work, anyway)—and assuming comparable states of disrepair, the West Enders were paying $6 or $7 a month for a room that cost the Carry-outers at least $50 a month, and frequently more. Looking at housing costs as a percentage of income—and again ignoring what cannot be ignored: that what goes by the name of "housing" in the two areas is not at all the same thing—the median-income West Ender could get a six-room apartment for about 12 per cent of his income, while his 1963 Carry-out counterpart, with a weekly income of $60 (to choose a figure from the upper end of the income range), often paid 20–33 per cent of his income for one room. See Herbert J. Gans, *The Urban Villagers*, pp. 10–13.

[6] The higher amount is 1962 union scale for building laborers. According to the Wage Agreement Contract for Heavy Construction Laborers (Washington, D.C., and vicinity) covering the period from May 1, 1963 to April 30, 1966, minimum hourly wage for heavy construction laborers was to go from $2.75 (May, 1963) by annual increments to $2.92, effective November 1, 1965.

in the spring and tapering off as winter weather sets in.[7] And, even during the season, the work is frequently irregular. Early or late in the season, snow or temperatures too low for concrete frequently sends the laborers back home, and, during late spring or summer, a heavy rain on Tuesday or Wednesday, leaving a lot of water and mud behind it, can mean a two- or three-day workweek for the pick-and-shovel men and other unskilled laborers.[8]

The elements are not the only hazard. As the project moves from one construction stage to another, laborers—usually without warning—are laid off, sometimes permanently or sometimes for weeks at a time. The more fortunate or the better workers are told periodically to "take a walk for two, three days."

Both getting the construction job and getting to it are also relatively more difficult than is the case for the menial jobs in retailing and the service trades. Job competition is always fierce. In the city, the large construction projects are unionized. One has to have ready cash to get, into the union to become eligible to work on these projects, and, being eligible, one has to find an opening. Unless one "knows somebody"—say, a foreman or a laborer who knows the day before that they are going to take on new men in the morning—this can be a difficult and disheartening search.

Many of the nonunion jobs are in suburban Maryland or Virginia. The newspaper ads say "Report ready to work to the trailer at the intersection of Rte. 11 and Old Bridge Rd., Bunston, Virginia (or Maryland)," but this location may be ten, fifteen, or even twenty-five miles from the Carry-out. Public transportation would require two or more hours to get there, if it services the area at all. Without access to a car or to a car-pool arrangement, it is not worthwhile reading the ad. So the men do not. Jobs such as these are usually filled by word-of-mouth information, beginning with someone who knows someone or who is himself working there and looking for a paying rider. Furthermore, nonunion jobs in outlying areas tend to be smaller projects of relatively short duration and to pay somewhat less than scale.

[7] "Open-sky" work, such as building overpasses, highways, etc., in which the workers and materials are directly exposed to the elements, traditionally begins in March and ends around Thanksgiving. The same is true for much of the street repair work and the laying of sewer, electric, gas, and telephone lines by the city and public utilities, all important employers of laborers. Between Thanksgiving and March, they retain only skeleton crews selected from their best, most reliable men.

[8] In a recent year, the crime rate in Washington for the month of August jumped 18 per cent over the preceding month. A veteran police officer explained the increase to David L. Bazelon, Chief Judge, U.S. Court of Appeals for the District of Columbia. "It's quite simple. . . . You see, August was a very wet month. . . . These people wait on the street corner each morning around 6:00 or 6:30 for a truck to pick them up and take them to a construction site. If it's raining, that truck doesn't come, and the men are going to be idle that day. If the bad weather keeps up for three days . . . we know we are going to have trouble on our hands—and sure enough, there invariably follows a rash of purse-snatchings, house-breakings and the like. . . . These people have to eat like the rest of us, you know." David L. Bazelon, Address to the Federal Bar Association, p. 3.

Still another objective factor is the work itself. For some men, whether the job be digging, mixing mortar, pushing a wheelbarrow, unloading materials, carrying and placing steel rods for reinforcing concrete, or building or laying concrete forms, the work is simply too hard. Men such as Tally and Wee Tom can make such work look like child's play; some of the older work-hardened men, such as Budder and Stanton, can do it, too, though not without showing unmistakable signs of strain and weariness at the end of the workday. But those who lack the robustness of a Tally or the time-inured immunity of a Budder must either forego jobs such as these or pay a heavy toll to keep them. For Leroy, in his early twenties, almost six feet tall but weighing under 140 pounds, it would be as difficult to push a loaded wheelbarrow, or to unload and stack 96-pound bags of cement all day long, as it would be for Stoopy with his withered leg.

Heavy, backbreaking labor of the kind that used to be regularly associated with bull gangs or concrete gangs is no longer characteristic of laboring jobs, especially those with the larger, well-equipped construction companies. Brute strength is still required from time to time, as on smaller jobs, where it is not economical to bring in heavy equipment, or where the small, undercapitalized contractor has none to bring in. In many cases, however, the conveyor belt has replaced the wheelbarrow or the Georgia buggy, mechanized forklifts have eliminated heavy, manual lifting, and a variety of digging machines have replaced the pick and shovel. The result is fewer jobs for unskilled laborers and, in many cases, a work speed-up for those who do have jobs. Machines now set the pace formerly set by men. Formerly, a laborer pushed a wheelbarrow of wet cement to a particular spot, dumped it, and returned for another load. Another laborer, in hip boots, pushed the wet concrete around with a shovel or a hoe, geting it roughly level in preparation for the skilled finishers. He had relatively small loads to contend with and had only to keep up with the men pushing the wheelbarrows. Now, the job for the man pushing the wheelbarrow is gone, and the wet concrete comes rushing down a chute at the man in the hip boots, who must "spread it quick or drown."

Men who have been running an elevator, washing dishes, or "pulling trash" cannot easily move into laboring jobs. They lack the basic skills for "unskilled" construction labor, familiarity with tools and materials, and tricks of the trade without which hard jobs are made harder. Previously unused or untrained muscles rebel in pain against the new and insistent demands made upon them, seriously compromising the man's performance and testing his willingness to see the job through.

A healthy, sturdy, active man of good intelligence requires from two to four weeks to break in on a construction job.[9] Even if he is willing somehow to bull his way through the first few weeks, it frequently happens that

[9] Estimate of Mr. Francis Greenfield, President of the International Hod Carriers, Building and Common Laborers' District Council of Washington, D.C. and vicinity. I am indebted to Mr. Greenfield for several points in these paragraphs dealing with construction laborers.

his foreman or the craftsman he services with materials and general assistance is not willing to wait that long for him to get into condition or to learn at a glance the difference in size between a rough 2″ x 8″ and a finished 2″ x 10″. The foreman and the craftsman are themselves "under the gun" and cannot "carry" the man when other men, who are already used to the work and who know the tools and materials, are lined up to take the job.

Sea Cat was "healthy, sturdy, active, and of good intelligence." When a judge gave him six weeks in which to pay his wife $200 in back child-support payments, he left his grocery-store job in order to take a higher-paying job as a laborer, arranged for him by a foreman friend. During the first week, the weather was bad, and he worked only Wednesday and Friday, cursing the elements all the while for cheating him out of the money he could have made. The second week, the weather was fair, but he quit at the end of the fourth day, saying frankly that the work was too hard for him. He went back to his job at the grocery store and took a second job working nights as a dishwasher in a restaurant,[10] earning little, if any, more at the two jobs than he would have earned as a laborer and keeping at both of them until he had paid off his debts.

Tonk did not last as long as Sea Cat. No one made any predictions when he got a job in a parking lot; but, when the men on the corner learned he was to start on a road construction job, estimates of how long he would last ranged from one to three weeks. Wednesday was his first day. He spent that evening and night at home. He did the same on Thursday. He worked Friday and spent Friday evening and part of Saturday draped over the mailbox on the corner. Sunday afternoon, Tonk decided he was not going to report on the job the next morning. He explained that, after working three days, he knew enough about the job to know that it was too hard for him. He knew he wouldn't be able to keep up, and he'd just as soon quit now as get fired later.

Logan was a tall, two-hundred-pound man in his late twenties. His back used to hurt him only on the job, he said, but now he can't straighten up for increasingly longer periods of time. He said he had traced this to the awkward walk he was forced to adopt by the loaded wheelbarrows, which pull him down into a half-stoop. He's going to quit, he said, as soon as he can find another job. If he can't find one real soon, he guesses he'll quit anyway. It's not worth it, having to walk bent over and leaning to one side.

Sometimes, the strain and effort is greater than the man is willing to admit, even to himself. In the early summer of 1963, Richard was rooming at Nancy's place. His wife and children were "in the country" (his grandmother's home in Carolina), waiting for him to save up enough money so that he could bring them back to Washington and start over again after a disastrous attempt to "make it" in Philadelphia. Richard had gotten a job with a fence company in Virginia. It paid $1.60 an hour. The first few evenings, when he came home from work, he looked ill from exhaustion and the heat. Stanton said Richard would have to quit, "he's too small

[10] Not a sinecure, even by street-corner standards.

[thin] for that kind of work." Richard said he was doing O.K. and would stick with the job.

At Nancy's one night, when Richard had been working about two weeks, Nancy and three or four others were sitting around talking, drinking, and listening to music. Someone asked Nancy when was Richard going to bring his wife and children up from the country. Nancy said she didn't know, but it probably depended on how long it would take him to save up enough money. She said she didn't think he could stay with the fence job much longer. This morning, she said, the man Richard rode to work with knocked on the door, and Richard didn't answer. She looked in his room. Richard was still asleep. Nancy tried to shake him awake. "No more digging!" Richard cried out. "No more digging! I can't do no more God-damn digging!" When Nancy finally managed to wake him, he dressed quickly and went to work.

Richard stayed on the job two more weeks, then suddenly quit, ostensibly because his pay check was three dollars less than what he thought it should have been.

In summary of objective job considerations, then, the most important fact is that a man who is able and willing to work cannot earn enough money to support himself, his wife, and one or more children. A man's chances for working regularly are good only if he is willing to work for less than he can live on, and sometimes not even then. On some jobs, the wage rate is deceptively higher than on others; but the higher the wage rate, the more difficult it is to get the job, and the less the job security. Higher-paying construction work tends to be seasonal, and, during the season, the amount of work available is highly sensitive to business and weather conditions and to the changing requirements of individual projects.[11] Moreover, high-paying construction jobs are frequently beyond the physical capacity of some of the men, and some of the low-paying jobs are scaled down even lower in accordance with the self-fulfilling assumption that the man will steal part of his wages on the job.[12]

Bernard assesses the objective job situation dispassionately over a cup of coffee, sometimes poking at the coffee with his spoon, sometimes staring at it as if, like a crystal ball, it holds tomorrow's secrets. He is twenty-seven years old. He and the woman with whom he lives have a baby son, and she

[11] The over-all result is that, in the long run, a Negro laborer's earnings are not substantially greater—and may be less—than those of the busboy, janitor, or stock clerk. Herman P. Miller, for example, reports that, in 1960, 40 per cent of all jobs held by Negro men were as laborers or in the service trades. The average annual wage for nonwhite, nonfarm laborers was $2,400. The average earning of nonwhite service workers was $2,500 (*Rich Man, Poor Man,* p. 90). Francis Greenfield estimates that, in the Washington vicinity, the 1965 earnings of the union laborer who works whenever work is available will be about $3,200. Even this figure is high for the man on the street corner. Union men in heavy construction are the aristocrats of the laborers. Casual day labor and jobs with small firms in the building and construction trades, or with firms in other industries, pay considerably less.

[12] For an excellent discussion of the self-fulfilling assumption (or prophecy) as a social force, see "The Self-Fulfilling Prophecy," Chap. 11, in Robert K. Merton's *Social Theory and Social Structure.*

has another child by another man. Bernard does odd jobs—mostly painting —but here it is the end of January, and his last job was with the Post Office during the Christmas mail rush. He would like postal work as a steady job, he says. It pays well (about $2.00 an hour), but he has twice failed the Post Office examination (he graduated from a Washington high school) and has given up the idea as an impractical one. He is supposed to see a man tonight about a job as a parking attendant for a large apartment house. The man told him to bring his birth certificate and driver's license, but his license was suspended because of a backlog of unpaid traffic fines. A friend promised to lend him some money this evening. If he gets it, he will pay the fines tomorrow morning and have his license reinstated. He hopes the man with the job will wait till tomorrow night.

A "security job" is what he really wants, he said. He would like to save up money for a taxicab. (But, having twice failed the postal examination, and having a bad driving record as well, it is highly doubtful that he could meet the qualifications or pass the written test.) That would be "a good life." He can always get a job in a restaurant or as a clerk in a drugstore, but they don't pay enough, he said. He needs to take home at least $50–$55 a week. He thinks he can get that much driving a truck somewhere. . . . Sometimes, he wishes he had stayed in the army. . . . A security job, that's what he wants most of all, a real security job. . . .

Black Power

An Advocate of Black Power Defines It[*]

Charles V. Hamilton

Black power has many definitions and connotations in the rhetoric of race relations today. To some people, it is synonymous with premeditated acts of violence to destroy the political and economic institutions of this country. Others equate Black Power with plans to rid the civil-rights movement of whites who have been in it for years. The concept is understood by many to mean hatred of, and separation from, whites; it is associated with calling whites "honkies" and with shouts of "Burn, baby, burn!" Some understand it to be the use of pressure-group tactics in the accepted tradition of the American political process. And still others say that Black Power must be seen first of all as an attempt to instill a sense of identity and pride in black people.

[*] From the *New York Times Magazine*, April 14, 1968. Copyright 1968 by the New York Times Company. Reprinted by permission.

Ultimately, I suspect, we have to accept the fact that, in this highly charged atmosphere, it is virtually impossible to come up with a single definition satisfactory to all.

Even as some of us try to articulate our idea of Black Power and the way we relate to it and advocate it, we are categorized as "moderate" or "militant" or "reasonable" or "extremist." "I can accept your definition of Black Power," a listener will say to me. "But how does your position compare with what Stokely Carmichael said in Cuba, or with what H. Rap Brown said in Cambridge, Maryland?" Or, just as frequently, some young white New Left advocate will come up to me and proudly announce: "You're not radical enough. Watts, Newark, Detroit—that's what's happening, man! You're nothing but a reformist. We've got to blow up this society. Read Ché or Debray or Mao." All I can do is shrug and conclude that some people believe that making a revolution in this country involves rhetoric, Molotov cocktails, and being under thirty.

To have Black Power equated with calculated acts of violence would be very unfortunate. First, if black people have learned anything over the years, it is that he who shouts revolution the loudest is one of the first to run when the action starts. Second, open calls to violence are a sure way to have one's ranks immediately infiltrated. Third—and this is as important as any reason—violent revolution in this country would fail; it would be met with the kind of repression used in Sharpeville, South Africa, in 1960, when 67 Africans were killed and 186 wounded during a demonstration against apartheid. It is clear that America is not above this. There are many white bigots who would like nothing better than to embark on a program of black genocide, even though the imposition of such repressive measures would destroy civil liberties for whites as well as for blacks. Some whites are so panicky, irrational, and filled with racial hatred that they would welcome the opportunity to annihilate the black community. This was clearly shown in the senseless murder of Dr. Martin Luther King, Jr., which understandably—but nonetheless irrationally—prompted some black militants to advocate violent retaliation. Such cries for revenge intensify racial fear and animosity, when the need—now more than ever—is to establish solid, stable organizations and action programs.

Many whites will take comfort in these words of caution against violence. But they should not. The truth is that the black ghettos are going to continue to blow up out of sheer frustration and rage, and no amount of rhetoric from professors writing articles in magazines (which most black people in the ghettos do not read, anyway) will affect that. There comes a point beyond which people cannot be expected to endure prejudice, oppression, and deprivation, and they *will* explode.

Some of us can protect our positions by calling for "law and order" during a riot or by urging "peaceful" approaches, but we should not be confident that we are being listened to by black people legitimately fed up with intolerable conditions. If white America wants a solution to the violence in the ghettos by blacks, then let white America end the violence done to the ghettos by whites. We simply must come to understand that there can be no social order without social justice. "How long will the violence in the summers last?" another listener may ask. "How intransigent is white America?" is my answer. And the answer to that could be just more rhetoric, or it could be a sincere response to legitimate demands.

Black power must not be naïve about the intentions of white decision-makers to yield anything without a struggle and a confrontation by organized power. Black people will gain only as much as they can win through their ability to organize independent bases of economic and political power —through boycotts, electoral activity, rent strikes, work stoppages, pressure-group bargaining. And it must be clear that whites will have to bargain with blacks or continue to fight them in the streets of the Detroits and the Newarks. Rather than being a call to violence, this is a clear recognition that the ghetto rebellions, in addition to producing the possibility of apartheid-type repression, have been functional in moving *some* whites to see that viable solutions must be sought.

Black Power is concerned with organizing the rage of black people and with putting new, hard questions and demands to white America. As we do this, white America's responses will be crucial to the questions of violence and viability. Black Power must (1) deal with the obviously growing alienation of black people and their distrust of the institutions of this society, (2) work to create new values and to build a new sense of community and of belonging, and (3) to work to establish legitimate new institutions that make participants, not recipients, out of a people traditionally excluded from the fundamentally racist processes of this country. There is nothing glamorous about this; it involves persistence and hard, tedious, day-to-day work.

Black Power rejects the lessons of slavery and segregation that caused black people to look upon themselves with hatred and disdain. To be "integrated," it was necessary to deny one's heritage, one's own culture; to be ashamed of one's black skin, thick lips, and kinky hair. In their book, *Racial Crisis in America,* two Florida State University sociologists, Lewis M. Killian and Charles M. Grigg, wrote: "At the present time, integration as a solution to the race problem demands that the Negro forswear his identity as a Negro. But for a lasting solution, the meaning of 'American' must lose its implicit racial modifier, 'white.'" The black man must change his demeaning conception of himself; he must develop a sense of pride and self-respect. Then, if integration comes, it will deal with people who are psychologically and mentally healthy, with people who have a sense of their history and of themselves as whole human beings.

In the process of creating these new values, Black Power will, its advocates hope, build a new sense of community among black people. It will try to forge a bond in the black community between those who have "made it" and those "on the bottom." It will bring an end to the internal backbiting and suspicious bickering, the squabbling over tactics and personalities so characteristic of the black community. If Black Power can produce this unity, that in itself will be revolutionary—for the black community and for the country.

Black power recognizes that new forms of decision-making must be implemented in the black community. One purpose, clearly, is to overcome the alienation and distrust.

Let me deal with this specifically by looking at the situation in terms of "internal" and "external" ghetto problems and approaches. When I speak of internal problems, I refer to such things as exploitative merchants who invade the black communities, to absentee slumlords, to inferior schools and arbitrary law enforcement, to black people unable to develop their own independent economic and political bases. There are, of course, many problems facing black people that must be dealt with outside the ghettos—jobs, open occupancy, medical care, higher education.

The solution of the internal problems does not require the presence of massive numbers of whites marching arm in arm with blacks. Local all-black groups can organize boycotts of disreputable merchants and of those employers in the black communities who fail to hire and promote black people. Already, we see this approach spreading across the country with Operation Breadbasket, initiated by Dr. King's Southern Christian Leadership Conference. The national director of the program, the Reverend Jesse Jackson, who was with Dr. King when he was murdered in Memphis, has established several such projects from Los Angeles to Raleigh, North Carolina.

In Chicago alone, in fifteen months, approximately 2,000 jobs, worth more than $15 million in annual income, were obtained for black people. Negotiations are conducted on hiring and upgrading black people, marketing the products of black manufacturers and suppliers, and providing contracts to black companies. The operation relies heavily on the support of black businessmen, who are willing to work with Operation Breadbasket because it is mutually beneficial. They derive a profit and, in turn, contribute to the economic development of the black community.

This is Black Power in operation. But there is not nearly enough of this kind of work going on. In some instances, there is a lack of technical know-how coupled with a lack of adequate funds. These two defects constantly plague constructive pressure-group activity in the black communities.

CORE (Congress of Racial Equality) has developed a number of co-operatives around the country. In Opelousas, Louisiana, it has organized over 300 black farmers, growers of sweet potatoes, cabbages, and okra, in the Grand-Marie Co-op. They sell their produce, and some of the income goes back into the co-op as dues. Initially, 20 per cent of the cooperative's members were white farmers, but most of the whites dropped out as a result of social and economic pressures from the white community. An offshoot of the Grand-Marie group is the Southern Consumers' Cooperative in Lafayette, Louisiana, which makes and sells fruit cakes and candy. It has been in existence for more than a year, employs approximately 150 black people, and has led to the formation of several credit unions and buying clubs.

The major effort of Black Power—oriented CORE is in the direction of economic development. Antoine Perot, program director of CORE, says: "One big need in the black community is to develop capital-producing instruments which create jobs. Otherwise we are stuck with the one-crop commodity—labor—which does not produce wealth. Mere jobs are not enough. These will simply perpetuate black dependency."

Thus, small and medium-sized businesses are being developed in the black communities of Chicago, San Francisco, Detroit, Cleveland, New York, and several other urban centers. CORE hopes to call on some successful black businessmen around the country as consultants, and it is optimistic that they will respond favorably with their know-how and, in some instances, their money. The goal is to free as many black people as possible from economic dependency on the white man. It has been this dependency in many places that has hampered effective, independent political organizing.

In New York, Black Power, in the way we see it, operates through a group called NEGRO (National Economic Growth and Reconstruction Organization). Its acronym does not sit too well with some advocates of black consciousness who see in the use of the term "Negro" an indication of less than sufficient racial pride. Started in 1964, the group deals with economic self-help for the black community: a hospital in Queens, a chemical corporation, a textile company, and a construction company. NEGRO, with an annual payroll of $1 million and assets of $3 million, is headed by Dr. Thomas W. Matthew, a neurosurgeon who has been accused of failing to file federal income-tax returns for 1961, 1962, and 1963. He has asserted that he will pay all the Government says he owes, but not until "my patient is cured or one of us dies." His patient is the black community, and the emphasis of his group is on aiding blacks and reducing reliance on the white man. The organization creates a sense of identity and cohesiveness that is painfully lacking in much of the black community.

In helping oneself and one's race through hard work, NEGRO would appear to be following the Puritan ethic of work and achievement: If you work hard, you will succeed. One gets the impression that the organization is not necessarily idealistic about this. It believes that black people will never develop in this country as long as they must depend on handouts from the white man. This is realism, whatever ethic it is identified with. And this, too, is Black Power in operation.

More frequently than not, projects will not use the term "Black Power," but that is hardly necessary. There is, for instance, the Poor People's Corporation, formed by a former SNCC (Student Nonviolent Coordinating Committee) worker, Jessie Norris, in August, 1965. It has set up 15 cooperatives in Mississippi, employing about 200 black people. The employees, all shareholders, make handbags, hats, dresses, quilts, dolls, and other handcraft items that are marketed through Liberty House in Jackson, Mississippi. Always sensitive to the development of the black community, the Poor People's Corporation passed a rule that only registered voters could work in the co-ops.

These enterprises are small; they do not threaten the economic structure of this society, but their members look upon them as vital for the development of the black people. Their purpose is to establish a modicum of economic self-sufficiency without focusing too much attention on the impact they will have on the American economic system.

Absolutely crucial to the development of Black Power is the black middle class. These are people with sorely needed skills. There has been a lot of discussion about where the black middle class stands in relation to Black Power. Some people adopt the view that most members of the class opt out of the race (or at least try to do so); they get good jobs, a nice home, two cars, and forget about the masses of blacks who have not "made it." This has been largely true. Many middle-class blacks simply do not feel an obligation to help the less fortunate members of their race.

There is, however, a growing awareness among black middle-class people of their role in the black revolution. On January 20, [1968,] a small group of them (known, appropriately enough, as the Catalysts) called an all-day conference in a South Side Chicago church to discuss ways of linking black middle-class professionals with black people in the lower class. Present were about 370 people of all sorts—teachers, social workers, lawyers, accountants, three physicians, housewives, writers. They met in workshops to discuss ways of making their skills and positions relevant to the black society, and they held no press conferences. Although programs of action developed, the truth is that they remain the exception, not the rule, in the black middle class.

Another group has been formed by black teachers in Chicago, Detroit, and New York, and plans are being made to expand. In Chicago, the organization is called the Association of Afro-American Educators. These are people who have traditionally been the strongest supporters of the status quo. Education is intended to develop people who will support the existing values of the society, and "Negro" teachers have been helping this process over the years. But now some of them (more than 250 met on February 12 in Chicago) are organizing and beginning to redefine, first, their role as black educators vis-à-vis the black revolution and, second, the issues as they see them. Their motivation is outlined in the following statement:

> By tapping our vast resources of black intellectual expertise, we shall generate new ideas for *meaningful* educational programs, curricula and instructional materials that will contribute substantially toward raising the educational achievement of black children.
>
> Our purpose is to extricate ourselves momentarily from the dominant society in order to realign our priorities, to mobilize, and to "get ourselves together" to do what must be done by those best equipped to do it.

This is what they *say;* whether they can pull it off will depend initially on their ability to bring along their black colleagues, many of whom, admittedly, do not see the efficacy of such an attitude. Unless the link is made between the black middle-class professionals and the black masses, Black Power will probably die on the speaker's platform.

Another important phenomenon in the development of Black Power is the burgeoning of black students' groups on college campuses across the country. I have visited seventeen such campuses—from Harvard to Virginia to Wisconsin to UCLA—since October [, 1967]. The students are discussing problems of identity, of relevant curricula at their universities, of ways of helping their people when they graduate. Clearly, one sees in these hundreds (the figure could be in the thousands) of black students a little bit of Booker T. Washington (self-help and the dignity of common labor) and a lot of W. E. B. DuBois (vigorous insistence on equality and the liberal education of the most talented black men).

These are the people who are planning to implement social, political, and economic Black Power in their home towns. They will run for public office, aware that Richard Hatcher started from a political base in the black community. He would not be Mayor of Gary, Indiana, today if he had not first mobilized the black voters. Some people point out that he had to have white support. This is true; in many instances, such support is necessary, but internal unity is necessary first.

This brings us to a consideration of the external problems of the black community. It is clear that black people will need the help of whites at many places along the line. There simply are not sufficient economic resources —actual or potential—in the black community for a total, unilateral, bootstrap operation. Why should there be? Black people have been the target of deliberate denial for centuries, and racist America has done its job well. This is a serious problem that must be faced by Black Power advocates. On the one hand, they recognize the need to be independent of the "white power structure." And, on the other, they must frequently turn to that structure for help—technical and financial. Thus, the rhetoric and the reality often clash.

Resolution probably lies in the realization by white America that it is in her interest not to have a weak, dependent, alienated black community inhabiting the inner cities and blowing them up periodically. Society needs stability, and, as long as there is a sizable, powerless, restless group within it that considers the society illegitimate, stability is not possible. However it is calculated, the situation calls for a black-white rapprochement, which may well come only through additional confrontations and crises. More frequently than not, the self-interest of the dominant society is not clearly perceived until the brink is reached.

There are many ways whites can relate to this phenomenon. First, they must recognize that blacks are going to insist on an equitable distribution of *decision-making power.* Anything less will simply be perpetuating a welfare mentality among blacks. And, if the society thinks only in terms of *giving* more jobs, better schools, and more housing, the result will be the creation of more black recipients still dependent on whites.

The equitable distribution of power must result from a conviction that it is a matter of mutual self-interest, not from the feelings of guilt and altruism that were evident at the National Conference of New Politics convention in Chicago in August. An equitable distribution means that black men will have to occupy positions of political power in precincts, counties, Congressional districts, and cities where their numbers and organization warrant. It means the end of absentee white ward committeemen and precinct captains in Chicago's black precincts.

But this situation is much easier described than achieved. Black Americans generally are no more likely to vote independently than other Americans. In many Northern urban areas, especially, the job of wooing the black vote away from the Democratic party is gigantic. The established machine has the resources—patronage, tradition, apathy. In some instances, the change will take a catalytic event—a major racial incident, a dramatic black candidate, a serious boner by the white establishment (such as splitting the white vote). The mere call to "blackness" simply is not enough, even where the numbers are right.

In addition, many of the problems facing black people can be solved only to the extent that whites are willing to see such imperatives as an open-housing market and an expanding job market. White groups must continue to bring as much pressure as possible on local and national decision-makers to adopt sound policy in these fields. These enlightened whites *will* be able to work with Black Power groups.

There are many things that flow from this orientation to Black Power. It is not necessary that blacks create parallel agencies—political or economic —in all fields and places. In some areas, it is possible to work within, say, the two-party system. Richard Hatcher did so in Gary, but he first had to organize black voters to fight the Democratic machine in the primary. The same is true of Mayor Carl Stokes in Cleveland. At some point it may be wise to work with the existing agencies, but this must be done only from a base of independent, not subordinated, power.

On the other hand, dealing with a racist organization like George Wallace's Democratic party in Alabama would require forming an independent group. The same is true with some labor unions, especially in the South, that still practice discrimination, despite the condemnation of such a policy by their parent unions. Many union locals are willing to work with their black members on such matters as wages and working conditions but refuse to join the fight for open-housing laws.

The point is that black people must become much more pragmatic in their approach. Whether we try to work within or outside a particular agency should depend entirely on a hard-nosed, calculated examination of potential success in each situation—a careful analysis of cost and benefit. Thus, when we negotiate, the test will be: How will black people, not some political machine downtown or some labor union boss across town, benefit from this?

Black Power must insist that the institutions in the black community be led by, and, wherever possible, staffed by, blacks. This is advisable psychologically, and it is necessary as a challenge to the myth that black people are incapable of leadership. Admittedly, this violates the principle of egalitarianism ("We hire on the basis of merit alone, not color"). What black and white America must understand is that egalitarianism is just a *principle,* and [that] it implies a notion of "colorblindness" that is deceptive. It must be clear by now that any society that has been color-conscious all its life, to the detriment of a particular group, cannot simply become color-blind and expect that group to compete on equal terms.

Black Power clearly recognizes the need to perpetuate color consciousness, but in a positive way—to improve a group, not to subject it. When principles like egalitarianism have been so flagrantly violated for so long, it does not make sense to think that the victim of that violation can be equipped to benefit from opportunities simply upon their pronouncement. Obviously, some positive form of special treatment must be used to overcome centuries of negative special treatment.

This has been the argument of the Nation of Islam (the so-called Black Muslims) for years; it has also been the position of the National Urban League since its proposal for preferential treatment (the Domestic Marshall Plan, which urged a "special effort to overcome serious disabilities resulting from historic handicaps") was issued at its 1963 Denver convention. This is not racism. It is not intended to penalize or subordinate another group; its goal is the positive uplift of a deliberately repressed group. Thus, when some Black Power advocates call for the appointment of black people to head community-action poverty programs and to serve as school principals, they have in mind the deliberate projection of blacks into positions of leadership. This is important to give other black people a feeling of ability to achieve, if nothing else. And it is especially important for young black children.

An example of concentrated special treatment is the plan some of us are proposing for a new approach to education in some of the black ghettos. It goes beyond the decentralization plans in the Bundy Report; it goes beyond the community involvement at I.S. 201 in Harlem. It attempts to build on the idea proposed by Harlem CORE last year for an independent Board of Education for Harlem.

Harlem CORE and the New York Urban League saw the Bundy Report as a "step toward creating a structure which would bring meaningful education to the children of New York." CORE, led by Roy Innis, suggested an autonomous Harlem school system, chartered by the State Legislature and responsible to the state. "It will be run by an elected school board and an appointed administrator, as most school boards are," CORE said. "The elected members will be Harlem residents. It is important that much of the detailed planning and structure be the work of the Harlem community." Funds would come from city, state, and federal governments and from private sources. In describing the long-range goal of the proposal, CORE says: "Some have felt it is to create a permanently separate educational system. Others have felt it is a necessary step toward eventual integration. In any case, the ultimate outcome of this plan will be to make it possible for Harlem to choose."

Some of us propose that education in the black community should be family-oriented, not simply child-oriented. In many of the vast urban black ghettos (which will not be desegregated in the foreseeable future) the school should become the focal point of the community. This we call the Family-Community-School Comprehensive Plan. School would cease to be a 9-to-3, September-to-June, time-off-for-good-behavior institution. It would involve education and training for the entire family—all year round, day and evening. Black parents would be intimately involved as students, decision-makers, teachers. This is much more than a revised notion of adult education courses in the evening or the use of mothers as teachers' aides.

This plan would make the educational system the center of community life. We could have community health clinics and recreational programs built into the educational system. Above all, we could reorient the demeaning public welfare system, which sends caseworkers to "investigate" families. Why could we not funnel public assistance through the community educational program?

One major advantage would be the elimination of some of the bureaucratic chaos in which five to ten governmental agencies zero in on the black family on welfare, seldom if ever coordinating their programs. The welfare department, for one, while it would not need to be altered in other parts of the state, would have to work jointly with the educational system in the black community. This would obviously require administrative reorganization, which would not necessarily reduce bureaucracy but would consolidate and centralize it. In addition to being "investigators," for example, some caseworkers (with substantially reduced case loads) could become teachers of budgetary management, and family health consultants could report the economic needs of the family.

The teachers for such a system would be specially trained in a program similar to the National Teacher Corps, and recruits could include professionals as well as mothers who could teach classes in child rearing, home economics, art, music, or any number of skills they obviously possess. Unemployed fathers could learn new skills or teach the ones they know. The curriculum would be both academic and vocational, and it would contain courses in the culture and history of black people. The school would belong to the community. It would be a union of children, parents, teachers, social workers, psychologists, urban planners, doctors, community organizers. It would become a major vehicle for fashioning a sense of pride and group identity.

I see no reason why the local law-enforcement agency could not be integrated into this system. Perhaps this could take the form of training "community service officers," or junior policemen, as suggested in the report of the President's Commission on Civil Disorders. Or the local police precinct could be based in the school, working with the people on such things as crime prevention, first aid, and the training of police officers. In this way, mutual trust could be developed between the black community and the police.

Coordinating these programs would present problems to be worked out on the basis of the community involved, the agencies involved, and the size of the system. It seems quite obvious that, in innovations of this sort, there will be a tremendous amount of chaos and uncertainty, and there will be mistakes. This is understandable; it is the price to be paid for social change under circumstances of widespread alienation and deprivation. The recent furor about the Malcolm X memorial program at I.S. 201 in Harlem offers an example of the kind of problem to be anticipated. Rather than worrying about what one person said from a stage at a particular meeting, the authorities should be concerned about how the Board of Education will cooperate to transfer power to the community school board. When the transfer is made, confusion regarding lines of authority and program and curriculum content can be reduced.

The longer the delay in making the transfer, however, the greater the likelihood of disruption. One can expect misunderstanding, great differences of opinion, and a relatively low return on efforts at the beginning of such new programs. New standards of evaluation are being set, and the experimental concept developed at I.S. 201 should not be jeopardized by isolated incidents. It would be surprising if everything went smoothly from the outset.

Some programs *will* flounder, some will collapse out of sheer incompetence and faulty conception, but this presents an opportunity to build on mistakes. The precise details of the Comprehensive Plan would have to be worked out in conjunction with each community and agency involved. But the *idea* is seriously proposed. We must begin to think in entirely new terms of citizen involvement and decision-making.

Black power has been accused of emphasizing decentralization, of overlooking the obvious trend toward consolidation. This is not true with the kind of Black Power described here, which is ultimately not separatist or isolationist. Some Black Power advocates are aware that this country is simultaneously experiencing centralization and decentralization. As the federal government becomes more involved (and it must) in the lives of people, it is imperative that we broaden the base of citizen participation. It will be the new forms, new agencies and structures, developed by Black Power that will link these centralizing and decentralizing trends.

Black Power structures at the local level will activate people, instill faith (not alienation), and provide a habit of organization and a consciousness of ability. Alienation will be overcome and trust in society restored. It will be through these local agencies that the centralized forces will operate, not through insensitive, unresponsive city halls. Billions of dollars will be needed each year, and these funds must be provided through a more direct route from their sources to the people.

Black Power is a developmental process; it cannot be an end in itself. To the extent that black Americans can organize, and to the extent that white Americans can keep from panicking and begin to respond rationally to the demands of that organization—to that extent can we get on with the protracted business of creating not just law and order but a free and open society.

6. SUGGESTIONS FOR FURTHER READING

ADORNO, T. W., et al. The Authoritarian Personality (New York: Harper, 1950).*

ALLPORT, GORDON. The Nature of Prejudice (Garden City, N.Y.: Doubleday, 1958).*

DE BEAUVOIR, SIMONE. The Coming of Age (New York: Putnam, 1972).*

CAHN, EDGAR (ed.). Our Brothers' Keeper: The Indian in White America (Washington, D.C.: New Community Press, 1969).*

CARMICHAEL, S., and C. HAMILTON. Black Power (New York: Random House, 1967).*

CLEAVER, ELDRIDGE. Soul on Ice (New York: McGraw-Hill, 1968).*

DOLLARD, JOHN. Class and Caste in a Southern Town (New Haven, Conn.: Yale University Press, 1937).*

FANON, FRANTZ. The Wretched of the Earth (New York: Grove Press, 1963).*

GLAZER, N., and D. P. MOYNIHAN. Beyond the Melting Pot (Cambridge, Mass.: MIT Press, 1963).*

GORDON, MILTON. Assimilation in American Life (New York: Oxford University Press, 1964).*

GRIER, W., and P. COBB. Black Rage (New York: Basic Books, 1968).*

HANDLIN, OSCAR. The Newcomers (Garden City, N.Y.: Doubleday, 1962).*

HERBERG, WILL. Protestant, Catholic, Jew (Garden City, N.Y.: Doubleday, 1955.)*

HUBER, JOAN (ed.). Changing Women in a Changing Society (Chicago: University of Chicago Press, 1973).*

KOZOL, JONATHAN. Death at an Early Age (Boston: Houghton Mifflin, 1967).*

LIEBOW, ELLIOT. Tally's Corner (Boston: Little, Brown, 1967).*

LOPREATO, JOSEPH. Italian Americans (New York: Random House, 1970).*

LYMAN, STANFORD. Chinese Americans (New York: Random House, 1974).*

MCWILLIAMS, CAREY. Mexicans in America (New York: Teachers College Press, 1968).*

MILLET, KATE. Sexual Politics (Garden City, N.Y.: Doubleday, 1970).*

MORGAN, ROBIN (ed.). Sisterhood Is Powerful (New York: Random House, 1970).*

PARSONS, T., and K. CLARK (eds.). The Negro American (Boston: Houghton Mifflin, 1965).*

ROSE, A., and C. ROSE (eds.). Minority Problems (New York: Harper, 1965).*

SIMPSON, G., and J. YINGER. Racial and Cultural Minorities (New York: Harper, 1965).

SKLARE, MARSHALL (ed.). The Jews: Social Patterns of an American Group (Glencoe, Ill.: The Free Press, 1958).

*Available in paperback.

7. The Family

INTRODUCTION

If we define the family as a structural unit composed of at least a man and a woman joined in a socially recognized union (marriage) with their children (i.e., biological or adopted offspring), every known society can be said to have a family. In actuality, in most of the world's societies, the family unit is composed of a greater number of individuals than are included in our definition. Other kin, possibly including grandparents, uncles, aunts, and cousins, among others, live together with parents and children in what sociologists call an extended family. Within any given society, there are also families composed of a mother (or father) with children but no spouse or of spouses without children. While these varying patterns are usually accepted in the societies where they may occur, in no society are they the norm, nor do they represent the cultural ideal. In all societies, the preferred family pattern conforms to our definition.

The family is a basic and universal institution. The survival of every society depends upon the continued existence and functioning of the family, not only to ensure the replacement of defunct members, but also to provide for the care, training, and role development of its infant population, enabling them to assume functioning positions in the social order. In every known society, the replacement function is performed in the context of the family. Although it is conceivably possible that sexual relations and child rearing could be deregulated or governed by norms that do not entail a family institution, everywhere in the world they are connected with the family. Except for a few communal societies, such as the Israeli kibbutz, socialization is performed primarily, if not exclusively, within the organization of the family.

In "The Attempt to Abolish the Family in Russia," Nicholas Timasheff describes a plan to correct inequities in the treatment of Soviet women and children. Although well intentioned, the plan proved unsuccessful. Why it failed, and why the Soviets found it necessary to resurrect the family institution almost as it was prior to the antifamily policies, may perhaps reflect the societal need to have these critical functions performed within the family.

In America, the family system is typically nuclear (spouses and their children), neolocal (the family lives apart from both spouses' kin groups), monogamous (the family consists of one husband and one wife), and patriarchal (power and authority are vested chiefly in the male). Compared with most of the world's societies, our family system is unusual.

In the overwhelming majority of societies, extended family life is most common. This is especially true among preindustrial societies, nearly universal among hunting and gathering societies, and very common among agricultural peoples. It appears that, as societies become more urban and industrial, family patterns move toward the nuclear structure.

Neolocal residence is also uncommon from a worldwide perspective. In most of the world's societies, patrilocal residence (living with or near the husband's kin group) is most popular. Where the family acts as the key economic unit—as is true in most of the preindustrial world—it is of fundamental importance to live near one's kin group.

Monogamy is not the most widely preferred marital form. The people of four-fifths of the world's societies, if they could chose, would prefer to live in polygynous society (in which one husband has several wives). However, in most polygynous societies, most members live in monogamy, mainly because they are financially unable to support more than one wife.

Polyandry (one wife with several husbands) and group marriage are the most uncommon patterns of all; fewer than 5 per cent of the world's societies live according to these modes.

Patriarchal society is most common throughout the world. Patriarchy still exists in American family life, especially among the working and upper classes. However, it appears that America is moving away from this pattern toward an equalitarian pattern, especially among the middle classes. As women participate to a growing extent in the labor force, the trend toward equalitarian family life will continue. The 1970 census found that nearly half of the married female population were holding jobs.

In the wake of the great urban industrial transformation, the modern American family has changed considerably since colonial days. Many functions once performed within the context of the family are now performed outside the home. The economic needs of the individual are no longer met within the family; it is now the corporation to which

254 The Family

he looks for a livelihood. No longer is the home the place to learn specialized skills; the educational system now provides training. The state, organized religion, and professional caretakers (i.e., physicians, psychiatrists, social workers) also play a significant role in providing for the needs of people, furnishing many services that were once exclusively, or almost exclusively, provided within the family.

While the family has lost some important functions, it has become more specialized in function. Burgess and Locke argue that the family has changed from being an institution to a companionship. This transition implies that marriage is no longer a social "have to"; rather, it has become a "want to." One marries not simply for social propriety and social acceptance, but because marriage meets one's personal needs for friendship and companionship. In a world that has become ever more rationalized (codified in legal and official regulations), bureaucratized, and impersonal, the family is increasingly expected to provide for the emotional needs of the individual. The family is becoming the central, if not the only, place for the expression of intimacy and primary-group life. (Sociologists define primary groups as relatively small, durable, face-to-face, unspecialized groups within which relationships are highly personal and emotionally laden. In primary groups, free and extensive communication prevails, and individuals react to one another as whole personalities. Primary groups are believed to be the "cradle of personality development" and are vitally necessary for the maintenance of ego strength.)

In response to these factors, some trends have been noted. It appears that interest in family life has never been more widely shared; over the twentieth century, there have been continuous increases in the percentage of the population who marry. People are also marrying younger than they used to. And divorce and remarriage have reached new heights. All these changes could be related to the changing functions of the family and its increasing socio-emotional significance. Perhaps, too, the modern family has been emotionally overloaded by its members. It is also possible that we are moving toward what Bernard Farber calls the "permanent availability" model, where individuals are available to marry anyone at any time during their adulthood, thus reducing the durability of marital bonds and increasing voluntarism and fluidity in family life.

Intrafamily relationships are an important focus of the sociologist's interest in the family. In "The Split-Level American Family," reprinted here in Chapter 4, Urie Bronfenbrenner reviews the diminution in the role of the extended family with the advent of modern urban-industrial society. It is Bronfenbrenner's contention that suburbanization—which, among other effects, increases the father's commuting time to and from his workplace and hence decreases the time available to spend with his family—and the increase in the number of married women who hold jobs or pursue other interests outside the home have contributed toward fracturing normal family relationships, depriving children of necessary association with their parents and kin, relegating them to their peers, and leading to abnormally great exposure to television. It is Bronfenbrenner's view that these factors, together, are producing deleterious consequences for personality development and possibly contributing to the widening gap between the generations.

Another important aspect of the sociology of the family is the subject of courtship and mating. With the advent of industrial society, probably the most significant change in courtship patterns has been the diminution of arranged marriages, accompanied by a rise in marriage by individual choice and the development of romantic love as a basis for mate selection. When arranged marriage was the leading form of mate selection, considerable homogamy (marriage between individuals possessing similar characteristics) prevailed. In recent years, there has been increasing intermarriage, particularly across religious and ethnic lines. Class and racial intermarriage, while increasing somewhat, has shown the least change.

Postindustrial society will inevitably produce changes in family patterns. The contemporary rise of feminism is in some way related to the development of a machine-dominated technology that diminishes the importance of physical strength. The women's movement, a product of, as well as a contributor to, such larger social changes, has already had an immense impact on family patterns. It is likely to be even more influential in the years ahead.

One of the things that is clear from Komarovsky's research is that men seem to accept female liberation more readily in the work sphere than in their home lives. Undoubtedly, the women's movement will serve as a major source of future domestic strife. On the one hand, many wives are encouraged to be their husbands' intellectual equals, to have careers, and to be involved in creative endeavors outside the home. On the other hand, wives are still felt to be indispensable in child care and household duties. Such contradictions will inevitably produce role strains for husband and wife alike, with neither receiving adequate support from his or her partner for fulfilling the expectations of self and others.

In postindustrial societies such as our own, the family is in a state of transition. Premarital sex and courtship patterns have changed greatly. After a century-long trend toward more youthful marriage and greater popularity of the institution of marriage itself, these patterns have recently stabilized and may be showing signs of decline. Family size continues to diminish; divorce and remarriage rates continue to rise. Growing numbers of Americans have become disenchanted with the conventional nuclear family and have formed communes, joint families, and open marriages, in which power, resources, and sexual privileges are shared more widely than ever before. Rosabeth Kanter's article in Chapter 10 is an interesting and informative portrayal of urban communal patterns. Increasing numbers of couples also are altering the accepted biological model of family formation; there has been an upsurge of childless marriages, adoptions by fertile couples, and transracial adoptions. Today we are observing growing innovation and experimentation with family forms. In light of all this, it seems especially difficult to predict the family forms that will be prevalent in the future.

Is the Family a Universal Societal Institution?

The Attempt to Abolish the Family in Russia *

Nicholas S. Timasheff

In their attempts to create a new culture, the revolutionists always meet resistance. This resistance is displayed by individuals, but they resist because they have been molded by mighty institutions through which social structure and culture are perpetuated. In modern society, these pillars of society are the family, the school, and the church. From the standpoint of the revolutionists, two of them, the family and the church, are hopeless, for it is their very nature to preserve tradition. But the school might, perhaps, be transformed into an instrument of cultural revolution.

Hence, for those who are eager to endow a nation with a new culture, a definite program of action follows: They must loosen the family ties; they must destroy, or at least weaken, the church; and they must transform the school into an accelerator of cultural revolution. This was the natural program of the Communists while they performed their Great Experiment.

With respect to the family, the destructive attitude is sometimes denied by pro-Communist writers outside of Russia.[1] The reason is obvious; the value of the family is beyond question, say, in this country, and a regime that is hostile to it cannot count on many sympathizers. But, in 1919, an authoritative representative of the regime said: "The family has ceased to be a necessity, both for its members and for the State." A few years later, another high dignitary declared that the Communists had to undermine the

* From *The Great Retreat*, by Nicholas S. Timasheff. Copyright 1946 by E. P. Dutton & Co., Inc., and used with their permission.
[1] See, for instance, Nathan Berman, "Juvenile Delinquency in the Soviet Union," *American Journal of Sociology*, March, 1937.

family, "this formidable stronghold of all the turpitudes of the old regime."[2] And acts were still more conclusive than words.

The family, which was to be destroyed, was of the patriarchal type. In old Russia, marriage was a religious institution. Only religious marriage and divorce were recognized, so that the rules of the corresponding religious communities were exclusively applied. The superiority of the husband over the wife was legally recognized, but there was no joint property of the consorts.[3] The wife received the husband's last name, but the Russians emphasized that, in contradistinction to the West, their women never were addressed as "Mrs. John Doe"; their first names had to be used. Parental authority was strong; up to the age of twenty-one, children needed parental consent for marriage and quite a few other significant acts. Naturally, the institution of inheritance existed. Thus, the strong family structure prevailed; this was especially the case among the peasants and the lower middle class, whereas, among the upper classes, the intellectuals, and the workers, there was a well-expressed tendency to weaken the family ties.

This stronghold of the old order, this instrument of culture tradition, was attacked by the Communists from the very start of their rule.[4] The general tendency was to destroy the stable character of marital relations and make marriage as easily soluble as possible. Naturally, marriage was liberated from all bonds with religion: After a certain date, church weddings ceased to be accorded any legal effect. Instead of going to church, the prospective consorts had to apply for "registration" of their marriage to local boards established for that purpose. Measures were taken to deprive the registration of the character of an impressive ceremony. The boards were usually located in some dark and abject room of an office building, and no words about the significance of marriage were uttered by the officials.

The most drastic change concerned divorce: In contradistinction to the old law, which made it so difficult, the decrees of December 17 and 18, 1917, permitted every consort to declare that he wanted his marriage to be canceled. No reasons were to be given to the board. Receiving the application, it had to grant the cancellation immediately, if there was mutual consent; if this was not the case, divorce was to be granted by the court, but this was a meaningless formality, since the court had to do it at the request of each consort, even if the other one opposed it. If one of the consorts was absent, he or she was notified by a postcard.

In addition to this, incest, bigamy, and adultery were dropped from the list of criminal offenses. Abortion was explicitly permitted by the decree of November 20, 1920, provided that it was performed by an approved

[2] A. Kollontay, "The Family and the Communist State" (Russian; 1919), p. 8; N. Bukharin, *Proceedings of the XIII Congress of the Communist Party* (Russian; 1924), p. 545.

[3] Cf. John Hazard in "Law and the Soviet Family," *Wisconsin Law Review,* 1939, p. 245.

[4] First by the decree of December 17 and 18, 1917, later on consolidated and expanded by the Family Code of October 22, 1918.

physician in a state hospital. Under these conditions, the physician had to accede to requests for abortion, even if no valid reasons could be established. Under war Communism, inheritance ceased to exist.

When marriage can be canceled by means of a postcard, when there is no distinction between legitimacy and illegitimacy, when inheritance is unknown, parental authority is naturally weakened, and this effect was one of the purposes of the measures described. In official propaganda, the idea was persistently emphasized that children had to obey their parents only insofar as the parents complied loyally with the directions of those in power. This signified, among other things, that, unless they wanted to risk placing themselves in a dangerous position, parents could not oppose the propaganda of the Marxist doctrine, including atheism, to which the children were exposed at school. There, they were taught to do their best to re-educate their parents in the Communist spirit and denounce them to the authorities if they displayed a marked counterrevolutionary attitude. Numerous family tragedies evolved on that basis, the state backing the children against the parents. Time and again the idea was publicly discussed as to whether family education ought not to be abolished and replaced by education in state institutions. Reluctantly, the idea was rejected as impractical, at least for the period of transition.

During the NEP[5] a partial restoration of the family could be expected, if the Marxist doctrine were correct and monogamy and the strong family were the counterpart of the individualistic manner of production. There was actually one almost unavoidable concession; this was the restoration of inheritance. But, in contrast with the Marxist scheme, the attack on the family was rather strengthened. A new Family Code was prepared in 1925, and the draft was submitted to an informal discussion. Voices from the countryside were unfavorable, but this did not stop the government, and the new code was enacted as of January 1, 1927. The main innovation was the introduction of the institution of the "nonregistered marriage," legally equal to the registered one. This meant that courts and boards were obliged to consider every union of a man and woman as marriage, provided that at least one of the following conditions were present: (1) durable cohabitation, (2) common menage, (3) declaration of the relationship before third persons, or (4) mutual support and common education of the children. The unforeseen effect was the legalization of bigamy: Applying the new law, the Supreme Court prescribed the division of the estate of a deceased man between his registered and nonregistered wife.[6]

The period of the Second Socialist Offensive was characterized by additional efforts to uproot the traditional structure of the family. The labor law of the period made it obligatory to accept any job imposed on the individual, and often husband and wife were assigned work in different towns. To the complaint of a teacher that she was artificially separated

[5] New Economic Policy.
[6] Decision of the Supreme Court of the RSFSR, reported in *Sudebnaya Praktika,* 1929, No. 20.

from her husband, the Labor Board replied that divorce was easy, and that she probably could find another husband in the place of her occupation. In Stalingrad, it was decided to create "socialist suburbs" consisting of houses without apartments for family life, replaced by single rooms, refectories, and nurseries. The plan fell through, because nobody but bachelors agreed to live in such suburbs.

The antifamily policy was crowned by partial success: Around 1930, on the average, family ties were substantially weaker than they had been before the revolution. But this partial success was more than balanced by a number of detrimental effects unforeseen by the promoters of the Communist Experiment. About 1934, these detrimental effects were found to endanger the very stability of the new society and its capacity to stand the test of war. Let us review these effects:

1. The abuse of the freedom of divorce and abortion resulted in an ominous decrease of the birth rate. No natality figures have ever been published for the crucial years, but, in 1937, the population proved to be 13 million behind expectation, so that, around 1934, the deficit must already have been large. To what extent this was due to the freedoms just mentioned, cannot be established. But the following figures speak for themselves: In 1934, in the medical institutions of the city of Moscow, 57,000 children were born, but 154,000 abortions were performed; in 1935, already under changing conditions, the figures were 70,000 and 155,000. As to divorce, the frequency of which also pushes down the birth rate, the following figures were reported from Moscow: In 1934, in 100 marriages there were 37 divorces, and, in the first half of 1935, there were 38.3 divorces.[7]

2. The dissolution of family ties, especially of the parent-child relations, threatened to produce a wholesale dissolution of community ties, with rapidly increasing juvenile delinquency as the main symptom. In 1935, the Soviet papers were full of information and indignation about the rise of hooliganism—i.e., of crimes in which the sadistic joy of inflicting pain on somebody or destroying something of value was paramount. Everywhere, wrote the papers, gangs invaded workingmen's dwellings, ransacked them, and destroyed or spoiled what they did not take away; if somebody dared to resist, he was mercilessly killed. In trains, the hooligans sang obscene songs; to prolong the fun, they did not permit travelers to alight at their destinations if they had not finished singing. Sometimes, the schools were besieged by neglected children; other times, gangs beat the teachers and attacked women or regularly fought against one another.

3. Finally, the magnificent slogans of the liberation of sex and the emancipation of women proved to have worked in favor of the strong and reckless and against the weak and shy. Millions of girls saw their lives ruined by Don Juans in Communist garb, and millions of children had never known parental homes.

[7] *Izvestia,* July 7, 1935.

The disintegration of the family did not disturb the Communists, since this was precisely what they wanted to achieve; but they were disturbed by quite a few collateral effects of the disorganization. The unfavorable trend of the population figures threatened to undermine both the labor supply and the strength of the nation at arms—for wars to be waged by the next generation. In the specific circumstances of 1934, the waste of human energy in juvenile delinquency, the combat against it, and love affairs and the accumulation of unfavorable attitudes among the victims of the new family order—or perhaps disorder is the correct word—could no longer be tolerated: They undermined the strength of the nation for the war that was straight ahead. The unfavorable development had to be stopped, and, to achieve this, the government had no other choice than to re-enforce that pillar of society that is the family. These were the main lines of development:

1. Contrary to the teachings of the previous years, young people were instructed to consider marriage "as the most serious affair in life," since, in principle, it should be a union for life. Statements such as follow, which never could have appeared in the course of the Communist Experiment, now daily adorned the Soviet papers and magazines: "There are people who dare to assert that the Revolution destroys the family; this is entirely wrong: The family is an especially important phase of social relations in socialist society. . . . One of the basic rules of Communist morals is that of strengthening the family. . . . The right to divorce is not a right to sexual laxity. A poor husband and father cannot be a good citizen. People who abuse the freedom of divorce should be punished." And, actually, in 1935 the Soviet Government started to prosecute men for rape who "changed their wives as gloves," registering a marriage one day and divorce the next. *Pravda* told the following story:

Engineer P. seduced a girl by promising to marry her. When symptoms of pregnancy appeared, the girl reminded him of his promise. His reply was: "Look, dear, you are the seventh girl in my life to whom the same unpleasant thing has occurred. Here is a letter from another woman who is also bearing a child of mine. Could I marry her, too?" The girl insisted, but the engineer terminated the discussion by saying: "Forget about marriage. Do as you like. Here is money to pay for an abortion." Having told the story, the paper added: "This man should be tried, and his trial ought to be a 'demonstrative trial.' "[8]

In the official journal of the Commissariat of Justice these amazing statements may be found:

The State cannot exist without the family. Marriage is a positive value for the Socialist Soviet State only if the partners see in it a life-long union. So-called free love is a bourgeois invention and has nothing in common with the principles of conduct of a Soviet citizen.

[8] *Pravda,* June 4 and 26, 1935; *Molodaya Gvardiya,* 1935, No. 1.

Moreover, marriage receives its full value for the State only if there is progeny, and the consorts experience the highest happiness of parenthood.[9]

To inculcate the rediscovered value of marriage into the minds of the younger generation, not only the negative method of deterrence by trials and producing indignation by well-chosen stories was used but also the positive method of glorifying marriage by well-staged ceremonies; perhaps one could speak of "demonstrative marriage." Here is a story from *Izvestia*. The people involved are a *kolhoz* brigadier, V., and the first parachutist among *kolhoz* girls, B. The scene is Northern Caucasus, one of Russia's granaries.

The romance lasted about two years. In the beginning, V. hated B. He did his best to organize a shock brigade,[10] but she preferred dancing and diverted the energy of youth toward that futility. When V. saw that he was unable to discourage that attraction, he joined the movement, even started helping young people organize dances and athletic performances, and in return was helped by them in work. Then, suddenly, when B. made her first jump, V. decided that life without her would be valueless and proposed to her. She accepted. The secretaries of the regional and local party organizations decided to sponsor the marriage. Stimulated by them, the collective farm took over all preparations and decorated the village beautifully for the great day. The people's commissar for agriculture was invited to come. He could not accept, but congratulated the young people by wire and offered them a magnificent gift—a phonograph and a set of records.

The story is continued in *Pravda*. Early in the morning, guests started arriving. Among them were leaders of the party, the Soviets, and the economic organizations, as well as the champion of the girl parachutists of the Union. About noon, a score of airplanes appeared in the sky. The betrothed were offered a ride, after which they were enthusiastically acclaimed by the crowd. About five o'clock, 800 guests were invited to dinner. Tables were overloaded with mutton, hams, ducks, chickens, pies, and other dishes. After a while, the regional party secretary rose and made a speech congratulating the V.'s on their marriage, the most serious step in their lives. He expressed the hope that they would live in perfect unity and procreate an abundant Bolshevik progeny. The 800 present rose and drank to the health of the newlyweds. The people danced and rejoiced far into the night.[11]

Was not this an invitation to millions of young people to reconsider those ideas about marriage that, until quite recently, they were taught as belonging to the very essence of the Doctrine? To re-enforce the new ideas, very simple, but probably very effective symbolic means were used. The registration offices ceased to be filthy places. Now, young people found

[9] *Sotsialisticheskaya Zakonnost,* 1939, No. 2.
[10] A group of workers pledged to work substantially faster and better than required by regulations.
[11] *Izvestia,* September 9, 1935; *Pravda,* September 11, 1935.

them clean, comfortable, well furnished; the officers became polite, friendly, underlining the seriousness of the act. Marriage certificates started being issued on decent paper, no longer on wrapping paper, as was the case previously. For a small additional sum, the newlyweds could receive a marriage certificate designed by artists.[12] Then, in the fall of 1936, wedding rings started being sold in Soviet shops.[13] Since these rings are used in church weddings, this novelty could be interpreted as an invitation, on the part of the government, to have the civil marriage, or registration, re-enforced and made almost indissoluble by the Church.

2. The freedom of divorce was first curtailed and then almost abolished. The first phase appears in the law of June 27, 1936, which introduced a number of inhibitions. It calls for the summoning of both parties when a divorce is to be registered.

Moreover, according to the law of September 28, 1935, the fact of divorce must be marked in the passports and birth certificates of the consorts. Commenting on this regulation, *Izvestia* expressed the hope that, before marrying a "fluttering scoundrel," a girl would ask him to produce his papers and then perhaps renounce the honor of becoming his thirtieth bride.[14]

Finally, the fee for divorce, which previously had been rather nominal, was substantially raised; instead of three rubles, one had to pay 50 rubles for the first divorce, 150 for the second, and 300 for the third and each subsequent divorce.

The effect of the antidivorce drive may be measured by the following figures: In the course of the second half of the year 1936, the number of divorces in the Ukraine was 10,992, against 35,458 in the second half of 1935;[15] in other words, it decreased more than three times.

The second phase appears in the decree of July 8, 1944.

Prospective applicants for a divorce will henceforth be obliged to state their reasons and satisfy the courts that these reasons are serious and valid. Both parties must appear personally before a lower court, which hears all the evidence and then seeks to determine if it cannot effect a reconciliation. If this is believed impossible, the petition can be carried to a higher court. Witnesses must be heard in both courts. The divorce fees have been raised to 2,000 rubles.

It is probable that the courts, obeying the government's directions, will demand very good reasons and irrefutable evidence to grant a divorce. In consequence, obtaining a divorce in Russia will probably become more difficult than in many states of this country.

Moreover, the decree of July 8, 1944, abolished the institution of "unregistered marriage" introduced in 1926. Now, only "registered marriage"

[12] *Izvestia,* July 7, 1937; *Krasaya Gazeta,* November 4, 1934.
[13] *New York Times,* November 18, 1936.
[14] *Izvestia,* February 12, 1937.
[15] *New York Times,* July 11, 1944.

is legally recognized; as a corollary, the "bourgeois" distinction between legitimate and illegitimate children has reappeared in Soviet law. In addition to this, "the research of paternity" has been explicitly forbidden, so that illegitimate children and their mothers will receive no alimony. Very definitely, this will prove a mighty deterrent to extramarital relations, insofar as girls are concerned.

3. The freedom to dispose of unborn children through abortion no longer exists. Early in 1935, a campaign against abortion was started. Articles began to appear in Soviet papers written by high medical authorities, explaining the harm that abortion, especially repeated abortion, inflicts on women.[16] Praising maternity, these authorities declared that the longing for children had suddenly reappeared among the women of the Soviet Union —a manner of saying that now Stalin wanted them to bear as many children as possible. Trials resulting in severe sentences finished the careers of persons operating clandestine "abortaria": Their very emergence disclosed that, without change in the law, Soviet hospitals no longer performed abortion at the simple request of the pregnant woman. Finally, a draft law prohibiting abortion was published and offered for public discussion. Numerous objections were raised, mainly based on intolerable dwelling conditions. Nevertheless, the law of June 27, 1936, abolished the freedom of abortion, which had been considered one of the highest achievements of Communism by many pro-Communists.

Repealing the notorious law of November 20, 1920, the new law prohibited abortion in all cases except where there was danger to life or health of the pregnant woman or danger of hereditary transmission of serious sickness. As in the former law, only medical men were permitted to perform the operation. Pressure exerted on a woman to induce her into abortion was declared a crime punishable by two years in prison. To make more childbearing possible, the law promised a large extension of the network of maternity hospitals, day nurseries, and kindergartens. Maternity grants were increased, and special allowances were promised to mothers of six or more children.[17]

4. The peculiar parent-child relationship that had obtained under the Communist Experiment, and which granted superiority to the children, was reversed to one that is considered normal in the world; once more, children have to recognize the authority of their parents. Obviously, the change could not be effected through legal enactment, and the method of persuasion through propaganda was used exactly in the same manner as it was used to stabilize marriage. Statements like these could be found almost daily on the pages of Soviet papers, beginning with the spring of 1935:

[16] For instance, by Arkhangelski, member of the Academy of Sciences, *Izvestia*, June 5, 1935.

[17] The second antidivorce law (1944) substantially increased the advantages granted to mothers of numerous children. Honorary titles were granted to mothers of seven or more children.

Young people should respect their elders, especially their parents.
. . . The respect and care of parents is an essential part of the
Komsomol[18] morals. . . . One must respect and love his parents,
even if they are old-fashioned and do not like the Komsomol.[19]

In 1939, the official journal of the Union Prosecutor declared:

Sound moral ideas must be inculcated into the minds of young
persons. They must know that lack of care for their parents is found
only among savages, and that in every civilized society such conduct
is considered dishonest and base.[20]

To corroborate these ideas, the journal cited the laws of Solon and
Xenophon's works.

The method of positive demonstration was also used, and Stalin himself
found it necessary to set the example. In October, 1935, he paid a visit to
his old mother living in Tiflis,[21] and, in the detailed accounts of this visit,
signs of love and respect to the old lady by the leader of the World Proletariat were emphasized. A high degree of intimacy in family relations was
displayed through the reproduction of such questions as: How did Stalin's
children like the jam made for them by their grandmother? Another day,
Stalin appeared in one of Moscow's gardens with his children, something
he had never done previously. Up to that time, the majority of Soviet citizens did not even know that Stalin had any children.

Gradually, the unlimited freedom granted to young people under the
Communist Experiment was curbed. One of the most conspicuous items in
the process has been the decree of July 15, 1943, excluding children below
the age of sixteen from evening performances in theaters and movies.

To strengthen parental authority, an indirect method has been used in
the new inheritance law of March 20, 1945. While previous laws limited
possible heirs to direct or adopted descendants, consorts, and needy dependents, the new law broadens this list to include parents, brothers, sisters, and public organizations. Although, according to the new law, the
testator may not deprive his minor children or jobless heirs of their rightful
portion, its impact on the family is clear: The greater the freedom to dispose of one's estate, the greater is the authority of the head of the family relating to presumptive heirs.

[18] Young Communist League.
[19] *Komsomolskaya Pravda,* June 7 and September 29, 1935; *Pravda,* August 4, 1935.
[20] *Sovetskaya Yustitsia,* 1939, No. 4.
[21] *Izvestia,* December 23, 1935.

Women's Liberation and Family Life

Cultural Contradictions and Sex Roles: The Masculine Case*

Mirra Komarovsky

In a rapidly changing society, normative malintegration is commonly assumed to lead to an experience of strain. Earlier research (Komarovsky,
1946) on cultural contradictions and the feminine sex role showed that
women at an eastern college suffered uncertainty and insecurity because the
norms for occupational and academic success conflicted with norms for the
traditional feminine role. A replication (Wallin, 1950) at a western university reported agreement in the questionnaire data, but the interview material led the investigator to conclude that the problem was less important
to the women than the earlier study had suggested. However, Wallin
pointed out that, in his replication, the respondents were oriented to marriage, while the Komarovsky study had included an appreciable number of
women oriented to careers. This finding tended to support the view that
women who were satisfied with the traditional female role would show less
strain when confronted with contrary expectations than women who hoped
to have both a rewarding career and a rewarding marriage.

Men are also confronted with contradictory expectations. For example,
the traditional norm of male intellectual superiority conflicts with a newer
norm of intellectual companionship between the sexes. This research investigated the extent of masculine strain experienced by sixty-two college
males randomly selected from the senior class of an Ivy League male college. The study included a variety of status relationships, but the results reported here deal with intellectual relationships with female friends and attitudes toward working wives.

METHODS

Each of the sixty-two respondents contributed a minimum of three two-
hour interviews and also completed a set of five schedules and two psycho-

* From *American Journal of Sociology*, vol. 78, no. 4 (January, 1973), pp. 873–84.
Copyright © 1973, University of Chicago. Reprinted by permission.
 This research is supported by NIMH grant MH 14618. Associated with the author
in the interviewing were Mr. Wesley Fisher, Mrs. Susanne Riveles, and Dr. Edith
Sanders. Mrs. Ana Silbert analyzed the scored psychological tests and prepared the
sixty-two psychological profiles. The field work was done in 1969–70.

logical tests, the California Personality Inventory and the Gough Adjective Check List. The psychological tests were interpreted by a clinical psychologist. The thirteen-page interview guide probed for data on actual role performance, ideal role expectations and limits of tolerance, personal preferences, perception of role partner's ideal expectations, and relevant attitudes of significant others. Direct questions on strains came only at the end of this sequence. Extensive use was made of quasi-projective tests in the form of brief episodes. The total response rate of the original sample ($N = 79$) was 78 per cent.

INTELLECTUAL RELATIONSHIPS WITH FEMALE FRIENDS

When fewer women attended college, the norm of male intellectual superiority might have had some validation in experience. But today college women are more rigorously selected than men in terms of high school academic performance (*Princeton Alumni Weekly*, 1971). Nevertheless, social norms internalized in early childhood are resistant to change. The first question for this research was "How many men would show insecurity or strain in their intellectual relationships with women when confronted with both bright women and the traditional norm of male superiority?"

The Troubled Third. Of the fifty-three men for whom the data were available (six did not date, three could not be classified reliably), 30 per cent reported that intellectual insecurity or strain with dates was a past or current problem. This number included men who, having experienced stress, sought to avoid it by finding dates who posed no intellectual threat. The following excerpts from interviews illustrate the views of this troubled third:

I enjoy talking to more intelligent girls, but I have no desire for a deep relationship with them. I guess I still believe that the man should be more intelligent.

* * *

I may be a little frightened of a man who is superior to me in some field of knowledge, but if a girl knows more than I do, I resent her.

* * *

Once I was seeing a philosophy major, and we got along quite well. We shared a similar outlook on life, and while we had some divergent opinions, I seemed better able to document my position. One day, by chance, I heard her discussing with another girl an aspect of Kant that just the night before she described to me as obscure and confusing. But now she was explaining it to a girl so clearly and matter-of-factly that I felt sort of hurt and foolish. Perhaps it was immature of me to react this way.

The mode of strain exemplified by these men might be termed "a socially structured scarcity of resources for role fulfillment." Apart from the ever present problem of lack of time and energy, some social roles are intrinsically more difficult to fulfill, given the state of technical skills, the inherent risks, or other scarcities of facilities. The strain of a doctor called upon to treat a disease for which modern medicine has no cure is another case in point.

Selective dating and avoidance of superior women solved the problem for some troubled youths, but this offered no solution for six respondents who yearned for intellectual companionship with women but dreaded the risk of invidious comparisons. The newly emerging norm of intellectual companionship with women creates a mode of strain akin to one Merton and Barber (1963) termed "sociological ambivalence." Universalistic values tend to replace sex-linked desiderata among some male undergraduates who now value originality and intelligence in female as well as in male associates. The conflict arises when, at the same time, the norm of masculine intellectual superiority has not been relinquished, as exemplified in the following case: "I am beginning to feel," remarked one senior about his current girl friend, "that she is not bright enough. She never says anything that would make me sit up and say, 'Ah, that's interesting!' I want a girl who has some defined crystal of her own personality and does not merely echo my thoughts." He recently met a girl who fascinated him with her quick and perceptive intelligence but this new girl made him feel "nervous and humble."

The problem of this youth is to seek the rewards of valued attributes in a woman without arousing in himself feelings of inferiority. It may be argued that in a competitive society this conflict tends to characterize encounters with males as well. Nonetheless, if similar problems exist between two males, the utility curve is shaped distinctively by the norm of male intellectual superiority because mere equality with a woman may be defined as a defeat or a violation of a role prescription.

The Adjusted Majority. The thirty-seven students who said that intellectual relationships with dates were not a problem represented a variety of types. Eleven men felt superior to their female friends. In two or three cases, the relationships were judged equalitarian with strong emphasis on the rewards of intellectual companionship. In contrast, several men—and their dates—had little interest in intellectual concerns. In a few instances the severity of other problems overwhelmed this one. Finally, some eight men were happily adjusted despite the acknowledged intellectual superiority of their women friends. What makes for accommodation to this still deviant pattern?

In seven of the eight cases, the female friend had some weakness which offset her intellectual competence, such as emotional dependence, instability, or a plain appearance, giving the man a compensating advantage. A bright, studious, but relatively unattractive girl may be acceptable to a man who is not as certain of his ability to win a sexually desirable female as he is of his mental ability. In only one of the eight cases the respondent admitted that his steady girl was "more independent and less emotional, actually a little smarter than I. But she doesn't make me feel like a dunce." Her superiority was tolerable because she provided a supportive relationship which he needed and could accept with only mild, if any, emotional discomfort.

Another factor which may account for the finding that 70 per cent of the sample reported no strain is the fact that intellectual qualities are no longer considered unfeminine and that the imperative of male superiority is giving way to the ideal of companionship between equals. This interpretation is supported by responses to two standard questions and by the qualitative materials of the interviews. A schedule testing beliefs on sixteen psychological sex differences asked whether the reasoning ability of men is greater than that of women. Only 34 per cent of the respondents "agreed" or "agreed somewhat," while 20 per cent were "uncertain"; almost half "disagreed" or "disagreed somewhat."

Another question was put to all sixty-two respondents: what are for you personally the three or four most desirable characteristics in a woman (man) who is to be close to you? Of all the traits men desired in a woman, 33 per cent were in the "intellectual" cluster, in contrast with 44 per cent of such traits if the friend were male. The fact that the sex difference was not large seems significant. The major difference in traits desired in male and female intimates (apart from sexual attractiveness and love) was the relative importance of "social amenities and appearance" for women.

The qualitative data amply document the fact that the majority of the respondents ideally hoped to share their intellectual interests with their female as well as their male friends. To be sure, what men occasionally meant by intellectual rapport with women was having an appreciative listener: "I wouldn't go out," declared one senior, "with any girl who wasn't sharp and perceptive enough to catch an intellectual subtlety." But for the majority a "meaningful relationship" with a woman included also a true intellectual interchange and sharing. As one senior put it, "A guy leaving a movie with his date expects her to make a stimulating comment of her own and not merely echo his ideas." Another man wanted a date with whom he could "discuss things that guys talk about," and still a third man exclaimed: "What I love about this girl is that she is on my level, that I can never speak over her head."

It is this ideal of intellectual companionship with women, we suggest, that may explain the relative adjustment of the men in this sphere. As long as the expectation of male superiority persisted, anything near equality on the part of the woman carried the threatening message to the men: "I am not the intellectually *superior* male I am expected to be." But when the ideal of intellectual companionship between equals replaces the expectation of male superiority, the pressure upon the man eases and changes. Now he need only reassure himself that he is not inferior to his date, rather than that he is markedly superior to her. Once the expectation of clear superiority is relinquished, varieties of relationships may be accommodated. Given a generally similar intellectual level, comparative evaluations are blurred by different interests, by complementary strengths and weaknesses, and occasionally by rationalizations. ("she studies harder") and other devices.

One final explanation remains to be considered. May the intellectual self-confidence of the majority be attributed in part to women's readiness to play down their intellectual abilities? That such behavior occurs is attested by a number of studies (Komarovsky, 1946; Wallin, 1950).

When respondents were asked to comment upon a projective story about a girl "playing dumb" on dates, the great majority expressed indignation at such "dishonest," "condescending" behavior. But some three or four found the behavior praiseworthy. As one senior put it, "Her intentions were good; she wanted to make the guy feel important."

Although we did not interview the female friends of our respondents, a few studies indicate that such playing down of intellectual ability by women is less common today than in the 1940s. Questionnaires filled out in 1970 and 1971 by eighty-seven members of two undergraduate classes in sociology at an eastern women's college duplicated earlier studies by Wallin (1950) and Komarovsky (1946). The 1970 class was a course on the family, and the 1971 class probably recruited a relatively high proportion of feminists. Table 1 indicates that the occasional muting of intellectual

TABLE 1
Readiness of Women to Play Down Intellectual Abilities (%)

	Wallin 1950 (N = 163)	Sociology Class 1970* (N = 33)	Advanced Sociology Class 1971* (N = 55)
When on dates how often have you pretended to be intellectually inferior to the man?			
Very often, often, or several times. . . .	32	21	15
Once or twice.	26	36	30
Never	42	43	55
In general, do you have any hesitation about revealing your equality or superiority to men in intellectual competence?			
Have considerable or some hesitation.	35	21	13
Very little hesitation.	39	33	32
None at all.	26	46	55

* Mirra Komarovsky, unpublished study.

competence by women may have played some role in the adjustment of the men, but it would appear to be a minor and decreasing role.

The hypothesis that the emerging ideal of intellectual companionship serves as a buffer against male strain needs a test which includes (as our study did not) some index of intellectual ability as well as indices of norms and of strain. Of the twenty-seven men who disagreed with the proposition that the reasoning ability of men is greater than that of women, only five reported intellectual insecurity with women, whereas of the thirty-four men who believed in masculine superiority or were uncertain, nine experienced strain. Most troubled were the twelve men who were "uncertain"; four of them were insecure with women. Case analyses suggests that the interplay between a man's experience, personality, and beliefs is complex. For example, one traditional man, having confessed feelings of intellectual insecurity on dates, clung all the more tenaciously to the belief in superior male reasoning ability.

Some men took the "liberal" position on sex differences as a matter of principle. Of the nine black students, eight rejected the belief in male superiority, perhaps because they opposed group comparisons in intelligence. Again, in some cases, the direction of the causal relation was the reverse of the one we posited: men who felt in fact intellectually superior were hospitable to the "liberal" ideology. In view of these complexities, our suggestive results as to the positive association between egalitarian norms and the absence of strain remain to be tested in larger samples.

ATTITUDES TOWARD FUTURE WIVES' OCCUPATIONAL ROLES

The ethos on the campus of this study clearly demanded that men pay at least lip service to liberal attitudes toward working wives. If the initial responses to structured questions were accepted as final, the majority would have been described as quite feminist in ideology. But further probing revealed qualifications which occasionally almost negated the original response. For example, an affirmative answer to a proposition, "It is appropriate for a mother of a preschool child to take a full-time job," was, upon further questioning, conditioned by such restrictions as "provided, of course, that the home was run smoothly, the children did not suffer, and the wife's job did not interfere with her husband's career." The interview provided an opportunity to get an assessment of normative expectations, ideal and operative, as well as of actual preferences. The classification of attitudes to be presented in this report is based on the total interview. Preferences reported here assume that a wife's paycheck will not be an economic necessity. The overwhelming majority were confident that their own earnings would be adequate to support the family. Throughout the discussion of working, only two or three men mentioned the temptation of a second paycheck.

Four types of response to the question of wives' working may be identified. The "traditionalists," 24 per cent of the men, said outright that they intended to marry women who would find sufficient fulfillment in domestic, civic, and cultural pursuits without ever seeking outside jobs. "Pseudofeminists," 16 per cent of the men, favored having their wives work, at least when the question was at a high level of abstraction, but their approval was hedged with qualifications that no woman could meet.

The third and dominant response included almost half (48 per cent) of the respondents. These men took a "modified traditionalist" position which favored a sequential pattern: work, withdrawal from work for child rearing, and eventual return to work. They varied as to the timing of these stages and as to the aid they were prepared to give their wives with domestic and child-rearing functions. The majority saw no substitute for the mother during her child's preschool years. Even the mother of schoolage children, were she to work, should preferably be at home when the children return from school. Though they were willing to aid their wives in varying degrees, they frequently excluded specific tasks, for instance, "not the laundry," "not the cleaning," "not the diapers," and so on. Many hoped that they would be "able to assist" their wives by hiring maids. The greater the importance of the wife's work, the more willing they were to help her. (One senior, however, would help only if his wife's work were "peripheral," that is, not as important to her as her home.)

The last, the "feminist" type, was the smallest, only 7 per cent of the total. These men were willing to modify their own roles significantly to facilitate their future wives' careers. Some recommended a symmetrical allocation of tasks—"as long as it is not a complete reversal of roles." In the remaining 5 per cent of the cases, marriage was so remote that the respondents were reluctant to venture any views on this matter.

The foregoing summary of types of male attitude toward working wives fails to reveal the tangled web of contradictory values and sentiments associated with these attitudes. We shall presently illustrate a variety of inconsistencies. But underlying them is one basic problem. The ideological support for the belief in sharp sex role differentiation in marriage has weakened, but the belief itself has not been relinquished. Increasing skepticism about the innate character of psychological sex differences and some convergence in the ideas of masculinity and femininity (see McKee and Sheriffs, 1957, 1959) have created a strain toward consistency. The more similar the perceptions of male and female personalities (see Kammeyer, 1964), the more universalistic must be the principles of evaluation applied to both sexes. "If you could make three changes in the personality of the girl friend who is currently closest to you, what would they be?" we asked the seniors. Universalistic values were reflected in the following, as in many other responses: "I would like her to be able to set a goal for herself and strive to achieve it. I don't like to see people slacking off." Earlier cross-sex association in childhood and early adolescence (see Udry, 1966) has raised male expectation of enjoying an emotional and intellectual companionship with women. These expectations, however, coexist with the deeply rooted norm that the husband should be the superior achiever in the occupational world and the wife, the primary child rearer. One manifestation of this basic dilemma is the familiar conflict between a value and a preference. "It is only fair," declared one senior, "to let a woman do her own thing, if she wants a career. Personally, though, I would want my wife at home."

More interesting are the ambivalent attitudes manifested toward both the full-time homemaker and the career wife. The image of each contained both attractive and repellent traits. Deprecating remarks about housewifery were not uncommon, even among men with traditional views of women's roles. A conservative senior declared, "A woman who works is more interesting than a housewife." "If I were a woman," remarked another senior, "I would want a career. It must be boring sitting around the house doing the same thing day in, day out. I don't have much respect for the type of woman whom I see doing the detergent commercials on TV."

But the low esteem attached by some of the men to full-time homemaking coexisted with other sentiments and convictions which required just such a pattern for one's wife. For example, asked about the disadvantages of being a woman, one senior replied, "Life ends at forty. The woman has raised her children and all that remains is garden clubs and that sort of thing—unless, of course, she has a profession." In another part of the interview, this young man explained that he enjoyed shyness in a girl and detested aggressive and ambitious women. He could never be attracted to a career woman. It is no exaggeration to conclude that this man could not countenance in a woman who was to be his wife the qualities that he himself felt were necessary for a fulfilling middle age.

A similar mode of contradiction, incidentally, was also disclosed by some seniors with regard to women's majors in college. "There are no 'unfeminine' majors," declared one senior. "I admire a girl who is premed or prelaw." But the universalistic yardstick which led this senior to sanction and admire professional goals for women did not extend to the means for their attainment, as he unwittingly revealed in another part of the interview. Questioned about examples of "unfeminine" behavior, this senior answered, "Excessive grade consciousness." If a premed man, anxious about admission to a good medical school, should go to see a professor about a C in chemistry, this senior would understand although he would disapprove of such preoccupation with grades. But in a woman premed he would find such behavior "positively obnoxious."

If the image of the full-time homemaker contained some alienating features, the main threat of a career wife was that of occupational rivalry, as illustrated in the following excerpt from the interviews. A senior speaks:

> I believe that it is good for mothers to return to full-time work when the children are grown, provided the work is important and worthwhile. Otherwise, housewives get hung up with tranquilizers, because they have no outlet for their abilities. . . . Of course, it may be difficult if a wife becomes successful in her own right. A woman should want her husband's success more than he should want hers. Her work shouldn't interfere with or hurt his career in any way. He should not sacrifice his career to hers. For example, if he is transferred, his wife should follow—and not vice versa.

In sum, work for married women with grown children is approved by this young man, provided that the occupation is of some importance. But such an occupation is precisely one which carries a threat to the husband's pride.

The expectation that the husband should be the superior achiever appears still to be deeply rooted. Even equality in achievement of husband

and wife is interpreted as a defeat for the man. The prospect of occupational rivalry with one's wife seems intolerable to contemplate. "My girl friend often beats me in tennis," explained one senior. "Now, losing the game doesn't worry me. It in no way reduces my manhood. But being in a lower position than a woman in a job would hurt my self-esteem."

Another student, having declared his full support for equal opportunities for women in the occupational world, added a qualification: "A woman should not be in a position of firing an employee. It is an unpleasant thing to do. Besides, it is unfair to the man who is to be fired. He may be a very poor employee, but he is still a human being and it may be just compounding his unhappiness to be fired by a woman."

In sum, the right of an able woman to a career of her choice, the admiration for women who measure up in terms of the dominant values of our society, the lure but also the threat that such women present, the low status attached to housewifery but the conviction that there is no substitute for the mother's care of young children, the deeply internalized norm of male occupational superiority pitted against the principle of equal opportunity irrespective of sex—these are some of the revealed inconsistencies.

Such ambivalences on the part of college men are bound to exacerbate role conflicts in women. The latter must sense that even the men who pay lip service to the creativity of child rearing and domesticity reserve their admiration (if occasionally tinged with ambivalence) for women achievers who measure up in terms of the dominant values of our society. It is becoming increasingly difficult to maintain a system of values for women only (Komarovsky, 1953).

Nevertheless, to infer from this account of male inconsistencies that this is an area of great stress for them would be a mistake. It is not. By and large, the respondents assumed that the women's "career and marriage" issue was solved by the sequential pattern of withdrawal and return to work. If this doomed women to second-class citizenship in the occupational world, the outcome was consistent with the conviction that the husband should be the superior achiever.

Men who momentarily worried about the fate of able women found moral anchorage in their conviction that today no satisfactory alternative to the mother's care of young children can be found. Many respondents expressed their willingness to help with child care and household duties. Similarly, many hoped to spend more time with their own children than their fathers had spent with them. But such domestic participation was defined as assistance to the wife who was to carry the major responsibility. Only two or three of the men approved a symmetrical, rather than a complementary, allocation of domestic and occupational roles. An articulate senior sums up the dominant view:

> I would not want to marry a woman whose only goal is to become a housewife. This type of women would not have enough bounce and zest in her. I don't think a girl has much imagination if she just wants to settle down and raise a family from the very beginning. Moreover, I

want an independent girl, one who has her own interests and does not always have to depend on me for stimulation and diversion. However, when we both agree to have children, my wife must be the one to raise them. She'll have to forfeit her freedom for the children. I believe that, when a woman wants a child, she must also accept the full responsibility of child care.

When he was asked why it was necessarily the woman who had to be fully responsible for the children, he replied:

Biology makes equality impossible. Besides, the person I'll marry will want the child and will want to care for the child. Ideally, I would hope I'm not forcing her to assume responsibility for raising the children. I would hope that this is her desire and that it is the happiest thing she can do. After we have children, it will be her career that will end, while mine will support us. I believe that women should have equal opportunities in business and the professions, but I still insist that a woman who is a mother should devote herself entirely to her children.

The low emotional salience of the issue of working wives may also be attributed to another factor. The female partners of our respondents, at this particular stage of life, did not, with a few exceptions, force the men to confront their inconsistencies. Apparently enough women will freely make the traditional-for-women adjustments—whether scaling down their own ambitions or in other ways acknowledging the prior claims of the man's career. This judgment is supported by the results of two studies of female undergraduates done on the same campus in 1943 and 1971 (Table 2).

TABLE 2

College Women's Attitudes Toward Work and Family Patterns (%)

	Random Sample of Sophomore Class at Women's Liberal Arts College 1943 ($N = 78$)	Class in Introductory Sociology. Same College 1971 ($N = 44$)
Assume that you will marry and that your husband will make enough money so that you will not have to work unless you want to. Under these circumstances, would you prefer:		
1. Not to work at all, or stop after childbirth and decide later whether to go back.	50	18
2. To quit working after the birth of a child but definitely go back to work.	30	62
3. To continue working with a minimum of interruption for childbearing.	20	20

SOURCE.—Mirra Komarovsky, unpublished studies.

The big shift in postcollege preferences since 1943 was in the decline of women undergraduates who opted for full-time homemaking and volunteer activities. In 1971, the majority chose the sequential pattern, involving withdrawal from employment for child rearing. The proportion of committed career women who hope to return to work soon after childbirth has remained constant among freshmen and sophomores.

If women's attitudes have not changed more radically in the past thirty years, it is no doubt because society has failed to provide effective supports for the woman who wishes to integrate family life, parenthood, and work on much the same terms as men. Such an option will not become available as long as the care of young children is regarded as the responsibility solely of the mother. In the absence of adequate child-care centers, an acceptance of a symmetrical division of domestic and work responsibilities, or other facilitating social arrangements, the attitudes of the majority of undergraduates reflect their decision to make some kind of workable adjustment to the status quo, if not a heroic struggle to change it.

SUMMARY

Role conflicts in women have been amply documented in numerous studies. The problem underlying this study was to ascertain whether recent social changes and consequent malintegration with regard to sex roles have created stressful repercussions for men as well as for women. In a randomly selected sample of sixty-two male seniors in an eastern Ivy League college, nearly one-third experienced some anxiety over their perceived failure to live up to the norm of masculine intellectual superiority. This stressful minority suffered from two modes of role strain: scarcity of resources for role performance and ambivalence. The absence of strain in the majority may be explained by a changed role definition. Specifically, the normative expectation of male intellectual superiority appears to be giving way on the campus of our study to the ideal of intellectual companionship between equals. Attitudes toward working wives abounded in ambivalences and inconsistencies. The ideological supports for the traditional sex role differentiation in marriage are weakening, but the emotional allegiance to the modified traditional pattern is still strong. These inconsistencies did not generate a high degree of stress, partly, no doubt, because future roles do not require an immediate realistic confrontation. In addition, there is no gainsaying the conclusion that human beings can tolerate a high degree of inconsistency as long as it does not conflict with their self-interest.

REFERENCES

KAMMEYER, KENNETH. 1964. "The Feminine Role: An Analysis of Attitude Consistency." *Journal of Marriage and the Family* 26 (August): 295–305.
KOMAROVSKY, MIRRA. 1946. "Cultural Contradictions and Sex Roles." *American Journal of Sociology* 52 (November): 182–89.

————. 1953. *Women in the Modern World, Their Education and Their Dilemmas.* Boston: Little, Brown.

McKee, John P., and Alex C. Sherriffs. 1957. "The Differential Evaluation of Males and Females." *Journal of Personality* 25 (March): 356–63.

————. 1959. "Men's and Women's Beliefs, Ideals, and Self-Concepts." *American Journal of Sociology* 64 (4): 356–63.

Merton, Robert K., and Elinor Barber. 1963. "Sociological Ambivalence." In *Sociological Theory, Values and Socio-cultural Change,* edited by E. A. Tiryakian. Glencoe, Ill.: Free Press.

Princeton Alumni Weekly, February 23, 1971, p. 7.

Udry, J. Richard. 1966. *The Social Context of Marriage.* Philadelphia: Lippincott.

Wallin, Paul. 1950. "Cultural Contradictions and Sex Roles: A Repeat Study." *American Sociological Review* 15 (April): 288–93.

7. SUGGESTIONS FOR FURTHER READING

Bartell, Gilbert. *Group Sex* (New York: Peter H. Wyden, 1971).*

Bell, N. W., and E. Vogel (eds.). *A Modern Introduction to the Family* (Glencoe, Ill.: The Free Press, 1960).

Bell, Robert. *Premarital Sex in a Changing Society* (Englewood Cliffs, N.J.: Prentice-Hall, 1966).*

Billingsley, Andrew. *Black Families in White America* (Englewood Cliffs, N.J.: Prentice-Hall, 1968).*

Christensen, Harold (ed.). *Handbook of Marriage and the Family* (Chicago: Rand-McNally, 1964).

Farber, Bernard. *Family and Kinship in Modern Society* (Glenview, Ill.: Scott Foresman, 1973).*

Ford, C. S., and F. A. Beach. *Patterns of Sexual Behavior* (New York: Harper, 1951).*

Friedan, Betty. *The Feminine Mystique* (New York: Norton, 1963).*

Geiger, Kent. *The Family in Soviet Russia* (Cambridge, Mass.: Harvard University Press, 1968).

Goode, William J. *Women in Divorce* (Glencoe, Ill.: The Free Press, 1956).*

————. *World Revolution and Family Patterns* (New York: The Free Press, 1968).*

Hunt, Morton. *The World of the Formerly Married* (New York: McGraw-Hill, 1966).*

Komarovsky, Mirra. *Blue-Collar Marriage* (New York: Random House, 1962).*

Lewis, Oscar. *Five Families* (New York: John Wiley & Sons, 1962).*

Nye, I., and L. Hoffman. *The Employed Mother in America* (Chicago: Rand-McNally, 1963).

Rainwater, Lee. *And the Poor Get Children* (Chicago: Quadrangle Books, 1960).*

Skolnick, A., and J. Skolnick (eds.). *Family in Transition* (Boston: Little, Brown, 1971).*

———— (eds.). *Intimacy, Family and Society* (Boston: Little, Brown, 1974).*

Smith, J., and L. Smith (eds.). *Beyond Monogamy: Recent Studies of Sexual Alternatives in Marriage* (Baltimore: Johns Hopkins University Press, 1974).*

Spiro, Melford. *Kibbutz: Venture in Utopia* (Cambridge, Mass.: Harvard University Press, 1956).*

STEPHENS, WILLIAM. *The Family in Cross Cultural Perspective* (New York: Holt, Rinehart & Winston, 1963).*

WESTOFF, L., and C. WESTOFF. *From Now to Zero* (Boston: Little, Brown, 1968).*

WINCH, ROBERT. *The Modern Family,* 3rd ed. (New York: Holt, Rinehart & Winston, 1971).

YOUNG, M., and P. WILLMOTT. *Family and Kinship in East London* (Glencoe, Ill.: The Free Press, 1957).*

* *Available in paperback.*

8. Deviance

INTRODUCTION

Deviance may be defined as behavior that departs from societal expectations. It is viewed by the members of the social body with varying degrees of moral disapproval, depending on the nature of the act, the characteristics of the actor, and the values of the particular society. For example, our own society deviance embraces a broad range of phenomena, including mental illness, minority-group membership, political nonconformity, physical handicaps, criminal behavior, sexual aberrations, and drug use.

What is considered deviant in one society may be perfectly acceptable, if not socially desired, in another. For example, in our own society mate swapping, or "swinging," as it most recently has been called, is generally regarded as morally offensive or "perverse." However, among numerous Eskimo peoples, wife sharing does not signify deviance; it is an expression of hospitality and friendship. Deviance is a matter of social definition. Its content tends to reflect the values that are endorsed in a given society.

Because every society has a number of ideal values that are not generally achieved and prescriptions governing conduct that are logically contradictory, deviance is inevitable and universal. The renowned French sociologist Émile Durkheim argued that even a society of saints would detect deviance among its members; those whose behavior was somewhat divergent from the rest would be viewed with moral disapproval.

Durkheim argued that a certain amount of deviant behavior was not only inevitable but socially functional and indicative of a healthy society. He was one of the first to recognize that deviance may introduce needed social change; the deviant pattern may eventually become the socially accepted pattern, and the deviant may thus be transformed into an innovator or cultural hero. Deviance also helps to clarify and define the social rules shared within a group. Until a rule is broken, many members may be unaware of its existence or its importance to group life. Deviance may unify a group by bringing the members together in disapproval of the deviant. Punishment of the deviant may encourage other members of the society to abide by the social rules. However, when deviance increases dramatically, or is widely pervasive, the most likely result is social disorganization.

The origins of deviance are many and varied. As an introduction to this important question, we shall examine three leading sociological viewpoints. According to Robert Merton, every society has a set of culturally prescribed goals to which its members aspire as well as a set of socially approved means of obtaining or achieving these goals. When the goals and the means of realizing them are in correspondence, normal conforming behavior is encouraged. When the goals are emphasized far more than the means, then the regulatory agencies lose their credibility and authority, a moral breakdown (anomie) results, and deviance is engendered. This experience usually does not affect the whole social body; it may prevail for a sizable social segment, such as a social class or a minority group.

As an example of this imbalance in America, Merton observes that the gospel of financial success is emphasized to a great degree; yet, for many Americans, and for a great number of the American underclasses in particular, the means of obtaining success—getting an education, finding a good job, and advancing through a series of positions—are considerably few. This tends to produce anomie and deviance, particularly among those social segments that are most deprived.

One adaptation to the imbalance of socially approved goals and means is *innovation*—accepting the goals of society and rejecting the approved means of achieving them; for example, a bank teller may embezzle funds to buy a house in the suburbs. Another response may be *ritualism*—following the rules but losing sight of the goals; as exemplified by the overzealous clerk at the motor-vehicle bureau who sends an applicant back to the end of the queue—creating office chaos—because he failed to indicate his middle initial on one of the forms. Another response is *retreatism*—rejecting both goals and means; the skid-row alcoholic typifies this adaptation. A fourth possibility is *rebellion*—rejecting both ends and means and substituting new ones in their place; this is typified in the behavior of the revolutionary.

Edwin Sutherland's differential-association theory represents another perspective on deviant behavior. Sutherland argued that people are exposed to a variety of social influences, differing in values and attitudes and in the socializing techniques used. The groups in society with which one has the most extensive association have the greatest effect on one's personality and behavior patterns. According to this theory, an individual becomes deviant by being exposed to deviant patterns and having relatively little exposure to nondeviant patterns. Moreover, the individual with a preponderance of deviant or criminal role models is likely to internalize ideas favorable to deviance and to act in a deviant way. Essentially, deviance is learned in the same way conventional behavior patterns are acquired.

Many conceptions of deviance place the primary causative emphasis at least indirectly on the deviant person. By contrast, in labeling theory the social-sanctioning process is seen as the most important contributor to deviance. For Howard Becker, a leading proponent of labeling theory, a deviant act—or even a series of deviant acts—does not make a person deviant; to acquire that status, one's behavior must be perceived, defined, and labeled as deviant by society. Being publicly labeled a deviant (being arrested, reputed to be a "queer," etc.) is probably the most significant step in developing what Becker calls a "deviant career"—that is, adopting deviance as a way of life. A person who commits an improper act and is caught at it is placed in a new status and treated accordingly. The deviant is stigmatized; his freedom is curtailed; and opportunities available to the average citizen are now denied him. He must, therefore, develop illegitimate practices, thus moving toward increasing deviance. For example, lacking conventional employment prospects, the ex-convict returns to theft. Or the drug experimenter, once labeled an addict and rejected by his family and friends, is led to seek acceptance among the drug subculture. The final step in the development of a deviant career is movement into an organized deviant group. This has a powerful impact on the deviant's self-conception. As the members of a deviant group share an *esprit de corps,* they justify and rationalize their position with respect to the larger, nondeviant culture. The group ideology serves to insulate and protect them and makes the rewards of their deviant activities personally meaningful and gratifying. Membership in the deviant group also mobilizes the experiences and skills of the members, so that the deviant activity may be carried on with a minimum of trouble.

The notion of a deviant subculture is illustrated in Weinberg's essay on the nudist camp, in Chapter 2, "Culture." In such subculture, the deviant act is socially accepted and regarded as desirable; hence, in this context, it is no longer deviant. Weinberg's finding that single males tend to be rejected by nudist groups suggests, further, that the basis of social acceptance and ranking in the deviant subculture parallels in an inverted order the system found in the conventional world.

Another aspect of Becker's theory concerns the initiation of the labeling or social-sanctioning process. Enforcement of social rules is an enterprising act. Labeling requires "moral entrepreneurs," people who "blow the whistle" or call attention to the deviation. They may be "rule creators" (i.e., crusading reformers) or "rule enforcers" (i.e., the police and regulatory agencies). According to Becker, people may blow the whistle, making enforcement necessary, when they see some personal advantage in doing so. Within the moral community, there may be several competing groups, some of which want enforcement and others that do not. Enforcement is likely to be affected by the relative power of the groups opting for and against it, by their abilities to mobilize coordinate groups in their support, and by their access to the means of communication to facilitate a favorable climate of opinion.

D. L. Rosenhan's "Being Sane in Insane Places" clearly illustrates the process of labeling. On the basis of erroneous information provided by eight sane pseudopatients, psychiatrically stigmatizing labels were applied to them and were sustained in all cases despite ample behavioral evidence to the contrary. We see that once labels are assigned to people they exert a powerful influence on life chances, encouraging those who are labeled "deviant" actually to become deviant. The sociological literature is replete with evidence of how labeling influences deviance, particularly in the area of juvenile delinquency.[1]

Rosenhan's findings go beyond demonstrating the central precepts of labeling theory; his analysis raises serious questions about the adequacy of mental health care in the United States. The pseudopatient observers found that the staff generally tended to shun the patient population. They noted that the higher one's rank in the mental health staff hierarchy, the less contact he tended to have with patients. Rosenhan maintains that such avoidance tends to engender depersonalization among patients, or what amounts to the antithesis of good mental health care. Upon the publication of Rosenhan's findings an outpouring of rebuke appeared from the psychiatric community.[2] Despite the many arguments leveled against this study, Rosenhan's critics have yet to offer evidence that contradicts his major findings.

General theories are especially valuable for identifying common causal features in the multifarious types of deviant behavior. However, our knowledge can be greatly extended by focusing in depth on particular deviant patterns. With this proviso in mind, let us briefly explore two deviant activities, homosexuality and suicide.

In all modern industrial societies, homosexual behavior (relations with members of one's own sex) is viewed as morally disreputable, and in many places it is treated as a crime. Because of the highly privatized conception of sexual behavior in Western society, systematic sociological research has been most difficult. Consequently, to date, estimates of the incidence, prevalence, and increase of homosexuality are based, for the most part, on inadequate and unrepresentative data. Neverthe-

---

[1] Irving Piliavan and Scott Briar, "Police Encounters with Juveniles," *American Journal of Sociology*, vol. 70 (September, 1964), 206–14. Travis Hirschi, *Causes of Delinquency* (Berkeley: University of California Press, 1969).

[2] *Science*, vol. 180 (April 27, 1973), 356–69.

less, the best studies available[3] have found that about 5 per cent of American and British males are career homosexuals, and about a third have at least one homosexual experience some time between adolescence and old age. For women, the incidence of homosexuality is approximately half that for males. These differences between the sexes may be partly due to the widely shared belief in the West that males possess substantially greater interest in sex.

"Cruising" probably represents the major locus of male homosexual activity in urban areas. Homosexual contacts are frequently made around the shadowy places of public parks, public toilets, "gay bars," and the downtown city streets. The limited, yet steadily growing, body of research on the subject suggests that most male homosexual relationships are short-lived, and that there is considerable commercialism associated with homosexuality (homosexual prostitution).

Criminologist Laud Humphreys, in an article on "New Styles of Homosexual Manliness,"[4] suggests that there appears to be a trend away from the traditional cruising for pickups as the major activity in the homosexual market. Humphreys sees a polarization taking place between virilization of homosexuality, on the one hand, and impersonal homosexuality, on the other. He claims these changes may be caused by increasing crime in the streets, leaving the homosexual more vulnerable to assault and robbery; by the growing scarcity of leisure time; and by the development of a new morality among the youth counterculture.

Virilization refers to the increasingly masculine image of the "gay" scene. More male homosexuals evince traditional male characteristics in their dress, appearance, and manner. Homosexuality appears to be pursued increasingly along with heterosexual activities, accompanied by the advent of the "swinger" set and the orgy set. There is now more frank and open involvement in the cause of civil rights for homosexuals, as embodied in the growing and increasingly organized homophile movement.

At the same time, Humphreys feels that impersonal sex in public places is on the increase, furnishing an anonymous, short-term, immediate mode of homosexual gratification. Through a combination of ingenious and resourceful research methods, Humphreys was able to illuminate this behavior, providing us with a detailed, systematic understanding of its characteristics and its social bases. His work breaks new ground in delineating some of the identity problems faced by the career homosexual and those who are involved in homosexual activity but maintain a heterosexual style of life.

3 A. Kinsey *et al.*, *Sexual Behavior in the Human Male* (Philadelphia: W. B. Saunders, 1948); A. Kinsey *et al.*, *Sexual Behavior in the Human Female* (Philadelphia: W. B. Saunders, 1953); and Bryan Magee, *One in Twenty* (New York: Stein and Day, 1966).
4 *Trans-action*, vol. 8, nos. 5 and 6 (March–April, 1971), 38–46.

Ever since the publication of Émile Durkheim's *Suicide* in 1897, which illuminated for the first time the sociological factors involved in suicide, sociologists have exhibited continuing interest in this deviant behavior. In his research, which compared fluctuations in the rates of suicide throughout the provinces of France, Durkheim identified three types of suicide—altruistic, egoistic, and anomic suicide.

Altruistic suicide represents a willful act performed in behalf of others. Examples are the deliberate crashes of the Japanese Kamikaze pilots during World War II and the self-immolations of the Vietnamese Buddhist priests protesting the war. Altruistic suicide is the predominant type in folk societies. Among some Eskimo groups, old people who can no longer hunt or work kill themselves to help the group survive. In some folk societies, the death of a spouse customarily prompts an individual to commit suicide as part of religious observance. In modern industrial societies, some of the elderly and incurably ill may end their lives so as not to be a burden to others.

Egoistic suicide represents the polar opposite of the altruistic type; it is a form of suicide that results from a diminished attachment to others and is most pervasive in modern industrial societies. Durkheim identified three dimensions of estrangement from society—family, religious, and political. He noted the relatively high likelihood of suicide among single people and those belonging to small families. Protestants have higher rates of suicide than Catholics or Jews. Suicide is higher in peacetime than during periods of war, when people are united against a common enemy and need to solve common problems.

Anomic suicide results from a disruption in the group-affiliational networks of the individual, which presents him with conflicting and competing norms, thrusting him into a mood of profound moral ambiguity and confusion. Durkheim notes that anomic suicide is exemplified in rapid and abrupt social change, such as during periods of economic catastrophe or marked spurts of prosperity, and is more likely among the divorced than the married.

Most of the Durkheim's hypotheses have been supported by contemporary suicide research. Some research[5] indicates a very problematic disparity between those who actually commit suicide and those who receive care from suicide-prevention agencies; those who succeed in killing themselves have not generally received prior treatment from prevention services.

This disparity may be caused in part by the different motives and methods of "successful" suicides and those "attempting" suicide. It may also reflect discrimination against the aged, who, Maris finds, are overrepresented among successful suicides and who receive relatively few educational, rehabilitative, or economic benefits from social ser-

[5] Ronald W. Maris, "The Sociology of Suicide Prevention: Policy Implications of Differences Between Suicidal Patients and Completed Suicides," *Social Problems*, vol. 17, no. 1 (Summer, 1969), 132–49.

vice agencies.[6] Possibly, also, the precarious economic status and prestige of many social-service agencies promote a preoccupation with organizational maintenance, diverting them from pursuing their stated objectives. Accurate social-science knowledge and adequate public support are essential for effective remedial social action in suicide prevention and other deviant-treatment programs or social-problem reform.

Homosexuality

Tearoom Trade: Impersonal Sex in Public Places[*]

Laud Humphreys

At shortly after five o'clock on a weekday evening, four men enter a public restroom in the city park. One wears a well-tailored business suit; another wears tennis shoes, shorts, and teeshirt; the third man is still clad in the khaki uniform of his filling station; the last, a salesman, has loosened his tie and left his sports coat in the car. What has caused these men to leave the company of other homeward-bound commuters on the freeway? What common interest brings these men, with their divergent background, to this public facility?

They have come here not for the obvious reason but in a search for "instant sex." Many men—married and unmarried, those with heterosexual identities and those whose self-image is a homosexual one—seek such impersonal sex, shunning involvement, desiring kicks without commitment. Whatever reasons—social, physiological, or psychological—might be postulated for this search, the phenomenon of impersonal sex persists as a widespread but rarely studied form of human interaction.

There are several settings for this type of deviant activity—the balconies of movie theaters, automobiles, behind bushes—but few offer the advantages for these men that public restrooms provide. "Tearooms," as these facilities are called in the language of the homosexual subculture, have several characteristics that make them attractive as locales for sexual encounters without involvement.

[6] Robert Scott, "Selecting Clients for Welfare Agencies," *Social Problems,* XIV, no. 3 (Winter, 1967), 248–57.

[*] From Laud Humphries, *Tearoom Trade* (Chicago: Aldine Publishing Company, 1970); copyright © 1970 by R. A. Laud Humphreys. Reprinted by permission of Aldine-Atherton, Inc.

Like most other words in the homosexual vocabulary, the origin of *tearoom* is unknown. British slang has used "tea" to denote "urine." Another British usage is as a verb, meaning "to engage with, encounter, go in against." According to its most precise meaning in the argot, the only "true" tearoom is one that gains a reputation as a place where homosexual encounters occur. Presumably, any restroom could qualify for this distinction, but comparatively few are singled out at any one time. For instance, I have researched a metropolitan area with more than 90 public toilets in its parks, only 20 of which are in regular use as locales for sexual games. Restrooms thus designated join the company of automobiles and bathhouses as places for deviant sexual activity, second only to private bedrooms in popularity. During certain seasons of the year—roughly, that period from April through October that Midwestern homosexuals call "the hunting season"— tearooms may surpass any other locale of homoerotic enterprise in volume of activity.

Public restrooms are chosen by those who want homoerotic activity without commitment for a number of reasons. They are accessible, easily recognized by the initiate, and provide little public visibility. Tearooms thus offer the advantages of both public and private settings. They are available and recognizable enough to attract a large volume of potential sexual partners, providing an opportunity for rapid action with a variety of men. When added to the relative privacy of these settings, such features enhance the impersonality of the sheltered interaction.

In the first place, tearooms are easily accessible to the male population. They may be located in any sort of public gathering place—department stores, bus stations, libraries, hotels, YMCA's, or courthouses. In keeping with the drive-in craze of American society, however, the more popular facilities are those readily accessible to the roadways. The restrooms of public parks and beaches—and, more recently, the rest stops set at programmed intervals along superhighways—are now attracting the clientele that, in a more pedestrian age, frequented great buildings of the inner cities. My research is focused on the activity that takes place in the restrooms of public parks, not only because (with some seasonal variation) they provide the most action but also because of other factors that make them suitable for sociological study.

There is a great deal of difference in the volumes of homosexual activity that these accommodations shelter. In some, one might wait for months before observing a deviant act (unless solitary masturbation is considered deviant). In others, the volume approaches orgiastic dimensions. One summer afternoon, for instance, I witnessed twenty acts of fellatio in the course of an hour while waiting out a thunderstorm in a tearoom. For one who wishes to participate in (or study) such activity, the primary consideration is finding where the action is.

Occasionally, tips about the more active places may be gained from unexpected sources. Early in my research, I was approached by a man (whom I later surmised to be a park patrolman in plain clothes) while waiting at the window of a tearoom for some patrons to arrive. After finishing his business at the urinal and exchanging some remarks about the weather (it had been raining), the man came abruptly to the point: "Look, fellow, if you're looking for sex, this isn't the place. We're clamping down on this park because of trouble with the niggers. Try the john at the northeast corner of [Reagan] Park. You'll find plenty of action there." He was right. Some of my best observations were made at the spot he recommended. In most cases, however, I could only enter, wait, and watch—a method that was costly in both time and gasoline. After surveying a couple of dozen such rooms in this way, however, I became able to identify the more popular tearooms by observing certain physical evidence, the most obvious of which is the location of the facility. During the warm seasons, those restrooms that are isolated from other park facilities, such as administration buildings, shops, tennis courts, playgrounds and picnic areas, are the more popular for deviant activity. The most active tearooms studied were all isolated from recreational areas, cut off by drives or lakes from baseball diamonds and picnic tables.

I have chosen the term "purlieu" (with its ancient meaning of land severed from a royal forest by perambulation) to describe the immediate environs best suited to the tearoom trade. Drives and walks that separate a public toilet from the rest of the park are almost certain guides to deviant sex. The ideal setting for homosexual activity is a tearoom situated on an island of grass, with roads close by on every side. The getaway car is just a few steps away; children are not apt to wander over from the playground; no one can surprise the participants by walking in from the woods or from over a hill; it is not likely that straight people will stop there. According to my observations, the women's side of these buildings is seldom used at all.

WHAT THEY WANT, WHEN THEY WANT IT

The availability of facilities they can recognize attracts a great number of men who wish, for whatever reason, to engage in impersonal homoerotic activity. Simple observation is enough to guide these participants, the researcher, and, perhaps, the police to active tearooms. It is much more difficult to make an accurate appraisal of the proportion of the male population who engage in such activity over a representative length of time. Even with good sampling procedures, a large staff of assistants would be needed to make the observations necessary for an adequate census of this mobile population. All that may be said with some degree of certainty is that the percentage of the male population who participate in tearoom sex in the United States is somewhat less than the 16 per cent of the adult white male population Kinsey found to have "at least as much of the homosexual as the heterosexual in their histories."

Participants assure me that it is not uncommon in tearooms for one man to fellate as many as ten others in a day. I have personally watched a fellator take on three men in succession in a half hour of observation. One respondent, who has cooperated with the researcher in a number of taped interviews, claims to average three men each day during the busy season.

I have seen some waiting their turn for this type of service. Leaving one such scene on a warm September Saturday, I remarked to a man who left close behind me: "Kind of crowded in there, isn't it?" "Hell, yes," he answered. "It's getting so you have to take a number and wait in line in these places!"

There are many who frequent the same facility repeatedly. Men will come to be known as regular, even daily, participants, stopping off at the same tearoom on the way to or from work. One physician in his late fifties was so punctual in his appearance at a particular restroom that I began to look forward to our daily chats. This robust, affable respondent said he had stopped at this tearoom every evening of the week (except Wednesday, his day off) for years "for a blow job." Another respondent, a salesman whose schedule is flexible, may "make the scene" more than once a day—usually at his favorite men's room. At the time of our interview, this man claimed to have had four orgasms in the past twenty-four hours.

According to the participants I have interviewed, those who are looking for impersonal sex in tearooms are relatively certain of finding the sort of partner they want—

> You go into the tearoom. You can pick up some really nice things in there. Again, it is a matter of sex real quick; and, if you like this kind, fine—you've got it. You get one and he is done; and, before long, you've got another one.

—and when they want it:

> Well, I go there; and you can always find someone to suck your cock, morning, noon, or night. I know lots of guys who stop by there on their way to work—and all during the day.

It is this sort of volume and variety that keeps the tearooms viable as market places of the one-night-stand variety.

Of the bar crowd in gay (homosexual) society, only a small percentage would be found in park restrooms. But this more overt, gay bar clientele constitutes a minor part of those in any American city who follow a predominantly homosexual pattern. The so-called closet queens and other types of covert deviants make up the vast majority of those who engage in homosexual acts—and these are the persons most attracted to tearoom encounters.

Tearooms are popular, not because they serve as gathering places for homosexuals, but because they attract a variety of men, a *minority* of whom are active in the homosexual subculture and a large group of whom have no homosexual self-identity. For various reasons, they do not want to be seen with those who might be identified as such or to become involved with them on a "social" basis.

SHELTERING SILENCE

There is another aspect of the tearoom encounter that is crucial. I refer to the silence of the interaction.

Throughout most homosexual encounters in public restrooms, nothing is spoken. One may spend many hours in these buildings and witness dozens of sexual acts without hearing a word. Of 50 encounters on which I made extensive notes, only in 15 was any word spoken. Two were encounters in which I sought to ease the strain of legitimizing myself as lookout by saying, "You go ahead—I'll watch." Four were whispered remarks between sexual partners, such as "Not so hard!" or "Thanks." One was an exchange of greetings between friends.

The other eight verbal exchanges were in full voice and more extensive, but they reflected an attendant circumstance that was exceptional. When a group of us were locked in a restroom and attacked by several youths, we spoke for defense and out of fear. This event ruptured the reserve among us and resulted in a series of conversations among those who shared this adventure for several days afterward. Gradually, this sudden unity subsided, and the encounters drifted back into silence.

Barring such unusual events, an occasionally whispered "thanks" at the conclusion of the act constitutes the bulk of even whispered communication. At first, I presumed that speech was avoided for fear of incrimination. The excuse that intentions have been misunderstood is much weaker when those proposals are expressed in words rather than signaled by body movements. As research progressed, however, it became evident that the privacy of silent interaction accomplishes much more than mere defense against exposure to a hostile world. Even when a careful lookout is maintaining the boundaries of an encounter against intrusion, the sexual participants tend to be silent. The mechanism of silence goes beyond satisfying the demand for privacy. Like all other characteristics of the tearoom setting, it serves to guarantee anonymity, to assure the impersonality of the sexual liaison.

Tearoom sex is distinctly less personal than any other form of sexual activity, with the single exception of solitary masturbation. What I mean by "less personal" is simply that there is less emotional and physical involvement in restroom fellatio—less, even, than in the furtive action that takes place in autos and behind bushes. In those instances, at least, there is generally some verbal involvement. Often, in tearoom stalls, the only portions of the players' bodies that touch are the mouth of the insertee and the penis of the insertor; and the mouths of these partners seldom open for speech.

Only a public place, such as a park restroom, could provide the lack of personal involvement in sex that certain men desire. The setting fosters the necessary turnover in participants by its accessibility and visibility to the "right" men. In these public settings, too, there exists a sort of democracy that is endemic to impersonal sex. Men of all racial, social, educational, and physical characteristics meet in these places for sexual union. With the lack of involvement, personal preferences tend to be minimized.

If a person is going to entangle his body with another's in bed—or allow his mind to become involved with another mind—he will have certain standards of appearance, cleanliness, personality, or age that the prospective partner must meet. Age, looks, and other external variables are germane to the sexual action. As the amount of anticipated contact of body and mind in the sex act decreases, so do the standards expected of the partner. As one respondent told me:

> I go to bed with gay people, too. But if I am going to bed with a gay person, I have certain standards that I prefer them to meet. And in the tearooms you don't have to worry about these things—because it is just a purely one-sided affair.

Participants may develop strong attachments to the settings of their adventures in impersonal sex. I have noted more than once that these men seem to acquire stronger sentimental attachments to the buildings in which they meet for sex than to the persons with whom they engage in it. One respondent tells the following story: We had been discussing the relative merits of various facilities, when I asked him: "Do you remember that old tearoom across from the park garage—the one they tore down last winter?"

> Do I ever! That was the greatest place in the park. Do you know what my roommate did last Christmas, after they tore the place down? He took a wreath, sprayed it with black paint, and laid it on top of the snow—right where that corner stall had stood. . . . He was really broken up!

The walls and fixtures of these public facilities are provided by society at large, but much remains for the participants to provide for themselves. Silence in these settings is the product of years of interaction. It is a normative response to the demand for privacy without involvement, a rule that has been developed and taught. Except for solitary masturbation, sex necessitates joint action; but impersonal sex requires that this interaction be as unrevealing as possible.

PEOPLE NEXT DOOR

Tearoom activity attracts a large number of participants—enough to produce the majority of arrests for homosexual offenses in the United States. Now, employing data gained from both formal and informal interviews, we shall consider what these men are like away from the scenes of impersonal sex. "For some people," says Evelyn Hooker, an authority on male homosexuality, "the seeking of sexual contacts with other males is an activity isolated from all other aspects of their lives." Such segregation is apparent with most men who engage in the homosexual activity of public restrooms; but the degree and manner in which "deviant" is isolated from "normal" behavior in their lives will be seen to vary along social dimensions.

For the man who lives next door, the tearoom participant is just another neighbor—and probably a very good one at that. He may make a little more money than the next man and work a little harder for it. It is likely that he will drive a nicer car and maintain a neater yard than do other neighbors in the block. Maybe, like some tearoom regulars, he will work with Boy Scouts in the evenings and spend much of his weekend at the church. It may be more surprising for the outsider to discover that most of these men are married.

Indeed, 54 per cent of my research subjects are married and living with their wives. From the data at hand, there is no evidence that these unions are particularly unstable; nor does it appear that any of the wives are aware of their husbands' secret sexual activity. Indeed, the husbands choose public restrooms as sexual settings partly to avoid just such exposure. I see no reason to dispute the claim of a number of tearoom respondents that their preference for a form of concerted action that is fast and impersonal is largely predicated on a desire to protect their family relationships.

Superficial analysis of the data indicates that the maintenance of exemplary marriages—at least in appearance—is very important to the subjects of this study. In answering questions such as "When it comes to making decisions in your household, who generally makes them?" the participants indicate they are more apt to defer to their mates than are those in the control sample. They also indicate that they find it more important to "get along well" with their wives. In the open-ended questions regarding marital relationships, they tend to speak of them in more glowing terms.

TOM AND MYRA

This handsome couple live in ranch-style suburbia with their two young children. Tom is in his early thirties—an aggressive, muscular, and virile-looking male. He works "about 75 hours a week" at his new job as a chemist. "I am *wild* about my job," he says. "I really love it!" Both of Tom's "really close" friends he met at work.

He is a Methodist, and Myra a Roman Catholic, but each goes to his or her own church. Although he claims to have broad interests in life, they boil down to "games—sports like touch football or baseball."

When I asked him to tell me something about his family, Tom replied only in terms of their "good fortune" that things are not worse:

We've been fortunate that a religious problem has not occurred. We're fortunate in having two healthy children. We're fortunate that we decided to leave my last job. Being married has made me more stable.

They have been married for eleven years, and Myra is the older of the two. When asked who makes what kinds of decisions in his family, he said: "She makes most decisions about the family. She keeps the books. But I make the *major* decisions."

Myra does the household work and takes care of the children. Perceiving his main duties as those of "keeping the yard up" and "bringing home the bacon," Tom sees as his wife's only shortcoming "her lack of discipline in organization." He remarked: "She's very attractive . . . has a fair amount of poise. The best thing is that she gets along well and is able to establish close relationships with other women."

Finally, when asked how he thinks his wife feels about him and his behavior in the family, Tom replied: "She'd like to have me around more— would like for me to have a closer relationship with her and the kids." He believes it is "very important" to have the kind of sex life he needs. Reporting that he and Myra have intercourse about twice a month, he feels that his sexual needs are "adequately met" in his relationships with his wife. I also know that, from time to time, Tom has sex in the restrooms of a public park.

As an upwardly mobile man, Tom was added to the sample at a point of transition in his career as a tearoom participant. If Tom is like others who share working-class origins, he may have learned of the tearoom as an economical means of achieving orgasm during his navy years. Of late, he has returned to the restrooms for occasional sexual "relief," since his wife, objecting to the use of birth control devices, has limited his conjugal outlets.

Tom still perceives his sexual needs in the symbolic terms of the class in which he was socialized: "About twice a month" is the frequency of intercourse generally reported by working-class men; and, although they are reticent in reporting it, they do not perceive this frequency as adequate to meet their sexual needs, which they estimate are about the same as those felt by others of their age. My interviews indicate that such perceptions of sexual drive and satisfaction prevail among respondents of the lower-middle to upper-lower classes, whereas they are uncommon for those of the upper-middle and upper classes. Among the latter, the reported perception is of a much higher frequency of intercourse, and they estimate their needs to be greater than those of "most other men."

AGING CRISIS

Not only is Tom moving into a social position that may cause him to reinterpret his sexual drive, he is also approaching a point of major crisis in his career as a tearoom participant. At the time when I observed him in an act of fellatio, he played the insertor role. Still relatively young and handsome, Tom finds himself sought out as "trade"—that is, those men who make themselves available for acts of fellatio, but who, regarding themselves as "straight," refuse to reciprocate in the sexual act. Not only is that the role he expects to play in the tearoom encounters, it is the role others expect of him.

"I'm not toned up anymore," Tom complains. He is gaining weight around the middle and losing hair. As he moves past 35, Tom will face the aging crisis of the tearooms. Less and less frequently will he find himself the one sought out in these meetings. Presuming that he has been sufficiently reinforced to continue this form of sexual operation, he will be forced to seek other men. As trade, he was not expected to reciprocate, but he will soon be increasingly expected to serve as insertee for those who have first taken that role for him.

In most cases, fellatio is a service performed by an older man upon a younger. In one encounter, for example, a man appearing to be around forty was observed as insertee with a man in his twenties as insertor. A few minutes later, the man of forty was being sucked by one in his fifties. Analyzing the estimated ages of the principal partners in 53 observed acts of fellatio, I arrived at these conclusions: The insertee was judged to be older than the insertor in 40 cases; they were approximately the same age in 3; and the insertor was the older in 10 instances. The age differences ranged from an insertee estimated to be twenty-five years older than his partner to an insertee thought to be ten years younger than his insertor.

Strong references to this crisis of aging are found in my interviews with cooperating respondents, one of whom had this to say:

Well, I started off as the straight young thing. Everyone wanted to suck my cock. I wouldn't have been caught dead with one of the things in my mouth! . . . So, here I am at forty—with grown kids—and the biggest cocksucker in [the city]!

Similar experiences were expressed, in more reserved language, by another man, some 15 years his senior:

I suppose I was around thirty-five—or thirty-six—when I started giving out blow jobs. It just got so I couldn't operate any other way in the park johns. I'd still rather have a good blow job any day, but I've gotten so I like it the way it is now.

Perhaps by now there is enough real knowledge abroad to have dispelled the idea that men who engage in homosexual acts may be typed by any consistency of performance in one or another sexual role. Undoubtedly, there are preferences: Few persons are so adaptable, their conditioning so undifferentiated, that they fail to exercise choice between various sexual roles and positions. Such preferences, however, are learned, and sexual repertories tend to expand with time and experience. This study of restroom sex indicates that sexual roles within these encounters are far from stable. They are apt to change within an encounter, from one encounter to another, with age, and with the amount of exposure to influences from a sexually deviant subculture.

It is to this last factor that I should like to direct the reader's attention. The degree of contact with a network of friends who share the actor's sexual interests takes a central position in mediating not only his preferences for sex roles but his style of adaptation to—and rationalization of—the deviant activity in which he participates. There are, however, two reasons why I have not classified research subjects in terms of their participation in the homosexual subculture. It is difficult to measure accurately the degree of such involvement; and such subcultural interaction depends upon other social variables, two of which are easily measured.

Family status has a definitive effect on the deviant careers of those whose concern is with controlling information about their sexual behavior. The married man who engages in homosexual activity must be much more cautious about his involvement in the subculture than his single counterpart. As a determinant of life-style and sexual activity, marital status is also a determinant of the patterns of deviant adaptation and rationalization. Only those in my sample who were divorced or separated from their wives were difficult to categorize as either married or single. Those who had been married, however, showed a tendency to remain in friendship networks with married men. Three of the four were still limited in freedom by responsibilities for their children. For these reasons, I have included all men who were once married in the "married" categories.

The second determining variable is the relative autonomy of the respondent's occupation. A man is "independently" employed when his job allows him freedom of movement and security from being fired; the most obvious example is self-employment. Occupational "dependence" leaves a man little freedom for engaging in disreputable activity. The sales manager or other executive of a business firm has greater freedom than the salesman or attorney who is employed in the lower echelons of a large industry or by the federal government. The sales representative whose territory is far removed from the home office has greater independence, in terms of information control, than the minister of a local congregation. The majority of those placed in both the married and unmarried categories with *dependent* occupations were employed by large industries or the government.

Median education levels and annual family incomes indicate that those with dependent occupations rank lower on the socio-economic scale. Only in the case of married men, however, is this correlation between social class and occupational autonomy strongly supported by the ratings of these respondents on Warner's Index of Status Characteristics. Nearly all the married men with dependent occupations are of the upper-lower or lower-middle classes, whereas those with independent occupations are of the upper-middle or upper classes. For single men, the social-class variable is neither so easily identifiable nor so clearly divided. Nearly all single men in the sample can be classified only as "vaguely middle class."

As occupational autonomy and marital status remain the most important dimensions along which participants may be ranked, we shall consider four general types of tearoom customers: (1) married men with dependent occupations, (2) married men with independent occupations, (3) unmarried men with independent occupations, and (4) unmarried men with dependent occupations. As will become evident with the discussion of each type, I have employed labels from the homosexual argot, along with pseudonyms, to designate each class of participants. This is done not only to facilitate reading but to emphasize that we are describing persons rather than merely "typical" constructs.

TYPE I: TRADE

The first classification, which includes 19 of the participants (38 per cent), may be called "trade," since most would earn that appellation from the gay subculture. All of these men are, or have been, married—one was separated from his wife at the time of interviewing and another was divorced.

Most work as truck drivers, machine operators, or clerical workers. There is a member of the armed forces, a carpenter, and the minister of a pentecostal church. Most of their wives work, at least part time, to help raise their median annual family income to $8,000. One in six of these men is black. All are normally masculine in appearance and mannerism. Although 14 have completed high school, there are only 3 college graduates among them, and 5 have had less than twelve years of schooling.

George is representative of this largest group of respondents.

* * *

At the age of twenty, he married a Roman Catholic girl and has since joined her church, although he classifies himself as "lapsed." In the fourteen years of their marriage, they have had seven children, one of whom is less than a year old. George doesn't think they should have more children, but his wife objects to using any type of birth control other than the rhythm method. With his wife working part time as a waitress, they have an income of about $5,000.

"How often do you have intercourse with your wife?" I asked. "Not very much the last few years," he replied. "It's up to when she feels like giving it to me—which ain't very often. I never suggest it."

* * *

While more open than most in his acknowledgment of marital tension, George's appraisal of sexual relations in the marriage is typical of those respondents classified as trade. In 63 per cent of these marriages, the wife, husband, or both are Roman Catholic. When answering questions about their sexual lives, a story much like George's emerged: At least since the birth of the last child, conjugal relations have been very rare.

These data suggest that, along with providing an excuse for diminishing intercourse with their wives, the religious teachings to which most of these families adhere may cause the husbands to search for sex in the tearooms. Whatever the causes that turn them unsatisfied from the marriage bed, however, the alternate outlet must be quick, inexpensive, and impersonal. Any personal, ongoing affair—any outlet requiring money or hours away from home—would threaten a marriage that is already shaky and jeopardize the most important thing these men possess, their standing as father of their children.

Around the turn of the century, before the vice squads moved in (in their never-ending process of narrowing the behavioral options of those in the lower classes), the Georges of this study would probably have made regular visits to the two-bit bordellos. With a madam watching a clock to limit the time, these cheap whorehouses provided the same sort of fast, impersonal service as today's public restrooms. I find no indication that these men seek homosexual contact as such; rather, they want a form of orgasm-producing action that is less lonely than masturbation and less involving than a love relationship. As the forces of social control deprive them of one outlet, they provide another. The newer form, it should be noted, is more stigmatizing than the previous one—thus giving "proof" to the adage that "the sinful are drawn ever deeper into perversity."

* * *

For George, no doubt, the aging crisis is also an identity crisis. Only with reluctance—and perhaps never—will he turn to the insertee role. The threat of such a role to his masculine self-image is too great. Like others of his class with whom I have had more extensive interviews, George may have learned that sexual game as a teen-age hustler, or else when serving in the army during the Korean war. In either case, his socialization into homosexual experience took place in a masculine world where it is permissible to accept money from a "queer" in return for carefully limited sexual favors. But to use one's own mouth as a substitute for the female organ, or even to express enjoyment of the action, is taboo in the trade code.

Moreover, for men of George's occupational and marital status, there is no network of friends engaged in tearoom activity to help them adapt to the changes aging will bring. I found no evidence of friendship networks among respondents of this type, who enter and leave the restrooms alone, avoiding conversation while within. Marginal to both the heterosexual and homosexual worlds, these men shun involvement in any form of gay subculture. Type I participants report fewer friends of any sort than do those of other classes. When asked how many close friends he has, George answered: "None. I haven't got time for that."

TYPE II: AMBISEXUALS

* * *

Three-fourths of the married participants with independent occupations were observed, at one time or another, participating as insertees in fellatio, compared to only one-third of the trade. Not only do the Type II participants tend to switch roles with greater facility, they seem inclined to search beyond the tearooms for more exotic forms of sexual experience. Dwight, along with others in his class, expresses a liking for anal intercourse (both as insertee and insertor), for group activity, and even for mild forms of sadomasochistic sex. . . . Two-thirds of the married participants with occupational independence are college graduates.

. . . Although the upper-class deviants may have more to lose from exposure (in the sense that the mighty have farther to fall), they also have more means at their disposal with which to protect their moral histories.

Some need only tap their spending money to pay off a member of the vice squad. In other instances, social contacts with police commissioners or newspaper publishers make it possible to squelch either record or publicity of an arrest. One respondent has made substantial contributions to a police charity fund, while another hired private detectives to track down a black-mailer. Not least in their capacity to cover for errors in judgment is the fact that their word has the backing of economic and social influence. Evidence must be strong to prosecute a man who can hire the best attorneys. Lower-class men are rightfully more suspicious, for they have fewer resources with which to defend themselves if exposed.

This does not mean that Type II participants are immune to the risks of the game, but simply that they are bidding from strength. To them, the risks of arrest, exposure, blackmail, or physical assault contribute to the excite-ment quotient. It is not unusual for them to speak of cruising as an adven-ture, in contrast with the trade, who engage in a furtive search for sexual relief. On the whole, then, the action of Type II respondents is apt to be somewhat bolder and their search for "kicks" less inhibited than that of most other types of participants.

Dwight is not fleeing from an unhappy home life or sexless marriage to the encounters in the parks. He expresses great devotion to his wife and children: "They're my whole life," he exclaims. All evidence indicates that, as father, citizen, businessman and, church member, Dwight's behavior pat-terns—as viewed by his peers—are exemplary.

Five of the twelve participants in Dwight's class are members of the Episcopal church. Dwight is one of two who were raised in that church, although he is not as active a churchman as some who became Episcopali-ans later in life. In spite of his infrequent attendance to worship, he feels his church is "just right" for him and needs no changing. Its tradition and ceremony are intellectually and esthetically pleasing to him. Its liberal out-look on questions of morality round out a religious orientation that he finds generally supportive.

* * *

Unlike the trade, Type II participants recognize their homosexual ac-tivity as indicative of their own psychosexual orientations. They think of themselves as bisexual, or ambisexual, and have intellectualized their devi-ant tendencies in terms of the pseudopsychology of the popular press. They speak often of the great men of history, as well as of certain movie stars and others of contemporary fame, who are also "AC/DC." Erving Goffman has remarked that stigmatized Americans "tend to live in a literarily defined world." This is nowhere truer than of the subculturally oriented participants of this study. Not only do they read a great deal about homosexuality, they discuss it within their network of friends. For the Dwights, there is subcul-tural support that enables them to integrate their deviance with the re-mainder of their lives, while maintaining control over the information that could discredit their whole being. For these reasons, they look upon the gaming encounters in the parks as enjoyable experiences.

TYPE III: GAY GUYS

Like the ambisexuals, unmarried respondents with independent occupations are locked into a strong subculture, a community that provides them with knowledge about the tearooms and reinforcement in their particular brand of deviant activity. This open participation in the gay community distinguishes these single men from the larger group of unmarrieds with dependent occupations. These men take the homosexual role of our society and are thus the most truly "gay" of all participant types. Except for Tim, who was recruited as a decoy in the tearooms by the vice squad of a police department, Type III participants learned the strategies of the tearooms through friends already experienced in this branch of the sexual market.

Typical of this group is Ricky, a twenty-four-year-old university student whose older male lover supports him. Ricky stands at the median age of his type, who range from nineteen to fifty years. Half of them are college graduates, and all but one other are at least part-time students, a characteristic that explains their low median income of $3,000. Because Ricky's lover is a good provider, he is comfortably situated in a midtown apartment, a more pleasant residence than most of his friends enjoy.

* * *

Having met his lover in a park, Ricky returns there only when his mate is on a business trip or their relationship is strained. Then Ricky becomes, as he puts it, "horny," and he goes to the park to study, cruise, and engage in tearoom sex:

The bars are O.K.—but a little too public for a "married" man like me.
. . . Tearooms are just another kind of action, and they do quite well when nothing better is available.

Like other Type III respondents, he shows little preference in sexual roles. "It depends on the other guy," Ricky says, "and whether I like his looks or not. Some men I'd crawl across the street on my knees for—others I wouldn't piss on!" His aging crisis will be shared with all others in the gay world. It will take the nightmarish form of waning attractiveness and the search for a permanent lover to fill his later years, but it will have no direct relationship with the tearoom roles. Because of his socialization in the homosexual society, taking the insertee role is neither traumatic for him nor related to aging.

Ricky's life revolves around his sexual deviance in a way that is not true of George or even of Dwight. Most of his friends and social contacts are connected with the homosexual subculture. His attitudes toward, and rationalization of, his sexual behavior are largely gained from this wide circle of friends. The gay men claim to have more close friends than do any other type of control or participant respondents. As frequency of orgasm is reported, this class also has more sex than any other group sampled, averaging 2.5 acts per week. They seem relatively satisfied with this aspect of their lives and regard their sexual drive as normal—although Ricky perceives his sexual needs as less than most.

* * *

All three of the Unitarians in the sample are Type III men, although none was raised in that faith; and their jobs are uniformly of the sort to which their sexual activity, if exposed, would present little threat.

Although these men correspond most closely to society's homosexual stereotype, they are least representative of the tearoom population, constituting only 14 per cent of the participant sample. More than any other type, the Rickys seem at ease with their behavior in the sexual market, and their scarcity in the tearooms is indicative of this. They want personal sex —more permanent relationships—and the public restrooms are not where this is to be found.

That any of them patronize the tearooms at all is the result of incidental factors: They fear that open cruising in the more common homosexual market places of the baths and bars might disrupt a current love affair; or they drop in at a tearoom while waiting for a friend at one of the "watering places" where homosexuals congregate in the parks. They find the anonymity of the tearooms suitable for their purposes, but not inviting enough to provide the primary setting for sexual activity.

TYPE IV: CLOSET QUEENS

Another dozen of the 50 participants interviewed may be classified as single deviants with dependent occupations—"closet queens," in homosexual slang. Again, the label may be applied to others who keep their deviance hidden, whether married or single, but the covert, unmarried men are most apt to earn this appellation. With them, we have moved full circle in our classifications, for they parallel the trade in a number of ways.

1. They have few friends, only a minority of whom are involved in tearoom activity.
2. They tend to play the insertor role, at least until they confront the crisis of aging.
3. Half of them are Roman Catholic in religion.
4. Their median annual income is $6,000; and they work as teachers, postmen, salesmen, clerks—usually for large corporations or agencies.
5. Most of them have completed only high school, although there are a few exceptionally well-educated men in this group.
6. One in six is black.
7. Not only are they afraid of becoming involved in other forms of the sexual market, they share with the trade a relatively furtive involvement in the tearoom encounters.

. . . They report poorer childhood relationships with their fathers than do those of any other group. As is the case with Arnold's roommate, many closet queens seem to prefer teen-age boys as sexual objects. This is one of the features that distinguishes them from all other participant types. Although scarce in tearooms, teen-agers make themselves available for sexual activity in other places frequented by closet queens. A number of these men regularly cruise the streets where boys thumb rides each afternoon when school is over. One closet queen from my sample has been arrested for luring boys in their early teens to his home.

Interactions between these men and the youths they seek frequently results in the sort of scandal feared by the gay community. Newspaper reports of molestations usually contain clues of the closet-queen style of adaptation on the part of such offenders. Those respondents whose lives had been threatened by teen-age toughs were generally of this type. One of the standard rules governing one-night-stand operations cautions against becoming involved with such "chicken." The frequent violation of this rule by closet queens may contribute to their general disrepute among the bar set of the homosexual subculture, where "closet queen" is a pejorative term.

* * *

STYLES OF DEVIANT ADAPTATION

Social isolation is characteristic of Type IV participants. Generally, it is more severe even than that encountered among the trade, most of whom enjoy at least a vestigial family life. Although painfully aware of their homosexual orientations, these men find little solace in association with others who share their deviant interests. Fearing exposure, arrest, the stigmatization that might result from a participation in the homosexual subculture, they are driven to a desperate, lone-wolf sort of activity that may prove most dangerous to themselves and the rest of society. Although it is tempting to look for psychological explanations of their apparent preference for chicken, the sociological ones are evident. They resort to the more dangerous game because of a lack of both the normative restraints and adult markets that prevail in the more overt subculture. To them, the costs (financial and otherwise) of operating among street-corner youths are more acceptable than those of active participation in the gay subculture. Only the tearooms provide a less expensive alternative for the closet queens.

* * *

In delineating styles of adaptation, I do not intend to imply that these men are faced with an array of styles from which they may pick one or even a combination. No man's freedom is that great. They have been able to choose only among the limited options offered them by society. These sets of alternatives, which determine the modes of adaptation to deviant pressures, are defined and allocated in accordance with major sociological variables: occupation, marital status, age, race, amount of education. That is one meaning of social probability.

THE SOCIOLOGIST AS VOYEUR

The methods employed in this study of men who engage in restroom sex are the outgrowth of three ethical assumptions: First, I do not believe the social scientist should ever ignore or avoid an area of research simply because it is difficult or socially sensitive. Second, he should approach any aspect of human behavior with those means that least distort the observed phenomena. Third, he must protect respondents from harm—regardless of what such protection may cost the researcher.

Because the majority of arrests on homosexual charges in the United States result from encounters in public restrooms, I felt this form of sexual behavior to provide a legitimate, even essential, topic for sociological investigation. In our society, the social control forces, not the criminologist, determine what the latter shall study.

Following this decision, the question is one of choosing research methods that permit the investigator to achieve maximum fidelity to the world he is studying. I believe ethnographic methods are the only truly empirical ones for the social scientist. When human behavior is being examined, systematic observation is essential; so, I had to become a participant-observer of furtive, felonious acts.

Fortunately, the very fear and suspicion of tearoom participants produces a mechanism that makes such observation possible: A third man (generally one who obtains voyeuristic pleasure from his duties) serves as a lookout, moving back and forth from door to windows. Such a "watch-queen," as he is labeled in the homosexual argot, coughs when a police car stops nearby or when a stranger approaches. He nods affirmatively when he recognizes a man entering as being a "regular." Having been taught the watchqueen role by a cooperating respondent, I played that part faithfully while observing hundreds of acts of fellatio. After developing a systematic observation sheet, I recorded 50 of these encounters (involving 53 sexual acts) in great detail. These records were compared with another 30 made by a cooperating respondent who was himself a sexual participant. The bulk of information presented in "Tearoom Trade" results from these observations.

Although primarily interested in the stigmatized behavior, I also wanted to know about the men who take such risks for a few moments of impersonal sex. I was able to engage a number of participants in conversation outside the restrooms; and, eventually, by revealing the purpose of my study to them, I gained a dozen respondents who contributed hundreds of hours of interview time. This sample I knew to be biased in favor of the more outgoing and better educated of the tearoom population.

To overcome this bias, I cut short a number of my observations of encounters and hurried to my automobile. There, with the help of a tape recorder, I noted a brief description of each participant, his sexual role in the encounter just observed, his license number, and a brief description of his car. I varied such records from park to park . . . to correspond with previously observed changes in volume at various times of the day. This provided me with a time-and-place-representative sample of 134 participants. With attrition, chiefly of those who had changed address or who drove rented cars, and the addition of two persons who walked to the tearooms, I ended up with a sample of 100 men, each of whom I had actually observed engaging in fellatio.

At this stage, my third ethical concern impinged. I already knew that many of my respondents were married, and that all were in a highly discreditable position and fearful of discovery. How could I approach these covert deviants for interviews? By passing as deviant, I had observed their sexual behavior without disturbing it. Now, I was faced with interviewing these men (often in the presence of their wives) without destroying them. Fortunately, I held another research job that placed me in the position of preparing the interview schedule for a social-health survey of a random selection of male subjects throughout the community. With permission from the survey's directors, I could add my sample to the larger group (thus enhancing their anonymity) and interview them as part of the social-health survey.

To overcome the danger of having a subject recognize me as a watchqueen, I changed my hair style, attire, and automobile. At the risk of losing more transient respondents, I waited a year between the sample gathering and the interviews, during which time I took notes on their homes and neighborhoods and acquired data on them from the city and county directories.

Having randomized the sample, I completed 50 interviews with tearoom participants and added another 50 interviews from the social-health survey sample. The latter control group was matched with the participants on the bases of marital status, race, job classification, and area of residence.

This study, then, results from a confluence of strategies: systematic, firsthand observation, in-depth interviews with available respondents, the use of archival data, and structured interviews of a representative sample and a matched control group. At each level of research, I applied those measures that provided maximum protection for research subjects and the truest measurement of persons and behavior observed.

The Labeling Theory of Deviance

On Being Sane in Insane Places[*]

D. L. Rosenhan

If sanity and insanity exist, how shall we know them?

The question is neither capricious nor itself insane. However much we may be personally convinced that we can tell the normal from the abnormal, the evidence is simply not compelling. It is commonplace, for example, to read about murder trials wherein eminent psychiatrists for the defense are contradicted by equally eminent psychiatrists for the prosecution on the matter of the defendant's sanity. More generally, there are a great deal of conflicting data on the reliability, utility, and meaning of such terms as "sanity," "insanity," "mental illness," and "schizophrenia." Finally, as early as 1934, Benedict suggested that normality and abnormality are not universal. What is viewed as normal in one culture may be seen as quite aberrant in another. Thus, notions of normality and abnormality may not be quite as accurate as people believe they are.

To raise questions regarding normality and abnormality is in no way to question the fact that some behaviors are deviant or odd. Murder is deviant. So, too, are hallucinations. Nor does raising such questions deny the existence of the personal anguish that is often associated with "mental illness." Anxiety and depression exist. Psychological suffering exists. But normality and abnormality, sanity and insanity, and the diagnoses that flow from them may be less substantive than many believe them to be.

At its heart, the question of whether the sane can be distinguished from the insane (and whether degrees of insanity can be distinguished from each other) is a simple matter: do the salient characteristics that lead to diagnosis reside in the patients themselves or in the environments and contexts in which observers find them? From Bleuler, through Kretchmer, through the formulators of the recently revised *Diagnostic and Statistical Manual* of the American Psychiatric Association, the belief has been strong that patients present symptoms, that those symptoms can be categorized, and, implicitly, that the sane are distinguishable from the insane. More recently, however, this belief has been questioned. Based in part on theoretical and anthropological considerations, but also on philosophical, legal, and therapeutic ones,

* From *Science*, vol. 179 (January 19, 1973), 250–58. Copyright © 1973 by the American Association for the Advancement of Science.

the view has grown that psychological categorization of mental illness is useless at best and downright harmful, misleading, and pejorative at worst. Psychiatric diagnoses, in this view, are in the minds of the observers and are not valid summaries of characteristics displayed by the observed.

Gains can be made in deciding which of these is more nearly accurate by getting normal people (that is, people who do not have, and have never suffered, symptoms of serious psychiatric disorders) admitted to psychiatric hospitals and then determining whether they were discovered to be sane and, if so, how. If the sanity of such pseudopatients were always detected, there would be prima facie evidence that a sane individual can be distinguished from the insane context in which he is found. Normality (and presumably abnormality) is distinct enough that it can be recognized wherever it occurs, for it is carried within the person. If, on the other hand, the sanity of the pseudopatients were never discovered, serious difficulties would arise for those who support traditional modes of psychiatric diagnosis. Given that the hospital staff was not incompetent, that the pseudopatient had been behaving as sanely as he had been outside the hospital, and that it had never been previously suggested that he belonged in a psychiatric hospital, such an unlikely outcome would support the view that psychiatric diagnosis betrays little about the patient but much about the environment in which an observer finds him.

This article describes such an experiment. Eight sane people gained secret admission to twelve different hospitals.* Their diagnostic experiences constitute the data of the first part of this article; the remainder is devoted to a description of their experiences in psychiatric institutions. Too few psychiatrists and psychologists, even those who have worked in such hospitals, know what the experience is like. They rarely talk about it with former patients, perhaps because they distrust information coming from the previously insane. Those who have worked in psychiatric hospitals are likely to have adapted so thoroughly to the settings that they are insensitive to the impact of that experience. And while there have been occasional reports of researchers who submitted themselves to psychiatric hospitalization, these researchers have commonly remained in the hospitals for short periods of time, often with the knowledge of the hospital staff. It is difficult to know the extent to which they were treated as patients or as research colleagues. Nevertheless, their reports about the inside of the psychiatric hospital have been valuable. This article extends those efforts.

PSEUDOPATIENTS AND THEIR SETTINGS

The eight pseudopatients were a varied group. One was a psychology graduate student in his twenties. The remaining seven were older and "estab-

* Data from a ninth pseudopatient are not incorporated in this report because, although his sanity went undetected, he falsified aspects of his personal history, including his marital status and parental relationships. His experimental behaviors therefore were not identical to those of the other pseudopatients.

lished." Among them were three psychologists, a pediatrician, a psychiatrist, a painter, and a housewife. Three pseudopatients were women, five were men. All of them employed pseudonyms, lest their alleged diagnoses embarrass them later. Those who were in mental health professions alleged another occupation in order to avoid the special attentions that might be accorded by staff, as a matter of courtesy or caution, to ailing colleagues.* With the exception of myself (I was the first pseudopatient and my presence was known to the hospital administrator and chief psychologist and, so far as I can tell, to them alone), the presence of pseudopatients and the nature of the research program were not known to the hospital staffs.†

The settings were similarly varied. In order to generalize the findings, admission into a variety of hospitals was sought. The twelve hospitals in the sample were located in five different states on the East and West coasts. Some were old and shabby, some were quite new. Some were research-oriented, others not. Some had good staff-patient ratios, others were quite understaffed. Only one was a strictly private hospital. All of the others were supported by state or federal funds or, in one instance, by university funds.

After calling the hospital for an appointment, the pseudopatient arrived at the admissions office complaining that he had been hearing voices. Asked what the voices said, he replied that they were often unclear, but as far as he could tell they said "empty," "hollow," and "thud." The voices were unfamiliar and were of the same sex as the pseudopatient. The choice of these symptoms was occasioned by their apparent similarity to existential symptoms. Such symptoms are alleged to arise from painful concerns about the perceived meaninglessness of one's life. It is as if the hallucinating person were saying, "My life is empty and hollow." The choice of these symptoms was also determined by the *absence* of a single report of existential psychoses in the literature.

Beyond alleging the symptoms and falsifying name, vocation, and employment, no further alterations of person, history, or circumstances were made. The significant events of the pseudopatient's life history were presented as they had actually occurred. Relationships with parents and siblings, with spouse and children, with people at work and in school, con-

* Beyond the personal difficulties that the pseudopatient is likely to experience in the hospital, there are legal and social ones that, combined, require considerable attention before entry. For example, once admitted to a psychiatric institution, it is difficult, if not impossible, to be discharged on short notice, state law to the contrary notwithstanding. I was not sensitive to these difficulties at the outset of the project, nor to the personal and situational emergencies that can arise, but later a writ of habeas corpus was prepared for each of the entering pseudopatients and an attorney was kept "on call" during every hospitalization. I am grateful to John Kaplan and Robert Bartels for legal advice and assistance in these matters.

† However distasteful such concealment is, it was a necessary first step to examining these questions. Without concealment, there would have been no way to know how valid these experiences were; nor was there any way of knowing whether whatever detections occurred were a tribute to the diagnostic acumen of the staff or to the hospital's rumor network. Obviously, since my concerns are general ones that cut across individual hospitals and staffs, I have respected their anonymity and have eliminated clues that might lead to their identification.

sistent with the aforementioned exceptions, were described as they were or had been. Frustrations and upsets were described along with joys and satisfactions. These facts are important to remember. If anything, they strongly biased the subsequent results in favor of detecting sanity, since none of their histories or current behaviors was seriously pathological in any way.

Immediately upon admission to the psychiatric ward, the pseudopatient ceased simulating *any* symptoms of abnormality. In some cases, there was a brief period of mild nervousness and anxiety, since none of the pseudopatients really believed that he would be admitted so easily. Indeed, their shared fear was that they would be immediately exposed as frauds and greatly embarrassed. Moreover, many of them had never visited a psychiatric ward; even those who had nevertheless had some genuine fears about what might happen to them. Their nervousness, then, was quite appropriate to the novelty of the hospital setting, and it abated rapidly.

Apart from that short-lived nervousness, the pseudopatient behaved on the ward as he "normally" behaved. The pseudopatient spoke to patients and staff as he might ordinarily. Because there is uncommonly little to do on a psychiatric ward, he attempted to engage others in conversation. When asked by staff how he was feeling, he indicated that he was fine, that he no longer experienced symptoms. He responded to instructions from attendants, to calls for medication (which was not swallowed), and to dining-hall instructions. Beyond such activities as were available to him on the admissions ward, he spent his time writing down his observations about the ward, its patients, and the staff. Initially these notes were written "secretly," but as it soon became clear that no one much cared, they were subsequently written on standard tablets of paper in such public places as the dayroom. No secret was made of these activities.

The pseudopatient, very much as a true psychiatric patient, entered a hospital with no foreknowledge of when he would be discharged. Each was told that he would have to get out by his own devices, essentially by convincing the staff that he was sane. The psychological stresses associated with hospitalization were considerable, and all but one of the pseudopatients desired to be discharged almost immediately after being admitted. They were, therefore, motivated not only to behave sanely, but to be paragons of cooperation. That their behavior was in no way disruptive is confirmed by nursing reports, which have been obtained on most of the patients. These reports uniformly indicate that the patients were "friendly," "cooperative," and "exhibited no abnormal indications."

THE NORMAL ARE NOT DETECTABLY SANE

Despite their public "show" of sanity, the pseudopatients were never detected. Admitted, except in one case, with a diagnosis of schizophrenia,*

---

* Interestingly, of the twelve admissions, eleven were diagnosed as schizophrenic and one, with the identical symptomatology, as manic-depressive psychosis. This diagnosis has a more favorable prognosis, and it was given by the only private hospital in our sample.

each was discharged with a diagnosis of schizophrenia "in remission." The label "in remission" should in no way be dismissed as a formality, for at no time during any hospitalization had any question been raised about any pseudopatient's simulation. Nor are there any indications in the hospital records that the pseudopatient's status was suspect. Rather, the evidence is strong that, once labeled schizophrenic, the pseudopatient was stuck with that label. If the pseudopatient was to be discharged, he must naturally be "in remission"; but he was not sane, nor, in the institution's view, had he ever been sane.

The uniform failure to recognize sanity cannot be attributed to the quality of the hospitals, for, although there were considerable variations among them, several are considered excellent. Nor can it be alleged that there was simply not enough time to observe the pseudopatients. Length of hospitalization ranged from seven to fifty-two days, with an average of nineteen days. The pseudopatients were not, in fact, carefully observed, but this failure clearly speaks more to traditions within psychiatric hospitals than to lack of opportunity.

Finally, it cannot be said that the failure to recognize the pseudopatients' sanity was due to the fact that they were not behaving sanely. While there was clearly some tension present in all of them, their daily visitors could detect no serious behavioral consequences—nor, indeed, could other patients. It was quite common for the patients to "detect" the pseudopatients' sanity. During the first three hospitalizations, when accurate counts were kept, 35 of a total of 118 patients on the admissions ward voiced their suspicions, some vigorously. "You're not crazy. You're a journalist, or a professor [referring to the continual note-taking]. You're checking up on the hospital." While most of the patients were reassured by the pseudopatient's insistence that he had been sick before he came in but was fine now, some continued to believe that the pseudopatient was sane throughout his hospitalization.* The fact that the patients often recognized normality when staff did not raises important questions.

Failure to detect sanity during the course of hospitalization may be due to the fact that physicians operate with a strong bias toward what statisticians call the type 2 error. This is to say that physicians are more inclined to call a healthy person sick (a false positive, type 2) than a sick person healthy (a false negative, type 1). The reasons for this are not hard to find: it is clearly more dangerous to misdiagnose illness than health. Better to err on the side of caution, to suspect illness even among the healthy.

But what holds for medicine does not hold equally well for psychiatry. Medical illnesses, while unfortunate, are not commonly pejorative. Psychiatric diagnoses, on the contrary, carry with them personal, legal, and social stigmas. It was therefore important to see whether the tendency toward

* It is possible, of course, that patients have quite broad latitudes in diagnosis and therefore are inclined to call many people sane, even those whose behavior is patently aberrant. However, although we have no hard data on this matter, it was our distinct impression that this was not the case. In many instances, patients not only singled us out for attention, but came to imitate our behaviors and styles.

diagnosing the sane as insane could be reversed. The following experiment was arranged at a research and teaching hospital whose staff had heard these findings but doubted that such an error could occur in their hospital. The staff was informed that at some time during the following three months, one or more pseudopatients would attempt to be admitted into the psychiatric hospital. Each staff member was asked to rate each patient who presented himself at admissions or on the ward according to the likelihood that the patient was a pseudopatient. A 10-point scale was used, with a 1 and 2 reflecting high confidence that the patient was a pseudopatient.

Judgments were obtained on 193 patients who were admitted for psychiatric treatment. All staff who had had sustained contact with or primary responsibility for the patient—attendants, nurses, psychiatrists, physicians, and psychologists—were asked to make judgments. Forty-one patients were alleged, with high confidence, to be pseudopatients by at least one member of the staff. Twenty-three were considered suspect by at least one psychiatrist. Nineteen were suspected by one psychiatrist *and* one other staff member. Actually, no genuine pseudopatient (at least from my group) presented himself during this period.

The experiment is instructive. It indicates that the tendency to designate sane people as insane can be reversed when the stakes (in this case, prestige and diagnostic acumen) are high. But what can be said of the nineteen people who were suspected of being "sane" by one psychiatrist and another staff member? Were these people truly "sane," or was it rather the case that in the course of avoiding the type 2 error the staff tended to make more errors of the first sort—calling the crazy "sane"? There is no way of knowing. But one thing is certain: any diagnostic process that lends itself so readily to massive errors of this sort cannot be a very reliable one.

THE STICKINESS OF PSYCHODIAGNOSTIC LABELS

Beyond the tendency to call the healthy sick—a tendency that accounts better for diagnostic behavior on admission than it does for such behavior after a lengthy period of exposure—the data speak to the massive role of labeling in psychiatric assessment. Having once been labeled schizophrenic, there is nothing the pseudopatient can do to overcome the tag. The tag profoundly colors others' perceptions of him and his behavior.

From one viewpoint, these data are hardly surprising, for it has long been known that elements are given meaning by the context in which they occur. Gestalt psychology made this point vigorously, and Asch demonstrated that there are "central" personality traits (such as "warm" versus "cold") which are so powerful that they markedly color the meaning of other information in forming an impression of a given personality. "Insane," "schizophrenic," "manic-depressive," and "crazy" are probably among the most powerful of such central traits. Once a person is designated abnormal, all of his other behaviors and characteristics are colored by that label. Indeed, that label is so powerful that many of the pseudopatients' normal behaviors were overlooked entirely or profoundly misinterpreted. Some examples may clarify this issue.

Earlier I indicated that there were no changes in the pseudopatient's personal history and current status beyond those of name, employment, and, where necessary, vocation. Otherwise, a veridical description of personal history and circumstances was offered. Those circumstances were not psychotic. How were they made consonant with the diagnosis of psychosis? Or were those diagnoses modified in such a way as to bring them into accord with the circumstances of the pseudopatient's life, as described by him?

As far as I can determine, diagnoses were in no way affected by the relative health of the circumstances of a pseudopatient's life. Rather, the reverse occurred: the perception of his circumstances was shaped entirely by the diagnosis. A clear example of such translation is found in the case of a pseudopatient who had had a close relationship with his mother but was rather remote from his father during his early childhood. During adolescence and beyond, however, his father became a close friend, while his relationship with his mother cooled. His present relationship with his wife was characteristically close and warm. Apart from occasional angry exchanges, friction was minimal. The children had rarely been spanked. Surely there is nothing especially pathological about such a history. Indeed, many readers may see a similar pattern in their own experiences, with no markedly deleterious consequences. Observe, however, how such a history was translated in the psychopathological context, this from the case summary prepared after the patient was discharged.

> This white 39-year-old male . . . manifests a long history of considerable ambivalence in close relationships, which begins in early childhood. A warm relationship with his mother cools during his adolescence. A distant relationship to his father is described as becoming very intense. Affective stability is absent. His attempts to control emotionality with his wife and children are punctuated by angry outbursts and, in the case of the children, spankings. And while he says that he has several good friends, one senses considerable ambivalence embedded in those relationships also. . . .

The facts of the case were unintentionally distorted by the staff to achieve consistency with a popular theory of the dynamics of a schizophrenic reaction. Nothing of an ambivalent nature had been described in relations with parents, spouse, or friends. To the extent that ambivalence could be inferred, it was probably not greater than is found in all human relationships. It is true the pseudopatient's relationships with his parents changed over time, but in the ordinary context that would hardly be remarkable—indeed, it might very well be expected. Clearly, the meaning ascribed to his verbalizations (that is, ambivalence, affective instability) was determined by the diagnosis: schizophrenia. An entirely different meaning would have been ascribed if it were known that the man was "normal."

All pseudopatients took extensive notes publicly. Under ordinary circumstances, such behavior would have raised questions in the minds of observers, as, in fact, it did among patients. Indeed, it seemed so certain that the notes would elicit suspicion that elaborate precautions were taken to remove them from the ward each day. But the precautions proved needless. The closest any staff member came to questioning these notes occurred when one pseudopatient asked his physician what kind of medication he was receiving and began to write down the response. "You needn't write it," he was told gently. "If you have trouble remembering, just ask me again."

If no questions were asked of the pseudopatients, how was their writing interpreted? Nursing records for three patients indicate that the writing was seen as an aspect of their pathological behavior. "Patient engages in writing behavior" was the daily nursing comment on one of the pseudopatients who was never questioned about his writing. Given that the patient is in the hospital, he must be psychologically disturbed. And given that he is disturbed, continuous writing must be a behavioral manifestation of that disturbance, perhaps a subset of the compulsive behaviors that are sometimes correlated with schizophrenia.

One tacit characteristic of psychiatric diagnosis is that it locates the sources of aberration within the individual and only rarely within the complex of stimuli that surrounds him. Consequently, behaviors that are stimulated by the environment are commonly misattributed to the patient's disorder. For example, one kindly nurse found a pseudopatient pacing the long hospital corridors. "Nervous, Mr. X?" she asked. "No, bored," he said.

The notes kept by pseudopatients are full of patient behaviors that were misinterpreted by well-intentioned staff. Often enough, a patient would go "berserk" because he had, wittingly or unwittingly, been mistreated by, say, an attendant. A nurse coming upon the scene would rarely inquire even cursorily into the environmental stimuli of the patient's behavior. Rather, she assumed that his upset derived from his pathology, not from his present interactions with other staff members. Occasionally, the staff might assume that the patient's family (especially when they had recently visited) or other patients had stimulated the outburst. But never were the staff found to assume that one of themselves or the structure of the hospital had anything to do with a patient's behavior. One psychiatrist pointed to a group of patients who were sitting outside the cafeteria entrance half an hour before lunchtime. To a group of young residents he indicated that such behavior was characteristic of the oral-acquisitive nature of the syndrome. It seemed not to occur to him that there were very few things to anticipate in a psychiatric hospital besides eating.

A psychiatric label has a life and an influence of its own. Once the impression has been formed that the patient is schizophrenic, the expectation is that he will continue to be schizophrenic. When a sufficient amount of time has passed, during which the patient has done nothing bizarre, he is considered to be in remission and available for discharge. But the label endures beyond discharge, with the unconfirmed expectation that he will behave as a schizophrenic again. Such labels, conferred by mental health professionals, are as influential on the patient as they are on his relatives and friends, and it should not surprise anyone that the diagnosis acts on all of them as a self-fulfilling prophecy. Eventually, the patient himself accepts the diagnosis, with all of its surplus meanings and expectations, and behaves accordingly.

The inferences to be made from these matters are quite simple. Much as Zigler and Phillips have demonstrated that there is enormous overlap in the symptoms presented by patients who have been variously diagnosed, so there is enormous overlap in the behaviors of the sane and the insane. The sane are not "sane" all of the time. We lose our tempers "for no good reason." We are occasionally depressed or anxious, again for no good reason. And we may find it difficult to get along with one or another person—again for no reason that we can specify. Similarly, the insane are not always insane. Indeed, it was the impression of the pseudopatients while living with them that they were sane for long periods of time—that the bizarre behaviors upon which their diagnoses were allegedly predicated constituted only a small fraction of their total behavior. If it makes no sense to label ourselves permanently depressed on the basis of an occasional depression, then it takes better evidence than is presently available to label all patients insane or schizophrenic on the basis of bizarre behaviors or cognitions. It seems more useful, as Mischel has pointed out, to limit our discussions to *behaviors,* the stimuli that provoke them, and their correlates.

It is not known why powerful impressions of personality traits, such as "crazy" or "insane," arise. Conceivably, when the origins of and stimuli that give rise to a behavior are remote or unknown, or when the behavior strikes us as immutable, trait labels regarding the *behavior* arise. When, on the other hand, the origins and stimuli are known and available, discourse is limited to the behavior itself. Thus, I may hallucinate because I am sleeping, or I may hallucinate because I have ingested a peculiar drug. These are termed sleep-induced hallucinations, or dreams, and drug-induced hallucinations, respectively. But when the stimuli to my hallucinations are unknown, that is called craziness, or schizophrenia—as if that inference were somehow as illuminating as the others.

THE EXPERIENCE OF
PSYCHIATRIC HOSPITALIZATION

The term "mental illness" is of recent origin. It was coined by people who were humane in their inclinations and who wanted very much to raise the station of (and the public's sympathies toward) the psychologically disturbed from that of witches and "crazies" to one that was akin to the physically ill. And they were at least partially successful, for the treatment of the mentally ill *has* improved considerably over the years. But while treatment has improved, it is doubtful that people really regard the mentally ill in the same way that they view the physically ill. A broken leg is something one recovers from, but mental illness allegedly endures forever. A broken leg does not threaten the observer, but a crazy schizophrenic? There is by now a host of evidence that attitudes toward the mentally ill are characterized by fear, hostility, aloofness, suspicion, and dread. The mentally ill are society's lepers.

That such attitudes infect the general population is perhaps not surprising, only upsetting. But that they affect the professionals—attendants, nurses, physicians, psychologists, and social workers—who treat and deal with the mentally ill is more disconcerting, both because such attitudes are self-evidently pernicious and because they are unwitting. Most mental health professionals would insist that they are sympathetic toward the mentally ill, that they are neither avoidant nor hostile. But it is more likely that an exquisite ambivalence characterizes their relations with psychiatric patients, such that their avowed impulses are only part of their entire attitude. Negative attitudes are there too and can easily be detected. Such attitudes should not surprise us. They are the natural offspring of the labels patients wear and the places in which they are found.

Consider the structure of the typical psychiatric hospital. Staff and patients are strictly segregated. Staff have their own living space, including their dining facilities, bathrooms, and assembly places. The glassed quarters that contain the professional staff, which the pseudopatients came to call "the cage," sit out on every dayroom. The staff emerge primarily for caretaking purposes—to give medication, to conduct a therapy or group meeting, to instruct or reprimand a patient. Otherwise, staff keep to themselves, almost as if the disorder that afflicts their charges is somehow catching.

So much is patient-staff segregation the rule that, for four public hospitals in which an attempt was made to measure the degree to which staff and patients mingle, it was necessary to use "time out of the staff cage" as the operational measure. While it was not the case that all time spent out of the cage was spent mingling with patients (attendants, for example, would occasionally emerge to watch television in the dayroom), it was the only way in which one could gather reliable data on time for measuring.

The average amount of time spent by attendants outside the cage was 11.3 percent (range, 3 to 52 percent). This figure does not represent only time spent mingling with patients, but also includes time spent on such chores as folding laundry, supervising patients while they shaved, directing ward clean-up, and sending patients to off-ward activities. It was the relatively rare attendant who spent time talking with patients or playing games with them. It proved impossible to obtain a "percent mingling time" for nurses, since the amount of time they spent out of the cage was too brief. Rather, we counted instances of emergence from the cage. On the average, daytime nurses emerged from the cage 11.5 times per shift, including instances when they left the ward entirely (range, 4 to 39 times). Late afternoon and night nurses were even less available, emerging on the average 9.4 times per shift (range, 4 to 41 times). Data on early morning nurses, who arrived usually after midnight and departed at 8:00 A.M., are not available because patients were asleep during most of this period.

Physicians, especially psychiatrists, were even less available. They were rarely seen on the wards. Quite commonly, they would be seen only when they arrived and departed, with the remaining time being spent in their offices or in the cage. On the average, physicians emerged on the ward 6.7 times per day (range, 1 to 17 times). It proved difficult to make an accurate estimate in this regard, since physicians often maintained hours that allowed them to come and go at different times.

The hierarchical organization of the psychiatric hospital has been commented on before, but the latent meaning of that kind of organization is worth noting again. Those with the most power have least to do with patients, and those with the least power are most involved with them. Recall, however, that the acquisition of role-appropriate behaviors occurs mainly through the observation of others, with the most powerful having the most influence. Consequently, it is understandable that attendants not only spend more time with patients than do any other members of the staff—that is required by their station in the hierarchy—but also, insofar as they learn from their superiors' behavior, spend as little time with patients as they can. Attendants are seen mainly in the cage, which is where the models, the action, and the power are.

I turn now to a different set of studies, these dealing with staff response to patient-initiated contact. It has long been known that the amount of time a person spends with you can be an index of your significance to him. If he initiates and maintains eye contact, there is reason to believe that he is considering your requests and needs. If he pauses to chat or actually stops and talks, there is added reason to infer that he is individuating you. In four hospitals, the pseudopatient approached the staff member with a request which took the following form: "Pardon me, Mr. [or Dr. or Mrs.] X, could you tell me when I will be eligible for grounds privileges?" (or ". . . when I will be presented at the staff meeting?" or ". . . when I am likely to be discharged?"). While the content of the question varied according to the appropriateness of the target and the pseudopatient's (apparent) current needs the form was always a courteous and relevant request for information. Care was taken never to approach a particular member of the staff more than once a day, lest the staff member become suspicious or irritated. In examining these data, remember that the behavior of the pseudopatients was neither bizarre nor disruptive. One could indeed engage in good conversation with them.

The data for these experiments are shown in Table 1, separately for physicians (column 1) and for nurses and attendants (column 2). Minor differences between these four institutions were overwhelmed by the degree to which staff avoided continuing contacts that patients had initiated. By far, their most common response consisted of either a brief response to the question, offered while they were "on the move" and with head averted, or no response at all.

TABLE 1

Self-Initiated Contact by Pseudopatients with Psychiatrists and Nurses and Attendants, Compared to Contact with Other Groups.

Contact	Psychiatric hospitals		University campus (nonmedical)		Physicians at University medical center	
	(1) Psychiatrists	(2) Nurses and attendants	(3) Faculty	(4) "Looking for a psychiatrist"	(5) "Looking for an internist"	(6) No additional comment
Responses						
Moves on, head averted (%)	71	88	0	0	0	0
Makes eye contact (%)	23	10	0	11	0	0
Pauses and chats (%)	2	2	0	11	0	10
Stops and talks (%)	4	0.5	100	78	100	90
Mean number of questions answered (out of 6)	*	*	6	3.8	4.8	4.5
Respondents (No.)	13	47	14	18	15	10
Attempts (No.)	185	1283	14	18	15	10

* Not applicable.

The encounter frequently took the following bizarre form:

PSEUDOPATIENT: Pardon me, Dr. X. Could you tell me when I am eligible for grounds privileges?
PHYSICIAN: Good morning, Dave. How are you today? [*Moves off without waiting for a response.*]

It is instructive to compare these data with data recently obtained at Stanford University. It has been alleged that large and eminent universities are characterized by faculty who are so busy that they have no time for students. For this comparison, a young lady approached individual faculty members who seemed to be walking purposefully to some meeting or teaching engagement and asked them the following six questions.

1. "Pardon me, could you direct me to Encina Hall?" (at the medical school: ". . . to the Clinical Research Center?").
2. "Do you know where Fish Annex is?" (there is no Fish Annex at Stanford).
3. "Do you teach here?"
4. "How does one apply for admission to the college?" (at the medical school: ". . . to the medical school?").
5. "Is it difficult to get in?"
6. "Is there financial aid?"

Without exception, as can be seen in Table 1 (column 3), all of the questions were answered. No matter how rushed they were, all respondents not only maintained eye contact, but stopped to talk. Indeed, many of the respondents went out of their way to direct or take the questioner to the office she was seeking, to try to locate "Fish Annex," or to discuss with her the possibilities of being admitted to the university.

Similar data, also shown in Table 1 (columns 4, 5, and 6), were obtained in the hospital. Here too, the young lady came prepared with six questions. After the first question, however, she remarked to eighteen of her respondents (column 4), "I'm looking for a psychiatrist," and to fifteen others (column 5), "I'm looking for an internist." Ten other respondents received no inserted comment (column 6). The general degree of cooperative responses is considerably higher for these university groups than it was for pseudopatients in psychiatric hospitals. Even so, differences are apparent within the medical school setting. Once having indicated that she was looking for a psychiatrist, the degree of cooperation elicited was less than when she sought an internist.

POWERLESSNESS AND DEPERSONALIZATION

Eye contact and verbal contact reflect concern and individuation; their absence, avoidance and depersonalization. The data I have presented do not do justice to the rich daily encounters that grew up around matters of depersonalization and avoidance. I have records of patients who were beaten by staff for the sin of having initiated verbal contact. During my own experience, for example, one patient was beaten in the presence of other patients for having approached an attendant and told him, "I like you." Occasionally, punishment meted out to patients for misdemeanors seemed so excessive that it could not be justified by the most radical interpretations of psychiatric canon. Nevertheless, they appeared to go unquestioned. Tempers were often short. A patient who had not heard a call for medication would be roundly excoriated, and the morning attendants would often wake patients with, "Come on, you m—f—s, out of bed!"

Neither anecdotal nor "hard" data can convey the overwhelming sense of powerlessness which invades the individual as he is continually exposed to the depersonalization of the psychiatric hospital. It hardly matters *which* psychiatric hospital—the excellent public ones and the very plush private hospital were better than the rural and shabby ones in this regard, but, again, the features that psychiatric hospitals had in common overwhelmed by far their apparent differences.

Powerlessness was evident everywhere. The patient is deprived of many of his legal rights by dint of his psychiatric commitment. He is shorn of credibility by virtue of his psychiatric label. His freedom of movement is restricted. He cannot initiate contact with the staff, but may only respond to such overtures as they make. Personal privacy is minimal. Patient quarters and possessions can be entered and examined by any staff member, for whatever reason. His personal history and anguish is available to any staff member (often including the "gray lady" and "candy striper" volunteer) who chooses to read his folder, regardless of their therapeutic relationship to him. His personal hygiene and waste evacuation are often monitored. The water closets may have no doors.

At times, depersonalization reached such proportions that pseudopatients had the sense that they were invisible, or at least unworthy of account. Upon being admitted, I and other pseudopatients took the initial physical examinations in a semipublic room, where staff members went about their own business as if we were not there.

On the ward, attendants delivered verbal and occasionally serious physical abuse to patients in the presence of other observing patients, some of whom (the pseudopatients) were writing it all down. Abusive behavior, on the other hand, terminated quite abruptly when other staff members were known to be coming. Staff are credible witnesses. Patients are not.

A nurse unbuttoned her uniform to adjust her brassiere in the presence of an entire ward of viewing men. One did not have the sense that she was being seductive. Rather, she didn't notice us. A group of staff persons might point to a patient in the dayroom and discuss him animatedly, as if he were not there.

One illuminating instance of depersonalization and invisibility occurred with regard to medications. All told, the pseudopatients were administered nearly 2100 pills, including Elavil, Stelazine, Compazine, and Thorazine, to name but a few. (That such a variety of medications should have been administered to patients presenting identical symptoms is itself worthy of note.) Only two were swallowed. The rest were either pocketed or deposited in the toilet. The pseudopatients were not alone in this. Although I have no precise records on how many patients rejected their medications, the pseudopatients frequently found the medications of other patients in the toilet before they deposited their own. As long as they were cooperative, their behavior and the pseudopatients' own in this matter, as in other important matters, went unnoticed throughout.

Reactions to such depersonalization among pseudopatients were intense. Although they had come to the hospital as participant observers and were fully aware that they did not "belong," they nevertheless found themselves caught up in and fighting the process of depersonalization. Some examples: a graduate student in psychology asked his wife to bring his textbooks to the hospital so he could "catch up on his homework"—this despite the elaborate precautions taken to conceal his professional association. The same student, who had trained for quite some time to get into the hospital, and who had looked forward to the experience, "remembered" some drag races that he had wanted to see on the weekend and insisted that he be discharged by that time. Another pseudopatient attempted a romance with a nurse. Subsequently, he informed the staff that he was applying for admission to graduate school in psychology and was very likely to be admitted, since a graduate professor was one of his regular hospital visitors. The same person began to engage in psychotherapy with other patients—all of this as a way of becoming a person in an impersonal environment.

THE SOURCES OF DEPERSONALIZATION

What are the origins of depersonalization? I have already mentioned two. First are attitudes held by all of us toward the mentally ill—including those who treat them—attitudes characterized by fear, distrust, and horrible expectations on the one hand, and benevolent intentions on the other. Our ambivalence leads, in this instance as in others, to avoidance.

Second, and not entirely separate, the hierarchical structure of the psychiatric hospital facilitates depersonalization. Those who are at the top have least to do with patients, and their behavior inspires the rest of the staff. Average daily contact with psychiatrists, psychologists, residents, and physicians combined ranged from 3.9 to 25.1 minutes, with an over-all mean of 6.8 (six pseudopatients over a total of 129 days of hospitalization). Included in this average is time spent in the admissions interview, ward meetings in the presence of a senior staff member, group and individual psychotherapy contacts, case presentation conferences, and discharge meetings. Clearly, patients do not spend much time in interpersonal contact with doctoral staff. And doctoral staff serve as models for nurses and attendants.

There are probably other sources. Psychiatric installations are presently in serious financial straits. Staff shortages are pervasive, staff time at a premium. Something has to give, and that something is patient contact. Yet, while financial stresses are realities, too much can be made of them. I have the impression that the psychological forces that result in depersonalization are much stronger than the fiscal ones and that the addition of more staff would not correspondingly improve patient care in this regard. The incidence of staff meetings and the enormous amount of record-keeping on patients, for example, have not been as substantially reduced as has patient contact. Priorities exist, even during hard times. Patient contact is not a significant priority in the traditional psychiatric hospital, and fiscal pressures do not account for this. Avoidance and depersonalization may.

Heavy reliance upon psychotropic medication tacitly contributes to depersonalization by convincing staff that treatment is indeed being conducted and that further patient contact may not be necessary. Even here, however, caution needs to be exercised in understanding the role of psychotropic drugs. If patients were powerful rather than powerless, if they were viewed as interesting individuals rather than diagnostic entities, if they were socially significant rather than social lepers, if their anguish truly and wholly compelled our sympathies and concerns, would we not *seek* contact with them, despite the availability of medications? Perhaps for the pleasure of it all?

THE CONSEQUENCES OF LABELING AND DEPERSONALIZATION

Whenever the ratio of what is known to what needs to be known approaches zero, we tend to invent "knowledge" and assume that we understand more than we actually do. We seem unable to acknowledge that we simply don't know. The needs for diagnosis and remediation of behavioral and emotional problems are enormous. But rather than acknowledge that we are just embarking on understanding, we continue to label patients schizophrenic, manic-depressive, and insane, as if in those words we had captured the essence of understanding. The facts of the matter are that we have known for a long time that diagnoses are often not useful or reliable, but we have nevertheless continued to use them. We now know that we cannot distinguish insanity from sanity. It is depressing to consider how that information will be used.

Not merely depressing, but frightening. How many people, one wonders, are sane but not recognized as such in our psychiatric institutions? How many have been needlessly stripped of their privileges of citizenship, from the right to vote and drive to that of handling their own accounts? How many have feigned insanity in order to avoid the criminal consequences of their behavior, and, conversely, how many would rather stand trial than live interminably in a psychiatric hospital—but are wrongly thought to be mentally ill? How many have been stigmatized by well-intentioned, but nevertheless erroneous, diagnoses? On the last point, recall again that a "type 2 error" in psychiatric diagnosis does not have the same consequences it does in medical diagnosis. A diagnosis of cancer that has been found to be in error is cause for celebration. But psychiatric diagnoses are rarely found to be in error. The label sticks, a mark of inadequacy forever.

Finally, how many patients might be "sane" outside the psychiatric hospital but seem insane in it—not because craziness resides in them, as it were, but because they are responding to a bizarre setting, one that may be unique to institutions which harbor nether people? Goffman calls the process of socialization to such institutions "mortification"—an apt metaphor that includes the processes of depersonalization that have been described here. And while it is impossible to know whether the pseudopatients' responses to these processes are characteristic of all inmates—they were, after all, not real patients—it is difficult to believe that these processes of socialization to a psychiatric hospital provide useful attitudes or habits of response for living in the "real world."

SUMMARY AND CONCLUSIONS

It is clear that we cannot distinguish the sane from the insane in psychiatric hospitals. The hospital itself imposes a special environment in which the meanings of behavior can easily be misunderstood. The consequences to patients hospitalized in such an environment—the powerlessness, depersonalization, segregation, mortification, and self-labeling—seem undoubtedly countertherapeutic.

I do not, even now, understand this problem well enough to perceive solutions. But two matters seem to have some promise. The first concerns the proliferation of community mental health facilities, of crisis intervention centers, of the human potential movement, and of behavior therapies that, for all of their own problems, tend to avoid psychiatric labels, to focus on specific problems and behaviors, and to retain the individual in a relatively nonpejorative environment. Clearly, to the extent that we refrain from sending the distressed to insane places, our impressions of them are less likely to be distorted. (The risk of distorted perceptions, it seems to me, is always present, since we are much more sensitive to an individual's behaviors and verbalizations than we are to the subtle contextual stimuli that often promote them. At issue here is a matter of magnitude. And, as I have shown, the magnitude of distortion is exceedingly high in the extreme context that is a psychiatric hospital.)

The second matter that might prove promising speaks to the need to increase the sensitivity of mental health workers and researchers to the *Catch 22* position of psychiatric patients. Simply reading materials in this area will be of help to some such workers and researchers. For others, directly experiencing the impact of psychiatric hospitalization will be of enormous use. Clearly, further research into the social psychology of such total institutions will both facilitate treatment and deepen understanding.

I and the other pseudopatients in the psychiatric setting had distinctly negative reactions. We do not pretend to describe the subjective experiences of true patients. Theirs may be different from ours, particularly with the passage of time and the necessary process of adaptation to one's environment. But we can and do speak to the relatively more objective indices of treatment within the hospital. It could be a mistake, and a very unfortunate one, to consider that what happened to us derived from malice or stupidity on the part of the staff. Quite the contrary, our overwhelming impression of them was of people who really cared, who were committed and who were uncommonly intelligent. Where they failed, as they sometimes did painfully, it would be more accurate to attribute those failures to the environment in which they, too, found themselves than to personal callousness. Their perceptions and behavior were controlled by the situation, rather than being motivated by a malicious disposition. In a more benign environment, one that was less attached to global diagnosis, their behaviors and judgments might have been more benign and effective.

8. SUGGESTIONS FOR FURTHER READING

BECKER, HOWARD (ed.). *The Other Side* (New York: The Free Press, 1964).*
————. *Outsiders: Studies in the Sociology of Deviance* (New York: The Free Press, 1963).*
CLINARD, MARSHALL. *Sociology of Deviant Behavior,* 3rd ed. (New York: Holt, Rinehart & Winston, 1968).
COHEN, ALBERT. *Deviance and Control* (Englewood Cliffs, N.J.: Prentice-Hall, 1966).*
DOUGLAS, JACK (ed.). *Observations of Deviance* (New York: Random House, 1970).*
DURKHEIM, ÉMILE. *Suicide* (Glencoe, Ill.: The Free Press, 1951).*
ERIKSON, KAI. *Wayward Puritans* (New York: John Wiley & Sons, 1966).*
GOFFMAN, ERVING. *Stigma: Notes on the Management of Spoiled Identity* (Englewood Cliffs, N.J.: Prentice-Hall, 1963).*
HENRY, ANDREW, and JAMES SHORT. *Suicide and Homicide* (Glencoe, Ill.: The Free Press, 1954).*
HUMPHREYS, LAUD. *Tearoom Trade: Impersonal Sex in Public Places* (Chicago: Aldine-Atherton, 1970).
IANNI, FRANCIS. *A Family Business: Kinship and Social Control in Organized Crime* (New York: Russell Sage, 1972).*
JACKSON, GEORGE. *Soledad Brothers: The Prison Letters of George Jackson* (New York: Coward, McCann & Geoghegan, 1970).*
KLOCKARS, CARL. *The Professional Fence* (New York: The Free Press, 1974).
MATZA, DAVID. *Delinquency and Drift* (New York: John Wiley & Sons, 1964).*
MITFORD, JESSICA. *Kind and Unusual Punishment: The Prison Business* (New York: Alfred A. Knopf, 1973).*
MURTON, TOM, and JOE HYAMS. *Accomplices to the Crime* (New York: Grove Press, 1969).*
SCHUR, EDWIN. *Crimes Without Victims* (Englewood Cliffs, N.J.: Prentice-Hall, 1965).*
————. *Our Criminal Society* (Englewood Cliffs, N.J.: Prentice-Hall, 1969).*
SKOLNICK, JEROME. *Justice Without Trial* (New York: John Wiley & Sons, 1966).*
STENGEL, ERWIN. *Suicide and Attempted Suicide* (New York: Humanities Press, 1964).*
SUTHERLAND, EDWIN. *The Professional Thief* (Chicago: University of Chicago Press, 1937).*
————. *White Collar Crime* (New York: Holt, Rinehart & Winston, reissue 1960).*
SYKES, GRESHAM. *The Society of Captives* (Princeton, N.J.: Princeton University Press, 1958).*
THRASHER, FREDERIC. *The Gang* (Chicago: University of Chicago Press, 1927).*
* *Available in paperback.*

9. Political Sociology

INTRODUCTION

To understand the field of interest of the political sociologist, one must be familiar with several basic terms. *Power refers to a relationship in which one person is able to exercise his will in determining the behavior of another.* Power may be exerted by force, domination, manipulation, or any combination of these—for example, by the gunman who insists that the storekeeper open his cash drawer, the parent who demands that the child go to bed at a certain hour, the advertiser who convinces the public of the worth of his product.

Authority refers to legitimate power—that is, influence exercised by persons entitled to give commands to others obliged to obey them. When we say that power is legitimate, we mean that it is recognized as socially right and proper. For example, the policeman has the authority to stop traffic; the judge has the authority to order that a convicted offender pay a fine or spend a certain period of time in confinement.

We may define *government* as a social institution consisting of an enduring complex of norms and statuses through which the functions of maintaining order and enforcing norms are performed. Thus, the American Government includes the Constitution and the laws; the structure of the legislative, executive, and judiciary branches; the statuses of senator, congressman, President, Supreme Court justice, cabinet member, Federal Bureau of Investigation personnel, member of the U.S. Army, and the many other elected and appointed officials. The *state*, the agency that performs governmental functions, may be defined as having a "monopoly of the legitimate use of physical force within a given territory."[1] Thus, the state possesses the supreme power within a society.

The transition from one ruling group or system to another within a given society may take place over so extended a period of time and be so unceremonious that the members of the society find it difficult to discern when it has taken place. On the other hand, the transfer of power may be very abrupt and may involve considerable violence, in which case it is termed a revolution. In Chapter 10, "Social Change," James Davies examines a number of leading causal explanations of revolutionary political change, in addition to offering his own theory.

The political sociologist is especially interested in the underlying social conditions that affect government and power. According to Broom and Selznick,[2] three main areas within political sociology may be distinguished: (1) the social foundations of political institutions, especially the way in which political structures depend upon social organization and cultural values; (2) the social bases of political behavior—that is, why and how individuals vote, hold political opinions, support political associations and movements; and (3) the social aspect of political process, involving the identification of types of organized groups in politics and their patterns of association, in order to evaluate how interest groups, parties, and political movements affect political life.

In order for any society to remain in existence, there must be provisions for the accommodation of conflicts, the protection of the members, and the maintenance of order. Since every society must deal with these basic sociopolitical problems, political institutions, in some form, are universal phenomena. Differentiated political institutions are not often found in preindustrial societies, where political structures are likely to be inseparable from the system of kinship. In these simpler societies, social control is most often maintained informally, through the mores and the folkways, rather than regulated through judicial and police systems. The relative paucity of specialized political and legal institutions in simpler societies is examined more closely in Robert Redfield's discussion of "The Folk Society," presented in Chapter 3, "Social Organization." By contrast, in modern industrial societies one finds the nation-state, a formally organized, specialized, and highly differentiated political institution. In such complex and heterogeneous societies, social control is most often exercised by law.

Claude Lévi-Strauss asserts that, in studying simple societies, one can identify generic patterns of behavior that are invaluable for understanding more complex social worlds. Using this approach and the method he calls structuralism, he examines political institutions among the Nambikuara of Brazil in an effort to shed light on our own political arrangements. His research uncovers a basic feature of political rela-

[1] H. H. Gerth and C. Wright Mills, eds., *From Max Weber: Essays in Sociology* (New York: Oxford University Press, 1958), p. 78.
[2] L. Broom and P. Selznick, *Sociology* (New York: Harper & Row, 1963), p. 670.

tions everywhere: the reciprocity between the leaders of society and the led. The Nambikuara tribesmen receive numerous benefits from the chief in exchange for their deferential behavior. The chief, while receiving the benefits of polygyny and other rewards, is obliged to demonstrate unremitting generosity and especial hunting proficiency. These pressures have made this role a somewhat unattractive social position to the Nambikuara. Lévi-Strauss's findings appear to support the views of a number of political theorists of the Enlightenment, including Rousseau and Locke, who advanced the idea of a "social contract" between rulers and ruled as essential for stable political relations. No society, no matter how effective its coercive powers, can maintain its existence for very long without some modicum of consent on the part of those governed.

The stabilization of power relationships in society revolves around the nature of authority. The legitimation of power comes from many sources. The late German sociologist Max Weber classified authority into three main types, suggesting the most common and important sources of each:

Charismatic authority is based on the extraordinary personal characteristics of the leader. For example, the authority of Mao Tse-tung, Mahatma Gandhi, or the Nambikuara chief more or less typifies the charismatic type.

Traditional authority, by contrast, bases its legitimacy on custom and accepted practice. The ascribed power of the king in a monarchy or of the tribal chief who inherits his status are examples of legitimacy based on tradition.

In the third type, *rational-legal* authority, a body of generalized rules that apply impersonally to both the ruler and the ruled is the basis of legitimacy. Authority accompanies a particular office or status and is distinct from the person who occupies it at a given time. For instance, the Presidency of the United States or the executives of any corporation exemplify rational-legal authority.

In most societies, all three types of authority are represented, although one type usually is the most pervasive, as rational-legal authority is in the United States. But no recent American president has relied exclusively on rational-legal authority: Most have attempted to achieve some degree of charismatic authority by presenting themselves to the public in an attractive personal manner; most have followed their predecessors' policies, to varying degrees, in an effort to maintain a semblance of traditional continuity.

It was Weber's belief that the long-run trend will be marked by the increasing development of rational-legal authority. This form of authority corresponds most closely with bureaucratization. While there will be occasional eruptions of the charismatic, associated with revolutionary social movements, this basis of authority will eventually decline because of its inherent instability. Like charismatic authority, traditional authority, embodied as it is in the person of the monarch or the patriarch, presents problems of succession and expansion that will ultimately lead to its transformation into rational-legal authority.

Political sociologists have pursued other lines of inquiry, including, as we have noted, the social bases of individual political behavior. In this venture, probably the greatest effort has been expended in the area of voting behavior.

The extensive research on voting patterns in the United States has produced a great fund of knowledge on Americans' voting behavior.[3] In presidential elections, voter participation is approximately 60 per cent of the eligible electorate; in regional and local elections, participation is usually lower. The social factors associated with voting include high income, high educational attainment, white-collar occupation, government employment, long-term residence in the community, and membership in voluntary associations. Men vote more frequently than women; whites, more frequently than blacks; middle-aged citizens, more frequently than the young or old. Married people vote more regularly than nonmarried. Jews vote more often than Catholics, with Protestants occupying an intermediate position. Voting is more frequent among those whose personal interests are strongly affected by government policies. For example, during periods of national crisis, the electorate as a whole takes a greater interest in politics.

Political sociologists have noted a number of social correlates associated with political-party membership. In general, the higher one's occupational status, income, and educational attainment, the greater one's support for conservative political parties. Males somewhat more than females, blacks more than whites, Jews and Catholics, and labor-union members—all are more inclined to endorse the parties of the left. While there are shifts from time to time, those whose views would be classified as "conservative" generally are more likely to support the Republican Party; those with more "liberal" views tend to be aligned with the Democratic Party.

As people move up the social ladder, they tend to adopt more conservative political positions. This tendency appears to be more pronounced in the United States than in many European countries. Lipset and Bendix suggest that European men who move up in the economic hierarchy find it difficult to adjust their life-style to a higher level, while American men do so more readily.[4] Perhaps European men identify more closely with the political ideology of their original class affiliation than is true of the less class-conscious American.

[3] For excellent summaries of these findings, upon which the following discussion relies heavily, see Angus Campbell *et al.*, *The American Voter* (New York: John Wiley & Sons, 1960); and S. M. Lipset, *Political Man* (Garden City, N.Y.: Doubleday, 1960).

[4] S. M. Lipset and R. Bendix, *Social Mobility in Industrial Society* (Berkeley: University of California Press, 1959), p. 68.

Those who are mobile in social status as well as those who are torn by conflicting sociopolitical memberships—e.g., being both a Catholic (Democratic influence) and a bank president (Republican influence)—are more likely to consider themselves political independents, to shift their vote from one election to the next, and to abstain from electoral participation.

Political life and political decision-making consist of more than the sum of individual political actions or electoral results. The activities of a vast array of groups, organized for the pursuit of political goals, have considerable importance in determining political affairs. The political sociologist has a deep interest in the variety of group life and how it affects political action.

In characterizing American political life, there appear to be two widely shared, competing views of the political process. Some students of American politics have advanced a "pluralist" theory of national power, in which political action is seen as a result of the diversified and balanced plurality of interest groups, each of which is chiefly concerned with protecting its own interests and blocking the threatening actions of others. On some issues, coalitions of various groups are formed to pursue specific aims or goals, which may be opposed by other coalitions. In this perspective, as the issues change, accompanying changes take place in the structure of coalition forces. There is no stable structure of power; power is ever shifting, changing with the issues involved and affected by the varying success of groups in mobilizing their resources against others.

In contrast to this view is the "power-elite" thesis advocated by the late C. Wright Mills and G. William Domhoff, among others. In this conception, political affairs are determined by a very small number of individuals and groups. Decisions are frequently made outside the formal structures of government. According to Mills, the real rulers of America come from among three groups: leading corporate executives, military leaders, and high-ranking politicians. These individuals have similar socialization experiences (they attend the same private schools, academies, and ivy-league colleges) and travel in the same social circles. They share similar outlooks and form an interlocking directorate of power. These individuals comprise a stable and enduring power base whose power is not diminished by electoral process; they are subject to little control by others, least of all by the average citizen.

There are still other views of the American political scene, such as the argument advanced by Theodore Roszak in his popular *The Making of a Counter-Culture* (Doubleday, 1969). Roszak argues that a new kind of political cleavage is beginning to appear in America and other advanced industrial societies—adult-youth conflict. Further technological development, he claims, has rendered some of the previous political cleavage points—conservative versus liberal, right-wing versus left-wing, capitalist versus socialist—less meaningful. The new conflict groups are beginning to consist of a "militant minority of dissenting youth" versus "the sluggish, consensus-and-coalition politics of their middle-aged elders."

In *The Making of a Counter-Culture,* Roszak asserts that the newly emerging conflict between youth and adults is not simply political but represents an almost total opposition, in which most of the components of culture—fundamental values, moral prescriptions, and institutional matrix—are matters of contention. The youthful counterculture includes opposition to rationality, bureaucracy, authority, and technology, combined with an emphasis on spontaneity, immediacy, self-expression, and self-actualization. The outlook highlights authenticity, commitment, and a quest for community. Whether these values will become more widely shared and will come to represent a major axis of political cleavage, only the future will reveal.

Perhaps the most significant event in American political life during the mid-seventies was the Watergate scandal, which brought down President Richard Nixon and resulted in criminal charges against nearly all of his close aides. Watergate has inspired an almost endless array of questions about political life in democratic-industrial societies. What should be the ethical standards of political office holders? How much power should be vested in the office of the chief executive? What interests and concerns rightfully comprise national security? How should a nation's well-being be safeguarded? These are but a few of the many questions now being discussed throughout the halls of Congress and the courts, in the press, and among the political body at large. In the post-Watergate period serious objections have been raised by many against the CIA and the FBI, dispelling the uncriticizable aura these investigative bodies formerly enjoyed.

Kirkpatrick Sale's "World Behind Watergate" attempts to probe into the sociological causes of Watergate. His provocative thesis is that Nixon's reign signaled the emergence of a new elite in American politics, composed of the newly wealthy, aerospace and defense interests, and groups with holdings in oil, gas, and real estate. These southern-rim people, or "cowboys," as others have called them, are insecure in their new power and have felt obliged to act in shady ways to bolster their ascendancy over the previously dominant eastern establishment. Sale contends that this group has assumed a pivotal position in the conservative movement in American politics and that it promises to continue to exercise a great deal of power for a long time to come. On the other hand, it is possible that public indignation about Watergate crimes and today's unstable economic conditions may divert public interest away from conservatism.

Sale's viewpoint shows a close affinity to Mills's theory of American politics. Whether the current reformist mood will ultimately succeed in bringing down the elite-led politics of the past, and whether it will give rise to substantial reforms that will make future Watergates unlikely—revitalizing our democracy—remains to be seen.

The Social and Psychological Aspects of Chieftainship in a Primitive Tribe*

Claude Lévi-Strauss

. . . **I do not** believe that the data I am going to present, if considered only as data on chieftainship among a hitherto little known group, would honestly deserve one hour of attention. Similar facts have been recorded many times, either joined or separately. The particular interest offered by the Nambi-kuara is that they confront us with one of the simplest conceivable forms of social and political organization. Chiefs and chieftainship exist, among all human groups, under very different forms, but it would be vain to assign a special functional value to each of the modalities down to their smallest details. There is, undoubtedly, a function in chieftainship. This can, however, be reached only through analysis as the underlying principle of the institution. In other words, the differing structure of the digestive organs in man, ox, fish, and clam do not point toward different functions of the digestive system. The function is always and everywhere the same and can be better studied, and more fully understood, where it exists under a simple form—for instance, in a mollusc. Similarly, and as Professor Lowie once wrote, if anthropology is to be considered as a scientific study, its subject matter cannot be individual cultures but culture taken as a whole; the role of individual cultures being to offer, according to their own characteristics, special angles from which the basic functions of culture, although universal in application, can be more easily reached.

This will, perhaps, help us to eliminate preliminary questions that otherwise could have proved very difficult. Anthropologists in South America and elsewhere have been eagerly debating the question of whether these South American tribes—nomadic, relying mostly on collecting and gathering, with little or no agriculture, little or no pottery, and, in some cases, with no dwelling other than crude shelters—should be considered as truly primitive and as having preserved their exceptionally low cultural level through tarriance, or whether they did not previously possess a higher type of social and material organization and have regressed to a pseudoarchaism under unfavorable circumstances. The Nambikuara are one of those tribes

* From *Transactions of the New York Academy of Sciences,* Section of Anthropology, vol. 7 (October 23, 1944), pp. 16–32. Reprinted by permission of the author and The New York Academy of Sciences.

that, together with the Siriono, on the other side of the Guaporé valley, the Cayapo, Bororo, Karaja of central Brazil, the so-called *Gé* of Central and Eastern Brazil, and some others, form a kernel of primitiveness surrounded, in the West, by the higher tribes of the upper Amazon, the Bolivian plain and the Chaco, and from the Orinoco's to the La Plata's estuaries, by a coastal strip inhabited mostly by the Arawak, Carib, and Tupi-Guarani linguistic families. An independent linguistic stock divided into several dialects, the Nambikuara seem to display one of the more backward cultures in South America. At least, some of their bands do not build huts and are wholly ignorant of pottery—and, even among the others, these two arts are exceedingly poor. There is no weaving, except for the narrow arm and leg bands that are made of cotton; no dress whatsoever, either for the men or for the women; no sleeping contrivances, such as hammocks or platforms, the natives being used to sleeping on the bare ground without the protection of blankets, mats, or hides. Gardening exists only during the rainy season and does not free the Nambikuara from wandering during the seven months of the dry season, looking for wild roots, fruits, and seeds, small animals such as lizards, snakes, bats, spiders, and grasshoppers, and, generally speaking, anything that may prevent them from starving. As a matter of fact, their geographical surroundings, which are located in the northwestern part of the state of Mato Grosso and include the headwaters of the Tapajoz, Rio Roosevelt, and Rio Gi-Parana, consist of a desolated savanna with few vegetal resources and still less game.

Had I approached my subject from a point of view other than the one outlined above, I could not have avoided a long discussion in South American cultural history, aimed at clearing up this apparent primitiveness, on the question as to whether the survival of early conditions of life in South America is genuine, or whether we should consider it as a more recent—though undoubtedly pre-Columbian—result of culture clashes and processes of acculturation. Whatever the answer may be, it cannot substantially change our problem: Whether tarriant or recessive, the Nambikuara society functions, in the present, as one of the simplest forms of human society to be conceived. We shall not seek information from the particular history that kept them in their exceptionally crude organization or brought them back to it. We shall only look at the experiment in social anthropology that they now enact under our very eyes.

This holds especially true in respect to their social and political life. For, if we do not know what was the material culture of the Nambikuara forty years ago (they were discovered only in 1907), we do know that their numbers became tremendously reduced after their contact with white civilization. General (then Colonel) Candido Mariano da Silva Rondon, who discovered and studied them, first stated that their number was about 20,000. This was around 1915. I take this figure as greatly exaggerated; but, even if reduced by one-half, it considerably exceeds the present number, which is hardly more than 2,000. Epidemics have taken care of difference. What does this mean, from the point of view of our study? During the dry season, the Nambikuara live in nomadic bands, each one under the leadership of a chief, who, during the sedentary life of the rainy months, may be either a village chief or a person of position. General Rondon wrote that, at the time he was exploring the country, it was not rare to see bands averaging two or three hundred individuals. Now, sixty or seventy people are seldom met together, the average size of the bands being twenty individuals, women and children included. This demographic collapse cannot possibly have taken place without affecting the structure of the band. But here, too, we do not need to concern ourselves with such questions as the type of political organization in earlier times. It is probably more difficult to understand Nambikuara sociology now than it was thirty years ago. Perhaps, on the contrary, the much reduced Nambikuara band offers, better than in the past, a privileged field for a study in social anthropology. My contention is that, precisely on account of its extreme impoverishment, Nambikuara political structure lays bare some basic functions that may remain hidden in more complex and elaborate systems of government.

Each year, at the end of the rainy season—that is, in April or in early May —the semipermanent dwellings laid in the vicinity of the gallery-forest where the gardens are cleared and tilled are abandoned, and the population splits into several bands formed on a free-choice basis. Each band includes from two to about ten families usually tied by kinship. This may be misleading when a band is met, for one easily gets the impression that it is formed as an extensive family. It does not take long to discover, however, that the kinship tie between two families belonging to separate bands may be as close [as], and eventually closer than, between two families inside the same band. The Nambikuara have a simple kinship system based on cross-cousin marriage and the subsequent dichotomy between "cross" and "parallel" in every generation. Therefore, all the men in one generation are either "brothers" or "brothers-in-law," and men and women are to one another either siblings (true or classificatory) or spouses (true or classificatory). Similarly, children are, in relation to the adults, either sons and daughters (true or classificatory) or nephews and nieces, which is the same as actual or potential children-in-law.[1] As a result, there is no great choice of terms to express kinship, and this explains why kinship inside the band may appear closer than it actually is, and kinship between people belonging to different bands more remote than shown by genealogies. Furthermore, a bilateral, cross-cousin marriage system functioning in a relatively small tribe must produce a progressive narrowing, and even a multiplication, of the kinship ties between any two individuals. This is a supplementary reason preventing family relationship from becoming really operative in the constitution of the band. It can be said that, inside the band as well as between the different bands that are the offspring of the same temporary village, everybody is everybody's kin, in pretty much the same fashion.

Why, then, the splitting-up process? Two different considerations must

[1] Claude Lévi-Strauss, "The Social Use of Kinship Terms Among Brazilian Indians." *American Anthropologist*, XLV, no. 3 (1943).

be brought forth to answer this question. From an economic point of view, the scarcity of wild-food resources and the subsequent high square-mileage needed to feed one individual during the nomadic period make the division into small bands almost compulsory. The real question is not why there is a division but, rather, on what basis it takes place. I have said that this is done by free choice, but this freedom is not arbitrary. There are, in the initial group, several men acknowledged as leaders (who likely acquired this reputation from their behavior during the nomadic life), and who make the relatively stable nuclei around which the different aggregates center. The importance, as well as the permanence of the aggregate through successive years, depends largely upon the ability of each of these leaders to keep his rank and eventually to improve it. Thus, it may be said that leadership does not exist as a result of the band's needs, but, instead, that the band receives its shape, its size, and even its origin from the potential leader who antedates it.

There is, however, a continuous function of leadership, although not permanently assumed by the same individual. Among the Nambikuara, chieftainship is not hereditary. When a chief grows old or is taken ill, and when he does not feel able to fulfill his heavy duty any more, he himself designates his successor. "This one—this one will be the chief . . ." he says. It seems likely that this autocratic power to insure one's own succession is more apparent than real. We shall emphasize later . . . the small amount of authority enjoyed by the chief; and, in this case as in many others, the final decision is probably preceded by a careful survey of public opinion, the designated heir being, at the same time, the one with the greate[st] support from the members of the band. The appointment of the new chief is not only limited by the wishes or disapproval of the band; it needs also to correspond to the plans of the individual to be chosen. Not seldom does the offer of leadership meet with a vehement refusal: "I don't want to be the chief." Then, a new choice must be made. As a matter of fact, chieftainship does not seem to be coveted by many people, and the general attitude of the different chiefs I happened to know was less to brag about their importance and authority than to complain of their many duties and heavy responsibilities. What, then, are the privileges of the chief, and what are his obligations?

When, about 1560, the great French moralist of the sixteenth century, Montaigne, met in Rouen with three Brazilian Indians brought there by some navigator, he asked one of them what were the privileges of the chief (Montaigne said the "King") in his country; and the native, himself a chief, answered: "To walk ahead on the warpath." Montaigne related this story in a famous chapter of the *Essays* where he wondered a great deal about this proud definition;[2] but it was a greater wonder to me when, almost four centuries later, putting the same question to my informants, I was given the same answer. Civilized countries are certainly not accustomed to such con-

[2] Michel de Montaigne. "Des Cannibales." *Essais,* Livre I, XXXI (end of the chapter).

stancy in the field of political philosophy! Striking as it may be, this answer is less significant than the name by which the chief is designated in the Nambikuara language. *Uilikande,* the native word for chief, seems to mean "the one who unites" or "the one who joins together." This etymology suggests that the native mind is fully conscious of this extremely important phenomenon that I have pointed out from the beginning; namely, that the leader appears as the cause of the group's willingness to aggregate rather than as the result of the need for a central authority felt by a group already constituted.

Personal prestige and the ability to inspire confidence are thus the foundations of leadership in Nambikuara society. As a matter of fact, both are necessary in the man who will become the guide of this adventurous experiment—the nomadic life of the dry season. For six or seven months, the chief will be entirely responsible for the management of his band. It is he who orders the start of the wandering period, selects the routes, chooses the stopping points and the duration of the stay at each of them, whether a few days or several weeks. He also orders and organizes the hunting, fishing, collecting and gathering expeditions and determines the conduct of the band in relation to neighboring groups. When the band's chief is, at the same time, a village chief (taking the word village with the restricted meaning of semipermanent dwelling for the rainy season), his duties do not stop there. He will determine the moment when, and the place where, the group will settle; he will also direct the gardening and decide what plants are to be cultivated; and, generally speaking, he will organize the occupations according to the season's needs and possibilities.

These rather versatile duties, it should be pointed out from the start, are not facilitated by any fixed power or recognized authority. Consent is at the origin of leadership, and consent, too, furnishes the only measure of its legitimacy. Disorderly conduct (according to the native standards) and unwillingness to work on the part of one or two discontented individuals may seriously jeopardize the chief's program and the welfare of his small group. In this eventuality, however, the chief has no coercive power at his disposal. The eviction of the bad people can take place only insofar as the chief is able to make public feeling coincide with his own opinion. Thus, he must continuously display a skill belonging more to the politician trying to keep hold of his fluctuating majority than to an overpowering ruler. Furthermore, he does not only need to keep his group together. Although the band lives practically alone and by itself during the nomadic period, the existence of the other bands is not forgotten. It is not enough to do well; the chief must try—and his people count on him for that—to do better than the others.

No social structure is weaker and more fragile than the Nambikuara band. If the chief's authority appears too exacting, if he keeps too many women for himself (I shall later analyze the special features of the chief's polygamy), or if he does not satisfactorily solve the food problem in times of scarcity, discontent will very likely appear. Then, individuals, or families, will separate from the group and join another band believed to be better managed. For instance, this band may get better fare from the discovery of new hunting or gathering emplacements; or it may have become richer in ornaments or implements, through trade with neighboring groups, or more powerful as a result of a successful war expedition. The day will come when the chief finds himself heading a group too small to face the problems of daily life and to protect his women from the covetousness of other bands. In such cases, he will have no alternative but to give up his command and to rally, together with his last followers, a happier faction. Therefore, Nambikuara social structure appears continuously on the move. The bands take shape, then disorganize; they increase, and they vanish. Within a few months, sometimes, their composition, number, and distribution cannot be recognized. Political intrigues within the same band and conflicts between bands impose their rhythm upon these fluctuations, and the ascent [and] decline of individuals and groups follow each other in a rather surprising manner.

How will the chief be able to overcome these difficulties? The first instrumental force of his power lies in his generosity. Generosity—an all-important feature of chieftainship among most primitive peoples, especially in America—plays an outstanding part even on those crude cultural levels where worldly goods are limited to the most primitive weapons and tools, coarse ornaments made of feathers, shells and bones, and raw materials, such as lumps of rosin and wax, hanks of fiber and splinters of bamboo for arrow-making. There cannot be great economic distinctions between families, each of which can pack all of its belongings in the baskets carried along by the women during the long travels of the dry season. But, although the chief does not seem to fare better, in this respect, than the others, he must always have at hand surpluses of food, tools, weapons, ornaments that, while being small indeed, acquire great value because of the scarcity that is the prevalent condition. When an individual, a family, or the band itself needs or covets something, the chief is called upon to secure the desired article. Generosity is the quality, much speculated on, that is expected of a new chief. Generosity is the string constantly struck that makes the general consent to one's leadership sound clear or out of tune. There is little doubt that, in this respect, the chief's ability to give is exploited to the utmost. Band chiefs used to be my best informants, and, well aware of their difficult position, I liked to reward them liberally; but I seldom saw one of my many gifts remain in their hands for more than a few days. Each time I took leave of a band, after a few weeks or a few months, its members had time to become the happy hoarders of axes, knives, beads, and so on. As a rule, however, the chief was exactly as poor as at my first arrival. Everything he had received from me (and this was considerably more than the average) had already been squeezed out of him. This collective greediness not seldom drives the chief to an almost desperate position; then the refusal to give plays about the same part, in this primitive democracy, as the threat to resign followed by a vote of confidence in a modern parliament. When a chief reaches the point where he must say, "To give away is over! To be generous is over! Let another be generous in my place!" he must, indeed, be sure of his power and prestige, for his rule is undergoing its severest crisis.

Ingenuity is but the intellectual form of generosity. A great deal of skill and initiative are the prerequisites of a good leader. It is he who makes the arrow-poison, although the preparation of *curare* among the Nambikuara is a purely profane activity surrounded by no ceremonial taboos or magic prescriptions. It is he, also, who makes the rubber ball used in the head-ball games that are played occasionally. The chief must be a good singer and dancer, a merrymaker always ready to cheer up the band and to brighten the dullness of daily life. This could easily lead to shamanism; and, in some cases, I have met with chiefs who were at the same time healers and trance addicts. Mystical life, however, is kept in the background among the Nambikuara, and, wherever they exist, magical functions are only secondary attributes of the leader. More often, chieftainship and sorcery are divided between two different individuals. In this respect, there is a strong difference between the Nambikuara and their northwestern neighbors, the Tupi-Kawahib, among whom the chief is, first of all, a shaman, usually a psychotic addicted to dreams, visions, trances, and impersonations.

But, although they are oriented in a more positive direction, the Nambikuara chief's skill and ingenuity are nonetheless amazing. He must have a perfect knowledge of the territories haunted by his and other groups; be familiar with the hunting grounds, the location of fruit-bearing trees, and the time of their ripening; have some idea of the itineraries followed by other bands, whether hostile or friendly. Therefore, he must travel more, and more quickly, than his people, have a good memory, and sometimes gamble his prestige on hazardous contacts with foreign and dangerous people. He is constantly engaged in some task of reconnoitering and exploring and seems to flutter around his band rather than lead it.

Except for one or two men without actual power, but eager to cooperate and to receive occasional rewards, the passivity of the band makes a strong contrast with its dynamic leader. It seems as if the band, having relinquished certain advantages to the chief, were in exchange relying entirely upon him for its interests and safety. I received a particularly striking demonstration of this under rather strange circumstances. After several weeks' discussion, I had obtained from a chief the favor of taking me, together with a few companions and some animals loaded with presents, to the semipermanent dwellings of his band, which were uninhabited at that time. This was a chance for me to penetrate more deeply into the unexplored Nambikuara territory and to meet groups too shy to venture forth on the outer fringe. The native band and my own group set out together on a journey supposed to be short; but, because of the animals I had taken, the chief had decided that the usual route through a dense forest could not be used. He led us through the open country, lost his way several times, and we did not reach our destination on the scheduled day. Supplies were exhausted and no game was in sight. The not unfamiliar prospect of a foodless day fell gloomily upon the natives. But, this time, it was the chief's responsibility. The whole project was his own, as well as the attempt to find an easier route. So, instead of trying to discover food, the hungry natives simply lay down in the shadow of the brush and waited for their leader to take them out of this most unpleasant situation. He did not wait or discuss; but, taking the incident as a matter of course, he simply left the camp accompanied by one of his wives. At the camp, the day was spent sleeping, gossiping, and complaining. There was no lunch or dinner. But, late at dusk, the chief and his wife reappeared, both heavily laden with baskets filled to the brim. They had hunted grasshoppers the entire day, and, although the expression "to eat grasshoppers" has approximately the same meaning in Nambikuara as the French *manger de la vache enragée*,[3] this food was enthusiastically received, shared, and consumed amidst restored good humor. The following morning, everybody armed himself or herself with a leafless twig and went grasshopper-hunting.

I have several times referred to the chief's wives. Polygamy, which is practically the chief's privilege, brings him a moral and sentimental reward for his heavy duties, together with the practical means of fulfilling them. In the Nambikuara band, apart from rare exceptions, only the chief and the sorcerer (when these functions are divided between two individuals) may have several wives. The chief's polygamy, however, presents special features. It does not constitute a plural marriage but rather a monogamous marriage to which relations of a different nature are added. I have already mentioned the fact that cross-cousin marriage is the usual pattern among the Nambikuara. Another type of marriage also exists, between a man and a woman belonging to the generation following his own, either a wife's "daughter" (true or classificatory) or a sister's niece. Both forms are not uncommon in South America, and, together or separately, they have been recorded among many tribes. Now, what do we find in the chief's case? There is first a monogamous marriage of the cross-cousin type, that is, where the wife belongs to the same generation as her husband. This first wife plays the same part as the monogamous wife in ordinary marriages. She follows the sexual pattern of the division of labor, taking care of the children, doing the cooking, and collecting and gathering wild food. To this marriage are added one or several unions, which, technically, are true marriages but of a different type. Usually, the secondary wives belong to a younger generation. The first wife calls them daughters or nieces. Besides, they do not follow the sexual pattern of the division of labor but share indifferently in men's or women's activities. At the camp, they disdain domestic tasks and remain idle, either playing with the children to whose generation they belong or flirting with their husband, while the first wife keeps busy with the food and the fire. On the contrary, when the chief leaves on an exploration, a hunt, or some other manly task, they will accompany

---

[3] Closest English equivalent: "to have a rough time of it," "to go through the mill."

him and bring him their moral and physical help. These somewhat "tom-boy" girls, elected by the chief from among the prettiest and healthiest of the group, are to him rather "girl-friends" than spouses. They live on the basis of an amorous friendship that contrasts strongly with the more con-jugal atmosphere of the first marriage.

This system exerts a tremendous influence upon the whole life of the group. The periodical withdrawal by the chief of young women from the regular cycle of marriages creates a permanent unbalance within the group, between the number of boys and girls of marriageable age. Young men are the chief victims of that situation and must either remain bachelors for sev-eral years or marry widows or old women discarded by their husbands. Thus, the right to plural marriages represents a concession of considerable importance made by the group to its leader. What does it mean from the latter's point of view? There is little doubt that access to young and pretty girls brings him a much appreciated gratification, not so much from the physical side (as the Nambikuara share in the quiet dispositions of most South American tribes) as from the psychological and sentimental one. But, above all, plural marriage, together with its distinctive features, con-stitutes the technical means and the functional device placed at the chief's disposal by the group to enable him to carry out his exacting duties. Left by himself, he could hardly do more than the others. His secondary wives, freed by their special status from the customary liabilities of their sex, are his helpers, comforters and assistants. They are, at the same time, leader-ship's prize and instrument. Can it be said, from the native point of view, that the prize is worth the trouble? To answer that question, I shall now have to consider the problem from a broader angle—namely, what does this elementary social structure, the Nambikuara band, teach us about leader-ship, its basis and its function?

There is a first point that does not require great elaboration. Nambi-kuara data contribute, with many others, to destroy the belief originated by early anthropologists, and temporarily revived by psychoanalysis, that the primitive chief could find his prototype in a symbolical father, and that the simpler forms of the state could progressively have grown out of the family. We have found at the root of the crudest forms of chieftainship a decisive step, which introduced something entirely new in respect to biological rela-tions—and this step consists of *consent*. Consent, we have seen, is at the same time the origin and the limit of leadership. Unilateral relations, such as right of age, autocratic power, or others, may appear in groups having an already complex structure. In simple forms of social organization, such as the one I have tried to describe, they are inconceivable. Here, on the contrary, the relationship between the chief and the group can be seen as a perpetual process of arbitration, where the chief's talents and authority, on the one hand, and the group's size, cohesion, and willingness, on the other, constantly react on, and influence, each other. If I had the time, and if it were not so far removed from my topic, I would have liked to show what considerable support modern anthropological observations bring, in this respect, to the analysis of the eighteenth-century social philosophers. I am well aware of the fact that Rousseau's "social contract," which is the step by which individuals resign their autonomy in favor of the General Will, is entirely different from the nearly contractual relations existing between the chief and his followers. It remains true, however, that Rousseau and his contemporaries displayed a keen sociological feeling when they understood that cultural attitudes and elements such as "contract" and "consent" are not the result of secondary processes, as claimed by their opponents; they are culture's raw materials, and it is impossible to conceive a political or social organization in which they would not already be present. If I understand correctly, the recent analysis, by modern American anthropologists, of the state-growth significance of military societies among the Plains Indians leads to exactly the same conclusion.[4]

My second point is but an exemplification of the first: Consent is the psychological basis of leadership; but, in daily life, it expresses itself in, and is measured by, a game of give-and-take played by the chief and his followers, . . . which brings forth, as a basic attribute of leadership, the notion of reciprocity. The chief has power, but he must be generous. He has duties, but he is entitled to several wives. Between him and the group, there is a perpetual balance of prestations, privileges, services, and obligations. The notion of reciprocity, originated by Marcel Mauss, was brillantly analyzed by Malinowski in his "Crime and Custom in Savage Society." In respect to leadership, he says: "The claims of chief over commoners, husband over wife, parent over child and vice versa are not exercised arbitrarily and onesidedly, but according to definite rules, and arranged into well-balanced chains of reciprocal services."[5] This statement needs somewhat to be completed. Malinowski is right when he points out that the chief-commoner's relationship, as every relationship in primitive society, is based on reciprocity. In the first case, however, the reciprocity is not of the same type as in the others. In any human society, whether primitive or civilized, two different cycles of reciprocity are constantly at work: first, the chain of individual prestations linking the isolated members of the group; and, next, a relation of reciprocity binding the group considered as group (not as a collection of individuals) and its ruler. In the case we have studied, this is well illustrated by the rules of marriage. Taken in its broadest sense, the incest prohibition means that everybody in the group is obliged to deliver his sister or daughter to an individual; and, conversely, is entitled to receive his wife from the latter (whether from the same man, as in exchange-marriage, or from a different one). Thus, a continuous chain of reciprocal prestations is directly or indirectly set up between all the collective or individual members of the group.[6] This may be called qualitative reciprocity;

[4] R. H. Lowie, *The Origin of the State* (reprint of 1927 edition; New York: Russell & Russell, 1962), pp. 76–107, and K. N. Llewellyn and E. A. Hoebbel, *The Cheyenne* pt. 2 (Norman: University of Oklahoma Press, 1941), chap. 5.

[5] B. Malinowski, *Crime and Custom in Savage Society*: 46. New York, 1940. (Third Printing.)

[6] See the late F. E. Williams' remarkable analysis in *Papuans of the Trans-Fly* (Oxford: Clarendon Press, 1936), pp. 167–69.

but incest prohibition also provides the basis for a quantitative reciprocity. We may consider it as a "freezing" measure, which, while it forbids the appropriation of women who are at one's natural disposal, prepares the formulation of marriage rules allowing every man to get a wife. Therefore, a close relationship exists in a given society between the forbidden degrees and the extent to which polygamy is allowed. How does the preceding apply to the Nambikuara? If they had cross-cousin marriage associated exclusively with monogamy, there would be a perfectly simple system of reciprocity (from the individual's point of view), both qualitative and quantitative. This theoretical formula is, however, upset by the chief's privilege to polygamy. The withholding of the simpler rule, in a favor of the chief, creates for each individual an element of insecurity that would otherwise not exist. Let us state this in other terms: The granting of polygamous privilege to the chief means that the group has exchanged *individual elements of security* resulting from monogamous rule for *collective security* provided by leadership. Each man receives a wife from another man, but the chief receives several wives from the group. In exchange, he offers to guarantee against need and danger, not to the individuals whose sisters or daughters he marries; not to those who will be deprived of a spouse by his polygamous right; but to the group, taken as a whole. For it is the group, taken as a whole, that has withheld the common law in his favor. The preceding considerations may have some bearing upon the theory of plural marriage; but, most of all, they remind us that the interpretation of the state, conceived as a security system, recently revived by discussions about a national insurance policy (such as the Beveridge plan and others), is not a modern development. It is a return to the basic nature of social and political organization.

So much for the group's point of view on leadership. What about the chief's own attitude in relation to his function? What is his incentive in assuming duties of which I have given a not too favorable account? We saw that the Nambikuara band leader has a tiresome and exacting role; that he must exert himself without pause to maintain his position. What is more, if he does not constantly improve it, he runs the risk of losing what he has taken months or years to achieve. This explains why many men, as I have already said, shun leadership. But why do others accept and even seek it? It is always difficult to appraise psychological motives; and the task is almost impossible when a culture totally alien to our own is considered. I venture to say, however, that the polygamous privilege, highly valued as it may be from the point of view of sexual gratification, sentimental appeal, and social prestige, would not suffice to determine a leader's vocation. Plural marriage is but a technical prerequisite of chieftainship; its individual value can only be residual. There must be something more; and, going over the moral and psychological features of the Nambikuara chiefs I knew, and trying to hold on to those fugitive and irreplaceable glimpses at their intimate selves (of which no scientific approach may certify the accuracy, but which gain, from a deep feeling of friendship and human communication, some sort of intuitive value), I feel imperiously led to this answer: There are chiefs because there are, in any human group, men who, unlike most of their companions, enjoy prestige for its own sake, feel a strong appeal to responsibility, and to whom the burden of public affairs brings its own reward. These individual differences are certainly emphasized and "played up" by the different cultures, and to unequal degrees. But their clear-cut existence in a society as little competitive as the Nambikuara strongly suggests to my mind that their origin itself is not cultural. They are rather part of those psychological raw materials out of which any given culture is made. Men are not all alike; and, in primitive societies, believed by early anthropologists to be overwhelmed by the crushing power of custom, these individual differences are as keenly perceived and worked out as in our so-called individualistic civilization.

It is remarkable how far the practical experience of colonial administrators has outgrown, in relation to the previous considerations, anthropologists' theoretical studies. During the past twenty years, Lowie's pessimistic appraisal of anthropological work in the field of political institutions[7] has certainly not lost its value. We have much to learn from the scientifically untrained who deal with native institutions. I shall not here record Lyautey's testimony without reservation: "In every society, there is a leading class born for leadership and without which nothing can be accomplished."[8] What may be true for the simpler structures cannot be considered equally valid when considering the complex ones, where the function of leadership does not manifest itself any more in a "pure" state. But let us listen to Eboué, who passed away a few months ago. Himself a full-blooded Negro, he wrote the following when he was Governor-General of French Equatorial Africa in special relation to those nomadic tribes that, as he put it, "live under a regime of organized anarchy." I quote: "Who is to be chief? I shall not answer, as was the custom in Athens, 'the best.' There is no best chief, there is just a chief"; and further, "the chief is not interchangeable . . . the chief pre-exists."[9] This is precisely what was suggested to us from the start of our analysis of Nambikuara society.

In conclusion, I submit that, when developing the study of political institutions, anthropologists will have to pay more and more attention to the idea of "natural leadership." I am well aware that this expression is almost contradictory. There is no possible form of leadership that does not receive its shape and specification inside of a given cultural context. But this expression can be taken as a borderline case, or as a limit—as say the mathematicians. While the limit can never be reached, simple social structures give us, in the order of their simplicity, an even closer approximation of it. In such studies, we may accordingly foresee a privileged field for close, cooperative work between anthropology and individual psychology.

[7] At the beginning of chapter 13 of *Primitive Society*.

[8] Quoted in Governor-General Felix Eboué's memorandum on "Native Policy," issued on November 8, 1942.

[9] *Ibid*.

Political Crimes and Abuses of Power

The World Behind Watergate*

Kirkpatrick Sale

The bedfellows politics makes are never strange; it only seems that way to those who have not watched the courtship. In Richard Nixon's case, notwithstanding his presence in national politics for the last twenty-five years, those courtships have remained remarkably unexamined—or, when examined, remarkably misunderstood—and as a result the bedfellows he has acquired have remained unusually obscure both to the public and to the political pundits who are supposed to conjure with such things. Certain obvious relationships, to be sure, have been given attention—the back-scratching of Nixon and his old friend and Pepsico chairman Donald Kendall, for example, the latest evidence of which is Washington's gift of the Soviet soft-drink franchise to Pepsi-Cola. But the wider pattern of his associations, the character of his power base, remains essentially obscure. This seems particularly dangerous in view of the evidence that these people will be influential in American government not only for the next four years but for the foreseeable future.

The Nixonian bedfellows, the people whose creed the president expresses and whose interests he guards, are, to generalize, the economic sovereigns of America's southern rim, the "sunbelt" that runs from Southern California, through Arizona and Texas, down to the Florida keys. They are for the most part new-money people, without the family fortunes and backgrounds of eastern wealth (Rockefellers, DuPonts, etc.), people whose fortunes have been made only in the postwar decades, mostly in new industries such as aerospace and defense contracting, in oil, natural gas, and allied businesses, usually domestic rather than international, and in real-estate operations during the postwar sun-belt population boom.

They are "self-made" men and women, in the sense that they did not generally inherit great riches (though of course in another sense they are government-made, depending, as in oil and aerospace, on large favors from Washington, but they hardly like to think of it that way), and they tend to

* This article first appeared in the *New York Review of Books,* vol. 20, no. 7 (May 3, 1973), 9–16. Reprinted by permission of International Creative Management and Kirkpatrick Sale. Copyright © 1973 by *New York Review.*

a notable degree to be politically conservative, even retrograde, usually anti-union, anti-black, anti-consumer, and anti-regulation, and quite often associated with professional "anti-communist" organizations. Whether because of the newness of their position, their frontier heritage, or their lack of old-school ties, they tend to be without particular concerns about the niceties of business ethics and morals, and therefore to be connected more than earlier money would have thought wise with shady speculations, political influence-peddling, corrupt unions, and even organized crime.

The political ascendancy of these southern-rim people—those whom Carl Oglesby once called "the cowboys," as distinct from "the yankees" of old eastern money—has taken place coincidentally with their economic growth in the last generation. Their power on a state level was solidified a decade or so ago, and they made certain inroads to national influence with Johnson's assumption of the presidency in 1963.* But it was not until the election of Richard Nixon in 1968—and even more now during a second term in which he seems far beyond mediating pressure from the press, Congress, and public—that the southern-rim bedfellows were firmly installed in the bedrooms of political power in Washington. It is a fitting symbol of this that Nixon has established White Houses at the two extremes of the southern rim, San Clemente and Key Biscayne.

Now it is certainly true that the yankees retain considerable power in national politics, that the Wall Street investment houses and the family banks and the well-established holding and insurance companies still have influence throughout local and federal government. No one would want to suggest that David Rockefeller or the First National City Bank was inconsequential in guiding the affairs of state—and the important position of Henry Kissinger, a man with authentic yankee ties (Harvard, Rockefeller Brothers Fund, Council on Foreign Relations) attests to their continuing influence. What is important to note, however, is the *relative* decline of the yankees in recent years and their relinquishment of important powers to cowboy hands. Moreover, as the economic importance of the southern rim has increased, New York banks and investment houses (notably Loeb Rhoades and Lehman Brothers) have bought into its businesses, with the result that to a greater extent than before the interests and wishes of the cowboys have become of serious concern to the moguls of Wall Street.

One rough measure of the political ascendancy of the cowboys is the number of them who actually occupy high positions in Washington. Of the four members of what Nixon likes to call his "super-super cabinet," three of them—the three with the highest authority in domestic affairs (the fourth is Kissinger)—are from the southern rim: Roy Ash (California: millionaire

* Johnson's assumption of power had several consequences beyond the enthronement of a man heavily in political debt to conservative Texas oil, among them the squelching of the Bobby Baker and TFX-Convair (Dallas) investigations, the exercise of American pressure to forestall a threatened nationalization of American oil interests in Argentina, and the reversal of Kennedy's announced plans to begin withdrawing troops from Vietnam.

defense contractor), John Ehrlichman (California, out of Seattle: lawyer, politico), and Bob Haldeman (California: PR man). On the cabinet level there are Anne Armstrong (Texas: Republican politico), Claude Brinegar (California: Union Oil executive), Frederick Dent (South Carolina: textile millionaire), Richard Kleindienst (Arizona: Goldwater crony), and Caspar Weinberger (California: Republican politico and ex-Reagan aide).

Of the five Nixon nominees to the Supreme Court, three (Rehnquist, Carswell, and Haynesworth) were wool-died southern-rim conservatives and one (Powell) was a right-wing Virginian who was also a director of oil and gas corporations. The key appointments to the increasingly powerful Republican National Committee have all been from the southern-rim—co-chairpersons George Bush (Texas: oil company co-founder) and Janet Johnston (California: rancher) and general counsel Harry Dent (South Carolina: lawyer, ex-GOP state head). The rim influence is here so strong that there have even been published complaints from midwestern Republicans about a "southern Mafia."

And peppered throughout the government are such key cowboys as press secretary Ronald Ziegler (California: public relations), Frederic Malek, second-in-command of the budget (South Carolina: tool-manufacturing millionaire), Commissioner of Education John Ottina (California: defense industry consultant), Director of Communications Herbert Klein (California: Copley Press executive), Deputy Secretary of Defense William Clements (Texas: oil millionaire), Assistant Agriculture Secretary Robert Long (California: Bank of America executive), Undersecretary of State William Casey (a New Yorker, but director and counsel of a southern-rim agribusiness corporation). . . . And on and on, scores more throughout the top levels of the administration, not even balanced this term by very many liberals and easterners.

A second measure of cowboy penetration is their preponderance among Nixon's major financial supporters. Though the loopholed campaign-spending laws permit only partial identification of the top money men, it seems clear at least that the chief sources of Nixon's campaign finances—and therefore presumably the people whose interests the president will try to keep dominant—are independent oil producers, defense contractors, right-wing unions, rich conservative businessmen, and various southern-rim manufacturers. This does not mean, of course, that the more traditional sources of Republican money, such as the old-money families and yankees new and old throughout the financial world, have been thoroughly displaced or no longer make big contributions, but only that their position is being steadily narrowed and their importance therefore steadily decreased.

Oil money, for example, has always found its way into politics, as much from the old corporations with chiefly international interests as from the new independents who have sprung up along the southern rim. But it has been the latter who have been most important in Nixon's career, from such supporters as Union Oil, Superior Oil, and Texas ultraconservative H. L.

Hunt, who helped finance his early campaigns, through California right-winger Henry Salvatori, the Texas Murchison family, and at least a third of the backers in the 1952 "slush fund." In this last campaign there were some large contributions from old oil—Richard Mellon Scaife (Gulf Oil, among other interests) gave $1 million, the Phipps family (Texaco among others) gave at least $55,000—but the striking fact is the number of domestic oil donors, rimsters or with rim interests, people like Kent Smith (Lubrizol, $224,000), Francis Cappeart (southern oil and agribusiness, $174,000), John Paul Getty (Getty Oil, $97,000), John J. Shaheen (Shaheen Natural Resources, $100,000), Elisha Walker (Petroleum Corporation of America, $100,000), Max Fisher (Marathon Oil, $60,000), the O'Connor family (Texas Oil, $60,000), and the Osea Wyatt family (Coastal States Gas, $41,000).*

Other major sources of support in the last campaign can be traced, too, and they follow the same general pattern: some sizable donors from the old-money families and new-money easterners, but surprising strength from the southern rim. Among the largest donors with defense interests last year were yankees like Arthur Watson (IBM, $303,000) and Saul Steinberg (Leasco, $250,000), but they were matched by the rimsters, people like Charles and Sam Wyly (Dallas computer company, $172,000), Thomas Marquez (Electronic Data Systems, Dallas, $88,000), Howard Hughes (Hughes Tool, etc., Houston, $100,000), Ling–Temco–Vought (Texas, $60,000), and Litton Industries ($18,000).

Southern-rim new-money businessmen included Walter T. Duncan (Texas, real estate, $305,000), Sam Schulman (California, National General conglomerate, $257,000), John and Charles Williams (Oklahoma manufacturers, $98,000), M. B. Seretean and Eugene Barwick (southern textile manufacturers, $200,000), Anthony Rossi (Florida, Tropicana, $100,000), C. Arnholt Smith (California financier, $50,000), and L. B. Maytag (Florida, National Airlines, $50,000). Donors among the major organizations include three with extensive rim contracts, the Texas-based Associated Milk Producers ($782,000), and the two right-wing unions, the Seafarers (with direct oil and agribusiness links, $100,000) and the Teamsters (with heavy investments from Southern California and Las Vegas to Miami, an estimated $100,000).

Perhaps an even more revealing measure of the rimsters' influence is their dominance of the Nixon inner circle. Now their numbers are hardly legion, because this president is an essentially friendless man, a distrustful person with few close cronies, but the few that exist are, almost to a man (no

---

* These figures are from the Citizens Research Foundation of Princeton, New Jersey, a group that tries to keep track of all the sources of campaign money. They are generally only estimates and often represent only a small part of what was actually given. Other major oil donors and fund raisers on the CRF lists include Arthur E. Johnson (Midwest Oil), Thomas Pappas (ESSO-Pappas), the Pew family (Sun Oil), William Liedtke (Pennzoil), J. A. Vickers (Vickers Petroleum), and H. W. McCollum, Philip Kramer, and J. D. Callender (Amerada Hess).

women), from the sun-belt states. The only visible exceptions are Donald Kendall and Secretary of State William Rogers, both solid easterners, and even they are new-money, up-from-poverty types.

The rest are people like Southern California businessmen Jack Drown, Ray Arbuthnot and C. Arnholt Smith, California politician Robert Finch (a friend, apparently, even after his fall from office), and four men who seem to be closest of all to the president: Herbert Kalmbach, a rich Los Angeles lawyer who is the president's personal counsel and was his chief fund-raiser during 1971; John Connally, the oil-tied Texas politician who is Nixon's financial guru and reportedly his choice as successor; Murray Chotiner, the California lawyer who has been with Nixon since the beginning and during 1971 and 1972 was with him in the White House; and Bebe Rebozo, the Florida millionaire who is reckoned to be the most intimate of all with the president. All of these are fairly typical southern rimsters, all are new-money people, all are well-off, and all of them (except maybe Finch) are politically conservative. Most disturbing of all, several of these people have had the taint, and sometimes the full stigma, of scandal around them.

This last attribute deserves somewhat more attention, for it is inevitably one of the most striking features of the political cowboys and one with very serious implications for our national life. Without going into a full portrait of the noisome character of so much of the southern rim—home of well-established organized-crime centers in such places as Las Vegas, New Orleans, and Miami, the last having lately become a veritable Marseilles—one can still note that many of Nixon's closest friends from this region are, to a remarkable and unhealthy degree, guilty of improprieties in business, a certain disregard for public trust, a general lack of ethical sophistication, or in some cases direct association with criminal figures. To cite a few examples:

Herbert Kalmbach has been identified as one of the five people in charge of funds for the million-dollar Republican operation to sabotage the Democratic campaign last year, and according to the FBI he personally gave Republican funds to Donald Segretti, the California lawyer who by all accounts (none denied) was the West Coast leader of that operation; Kalmbach has also been identified in sworn court papers as the strong-man in the Republicans' efforts to squeeze some $700,000 out of the large milk producers in return for a government-approved price raise.

Connally, whose service on behalf of rich Texas oilmen has been well documented, was attorney for Texas millionaire Sid Richardson when he engineered a million-dollar payment to Texas oilman Robert Anderson in the mid-fifties; and while governor of Texas he trickily denied the fact that he had received at least $225,000 from the multimillion-dollar Richardson estate, a payment that was possibly in violation of the Texas constitution.

Chotiner has also had a career of slimy dealings ever since he first invented the pink-lady attack on Helen Gahagan Douglas: between 1949 and 1952 he handled some 221 gambler-bookmaker cases in Los Angeles; he was instrumental in getting a deportation order rescinded for Philadelphia mobster Marco Reginelli in the 1950s; in 1956 the McClellan Senate committee investigated his role as attorney for a convicted clothing racketeer and exposed (but did not fully explore) his influence-peddling activities in Washington; and most recently he has acknowledged in court papers his own role in the milk scandal by admitting he intervened with Ehrlichman and others in the White House to get the price increase for the milk producers and subsequently arranged the channeling of their contributions to the Nixon campaign.

Whatever else you want to say about these presidential pals, they hardly seem to be the kind that Billy Graham, let's say, should approve of.

Rebozo, the inscrutable man who is closest of all to Nixon—the latest example of his intimacy being the donation of his $100,000 Bethesda home to Julie Nixon Eisenhower—deserves a somewhat closer examination here, for in some ways he personifies the cowboy type.* Rebozo, Cuban-born of American parents, grew up in relative poverty, and at the start of World War II he was a gas-station operator in Florida. With the wartime tire shortage Rebozo got it into his head to expand his properties and start a recapping business, so he got a loan from a friend who happened to be on the local OPA tire board (a clear conflict of interest) and before long was the largest recapper in Florida. In 1951, he met Richard Nixon on one of the latter's trips to Miami and the two seem to have hit it off: both the same age, both quiet, withdrawn, and humorless, both aggressive success-hunters, both part of the new southern-rim milieu.

Rebozo later expanded into land deals and in the early 1960s established the Key Biscayne Bank, of which he is president and whose first savings-account customer was Nixon. This bank in 1968 was the repository of stolen stocks, originally taken and channeled to the bank by organized-crime sources. Rebozo clearly suspected there was something dubious about these stocks (he even told an FBI agent that he had called up Nixon's brother Donald to check on their validity), but he subsequently sold them for cash, even after an insurance company circular was mailed out to every bank listing them as stolen. Small wonder that the bank was thereupon sued by the company which had insured those stocks. (The case was eventually tried before a Nixon-appointed federal judge, James Lawrence King, who himself had some interesting banking experience as a director in 1964 of the Miami

---

* Rebozo's career has been examined in at least three recent studies which also spell out other unsavory aspects of those in the Nixon circle and cast doubt upon the president's own behavior. *Newsday* published a series of articles on Nixon's Florida connections in the fall of 1971 (available as a "Special Report" from *Newsday,* 550 Stewart Avenue, Garden City, New York 11530); a New Leftist magazine called *SunDance* (1913 Fillmore Street, San Francisco, California 94115) ran an article by Journalist Jeff Gerth in its issue of November–December, 1972; and the North American Congress on Latin America (Box 57, Cathedral Station, New York, New York 10025) published a booklet on Nixon's links to organized crime and the Watergate affair in October 1972. In constructing this portrait of Rebozo, as in other sections in this article, I have also used the copious and careful researches of Peter Dale Scott.

National Bank, cited by the *New York Times* [December 1, 1969, p. 42] as a conduit for the Meyer Lansky syndicate's "shady money" from 1963 to 1967. King decided against the insurance company, but the case is now being appealed to a higher court.)

At about the same time as the stolen stocks episode came the shopping-center deal. Rebozo, by now a very rich man, still managed to get a loan out of the federal Small Business Administration—one of five which he somehow was lucky enough to secure in the 1960s, perhaps because of his friendship with ex-Senator George Smathers (who had been on the Senate Small Business Committee and who wrote the SBA to help Rebozo get another loan), or perhaps because the chief Miami officer of the SBA also happened to be a close friend of Rebozo and a stockholder in his bank. This, coupled with the fact that Rebozo never fully disclosed his business dealings in making applications to the SBA, led *Newsday,* in a prominent editorial, to denounce the SBA for "wheeling and dealing . . . on Rebozo's behalf," and it led Representative Wright Patman to accuse the SBA publicly of wrongdoing in making Rebozo a "preferred customer."

With one of the SBA grants Rebozo proceeded to build an elaborate shopping center, to be leased to members of the right-wing Cuban exile community, and he let out the contracting bid for that to one "Big Al" Polizzi, a convicted black marketeer and a man named by the Federal Bureau of Narcotics as "one of the most influential members of the underworld in the United States."

Rather unsavory, all that, if not precisely criminal, and a rather odd career for an intimate of our moralistic president. But Nixon seems not to mind. In fact he has even gone in with Rebozo on at least one of his deals, a Florida real-estate venture called Fisher's Island Inc., in which Nixon invested some $185,891 around 1962, and which he sold for exactly twice the value, $371,782, in 1969. It seems to have been a peculiarly shrewd deal, since the going rate for Fisher's Island stock had not in fact increased by a penny during those years and certainly hadn't doubled for anyone else —but happily for the stockholders, Nixon shortly thereafter signed a bill paving the way for $7 million worth of federal funds for the improvement of the Port of Miami, in which Fisher Island just happens to be located. In any case, that's small enough potatoes for a man in Nixon's position, and seems to reflect the fact that, no matter how many rich wheeler-dealers he has around him, Nixon himself is not out to make a vast personal fortune as his predecessor did.

But the unsavoriness surrounding Bebe Rebozo does not stop there. For in the mid-1960s Rebozo was also a partner in a Florida real-estate company with one Donald Berg, an acquaintance of Nixon and the man from whom Nixon bought property in Key Biscayne less than a mile from the Florida White House. This same Donald Berg, who has been linked with at least one associate of mobster Meyer Lansky, has a background so questionable that after Nixon became president the Secret Service asked him to stop eating at Berg's Key Biscayne restaurant.* Finally, according to Jack Anderson, Rebozo was "involved" in some of the real-estate deals of Bernard Barker—the former CIA operative who was the convicted payoff man for the Watergate operation last year.

It is not surprising that *Newsday,* among many others, has concluded: "The deals made by Bebe Rebozo . . . have tarnished the presidency."

Mention of Bernard Barker brings up the Watergate scandal, perhaps even more interesting because it is so complicated and revealing of the interlocking relations along the southern rim. We are far from knowing all the details as yet, but an examination of the people known to have been involved does provide a clear window on the Nixon milieu.

Watergate, and at least some of the other operations against the Democrats and radical political groups last year, was paid for by cowboy money. Most of it came from Texas oil, channeled through Nixon fund-raiser Robert Allen (Gulf Resources), "laundered" in a Mexican bank, and then carried to Republican finance chairman Maurice Stans by an executive of Penzoil. The rest came from a Minneapolis "soybean king," Dwayne Andreas, with a home and investments in Florida and ties to southern money, and was delivered to Stans by a crony of Andreas with Florida investments of his own.† The money stayed for a time in Stans's safe and then was deposited in a Miami bank for Bernard Barker, Rebozo's business associate, a man who had worked for the CIA, had been paymaster of the Bay of Pigs operation, was close to the anti-Castro–pro-Batista Cuban community in Miami, and masterminded at least three forays by Cuban emigres to attack antiwar protesters in Washington last spring.

---

* Two mortgages on a part of the property Nixon bought from Berg were held, from 1967 to 1971, by Arthur Desser, a Florida real-estate operator who was another director of the Miami National Bank during the time it was a Lansky syndicate conduit. Nixon let this property go unrecorded in the Dade County Clerk's office for four years, until the mortgages were paid off in March, 1971, presumably because he wanted no public record of his connection with a man like Desser (*SunDance,* p. 64).

† To get an idea of how complicated southern-rim contacts can be, try this. Andreas's crony, Kenneth Dahlberg, a Nixon fund-raiser, was also a director of a Florida bank whose co-chairman was a major stockholder in an investment group called Penphil and who has benefitted enormously from Penphil's favors. Penphil has since been accused by a congressional committee of helping to bankrupt the Penn Central Railroad, and two of its organizers and one of its key shareholders have been indicted for criminal conspiracy in manipulating more than $85 million of Penn Central investments for their own personal profit. (*New York Times,* January 5, 1972, p. 1).

Among Penphil's major investments were a Florida gas company, two Florida banks, and a Dallas investment corporation, which also owned a California real-estate operation—a rather neat sweep of the southern rim. This last outfit, Macco Corporation, had—are you ready?—Herbert Kalmbach as its vice-president, and Maurice Stans as an investor with stock options that turned out to be worth $570,000. How's that for full circle? (The Penphil story is told in full in Joseph R. Daughen and Peter Blinzen, *The Wreck of the Penn Central* [Little, Brown, 1971], pp. 148–175. For the role of the congressional committee, see House Committee on Banking and Currency, *The Penn Central Failure and the Role of Financial Institutions,* Staff Report, January 3, 1972.)

Barker was paymaster this time around, too, and personally recruited three others, all of whom subsequently pleaded guilty at the Watergate trial: Eugenio Martinez, another old CIA operative and a real-estate business partner of Barker's, and also vice-president of another real-estate firm with whom both Nixon and Rebozo have done business; Frank Sturgis, a CIA operative, who lost his citizenship at one time for his Caribbean gun-running activities (first for Castro in 1958, then against him in 1962), and organizer of a "Cubans for Nixon" demonstration at Miami Beach last year;* and Virgilio Gonzalez, also a CIA operative in on the Bay of Pigs, and a member of a right-wing anti-Castro organization run by the same people who ran the "Cubans for Nixon" operation both last year and in 1968.

These four men were guided in their operations by at least three others with close connections to the Nixon inner circle, all of whom have been convicted for their part in Watergate: Gordon Liddy, a former FBI agent who had worked on espionage matters in the White House under Ehrlichman, who was assigned by White House counsel John Dean to Nixon's Committee to Re-elect the President (CRP), and who thereupon, according to trial testimony, set up the Republican sabotage campaign; James McCord, a twenty-year CIA Agent with extensive contacts among the anti-Castro community, who was "security coordinator" for CRP and who says that Dean cleared him for the job;† and Howard Hunt, another career CIA agent (chief operations officer for the Bay of Pigs) and former White House consultant, who became a CRP operative in 1971. Having spooks right in the White House seems bad enough, but the sorry trail goes on—in fact goes on for two more steps.

The first step involves at least three other men besides Dean who were White House aides to Nixon: Charles Colson, Hunt's supervisor at the White House and head of a White House anti-Democrat committee known as the "attack group";** Gordon Strachan, a Haldeman assistant who (according to an FBI file) was the chief link to the reported California saboteur, Donald Segretti, and according to the *New York Times* was the White

* Senate Committee of the Judiciary, *Communist Threat to the United States through the Caribbean*, Hearings, 1965, pp. 918–920, 946, 951, 963–964; *New York Times*, June 28, 1972; NACLA, p. 24; *Washington Post*, June 18, 1972. Sturgis (then using the name Fiorini) was also involved in a scheme—aborted by the Miami police —to supply arms for a Nicaragua rebellion in 1959, using planes bought in his name originally for Castro (Senate Hearings, pp. 963–964); that same year he also flew a plane over Havana to drop anti-Castro leaflets, provoking a major diplomatic incident (*New York Times*, October 3, 1959, p. 12).

† Dean's assignment of Liddy emerged from testimony at the Gray hearings (e.g., *New York Times*, March 10, 1973, p. 1, and *Newsweek*, March 19, 1973, p. 21). Trial testimony was reported in the *New York Times*, January 24, 1973, p. 1. The *New York Times*, April 7, 1973, reported his "clearing" McCord.

** *Washington Post*, February 8, 1973, p. 1. Colson has produced his own private lie detector test claiming that, in spite of McCord's impression, he was not involved specifically in Watergate. The *New York Times* reported, however, that "the examination did not deal with the campaign of espionage and disruption that was reportedly directed from the White House" (April 7).

House contact for the Watergate people; and Dwight Chapin, another White House Californian and Haldeman aide who, according to L. Patrick Gray III, transmitted funds to his old college friend Segretti, mostly through—here he is again—Herbert Kalmbach. (In the recent hearsay testimony of McCord to the Senate Watergate Committee Haldeman himself is said to have known "what was going on" at CRP.)

The second step leads to two men close to Nixon, personally and professionally, CRP treasurer Stans and CRP chairman John Mitchell. Though things get pretty shadowy at this point—partly because Nixon's FBI hasn't investigated much here—it seems obvious that both men condoned the anti-Democratic operations, and trial testimony indicates that both men approved specific payments to spy-master Liddy out of Stans's own office safe. In addition, Mitchell as CRP chairman was so implicated in the scandal—not least by his loquacious wife, who complained of John's "dirty things"—that he resigned his CRP position in July; it has since emerged that he met daily with McCord while running the CRP and according to McCord was the "overall boss" of the operation.

Stans, who stayed on, has since been shown to be directly involved in at least one other piece of chicanery having to do with a secret $200,000 campaign gift he accepted in cash from Robert Vesco of Investors Overseas Service (heavily invested, incidentally, in the Bahamas), a man then (and now) being sued by the SEC for having "spirited away" some $224 million from four mutual funds.

There can be little doubt finally that the entire sabotage campaign was at least tacitly approved, if not actually orchestrated, by the president himself—a conclusion which subsequent presidential actions seem only to confirm, from the hasty attempt at a "no-one-was-involved" coverup to the testy erection of "executive privilege" barriers. And so there it is: from the top level of the government, through two of Nixon's closest advisers and the "California Mafia" in the White House, through CIA career men and right-wing Miami exiles, down to Florida businessmen and Texas oil millionaires. This is the world of the thirty-seventh president.

Maybe Nixon's Quaker brethren were right all along. One leader of the Whittier, California, Quaker meeting—of which Richard Nixon is still a member—has gone on record as being "quite concerned personally for the spiritual life of Richard Nixon"; the entire body once debated "the removal of Richard Nixon from membership" for his un-Quakerly prosecution of the Vietnam War; and his own mother, Hannah Milhous Nixon, a member of the committee charged with members' "spiritual health," even had serious enough doubts about her son to advise him "not to run for president."

The purpose of examining all of this is not, of course, to sling more mud on a figure already as splattered as a happy hippopotamus, but to try to clarify the shadowy world of Nixon's bedfellows and to examine the extent of what is almost a second government, an unofficial but very important nexus of power behind the acknowledged civics–textbook institutions. This second government, as we have begun to see, is a combination of vast and complicated interlocking forces, pulling in the CIA here and organized crime there, using politicians one time and emigre thugs the next, which seems to regard government as a tool for financial enrichment, and is to a large extent financed by and working to the benefit of the newer exploitative businesses, chiefly in the southern rim.

Perhaps because they are new to the game, perhaps because they just feel they can get away with it, the more recent operatives of this second government seem to have been a little clumsy, inadvertently supplying several revealing glimpses into their world.*

Take the Soviet wheat deal, a bonanza for certain American shippers and agricultural middlemen, oddly enough with Republican ties. Or the cost-plus banditry which such defense giants as Litton and Ling–Temco–Vought have been allowed to get away with. Or the funny dealings of Under Secretary of State and former SEC chairman William Casey, who is one of seventeen defendants in a $2.1 million federal damage suit, charged, in the words of the court-appointed trustee, with "self-dealings among themselves for their own personal self-gain but to the utmost detriment and damage" to a southern-rim agribusiness corporation which went bankrupt a week after Casey was nominated for the SEC. Or the charges against California businessman and former Assistant Attorney General Robert Mardian, a leader of Nixon's CRP whom McCord has linked to Watergate and whom the *New York Times* has accused of getting confidential information from the Justice Department to use in the Republican campaign.

Or the findings of "profound immorality and corruption" by a nonpartisan investigating committee of the Argentine legislature against Texan William Clements, now deputy secretary of defense, for his very profitable role in a multimillion-dollar oil deal, a deal in which he was partners with one man who is suing him for fraudulent conspiracy and two others who have skipped the U.S. to avoid paying taxes on their profits. Or the neat little deal by which Director of the Budget Roy Ash and a partner in 1969 traded twenty-two acres of land in California with the Federal Bureau of Lands for 14,145 acres of government-owned land in Nevada, or his even neater dumping of some $2.6 million worth of Litton stock in 1970, not long before it became public that Litton's shipbuilding program was in deep trouble and the price of the stock dropped by half, the implications of which are now being looked into by the SEC. Or, . . . but just wait until tomorrow morning's paper.

---

* Even one of the old operators of this type has recently misstepped. ITT, which has been quietly cozy with the CIA since World War II, recently had to acknowledge its attempt to pay a million dollars to the White House and the CIA to prevent Allende's election in Chile, and this followed not long after its public embarrassment in being caught bribing and arm-twisting to pave the way for its multibillion dollar Hartford Fire Insurance merger.

All of these glimpses into the world of the second government—and they are obviously only tip-of-the-iceberg glimpses—suggest that there are important operations going on beyond the reach of ordinary citizens or of party politics, in many ways beyond even the control of Congress. And though these operations involve men at the top levels of government, they do not seem to indicate any great attachment to democratic processes, as the acknowledged campaign to sabotage one major political party bears witness, or to the constitutional exercise of foreign policy, as the acknowledged attempt to forestall Allende makes clear. Who knows what other schemes ITT may be hatching right now in some other part of the world? Who knows what other secret plans the Republican party has ready to serve its own narrow purposes?

On a somewhat less sordid level, we can also get a glimpse of how the second government operates by looking at the recent "energy crisis" furor. Now the fuel resources of this country are quite possibly being dangerously depleted—though, as James Ridgeway has pointed out, since few independent surveys have been made, it's almost impossible to tell—but the evidence indicates that the recent "crisis" was created not so much by diminishing supplies as by the oil interests, both those with international ties who wanted to increase shipments from abroad and domestic producers along the southern rim. With winter coming on and the refineries having concentrated on gasoline rather than heating fuel over the summer, the industry last year launched a $3 million PR campaign to create panic buying at higher rates and force a relaxation of unwanted pollution standards ("buy dirty or freeze"). As a Ford Foundation energy consultant, S. David Freeman, recently put it, "The 'energy crisis' could well serve as a smoke screen for a massive exercise in picking the pocket of the American consumer to the tune of billions of dollars a year."

The Nixon administration, as might be expected, considering its enormous debt to oil, bought the "energy crisis" line and pushed it upon the public with all the skill of the Petroleum Institute itself. It has made provisions in the new budget for considerable money to be given to domestic producers for "technical assistance"—especially to develop oil-from-coal extraction—and this is likely to increase in future budgets. It permitted a hefty 8 percent rise in heating-oil costs in the middle of January, right after price controls were lifted (thus making its ballyhooed 1 percent price freeze in March almost pointless). And it has just proposed a new energy program which, while allowing more foreign oil imports, to the benefit of the larger international concerns, is explicitly designed for the advantage of domestic producers through the imposition of a set of tariff-like "fees" on imports and the official encouragement of domestic resource development and refinery construction. Its net effect is to increase the value of in-ground resources in this country, which will be vital in case of future international troubles or eventual shortages.

More of the same governmental largesse can be expected in the future. The administration, disregarding its recent setback by the Supreme Court, will step up pressure in Congress to pass laws permitting the Alaskan pipe-line favored by oilmen and damned by environmentalists (one source has already said the latter are fighting a lost cause). It is likely to open up the eastern seaboard's continental shelf to oil explorers and exploiters. It will press for the no-control strip-mining bill already in Congress on the grounds that quick coal-gathering, even if ecologically disastrous, is necessary to meet energy needs, a conclusion that chiefly benefits the western and south-western coal operators. And it is more than likely to postpone enforcement of the federal pollution standards which, much to the dismay of the fuel corporations, were supposed to have gone into effect in 1975.

Other examples of the influence of the southern rim, operating through this shadowy second government, are sure to emerge in the coming months: more money for defense industries, for example, following the $4.1 billion increase in the new budget even after the Vietnam cease-fire; support for road building over mass transportation, satisfying boom-area industry, right-wing construction unions, Detroit, oil interests, and the Teamsters all at once; continued encouragement for TV and radio licensing challenges from conservative cowboys against yankee-owned stations; expansion of Ameri-can influence in the Caribbean, where so many of Nixon's friends have heavy investments (Connally, Rebozo, Robert Abplanalp, the Murchisons, etc.).

Other scandals—whether called by that name in the press or not, as with the Watergate "caper"—are also sure to follow, for it seems obvious that the kind of milieu in which the president has chosen to immerse himself will continue to produce policies self-serving at best, shady at average, and downright illegal at worst, and that at least some of this will break through to public attention. It also seems probable that the American public will continue to pay it all not much mind, despite worries from some Republi-cans now, and indeed that many people in the land identify themselves with—or at least dream themselves as—the new-money wheeler-dealers and seem to regard influence-peddling and back-scratching as the true stuff of the American dream. But that's another story.

The real trouble with such oil stains, not to mention spots of fetid dirt, is that they are very hard to wash off your hands. Some liberals, clucking with glee over the new Watergate disclosures, might like to believe that the power of the southern rimsters is going to vanish after Nixon and his im-mediate friends leave office. As I read it, however, this power is not likely to be washed away with a new administration, no matter what party it comes from, for the entrenched position of the southern rim in the Ameri-can economy is not likely to diminish—indeed, seems most likely to increase —in the decades to come.

There will certainly be more exploitation of its untapped energy re-sources, on shore and off, more dependence upon its defense expertise. There will be more reliance upon its (often) union-free labor, both in agriculture and textile manufacturing, more trade (legal and illegal) across its wide-open borders to Latin America. There will also continue to be more population growth in its undeveloped areas, automatically shifting political power (as with the House of Representatives), and more growth especially in its suburbs, where the Supreme Court's one-man-one-vote decision has so far had the largest effect and where political power has already been transferred to a considerable degree to Republicans and conservatives.

What is at work here is nothing less than Kevin Phillips's (and Richard Nixon's) southern strategy, the creation of a coalition of conservative forces within the Republican party so as to make it, for the first time since 1932, the majority party in the country. It is built on the population growth of the southern rim, the increased *voting* population of the new-money suburbs, the galloping desertions from the ever-blackening Democratic party in the South, the rampant I'm-all-right-Jackism of the established nonurban unions, and of course the financial wealth and shady dealings of the cowboys. If that strategy is correct, and every indication from the last two elections suggests that it is, the reversal of power that it has brought is likely to last just as long as the one that brought Roosevelt to power.

9. SUGGESTIONS FOR FURTHER READING

ALMOND, G., and J. COLEMAN. *The Politics of Developing Areas* (Princeton, N.J.: Princeton University Press, 1960).*

BARNET, RICHARD, and RONALD MULLER. *Global Reach: The Power of the Multi-National Corporations* (New York: Simon & Schuster, 1974).

BOTTOMORE, TOM. *Elites and Society* (New York: Basic Books, 1964).*

BRINTON, CRANE. *The Anatomy of Revolution,* rev. ed. (New York: Random House, 1957).*

CAMPBELL, ANGUS, *et al. The American Voter* (New York: John Wiley & Sons, 1960).*

DAHL, ROBERT. *Who Governs?* (New Haven, Conn.: Yale University Press, 1961).*

FROMM, ERICH. *Escape from Freedom* (New York: Henry Holt, 1941).*

HARRINGTON, MICHAEL. *Socialism* (New York: Saturday Review Press, 1972).*

HOFFER, ERIC. *The True Believer* (New York: Harper, 1951).*

HUNTER, FLOYD. *Community Power Structure* (Chapel Hill: University of North Carolina Press, 1953).*

KEY, V. O., JR. *Southern Politics* (New York: Random House, 1949).*

KORNHAUSER, WILLIAM. *The Politics of Mass Society* (Chicago: The Free Press, 1959).

LIPSET, S. M. *Political Man: The Social Bases of Politics* (Garden City, N.Y.: Doubleday, 1960).*

MARCUSE, HERBERT. *One Dimensional Man: Studies in the Ideology of Advanced Industrial Society* (Boston: Beacon Press, 1964).*

MICHELS, ROBERT. *Political Parties* (New York: Collier Books, 1962).*

MILLS, C. WRIGHT. *Power, Politics, and People* (New York: Oxford University Press, 1963).*

MOORE, BARRINGTON, JR. *Social Origins of Dictatorship and Democracy* (Boston: Beacon Press, 1966).*

OPPENHEIMER, MARTIN. *The Urban Guerilla* (Chicago: Quadrangle Books, 1969).*

ROSE, ARNOLD. *The Power Structure: Political Process in American Society* (New York: Oxford University Press, 1967).*

ROSZAK, THEODORE. *The Making of a Counter Culture* (Garden City, N.Y.: Doubleday, 1969).*

RULE, JAMES. *Private Lives and Public Surveillance: Social Control in the Computer Age* (New York: Schocken Books, 1974).

SWARTZ, MARC, *et al. Political Anthropology* (Chicago: Aldine-Atherton, 1966).

TOCQUEVILLE, ALEXIS DE. *Democracy in America* (New York: Alfred A. Knopf, 1945).*

VIDICH, A., and J. BENSMAN. *Small Town in Mass Society* (Garden City, N.Y.: Doubleday, 1960).*

* Available in paperback.

10. Social Change

INTRODUCTION

Social change may be defined as any transformation in the social structure, normative order, or behavior patterns typical of a given society. This definition embraces change in knowledge, beliefs, and values; in technology and material culture; in the various social institutions—e.g., the economy, government, the family, education, and religion; in the system of stratification and the patterns of intergroup relations; and in the conceptions members of society have of themselves.

Although the rate of change may vary considerably from one society to another, or from one time period to another within a given society, social change is inevitable and universal. Wilbert Moore has identified a number of the factors that account for this: movement through the life cycle, differing physiological potentialities and socialization experiences, variations in fertility and mortality rates, the changing physical and social environment, the ubiquity of nonconformity, and the failure to achieve ideal values.[1]

There has been a phenomenal acceleration of social change during the past several hundred years. Nowadays, novelty and upheaval characterize our everyday reality. Alvin Toffler articulately discusses the unparalleled rate of contemporary change:

> It has been observed, for example, that, if the last 50,000 years of man's existence were divided into lifetimes of approximately sixty-two years each, there have been about 800 such lifetimes. Of these 800, fully 650 were spent in caves.
>
> Only during the last seventy lifetimes has it been possible to

[1] Wilbert Moore, *Social Change* (Englewood Cliffs, N.J.: Prentice-Hall, 1963), pp. 11–21.

communicate effectively from one lifetime to another—as writing has made it possible to do. Only during the last six lifetimes did masses of men ever see a printed word. Only during the last four has it been possible to measure time with any precision. Only in the last two has anyone anywhere used an electric motor. And the overwhelming majority of all the material goods we use in daily life today have been developed within the present, the 800th, lifetime.

This 800th lifetime marks a sharp break with all past human experience, because during this lifetime man's relationship to resources has reversed itself. This is most evident in the field of economic development. Within a single lifetime, agriculture, the original basis of civilization, has lost its dominance in nation after nation. Today in a dozen major countries agriculture employs fewer than 15 per cent of the economically active population.[2]

This avalanche of social change is being experienced everywhere—in the peasant societies of the world that are becoming urbanized as well as in the modern industrial world that is being transformed into the little-understood postindustrial societies of the future.

Social change makes man uneasy; it uproots him from familiar surroundings, meanings, habits, and relationships, creating fear and anxiety. Toffler calls man's response to social change "future shock," akin to the phenomenon of culture shock—the sense of bewilderment, frustration, and disorientation that people experience when they confront an unfamiliar culture.

The ambiguity and psychologically threatening potential of change may spur many to resist innovation. Sometimes, resistance to change is based on the protection of vested interests. For example, the owners of barge canals and stagecoach lines were among the most active opponents of railroads. A century later, the shift from coal-burning engines to diesels was opposed by coal miners, who were threatened with reduction of work, and by railroad firemen, whose occupations were menaced with complete extinction.

Sociologists have observed that social change does not occur in a coordinated way. Frequently, changes take place at uneven rates throughout the different parts of the culture and social structure. About fifty years ago, W. F. Ogburn posited the theory of "cultural lag," which argues that material culture (technology and its artifacts) changes more readily than adaptive culture (customs, values, beliefs, and laws). He cited as an example the development of conservation laws in the United States, which has lagged behind the development of the technology that threatens to destroy most forest lands. We might also consider the development of nuclear weapons and the many other technical improvements in weaponry and warfare that appear to have far surpassed techniques of diplomacy and statesmanship.

2 Alvin Toffler, *Future Shock* (New York: Random House, 1970), pp. 15–16.

Another element that determines whether change is opposed or welcomed within a society are the values shared by the social membership. In folk societies, where one usually finds greater endorsement of traditional authority, there tends to be a general resistance to social change. The time-honored way is considered to be the best way. By contrast, in urban-industrial societies, change is regarded as an everyday fact of life, socially desirable for its own sake, as well as an indication of progress. Perhaps this difference in resistance to change may reflect the fact that the peoples of folk societies are being exposed to substantially greater change than the peoples of the urban-industrial world. Those living in the folk societies of the world are facing the prospect of being catapulted from the Middle Ages to modernity in less than a generation —a change of the most colossal and staggering dimensions.

Space limitations require that we focus our examination on a selected few areas of social change. The demographic dimension—population—represents a most significant source of social change. The importance of the "population explosion" cannot be overemphasized.[3]

The total human population at the birth of Christ was approximately 250 million; it increased to 500 million by 1650, doubled to about 1 billion by 1850, and doubled again 80 years later, reaching two billion by 1930. Demographers today estimate that the world population had doubled again by 1975, reaching four billion. This represents an overwhelming rate of increase in population. It now takes approximately 45 years to double the world's population, compared to over 1,600 years at the dawn of the Christian era!

This growth has not occurred uniformly throughout the world. It has been most accelerated in the so-called underdeveloped societies. In the industrialized countries, the doubling time falls within the 50- to 200-year range; among underdeveloped nations, it falls between 20 and 35 years. For example, the population of Kenya is currently doubling every 24 years.

Rapid population growth is attributable not to any significant rise in the birth rate but to a dramatic drop in the number of early deaths. For example, in Ceylon the introduction of DDT, which controlled the malaria-carrying mosquito, resulted in a 34-per-cent drop in the death rate in the year following its wide-scale application.

Although estimates vary, many experts judge that at least half of the world's population today is improperly nourished. Even the most accelerated economic development imaginable for the next two generations probably would not result in a sufficient supply of food for our present population; and, by that time, the population will have more than doubled and perhaps even quadrupled.

[3] For authoritative and up-to-date assessments of the population problem see Paul Ehrlich and Anne Ehrlich, *Population, Resources, Environment,* 2d ed. (San Francisco: W. H. Freeman, 1972 and the Editors of *Scientific American, The Human Population* (San Francisco: W. H. Freeman, 1974).

Calculations show that Asia, merely to maintain her present low level of living standards, must increase her aggregate product by 60 per cent between now and 1975, and by an additional 75 per cent between 1975 and 2000.[4]

If nothing is done to control the population explosion, alarming increases in the death rate appear to be inevitable. In "The Population Explosion: Facts and Fiction," Paul Ehrlich summarizes the most important aspects of the problem and demonstrates the fallacy of believing that population problems will not affect the peoples of the developed world. He examines several of the remedies proposed to rectify the population–food imbalance—e.g., the use of resources from the sea, outer space, and synthetic food—to underscore the staggering dimensions of the problem, as well as the need for immediate action.

Next to the threat posed by thermonuclear war, the problem of worldwide hunger represents today's most dramatic challenge. With half of the world population underfed, the need to increase mankind's productive capacity has great urgency. In the underdeveloped world, the revolution in transportation and communications has brought greater familiarity with the ways of urban-industrial society, awakening new desires for economic improvement and well-being. A revolution of rising expectations is beginning to eclipse the fatalistic resignation and traditionalism of folk-peasant societies. The question facing the student of social change, then, is how this tremendous economic transformation can be brought about most speedily and with the least disruption.

Robert Heilbroner has identified a number of factors that are necessary for economic development.[5] A nation must possess a sufficient number of natural resources. These assets are vital for the nation's own developmental needs as well as for attracting partners to provide whatever necessary materials may be lacking. Secondly, a nation needs funds for capital investment. Only by deferring consumption and increasing savings and investment can it create the necessary capital to bring about growth. Once acquired, machines, electrical power, factories, and the like present opportunities for revolutionizing productivity. The pace of industrialization depends heavily upon capital goods obtained from the developed world, whether by trade, investment, or aid. Vast changes in attitudes will be required to build and attract capital; the rich must refrain from conspicuous consumption and nepotism; peasant cultivators must be more amenable to innovation, the application of scientific farming, and the idea of producing beyond their family's daily living requirements; caste barriers will have to yield in order to create more fluidity in the system of stratification.

The population explosion presents an obvious handicap to economic

[4] Robert Heilbroner, *The Great Ascent: The Struggle for Economic Development in Our Time* (New York: Harper & Row, 1963), p. 56.

[5] *Ibid.*, pp. 33–141.

growth, not only because of the vastly increasing numbers of people who must be supported, but also because the fastest-growing societies are most likely to have high proportions of youthful members who can contribute very little to productivity and who are economically dependent. For example, in Costa Rica some 50 per cent of the population is under fifteen years of age.

A nationalistic spirit and leadership deeply committed to economic development are especially valuable elements for bringing about economic transformation. Yet, nationalist feeling among the members of society in itself is insufficient to carry the development along; social capital has to be created—schools and hospitals built, technicians and professionals trained—so as to set the course of development in a self-sustaining direction. In the past, many attempts to parlay social capital failed to yield results; young people sent abroad for specialized training all too often never return to deliver the benefits of their studies to their homelands.

Coordinated land reform is also necessary; in some cases, large land holdings will have to be broken up into smaller units; in other cases, small holdings will have to be consolidated into larger sectors. Central government authority must assume a pivotal role in planning and coordinating economic development. Forceful political leadership will be needed to inspire the sacrifices necessary to carry the economic development along.

William Pratt's "Anabaptist Explosion" is most instructive for our understanding of economic development. The Anabaptists are unique, in that their rate of population increase is possibly the fastest on earth. Although they by no means represent a "typical" Third World people, their phenomenal population growth highlights the fact that development is taking place in the context of a tremendous population explosion. Pratt's findings suggest that there may be advantages in centralized planning over a decentralized, laissez-faire economic system. The centrally coordinated Hutterite economy adequately supports the needs of its members. And the economic success of these people may contribute to the infrequently observed defections from the group and their high fertility, the highest of any Anabaptist sect. The less economically successful Amish, on the other hand, are sustaining more defections and appear to be less closely approximating the Anabaptist cultural ideal of large families. There are, however, a number of confounding factors that make this a less than satisfactory comparison of collective-versus-individual—based economies.

Another condition encouraging the economic-development process seems to be the existence of a stable political system. Political stability, it seems, helps to generate both a climate favorable for the growth of nationalism and the requisite altruistic behavior for developing national capital. It also attracts foreign capital, offering the prospect of greater security to would-be investors and benefactors. However, the reality of politics in the underdeveloped world falls far short of stability; revolution and political upheaval are very frequent events. Why is revolution apparently more common in transitional societies? What are the social factors associated with revolutionary political change?

James Davies, in "Toward a Theory of Revolution," addresses both questions. Drawing upon the events of Doar's Rebellion of 1842 in New England, the Russian Revolution of 1917, and the Egyptian Revolution of 1952, Davies posits a theory of rising expectations to account for revolutionary action. He maintains that revolutions are most likely to occur when a prolonged period of social and economic development is followed by a short period of deep reversal. Revolution is generated by the expectation that past progress, now blocked, can and must continue in the future. Underdeveloped societies, especially as they come into closer contact with the developed world, have become unusually susceptible to a climate of rising expectations. Societies that have recently thrown off the yoke of colonial status, that are experiencing rapid social change, and whose economic development is occurring at a phenomenal rate—conditions that describe many transitional societies—are very likely to generate rising expectations.

A closely related theory, originally presented by Alexis de Tocqueville and more recently by the late Crane Brinton, is the theory of "relative deprivation." Actual or objective deprivation is not so important in motivating revolutionary sentiment as subjective or relative deprivation—that is, how deprived a person feels himself to be in relation to others. Thus, the greatest support for the French Revolution came from the ranks of affluent farmers and urban merchants who were resentful because their political power and social prestige were not commensurate with their material wealth. Seemingly affluent, they felt deprived and envious. It was not that they opposed the feudal estate system as an inequitable and morally offensive institution so much as that they wished to enjoy the privileges and distinctions of the nobility.

This theory raises some important questions about what social types are likely to be among the revolutionaries, especially the revolutionary leadership. Davies suggests that the poorest and most oppressed are unlikely to be among the revolutionary forces, because they are so absorbed with the struggle for survival that they are unlikely to have energy left for politicizing. Examination of several revolutions shows that the revolutionary ranks have a rather broad and varied social base. Many studies, including the Kerner Commission Report on urban ghetto disorder in the United States, have found that revolutionary leaders are ordinarily drawn from relatively high social ranks, more affluent and more highly educated than their constituencies. Conceivably, this finding could be interpreted as evidence for the relative-deprivation theory. It also concurs with sociologists' findings regarding organized action in general; leaders usually possess more social skills, rank, and esteem than are found among their supporters.

In transitional societies, glaring social inequities also play a role in generating revolutionary sentiment. Bruce Russett finds that the higher the concentration of land ownership and the higher the rate of tenancy, the greater the likelihood of political instability.[6] The rapidity of change also affects the probability of revolution in underdeveloped societies. As rapid change liberates men from their traditional social statuses, it creates social dislocations that make men more susceptible to the revolution-initiating potential of rising expectations and relative deprivation.

Where do we go from here? What will be the direction of social change in postindustrial society? What will be the life-styles of the future? If present trends offer an indication of what is to come, the commune may be an integral part of our future social life. In our contemporary society an unprecedented interest in communes has arisen; some estimate that the number of communes in the United States now exceeds two thousand. Rosabeth Kanter's exhaustive research provides a very detailed picture of urban communal living patterns, which could become more commonplace among postindustrial citizens in the years ahead. Kanter herself is uncertain of the future of communes. It is her contention that the commune itself is not so important as the diminished significance of blood ties, age and sex differentiation, and authority relationships. In the future, she anticipates, there will be more negotiated, egalitarian, and intentional relationships. So far, this has been the thrust of the transition from folk to urban societies, and it seems plausible that it could continue into the postindustrial era.

The Demographic Dimension of Social Change

The Population Explosion: Facts and Fiction*

Paul R. Ehrlich

The facts of today's population crisis are appallingly simple. Mankind at first gradually, but recently with extreme rapidity, has intervened artificially

---

[6] Bruce Russett, "Inequality and Instability: The Relation of Land Tenure to Politics," *World Politics*, XVI, no. 3 (April, 1964), 442–54.

* Copyright 1968 *Sierra Club Bulletin*. Reprinted by permission of the author and the editors of the *Sierra Club Bulletin*.

to lower the death rate in the human population. Simultaneously, we have not—repeat, *have not*—intervened to lower the birth rate. Since people are unable to flee from our rather small planet, the inevitable result of the wide discrepancy between birth and death rates has been a rapid increase in the numbers of people crowded onto the earth.

The growth of the population is now so rapid that the multitude of humans is doubling every 35 years. Indeed, in many undeveloped countries, the doubling time is between 20 and 25 years. Think of what it means for the population of a country like Colombia to double in the next 22 years. Throughout its history, the people of Colombia have managed to create a set of facilities for the maintenance of human beings: buildings, roads, farms, water systems, sewage systems, hospitals, schools, churches, and so forth. Remember that, just to remain even, just to maintain today's level of misery, Colombia would have to duplicate all of those facilities in the next 22 years. It would have to double its human resources as well—train enough doctors, lawyers, teachers, judges, and all the rest so that, in 22 years, the number of all these professionals would be twice that of today. Such a task would be impossible for a powerful, industrialized country with agricultural surpluses, high literacy rate, fine schools and communications, etc. The United States couldn't hope to accomplish it. For Colombia, with none of these things, with 30–40 per cent of its population illiterate, with 47 per cent of its population under fifteen years of age, it is inconceivable.

Yes, it will be impossible for Colombia to maintain its present level of misery for the next 22 years—and misery it is. Death control did not reach Colombia until after World War II. Before it arrived, a woman could expect to have two or three children survive to reproductive age if she went through ten pregnancies. Now, in spite of malnutrition, medical technology keeps seven or eight alive. Each child adds to the impossible financial burden of the family and to the despair of the mother. According to Dr. Sumner M. Kalman, the average Colombian mother goes through a progression of attempts to limit the size of her family. She starts with ineffective native forms of contraception and moves on to quack abortion, infanticide, frigidity, and all too often to suicide. The average family in Colombia, after its last child is born, has to spend 80 per cent of its income on food. And the per capita income of Colombians is $237 per year, less than one-tenth that of Americans. That's the kind of misery that's concealed behind the dry statistic of a population doubling every 22 years.

But it seems highly unlikely that, 22 years from now, Colombia will have doubled its present population of 20 million to 40 million. The reason is quite simple. The earth is a spaceship of limited carrying capacity. The 3.5 billion people who now live on our globe can do so only at the expense of the consumption of nonrenewable resources, especially coal and petroleum. Today's technology could not maintain 3.5 billion people without "living on capital," as we are now doing. Indeed, it is doubtful if any technology could permanently maintain that number. And note that, even living on capital, we are doing none too well. Somewhere between 1 and 2 billion people are *today* undernourished (have too few calories) or malnourished (suffer from various deficiencies, especially protein deficiencies). Somewhere between 4 and 10 million of our fellow human beings will starve to death this year. Consider that the average person among some 2 billion Asians has an annual income of $128, a life expectancy at birth of only 50 years, and is illiterate. A third of a billion Africans have an average life expectancy of only 43 years, and an average annual income of $123. Of Africans over fifteen years of age, 82 per cent are illiterate. Look at the situation in India, where Professor Georg Borgstrom estimates that only about one person in fifty has an adequate diet. For the vast majority, the calorie supply "is not sufficient for sustaining a normal workday. Physical exhaustion and apathy [are] the rule."

No, we're not doing a very good job of taking care of the people we have in 1968—and we are adding to the population of the earth 70 million people per year. Think of it—an equivalent of the 1968 population of the United States *added* to the world every three years! We have an inadequate loaf of bread to divide among today's multitudes, and we are quickly adding more billions to the bread line.

As I said at the beginning, the facts are indeed simple. We are faced by a most elementary choice. Either we find a way to bring the birth rate down or the death rate will soon go back up. Make no mistake about it—mankind has not freed itself on the tyranny of arithmetic! Anyone, including Pope Paul VI, who stands in the way of measures to bring down the birth rate is automatically working for a rise in the death rate.

The death rate could rise in several ways. Perhaps the most likely is through famine. The world has very nearly reached its maximum food production capacity—even with the expenditure of our nonrenewable resources. Agricultural experts, such as Professor Borgstrom and the Paddock brothers, present a dismal picture indeed. The Paddocks' best estimate of the onset of the "Time of Famines," the time when many tens of millions will starve to death annually, is 1975. How accurate their prediction is will depend on many factors, such as the weather, over which we have no control. It will also depend, in part, on what actions mankind takes to attempt an amelioration of the situation. I must, however, agree with the Paddocks that massive famines are now inevitable.

Plague presents another possibility for a "death rate solution" to the population problem. It is known that viruses may increase their virulence when they infect a large population. With viruses circulating in a weakened population of unprecedented size, and with modern transport capable of spreading infection to the far corners of the globe almost instantly, we could easily face an unparalleled epidemic. Indeed, if a man-made germ should escape from one of our biological warfare labs, we might see the extinction of *Homo sapiens*. It is now theoretically possible to develop organisms against which man would have no resistance—indeed, one Nobel laureate was so appalled at the possibility of an accidental escape that he quit research in this field.

Finally, of course, thermonuclear war could provide us with an instant death-rate solution. Nearly a billion people in China are pushing out of their biologically ruined country toward Siberia, India, and the Mekong rice bowl. The suffering millions of Latin America are moving toward revolution and Communist governments. An Arab population boom, especially among Palestinian refugees, adds to tensions. The competition to loot the sea of its fishes creates international incidents. As more and more people have less and less, as the rich get richer and the poor poorer, the probability of war increases. The poor of the world know what we have, and they want it. They have what is known as rising expectations. For this reason alone, a mere maintenance of current levels of living will be inadequate to maintain peace.

Unfortunately, we will not need to kill outright all human beings to drive mankind to extinction. Small groups of genetically and culturally impoverished survivors may well succumb to the inevitably harsh environment of a war-ravaged planet. War not only could end this population explosion, it has the potential for removing the possibility of any future population growth.

Faced with this dismal prospect, why haven't people, especially in an educated country like the United States, taken rational action to bring the birth rate down? Why haven't we led the way toward a world with an optimum population living in balance with its resources? Why, indeed, have most Americans remained unaware of the gravity of the entire problem? The answers to these questions are many and complex. In the rest of this talk, I'd like to discuss one major reason why we have not managed to defuse the population bomb. This reason is the perpetuation of a series of fictions that tend to discount the problem or present fantasy solutions to it. These fictions are eagerly believed by many people who show an all-too-human wish to avoid facing unpleasant realities. Let's look at some of the fictions, and some of the unpleasant realities.

FICTION: The population explosion is over, at least in the United States, because the birth rate is at an all-time low.

FACT: Although the birth rate of the United States has hit record lows (around 16 per thousand per year) for brief periods this year, it has not approached the death rate, which is down around 9 per thousand per year. Even at the record low rate (if it were to continue), the population of the United States would double in about 100 years. But the low birth rate will not persist, since the large group of women born in the post–World War II baby boom move into their peak reproductive period in the next few years. Birth rates are subject to short-term fluctuations, according to the number of women in their reproductive years, the condition of the economy, the occurrence of wars, etc. Viewing a temporary decline of the birth rate as a sign of the end of the population explosion is like considering a warm December 26th as a sign of spring. The ballyhooing of the temporary decline of birth rate (with, if you recall, no mention of death rate) has done great harm to the cause of humanity.

FICTION: The United States has no population problem—it is a problem of the undeveloped countries.

FACT: Considering the problems of air and water pollution, poverty, clogged highways, overcrowded schools, inadequate courts and jails, urban blight, and so on, it is clear that the United States has more people than it can adequately maintain. But, even if we were not overpopulated at home, we could not stand detached from the rest of the world. We are completely dependent on imports for our affluence. We use roughly one-half of all the raw materials consumed on the face of the earth each year. We need the ferroalloys, tin, bauxite, petroleum, rubber, food, and other materials we import. We, one-fifteenth of the population, grab one-half as our share. We can afford to raise beef for our own use in protein-starved Asia. We can afford to take fish from protein-starved South America and feed it to our chickens. We can afford to buy protein-rich peanuts from protein-starved Africans. Even if we are not engulfed in worldwide plague or war, we will suffer mightily as the "other world" slips into famine. We will suffer when they are no longer willing or able to supply our needs. It has been truly said that calling the population explosion a problem of undeveloped countries is like saying to a fellow passenger, "Your end of the boat is sinking."

FICTION: Much of the earth is empty land that can be put under cultivation in order to supply food for the burgeoning population of the planet.

FACT: Virtually all of the land that can be cultivated with known or easily foreseeable methods already is under cultivation. We would have to double our present agricultural production just to feed today's billions adequately—and the population of the earth is growing, I repeat, by some *70 million people* per year. No conceivable expansion of arable land could take care of these needs.

FICTION: Although land agriculture cannot possibly take care of our food needs, we still have "unmeasurable" resources of the sea that can be tapped so that we can populate the earth until people are jammed together like rabbits in a warren.

FACT: The resources of the sea have been measured and have been found wanting. Most of the sea is a biological desert. Our techniques for extracting what potential food there is in the sea are still very primitive. With a cessation of pollution, complete international cooperation, and ecologically intelligent management, we might manage to double our present yield from the sea or do even better on a sustained basis. But even such a miracle would be inadequate to meet the needs of the population growth. And there is no sign of such a miracle. Indeed, there is increasing pollution of the sea with massive amounts of pesticides and other biologically active compounds. In addition, a no-holds-barred race to harvest the fish of the sea has developed among China, Japan, Russia, the United States, and others. This race is resulting in the kind of overexploitation that led to the decline of the whaling industry. All the signs point to a *reduction* of the food yield of the sea in the near future—not to a bonanza from the sea.

FICTION: Science (with a capital S) will find a new way to feed everyone —perhaps by making food synthetically.

FACT: Perhaps, in the distant future, some foods will be produced synthetically in large quantity, but not in time to help mankind through the crisis it now faces. The most-discussed methods would involve the use of micro-organisms and fossil fuels. Since fossil fuels are limited in supply, and much in demand for other uses, their use as a food source would be a temporary measure, at best. Direct synthesis, even should it eventually prove possible, would inevitably present problems of energy supply and materials supply—it would be no simple "food for nothing" system. But, I repeat, science holds no hope of finding a synthetic solution to the food problem at this time.

FICTION: We can solve the crowding problem on our planet by migrating to other planets.

FACT: No other planet of the solar system appears to be habitable. But, if all of them were, we would have to export to them 70 million people a year to keep our population constant. With our current technology and that foreseeable in the next few decades, such an effort would be economically impossible—indeed, the drain on our mineral resources and fossil fuels would be unbelievable. Suppose that we built rockets immeasurably larger than any in existence today—capable of carrying 100 people and their baggage to another planet. Almost 2,000 of such monster ships would have to leave each day. The effects of their exhausts on the atmosphere would be spectacular, to say the least. And what if, through miracles, we did manage to export all those people and maintain them elsewhere in the solar system? In a mere 250 years, the entire system would be populated to the same density as the earth. Attempting to reach the planets of the stars raises the prospect of space ships taking generations to reach their destinations. Since population explosions could not be permitted on the star ships, the passengers would have to be willing to practice strict birth control. In other words, the responsible people will have to be the ones to leave, with the irresponsible staying at home to breed. On the cheery side, getting to the stars might not be so difficult. After all, in a few thousand years, at the current growth rate, all the material in the visible universe will have been converted into people, and the sphere of people will be expanding outward at better than the speed of light!

FICTION: Family planning is the answer to the population explosion. It has worked in places like Japan; it will work in places like India.

FACT: No country, including Japan, has managed to bring its population under rational control. After World War II, Japan employed abortion to reduce its birth rate, but it did not stop its growth. Indeed, in 1966, with its birth rate at a temporary low because it was the "Year of the Fiery Horse" (considered inauspicious for births), Japan's population was still growing at a rate that would double it in 63 years. Japan is in desperate straits. Today, it must import food equivalent to its entire agricultural production. In addition, it depends heavily on its fisheries, from which it gets food equivalent to more than one and one half times its agricultural production. Japan is so overpopulated that, *even if her population growth stopped,* she would succumb to disaster as her sources of food imports dry up and as her share of the yield from the sea shrinks. But, remember, grossly overpopulated Japan is continuing to grow at a rapid rate.

Family planning in India has had no discernible effect, even though it has had government support for some seventeen years. During those years, the population has increased by more than one half, and the growth rate itself has increased. The IUD (intrauterine device) was promoted by the professional optimists as the panacea for India, but the most recent news from that country indicates a recognition of the failure of the IUD campaign and a return to the promotion of condoms.

Most depressing of all is the point that family planning promotes the notion that people should have only the number of children they *want* and can support. It does not promote family sizes that will bring about population control. As Professor Kingsley Davis has often pointed out, people *want* too many children. Family planning has not controlled any population to date, and by itself it is not going to control *any* population.

These fictions are spread by a wide variety of people and organizations, and for a wide variety of reasons. Some have long-term emotional commitments to outmoded ideas, such as population control through family planning. Others wish to disguise the failure of the government agencies they run. Still others have simple economic interests in the sale of food or agricultural chemicals and equipment. Almost all also have genuine humanitarian motives. Most of these people have an incomplete view of the problem, at best. The less well informed simply have no grasp of the magnitude of the problem—these are the ones who propose solutions in outer space or under the sea. More sophisticated are those who hold out great hopes for agricultural changes (now often referred to as a "green revolution"), which will at least temporarily solve the problem. Such people are especially common in our government.

This sophisticated group tends to be ignorant of elementary biology. Our desperate attempts to increase food yields are promoting soil deterioration and contributing to the poisoning of the ecological systems on which our very survival depends. It is a long and complex story, but the conclusion is simple—the more we strive to obtain increased yields in the short run, the smaller the yields are likely to be in the long run. No attempt to increase food yields can solve the problem. How much, then, should we mortgage our future by such attempts?

I've concentrated, in my discussion, on the nature of the population explosion rather than attempting to detail ways of reaching a birth-rate solution. That is because the first step toward any solution involves a realistic facing of the problem. We must, as that first step, get a majority of Americans to recognize the simple choice: *Lower the birth rate or face a drastic rise in the death rate.* We must divert attention from the treatment of symptoms of the population explosion and start treating its cause. We have no more time; we must act now. Next year will not do. It is already too late for us to survive unscathed. Now we must make decisions designed to minimize the damage. America today reminds me of the fabled man who jumped off the top of a fifty-story building. As he passed the second floor, he was heard to say, "Things have gone pretty well so far."

The Economic Dimension of Social Change

The Anabaptist Explosion*

William F. Pratt

The survival of the Hutterites and the Amish, two religious sects whose communities are found in various parts of the United States and Canada, is a cultural anachronism. That these Anabaptist societies have persevered over several hundred years fraught with persecution and rejection is surprising enough. That they have maintained their medieval faith and their unsophisticated styles of life in a rapidly changing urban-industrial environment, is an ecological phenomenon of considerable moment. But of particular interest is their traditionally high level of fertility, which has persisted while their mortality rates have approximated that of the surrounding society. Consequently, they have experienced a phenomenal growth from natural increase, which has created portentous problems for them.

The Hutterites, settled in South Dakota, Montana, and the prairie provinces of Canada, and the Amish, formerly centered in Pennsylvania and Ohio, have birth rates of 46 and 33 per 1,000 population, respectively. A century and a half ago, the United States birth rate was a lofty 55—over three times higher than its present level; in 1967, it had dropped to an all-time low of 17.9 births per 1,000 population. It is against this shifting background that the continuing high fertility of the Hutterites and Amish is so startling.

Comparable fertility rates show that, from age twenty, Hutterite women have much higher birth rates than those of American women in general. Even in their late childbearing years (forty to forty-four), their birth rate

* Reprinted from *Natural History Magazine*, February, 1969. Copyright © 1969 The American Museum of Natural History.

exceeds that of American women in their peak childbearing years (twenty to twenty-four). (The Amish women, in a somewhat freer society, have birth rates about midway between those of Hutterites and of American women in general.) It may be that two centuries of high fertility, combined with the inbreeding brought about by the social isolation of the Hutterites, has created a unique strain of the human species—a strain distinct in its fertility from any other people. Indeed, the Hutterites, with an annual natural increase of about 4 per cent, are possibly the fastest-growing population on earth. Between 1950 and 1965, their numbers almost doubled, from 8,500 to 15,000. The United States growth rate, by contrast, is only .79. This would double the population in about 90 years, compared with a doubling among Hutterites about every 17 years.

The fertility of the two Anabaptist sects is one reflection of their rigidly theocratic cultures, which have managed to survive in an urban-industrial nation of 200 million that is wholly alien in outlook to the sects' own beliefs. At the same time, their rigid separatism, their being conscientious objectors, and their rapid growth have made these sects a focal point of hostility among their neighbors. The problems of the Amish families with respect to public education are familiar. As for Hutterite colonies, land laws have been proposed several times—and, in some cases passed—to restrict their spread. At their present growth rate, Hutterites would number 64,500 by the year 2000 and more than 55 million by 2168. Today, their colonies occupy about 1,000 square miles; by the year 2000, they would occupy an area almost equaling Connecticut.

The difference in birth rates of the two sects is intriguing. It undoubtedly reflects differences in social organization and comparative success in adapting to the secular milieu of modern America. Despite their common origins and life-style, they differ significantly in important respects.

HUTTERITES: A DISSIDENT SECT

The Anabaptists of the Reformation comprised several quite different sects, from the radical and violent Munsterites to the equally radical but wholly nonviolent Hutterites. What they shared was the label "Anabaptist"; it referred to their central belief in adult "rebaptism," baptism upon confession of faith. All these Protestant sects were religious responses of the socially disinherited of the Holy Roman Empire in the late fifteenth and sixteenth centuries.

Peasants, journeymen, and the landless were the most abject victims of that period's crises. Many turned from a cheerless reality to the comforts of a religion that made a virtue of their poverty and built a brotherhood on their passive suffering. But then Martin Luther and Huldrich Zwingli alike, having gained their patrimony from the state, turned upon the rabble. In 1527, the Swiss Anabaptists responded by formalizing many of the tenets that still characterize Hutterites and Amish. Among these are adult baptism, separation of church and state by the withdrawal of believers, and an emphatic rejection of violence. From the outset, then, Anabaptism was regarded as a threat to the established religious and secular authorities, both old and new.

Unsafe in Zurich, the Swiss Brethren—the main body of Swiss Anabaptists—found refuge in Nikolsburg, Moravia, where their mounting numbers undoubtedly created severe economic strains. These were soon reflected in doctrinal disputes between a liberal majority and a strict, radical minority. The radicals, proclaiming Christian communism, worshipping separately, holding fast to adult baptism, and rejecting military violence even to defend themselves, were expelled in 1528. At that time, they symbolically spread a cloak upon the ground to receive their worldly goods. This formally inaugurated the practice of "community of goods," which made them unique among sects descending from the Swiss Brethren. Under the organizational genius of Jacob Hutter (martyred in 1536), this radical group became known as Hutterites.

Although their communities flourished and increased through the first hundred years, they stood constantly in the shadow of persecution and dispersal. Between 1529 and 1622, an estimated 85 communal households, averaging from 300 to 400 members, had been established. But, by 1625, the sect had almost completely migrated to Hungary. There, the re-establishment of Catholic authority and the rise of the Jesuits overcame the reluctance of the nobility to persecute the Hutterites. Invasion by the Turks added to their troubles. Also, considerable internal discord arose, and, by the end of the seventeenth century, membership had been greatly reduced by apostasy to Catholicism.

Of the faithful, most migrated to Slovakia, Transylvania, and Walachia, and later to Russia. Here, unable to re-establish communal life, they accepted the individual family culture practiced by the Mennonites, an independent Anabaptist movement that also had set up some communities in Russia. In the 1870's, fearing Czarist persecution, most Hutterites migrated to the United States, where, returning to their former, communal order, they established three colonies, comprising about 440 persons.

HUTTERITES OF NORTH AMERICA

Thus began a demographic epic. As of January, 1965, there were 162 organized communities, averaging 94 "souls," in the United States and Canada. This growth to over 15,000 people is about a 33-fold increase, or over five doublings of population in less than a century.

These figures are the more remarkable because the Hutterites have been a "closed population" since arrival in America. Their growth has come entirely from natural increase, the excess of births over deaths.

Even when adjusted for differences in age distribution, the Hutterite death rate is only 85 per cent of the United States figure. The Hutterite rate for infant mortality in the past was above the national figure, but, with improving medical care and health practices, this, too, may now be equal to, or less than, for the nation as a whole.

Some practices, such as considerable reliance upon midwives, remain old-fashioned, but, in general, the Hutterites have adopted modern medical facilities. Although their anti-intellectualism and separation from the world have deprived them of the outstanding medical personnel they had in an earlier era, Hutterites do not hesitate to send ailing members to the Mayo Clinic and other medical centers. A recent study suggests that they may be spending more per capita on drugs and medical care than do most Americans. If their favorable mortality has been purchased at the cost of greater dependence upon the outside, it is nonetheless consistent with their historical emphasis on health and medical practice.

The exceptionally high fertility of Hutterite women is most sharply seen in their average completed fertility. It totals 10.4 live births, owing partly to the remarkably high rates of childbearing in the later fertile years. According to sociologists J. W. Eaton and A. J. Mayer, the fertility rate of over 425 per 1,000 for Hutterite women aged 35–39 exceeds that for women in any other culture now on record. Even at ages 40–44, Hutterites have a fertility rate higher than women in France, Sweden, and the United States during their years of maximum fertility, ages 20–29.

So striking a deviation suggests that something more than social or theocratic mores [is] involved. The inbreeding within the Hutterite population must be considerable. Since the 440 original brethren with only 15 patronyms among them (70 per cent had only five patronyms) came to America a century ago, they have attracted no "new blood." In view of the higher mortality of Hutterite women in the childbearing years and the continued reproduction of those women rugged enough to stay the course, genetic components favoring a superfecund strain in the species must have been added to the Hutterite gene pool. The degree to which inbreeding may have made this population genetically more uniform (homozygous) would depend on birth and marriage patterns within the colonies. Until a detailed genetic analysis of the Hutterite pedigree becomes available, it is impossible to derive accurate inbreeding coefficients and thereby add greatly to our knowledge of what inbreeding does to human populations.

At any rate, Hutterite fertility has few restrictions and strong positive encouragement from the culture. Hutterites take literally the Biblical injunction to "be fruitful and multiply": sex as pleasure is devalued and confined to marriage, the chief end of which is to beget children. Birth control, including the rhythm method, is prohibited. All but a very few Hutterites marry, divorce is unknown, and remarriage after the death of a spouse is frequent. The only major restraint upon fertility is the relatively late age at marriage, combined with prohibition of premarital sexual intercourse. Sociologist John A. Hostetler reports that, in 1965, the average age at marriage was 23.5 for men and 22.0 for women, compared with the national averages of 22.8 and 20.6 for men and women, respectively.

These direct factors are supported by the general cultural patterns of community life. Lack of privacy in one's household and possessions would make difficult the use of most mechanical or chemical contraceptive methods; and failure to bear children within a reasonably short time after marriage or the last birth starts gossip and insinuations about one's health and the health of one's marriage. The same lack of privacy makes premarital sexual adventures unlikely, not to mention the severe guilt and ostracism that a premarital pregnancy would bring.

In any case, there is little, if any, motivation for birth control. Unlike outsiders, the Hutterite family does not face the economic uncertainties that attend death and unemployment; it does not have the responsibilities of maintaining its own separate household and facilities; above all, it escapes "keeping up with the Joneses." The simplicity of Hutterite consumer needs, the economies of communal life, the low educational costs, and the early age at which youth enter the colony's productive enterprise all keep the costs of childbearing very low compared to the general population. This would seem to leave the state of the woman's health and the strains of childbearing as the only plausible focus for trying to limit the number of children, and, so far, these considerations have had no observable impact on fertility.

In view of its remarkably high fertility and rapid natural increase, the intriguing question is: How has this anti-intellectual, medieval communal order managed to adapt itself to a highly secular, urban-industrial environment and its rapidly changing technology? Other Anabaptist groups have clearly not resisted surrounding secular influences so well.

No longer subject to the whimsies of noble patrons, as in Europe, each Hutterite colony is an independent corporate enterprise integrated with the larger American economy. Hutterite economy is more specialized in agriculture today than when they were in Europe; they have sacrificed many of their former crafts and trades for modern mechanical skills and the economies of wholesale purchasing.

But their assimilation is exclusively at the economic and corporate level. Life within the contemporary colony is a revitalized communal order. Esthetic and individualizing interests are suppressed, as of old, by a common style in all things—a style marked by simplicity and sturdiness of materials. Thus, active economic choice does not intrude, and invidious status differences do not arise. Financial matters and control of funds are strictly communal. Although not motivated by profit, Hutterites are shrewd businessmen who must maintain a substantial level of savings for contingencies and for building new colonies every generation or less.

So far as possible, labor remains communal, and responsibilities are divided according to age, sex, and "election," as in former times. Cooking is done in a communal kitchen; eating is in a common dining hall. Although each family has one to two rooms in a communal apartment, toilet facilities are shared.

By isolating themselves socially, Hutterites sustain a strong sense of solidarity and a remarkable integrity of their communal life. Their rural location, the restrictions on working for outsiders, their language and quaint clothing, all help to separate them from the world. Information about the outside is primarily through the daily newspaper and farm journals, plus infrequent trips to town; but radios, TV, and movies are forbidden. Although bilingual and maintaining their level of literacy, they refuse state education beyond the legal required age, and maintain a parochial school in the colony to keep the children at home. The "English" teacher, certified by the state or province, generally lives in the colony but is as physically and socially isolated as Hutterite courtesy and hospitality will allow.

This social isolation of the Hutterite group itself is reinforced by a psychological turning inward. By constant reflection on their historical persecution and references to it, Hutterites maintain a fearful view of the outside world. The conditioning begins in earliest childhood, when Santa Claus is described as a bogeyman who kidnaps naughty children; consequently, the youngster shrinks from strangers. Also, the fundamentalist religious message stresses God's wrath and vengeance upon those who enter the world, or behave in worldly ways (against the community rules), and his forgiving love for those who repent. These teachings begin in the communal kindergarten and continue in the "German" school to age 15, where they are reinforced by the strict teacher. In sum, a somewhat paranoid fear of, and prejudice toward, the larger society is ritually induced from childhood, while the ascetic discipline of the community life comes to be viewed as the comforting, forgiving, God-given haven.

Contemporary Hutterites are keenly aware that colony size is also basically important. By limiting colonies to a maximum of about 150 members, they can preserve close interpersonal relations, with privacy nearly impossible and competing cliques seldom arising. When the colony population becomes too large, however, stresses do occur and feelings polarize along family and kinship lines.

This internal source of disruption is normally muted in several ways that characterize Hutterite communal life: The economic independence of the family is eliminated; family-centered activities are minimized; men and women are separated in labor, dining, and worship; and household privacy is limited.

North American society also fosters their internal solidarity. From time to time, their colonies have been harassed by neighbors and by attempted legislative restrictions; these, plus the jibes and prejudice of outsiders, suffice to keep their fears very much alive, even though their rights have been strongly protected.

Most significant, perhaps, is that the outside no longer offers a viable living alternative for the individual Hutterite or family. Neither by education, social skills, nor psychology is the Hutterite prepared to compete in the larger society. Since 1918, no more than 2 per cent of all Hutterites have ever forsaken their colonies. The young man who does "try the world" almost invariably feels a keen sense of loneliness and returns in short order, expressing a sense of guilt toward his parents.

STRESSES AND STRAINS

To the casual observer, Hutterite society may present the illusion of unchangeability over 400 years of history. A paradox is closer to the truth: They have changed, and in fundamental ways, in order to remain the same. A simple example is the principle of adult baptism. Although it is still observed in form, and plays a crucial part in Hutterite socialization, it has long since lost its original meaning. Today's young Hutterite adult does not "choose" the community life after having experienced and rejected the "world" on its own terms. He has been very successfully conditioned to fear the outside, to feel inadequate in the face of it, to cherish the psychological shelter of the community.

Will the adaptive processes that have so far preserved the Hutterite culture continue to operate in the indefinite future? This will depend on how much the stresses and strains are intensified by the phenomenal population growth.

The communal operation has an ideal or optimal labor demand that implies a population of about 100 persons in all ages. As sociologist Victor Peters observes: "A new colony with a population of about 100 persons will have an adult labor pool . . . of about 30 men and women. Approximately 15 . . . will be male, which means that almost all of them will be in charge of an office or enterprise. . . . As the population increases, there are duplications in the various enterprises (by a system of assistants)."

This is the stage at which invidious distinctions among equals arise and cause tensions; the basis for cliques and divisions along family lines now begins to emerge. The resulting tensions play upon the problem of esthetics and the adoption of consumer conveniences. In short, the intimate, primary relations of colony life begin to give way to more formal regulations and supervision. However, when colony size reaches about 150 members, the more informal, brotherly atmosphere of community life is re-established in Hutterite fashion. The oversize community splits, amoebalike, into two communities: one new and one old.

The rapid increase in colonies provides a classic illustration of ecological competition for territory and of population's role in intersocietal conflict. Hutterite aloofness is a source of prejudice; their economic efficiency is a source of envy; their refusal to bear arms can raise hostility to the boiling point. More direct and basic, the colonies, like corporate farms elsewhere, have reduced the population base that formerly provided support for the economies of local towns. The Hutterite ability to purchase wholesale from more distant centers further depresses the economy of these nearby towns. In some instances, Hutterite refusal to participate in local programs, such as rural electrification, has denied these services to other local farmers.

Against the resulting hostility, Hutterite protestations about contributing to the health of state and national economies, about paying school taxes from which they receive little benefit, about not drawing upon outside welfare funds to which they contribute, and about not contributing to problems of crime or mental illness are of little avail.

True, opposition so far has not blunted either their financial security in the general economy or their constitutional protections as citizens. Nonetheless, they have experienced outbreaks of vandalism against some of their colonies, especially in wartime, and there have been numerous proposals to restrict their land buying. A land law in Alberta requires that Hutterites purchase new colonies at least 40 miles away from any other and not exceeding 64,000 acres. To challenge such laws, Hutterites have been obliged to set up something hitherto alien to them—a national church. Although this secondary organization has had little effect on the daily operations of the colonies, it contains the seeds for wielding financial power and regulating communal life in a non-Hutterite way.

Given that this sect will number about 64,500 people in the year 2000, it is reasonable to expect that outside opposition will press harder for changes in Hutterite life. Moreover, given that Hutterites would number 55 million in another 168 years, it is clear that either their growth rate or their way of life, and probably both, must give way to change before that time. A fascinating experimental case study in the social consequences of demographic patterns appears to be rapidly unfolding before our eyes.

THE BELEAGUERED AMISH

Despite various similarities between the two sects, the story of the Amish is far more of a contrast with that of the Hutterites, especially in modern times.

The Amish arose as a branch from the Mennonites, an independent Anabaptist movement centering in the Netherlands. The Mennonites envisaged small, homogeneous, and self-sufficient communities living a scriptural way of life. Unlike Hutterites, they advocated no theocratic communism or any other economic mode of community life. In practice, like the majority of Swiss Brethren, they embraced the doctrine of Christian stewardship of private property and made the family the basic economic unit of their society.

However, the fanatical Mennonite preacher, Jakob Ammann, preached a harsher system of discipline. In 1693, angered by the refusal of a group of ministers to confer on this issue, he censured the lot of them and founded his own sect, the Amish. Thus was Amish life rigorously formalized and made more repressive.

Also for comparison: The migrations of the Amish—unlike those of Hutterites—have always occurred within the sphere of advancing Western culture rather than its backwash.

From communities widely scattered over Western Europe, the Amish emigrated to the United States over a long period of time, beginning with the first settlement, in Pennsylvania, in 1727. After the Napoleonic wars, large numbers of Amish fled Alsace and Bavaria, settling in Ontario, Illinois, and Ohio. Shortly, they were followed by others from central Germany, who settled in Ohio, Pennsylvania, and Maryland. By 1900, the Amish had either abandoned Europe or been reabsorbed by the Mennonites.

Through exceptional frugality, industry, and farming skill, the Amish prospered in their earlier years in America, compared with their neighbors. Today, the economic situation is reversed. The modern non-Amish farmer, utilizing farm machinery forbidden to the Old Order Amishman, is far more productive and also much less burdened by a large family. (Reference to the "Old Order Amish" reflects the fact that, over more recent times, the traditional order of Amish life has eroded and produced several schisms.)

By 1960, there were 258 loosely defined Amish "districts" in 19 states, with a total Amish population of about 43,000. Six years later, the population had grown to 49,370—an increase of just under 15 per cent, compared with 9 per cent for the United States as a whole. The Amish increase would be even greater were it not for their steady loss of members, who "emigrate" to the larger secular society.

In any case, the noticeably higher increase in the Amish population results almost exclusively from their higher fertility. Interestingly, the Amish apparently have a higher rate of twin births compared with the general population, suggesting the presence of a distinct genetic factor. Equally interesting is the lower fertility of the Amish compared with the Hutterites. Any superfecundity among the Hutterites might explain part of this difference. But, since the Amish have lower fertility than many other contemporary populations, a significant portion of the difference with the Hutterites must come from the spread of birth-control methods among the Amish.

Their higher fertility compared with that of the United States reflects a continuing influence of their fundamentalist views, but their lower fertility compared with Hutterites reflects the erosion of their large-family ideal. Although Amish couples marry somewhat younger than Hutterites, they produce fewer children per family. The median number of children in an Amish family is 6.7; it is 10.4 among the Hutterites. Yet, Amish doctrine, no less than that of the Hutterites, prohibits contraception and promotes the large-family ideal. Moreover, unlike Hutterites, they reject modern technology. This difference theoretically promotes the need for many farmhands, and these must come from the young. The Amish youth, like his Hutterite counterpart, enters the economic life of his community at about age fifteen.

In relations with the larger society, the Amish have probably been hurt less by population growth than the Hutterites. They have been less of a competitive threat to their neighbors, because their farming methods are less efficient and they do business in the local community rather than through their own communal organization, as Hutterites prefer to do. On the other hand, the simple mode of Amish life undoubtedly restricts the growth of local business, especially in farm equipment and through a wide range of consumer goods.

It is in relation to the internal life of their communities that population growth has undoubtedly been more distressing for the Amish than for the Hutterites. The family basis of Amish economy means that, as population increases, the community must spread geographically. This makes it increasingly difficult for each member to be equally well acquainted with all the others; consequently, those who see each other more often tend to form cliques. Moreover, the young people are forced to move away from the family home and seek new land when the family farm can no longer be subdivided. This development breaks down the positive controls with which kinship maintains conformity. In addition, high fertility increases the proportion of young dependents.

Actually, a population increase only creates pressure for change, and it is the type of community organization that determines the form of change. The small size of the Amish economy unit—the family—has severely restricted adaptability.

Unable to supply all its needs, either from its own resources or those of the Amish community, each family is compelled to operate directly in the larger market. Moreover, refusal to adopt fully modern farm technology restricts productivity and, therefore, family income. In turn, the income has to be spread among family members who include a higher proportion of nonproductive dependents.

Equally significant, the family system involves transmission of property through inheritance. With large numbers of children (an average of three or four sons), the size of an inheritance naturally decreases, providing a smaller income base for the next generation. The average size of an Amish farm has declined from several hundred acres in the eighteenth century to less than fifty acres today.

In turn, smaller home farms compel many unemployed young Amish to seek labor on other farms or in industry. Recent studies in Middlefield, Ohio, reveal that only 47 per cent of the Amish labor force was engaged in full-time agriculture. Employment outside the community exposes the Amish youth to worldly standards and friendships, and to more lucrative modes of livelihood. Even the young person who returns to farming brings an intense awareness of the advantages of modern methods.

It is the formation of cliques, combined with this exposure to outside influences, that generates considerable pressures for change, not only in farming methods but in all other areas of Amish life. This explains why, today, there are several different degrees of departure from standards of the Old Order Amish. In short, adaptation for the Amish has meant a progressive loss of members who have discarded many of the old ways, although many still call themselves Amish.

DOGMA IN A CHANGING WORLD

The story of the Hutterite and Amish offers a number of interesting things for contemporary man to think about. Two seem outstanding.

First, the impact of population on human affairs is dramatically demonstrated. Population movements do not enter human affairs only in the simplified Malthusian manner of too little food and too many people. Rather, the impact of population on human affairs is pre-eminently determined by social organization. For both the Hutterites and Amish, their very high levels of population increase have intensified competition with the larger society they prefer to avoid and have heightened intergroup conflict. Also for both, population increase has violated the primacy of informal, intimate social contact of each with all. This is most clearly seen among today's Amish; many of their people have spread geographically beyond the possibility of regular, daily interaction among all family members.

A similar process operated upon the Hutterites before their American adventure. Today, of course, Hutterites dull the effect of population growth by regularly dividing colonies when cliques arise and tensions become marked. But their conflict with the outside has sprouted the roots of a truly formalized secondary association: They have had to form a national church, with all its undesirable potential for regulation and control. This dynamic effect of population growth on social change seems everywhere unavoidable.

And this leads naturally to the second observation. Man does not live by ideology alone. Despite the rigid and unreflective character of their doctrines, these two groups have experienced fundamental changes in their social organization. It is this unreflective certainty in the rightness of their doctrines—and the blinders they place on the next generation—that blinds both sects to the dynamic causes of their tribulations and their successes. The Hutterites, for instance, do not attribute the successful revival of their life in America to the economic efficiency of corporate farming but to God's pleasure in their devotion. By the same token, they are unlikely to view their uncontrolled fertility as a principal factor in the probable unhappy course of future events. Perhaps they reflect a quite general human failing today: Our conventional ways of thinking no longer provide rational solutions for contemporary problems of human ecology, such as that of population pressure so well illustrated by the Hutterites and Amish.

The Political Dimension of Social Change

Toward a Theory of Revolution[*]
James C. Davies

In exhorting proletarians of all nations to unite in revolution, because they had nothing to lose but their chains, Marx and Engels most succinctly presented that theory of revolution that is recognized as their brain child. But

[*] From *American Sociological Review*, vol. 27, no. 1 (February, 1962). Reprinted by permission of The American Sociological Association.

this most famed thesis, that progressive degradation of the industrial working class would finally reach the point of despair and inevitable revolt, is not the only one that Marx fathered. In at least one essay, he gave life to a quite antithetical idea. He described, as a precondition of widespread unrest, not progressive degradation of the proletariat but rather an improvement in workers' economic condition that did not keep pace with the growing welfare of capitalists and, therefore, produced social tension.

> A noticeable increase in wages presupposes a rapid growth of productive capital. The rapid growth of productive capital brings about an equally rapid growth of wealth, luxury, social wants, social enjoyments. Thus, although the enjoyments of the workers have risen, the social satisfaction that they give has fallen in comparison with the increased enjoyments of the capitalist, which are inaccessible to the worker, in comparison with the state of development of society in general. Our desires and pleasures spring from society; we measure them, therefore, by society and not by the objects which serve for their satisfaction. Because they are of a social nature, they are of a relative nature.[1]

Marx's qualification here of his more frequent belief that degradation produces revolution is expressed as the main thesis by de Tocqueville in his study of the French Revolution. After a long review of economic and social decline in the seventeenth century and dynamic growth in the eighteenth, de Tocqueville concludes:

> So it would appear that the French found their condition the more unsupportable in proportion to its improvement. . . . Revolutions are not always brought about by a gradual decline from bad to worse. Nations that have endured patiently and almost unconsciously the most overwhelming oppression often burst into rebellion against the yoke the moment it begins to grow lighter. The regime which is destroyed by a revolution is almost always an improvement on its immediate predecessor. . . . Evils which are patiently endured when they seen inevitable become intolerable when once the idea of escape from them is suggested.[2]

On the basis of de Tocqueville and Marx, we can choose one of these ideas or the other, which makes it hard to decide just when revolutions are more likely to occur—when there has been social and economic progress, or when there has been regress. It appears that both ideas have explanatory

[1] The *Communist Manifesto* of 1848 evidently antedates the opposing idea by about a year. See Edmund Wilson, *To the Finland Station* (Garden City, N.Y.: Doubleday [Anchor Books ed.], n.d.), p. 157; Lewis S. Feuer, *Karl Marx and Friedrich Engels: Basic Writings on Politics and Philosophy*, (Garden City, N.Y.: Doubleday, 1959), p. 1. The above quotation is from Karl Marx and Frederick Engels, "Wage Labor and Capital," *Selected Works in Two Volumes* (Moscow: Foreign Languages Publishing House, 1955), vol. 1, p. 94.

[2] Alexis de Tocqueville, *The Old Regime and the French Revolution*, trans. by John Bonner (New York: Harper & Bros., 1856), p. 214. The Stuart Gilbert translation (Garden City, N.Y.: Doubleday, 1955), pp. 176–77, gives a somewhat less pungent version of the same comment. *L'Ancien régime* was first published in 1856.

and possibly predictive value, if they are juxtaposed and put in the proper time sequence.

Revolutions are most likely to occur when a prolonged period of objective economic and social development is followed by a short period of sharp reversal.[3] The all-important effect on the minds of people in a particular society is to produce, during the former period, an expectation of continued ability to satisfy needs—which continue to rise—and, during the latter, a mental state of anxiety and frustration when manifest reality breaks away from anticipated reality. The actual state of socio-economic development is less significant than the expectation that past progress, now blocked, can and must continue in the future.

Political stability and instability are ultimately dependent on a state of mind, a mood, in a society. Satisfied or apathetic people who are poor in goods, status, and power can remain politically quiet and their opposites can revolt, just as, correlatively and more probably, dissatisfied poor can revolt and satisfied rich oppose revolution. It is the dissatisfied state of mind, rather than the tangible provision of "adequate" or "inadequate" supplies of food, equality, or liberty, that produces the revolution. In actuality, there must be a joining of forces between dissatisfied, frustrated people who differ in their degree of objective, tangible welfare and status. Well-fed, well-educated, high-status individuals who rebel in the face of apathy among the objectively deprived can accomplish, at most, a coup d'état. The objectively deprived, when faced with solid opposition of people of wealth, status, and power, will be smashed in their rebellion as were peasants and Anabaptists by German noblemen in 1525 and East Germans by the Communist elite in 1953.

Before appraising this general notion in light of a series of revolutions, a word is in order as to why revolutions ordinarily do not occur when a society is generally impoverished—when, as de Tocqueville put it, evils that seem inevitable are patiently endured. They are endured in the extreme case because the physical and mental energies of people are totally employed in the process of merely staying alive. The Minnesota starvation studies conducted during World War II[4] indicate clearly the constant preoccupation of very hungry individuals with fantasies and thoughts of food. In extremis, as the Minnesota research poignantly demonstrates, the individual withdraws into a life of his own, withdraws from society, withdraws from any significant kind of activity unrelated to staying alive. Reports of behavior in Nazi concentration camps indicate the same preoccupation.[5] In less extreme and barbarous circumstances, where minimal survival

    [3] Revolutions are here defined as violent civil disturbances that cause the displacement of one ruling group by another that has a broader popular basis for support.

    [4] The full report is Ancel Keys et al., The Biology of Human Starvation (Minneapolis: University of Minnesota Press, 1950). See J. Brozek, "Semi-Starvation and Nutritional Rehabilitation," Journal of Clinical Nutrition, 1 (January, 1953), pp. 107–118, for a brief analysis.

    [5] E. A. Cohen, Human Behavior in the Concentration Camp (New York: W. W. Norton, 1953), pp. 123–25, 131–40.

is possible but little more, the preoccupation of individuals with staying alive is only mitigated. Social action takes place, for the most part, on a local, face-to-face basis. In such circumstances, the family is a—perhaps the major—solidary unit,[6] and even the local community exists primarily to the extent families need to act together to secure their separate survival. Such was life on the American frontier in the sixteenth through nineteenth centuries. In very much attenuated form, but with a substantial degree of social isolation persisting, such evidently is rural life even today. This is clearly related to a relatively low level of political participation in elections.[7] As Zawadzki and Lazarsfeld have indicated,[8] preoccupation with physical survival, even in industrial areas, is a force strongly militating against the establishment of the community-sense and consensus on joint political action that are necessary to induce a revolutionary state of mind. Far from making people into revolutionaries, enduring poverty makes for concern with one's solitary self or solitary family, at best, and resignation or mute despair, at worst. When it is a choice between losing their chains or their lives, people will mostly choose to keep their chains, a fact that Marx seems to have overlooked.[9]

It is when the chains have been loosened somewhat, so that they can be cast off without a high probability of losing life, that people are put in a condition of proto-rebelliousness. I use the term proto-rebelliousness because the mood of discontent may be dissipated before a violent outbreak occurs. The causes for such dissipation may be natural or social (including economic and political). A bad crop year that threatens a return to chronic hunger may be succeeded by a year of natural abundance. Recovery from sharp economic dislocation may take the steam from the boiler of rebellion.[10] The slow, grudging grant of reforms, which has been the political history of England since at least the Industrial Revolution, may effectively and continuously prevent the degree of frustration that produces revolt.

A revolutionary state of mind requires the continued, even habitual, but dynamic expectation of greater opportunity to satisfy basic needs, which may range from merely physical (food, clothing, shelter, health, and safety from bodily harm) to social (the affectional ties of family and friends) to

[6] For community life in such poverty, in Mezzogiorno Italy, see E. C. Banfield, *The Moral Basis of a Backward Society* (Glencoe, Ill.: The Free Press, 1958). The author emphasizes that the nuclear family is a solidary, consensual, moral unit (see p. 85), but, even within it, consensus appears to break down, in outbreaks of pure, individual amorality—notably between parents and children (see p. 117).

[7] See Angus Campbell *et al., The American Voter* (New York: John Wiley & Sons, 1960), chap. 15, "Agarian Political Behavior."

[8] B. Zawadzki and P. F. Lazarsfeld, "The Psychological Consequences of Unemployment," *Journal of Social Psychology,* 6 (May, 1935), pp. 224–51.

[9] A remarkable and awesome exception to this phenomenon occurred occasionally in some Nazi concentration camps—e.g., in a Buchenwald revolt against capricious rule by criminal prisoners. During this revolt, one hundred criminal prisoners were killed by political prisoners. See Cohen, *op. cit.,* p. 200.

[10] See W. W. Rostow, "Business Cycles, Harvests, and Politics: 1790–1850," *Journal of Economic History,* 1 (November, 1941), pp. 206–21, for the relation between economic fluctuation and the activities of the Chartists in the 1830's and 1840's.

the need for equal dignity and justice. But the necessary additional ingredient is a persistent, unrelenting threat to the satisfaction of these needs: not a threat that actually returns people to a state of sheer survival, but which puts them in the mental state where they believe they will not be able to satisfy one or more basic needs. Although physical deprivation in some degree may be threatened on the eve of all revolutions, it need not be the prime factor, as it surely was not in the American Revolution of 1775. The crucial factor is the vague or specific fear that ground gained over a long period of time will be quickly lost. This fear does not generate if there is continued opportunity to satisfy continually emerging needs; it generates when the existing government suppresses, or is blamed for suppressing, such opportunity.

Three rebellions or revolutions are given considerable attention in the sections that follow: Dorr's Rebellion of 1842, the Russian Revolution of 1917, and the Egyptian Revolution of 1952. Brief mention is then made of several other major civil disturbances, all of which appear to fit the J-curve pattern.[11] After considering these specific disturbances, some general theoretical and research problems are discussed.

No claim is made that all rebellions follow the pattern, but just that the ones here presented do. All of these are "progressive" revolutions in behalf of greater equality and liberty. The question is open whether the pattern occurs in such markedly retrogressive revolutions as Nazism in Germany or the 1861 Southern rebellion in the United States. It will surely be necessary to examine other progressive revolutions before one can judge how universal the J-curve is. And it will be necessary, in the interests of scientific validation, to examine cases of serious civil disturbance that fell short of producing profound revolution—such as the Sepoy Rebellion of 1857 in India, the Pullman Strike of 1894 in America, the Boxer Rebellion of 1900 in China, and the Great Depression of the 1920's and 1930's as it was experienced in Austria, France, Great Britain, and the United States. The explanation for such still-born rebellions—for revolutions that might have occurred—is inevitably more complicated than for those that come to term in the "normal" course of political gestation.

DORR'S REBELLION OF 1842

Dorr's Rebellion[12] in nineteenth-century America was perhaps the first of many civil disturbances to occur in America as a consequence, in part, of the Industrial Revolution. It followed by three years an outbreak in Eng-

[11] This curve is, of course, not to be confused with its prior and altogether different use by Floyd Allport in his study of social conformity. See F. H. Allport, "The J-Curve Hypothesis of Conforming Behavior," *Journal of Social Psychology,* 5 (May, 1934), pp. 141–83, reprinted in T. H. Newcomb and E. L. Hartley, *Readings in Social Psychology,* (New York: Henry Holt, 1947), pp. 55–67.

[12] I am indebted to Beryl L. Crowe for his extensive research on Dorr's Rebellion while he was a participant in my political-behavior seminar at the University of California, Berkeley, Spring, 1960.

land that had similar roots and a similar program—the Chartist agitation. A machine-operated textile industry was first established in Rhode Island in 1790 and grew rapidly as a consequence of domestic and international demand, notably during the Napoleonic wars. Jefferson's Embargo Act of 1807, the War of 1812, and a high tariff in 1816 further stimulated American industry.

Rapid industrial growth meant the movement of people from farms to cities. In Massachusetts, the practice developed of hiring mainly the wives and daughters of farmers, whose income was thereby supplemented but not displaced by wages. In Rhode Island, whole families moved to the cities and became committed to the factory system. When times were good, industrialized families earned two or three times what they got from the soil; when the mills were idle, there was not enough money for bread.[13] From 1807 to 1815, textiles enjoyed great prosperity; from 1834 to 1842, they suffered depression, most severely from 1835 to 1840. Prosperity raised expectations and depression frustrated them, particularly when accompanied by stubborn resistance to suffrage demands that first stirred in 1790 and recurred in a wave-like pattern in 1811 and then in 1818 and 1820, following suffrage extension in Connecticut and Massachusetts. The final crest was reached in 1841, when suffrage associations met and called for a constitutional convention.[14]

Against the will of the government, the suffragists held an election in which all adult males were eligible to vote, held a constitutional convention composed of delegates so elected, and, in December, 1841, submitted the People's Constitution to the same electorate, which approved it and the call for an election of state officers the following April, to form a new government under this unconstitutional constitution.[15]

These actions joined the conflict with the established government. When asked—by the dissidents—the state supreme court rendered its private judgment in March, 1842, that the new constitution was "of no binding force whatever," and [that, therefore,] any act "to carry it into effect by force will be treason against the state." The legislature passed what became known as the Algerian law, making it an offense punishable by a year in jail to vote in the April election and by life imprisonment to hold office under the People's Constitution.

[13] Joseph Brennan, *Social Conditions in Industrial Rhode Island: 1820–1860* (Washington, D.C.: Catholic University of America, 1940), p. 33.
[14] The persistent demand for suffrage may be understood in light of election data for 1828 and 1840. In the former year, only 3,600 votes were cast in Rhode Island, whose total population was about 94,000. (Of these votes, 23 per cent were cast for Jackson and 77 per cent for Adams, in contrast to a total national division of 56 per cent for Jackson and 44 per cent for Adams.) All votes cast in the 1828 election amount to 4 per cent of the total Rhode Island population and 11 per cent of the total U.S. population, excluding slaves. In 1840, with a total population of 109,000, only 8,300 votes—8 per cent—were cast in Rhode Island, in contrast to 17 per cent of the national population excluding slaves.
[15] A. M. Mowry, *The Dorr War* (Providence, R.I.: Preston & Rounds, 1901), p. 114.

The rebels went stoutly ahead with the election, and, on May 3, 1842, inaugurated the new government. The next day the People's legislature met and respectfully requested the sheriff to take possession of state buildings, which he failed to do. Violence broke out on the 17th of May in an attempt to take over a state arsenal with two British cannon left over from the Revolutionary War. When the cannon misfired, the People's Government resigned. Sporadic violence continued for another month, resulting in the arrest of over 500 men, mostly textile workers, mechanics, and laborers. The official legislature called for a new constitutional convention, chosen by universal manhood suffrage, and a new constitution went into effect in January, 1843. Altogether, only one person was killed in this little revolution, which experienced violence, failure, and then success within the space of nine months. . . .

THE RUSSIAN REVOLUTION OF 1917

In Russia's tangled history, it is hard to decide when began the final upsurge of expectations that, when frustrated, produced the cataclysmic events of 1917. One can truly say that the real beginning was the slow modernization process begun by Peter the Great over two hundred years before the revolution. And, surely, the rationalist currents from France that slowly penetrated Russian intellectual life during the reign of Catherine the Great a hundred years before the revolution were necessary, lineal antecedents of the 1917 revolution.

Without denying that there was an accumulation of forces over at least a two-hundred-year period,[16] we may nonetheless date the final upsurge as beginning with the 1861 emancipation of serfs and reaching a crest in the 1905 revolution.

The chronic and growing unrest of serfs before their emancipation in 1861 is an ironic commentary on the Marxian notion that human beings are what social institutions make them. Although serfdom had been shaping their personality since 1647, peasants became increasingly restive in the second quarter of the nineteenth century.[17] The continued discontent of peasants after emancipation is an equally ironic commentary on the belief that relieving one profound frustration produces enduring contentment. Peasants rather quickly got over their joy at being untied from the soil after two hundred years. Instead of declining, rural violence increased.[18] Having gained freedom but not much free land, peasants now had to rent or buy land to survive: Virtual personal slavery was exchanged for financial servi-

[16] There is an excellent summary in B. Brutzkus, "The Historical Peculiarities of the Social and Economic Development of Russia," in R. Bendix and S. M. Lipset, *Class, Status, and Power* (Glencoe, Ill.: The Free Press, 1953), pp. 517–40.

[17] Jacqueries rose from an average of 8 per year in 1826–30 to 34 per year in 1845–49. T. G. Masaryk, *The Spirit of Russia* (London: Allen and Unwin, 1919), vol. 1, p. 130. This long, careful, and rather neglected analysis was first published in German in 1913 under the title *Zur Russischen Geschichts— und Religionsphilosophie*.

[18] Jacqueries averaged 350 per year for the first three years after emancipation. *Ibid.*, pp. 140–41.

tude. Land pressure grew, reflected in a doubling of land prices between 1868 and 1897.

It is hard, thus, to tell whether the economic plight of peasants was much lessened after emancipation. A 1903 government study indicated that, even with a normal harvest, average food intake per peasant was 30 per cent below the minimum for health. The only sure contrary item of evidence is that the peasant population grew, indicating, at least, increased ability of the land to support life. . . .

The land-population pressure pushed people into towns and cities, where the rapid growth of industry truly afforded the chance for economic betterment. One estimate of net annual income for a peasant family of five in the rich blackearth area in the late nineteenth century was 82 rubles. In contrast, a "good" wage for a male factory worker was about 168 rubles per year. It was this difference in the degree of poverty that produced almost a doubling of the urban population between 1878 and 1897. The number of industrial workers increased almost as rapidly. The city and the factory gave new hope. Strikes in the 1880's were met with brutal suppression but also with the beginning of factory legislation, including the requirement that wages be paid regularly and the abolition of child labor. The burgeoning proletariat remained comparatively contented until the eve of the 1905 revolution.[19]

There is additional, noneconomic evidence to support the view that 1861–1905 was the period of rising expectations that preceded the 1917 revolution. The administration of justice before the emancipation had largely been carried out by noblemen and landowners, who embodied the law for their peasants. In 1864, justice was, in principle, no longer delegated to such private individuals. Trials became public, the jury system was introduced, and judges got tenure. Corporal punishment was alleviated by the elimination of running the gauntlet, lashing, and branding; caning persisted until 1904. Public joy at these reforms was widespread. For the intelligentsia, there was increased opportunity to think and write and to criticize established institutions, even sacrosanct absolutism itself.

But Tsarist autocracy had not quite abandoned the scene. Having inclined, but not bowed, in granting the inevitable emancipation as an act not of justice but grace, it sought to maintain its absolutist principle by conceding reform without accepting anything like democratic authority. Radical political and economic criticism surged higher. Some strong efforts to raise the somewhat lowered floodgates began as early as 1866, after an unsuccessful attempt was made on the life of Alexander II, in whose name serfs had just gained emancipation. When the attempt succeeded fifteen

[19] The proportion of workers who struck from 1895 through 1902 varied between 1.7 per cent and 4.0 per cent per year. In 1903 the proportion rose to 5.1 per cent but dropped a year later to 1.5 per cent. In 1905 the proportion rose to 163.8 per cent, indicating that the total working force struck, on the average, closer to twice than to once during that portentous year. In 1906 the proportion dropped to 65.8 per cent; in 1907 to 41.9 per cent; and by 1909 was down to a "normal" 3.5 per cent. *Ibid.*, p. 175n.

years later, there was increasing state action under Alexander III to limit constantly rising expectations. By suppression and concession, the last Alexander succeeded in dying naturally in 1894.

When it became apparent that Nicholas II shared his father's ideas but not his forcefulness, opposition of the intelligentsia to absolutism joined with the demands of peasants and workers, who remained loyal to the Tsar but demanded economic reforms. Starting in 1904, there developed a "League of Deliverance" that coordinated efforts of at least seventeen other revolutionary, proletarian, or nationalist groups within the empire. Consensus on the need for drastic reform, both political and economic, established a many-ringed circus of groups sharing the same tent. These groups were geographically distributed from Finland to Armenia and ideologically from liberal constitutionalists to revolutionaries made prudent by the contrast between their own small forces and the power of Tsardom.

Events of 1904–5 mark the general downward turning point of expectations, which people increasingly saw as frustrated by the continuation of Tsardom. Two major and related occurrences made 1905 the point of no return. The first took place on the Bloody Sunday of January 22, 1905, when peaceful proletarian petitioners marched on the St. Petersburg palace and were killed by the hundreds. The myth that the Tsar was the gracious protector of his subjects, however surrounded he might be by malicious advisers, was quite shattered. The reaction was immediate, bitter, and prolonged and was not at all confined to the working class. Employers, merchants, and white-collar officials joined in the burgeoning of strikes that brought the economy to a virtual standstill in October. Some employers even continued to pay wages to strikers. University students and faculties joined the revolution. After the great October strike, the peasants ominously sided with the workers and engaged in riots and assaults on landowners. Until peasants became involved, even some landowners had sided with the revolution.

The other major occurrence was the disastrous defeat of the Russian Army and Navy in the 1904–5 war with Japan. Fundamentally an imperialist venture aspiring to hegemony over the people of Asia, the war was not regarded as a people's but as a Tsar's war, to save and spread absolutism. The military defeat itself probably had less portent than the return of shattered soldiers from a fight that was not for them. Hundreds of thousands, wounded or not, returned from the war as a visible, vocal, and ugly reminder to the entire populace of the weakness and selfishness of Tsarist absolutism.

The years from 1905 to 1917 formed an almost relentless procession of increasing misery and despair. Promising, at last, a constitutional government, the Tsar, in October, 1905, issued from on high a proclamation renouncing absolutism, granting law-making power to a duma, and guaranteeing freedom of speech, assembly, and association. The first two dumas, of 1906 and 1907, were dissolved for recalcitrance. The third was made pliant by reduced representation of workers and peasants and by the prosecution and conviction of protestants in the first two. The brief period of a free press was succeeded in 1907 by a reinstatement of censorship and confiscation of prohibited publications. Trial of offenders against the Tsar was now conducted by courts-martial. Whereas there had been only 26 executions of the death sentence, in the thirteen years of Alexander II's firm rule (1881–94), there were 4,449 in the years 1905–10, in six years of Nicholas II's soft regimen.[20]

But this "white terror," which caused despair among the workers and intelligentsia in the cities, was not the only face of misery. For the peasants, there was a bad harvest in 1906, followed by continued crop failures in several areas in 1907. To forestall action by the dumas, [Premier] Stolypin decreed a series of agrarian reforms designed to break up the power of the rural communes by individualizing land ownership. Between these acts of God and government, peasants were so preoccupied with hunger or self-aggrandizement as to be dulled in their sensitivity to the revolutionary appeals of radical organizers.

After more than five years of degrading terror and misery, in 1910 the country appeared to have reached a condition of exhaustion. Political strikes had fallen off to a new low. As the economy recovered, the insouciance of hopelessness set in. Amongst the intelligentsia, the mood was hedonism or despair that often ended in suicide. Industrialists aligned themselves with the government. Workers worked. But an upturn of expectations, inadequately quashed by the police, was evidenced by a recrudescence of political strikes that, in the first half of 1914—on the eve of war—approached the peak of 1905. They sharply diminished during 1915 but grew again in 1916 and became a general strike in February, 1917.[21]

. . . The final . . . [event leading to revolution], after the first year of war, was a consequence of the dislocations of the German attack [World War I] on all kinds of concerted activities other than production for the prosecution of the war. Patriotism and governmental repression for a time smothered discontent. The inflation that developed in 1916 when goods, including food, became severely scarce began to make workers self-consciously discontented. The conduct of the war, including the growing brutality against reluctant, ill-provisioned troops, and the enormous loss of life, produced the same bitter frustration in the army.[22] When civilian discontent reached the breaking point in February, 1917, it did not take long for it to spread rapidly into the armed forces. Thus began the second phase of the revolution [which] started in 1905 and ended in death to the Tsar and Tsar-

[20] *Ibid.*, p. 189n.

[21] In his *History of the Russian Revolution,* Leon Trotsky presents data on political strikes from 1903 to 1917. In his *Spirit of Russia,* Masaryk presents comparable data from 1905 through 1912. The figures are not identical, but the reported yearly trends are consistent. Masaryk's figures are somewhat lower, except for 1912. Cf. Trotsky, *op. cit.,* (Doubleday Anchor Books ed., 1959), p. 32, and Masaryk, *op. cit., supra,* p. 197n.

[22] See Trotsky, *op. cit.,* pp. 18–21, for a vivid picture of rising discontent in the army.

dom—but not to absolutism—when the Bolsheviks gained ascendancy over the moderates in October. A centuries-long history of absolutism appears to have made this post-Tsarist phase of it tragically inevitable.

THE EGYPTIAN REVOLUTION OF 1952

The final slow upsurge of expectations in Egypt that culminated in the revolution began when the society became a nation in 1922, with the British grant of limited independence. British troops remained in Egypt not only to protect the Suez Canal but also, ostensibly, to prevent foreign aggression. The presence of foreign troops served only to heighten nationalist expectations, which were excited by the Wafd, the political organization that formed public opinion on national rather than religious grounds and helped establish a fairly unified community—in striking contrast to late-nineteenth century Russia.

But nationalist aspirations were not the only rising expectations in Egypt of the 1920's and 1930's. World War I had spurred industrialization, which opened opportunities for peasants to improve, somewhat, their way of life by working for wages in the cities and also opened great opportunities for entrepreneurs to get rich. The moderately wealthy got immoderately so in commodity market speculation, finance, and manufacture, and the uprooted peasants who were now employed, or at any rate living, in cities were relieved of at least the notion that poverty and boredom must be the will of Allah. But the incongruity of a money-based modern semifeudality that was like a chariot with a gasoline engine evidently escaped the attention of ordinary people. The generation of the 1930's could see more rapid progress, even for themselves, than their parents had even envisioned. If conditions remained poor, they could always be blamed on the British, whose economic and military power remained visible and strong.

Economic progress continued, though unevenly, during World War II. Conventional exports, mostly cotton, actually declined, not even reaching depression levels until 1945, but direct employment by Allied military forces reached a peak of over 200,000 during the most intense part of the African war. Exports after the war rose steadily until 1948, dipped, and then rose sharply to a peak in 1951 as a consequence of the Korean war. But, in 1945, over 250,000 wage earners[23]—probably over a third of the working force—became jobless. The cost of living by 1945 had risen to three times the index of 1937.[24] Manual laborers were hit by unemployment; white-collar workers and professionals, probably more by inflation

[23] C. Issawi, *Egypt at Mid-Century: An Economic Survey* (London: Oxford University Press, 1954), p. 262. J. and S. Lacouture in their *Egypt in Transition* (New York: Criterion Books, 1958), p. 100, give a figure of over 300,000. Sir R. Bullard, (ed.), *The Middle East: A Political and Economic Survey* (London: Oxford University Press, 1958), p. 221, estimates total employment in industry, transport, and commerce in 1957 to have been about 750,000.

[24] International Monetary Fund, *International Financial Statistics* (Washington, D.C.). See monthly issues of this report, 1950–53.

than unemployment. Meanwhile, the number of millionaires in pounds sterling had increased eight times during the war.[25]

Frustrations, exacerbated during the war by German and thereafter by Soviet propaganda, were at first deflected against the British[26] but gradually shifted closer to home. Egyptian agitators began quoting the Koran in favor of a just, equalitarian society and against great differences in individual wealth. There was an ominous series of strikes, mostly in the textile mills, from 1946 to 1948.

At least two factors stand out in the postponement of revolution. The first was the insatiable postwar world demand for cotton and textiles, and the second was the surge of solidarity with king and country that followed the 1948 invasion of the new state of Israel. Israel now supplemented England as an object of deflected frustration. The disastrous defeat a year later, by a new nation with but a fifteenth of Egypt's population, was the beginning of the end. This little war had struck the peasant at his hearth, when a shortage of wheat and of oil for stoves provided a daily reminder of a weak and corrupt government. The defeat frustrated popular hopes for national glory and—with even more portent—humiliated the army and solidified it against the bureaucracy and the palace, which had profiteered at the expense of national honor. In 1950 began, for the first time, a direct and open propaganda attack against the king himself. A series of peasant uprisings, even on the lands of the king, took place in 1951, along with some forty-nine strikes in the cities. The skyrocketing demand for cotton after the start of the Korean war in June, 1950, was followed by a collapse in March, 1952. The uncontrollable or uncontrolled riots in Cairo, on January 26, 1952, marked the fiery start of the revolution. The officers' coup in the early morning of July 23 only made it official.

* * *

SOME CONCLUSIONS

The notion that revolutions need both a period of rising expectations and a succeeding period in which they are frustrated qualifies substantially the main Marxian notion that revolutions occur after progressive degradation and the de Tocqueville notion that they occur when conditions are improving. By putting de Tocqueville before Marx, but without abandoning either theory, we are better able to plot the antecedents of at least the disturbances here described.

Half of the general, if not common, sense of this revised notion lies in the utter improbability of a revolution occurring in a society where there is the continued, unimpeded opportunity to satisfy new needs, new hopes, new expectations. Would Dorr's rebellion have become such if the established electorate and government had readily acceded to the suffrage de-

[25] J. and S. Lacouture, *op. cit.,* p. 99.

[26] England threatened to depose Farouk in February, 1942, by force if necessary, if Egypt did not support the Allies. Capitulation by the government and the Wafd caused widespread popular disaffection. When Egypt finally declared war on the Axis in 1945, the prime minister was assassinated. See J. and S. Lacouture, *op. cit.,* pp. 97–98, and Issawi, *op. cit.,* p. 268.

mands of the unpropertied? Would the Russian Revolution have taken place if the Tsarist autocracy had, quite out of character, truly granted the popular demands for constitutional democracy in 1905? Would the Cairo riots of January, 1952, and the subsequent coup actually have occurred if Britain had departed from Egypt, and if the Egyptian monarchy had established an equitable tax system and in other ways alleviated the poverty of urban masses and the shame of the military?

The other half of the sense of the notion has to do with the improbability of revolution taking place where there has been no hope, no period in which expectations have risen. Such a stability of expectations presupposes a static state of human aspirations that sometimes exists but is rare. Stability of expectations is not a stable social condition. Such was the case of American Indians (at least from our perspective) and perhaps Africans before white men with Bibles, guns, and other goods interrupted the stability of African society. Egypt was in such a condition, vis-à-vis modern aspiration, before Europe became interested in building a canal. Such stasis was the case in Nazi concentration camps, where conformism reached the point of inmates cooperating with guards even when the inmates were told to lie down so that they could be shot.[27] But, in the [last] case, there was a society with externally induced complete despair, and even in these camps there were occasional rebellions of sheer desperation. It is, of course, true that, in a society less regimented than concentration camps, the rise of expectations can be frustrated successfully, thereby defeating rebellion just as the satisfaction of expectations does. This, however, requires the uninhibited exercise of brute force as it was used in suppressing the Hungarian rebellion of 1956. Failing the continued ability and persistent will of a ruling power to use such force, there appears to be no sure way to avoid revolution short of an effective, affirmative, and continuous response on the part of established governments to the almost continuously emerging needs of the governed.

To be predictive, my notion requires the assessment of the state of mind —or, more precisely, the mood—of a people. This is always difficult, even by techniques of systematic public-opinion analysis. Respondents interviewed in a country with a repressive government are not likely to be responsive. But there has been considerable progress in gathering firsthand data about the state of mind of peoples in politically unstable circumstances. One instance of this involved interviewing in West Berlin, during and after the 1948 blockade, as reported by Buchanan and Cantril. They were able to ascertain, however crudely, the sense of security that people in Berlin felt. There was a significant increase in security after the blockade.[28]

Another instance comes out of the Middle Eastern study conducted by the Columbia University Bureau of Applied Social Research and reported

[27] Eugen Kogon, *The Theory and Practice of Hell* (New York: Farrar, Straus, 1950), pp. 284–86.

[28] W. Buchanan, "Mass Communication in Reverse," *International Social Science Bulletin*, 5 (1953), pp. 577–83, at p. 578. The full study is W. Buchanan and H. Cantril, *How Nations See Each Other* (Urbana: University of Illinois Press, 1953), esp. pp. 85–90.

by Lerner.[29] By directly asking respondents whether they were happy or unhappy with the way things had turned out in their life, the interviewers turned up data indicating marked differences in the frequency of a sense of unhappiness between countries and between "traditional," "transitional," and "modern" individuals in these countries.[30] There is no technical reason why such comparisons could not be made chronologically as well as they have been geographically.

Other than interview data are available with which we can, from past experience, make reasonable inferences about the mood of a people. It was surely the sense for the relevance of such data that led Thomas Masaryk, before World War I, to gather facts about peasant uprisings and industrial strikes and about the writings and actions of the intelligentsia in nineteenth-century Russia. In the present report, I have used not only such data—in the collection of which other social scientists have been less assiduous than Masaryk—but also such indexes as comparative size of vote as between Rhode Island and the United States, employment, exports, and cost of living. Some such indexes, like strikes and cost of living, may be rather closely related to the mood of a people; others, like value of exports, are much cruder indications. Lest we shy away from the gathering of crude data, we should bear in mind that Durkheim developed his remarkable insights into modern society, in large part, by his analysis of suicide rates. He was unable to rely on the interviewing technique. We need not always ask people whether they are grievously frustrated by their government; their actions can tell us as well and sometimes better.

In his *Anatomy of Revolution*, Crane Brinton describes "some tentative uniformities" that he discovered in the Puritan, American, French, and Russian revolutions.[31] The uniformities were: an economically advancing society, class antagonism, desertion of intellectuals, inefficient government, a ruling class that has lost self-confidence, financial failure of government, and the inept use of force against rebels. All but the last two of these are long-range phenomena that lend themselves to studies over extended time periods. The first two lend themselves to statistical analysis. If they serve the purpose, techniques of content analysis could be used to ascertain trends in alienation of intellectuals. Less rigorous methods would perhaps serve better to ascertain the effectiveness of government and the self-confidence of rulers. Because tensions and frustrations are present at all times in every society, what is most seriously needed [is] data that cover an extended time period in a particular society, so that one can say there is evidence that tension is greater or less than it was *n* years or months previously.

We need also to know how long is a long cycle of rising expectations and

[29] Daniel Lerner, *The Passing of Traditional Society* (Glencoe, Ill.: The Free Press, 1958).

[30] *Ibid.*, pp. 101–103. See also F. P. Kilpatrick and H. Cantril, "Self-Anchoring Scaling: A Measure of Individuals' Unique Reality Words," *Journal of Individual Psychology*, 16 (November, 1960), pp. 158–73.

[31] See the revised edition of 1952, as reprinted by Vintage Books (1957), pp. 264–75.

how long is a brief cycle of frustration. We noted a brief period of frustration in Russia after the 1881 assassination of Alexander II and a longer period after the 1904 beginning of the Russo-Japanese War. Why did not the revolution occur at either of these times rather than in 1917? Had expectations before these two times not risen high enough? Had the subsequent decline not been sufficiently sharp and deep? Measuring techniques have not yet been devised to answer these questions. But their unavailability now does not forecast their eternal inaccessibility. Physicists devised useful temperature scales long before they came as close to absolute zero as they have recently in laboratory conditions. The far more complex problems of scaling in social science inescapably are harder to solve.

We therefore are still not at the point of being able to predict revolution, but the closer we can get to data indicating by inference the prevailing mood in a society, the closer we will be to understanding the change from gratification to frustration in people's minds. That is the part of the anatomy, we are forever being told with truth and futility, in which wars and revolutions always start. We should eventually be able to escape the embarrassment that may have come to Lenin six weeks after he made the statement in Switzerland, in January, 1917, that he doubted whether "we, the old, [will] live to see the decisive battles of the coming revolution."[32]

Postindustrial Society: New Life-Styles

Communes in Cities [*]

Rosabeth Moss Kanter

In the early days of the contemporary commune movement, urban communes saw themselves as wayside inns on the route to the country.[†] City

[32] Quoted in E. H. Carr, *A History of Soviet Russia,* vol. 1, *The Bolshevik Revolution: 1917–23* (London: Macmillan, 1950), p. 69.
[*] Reprinted with permission from *Working Papers for a New Society,* vol. 2, no. 1 (Summer, 1974), © The Cambridge Policy Studies Institute.
Rosabeth Moss Kanter is author of *Commitment and Community* (Harvard University Press, 1972).
[†] I define communes as households of five or more unrelated adults, with or without children, sharing a common kitchen and household expenses and who define themselves in collective terms (as a "commune," "collective," or "extended family"). They are located in or near a metropolitan area, and members work in urban institutions.
I have been studying urban communes for over two years under a grant from the National Institute of Mental Health, MH 23030. Members of five households in Boston and New Haven were interviewed and observed over a period of seven months to two years. Members of another thirty groups were interviewed and/or surveyed. Names of individuals and communes are fictitious.

houses looked like country communes once you were past the front door: windows full of plants; batches of drying herbs; tattered oriental carpets; clutter of furniture; pets; smells of incense and marijuana; old barn boards and rough wood shelves in the kitchen holding mason jars of organic grains. And long-haired people mused about when they'd have their piece of land. But gradually the city commune lost its back-to-the-land nostalgia and attracted a different constituency: young professionals, single parents, and a few middle-class families.

Urban communes now have little in common with their rural or spiritual counterparts. Their purpose is not a return to the land and a retreat from technology. Nor do they plan to build a new community or to further particular spiritual ideals. Urban communes exist to create a collective household, a shared home, an augmented family. Like traditional families, the members of these "domestic" communes often share no specific values beyond intimacy, no activities beyond domestic chores and companionship, and no time together beyond evenings and weekends. Members commute to city jobs like other workers. While they may participate in the urban counterculture, their involvement with city life itself is conventional.

Urban communes have their roots in traditional family values as well as in America's long communal history. Outwardly they resemble nineteenth-century families-with-boarders and twentieth-century cooperative houses. Before 1969, those few urban groups that created communes solely for domestic purposes were virtually invisible. Today, the Boston area alone has over two hundred identifiable communal households. One prestigious, country-like suburb of two thousand families had at least twelve groups in 1973.

The crisis in the nuclear family is often blamed for the rapid rise of collective households. This in turn leads to speculation that future family forms will be radically different from traditional conjugal family structures. I doubt it. I think the outward form is less the issue than the change in underlying relationships among family members, whether communes or conventional nuclear families.

Long-term family trends have made urban communes possible, and at the same time have made traditional families more vulnerable to dissolution. But communes have not invented new family relationships. Rather, they bring into focus and speed up the process of change in family norms that has been taking place over many years. Assumptions of not so long ago no longer ring true for many, perhaps most, American families: "A woman's place is in the home." "Children should be seen but not heard." "That's women's work." Communes take these trends beyond what most American families would find comfortable today. But families based on intentionally created relationships of mutual support, rather than rigid roles determined by the biology of sex and age, may well be the norm in the future, whether the families are communal or nuclear. Urban communes may be the forerunners of "postbiological" families, where biology no longer determines status, role, who lives with whom, and how decisions are made within a family grouping.

Urban communes themselves are unlikely to be the family form of the future. They are too temporary, transient, and conflict-ridden. But they do signal shifts in family process, and they are laboratories for new kinds of family relationships.

The first urban communes were in hip-bohemian-student parts of the city. Now they can also be found in quiet suburban and exurban neighborhoods where large old houses provide comfortable settings for eight or ten increasingly affluent people. As often as not the size of a commune is determined by the number the house will hold. Each adult, coupled or not, generally has his or her own room, and small children often share a room. The amount and use of space in urban communes is important, for they are *places,* settings for family life, more than they are groups of specific people. Most communes take their names from their addresses, like "Cushing Street" or "Greenbrook Road." They refer to their living arrangements as a "house," as in "house meeting," or "friend of the house" (a friend of everyone), or "I'm taking my house out for dinner."

A few countercultural communes are centered around enterprises (a Cambridge commune runs a bookstore and craft shop) or shared religious tradition (Jewish communes in many cities, Mennonite communes in Kansas). For the most part, however, the house itself is the drawing card. Membership is surprisingly varied, but the young, the uncommitted, and the recently separated are most likely to have the opportunity or feel the need for urban communal living.

The Redbird Street commune was formed by a political group. The renovated multiple-family city building was financed by a married couple with inherited wealth, Sharon, twenty-six, and Carly, twenty-seven, parents of a three-year-old. The other adults are in their twenties and thirties, and include the divorced father of an eight-year-old boy. Two women in their late thirties, both with daughters, left Redbird last year because of lifestyle conflicts. For one it was too organized; for the other, too disorganized. Occupations of the present Redbirds run from teacher to part-time construction worker. Sharon and Carl have the strongest ideological commitment to communal living. They are thinking of starting a new community on a larger scale, and without them it is unlikely that Redbird Street will survive. Not surprisingly, single people often join communes to meet practical needs couples don't share. Like Sharon and Carl, couples more often join for ideological reasons.

The Brills' commune represents another configuration altogether, the augmented family. Jean and Harry Brill, both thirty-seven and parents of three daughters, fourteen, ten, and six, began to add other people to their rambling fourteen-room urban house in 1969. Several couples and individuals have since come and gone. Present members include a fifty-year-old divorcee, now back in school; two men, a law student and a priest, twenty-six and thirty-six, and a twenty-three-year-old woman artist. The Brills, including the children, enjoy sharing their lives and household chores with other people, and they miss those who leave.

Much rarer is a family cluster such as Blue Stream Farm. It was started in 1970 by five families from a Unitarian church group on fifteen acres in a wealthy shoreline suburb. Ten children, ages four to seventeen, and nine adults, twenty-nine to fifty-six, now live there. Blue Stream resembles a traditional utopian community more than an urban rooming house (one of the outbuildings around the big white farmhouse is even called Utopia), for members have strong beliefs in a committed community. They are very sad when members leave. One night recently they brainstormed eighty-two ideas for their future, and they changed the name from Blue Stream Farm to Blue Stream Community, hoping to attract more prospective members. The commune also responds to midlife-change rumblings. Two couples have switched partners and one of the new couples plans to remain at Blue Stream.

COMMUNAL STYLES

Though people seek communal settings for a variety of individual reasons, the communes themselves have in common certain styles of living that anticipate a change in what we mean by "family." Family life is more public, and the boundaries between nuclear families are blurred. The closest human relationships, especially man-woman and parent-child, are less private. Outsiders within a household who are privy to the most intimate details of family life are not new, of course. In the late nineteenth century, taking in boarders was common, and upper-class families have had live-in servants throughout the ages. But the particular mixture of strangers who themselves try to *create* a family in the city and witness each other's private lives not as outsiders with limited privileges, but as full-fledged members with equal rights, is new. It belongs to the same contemporary era that can broadcast "An American Family" coast-to-coast and turn encounter groups into weekend recreation.

The "publicness" of family is reflected in the way communes use space. For example, the bedroom, a private single-functioned preserve in the ideal, typical, one-family household, becomes a multi-purposed room for sleeping, working, and individual entertaining, since each member has only one private room. Because all members are free to invite guests, if not to the common rooms then always to their own, no individual or "head of household" or nuclear family can control the flow of people in and out of the house. There are frequent grumblings about other people's guests, especially strangers who appear at breakfast. In Greenbrook Road one woman complains that if she makes bacon for herself in the morning and leaves the room, someone else's visitor is apt to eat it. Visitors respond to the public character of the house by treating it less like a home than like a museum (the "house tour" is nearly universal) or a hotel (wandering around the bedrooms looking for a bathroom or opening the refrigerator in search of a snack).

Another theme shared by urban communes is the notion that family feeling can be intentionally created. A basic premise is that a group of strangers or casual friends, recruited from referral services, newspaper ads, or mutual acquaintances, can develop not only the external supports families provide their members but also the special, close, loving feelings. A new technology of instant intimacy developed in the sixties, along with an examination of the pathologies of that "ideal" human group, the family. At the same time, an increasing separation of two classical meanings of "family" developed. One is a set of specific biologically bonded, age- and sex-differentiated relationships, irreplaceable and obligatory. The other use of "family" is a metaphor for a quality in relationships—supportive, sentimental, warm, loyal, self-disclosing—regardless of the kinds of ties and the kinds of people who share the feelings. Homosexual marriages, single-parent families, artificial "kin" networks, childless couples: all compete for inclusion in the definition of family through a stress on quality of relationship rather than structure or biological base.

Urban communes deliberately try to develop family feeling within their households. Whatever their other shortcomings, most communes succeed admirably in making dinner a warm, fulfilling event, nourishing in emotional and spiritual as well as physical sense. Many groups begin dinner holding hands in a ritual moment of silence. Members take turns cooking, and ordinarily no one has to cook more than once a week. As a result, much energy goes into preparing dinner, and meals are often feast-like. People linger around the table long after dinner exchanging stories, laughing, sometimes discussing household business.

In most urban communes members take care of each other in ways common to any family group. To be sick in a commune means there is company around and someone to make chicken soup, which someone inevitably does. Occasionally a member asks for a meeting to discuss a personal problem. Advice, help with tire-changing or painting a room, and transportation are always nearby. Though members of urban communes typically do not pool incomes, they tend to help out-of-work members. Greenbrook Road has its own "medical insurance" that pays members' medical bills. Communes also talk about providing emotional support, but the success of this depends on the particular house. Communal living itself sparks emotional and interpersonal conflicts.

Holidays and celebrations—classic "family occasions"—punctuate the life of the more "together" urban communes. Usually such holidays are for the "family" alone; outside friends are not invited. Greenbrook Road, currently in its sixth year, has four yearly holidays, including an ecumenical Easter-Seder every spring and the celebration of Epiphany, a combined Chanukah and Christmas, every January. By now a rich body of tradition has accumulated: a mimeographed Seder, special foods, a traditional rhythm to the day of Epiphany. Former Greenbrookers often return to be with the "family."

Along with traditions and rituals, urban communes also develop stories, legends, myths, family portraits, family albums, and collective symbols. Greenbrookers' photographs line a kitchen wall. On another wall is a large mandala, a circular painting in twelve parts, each section drawn by one of the members. Another group took a collective name from a television program they watched together early in their existence and became known as the "Swan family." During an evening of joking around the dinner table, one house invented a character, Steve Thoreau, named after their street and a dinner guest. From then on he was the symbolic "head of the family." Postcards from traveling members and internal messages are sent to and from Steve Thoreau. Magazines come in his name, and Christmas gifts are given to and by him.

Negotiation rather than authority is the basis of relationships in urban communes. Role distinctions are blurred, as they often are in communal settlements historically and cross-culturally. Communes try to equalize the status of men and women and the status of adults and children. Decisions are usually made by the whole group at weekly or bi-weekly house meetings, which last until a consensus is reached. One group I visited stayed up all night to agree on admitting a new member. Formal authority is not recognized in most urban communes. Even when some people have more influence than others, that influence has to be negotiated, and it may not even be overtly acknowledged by others. Couples sometimes play a parent-like role toward other members, particularly if they have a special stake in the house, but "parent" is a pejorative word when used by one commune member to another. One group puts its cat as "head of household" on census forms rather than single out a member. Another commune, a stable group with several members in their forties, tries to acknowledge each member's influence in special areas and to give each equal credit. I observed several house meetings where Laura played an especially strong role. She checked consensus, restated issues, and generally policed the interaction. Her opinion obviously carried much weight, but when I asked the group who their leaders were, they said that Laura is good at meetings; Jim makes decisions about the kitchen, and so forth. They named every member, including, "John leads us in drinking and having a good time."

Changes in family norms are most clearly reflected in the equal work sharing of communal households. Everyone, sometimes even young children, cooks and does the dishes once a week. Shopping responsibilities are rotated. And everyone has a piece of the house to clean, sometimes a long-term speciality, sometimes a weekly rotation. Work assignments are usually posted prominently near the refrigerator, a common communication center in urban communes.* Greenbrook Road has "area committees," like its kitchen committee of two men and a woman. Nightly kitchen cleanup rotates among everyone, but the kitchen committee takes larger responsibility

---

* An intentional division of labor promotes egalitarianism. When tasks are left to be done spontaneously, they may reflect traditional sex-role socialization. I found in one study no differences in the participation of women and men in household work divided intentionally. But where one person more often than others "fell into" a particular one-time-only job, sex differences emerged. Handling money was more often male. Cleaning the bathroom was more often female.

for cupboards, the inside of the refrigerator, and the stove. Denny, self-named "Ecology Man," looks after garbage, trash, an recycling. Other houses mount collective cleanups reminiscent of the work "bees" in nineteenth-century communes. On Saturday mornings the vacuum cleaner hums in the background as men and women interchangeably push brooms and wax floors. Blue Stream Farm combines work with outreach. Every weekend they invite friends and visitors for a workday of repairs and projects, like the barn they are currently building.

Despite attempts to devise egalitarian work systems, however, house cleaning is the one aspect of domestic routine communes struggle with least successfully. There are more fights about cleaning than about any other single issue in urban communes. Family therapists tell me that cleaning fights also occur with increasing frequency in "liberated" couples. Because relationships in communal households are negotiated rather than authoritative, and because little besides the basic space-in-the-house is shared, the cleaning issue is the principal arena for power struggles—how to make order, whose standards prevail. Proponents of "clean" and "neat" are also proponents of order and collective responsibility. Those who are messy tend to resist order and deny the legitimacy of collective demands. This is a political issue and not entirely one of differing standards of cleanliness. One woman whose own room is spotless, for example, is among the messiest users of common space.

In the Colorado Avenue house issues of dominance and commitment were played out in seven months' worth of fights over cleaning. Jim was the central figure. At meetings he would declare, "I want this house clean!" Others interpreted this as, "I am committed to this house, and I want it my way." His "commitment" won over two others. His "power move" alienated him from the other three, and the house was spit, three-three. Jim finally presented the issue as one of caring. "Do you care about the house? Do you care about me? If you cared about me, you'd keep the house clean." This plea won over the dominant member of the opposition, a man who prides himself on his concern for others. Now the house is much cleaner, though not to Jim's complete satisfaction. This outcome is rare, however, and occurs primarily in highly committed groups. More typically anarchy drives out order.

Similar themes emerge in house after house. Many commune people respond to the state of the physical house as a symbol for the state of the group, the state of relationships. Sherry of Greenbrook Road reported:

> When I get fed up with people, sometimes I get very down. When we first got back from Christmas, the kitchen stayed in a perpetual mess, and I got so I just didn't want to go there, so I didn't. I'd eat my breakfast in my room and just go up there for dinner, and by then it'd be cleaned up. When it started to get cleaned up, I felt better and better about people, and then I started to feel good about the house again.

People also respond to the cleaning issue in terms of equity, a difficult problem for a supposedly participatory group. The "clean" people resent the fact that they must do more to make a comfortable environment for themselves than the "messy" folks. Said Don:

> I assumed that in any communal situation I am going to have to do a hundred-and-ten or a hundred-and-twenty percent of my share in order to make it work. When it gets to be three and four hundred percent, I start to feel bitter. Also when I feel like someone else is doing only fifty percent.

KIDS AS PEOPLE

Living in an urban commune is a mixed blessing for kids, but the egalitarian ethos seems to be a good thing for them. Children of school age and even younger are treated as separate people able to make their own decisions, obey the norms of the group, speak for themselves, contribute to the work of the household, confront, and be confronted. Parents in communal households tend to set few directions for kids other than self-discovery and learning to trust. More than one parent stressed in interviews that adults should be honest and open with children but that the children are entitled to form their own relationships. Says a mother of two small girls, "I want people to really care about the kids, to be straight with them. I don't care *how* they deal with them—that's their relationship, and I don't get involved." Another mother of a six-year-old boy sees her child's separate relationships as a problem for her, but feels she cannot interfere. "I lack control over other people and how they relate to him. Living here means he can learn anything from anybody, and I can't tell them how to relate.

The parent's role as intermediary for the child declines. People are encouraged to go directly to the child if they have an issue with him or her. "He's a human being and doesn't need me to intercede." Further, commune parents try to influence their children, but rarely coerce them to do something for their own good. "Benjamin's a fussy eater," one mother reports about her nine-year-old son, "but I finally stopped shoving food down him. It's his body, I decided. I've told him what's healthy, and now he's got to make the decision."

Formal demands on children and adults tend to be equal. Children have their chores to do from an early age and may be included in the regular job rotation. In the Brill family commune everyone, age six to fifty, cooks once a week, though each child has an adult assistant. On a recent visit, six-year-old Barbara was making cheeseburgers for dinner. At suburban Hilltop House, chores are divided by spinning a job wheel with Benjamin's as well as everyone else's name around the periphery. His favorite room to clean is the living room, and he sometimes volunteers three times a week to do the dishes (to his mother's dismay, since she is his back-up person). No less but also no more is demanded of Benjamin than other house members. According to his mother,

He's not going to do the living room as well as I could do it, but I think it's important to give equal responsibility. Unfortunately, all the adult members don't do their jobs, so it's hard for me to say, "Benjamin, this house is clean except for your room." I can't come down hard on him when he looks around and sees others haven't finished their jobs.

Children have a public role in urban communes, and they also have a public voice, or at least learn how to make their voices heard. They are encouraged to attend house meetings, and they learn to bring up their issues directly with other members of the household. Seven-year-old Mary came to a house meeting in her nine-person suburban commune to complain that adults were eating the ice cream and cones, supposedly "kids' food." She confronted people individually and responded to one person's remark that he never eats ice cream by insisting, "But that's not the issue. There is never enough. . . ." And later, "Don't be defensive with me!" She won her point. Benjamin routinely brings up house issues at meetings, like when the living room needs new light bulbs. Roger, six, knows he can go to house meetings when he wants to but usually doesn't. "It's boring," he says. "They just talk and make rules."

Experienced commune kids develop a noticeable ease in relating to people, especially adults. I first met five-year-old Janet when I arrived with a friend for dinner at the commune. No one was on the first floor except two adults and Janet. At first she looked coy, didn't come too close, and swung her body with her hands behind her back. Then she took my friend by the hand out of the room, saying, "I want to show you something." When they returned she repeated the same routine with me, led me from the dining room, where drinks were being prepared, to the pantry, and pointed out the glasses in the cabinet. Then she took me to her favorite couch and told me to sit in it. "Isn't it comfortable?" I agreed, we rejoined the others, and she brushed my hair until dinner was ready.

Other children seem equally at ease in their relationships with adults. Roger's teachers tell his mother, Linda, that he is a strong but benevolent leader in school. Roger, like most of the children in my research, attends public school. Linda herself notices that the commune has "given him many skills in dealing with people, getting in touch with what his needs are, and asking for things. He's easily accepted into a new group and very accepting of other people." Benjamin, according to other adults in his commune, was "just a closed-up little boy when he came. Now he's more open, more trusting, talks more, and can be drawn out more easily."

Kids in city communes live in adult-dominated worlds. Roger is six and lives with Linda (divorced), eleven other adults, and a newborn baby. The large, cleverly renovated two-family house was formed in 1970 and is in a dense urban area. Since he was two-and-a-half, Roger has been the only child. Sometimes grown-ups do special things for him, such as the candle-light breakfast with boiled eggs two of the women made to celebrate his first day of school. When Linda makes a special request, other people do take him out or put him to bed, but she is reluctant to ask. She feels that others don't really want to do things for Roger, and she complains that the men especially ignore him. Other single mothers also join communes to find father surrogates, apparently a rare commodity thus far. Roger, for his part, feels very close to Linda and feels especially happy "that my Momma makes me breakfast every morning, and when it's her turn to cook, she makes me dinner, and Saturdays we might go out or she might make me dinner here."

The parent-child bond is close and strong in urban communes. The parent is the chief "honcho," as one mother put it, for the care of his or her child. But Roger also feels sad that there are no other children his age living in the house, and that none of the other adults offers companionship. He says that his best friends are the television and the boy across the street. Benjamin, who is nine, feels lonely sometimes in his house of five adults and two teenage girls. A football addict, he wanders around the house in his helmet, roughhouses with the teenagers, but finds no one who'll throw the ball around with him. The other mother in the house did take him to a football game once, but the men always seem too busy for Benjamin.

From a child's viewpoint, living alone or virtually alone with many grown-ups means that many more authorities tell him or her what to do. For Roger, communal living is having "lots of bosses." Benjamin sees it as "two mothers, four fathers, and two sisters." Adults make rules, and any adult can call a kid on violations. Some adults, a distinct minority, have little to do with the children in their households except to tell them to be quiet or stop interrupting. Benjamin says that when he breaks a rule, the adults respond by making a bigger one. Commune members seem to release around children otherwise suppressed authoritative, demanding behavior, even if children are supposedly equal. Roger's fantasies of what he would change in the house are revealing:

> I'd want the inside of the whole house to look like a castle, with a throne for me and my mother, because she's the only one that has a grown-up kid, and I'd sit in one and she'd sit in the other, and we'd have servants.

The situation is different when there are more children, older children, or the adults are genuinely interested in children. Some people join communes especially to be with children, like the middle-aged woman new to the city who immediately became a grandmother surrogate to the young children in the Brill family, or the divorced medical student who says, "I don't want to be a father; I want to be an uncle." It is not surprising that people who are or have been parents themselves are generally more responsive to children than younger unattached residents who may not know how to react to a child. When asked who they would go to with a problem, children often name adults with parenting experience.

Kate lives with her five- and seven-year-old daughters in a suburban house where child care works particularly well even though the girls are the only children currently in the house. The other adults include three people in their forties who have had children. The seven-year-old expresses her warm feelings toward the house in essays she writes in school: "A commune is not just one family. It is many families. . . . Dear House, I love you. . . ." Janet and Mary are fortunate in the love and attention they get from adults. After school, they read, paint pictures, listen to music, or help out in the kitchen, with Kate if she is there but with other people if she's not. Some evenings they put on plays after dinner and recruit grown-ups to be the characters, using children's records for the sound and setting up chairs to transform the living room into an auditorium. Kate is especially pleased with how the men in the house treat Janet and Mary.

I get the impression that the men are really concerned about their relationships with the kids. One man feels closer to them than to his own kids. That must be hard. He told me that the other day, as though to say, "Isn't that something?"

Kate feels that communal living makes her a better parent.

The house took the pressure off. When I was the only mommy I lost my temper a lot more. There was no relief. Living alone with them I was terrified that I'd get sick. There was absolutely no one else. Here if I have some problem, there is always someone to take care of them. So relating to the children is a lot freer. I do it because I want to, not because I have to.

For adolescents communal living poses a set of problems having nothing to do with the commune itself, but rather with outside attitudes toward it. Several teenagers have reported nearly the same experience.

My friends thought it was a hippie commune. Everyone thought we were always having an orgy or smoking pot. It took me a while to convince them that it's just a place, and there are just more people there. After a while my friends came over and saw that the place wasn't weird. They weren't put off, once they saw it.

An eleven-year-old was teased by kids in school who assumed that "since we're in a commune, we share our bodies." Pressure from conformity-conscious peers is especially disturbing to some adolescents. One sixteen-year-old girl, living with her parents and sister in an augmented family-style commune in a wealthy suburb, denies to her friends that the house is a commune.

I tell them that we take in boarders for the money. When they ask me how we can afford such a big house in that case, I say that it is mortgaged to the hilt.

This particular teenager is as much bothered by her parents' lack of image consciousness as she is by the presence of other people in her home. Like the many adolescents who wish their parents "looked better" for their friends, she wants a *House Beautiful* furnished home instead of pillows on the floor for seating.

The status and participation of children in urban communes is probably as egalitarian as anywhere in America today, and in most cases the opportunity to relate to many adults seems good for the children. Otherwise, communal households are no different from other permissive families, and children are surrounded by universal middle-class cultural items: footballs, "Sesame Street," gerbils, trips to the dentist, ballet lessons, Brownies, sleeping over at friends' houses, posters of rock stars. Organic food isn't even particularly common.

HIGHS AND LOWS

How well do communes work? As the man in the old story answered about his wife, "Compared to what?" To the best or the worst in our family history? Communes are usually evaluated against an idealized picture of the stable, loving, child-centered family of "and they lived happily ever after" lore.* Questions are raised about the problems inherent in communal living as though nuclear families never faced such issues. Rarely are these questions addressed as more universal problems of the society. An example is the issue of how high turnover in communes affects children. Kate, divorced mother of Janet and Mary and refugee from a difficult suburban marriage, talks about the great loss her daughters suffered in their pre-commune days, when the family with four young kids next door moved away and there was no one else at home to substitute or to help cushion the blow. Now, in their "big family" of the commune, they feel sad when someone leaves but handle the loss with much less storm and stress.

Many people who ask how well communes work seek confirmation of their belief that group living is impossible, unworkable, destroys freedom and privacy, and retards children. There's a not-so-remarkable defensiveness around any proposal to tamper with the family. And commune folks have their own stake in rejecting typical criteria of success like longevity and stability. "We're here as long as we continue to grow together" is a common response to questions about commitment and future plans. "Success is a matter of how much we learn, not how long we last" is another response.

Nonetheless, turnover is an issue for collective households, and is an extreme version of the increasing fragility of families in the rest of society. Of sixty-three Boston-area groups contacted in the summer of 1972, only seven were more than a year old. Thirteen were continuing intact, six breaking up completely, and in thirty-eight houses, two or more people were leaving. (And these statistics are conservative, overrepresenting continuing

* By narrowly defining opportunities for family along biological lines, people momentarily or permanently without marital or blood ties are excluded from access to close human support. Beyond that, groups who do not fit the official definition of "family" face discrimination, from zoning laws to insurance.

groups where someone is likely to be available for an interview.) Relationships are often tentative and easily broken, which is reinforced by members' varied backgrounds and lack of shared work. In only a few groups do members seem solidly and deeply committed to one another as immediate family instead of distant relatives.

Indeed, the consensual, negotiated relationships characterizing these households almost preclude longevity. No one can assert too much influence or wield power without the risk of alienating the others. Few routines remain established for very long. Old issues recur and are debated again. New people represent subtle shifts in culture and organization, but old members are reluctant to claim the rights of seniority. All these things generate a feeling of living in an always changing, complex, emotionally charged atmosphere, where order is only temporarily accomplished and not to be regularly expected. One response is to move out of the house or to withdraw emotionally. The commune thus becomes institutionalized as a transient household where people continually move in and out, with the life cycle of an affair rather than a marriage. Cooperative houses of earlier periods also fit this pattern. Another response to fragility is the establishment of one family at the commune's core. The commune becomes their house, then, with others present at the family's sufferance, like the Brills' commune and those nineteenth-century families that took in lodgers. A less likely response for urban communes is to move toward an organizational rather than familial model, with rules, norms, and commitment mechanisms that make it difficult for people to leave. But the organizational response works only where there is a transcendent ideology to justify the social control and a strong, committed organizational core. Instead, in most of the urban communes I know, the most frequent response to easily breakable relationships is to break them.

Fragility is greater at some times than others, a function of group moods and rhythms that ebb and flow with the seasons (at least in the North). In January and February, for example, nearly everyone nourishes private thoughts of moving out. For two years running, several Greenbrook Road people told me confidentially that they would probably leave the house. None has. The cycles of group highs and lows are cultural: a greater scattering and transiency in the summer; a September sense of freshness; a partying and gift-giving atmosphere Thanksgiving through New Year's; the January-February-March slump accompanied by locked-in feelings of unrest. It is not hard to detect a group low, for its signs are nearly universal: the house is messier than usual; dishes are piled in the sink; communication is by notes left in public places rather than face-to-face; and attendance at dinner drops. Highs are marked by parties and spontaneous gatherings, by little extras such as a special dessert, games and surprises, and by people lingering at the table long after dinner is gone.

Some few people may live communally all of their lives, with or without mates and children. Even though urban communes as a social movement differentiated from rural cousins are only five years old, there are a number of people, both couples and singles, who have lived in one household throughout this period and intend to continue into the indefinite future. A somewhat larger group of urban migrants engages in the communal variant of serial monogamy: permanently committed to communal living but moving from group to group. One woman who has lived communally up and down the East Coast told me, "Of course communes work. I'm in my fifth." A surprising number of current commune residents express commitment to the communal way of life even if they are unhappy in their present group. Just as people with bad marriages blame it on their choice of mate and not on the institution, urban commune members insist that the idea is a good one even if their present group contains all the wrong people. In a Boston and New Haven study, which asked members about future plans, even those who were in the process of moving out said that they intended to live with another group some day.

A much larger number of people form communal households in response to a particular life-cycle issue. Young people who are out of school, new to a city, not attracted to marriage or perhaps divorced, find in communal living a way to create a family, live in a nice house, and lead a full, rich, family-like life. The recently separated and the single parent find communes a way to ease the pain of transition, to share the burdens, to develop a new life. People in midlife, perhaps part of a couple, perhaps divorced, with grown or nearly grown children, find in communal living an opportunity to open their horizons, to start a new set of adventures, to focus on self-development instead of the narrower responsibilities of running a nuclear family.

It is unlikely, however, that urban communes will be a dominant household form for more than a relatively few people and for more than a short period of people's lives. Yet descriptions of family structure seldom tell the whole story. The recent discoveries by demographic historians that the typical Western family has been nuclear for several centuries and has never been much larger than five or six people does not mean that the character of family life has stayed the same during that period. Similarly, the impact of communes is not in their form, their numbers, or the degree to which they become widespread. Rather, it is in how their existence reflects changing norms and expectations about the way all families, nuclear and otherwise, conduct their shared life. Urban communes reflect a general trend away from assumed biological imperatives of "family": the importance of blood ties, age and sex differentiation, authoritative relationships. If current trends persist, families of the most conventional nuclear variety will become more public. They will continue to minimize sex and age distinctions in favor of negotiated, egalitarian, intentional relationships. The experience and experiments of urban communes may be guideposts on the road that lies ahead.

10. SUGGESTIONS FOR FURTHER READING

APPLEBAUM, RICHARD. *Theories of Social Change* (Chicago: Markham, 1970).

BELL, DANIEL. *The Coming of Post-Industrial Society* (New York: Basic Books, 1973).

BOULDING, KENNETH. *A Primer on Social Dynamics* (New York: The Free Press, 1970).*

DALTON, GEORGE (ed.). *Economic Development and Social Change* (Garden City, N.Y.: Natural History Press, 1971).*

EHRLICH, PAUL. *The Population Bomb,* new rev. ed. (New York: Ballantine Books, 1971).*

EISENSTADT, S. N. (ed.). *Comparative Perspectives on Social Change* (Boston: Little, Brown, 1968).*

——— (ed.). *Readings in Social Evolution and Development* (London: Pergamon Press, 1970).*

ETZIONI, A., and E. ETZIONI (eds.). *Social Change* (New York: Basic Books, 1964).

FOSTER, GEORGE. *Tzintzuntzan: Mexican Peasants in a Changing World* (Boston: Little, Brown, 1967).*

HAGEN, EVERETT. *On the Theory of Social Change* (Homewood, Ill.: Dorsey Press, 1962).

HEILBRONER, ROBERT. *The Great Ascent: The Struggle for Economic Development in Our Time* (New York: Harper & Row, 1963).*

KANTER, ROSABETH MOSS. *Commitment and Community: Communes and Utopias in Sociological Perspective* (Cambridge, Mass.: Harvard University Press, 1972).*

KERR, CLARK, *et al. Industrialism and Industrial Man* (New York: Oxford University Press, 1964).*

LERNER, DANIEL. *The Passing of Traditional Society* (New York: The Free Press, 1958).*

LOPREATO, JOSEPH. *Peasants No More* (San Francisco: Chandler, 1967).

MACK, RAYMOND. *Transforming America* (New York: Random House, 1967).*

MEADOWS, DONELLA, *et al. The Limits to Growth* (New York: Universe Books, 1972).*

MILLIKAN, M., and D. BLACKMER (eds.). *The Emerging Nations* (Boston: Little, Brown, 1961).*

MOORE, BARRINGTON, Jr. *Political Power and Social Theory* (Cambridge, Mass.: Harvard University Press, 1958).*

MOORE, WILBERT. *Social Change* (Englewood Cliffs, N.J.: Prentice-Hall, 1963).*

NASH, MANNING. *Machine Age Maya* (Chicago: University of Chicago Press, 1958).*

POWDERMAKER, HORTENSE. *Coppertown: Changing Africa* (New York: Harper & Row, 1962).*

SLATER, PHILIP. *The Pursuit of Loneliness* (Boston: Beacon Press, 1970).*

TOFFLER, ALVIN. *Future Shock* (New York: Random House, 1970).*

* *Available in paperback.*